MEDITATIONS
IN THE
Messianic Psalms

WILLIAM McBRIDE

CRIMOND
HOUSE

CRIMOND HOUSE PUBLICATIONS

Published in 2017 by
Crimond House Publications
A division of
Ards Evangelical Bookshop
"Crimond House"
48 Frances Street
Newtownards
Co. Down
BT23 7DN
www.ardsbookshop.com

Printed in Glasgow by Bell & Bain Ltd.
Typesetting and cover design by Crimond House Publications.

ISBN: 978 1 908618 10 8

Dedication

This book is dedicated to the sweet memory of my beloved parents William and Eleanor McBride who from childhood taught me the Scriptures which at an early age were able to make wise unto salvation. Thereafter, they sacrificed much to ensure that my childhood dream of studying the Bible in its original languages was fulfilled.

Acknowledgements

I wish to record a special debt of thanks to my wife Esther for her constant spiritual support and encouragement in this project. I thank any who have read excerpts of the manuscript and commented thereupon. I thank my brother Samuel James McBride for helpful comments and allowing me access to some relevant publications and monographs. In addition, Crimond House Publications have been most helpful in bringing this book to publication. However, any errors in this volume are my own.

About the Author

Born in Lurgan, Northern Ireland, the author grew up on a farm in south Armagh. Saved in childhood he entered assembly fellowship in early teens. Godly parents and grandparents encouraged him to devote himself from childhood to a lifetime study of God's Word in the original languages. He also works in biomedical science and over many years has delivered presentations internationally in this field, mainly in Europe (in several European languages) and the Middle East, including Jerusalem, with several lectures in modern Hebrew. He lives in Lisburn, Northern Ireland with his wife Esther and two children.

Contents

Introduction

This book is a compilation of some of the author's meditations and studies in the Messianic Psalms over many years of Christian experience. Some of its content has been presented, in part, at ministry and gospel meetings in many assemblies of the Lord's people. Over the years, older believers have encouraged the author to commit some of these exercises to writing. Sadly, a number of these Christians have already passed on to their eternal reward and have not seen the completed book. Now they are singing heaven's New Song of redemption far from distress, sinful distraction or discouragement caused by life's frequent discordant notes. Every believer who expectantly awaits the moment of joining the throng of the redeemed ones already in heaven will find spiritual encouragement, solace and rest in tracing the glories of Christ in these precious passages of Scripture. Believers may also find spiritual challenge in these studies, effecting restoration of soul and owning the Lordship of Christ. Whatever the varied need of each believing reader, the end result of spending time in these passages should be a spontaneous response of praise to God for His Own Son, the Lord Jesus Christ. It is primarily with this desire that these meditations are now presented in a written form.

It is possible, and indeed hoped, that some who are not Christians may explore this book, curious as to why Christians hold Old Testament passages so dear. It is surely no coincidence that the first Messianic Psalm (Psalm 2) holds the key for any such friends who wish to embark on this study. It presents the **risen Christ** as an object of faith, through Whom alone true blessedness can be obtained. Only through trusting Him can salvation and forgiveness of sins be received as a free gift and, with this, the spiritual understanding to grasp the other Messianic Psalms. Apart from this, the rest of this book shall indeed be meaningless to you. It is the author's sincere prayer that many dear non-Christian friends will study carefully Psalm 2 and through its gospel message, clearly presented by the Psalmist, find the Messiah as their personal Lord and Saviour. If this becomes your experience through reading Psalm 2, then the rest of the subject matter of this book will become alive to you, as you will now be indwelt by the Holy Spirit!

The subject matter of this book

It could be said that almost all Psalms are Messianic, in that there is truth within them which speaks about the Messiah. However, to write about all of the Psalms was more than time or space permitted so, for the purposes of this book, two criteria have been used to determine what comprises a Messianic Psalm.

1 A Psalm is considered Messianic if excerpts which relate directly to the Lord Jesus Christ have been cited elsewhere in the Scriptures, either in the Old or New Testaments. Therefore, Psalm 72 is considered a Messianic Psalm because Psalm 72:8 is quoted in Zechariah 9:10 in relation to the

coming Kingdom of the Lord Jesus.

2 A Psalm is considered Messianic if it specifically refers to the coming King. Therefore, although Psalm 89 is not directly quoted in the New Testament, it is undoubtedly Messianic since it specifically refers to a coming day when the Messiah will sit upon the throne of David.

The context of the Messianic Psalms within the Psalter is of interest and for that reason some Psalms which precede and follow after a particular Messianic Psalm are considered, since such a meditation contributes to an understanding of the Messianic Psalm itself. This indicates that the order of the Psalms is not random but divinely arranged, and a careful study clearly validates this conclusion.

Similarly, understanding the context of New Testament quotations of the Messianic Psalms is of major importance to elucidate the overall meaning of entire passages of the New Testament. Accordingly, this matter is considered in *Meditations in the Messianic Psalms*. Since the epistle to the Hebrews quotes liberally from the Messianic Psalms, it is hoped that these meditations will encourage the exercised reader to be led of the Spirit of God to spend time on the mount with God in almost each chapter of Hebrews. Indeed, a grasp of the Messianic Psalms, begotten of the Spirit of God, will greatly enrich ones spiritual enjoyment of the sublime truths within the Hebrews epistle.

The objectives of this book

A particular objective of this book is to elucidate how the Messianic Psalms were understood by the early Hebrew Christians at the beginning of the New Testament era. For this reason, the main commentary on the Messianic Psalms used in this book is the New Testament itself. A guiding principle throughout these meditations is that the early New Testament writers, who quoted from and commented upon the Messianic Psalms, were writing with the supernatural enabling of the indwelling Holy Spirit. Undoubtedly, they were able to read the original Hebrew manuscripts fluently and without need for lexicons, concordances or grammatical aids. Accordingly, if we allow ourselves to be exclusively guided by their understanding of these ancient Hebrew writings, we will arrive at the intended meaning of the divine Author, Who inspired the various Psalmists to write.

This approach, by definition, sidesteps centuries of rabbinical scholarship and commentaries on these passages which have accumulated in the past 2000 years. This is because these writings, however learned, will not lead us to a direct understanding of how the New Testament Hebrew Christians understood the Messianic Psalms almost 2000 years ago. In fact, to elucidate this, it is best to go to the New Testament itself, and therein we discover that there is no shortage of material to clearly expound these ancient Hebrew passages. The author acknowledges that a comparison of the teachings of the New Testament Hebrew Christian writers on the Psalms with currently available rabbinical writings may be of interest to some. However, this is outside the scope of this present work.

Methods used in this book

An important principle underlying these meditations is that the Scriptures upon which they are based should not be studied in the same way as secular writings, because every word in the Bible is God-breathed, i.e. **God is the Author of each and every word**. Accordingly, if a word used in the earlier books of the Old Testament is quoted in the later books, it has not evolved into a different meaning because the divine Author has not changed. This conviction stands in contrast to recent liberal scholarship which contends that words at the end of the Old Testament need not necessarily mean the same as words at its beginning, due to alleged changes in meanings over the centuries, such as one might expect in a compilation of ancient secular writings spanning hundreds of years. Those who hold this liberal view may repudiate the method of study employed in *Meditations* where it is held that Hebrew words occurring early in the Old Testament retain the same meaning when used hundreds of years later. For any who have difficulties with identical words retaining the same meaning throughout the sacred canon, it is well to be reminded that the apostle Paul taught that the Bible should not be regarded as a secular book but rather be seen as authored by the Holy Ghost, allowing comparison of "spiritual things with spiritual".

1 Corinthians 2:13
"Which things also we speak, not in the **words which man's wisdom teacheth**, but which the Holy Ghost teacheth; comparing spiritual things with spiritual."

Throughout the Psalms, many metaphors are encountered which are not defined in the passage concerned. This has led to much and varied speculation as to their spiritual significance by Biblical commentators. The method used to obtain an understanding of such metaphors has been consistent in *Meditations in the Messianic Psalms*. It has been to look elsewhere in the Scriptures for use of similar or identical language where the meaning of the metaphor is defined. This can then be used to illuminate the meaning of the passage where the metaphor is not defined. Once again, this is based on Paul's words in 1 Corinthians 2:13 "comparing spiritual things with spiritual". An example to illustrate this is Psalm 91:3 where "the snare of the fowler" is not defined. However, in Hosea 9:8 it is used to describe a false prophet.

Hosea 9:8
"The watchman of Ephraim *was* with my God: *but* the prophet *is* a **snare of a fowler** in all his ways, *and* hatred in the house of his God."

This and other evidence is then used to elucidate that the first part of Psalm 91 refers to the future tribulation period when this world will be under the satanically energised influence of an evil individual called in Scripture "the false prophet".

This example illustrates that throughout the Psalms and indeed all of the Scriptures, elucidation of the meaning requires detailed study and comparison of Scripture with Scripture. Indeed, believers need to faithfully search after Biblical truth by comparing Scripture with Scripture. Peter tells us that no Scripture is of "any private interpretation", i.e. it needs to be read in context and in comparison with other relevant similar Scriptures.

2 Peter 2:19-21
> 19 "We have also a more sure word of prophecy; whereunto ye do well that ye take heed, as unto a light that shineth in a dark place, until the day dawn, and the day star arise in your hearts:
> 20 **Knowing this first, that no prophecy of the Scripture is of any private interpretation.**
> 21 For the prophecy came not in old time by the will of man: but holy men of God spake *as they were* moved by the Holy Ghost."

From time to time it is asked why God has presented His truth in Scripture in such an involved way. Solomon provides helpful insight into this:

Proverbs 25:2
> "*It is* the glory of God to conceal a thing: but the honour of kings *is* to search out a matter."

God's truth is concealed in His Word but is readily obtainable to the exercised soul who is prepared to prayerfully and reverently search it out in faith. It is this phenomenon which sets the Bible apart from all other human literature as being miraculous and divine and, above all, as **true**. **The Bible itself is a miraculous sign to all of humanity**. No other multi-author book spanning over a thousand years bears the hallmark of each word being God-breathed, as attested to by the breathtaking unity of thought and concept which prevails throughout its every page, "line upon line, here a little and there a little" (Isaiah 28:10), slowly and irrefutably revealing the excelling glories of Christ! *Meditations in the Messianic Psalms* will illustrate this for the believer and provide any atheist and secularist sincerely pursuing truth with a significant challenge to their unbelief.

Throughout this book, each verse in the original Hebrew has been carefully studied and, from time to time, details from the original Hebrew text, not immediately apparent in the English translation, are highlighted to facilitate the exposition.

The desired outcome for those who read this book

It is hoped that the reader will regard an understanding of these Messianic Psalms, based on their interpretation by New Testament writers two thousand years ago, to be of immediate relevance to us today. This is especially so, when we realise that much of the content of the Messianic Psalms is prophetic and is now approaching fulfilment as we near the end of the dispensation of grace, the impending rapture of the Church, the subsequent tribulation and the coming in manifestation of the Lord Jesus to set up His millennial Kingdom. In *Meditations in the Messianic Psalms*, prophetical aspects are carefully examined, with consideration of practical applications to present-day Christians. For example, the early Hebrew and Gentile Christians endured persecution, suffering and loss, yet these ancient passages from the Psalms brought them hope and comfort, strengthening their faith in the Lord Jesus Christ. Today, these passages of Scripture still carry the same intensely practical message of encouragement and hope which helped sustain early Christian testimony almost 2000 years ago.

It is impossible to study these sublime truths regarding the Lord Jesus, much less to endeavour to write about them, without feeling an overwhelming sense of one's own inadequacy to carry out such a written ministry. If, however, the believing reader is directed to a greater appreciation of the Lord Jesus Christ in his or her worship, these efforts will not have been in vain. Above all, may a younger generation of believers in our Lord Jesus Christ discover that sometimes Old Testament passages, which at first may seem remote and difficult to understand, still bear a startlingly relevant meaning in our day-to-day Christian lives, when we allow the inspired writers of the New Testament to guide us to the meaning.

Finally, I am sure that those of my fellow believers, known to God, who have been co-labourers in this work through their constant prayerful support, spiritual encouragement, timely proof reading and helpful comments and criticisms, will join with me in unreservedly acknowledging the unending truthfulness of the Lord's words to His indebted servants of Luke 17:10: "So likewise ye, when ye shall have done all those things which are commanded you, say, We are unprofitable servants: we have done that which was our duty to do."

William McBride
Lisburn
Northern Ireland
January 2017.

1

Psalm 2

1 Why do the heathen rage, and the people imagine a vain thing?
2 The kings of the earth set themselves, and the rulers take counsel together, against the Lord, and against His Anointed, saying,
3 Let us break Their bands asunder, and cast away Their cords from us.
4 He that sitteth in the heavens shall laugh: the Lord shall have them in derision.
5 Then shall He speak unto them in His wrath, and vex them in His sore displeasure.
6 Yet have I set My King upon My holy hill of Zion.
7 I will declare the decree: the Lord hath said unto Me, Thou art My Son; this day have I begotten Thee.
8 Ask of Me, and I shall give Thee the heathen for Thine inheritance, and the uttermost parts of the earth for Thy possession.
9 Thou shalt break them with a rod of iron; Thou shalt dash them in pieces like a potter's vessel.
10 Be wise now therefore, O ye kings: be instructed, ye judges of the earth.
11 Serve the Lord with fear, and rejoice with trembling.
12 Kiss the Son, lest He be angry, and ye perish from the way, when His wrath is kindled but a little. Blessed are all they that put their trust in Him.

Introduction

It was only a matter of weeks following the momentous events of the death, burial and resurrection of the Lord Jesus Christ that Peter and John were fearlessly preaching in Jerusalem the good news of His resurrection and the implications for mankind (Acts 4:1-31). Greatly perturbed by this turn of events, the Jewish council took them in for questioning. However, the council soon freed them on the condition that they no longer spoke or taught in the Name of Jesus. At once, the two apostles headed for their own company of disciples to share with them the latest developments. Their minds were in a quandary. Why ever did the world of religious and political leaders unite to reject the Lord's Anointed at Calvary? But, even more perplexing, why should their own learned leaders continue to reject

Him, in face of the overwhelming evidence of His bodily resurrection?

The way in which the early disciples handled this difficult question is most instructive for us. Firstly, they committed the whole matter to God in collective prayer. Secondly, they turned to the Scriptures for instruction and arrived at Psalm 2: 1-2. Similarly, when we are in times of difficulty and trial and do not understand the reason why, we have the twin resource of prayer and claiming the ever faithful promises of His Word.

It is evident that their understanding of Psalm 2:1-2 was most detailed.

Psalm 2:1-2

Acts 4:23-28
> 23 "And being let go, they went to their own company, and reported all that the chief priests and elders had said unto them.
> 24 And when they heard that, they lifted up their voice to God with one accord, and said, Lord, Thou *art* God, Which hast made heaven, and earth, and the sea, and all that in them is:
> 25 Who by the mouth of Thy servant David hast said, Why did the heathen rage, and the people imagine vain things?
> 26 The kings of the earth stood up, and the rulers were gathered together against the Lord, and against His Christ.
> 27 For of a truth against Thy Holy Child Jesus, **Whom Thou hast anointed**, both Herod, and Pontius Pilate, with the Gentiles, and the people of Israel, were gathered together,
> 28 For to do whatsoever Thy hand and Thy counsel determined before to be done."

In Acts 4: 27-28 we discover the meaning of the first two verses of Psalm 2:

1 His Anointed One is "Thy Holy Child Jesus Whom Thou has anointed". The phrase "His Anointed" is "His Messiah". The word "Christ" is the Greek word for the Hebrew "Messiah" meaning "Anointed One". The New Testament distinguishes between "Christ" and "the Christ" and this is discussed in **Appendix 1.**

2 The alliance of the heathen, the people, the kings of the earth and the rulers include "both Herod, and Pontius Pilate with the Gentiles and the people of Israel".

3 The rebellious action of this alliance had not taken God by surprise but rather was in fulfilment of Holy Scripture, including Psalm 2: 1-2.

The early disciples were confident in the purpose of God regarding these world leaders, whose actions were merely "...to do whatsoever Thy hand and Thy counsel determined before to be done".

All of this shows us that the first two verses of Psalm 2 have largely been fulfilled in the events surrounding His crucifixion and resurrection. The question arises, why did the early disciples stop at verse 2 and not go into verse 3 of Psalm 2?

Psalm 2:3

"Let us break Their bands asunder, and cast away Their cords from us."

We will discover in our studies of the Psalms that so often a section of Old Testament Scripture is only partially quoted in the New Testament and sometimes with slight modifications. It is important for us to notice these distinctions and then to ask why. The Old Testament is really only fully understood in light of New Testament revelation. When an Old Testament section is cut short in a New Testament quotation, this is often because the next verse is referring to a different event in God's prophetic scheme. A classic example is in Luke 4:17-21, when the Lord Himself, reading from Isaiah 61:1-2 about His anointing by the Spirit to preach the gospel, concluded with a dramatic note of grace by deliberately closing the book in the middle of the Isaiah passage so as not to read of "the day of vengeance of our God". The reason was that the day of vengeance was yet future, hence the accuracy of our Lord in concluding His reading at the point where He did.

The language of Psalm 2:3 is very emphatic. It implies complete rejection by world leaders of Who God is, His intrinsic holiness and His love. Let us examine these details.

"Let us break" and "Let us cast away".

The verse describes for us an objective of united world governments to completely sever all links with heaven. This dark day has not yet happened, which is why the disciples did not go on to quote Psalm 2:3 in the prayer meeting in Acts 4. We know from other passages that there will be intergovernmental unity during the future period of the tribulation after the rapture of the Church, when world leaders, who today struggle to agree on simple issues, will in that day unite in their opposition to God (Revelation 17:12-14).

Revelation 17:12-14

12 "And the ten horns which thou sawest are ten kings, which have received no kingdom as yet; but receive power as kings one hour with the beast.
13 **These have one mind**, and shall give their power and strength unto the beast.
14 These shall make war with the Lamb, and the Lamb shall overcome them: for He is Lord of lords, and King of kings: and they that are with Him *are* called, and chosen, and faithful."

Since this day is yet still future, it was appropriate that the disciples should pray for courage to proclaim the message of the risen Christ during this present day of opportunity, before the storm clouds of verse 3 of our Psalm descend. Such a prayer is still profitable for us today.

"Their bands"(mosrotemo) and "Their cords" (avotemo)

Notice the plural possessive "their" as indicated by the Hebrew word ending *emo*. Clearly, the doctrine of the Trinity is here being rejected, in other words the doctrine of "Who God is" – Father, Son and Holy Spirit. In a sense, the official rejection of "Who God is" by the nations awaits the arrival on this scene of the beast and the false prophet of Revelation 13, culminating in the blasphemous declaration by the former after 3 ½ years of the seven-year tribulation that he, in fact, is God. The activities of these two men emerge from the dragon (the devil) who controls them. When the world accepts the trinity of evil of the beast as God, the false prophet as Christ and the dragon (the devil) as the Holy Spirit (Who in contrast to the dragon appeared "in bodily shape as a dove" in Luke 3:22) the strong language of verse 3 will be fulfilled. This will take place in the future, in the final half of the seven-year tribulation period. More details regarding the trinity of evil in this dreadful period are discussed in **Appendix 2**.

"Bands" (*mosrotemo*) is very similar to the modern Hebrew word for "morals" or "restraining bands". Already this world is longing to be done with divine moral standards but cannot quite get away with it while the Church, which is His body, is still here. After the rapture of the Church, the mystery of iniquity, which is already working (2 Thessalonians 2:7), will rapidly come to fruition and the divine standards of holiness will be jettisoned completely by this world. "Cords" (**avotemo**) is another beautiful word which implies the methods by which God draws men to Himself – "constraining bands". This word is used of the entreaties of God towards Israel when, with bands (**avotot**) of love, He drew that nation.

Hosea 11:4
"I drew them with cords of a man, with bands (*avotot*) of love."

Today, God has a twofold message for men. Firstly, the **restraining** bands of His holy standard condemn man and show him his need of a Saviour. Secondly, the **constraining** cords of divine love tell man of a Saviour Who died to save and Who invites the sinner to come to Him for salvation. This world is soon to officially reject both!

The divine response to such ultimate rebellion is now unfolded to us in the Psalm.

Psalm 2:4
"He that sitteth in the heavens shall laugh: The Lord shall have them in derision."

The "laugh" and the "derision" which the Lord shall have in that coming day are His response to man's future global rebellion. Although, from the perspective of earth, the might of this anti-God alliance may appear impressive, from the perspective of heaven, it is utterly derisory and futile. Man cannot succeed in this rebellion against God.

Some would deny that a God of love would ever judge those who reject Him. In this section we discover that not only does He, Who sits on the throne, judge but His judgment is seen to be fair and righteous. All human argument and objection to God will melt away when the righteous Judge unveils His case.

Psalm 2:5

"Then shall He speak unto them in His wrath, and vex them in His sore displeasure."

Notice of the impending wrath of God is initially revealed to the rebellious earth dwellers in a verbal manner, "Then shall He speak unto them". The effect of this communication is dramatic. They are said to be "vexed". The Hebrew word, *yevahalemo* (vex), carries the idea "to vex, terrify and trouble". The first time we discover this word is in Genesis 45:3 when Joseph's brethren were "troubled" *nivhalu* (marginal rendering is "terrified") at the unavoidable presence of their estranged brother. The grammatical form of the word in Genesis 45:3 is called *Niphal* or simple passive. However, the particular grammatical form of the verb in Psalm 2:5 is called *Piel* or **intensive** active, signifying that the basic meaning of the word "to vex, terrify or trouble" has been considerably intensified. It now literally means that the Lord will "**mightily** vex, terrify or trouble" them in His sore displeasure. The word "sore displeasure" (*charono*) means "His burning wrath" and no doubt indicates the solemn fate of those who will be consumed at the "brightness of His coming" (2 Thessalonians 2:8). What is the nature of the communication which so fearfully troubles the earth dwellers? The answer is found in the next two verses.

Psalm 2:6

"Yet have I set My King upon My holy hill of Zion."

During the second half of the tribulation (a three and a half year period), Mount Zion becomes the scene of the greatest apostasy this world will have ever witnessed. The western leader (the first beast of Revelation 13) will declare himself to be God and will sit in the rebuilt temple in this capacity. At this time, what is described by the Lord as "the abomination of desolation, spoken of by Daniel the prophet" (Matthew 24:15), will be set up "in the holy place". Evidently, this is the image of the first beast of Revelation 13, which the earth dwellers worldwide shall be compelled to worship on pain of death. Meantime, his evil ally, the second beast of Revelation 13, the pseudo-messianic Israeli leader, shall acquiesce with this wicked scheme entirely and cause all to worship the first beast and his abominable image. It seems, at last, as if Mount Zion is completely under satanic control. But prophetic Scripture is adamant that this state of affairs is only transient. Appendix 2 considers these events in greater detail. At this point we should consider Isaiah 25:6, where Isaiah describes a wonderful future feast which will yet take place on Mount Zion **after** the satanic apostasy there has been destroyed.

Isaiah 25:6

"And in this mountain shall the LORD of hosts make unto all people a feast of fat things, a feast of wines on the lees, of fat things full of marrow, of wines on the lees well refined."

Isaiah did not understand the subject of the celebration, but he knew it would be unlimited in its scope, as "all people" would be involved. He must have understood that this tied in beautifully with many of his other glorious millennial prophecies when the nations would come up to Mount Zion to be taught of the LORD in that day (Isaiah 2). Before this delightful celebration can get underway, several key events will have to take place.

Firstly, God will "destroy in this mountain the face of the covering cast over all people, and the **veil** (*massechah*) that is spread (*nesuchah*) over all nations" (Isaiah 25:7). This translation in the Authorised Version is accurate. However, there is an alternative translation which the Hebrew text also allows. This is apparent when we observe that the Hebrew for "veil" (*massechah*) is also translated in Deuteronomy 9:12 as "molten image" for the purpose of idolatrous worship. Similarly, another form of the verb "spread over" (*nesuchah*) is also translated "molten an image" (Isaiah 44:10) or "set up" (Proverbs 8:23). Accordingly, the phrase could also accurately be translated that God will "destroy in this mountain the face of the covering cast over all people, and the molten image that is set up over all nations". Evidently, Isaiah as well as Daniel had this vision of an idolatrous image being set up on Mount Zion, the influence of which would tower over all the nations. Spine-chilling though this prospect may be, Isaiah assures us that the destruction of this is certain, in order to clear the way for the grand celebration on Mount Zion. We discover in the New Testament that this is the marriage supper of the Lamb. God has His answer for human rebellion. In the very mountain where the image of the beast is "set up", God shall "set up" His rightful King, the true Messiah, the Lord Jesus Christ Himself. The word "set" ("Have I set (*nasachti*) My King") in Psalm 2 verse 6, is the same root word as the image (*massechah*) which was set up (*nesuchah*) on Mount Zion as foretold by Isaiah in Isaiah 25. In other words, in the very place where the satanic counterfeit dominion held sway for the dreaded period of the tribulation, the triumphant Son of God shall reign supreme. A great wrong will have been righted at last.

Psalm 2:7

"I will declare the decree, the Lord hath said unto Me, 'Thou art My Son; this day have I begotten Thee.' "

"I will declare." **The public declaration** of this decree is still future, and evidently will be enforced in the government of this world when the Lord Jesus Christ returns to reign. As yet, this has not taken place. The decree itself, however, has already been made by the Father, albeit not yet publicly enforced ("The Lord **hath said**"). The honour of making the **declaration** of the decree is given to the Son Who will, in the future day of inauguration of His regal glory on earth, say, "I will declare the decree". This simply means that He will establish this decree as the foundational principle in the government of His Kingdom. This declaration of the decree which He will make in that coming day will look back to a moment in the past when the

Father said to Him, "Thou art My Son, this day have I begotten Thee". We need to establish when the Father said this to Him and what He meant.

Does the phrase, "this day have I begotten Thee", refer to His birth at Bethlehem or to His resurrection from the dead? Bible teachers have differed on this point. Here are some reasons why I hold that "this day have I begotten Thee" refers to His resurrection from the dead and was understood as such by first century A.D. Christians. Their understanding of the phrase becomes apparent when we study its quotation in three New Testament passages: Acts 13, Hebrews 1 and Hebrews 5.

Firstly, Paul quoted it while preaching in the synagogue in Antioch.

Acts 13:32-33

32 "And we declare unto you glad tidings, how that **the promise** which was made unto the fathers,
33 God hath fulfilled the same unto us their children in that He hath raised up Jesus again; as it is also written in the second Psalm, "Thou art My Son, this day have I begotten Thee." "

The Promise

All are agreed that the promise "made unto the fathers" (Acts 13:32) has been fulfilled "in that He hath raised up Jesus" (Acts 13:33). However, what does the promise of being "raised up" mean? There are two views.

The first view is that being "raised up" speaks of His upbringing following His incarnation, and carries the idea of "caused to flourish". The second view holds that "raised up" refers to His resurrection from the dead. Those who hold the first idea teach that Acts 13:32 is merely the promise of the birth and upbringing of the Messiah, and that the phrase, "He hath raised up Jesus", consequently refers only to His birth in Bethlehem and His upbringing in Nazareth. According to this argument, resurrection is not envisaged in the phrase, "He hath raised up Jesus", and, flowing from this logic, "This day have I begotten Thee" (Psalm 2:7) would refer to Bethlehem and Nazareth, not the empty tomb.

According to this view, "the promise" and its fulfilment in Acts 13:32-33 should be understood in the same sense as *"His* promise" and its fulfilment in Acts 13:22-23.

Acts 13:22-23

22 "And when He had removed him, He raised up unto them David to be their king; to whom also He gave testimony, and said, I have found David the *son* of Jesse, a man after Mine own heart, which shall fulfill all My will.
23 Of this man's seed hath God **according to *His* promise** raised unto Israel a Saviour, Jesus."

Here in Acts 13:22-23, there is no doubt that a general process of "raising" the Messiah to the throne is envisaged, i.e. "causing Him to flourish". However, there are good reasons to distinguish between Acts 13:22-23 and Acts 13:32-33. In verses 32 and 33, the promise is specific and has a specific fulfilment, whereas in verses 22 and 23 the promise is general and has a general fulfilment. In Acts 13:22 we read, "And when He had removed him (Saul), He raised (*egeiren*) up unto them David to be their king." Here the word "raise" (*egeiren*) clearly refers to the entire general process of establishing David upon the throne and causing him to flourish there. No one specific event is referred to. In the same sense, the word "raise" (*egeiren*) is used in Acts 13:23 of our Lord Jesus Christ – namely that God has "raised (*egeiren*) unto Israel a Saviour, Jesus."

It is important to note that the word for "His promise" (*epangelia*) is used here in a general sense because the definite article is omitted. Notice that in the Authorised Version, in the phrase "*His* promise," the "His" is in italics indicating it is not in the original. Consequently, no one specific promise is in view. Rather the "promise" in verses 22 and 23 is in a general sense and encompasses all the promises of God concerning His Son in providing Israel with a Saviour King. It follows, therefore, that the use of the word "raised up" in verses 22 and 23 cannot specifically refer to resurrection alone. Paul is still referring to the general divine movement in raising up the Messiah to sit upon the throne.

When we come to verse 32, Paul moves from general promise and general fulfilment to something very specific because this time the word "promise" has the definite article.

Acts 13:32-33
> 32 "And we declare unto you glad tidings, how that **the** promise which was made unto the fathers,
> 33 God hath fulfilled **the same** (literally, this particular one) unto us their children, in that He hath raised up (*anastesas*) Jesus. ("Again" is not in the original text)."

The very specific nature of the promise in Acts 13:32-33 cannot be understood in the same general sense of Acts 13:22-23.

An initial clue as to its meaning can be found in the verb translated "to raise up" in verse 33, where the word used is no longer *egeiren* (as in verse 22-23), but *anastesas* (root *anistemi*). Now *anistemi* in Acts 2:24 is used unambiguously, referring to His resurrection from the dead.

Acts 2:24
> "Whom God hath raised up (*anestesen*), having loosed the pains of death: because it was not possible that He should be holden of it."

This point is countered by some who point out that the verb *anestesen* can, on some occasions, be used in a general way in the sense of "raising up to an office" eg Acts 3:22;7:37 and that this is the sense intended in Acts 13:33. While it is indeed the case that *anestesen* can mean "raising up to an office", this seems highly unlikely in Acts 13:33 because *anestesen* appears again in verse 34 in the same context where it clearly is referring to resurrection from the dead.

Acts 13:34

> "And as concerning that He raised Him up (*anestesen*) from the dead, *now* no more to return to corruption, He said on this wise, I will give you the sure mercies of David."

If we acknowledge that it is unlikely for the same verb to carry separate meanings within the same passage, it becomes difficult to see that Acts 13:33 refers to the Lord Jesus being "raised up" in the general sense of His upbringing in Nazareth etc. Rather, we would anticipate *anestesen* in verse 33 to apply to His resurrection from the dead.

However, the incontrovertible proof that "to raise up" in Acts 13:33 refers to resurrection is found in the way in which Paul draws on three Old Testament passages, all of which explain to us aspects of "**the** promise" and which present to us key aspects of resurrection doctrine.

Psalm 2:7 "**Thou art My Son; this day have I begotten Thee**"
Isaiah 55:3 "**I will give you the sure mercies of David**"
Psalm 16:10 "**Thou shalt not suffer Thine Holy One to see corruption**"

These three Old Testament passages are presented in verses 33-37 and are used **together** to show us different aspects of "**the** promise".

Acts 13:32-37

> 32 "And we declare unto you glad tidings, how that **the** promise which was made unto the fathers,
> 33 God hath fulfilled the same unto us their children, in that He hath raised up Jesus again; as it is also written in the second psalm, **Thou art My Son, this day have I begotten Thee.**
> 34 And as concerning that He raised Him up from the dead, *now* no more to return to corruption, He said on this wise, **I will give you the sure mercies of David.**
> 35 Wherefore He saith also in another *psalm,* **Thou shalt not suffer Thine Holy One to see corruption.**
> 36 For David, after he had served his own generation by the will of God, fell on sleep, and was laid unto his fathers, and saw corruption:
> 37 But He, Whom God raised again, saw no corruption."

The way in which these three Old Testament passages are joined together in the New Testament Greek text strongly suggests that it is appropriate for us to consider their meaning within the context of the one specific promise which they are used to expound. What then is that promise? Of the three Old Testament passages Paul quotes, perhaps it is the third quotation, "**Thou shalt not suffer Thine Holy One to see corruption**" (Psalm 16:10), which answers this question for us by identifying the promise under discussion as being the resurrection of the Lord Jesus Christ from the dead. The detailed reasoning behind this conclusion is given when Psalm 16:10 is considered later in this book. The use of Psalm 16:10 at this point in Paul's message shows that "**the** promise" to which Paul alludes in Acts 13:32 was the promised resurrection from the dead of the Lord Jesus Christ. However, since the three Old Testament passages are giving us differing aspects of "**the** promise" it becomes apparent that Paul's quotations from Isaiah 55:3 and Psalm 2:7 must also refer to the resurrection of our Lord from the dead.

What each of these three Old Testament quotations teaches us about His resurrection from the dead shall now be considered.

(a) "Thou art My Son, this day have I begotten Thee" (Acts 13:33, quoted from Psalm 2:7).

"Thou art My Son" (*Bni atah*) literally reads, "My Son, Thou!" This statement presents to us the eternality of the relationship of the Father and the Son. In John's gospel, when the Lord Jesus spoke of Himself as the Son, the Jewish leadership of that day clearly understood that this placed Him on equality with the Father and for this reason they sought on three occasions to have Him killed for blasphemy (John 5:18, 8:59 and 10:31). These leaders had very good reason for understanding that the Son revealed in the Old Testament is on equality with the Father. In Isaiah 9:6, the prophet tells us that the Son was not born. The Son was given. It was the Child Who was born.

Isaiah 9:6

"For unto us a Child is born, unto us a Son is given: and the government shall be upon His shoulder: and His Name shall be called Wonderful, Counsellor, The Mighty God, The Everlasting Father (*Avi-Ad*), The Prince of Peace."

In other words, the Son existed **before** His birth. His eternal pre-existence is further emphasised by the title of the "Everlasting Father". In Hebrew this phrase *Avi-Ad* means "Father of Eternity." This majestic statement can only be appreciated when we realise afresh that eternity is infinite in its past expanses and has no beginning. Consequently, His title "Father of Eternity," eloquently reminds us that the Son is eternal and had no beginning. He is the Eternal Son.

"This day have I begotten Thee" *(ani hayyom yelidticha!)*

"Thou art My Son!" is a statement of fact. "This day have I begotten Thee," is the indisputable evidence of that fact which God has given to an unbelieving world. This statement is quoted three times in the New Testament – Acts 13:33, which we have just considered, Hebrews 1:5 and Hebrews 5:5.

This phrase directs the believer's attention
(i) in Acts 13 **to the past** and His resurrection ,
(ii) in Hebrews 1 **to the future** and His coming again and
(iii) in Hebrews 5 **to the present** and His high priestly ministry.

In Acts 13, the phrase presents the risen Son in the gospel as our Saviour. The believer **looks back** to these truths every time he or she recalls conversion to Christ.

The Hebrews 1 passage presents the risen Son as the future King Who will return in His glory and Who will unconditionally share His inheritance with us, something no angel could ever do. This presents Him as our Hope and a believer **looks forward** to these truths in anticipation of His coming.

In Hebrews 5, the quotation is for the believer today in the ever present vicissitudes of life. This encourages us today to **look up** to heaven to our Lord Jesus Christ as the risen Son in His role as our Great High Priest.

We have observed that the phrase, "This day have I begotten Thee", refers to His resurrection from the dead. However, is there additional scriptural evidence to support this view?

The resurrection from the dead of the Lord Jesus is metaphorically described in several other passages as a babe emerging from the womb. In this resurrection context, the Lord Jesus is described in Revelation 1:5 and Colossians 1:18 as the "First Begotten" (*prototokos*) which carries the significance of "Firstborn".

Revelation 1:5
"And from Jesus Christ, *Who is* the faithful Witness, *and* **the First Begotten** (*prototokos*) of the dead, and the Prince of the kings of the earth."

Colossians 1:18
"And He is the Head of the body, the Church: Who is the Beginning, **the Firstborn** (*prototokos*) from the dead; that in all *things* He might have the preeminence."

Also, in John 16:21-22, the Lord Jesus explained to His disciples that the joy attending the birth of a child is but a faint picture of the joy that would be theirs on the occasion of their joyful realisation of His resurrection.

John 16:21-22
21 "A woman when she is in travail hath sorrow, because her hour is come: but as soon as she is delivered of the child (*gennese*), she remembereth no more the anguish, for joy that a man is born (*egennethe*) into the world.
22 And ye now therefore have sorrow: but I will see you again, and your heart shall rejoice, and your joy no man taketh from you."

This passage is important because the phrases, "as soon as she is delivered of the child" and "a man is born", use the verb "*gennao*" meaning "to beget" where the meaning is clearly intended to be understood as metaphorically describing the resurrection of the Lord Jesus emerging from the womb of death and not His literal birth at Bethlehem. It is important to notice that it is the same verb (*gennao)* which is used in Acts 13:33: "Thou art My Son, this day have I begotten (*gennao*) Thee". Just as in John 16:21-22, *gennao* refers to being "begotten from the dead" similarly in Psalm 2:7 the verb "begotten Thee" carries the same significance.

In Psalm 110:3 this metaphor is again employed (see Psalm 110) and will be discussed in detail.

Psalm 110:3
"Thy people *shall be* willing in the day of Thy power, in the beauties of holiness **from the womb of the morning:** Thou hast the dew of Thy youth."

After His resurrection He became known as the "First Begotten" (*prototokos*) or "Firstborn of the dead". Perhaps it could be asked why the Lord Jesus is referred to as *prototokos* (firstborn) from the dead and not an alternative Greek word derived from the root *gennao*. The reason why *prototokos,* meaning "firstborn", must be used and not a word based on *gennao* is because the Lord Jesus is not the first Person **chronologically** to be raised from the dead. Resurrection was already seen in the Old Testament and He Himself had raised Lazarus, Jairus' daughter and the widow of Nain's son from the dead. However, He is unique in His resurrection. When we are raised from the dead, we are raised from corruption. He was raised from incorruption (Acts 13:34). In this sense, He is the "Firstborn" because the Biblical and Hebrew use of the word "firstborn" in Scripture does not mean "born first" chronologically but rather denotes rank. Others have been raised from the dead but since they were raised from corruption this was not evidence of them being divine. As the *prototokos* – "Firstborn" from the dead – He stands unique and it can now be seen that this is the evidence of His eternal Sonship.

At this point it needs to be stressed that He did not become the Son of God at His resurrection. Being begotten from the dead did not constitute Him the Only Begotten Son of God. He is eternally God's Son. This relationship with His Father is without beginning. However, being begotten from the dead is the **evidence** in our New Testament that He is the eternal Son of God.

For example, throughout the Acts of the Apostles and the Epistles, the resurrection is the proof of His eternal Sonship and that He is indisputably Who He said He was.

Romans 1:4
"And declared to be the Son of God with power, according to the Spirit of Holiness **by the resurrection from the dead**..."

The declaration of the Lord Jesus as the Son of God is based on His resurrection from the dead.

While our Lord was upon earth, men refused to accept that He was the Son of God. The resurrection of our Lord Jesus Christ has been the overwhelming evidence which God has provided to this fact.

In summary, the quotation "Thou art My Son, This day have I begotten Thee" shows us that the resurrection of our Lord Jesus Christ firstly attests to **Who He is**: God's Eternal Son.

(b) "I will give you the sure mercies of David" (Acts 13: 34, quoted from Isaiah 55:3)

Isaiah 55:3
"Incline your ear, and come unto Me: hear, and your soul shall live; and

I will make an everlasting covenant with you, *even* the sure mercies of David."

The word "sure" (*hanneemanim*) means simply "believable or worthy of faith". In Psalm 2, God has presented to us the resurrection of our Lord Jesus Christ as the supreme proof as to Who Christ is. He is God's Son. In Isaiah 55:3, He brings before us that God's Eternal Son, now risen from the dead, is truly worthy of the saving faith of every sin-sick individual seeking for salvation and pardon from God. What a joyful message emerges forth from the news of His resurrection! It is that the mercies of Jehovah can become the possession of every one who puts their trust in Him.

(c) "Thou shalt not suffer Thine Holy One to see corruption" (Acts 13:35, quoted from Psalm 16:10).

While our Lord was on earth, men were slow to accept the truth that He was born of the virgin in fulfilment of Isaiah's prophecy:

Isaiah 7:14
"Behold, a virgin shall conceive, and bear a Son, and shall call His Name Immanuel."

There are two examples of this denial by the Jewish leaders in the time of our Lord.

John 6:42
"Is not this Jesus, **the Son of Joseph**, Whose father and mother we know? how is it then that He saith, I came down from heaven?"

John 8:41
"Then said they to Him, We be not **born of fornication**; we have one Father, *even* God."

By so speaking, they were denying the virgin birth of our Lord Jesus Christ. However, His resurrection from the dead, as presented in Psalm 16, is the proof that He was indeed the Holy One spoken of by the angel to Mary in Luke 1:35.

Luke 1:35
"And the angel answered and said unto her, The Holy Ghost shall come upon thee, and the power of the Highest shall overshadow thee: therefore also **that Holy Thing** Which shall be born of thee shall be called the Son of God."

As the Holy One, He was born of the virgin and as a consequence of this He could not "see corruption". Death could not hold Him. If in Psalm 2, resurrection proves Who He is – the Son of God – in Psalm 16, His resurrection proves of what character He is – the Holy One of God, sinless and spotless.

We may wonder why the Isaiah 55 quotation, which presents Christ as an object of faith, comes between the Psalm 2 and Psalm 16 passages. If a present-day gospel preacher was taking up these three texts he would probably preach firstly Who Christ is, i.e. the Son of God, then secondly, he would proclaim of what character He is, i.e. the Holy One of God and, finally, based on these two preceding foundational truths, proclaim Him as an object of faith by presenting the "sure" (believable) mercies of David. Paul, under the guidance of the Spirit of God, did not do this. He presented Christ as an object of faith by proclaiming the "sure mercies of David" as a wonderful doctrinal fact bounded before and after by Psalms 2 and 16 respectively. In other words, the reliability of our Lord Jesus Christ as an object of our faith is completely surrounded by the truths of Who He is and of what character He is. Our faith in Christ is secure because He is none other than the Son of God and He is the Holy One of God.

In summary, then, His resurrection from the dead not only confirms to us the doctrines of His Person (His deity and sinless humanity), but as its **central message** presents Him to the "whosoever will" as an object of faith. Moreover, the fact that this blessing of salvation is obtained by faith alone, freely and not dependent on works of merit, is emphasised in the phrase, "I will **give you** the sure mercies of David..." Salvation is received alone as a **gift** from God, but at such a cost – the death, burial and resurrection of His own Son.

It is in light of His resurrection that Paul confidently declares:

Acts 13:38-39
> 38 "Be it known unto you **therefore**, men *and* brethren, that through this Man is preached unto you the forgiveness of sins:
> 39 And by Him all that believe are justified from all things, from which ye could not be justified by the Law of Moses."

The "therefore" in Acts 13:38 refers to the preceding arguments, namely that the Lord Jesus Christ through resurrection is attested to be:
1 The risen Son
2 The Holy One (i.e. His death was not for any sins of His own but rather on behalf of others)
3 Worthy of our faith
This great "therefore" provides us with the reason why Paul so confidently can present Christ to His audience as "this Man", i.e. this risen Man, through Whom forgiveness of sins is preached and received by "all that believe".

All gospel preachers should retain the resurrection as a vital part of any gospel message. Omission of the resurrection from a gospel message is contrary to the New Testament pattern of gospel preaching. This is the big practical lesson of the use of Psalm 2 in Acts 13.

The second quotation of the phrase, "**Thou art My Son, this day have I begotten Thee**", is found in Hebrews 1:5.

Hebrews 1:5
> "For unto which of the angels said He at any time, Thou art My Son, this day have I begotten Thee? And again, I will be to him a Father, and he shall be to Me a son?"

This is in the context of the Lord Jesus, on His return to this earth, being the legal Heir to the universe in general and this earth in particular. Any presumption that the Old Testament promises of a future millennial Kingdom might not be fulfilled constitutes an assault on the legal rights of the Person of Christ as the acclaimed Son of God to be the Heir. Indeed, as we will discuss in Psalm 95, there were those among the early Hebrew Christians who had lost sight of the literal fulfilment of the Old Testament promises of the coming Kingdom. A restatement in Hebrews 1 of His eternal Sonship, as attested to by His resurrection in Psalm 2, was a powerful frontal abuttal of such false teaching. It is because He is the Son, as attested to publicly by His resurrection, that He is the undisputed Heir. No angel can claim such majesty. However, could there have been false teachers denying the literality of the coming Kingdom? They may have argued against Sonship being a *sine qua non* claim (an indispensable condition) to a literal earthly inheritance by referring to Solomon, who had been denied the bequeathal of an undivided inheritance despite being the Son of David. Perhaps it is to counter such an idea that the promise to Solomon is introduced at this point in Hebrews 1:5, "And again, I will be to him a Father, and he shall be to Me a son".

2 Samuel 7:12-15
> 12 "And when thy days be fulfilled, and thou shalt sleep with thy fathers, I will set up thy seed after thee, which shall proceed out of thy bowels, and I will establish his kingdom.
> 13 He shall build an house for My Name, and I will stablish the throne of his kingdom for ever.
> 14 **I will be his Father (to him for a Father), and he shall be My son (to Me for a son)**. If he commit iniquity, I will chasten him with the rod of men, and with the stripes of the children of men:
> 15 But My mercy shall not depart away from him, as I took *it* from Saul, whom I put away before thee."

The literal translation of 2 Samuel 7:14 is as follows: "**I will be to him for a Father, and he shall be to Me for a son, that in his committing iniquity** I will chasten him with the rod of men, and with the stripes of the children of men". In the quotation of this section in Hebrews 1:5, the literal translation of the Greek is the same: "I will be to him for a Father and he shall be to Me for a son".

Contrasts between Solomon and Christ
The person in question in 2 Samuel 7: 14 is Solomon, the son of David, and

not the Lord Jesus Christ. The Lord tells David that He will be to Solomon "for a Father", and Solomon shall be to God "for a son". The phrase "for a son" suggests that Solomon will be treated as a son, even though he does not have the same nature as his Father God, because in the Old Testament, a believer was not indwelt by the Spirit of God. If God had said of Solomon, "I will be to him a Father and he will be to Me a son" that would imply that Solomon was an actual son with a divine nature within, due to the indwelling Holy Spirit. This was not the case, however, in common with all other Old Testament believers. When the Father says to the Lord Jesus, "Thou art My Son" He does not say, "Thou art to Me for a Son" since this would fall short of the Lord Jesus fully having the divine nature as God manifested in flesh. The Lord is explaining that after David's death, Solomon need not consider himself fatherless. God promises, "I **will** be to him for a Father, and he **shall** be to Me for a son". The use of the future tense indicates that the Lord's relationship with Solomon was something that would be particularly manifested **after** David's death when the Lord would apply to Solomon fatherly discipline to restore him to the right ways if he erred. This must have been very reassuring to David. He knew he could entrust his son Solomon to the safe care of his God. Therefore, David knew, even before his death, that God would treat Solomon just as a loving father would treat his son.

Interestingly, in the promise to David the context was the anticipated failures of Solomon. In the Authorised Version, the phrase, "if he commit iniquity", might suggest that Solomon's failures were merely an outside possibility. In the original text, Solomon's future failings are predicted with certainty. God's Father-like relationship with Solomon would be manifested when (not if) Solomon would commit iniquity. When this inevitable event occurred, God pledged to David that He would punish Solomon but it would always be as a father would train his son. Later, when Solomon comes to the end of his life and after periods of significant backsliding he, as an old man now restored to God, sits down to record and compile the inspired proverbs of Solomon. As one who had come to know a heavenly Father's chastening, he describes to us the training of the son by the Father.

Proverbs 1:8-9
> 8 "My son, hear the instruction of thy father, and forsake not the law of thy mother:
> 9 For they *shall be* an ornament of grace unto thy head, and chains about thy neck."

Proverbs 3:11-12
> 11 "My son, despise not the chastening of the Lord; neither be weary of His correction:
> 12 For whom the Lord loveth He correcteth; even as a Father the son *in whom* He delighteth."

In Hebrews 1:5, there are three note-worthy contrasts between the Lord Jesus and Solomon:

1 The **nature** of the Father-Son relationship is different between the Lord Jesus and Solomon. God did not say to the Lord Jesus, "Thou wilt be to Me **for** a Son". He said "Thou art My Son". This means that the Lord Jesus is God's Son eternally. In contrast to this, Solomon could not claim the same order of sonship. He was only to God "for a son".

2 The **timing** of the Father-Son relationship is different between the Lord Jesus and Solomon. As to the Father-son relationship of God and Solomon, the phrase, "I will be to him for a Father", suggests a finite time in Solomon's experience, when he could come to understand God as his Father. In contrast, the Lord Jesus always was, is and will be God's Son.

3 The **evidence** of the Father-Son relationship is different between the Lord Jesus and Solomon. God's relationship with Christ as the Eternal Father of the Eternal Son has been evidenced by His resurrection from the dead **and God** giving the world to Him as His inheritance. God's father-like relationship to Solomon is evidenced by God's pledge to correct him when he erred, leading ultimately to the dividing of Solomon's inheritance.

These observations show us that the Father-son relationship of Jehovah to Solomon is of a much lower order than the Father-Son relationship of the Father and the Lord Jesus Christ. Hebrews 1:5 presents us two distinct and **contrasting** orders of Father-Son relationship.

The thrust of the argument in Hebrews 1 is that although angels may be called "sons of God" in Job 38:7, they cannot be heirs to the universe because they do not possess the same Father-Son relationship of Christ to His Father – nor do they possess the same lower order of Father-son relationship such as Solomon enjoyed. When Solomon sinned, God punished him in a fatherly way to recover him and this involved taking half of the inheritance from Solomon. When angels sinned, they were punished but then there was no possibility of future recovery. Fallen angels are fallen forever. However, it is clear that the angels which did not fall are not possessors of the inheritance either. Rather they are "ministering spirits" to minister for those who will be the "heirs", namely sinners saved by grace who are sons of God by redemption.

Hebrews 1:14
> "Are they not all ministering spirits, sent forth to minister for them who shall be heirs of salvation?"

Later, the writer to the Hebrews shows that we can learn lessons from Solomon's relationship to God. Like Solomon, we are not perfect and we too can earn the displeasure and chastisement of our Heavenly Father. Therefore, the writer to the Hebrews quotes from the writings of Solomon in Proverbs 3:11-12.

Hebrews 12:5-8

> 5 "And ye have forgotten the exhortation which speaketh unto you as unto children, My son, despise not thou the chastening of the Lord, nor faint when thou art rebuked of Him:
> 6 For whom the Lord loveth He chasteneth, and scourgeth every son whom He receiveth.
> 7 If ye endure chastening, God dealeth with you as with sons; for what son is he whom the Father chasteneth not?
> 8 But if ye be without chastisement, whereof all are partakers, then are ye bastards, and not sons."

It is worth pointing out that Solomon, who was to Jehovah "for a son", due to failure had half of his inheritance taken from him. We have a son-Father relationship much higher than that which Solomon enjoyed. For example, a believer today does not say that she/he is "for a son". We are actual sons of God through being indwelt by God's Spirit thus being partakers of the divine nature. Moreover, in accordance with New Testament revelation, we can address God as Father (Luke 11), something we do not read of happening in the recorded prayers of Old Testament believers (see comment on Psalm 89 and also Appendix 3). Solomon did not have this wonderful experience of being indwelt by the Spirit of God which even the simplest New Testament believer enjoys, whereby we cry "Abba Father!" (Galatians 4:6, Romans 8:15).

Romans 8:15-17

> 15 "For ye have not received the spirit of bondage again to fear; but ye have received the Spirit of adoption, whereby we cry, Abba, Father.
> 16 The Spirit Itself beareth witness with our spirit, that we are the children of God:
> 17 And if children, then heirs; heirs of God, and joint-heirs with Christ; if so be that we suffer with *Him*, that we may be also glorified together."

Because we are joint heirs with Christ the Son, our inheritance, unlike Solomon's, cannot be divided and taken from us.

In summary, then, the quotation from Psalm 2 in Hebrews 1, "Thou art My Son, to day have I begotten Thee", is to show us that the Lord Jesus is God's Son, proven not only to be so by resurrection but also by standing peerless as the One Who only brought pleasure to His Father, in striking **contrast** to Solomon. If Solomon's kingdom –his inheritance –was glorious, how much more so will be that of God's **perfect** Son? In this inheritance we, who are God's sons by adoption, will share (Romans 8:15).

The third quotation of the phrase, "Thou art My Son, this day have I begotten Thee" is in Hebrews 5.

Hebrews 5:5

> "So also Christ glorified not Himself to be made an High Priest; but He that said unto Him, Thou art My Son, today have I begotten Thee."

This presents to us the Lord Jesus as our Great High Priest. Struggling saints need to hear once again that the power and compassions of our Great High Priest are beyond compare. It is in this context, in Hebrews 5, that the writer is contrasting and comparing the earthly and historical priesthood of Aaron with that of our Great High Priest Himself.

Contrasts between Aaron and Christ

Hebrews 5 shows that Aaron was taken from among men to represent men to God. Our High Priest likewise must be taken from among men. It is for this reason that some expositors hold that the quotation from Psalm 2, used in Hebrews 5:5, "Thou art My Son, today have I begotten Thee", must refer to His birth at Bethlehem since it was at Bethlehem that He became a Man in order to have human experience to qualify Him to be our Great High Priest. Unfortunately, this view loses sight of the fact that our Great High Priest must be more than a perfect Man. He must be a **risen** Man (this truth is further expanded in Psalm 110). This is the key to understanding Hebrews 5 and explains why the writer quotes from Psalm 2 which, as we have seen, is focused on His resurrection. The writer of Hebrews is showing that whereas Aaron was indeed a man, Christ is a **risen** Man!

The writer of Hebrews describes two great contrasts between Aaron and Christ:

(a) Every high priest is "taken from among men" and "is ordained..."

Hebrews 5:1
"For every high priest taken from among men is ordained for men in things *pertaining* to God, that he may offer both gifts and sacrifices for sins:"

The idea here is that the earthly priests were **constantly** being taken and ordained by men, because death so quickly terminated their office. In contrast, the heavenly High Priest has conquered death. He is risen!

(b) Earthly priests had limited "compassion on the ignorant and them that were out of the way".

Hebrews 5:2
"Who can have compassion on the ignorant, and on them that are out of the way; for that he himself also is compassed with infirmity."

This verse is presenting a further contrast between Christ and Aaron because the word used here to describe Aaron's compassions means literally "to have measured feeling" (*metriopathein*). The word *metriopathein* does not occur elsewhere in our New Testament but is a compound of *metrios* meaning "measured or moderate" and *pathos* meaning "passion or feeling". Apparently, in secular literature this "measured or moderate" feeling was considered a virtue in the heathen ancient Greek world, especially by the ancient Stoic philosophers, as it was thought to be preferable to extremes of emotions. No doubt, this so-called "virtue" could be used to logically exclude compassions in inopportune or inconvenient circumstances. An example might be in Luke 11:5-8 where a householder in bed at night could argue, perhaps legitimately, that getting up at an unsocial hour to provide bread for a friend was beyond reasonable compassion. The Hebrews writer chooses this word (*metriopathein*) to describe Aaron's attitude to the failing Israelites. Aaron's compassions were measured or limited because he too was "compassed with infirmity". What a delightful contrast with our risen High Priest! His compassions and feelings toward us are neither measured nor moderated. If they were, how often could we be disqualified from receiving those much-needed compassions! The ancient Stoics considered measured compassions as virtuous. The Scriptures do not commend Stoic philosophy (Acts 17:18). This word *metriopathein* is used of Aaron but is not applied to the Saviour by the writer of Hebrews. Christ was and is divine. Therefore, in contrast to Aaron, "His compassions fail not".

Lamentations 3:22-23
22 "*It is of* the Lord's mercies that we are not consumed, **because His compassions fail not**.
23 *They are* new every morning: great *is* Thy faithfulness."

In contrast to Aaron, our heavenly and risen High Priest is never weary of the cries of His own, whatever the time of day or night, or however insignificant our needs may be.

A comparison between Aaron and Christ

Hebrews 5:4-5
4 "And no man taketh this honour unto himself, but he that is called of God, as *was* Aaron.
5 So also Christ glorified not Himself to be made an High Priest; but He that said unto Him, Thou art My Son, today have I begotten Thee."

The writer of Hebrews now moves to a delightful comparison of the Aaronic priesthood with the Lord Jesus. Aaron, despite his own limitations, considered it an honour to be "a high priest called of God". Similarly, our risen Lord Jesus Christ considers it an honour to be called our High Priest, "So Christ glorified not Himself to be made an High Priest; but He that said unto Him, **Thou art My Son, today have I begotten Thee**". The quotation here from Psalm 2 is to emphasise to us that our High Priest, in contrast to Aaron, has endured death for us and now sits **in resurrection power** ministering for us at God's right hand. As an honour to Aaron, God granted him the privilege of representing men to God and God to men. How can God honour His risen Son in His resurrection Glory? The answer is by giving to Him the High Priestly ministry in His resurrection power. This is a truth which fills us with wonder and awe as to why the One Who, according to Romans 6:4, was "raised from the dead by the glory of the Father", and Who today is glorified in heaven, should still consider it an honour to be the High Priest of such feeble believers as ourselves. This simply means that every time we use His High Priestly ministry we give glory to Him. This may be in presenting prayer and praise to the Father through Him, as we are exhorted to do "for all things".

Ephesians 5:20
"Giving thanks always **for all things** unto God and the Father in the Name of our Lord Jesus Christ;"

In so doing, we are giving Him the glory due to His Name. Some believers worry that if we do not pray directly to the Lord Jesus we rob Him of glory. This is not the case. We should understand that each time we pray to the Father through Him, He takes our imperfect and failing praise and it is then presented by Him from His own lips to the Father, no longer imperfect or flawed but in all the perfection of His Person.

Just as Aaron partook of the peace offerings which he presented to God, and in so doing received his portion (see Psalm 16), so the Lord Jesus as our Great High Priest receives His portion every time we come before the Father presenting our praise to Him "in the Name of the Lord Jesus"(Colossians 3:17). As the risen Son, He is our Great High Priest. As we will see in Psalm 16, Aaron's **inheritance** was to eat of the offerings of the people. Our Risen Lord has been declared to be the Son of God with power. As the Son, He is the Heir of all things. He also is the Heir to our worship. Let us never forget, that because in Psalm 2 He is declared to be the risen Son of God, so now He is our Great High Priest and thus the rightful Heir to receive the worship of His people. Do we rob Him of the glory due to His Name by not taking time to commune with the Father through Him?

At this point, let us summarise the significance of the statement, "**Thou art My Son, this day have I begotten Thee**" as understood by New Testament believers:

a) It refers to Jehovah addressing the risen One on the occasion of His resurrection from the dead

b) It is the incontrovertible evidence to men of His eternal Sonship "declared to be the Son of God with power... by the resurrection from the dead"

c) It is a truth which the coming King will publicly declare as the basis of the constitution of the coming Kingdom –"I will declare the decree"

d) It forms the basis of the preaching of the Gospel to the unsaved (Acts 13)

e) It is the basis of our worship as each time we approach the Father through the risen Son, our High Priest, He receives the honour due to His Name (Hebrews 5).

The Son as Heir to the universe
The rebels of this world have refused to accept the evidence which God has given concerning His Son, namely, His resurrection from the dead. God

must and will set the record straight. His coming again to the earth will be the grand vindication of the Father and the Son. One can only imagine how aghast the unbelieving world will be when it sees the risen Son returning in power. "He is alive after all", they will cry in terror. Alas, for them the truth of His resurrection will no longer bring news of salvation, but rather spell their eternal judgment and doom. Today, His resurrection is the proof of free salvation through faith in Him (Acts 13). However, His resurrection is also proof that those who reject Him must meet Him as their Judge.

Acts 17:30-31
> 30 "And the times of this ignorance God winked at; but now commandeth all men every where to repent:
> 31 Because He hath appointed a day, in the which **He will judge the world** in righteousness by *that* Man whom He hath ordained; *whereof* He hath given assurance unto all *men*, in that He hath raised Him from the dead."

Psalm 2:8
> "Ask of Me and I will give Thee the heathen (*goyim* the nations) for Thine inheritance and the uttermost parts of the earth for Thy possession."

If "Thou art My Son" is a statement of the eternal relationship, and "This day have I begotten Thee" is the proof of that relationship, then the next section, on the rights of the Son as the Heir of the universe, is a direct result of the proving of this relationship. It is a principle in Scripture that the Son is the Heir. It was in open rebellion to this fact that, in the parable of the vineyard, the rebel workmen, on seeing the Son coming, said, "This is the Heir; come, let us kill Him, and the inheritance shall be ours" (Mark 12:7). This is what the raging nations and the kings of the earth did in the first two verses of Psalm 2. However, just as surely as resurrection proves Him to be the Son, it also establishes Him as the Heir. This is the theme of Hebrews chapter one which quotes Psalm 2.

Hebrews 1:1-2
> 1 "GOD, Who at sundry times and in divers manners spake in time past unto the fathers by the prophets,
> 2 Hath in these last days spoken **unto us by *His* Son, Whom He hath appointed Heir of all things, by Whom also He made the worlds (ages)**";

His inheritance will be "the heathen (*goyim* the nations)", i.e. Gentiles (Psalm 2:8). In Psalm 22, Psalm 40 and in more detail in Psalm 69 the doctrine of redemption is considered. One central aspect of the Biblical teaching on redemption is that God obtains **an inheritance in us,** i.e. we (the redeemed ones) are **God's inheritance** because we belong to Him. In those passages it will be shown that the significance of us being God's inheritance is that **we are in fact priests** functioning **in His immediate presence**. It will be seen in Psalms 22, 40 and 69 as well as Psalm 16 that not only are we as redeemed ones the Lord's inheritance i.e. His priests, but that the Lord Jesus is Heir to the praise we bring. As He presents our praise to the Father, He obtains

His portion, i.e. His inheritance, just as Aaron was able to eat of the peace offering which the Israelite brought to God, and regarded this as his priestly inheritance (explained in detail in Psalm 16). Thus the Lord Jesus is Heir to us as **persons (Psalm 2:8) (i.e. we become His priests functioning within the veil)**. However, He also has become Heir to our **praise (Psalm 16:5-6) as He presents it on our behalf to the Father.** Now we begin to appreciate why the Lord Jesus Who is the Heir to all of this by virtue of being the Son, is described as the One "By Whom also He made the worlds (ages)". In other words, the Lord Jesus as Son not only had the rights to full heirship (i.e. that we should be His priests and He should present our praise), He also has the power in the course of the ages to bring this goal to pass. The Lord Jesus not only created this physical universe, He also created the ages, i.e. the different phases of time through which this universe must run to achieve the goal for which it was ever created. The ultimate objective of this goal is that men should be God's inheritance i.e. be a priestly people **worshipping** in His presence forever. In this regard as far as angels are concerned the Lord Jesus "hath by inheritance obtained a more excellent Name than they" (Hebrews 1:4). Accordingly, Hebrews 1 elaborates this grand theme to show that in a coming day it is not merely angels which **worship** Him on His return (Hebrews 1:6; Psalm 97:7), it will be redeemed mankind (Psalm 97:12). Moreover as One "anointed" "with the oil of gladness above Thy fellows" (Hebrews 1:9) He obtains the **worship of His Bride**, the Church (Psalm 45:11). All of this stems from His death and resurrection, the means whereby the divine program of the ages is guaranteed. No amount of rebellion against the risen Son can hinder or delay God's programme by one millisecond.

One day the nations, which today are in open rebellion against God and His Son, will discover that He is alive and has the power to reclaim the "uttermost parts of the earth" as "His possession". In the coming Kingdom there shall be no pockets of resistance left, for the "uttermost parts of the earth" will be undisputably under His control. He is the rightful Owner, having paid the redemption price at Calvary as will be expanded further in Psalm 24. However, for the rebels who refuse to bow today to the claims of the Son, and who persist in rejection of Him, there will be no mercy in that day.

Psalm 2:9

"Thou shalt break them with a rod of iron; Thou shalt dash them in pieces like a potter's vessel."

They face being broken with a "rod of iron" (Hebrew: **sceptre** of iron). This powerfully symbolizes the authority of the divine King against Whom no power on earth can stand. As mere earthen vessels, evidently perceived as worthless by the potter, they will be smashed in pieces. This is heaven's verdict on the earthly rebellion against the Son of God, the rightful Heir.

The advice is clear in the next verse.

Psalm 2:10
"Be wise now therefore, O ye kings: be instructed, ye judges of the earth."

The Hebrew for "be wise" is the root word from which the Psalm title *"maschil"* or "giving instruction" is derived. It is worth noting that all wisdom and instruction which is of value is based alone upon right thoughts of God's Son. If one is wrong here everything else is "a vain thing"(Psalm 2:1). In his pleading with the kings and judges of the earth, the Psalmist is not merely challenging the world to accept the truth and the evidence concerning His Person, but he goes further. He invites a world of rebels to be reconciled to Him. The result will be undiluted service to Him, out of which comes joy (Psalm 2:11).

Psalm 2:11
"Serve the Lord with fear, and rejoice with trembling."

There is complete obeisance to the Lord in that coming day from all the kings and judges. The fear will be a healthy and holy dread of grieving the Son.

Psalm 2:12
"Kiss the Son, lest He be angry, and ye perish *from* the way, when His wrath is kindled but a little. Blessed *are* all they that put their trust in Him."

"Kiss the Son..." The word here for Son is not the usual Hebrew word *Ben* (used in "Thou art My Son"). It is the Hebrew word *Bar*. This is significant as *Bar* is understood not just in Hebrew, but also in Aramaic, as meaning "Son". Aramaic, as we discover in Ezra and Daniel, was the language of international decrees. When the appeal to be reconciled to Christ goes forth in this Psalm, the use of the internationally understood word *Bar*, indicates that God wants **all** mankind to know about His own Son and to be brought into vital relationship with Him through faith. This reconciliation leads to two results. The first is negative, i.e. that the wrath and anger of God will be escaped ("lest He be angry", "when His wrath is kindled but a little"). Today, the wrath of God in mercy is held back while the gospel news of salvation, through believing on the Son, is heralded forth. All unbelievers will eventually undergo the wrath of God because of their dual rejection of the risen Christ and of the appeal in the gospel to believe in Him for salvation.

The second outcome of being reconciled to the Son is gloriously positive: "... Blessed *are* all they that put their trust in Him" (Psalm 2:12). The phrase "all they" really is just the same as the "whosoever" of John 3:16, where we read that "…whosoever believeth in Him (the Son) should not perish, but have everlasting life".

Conclusion
The early Christians in Acts 4, who were facing persecution and a world

who rejected their Lord and Saviour, would clearly have found great comfort and strength in this Psalm. It presented to them the Risen Son of God as the basis of gospel preaching (Acts 13), the means of worship (Hebrews 5) and the prospect of future glory (Hebrews 1). In face of such a wonderful revelation of divine grace, this Psalm helped them to "serve the Lord with fear and rejoice with trembling" (verse 11). This should be the practical effect of a meditation of this Psalm upon believers in the twenty-first century.

2

Psalm 8

To the chief Musician upon Gittith, A Psalm of David.
1 O Lord our Lord, how excellent is Thy Name in all the earth! Who hast set Thy glory above the heavens.
2 Out of the mouth of babes and sucklings hast Thou ordained strength because of Thine enemies, that Thou mightest still the enemy and the avenger.
3 When I consider Thy heavens, the work of Thy fingers, the moon and the stars, which Thou hast ordained;
4 What is man (enosh), that Thou art mindful of him? and the son of man (ben-adam), that Thou visitest him?
5 For Thou hast made him Note 1 *a little lower than the angels* Note 2*, and hast crowned him*[1] *with glory and honour.*
6 Thou madest him Note 1 *to have dominion over the works of Thy hands; Thou hast put all things under his* Note 1 *feet:*
7 All sheep and oxen, yea, and the beasts of the field;
8 The fowl of the air, and the fish of the sea, and whatsoever passeth through the paths of the seas.
9 O Lord our Lord, how excellent is Thy Name in all the earth!

Introduction

Psalm 1:1

1 "O Lord our Lord, how excellent *is* Thy Name **in all the earth**! Who hast set Thy glory above the heavens".

While it is true throughout history that all believers in the Lord recognise His Name as "excellent", there are many unbelievers in this earth sadly, who still quite openly blaspheme that "excellent" Name. However, this Psalm begins with the Name of the Lord, being globally recognised as "excellent". This is what is meant by "Thy Name" being "excellent" "**in all the earth**". This suggests that the Psalm is envisaging a day when the Lord's Name will be universally glorified by all of earth's inhabitants and not just a faithful minority. We know that this will only happen during the millennial reign of our Lord Jesus Christ. Accordingly, verse 1 sets the scene for the remainder of the Psalm which will describe the wonderful conditions which will pertain when the Man Christ Jesus (1 Timothy 2:5) reigns supreme. In that day the glory of God above the heavens will harmonise with world wide obeisance to the Lord's Name. In that day Old Testament and Tribulation believers will enter into the millennial reign of the Lord Jesus. Satan will be bound and no longer able to influence this world. These aspects of millennial glory are described in Psalm 8:2.

Psalm 8:2

2 "Out of the mouth of babes and sucklings hast Thou ordained strength because of Thine enemies, that Thou mightest still the enemy and the avenger".

Echoes of this concept are found in the millennial vision of Isaiah 11:6 where little children will have power over the animal world.

Isaiah 11:6

"The wolf also shall dwell with the lamb, and the leopard shall lie down with the kid; and the calf and the young lion and the fatling together; and a little child shall lead them."

Clearly in that coming day the babes and sucklings have "power". It was clear then to Old Testament believers that Psalm 8:2 was a future prophecy answering to the millennial events of Isaiah 11:6. When the Lord Jesus quoted from this passage in Matthew 21:15-16, and referred to the "babes and sucklings" of Psalm 8, it was in the context of young children singing His praises as He came into the city. This shows that the phrase "babes and sucklings" in Psalm 8 has, as its primary meaning, children who will be able to have power over a healed creation. However, a detailed study of the scriptural use of the phrase "babes and sucklings" suggests that an even deeper significance is found in Psalm 8:2. For example, in the Old Testament, **the restored remnant** of the future tribulation period are metaphorically referred to as "sucklings" as they enter into the millennial Kingdom, and the Lord personally comforts them in restored Jerusalem.

Isaiah 66:10-13

10 "Rejoice ye with Jerusalem, and be glad with her, all ye that love her: rejoice for joy with her, all ye that mourn for her:
11 That ye **may suck**, and be satisfied with the breasts of her consolations; that ye may milk out, and be delighted with the abundance of her glory.
12 For thus saith the Lord, Behold, I will extend peace to her like a river, and the glory of the Gentiles like a flowing stream: **then shall ye suck**, ye shall be borne upon *her* sides, and be dandled upon *her* knees.
13 As one whom his mother comforteth, so will I comfort you; and ye shall be comforted in Jerusalem."

On the other hand, in the New Testament, a similar but quite distinct word "babe" is used many times to metaphorically refer to Old Testament believers, or New Testament believers in an Old Testament level of knowledge. However because there are several Greek words translated as "babe" a brief review of these words in the English New Testament is appropriate here. Although the intrinsic meaning of these different words is accurately translated "babe", there are some important doctrinal distinctions which emerge in a detailed study of the use of these words in the original Greek New Testament text.

The Hebrew word for "babe" used in Psalm 8:2 is *olel*. When quoted in Matthew 21:16, *nepios* is used, which is the equivalent New Testament Greek word for *olel*. A study of the New Testament occurrences of *nepios* reveals that first century AD Christians used this word **as a metaphorical description of believers equipped only with Old Testament understanding even if they lived in the early New Testament era**. Let us review the evidence.

Galatians 4:1-6
> 1 "Now I say, that the heir, as long as he is a child (*nepios*), differeth nothing from a servant, though he be lord of all;
> 2 But is under tutors and governors until the time appointed of the father.
> 3 Even so we, when we were children (*nepios*), were in bondage under the elements of the world:
> 4 But when the fullness of the time was come, God sent forth His Son, made of a woman, made under the Law,
> 5 To redeem them that were under the Law, that we might receive the adoption of sons.
> 6 And because ye are sons, God hath sent forth the Spirit of His Son into your hearts, crying, Abba, Father."

This passage shows that the word *nepios* includes all believers whose level of dispensational understanding does not go beyond that of Old Testament believers who lived under or prior to the Law, before the accomplishment of redemption at Calvary (verses 4 and 5). Accordingly all Old Testament believers, by this criterion were "babes". Furthermore, unbelievers in the Old Testament, whether Jew or Gentile, were not "babes". It would appear, therefore, from this passage that *nepios* describes the position of all believers prior to the day of Pentecost and those in the days after Pentecost who had not come into the full understanding of the New Testament mystery doctrines. In other words, Abraham, David, Daniel and their believing friends were all "babes". Although they were faithful men of God, they did not enjoy the full privileges of "Sonship" (Galatians 4:5) as every believer enjoys today in this Church age. Therefore, in a positional sense they were "babes" in God's prophetic programme. More importantly, they were unaware of the mystery doctrines revealed and expounded in the New Testament. Clearly, in Galatians 4:3, when Paul says, "Even so we, when we were children (*nepios*), were in bondage under the elements of the world" he is referring, by the use of "we", not primarily to himself but to the faithful element of the nation of Israel before the coming of Christ, i.e. those who were believers before "the fullness of the time was come" when "God sent forth His Son". However, Paul's use of "even so we" shows that there were believers in the era **after** "God sent forth His Son", including himself, who had not come immediately post-conversion into the good of the understanding of sonship and its attendant privileges. Arrival at this state of understanding required the revelation of New Testament mystery doctrines, something which the Lord gave and committed to Paul sometime **after his conversion**, with the charge to deliver onwards to the early Church.

Even before Paul's involvement in this great work the Lord rejoiced at the prospect of the "babes" being given divine revelation.

Luke 10:21
"In that hour **Jesus rejoiced** in spirit, and said, I thank Thee, O Father, Lord of heaven and earth, that Thou hast hid these things from the wise and prudent, and hast revealed them unto **babes**: even so, Father; for so it seemed good in Thy sight."

Here we discover that the Lord was describing the "babes" (*nepioi*) as those who were very soon to receive a divine revelation. In this passage, the "babes" were about to have revealed to them the truth of God as their Father in Luke chapter 11. In the equivalent passage in Matthew 11:25-27, the Lord was rejoicing at the imminent revelation to the "babes" of the mystery doctrines of Matthew 13 as taught in the Kingdom parables.

The opposite of *nepios* or "babe" is to be mature, fully equipped or "of full age" (Hebrews 5:14). It is often translated in the Authorized Version as "perfect" (*teleios*).

Hebrews 5:13-14
13 "For every one that useth milk is unskilful in the word of righteousness: for he is a babe (*nepios*).
14 But strong meat belongeth to them that are of full age (*teleios*), even those who by reason of use have their senses exercised to discern both good and evil."

This word (*teleios*) is used to describe, in a positional way, believers in this New Testament age of grace. These New Testament believers differ from Old Testament believers in that to them have been revealed the mystery doctrines of the New Testament. Key elements of the mystery doctrines include the unique dignity and position of the Church as the Bride and the Body of Christ. Even a believer saved for a short time, in this day of grace is *teleios* compared with Old Testament believers. This is because the New Testament now clearly reveals what had been hidden for centuries in the heart of God. When Paul in the prison epistles is challenging his believing readers to be no more "babes" (*nepioi*), he is calling on them to rise above the Old Testament position of babyhood. They knew nothing of Church privilege and responsibility, until the mystery of Christ and the Church was revealed to them.

Ephesians 4:13-14
> 13 "Till we all come in the unity of the faith, and of the knowledge of the Son of God, unto a **perfect (*teleios*) man**, unto the measure of the stature of the fullness of Christ:
> 14 That we *henceforth* be no more children (*nepios*), tossed to and fro, and carried about with every wind of doctrine, by the sleight of men, *and* cunning craftiness, whereby they lie in wait to deceive;"

At the beginning of the Church era, there were many believers who only understood the Old Testament Scriptures. The mystery doctrines of the New Testament were new to their understanding. God graciously backed up the revelations of the New Testament mystery doctrines by corroborative signs and wonders and miracles. These were, in a sense, used by God to bring these believers from positional "babyhood" (i.e. Old Testament standing) to positional "maturity" (i.e. New Testament standing). That is why Paul, when speaking of the miraculous New Testament gifts, tells us in 1 Corinthians 13:11:

1 Corinthians 13:11
> "When I was a child (*nepios*), I spake as a child (*nepios*), I understood as a child (*nepios*), I thought as a child (*nepios*): but when I became a man, I put away childish things (things of a *nepios*)."

Just as a child (*nepios*) uses toys to hasten its development into maturity and then puts them away, so Paul shows us that, in the early Church, miraculous gifts were needed in the transition from positional babyhood (not knowing the mystery doctrines) to the positional maturity (*teleios*) of knowing the mystery doctrines. The ink has long since dried on the precious parchments on which the prison epistles were written, revealing the mystery of Christ and the Church. As a result, the position of a believer of this dispensation is no longer that of a *nepios*. In other words, one major purpose for which miraculous gifts were given has long been fulfilled. Of course the question needs to be asked if there are still "babes" in Christ. The answer is yes. A new Christian is a babe with regard to **condition**, but no longer a babe as to **position**. He or she is in a position of already enjoying the full privilege of Sonship even though the new convert may not fully understand this! Scripture is exceedingly accurate, and when in 1 Peter 2:2 Peter tells us that "new born babes desire the sincere milk of the word" he is speaking of a new believer in a state of babyhood with respect to **condition** but not **position**. Consequently the word Peter uses is not *nepios*, it is *brephos*.

It appears, therefore, that Psalm 8 is viewing the day when Old Testament saints (**babes**) together with tribulation saints (**sucklings**) will together enter into their earthly inheritance in the millennial earth and will then have dominion over the healed creation. The restoration of the Jewish remnant (sucklings) after the rapture of the Church is considered in more detail in Appendix 3.

Why is the quotation of Psalm 8:2 in Matthew 21:16 changed?

Matthew 21:15-16

15 "And when the chief priests and scribes saw the wonderful things that He did, and the children crying in the temple, and saying, Hosanna to the Son of David; they were sore displeased,

16 And said unto him, Hearest Thou what these say? And Jesus saith unto them, Yea; have ye never read, **Out of the mouth of babes and sucklings Thou hast perfected praise?"**

On this momentous occasion, the leaders in Israel were condemning the children and common people for welcoming the Lord Jesus into Jerusalem as the promised Messiah. The Lord then quotes from Psalm 8: "Out of the mouth of babes and sucklings Thou hast perfected **praise**". He did not quote from the original Hebrew text in Psalm 8: "Thou hast ordained **strength**." "Strength" in Psalm 8, as we have seen, is describing future events in coming millennial glory when man will exhibit strength and power over the healed creation, just as unfallen Adam did in Eden's garden before the entry of sin. The "babes", the Lord was speaking of, included the true believers of His day who did not, at that time, have the privilege of exercising power over the untamed wild animals in creation, as Adam once enjoyed and as the millennial believers will enjoy. Therefore, the Lord used the slightly different Septuagint translation, "Out of the mouth of babes and sucklings Thou hast perfected praise". As the Lord rode into Jerusalem on that occasion it was the "babes" who praised Him although the day when they will have "strength" is still future in the coming Kingdom. Similarly when He comes the second time to Jerusalem it will be the "sucklings" (tribulation believers) who will praise Him even though they will not have the strength or power over the healed creation until the Kingdom is extablished. Thus the Lord's use of the phrase "Out of the mouth of babes and sucklings Thou hast perfected praise" will not be completely fulfilled until the "sucklings" welcome Him to earth in that coming day. It will be after this that the Psalm in the original Hebrew Old Testament passage will find fulfilment when the "babes **and** sucklings" will not only have **praise** but also **power** over all animate creation, reminiscent of conditions in Eden's Garden when Adam moved amongst the largest of living creatures in unchallenged total dominion. Tragically, Adam lost this revered position when he fell by sinning.

The enemy and avenger is stilled

In the millennial Kingdom, the privileges Adam lost in the garden will be restored, namely power over all animate creation including birds, land animals and sea creatures. These Eden Garden privileges before the fall are described in Genesis 1:26-28 and involved man (Adam) having "dominion over the fish of the sea, and over the fowl of the air, and over the cattle, and over all the earth, and over every creeping thing that creepeth upon the earth" (Genesis 1:26). Sadly this wonderful position of dominion was lost through Satan's intervention and man's fall. Psalm 8 tells how Satan, who is the "enemy and the avenger" (Psalm 8:2) will be "stilled" (literally: there will be a Sabbath **rest** from the enemy and the avenger). This will happen in millennial glory where there will be a Sabbath rest from Satan's activities. In the later chapter dealing with Psalm 95 it will become evident that it is to this future millennial Sabbath rest that the Hebrews' writer refers in Hebrews 4:9, "There remaineth therefore a rest (Sabbath Rest) to the people of God". What a day that will be!

Psalm 8:2 brings before us the future millennial events when Satan (the enemy and the avenger) is stilled and the millennial inhabitants again have power over a healed creation similar to the dominion Adam once held in the garden of Eden (Genesis 1:26). When that happens, then the vision of Psalm 8:1 is fulfilled when just as God's glory is set above the heavens i.e. unsurpassed and peerless, so His Name is revered on earth. However, the Psalm describes more than merely stilling "**the enemy** and the avenger" i.e. Satan. It is going to tell us how even the **last enemy**, namely death will be eradicated from the universe of God along with the cause of death, even sin itself. This emerges from the interpretation of the remaining verses of the Psalm provided in Hebrews 2 and 1 Corinthians 15:25 where in a quotation from Psalm 8:6 Paul indicates that "all things" (including death) are put under the feet of the risen and glorified Man, the Lord Jesus Christ.

1 Corinthians 15:25-26
> 25 "For He must reign, till He hath put all enemies under His feet.
> 26 The last enemy *that* shall be destroyed *is* death".

How God intervened to rightify the tragedy of the fall of man

The remaining part of the Psalm tells us how it is that the actions of Satan (the enemy and the avenger) in bringing about the fall of our first parents will be ultimately defeated and reversed. Vividly the Psalmist invites us to accompany him outside as he lifts his eyes heavenward, in what is clearly a cloudless night scene, and with him contemplate the moon and the stars of the middle eastern night sky. The Psalmist's commentary on what he sees is most beautiful. He sees beyond the splendour of the night sky to identify in it all the handywork of the fingers of an Almigthy Creator God. He goes further. He recognises that the universe was created for a purpose and not just a randomly produced phenomenon. Moreover, it is man who is central to the outworking of this purpose.

Psalm 8:3-4
> 3 "When I consider Thy heavens, the work of Thy fingers, the moon and the stars, which Thou hast ordained;
> 4 What is man (*enosh*), that Thou art mindful of him? and the son of man (*ben-adam*), that Thou visitest him?"

The moon and the stars are not just created, they are "ordained" which suggests that God has invested in this universe a **purpose** for its existence. Central to that purpose is that within a perfect universe, man, in fellowship with his God should manage God's fair creation in a sin-free, death free environment such as is described in the rest of the Psalm. That purpose would never be achieved if man were to be left out of God's programme. Sadly due to the fall of man in Eden's garden, this purpose for which the universe was "ordained" had been grievously attacked by the enemy and avenger – Satan. Far from man holding the Lord's Name as "excellent in all the earth", His Holy Name is blasphemed by men on a daily basis. This is all the outcome of the actions of the "enemy and the avenger". How tragic! Nevertheless, Psalm 8:1-3 provides a divine pledge to restore these Eden garden conditions to mankind and it is this which prompts the Psalmist to enquire in wonder as to why once **fallen man** should be returned to such a dignified position. We know that it is fallen man being restored to pre-fall conditions which the Psalmist is considering because the word "man" in Psalm 8:4 is *enosh* which, in its occurrence in the singular (as here), means "frail or mortal man" from the verb *anash* meaning "to be frail or feeble". This is well explained in the introduction to the Newberry Bible as well as in the Lexicon at the end of Strong's Exhaustive Concordance of the Bible. This use of *enosh* in Psalm 8:4 means that this particular verse in the Psalm cannot refer to Adam before the fall since he was not subject to death before sin entered (Romans 5:12). Moreover, the second occurrence of "man" in verse 4 is "son of man" (*adam*) which clearly shows us that the first man, Adam is not the subject of Psalm 8:4, but rather the **fallen posterity** of Adam. There is a tremendous pathos in Psalm 8:4 as it is inquiring as to why the God of heaven should remember and visit in blessing a fallen creature in Psalm 8:4 who had, due to his rebellion and sin, forfeited all the Eden garden dignity of dominion over God's fair creation, so eloquently described in this Psalm. What is there about such a creature that God should visit him in mercy despite all the dire consequences of sin to God's creation? This is the central question of the Psalm. This question is not directly answered in this particular Psalm, but will be addressed in Psalms 16, 69 and 110 where the significance of man being made in the image of God is considered. However, there is a hint as to the answer. It is that God not just created the universe, He "ordained" it, hence giving it purpose. If man was never to be restored to pre-fall conditions then the very purpose of creation itself would have been wholly thwarted. An omnipotent God cannot and would not allow this to happen. This is the reason for the intervention of God in the next verse.

The New Testament exposition of the Psalm in Hebrews 2 indicates that the "visitation" by God to this frail mortal creature (*enosh*) was not a passing encounter or random visit. It involved the Lord Jesus becoming Man in incarnation. The key to understanding the Psalm is in the New Testament interpretation of the "visitation" in the phrase "What is (frail mortal) man...... or the son of (posterity of) man (Adam) **that Thou visitest him**?"

This becomes clear in Hebrews 2:6-8 where Psalm 8:4-6 is quoted, and there the divinely inspired writer goes on to explain that the visitation of God to man in Psalm 8:4 was in fact the **visitation of Christ** to humanity in His incarnation with the objective of delivering frail mortal man from death and its effects so as to restore to man all the dignity of pre-fall conditions and much more besides! By so doing the destiny to which this universe was "ordained" would be achieved.

The Hebrews passage beginning at Hebrews 2:5-9 shows that this was accomplished through the incarnation, death, resurrection and ascension of our Lord Jesus Christ.

Hebrews 2:5-9

5 "For unto the angels hath He not put in subjection **the world to come, whereof we speak**.
6 But one in a certain place testified, saying, What is man, that Thou art mindful of him? or the son of man, that Thou visitest him?
7 Thou madest him Note 1 a little lower than the angels; Thou crownedst him Note 1 with glory and honour, and didst set him Note 1 over the works of Thy hands:
8 Thou hast put all things in subjection under his feet. For in that He put all in subjection under him Note 1, He left nothing *that is* not put under him Note 1. But now we see not yet all things put under him Note 1.
9 But we see Jesus, Who was made a little lower than the angels for the suffering of death, crowned with glory and honour; that He by the grace of God should taste death for every man".

Hebrews 2 shows how that the blissful conditions of Psalm 8:5-8 refer not just to a golden era long since lost in human history but to a future inevitable result of the Divine Visitation to humanity in incarnation. The **future aspect** of the era described in Psalm 8:5-8 is emphasised by it being called "the world to come" in Hebrews 2:5. Accordingly, Hebrews 2 uses Psalm 8:5-8 to emphasise the certainty of the prospect of a coming day when man, once subject to death (i.e. mortal), is now restored to the place of dominion once held by Adam and lost at the fall. This restoration of dominion to a creature previously described as *enosh* (i.e. subject to death) is accompanied by restoration of dignity, for he is "crowned … with glory and honour" (verse 5). This suggests that the era described by the Psalm will envisage human beings on this earth for whom death is now a thing of the past, and all the shame and dishonour attending their mortality (1 Corinthians 15:43-44) has now been replaced by honour.

1 Corinthians 15:43-44

43 "It is sown in **dishonour**; it is raised in **glory**: it is sown in weakness; it is raised in power:
44 It is sown a **natural** body; it is raised a **spiritual** body. There is a **natural** body, and there is a spiritual **body**."

This understanding of the Psalm requires an appreciation of death being vanquished before the ideal conditions described in these verses have become a reality. Of course, this was the triumph of the Lord Jesus' visitation to humanity 2000 years ago when He arose from the dead. Although Hebrews 2 ascribes a prophetic meaning to Psalm 8:5-8, would this future aspect be readily discernible to Old Testament readers or could they only have considered Psalm 8:5-8 as a nostalgic memory to Adam's pre-fall status and privileges? The present author is of the former view, namely that the prophetic aspect of Psalm 8:5-8 was already apparent to the Old Testament reader even before the New Testament inspired commentaries provided by Hebrews 2 and 1 Corinthians 15 clearly indicated a future aspect to Psalm 8:5-8. Firstly, it follows contextually that Psalm 8:5-8 refers to future events since Psalm 8:2 earlier describes a future day when the babes and sucklings would have divinely ordained strength (or power). Secondly it is apparent that it is fallen man (*enosh*) who is the object of the visitation of Psalm 8:4 which is obviously subsequent to Eden's garden. Thirdly, in relation to the statement that "all things are under his (man's) feet" Note 3, Hebrews 2:8 comments that "now we see **not yet** all things put under him" something which is readily apparent to anyone who walks through a zoo and understands the necessity to keep the lions and bears separated from human visitors!

Hebrews 2:8

"Thou hast put all things in subjection under his feet Note 3. For in that he put all in subjection under him, he left nothing that is not put under him. But now we see not yet all things put under him."

The phrase "not yet" indicates that these verses are yet to be fulfilled. However, a fourth reason comes at the end of the Psalm when at the end of the description of a world where man has dominion over a healed creation, the first verse of the Psalm is repeated, which as we have already observed is a vision of the future when Heaven and all of Earth's inhabitants will again be in perfect harmony. All of this future programme of glory flows out of the triumph of the divine visitation to man in Psalm 8:4.

A detailed look at the divine visitation

The transformation from *enosh,* i.e. a creature subject to the indignity of frailty and death and characterised by a body of humiliation (Philippians 3:21), to a creature "crowned with glory and honour" has all arisen from direct divine intervention. Firstly, God "was mindful of" (i.e. remembered) man his fallen creature and secondly, God "visited him". It is this visitation in blessing which ultimately will result in the restoration to man of conditions as they had been before the fall in the Garden of Eden, as well as deliverance from all the humiliation which human frailty involves.

Old Testament believers must have wondered when and how God would "visit" man to bring about these blessings, including victory over death. As we have already suggested their understanding of this may not have been quite as limited as we may sometimes imagine, particularly if we consider the message of Psalms 40 and 69 where David affirms how God would become Man in order to become Kinsman Redeemer to bring about this great deliverance. These passages will be considered later in subsequent chapters.

The profound implications of God visiting man in blessing ("Thou visitest him") (Hebrews 2:6)

How will the prophecies presented in this Psalm be fulfilled? How will Satan be bound and the earth liberated from his influence? The answer lies entirely in the Person of our Lord Jesus Christ and in these key words, "What is man (*enosh* = frail and mortal man) ... that Thou visitest him?"

How sad was man's situation under Satan's dominion and estrangement from God, living in a creation ravaged by sin's catastrophic effects! The good news in our Psalm is that God did not forget such a frail man (*enosh*). The Psalmist is exclaiming in wonder that God should firstly remember (be mindful) and secondly visit such a pathetic creature. The word *pakad* used here for "visit" is used either in visitation of blessing or of judgment. An example of visitation in blessing is in Ruth 1:6 when "the Lord had visited His people in giving them bread". In Psalm 8, the visitation in question is one of blessing which involves liberation of man from the bondage of sin and Satan, including the deeply adverse effects of sin on God's once fair creation. Man is, therefore, delivered from death since it is "frail, mortal man" (*enosh*) who is the objective of a divine blessing, which is so magnificent that it will not end until such a man is crowned with "glory and honour" i.e. all the dishonour of death ended forever (1 Corinthians 15:43-44).

Early christians would have easily understood how that the "visitation" of Psalm 8:4 was the incarnation of the Lord Jesus, followed by His life, death, resurrection and ascension to God's right hand.

However, after these events, and the Lord Jesus' return to His Father the expectation of early christians, especially Hebrew christians that the Kingdom would come quickly, seemed to face a challenge in face of the apparent delay in the fulfilment of so many Old Testament passages speaking of His return to reign. This must have led to some disquiet in their hearts. Would these Old Testament promises be literally fulfilled? The rest of the Psalm proves that the "visitation" of the Lord Jesus to humanity, in fact, **guarantees** the realisation of the divine purpose for man, namely that he should be a creature no longer frail and mortal but characterised by glory and honour, and in a position of dignity in the created universe. However, it is possible that this conclusion from Psalm 8 may have been missed by these early Jewish christians. They may have wondered, could not the Psalm have **already** been fulfilled while Christ was upon earth? Their reasoning may have been as follows: did Christ not clearly demonstrate while on earth that He had dominion over the fowls of the air (the cock crew at His bidding (Matthew 26:74)), the beasts of the field (He rode on the unbroken colt (Matthew 21:2-7)) and whatsoever passes through the paths of the sea (the fish with the tribute money came up at His bidding (Matthew 17:27))? If these historical events in the life of the Lord Jesus constituted the fulfilment of Psalm 8, then it did not carry a future Kingdom significance or so they may have thought. The outcome of such deliberations would have been the development of significant doubt in their minds as to whether the promise of a future Kingdom in manifestation should even be taken literally after all. Bearing in mind that the epistle to the Hebrews was initially addressed to Jewish christians who were being severely persecuted for their faith (Hebrews 10:32-34), any such questioning of a future literal fulfilment of the Old Testament prophecies must have been very discouraging. More worrying though, such amillennial teaching is later defined in Hebrews 3 and 4 as being seriously erroneous and dangerous. This will become especially apparent in our consideration of Psalm 95. The existence of these unscriptural ideas in their midst may well have constituted at least some of the "divers and strange doctrines" spoken of in Hebrews 13:9.

Hebrews 13:9
"Be not carried about with divers and strange doctrines."

Let us look again at the Hebrews quotation of Psalm 8:4-6 (Hebrews 2:6-9). As we read it, we will first of all consider it as a prophecy of man in a future day having dominion over a healed creation.

Hebrews 2:6-9
6 "But one in a certain place testified, saying, **What is man, that Thou art mindful of him? or the son of man, that Thou visitest him?**
7 Thou madest him a little lower than the angels; Thou crownedst him with glory and honour, and didst set him over the works of Thy hands:
8 Thou hast put all things in subjection under his feet. For in that He put all in subjection under him, He left nothing *that is* not put under him. But now we see not yet all things put under him.

Here we see how that a major element in the counter-argument of the Hebrews writer to any who doubted a literal coming earthly Kingdom of Christ, was to reaffirm that the era depicted in Psalm 8 of man, who once was frail, having his dignity restored and having Adamic dominion over all creation, **is yet future** and was not entirely fulfilled by our Lord while upon earth. There are at least two grounds for this argument:

1 "Frail mortal man" (*enosh*) must have a transformation to "glory and honour". Therefore, the Psalm is referring to a period when men (*enosh*), who by the very definition of the word *enosh,* were once subject to death, will be governing the restored millennial earth with physical death defeated, i.e. in resurrected bodies.

2 The second evidence to the future aspect of the Psalm lies in the words "not yet" in Hebrews 2:8.

Hebrews 2:8
"Thou hast put all things in subjection under his feet. For in that He put all in subjection under him, He left nothing *that is* not put under him. But now

we see **not yet** all things put under him."

The phrase "not yet" shows clearly that the conditions of all creation being subject to man have still to take place and were only partially illustrated by the Lord's demonstration of wild animals **obeying Him while on earth.**

The wonder of the divine visitation: that God should become Man

"Made a little lower than the angels" (Hebrews 2:9)

If the Hebrew believers were truly to grasp the wonder of the incarnation, that God should come into humanity, then any doubt as to His ability or sincerity in bringing to fruition all the Old Testament prophecies would vanish. The writer reminds us that man is made "a little lower than the angels".

Psalm 8:5

"For Thou hast made him a little lower (root *chisser*) than the angels Note 2"

A literal translation could be: "For Thou has caused him to experience lack (*chisser*) rather than angels." An example of the word "*chisser*" being used in the context of causing someone to experience "lack" is in Ecclesiastes 4:8 where it is translated "to deprive"

Ecclesiastes 4:8

"For whom do I labour, and **deprive (root *chisser*)** my soul of good?"

This verse shows us that a characteristic of humanity is the ability to experience lack. Hence it is very human to be hungry, thirsty, and in need of sustenance.

The exclamation by the Psalmist is not of wonder that God should have placed man in His creation as a lower order than angels. It is that God should "visit" such a lower rank within His creation. We know that the purpose of the visitation was to abolish death so that man would no longer be *enosh* and subject to death, in its threefold aspects, namely its **principle**, its **power** and its **presence** (see later in this chapter). How can this be? The threefold commentary provided by quotations of Psalm 8:6 in Hebrews 2, 1 Corinthians 15 and Ephesians 1 brings the answer. However, before this threefold problem of death can be addressed there must be a visitation in blessing to frail *enosh* which would involve the Lord Jesus Himself **becoming** man. If man is "a little lower than the angels" and if the Lord Jesus is to "visit" man to bless him, then He also must become "a little lower than the angels".

Hebrews 2:9

"But we see Jesus, **Who was made a little lower than the angels** for the suffering of death, crowned with glory and honour; that He by the grace of God should taste death for every man".

As we have observed, the idea of "becoming a little lower than" carries the literal meaning of "experiencing lack". The verse in the Hebrew does not mean being lower as to character or person, but rather as to circumstances, i.e. being in a situation of experiencing lack. Marvellously, our Lord Jesus experienced this in His life, and thus we read of Him saying "give Me to drink' (John 4:7) and being hungry (Matthew 4:2). Hebrews 2 indicates that if man is "a little lower than the angels" likewise the Lord Jesus voluntarily entered into this. His humanity was real, but sin apart. It is to further explain the nature of the "visitation" that the writer to the Hebrews explains:

Hebrews 2:16
> "For verily He took not on *Him the nature of* angels; but He took on *Him* the seed of Abraham."

This is more wonderful than the divine visit to Abraham in Genesis 18, which was a visitation in judgment to wicked Sodom and Gomorrah. When God visited this world in Christ to bless it, it involved taking on the seed of Abraham in incarnation in order to experience death to deliver us from death. O the wonder of Bethlehem! What a visitation to the human family!

The objective of the visitation: "the suffering of death" and "to taste death for every man"

Hebrews 2:9
> "But we see Jesus, Who was made a little lower than the angels **for the suffering of death,** crowned with glory and honour; that He by the grace of God should taste death for every man."

Arguably, this quotation is given in a poetic form and if we read it as follows perhaps the meaning is clearer:

"We see Jesus, Who was made a little lower than the angels for the suffering of death — that He by the grace of God should taste death for every man — crowned with glory and honour".

It is a cause of wonder to all believers that the visitation of the Lord Jesus Christ should involve Him "experiencing lack" relative to angels, but in no way refers to His intrinsic essential Being which never ceased to be on equality with the Father. However, Hebrews 2 shows us that **this step was necessary** in order that He should experience expiatory suffering and physical death.

"For the suffering of death"
His death would be a death of "suffering". It should be noted that the word "suffering" here is singular. It will be seen in the meditations on Psalm 22 that "suffering", in the singular form, refers to sin-expiating suffering. In contrast, "sufferings" include what He endured at the hands of men and in His "sufferings" believers are called to share (1 Peter 4:13).

1 Peter 4:13
> "But rejoice, inasmuch as ye are partakers of Christ's **sufferings**; that, when

His glory shall be revealed, ye may be glad also with exceeding joy."

Since a believer cannot participate in Christ's suffering (singular) to put away his sin, it is clear that the "suffering of Christ" is propitiating suffering and is finished, whereas the "sufferings of Christ" is a phrase used to describe what He endured at the hands of men and is not finished in as far as believers are still partakers of His sufferings. In Hebrews 2:10, His sufferings (plural) were experiences which qualify Him to be the One Who leads us to glory.

Hebrews 2:10
> "For it became Him, for Whom *are* all things, and by Whom *are* all things, in bringing many sons unto glory, to make the Captain of their salvation perfect through **sufferings**."

Accordingly, there are no sufferings or reproaches for His sake that believers sustain at the hands of men, but of which already He has had first-hand experience. For a detailed description of the definition of "expiation", "propitiation" and "atonement" please see Psalm 22.

"That He by the grace of God should taste death for (on the behalf of) every man"

The key to solving the problem of human mortality (*enosh*) was through His own voluntary death. This would involve destroying him that had the power of death, that is the devil and eventually to "still the enemy and the avenger" (Psalm 8:2).

Hebrews 2 14-16
> 14 "Forasmuch then as the children are partakers of flesh and blood, He also Himself likewise took part of the same; **that through death He might destroy him that had the power of death, that is, the devil;**
> 15 And deliver them who through fear of death were all their lifetime subject to bondage.
> 16 For verily He took not on *Him the nature of* angels; but He took on *Him* the seed of Abraham."

"Crowned with glory and honour"

Now we come to the phrase "crowned with glory and honour". Some suggest that this was fulfilled by our Lord Jesus Christ while upon earth, when, on several occasions, His dominion over His creation was clearly seen. But is this view really accurate? It is here where a careful study of the words used by the Psalmist is helpful. While reaffirming the absolute truth of the record of those occasions when His dominion over creation was seen, we must understand that this is not what is meant by the "glory and honour" (*ve chavod ve hadar*) referred to here. This becomes apparent from a careful study of the use of the Hebrew word for "honour" (*hadar*) in the Old Testament. The key questions we must ask ourselves are:

1 Did our Lord Jesus Christ demonstrate *hadar* while upon earth?

2 Did those occasions when He showed His dominion over animate creation amount to *hadar*?

Isaiah makes clear that in the eyes of Israel the Lord Jesus was not characterised by *hadar*. The prophet says,

Isaiah 53:2
> "…He hath no form nor comeliness (*hadar*); and when we shall see Him,
> *there is* no beauty that we should desire Him."

The word translated "comeliness" (*hadar*) in Isaiah 53:2 simply means "honour or outward majesty or splendour". The Authorised Version rendering – "no comeliness"– perhaps needs an accompanying caveat for the modern reader so as to disclaim any hint of there being limited beauty in our Lord Jesus Christ. The original text does not allow such a thought. Similarly, the following phrase "no beauty" (*lo-mareh*) literally means "no appearance". Scripture does not contradict itself, and when in Psalm 45:2 we read that "Thou art fairer than the children of men," the verse means just that. Why then does Isaiah tell us that the suffering Servant in Isaiah 53 had no *hadar*? We do not have to wait long for an answer. Isaiah goes on to tell us, "and we hid as it were *our* faces from Him; He was despised, and we esteemed Him not" (Isaiah 53:3). This could be equally accurately translated, "He hid as it were His face from us, He was despised, and we esteemed Him not!" What an amazing spectacle! Why was the Lord hiding Himself? Certainly this was not through fear of men. In the gospel account we read several times of Him hiding Himself (John 8:59;12:36) – but this is only in wondrous grace lest His majesty and splendour (His *hadar*) should burst forth and consume unbelievers around Him. Isaiah must have been filled with wonder and worship as he described how that the Throne Sitter of Isaiah chapter 6, should veil His *hadar* in chapter 53, to the extent of hiding His face from men, who really ought to be hiding from Him.

Of course His *hadar* is no longer veiled today. In the studies of other Messianic Psalms it will be seen that our Lord Jesus Christ on His **resurrection, ascension** (Psalm 110) and **return to reign** (Psalm 45) is characterised by *hadar* and the result will be catastrophic judgment for the Christ rejecters. However, in grace, while upon earth, He hid His face, and thus He was perceived as having no *hadar*. Today, though, He is risen and is in heaven. The writer to the Hebrews is happy to tell us that **now** He is "crowned with glory and honour" (*hadar*) – although Isaiah will remind us that He did not openly show His *hadar* to Israel prior to His crucifixion. Only at His transfiguration was there a private viewing of His *hadar* to the three apostles.

The meaning of Psalm 8 is beginning to emerge. As far as mankind is concerned, the day is coming, but "not yet", when during the millennial reign of our Lord Jesus Christ, this world will be populated by human beings, no longer in bodies of humiliation but characterised by "glory and honour" (*hadar*). However, Scripture is clear that the **first Person** to be crowned with glory and honour (*hadar*) after the fall of Adam in the Garden is the risen Man, the Lord Jesus Christ (Psalms 45 and 110). Hebrews 2 makes clear that only as a result of His visitation to mankind in incarnation, and His victory over death in arising from the dead as the risen Man Who is crowned with glory and honour can the rest of the Psalm be fulfilled in the experience of the redeemed believers. This fulfilment of the Psalm will be seen when redeemed mankind enters into the victory of the Lord Jesus by experiencing deliverance from mortality (i.e. resurrection) and all the indignity which sin, disease and death bring. The Psalmist is filled with wonder at the thought that frail man (*enosh*) should one day be like unto our Lord Jesus Christ, Who is today on the throne, crowned with glory and honour (*hadar*). In other words, just as the risen Lord Jesus is crowned with glory and honour, redeemed mankind will be also brought into this dignity with Him as a result of His victory.

J.N. Darby described it aptly in his hymn,

> And is it so, I shall be like Thy Son,?
> Is this the grace which He for me has won?
> Father of glory! Thought beyond all thought,
> In glory to His own blest likeness brought!

This will be evidenced by their having dominion over creation in conditions reminiscent of Eden's garden (Genesis 1:26). However, during the millennium death still will happen to those who rebel against the King, i.e. those who are born into the millennium who do not get saved and rebel against Christ. This means that in the millennium, Eden garden conditions have **not been fully restored** because death is ever a possibility in this specific context, and sin still happens. The millennium is not a sin-free environment. Psalm 8 tells us that in this future scene of Glory, with regard to the Ideal Man described in the Psalm it will be said "Thou hast put all things under His feet". Clearly throughout the long years of the millennium, death has not yet been subjugated. However, if the phrase "Thou has put all things under His feet" is to find complete fulfilment, then this final condition of death being obliterated from the presence of this universe has to happen. The person under Whose feet death will be subjugated, in all its aspects, is the Ideal Man, the Risen One, the Lord Jesus Christ! According to 1 Corinthians 15:25 this happens **at the end** of the millennium.

"All things under His Feet" and the victory over death

This quotation from the Psalm is presented three times in the New Testament, in 1 Corinthians 15:27, Hebrews 2:8 and Ephesians 1:22.

1 Corinthians 15:24-28

> 24 "Then *cometh* the end, when He shall have delivered up the Kingdom to God, even the Father; when He shall have put down all rule and all authority and power.

25 For He must reign, till He hath put all enemies under His feet.

26 The last enemy *that* shall be destroyed *is* death.

27 For **He hath put all things under His feet**. But when He saith, all things are put under *Him, it is* manifest that He is excepted, which did put all things under Him.

28 And when all things shall be subdued unto Him, then shall the Son also Himself be subject unto Him that put all things under Him, that God may be all in all."

Hebrews 2: 8

"**Thou hast put all things in subjection under His feet**. For in that He put all in subjection under Him, He left nothing *that is* not put under Him. But now we see not yet all things put under Him."

Ephesians 1:22

"And **hath put all *things* under His feet**, and gave Him *to be* the Head over all *things* to the Church"

In 1 Corinthians 15: 27 we read "He (i.e. God) hath put all things under His (Christ's) feet". Similarly in Ephesians 1:22 it is God Who "hath put all things under His feet". It is so delightful to note that in both these passages it is **the subjugation of death** which is in view. It is not just a Man Who has all things under His feet, it is a **Risen Man** Who has utterly defeated death itself. Accordingly, in Ephesians 1:22 the context is of the Lord Jesus **defeating death** on the occasion of His resurrection. In 1 Corinthians 15:27 the context is of the Lord Jesus **abolishing death** from this universe **at the end** of the millennium. Hebrews 2:8 again reminds us that to this Ideal Man, God has "put all things in subjection under His feet" and that this is an all inclusive decree. However Hebrews 2:8 also shows us that this decree is "not yet" completely fulfilled in the comment, "But now we see not yet all things put under Him." Thus Hebrews 2:8 straddles the promise of Ephesians 1:22 which found fulfilment in the resurrection and ascension of our Lord Jesus Christ 2000 years ago, as well as the future promise of death being abolished at the end of the millennium in 1 Corinthians 15:27. How encouraging it is for us to know that such an omnipotent Man, Who has defeated death in **principle** 2000 years ago (Ephesians 1:22), and Who will abolish **the presence of death** in a coming day (1 Corinthians 15:27) is our High Priest today Who has destroyed him who has the **power of death** namely the devil (Hebrews 2:14). To God be the glory!

When Adam was in the garden in his unfallen state, he was in dominion over all things and death was nowhere to be seen. Catastrophically, this position of honour was lost to Adam and the whole human family by the fall. Thereafter, man was described as *enosh* – subject to frailty and death. Hebrews 2:8 makes clear that to Christ alone, as the perfect Man, belongs the right to have all things put under His feet by God, His Father. However, just as Adam's fall robbed the whole human race of dominion in God's creation, so the death and resurrection of Christ, as the Perfect Man, restores this to the Old Testament and millennial saints (babes and sucklings). They will have made a transition from a state of mortality (*enosh* i.e. subjection to death) to a state of deliverance from death all because of the visitation of God in Christ. This will be manifest in that day when "out of the mouths of babes and sucklings" will come "strength" (power) (Psalm 8:2).

However, when we read in I Corinthians 15:27 that "He hath put all things under His feet", specifically what is in view is death itself. Living saints who enter the millennium cannot die. Those of their children who become saved during the millennium cannot die. This is because there is no further resurrection of the just. Why then does death still remain to be subjugated in the millennium? The reason is that the living saints who enter at the start of the millennium will have children, some of whom, sadly, will not get saved. Such individuals, if persistent in unbelief, are at risk of death. However, since we learn that God will put all enemies under His feet, and that death is the last enemy, this means that death must eventually be abolished from creation. This requires bringing an end to the millennial era so that no others can be born in an unsaved state who have the potential to refuse to trust Christ and thus die. Since putting "all things under His feet" must include death being banished from the environment of God's people, there is a requirement for this universe to be folded up and the eternal state to be inaugurated, where there shall be no sin or potential of sin or death. This is what is meant by:

1 Corinthians 15:24
"Then *cometh* the end, when He shall have delivered up the Kingdom to God, even the Father; when He shall have put down all rule and all authority and power."

1 Corinthians 15:55-56 indicates that the cause (sting) of death is sin.

1 Corinthians 15:55-56
55 "O death, where *is* thy sting? O grave, where *is* thy victory?
56 The sting of death *is* sin; and the strength of sin *is* the Law."

At the end of the millennium the Lord Jesus not merely obliterates death from the scene, He obliterates the cause of death, i.e. sin itself. If He is to put all things including the last enemy (death), beneath His feet, then the cause and sting of death, namely sin, must be abolished. This shows us how that the saints who entered the millennium with bodies capable of sinning albeit not permitted to die will eventually prior to the eternal state be delivered from the very possibility of sinning itself, something which those who are in the Church at the rapture before the tribulation and those who have been raised from the dead at the end of the tribulation will already have entered into at least 1000 years earlier. This is perhaps one of the positive aspects which will bring comfort to tribulation saints who die for their faith, that their battle with sin is over and in resurrection bodies in the millennium they will not have to conflict with sinful desires ever again.

Whether the victory over sin and death is entered into (1) at the rapture for the Church, or (2) the resurrection of Old Testament and tribulation saints at the end of the tribulation, or (3) the abolition of sin and death from the experience of the millennial saints in preparation for the eternal state, all will in unison acknowledge that this great triumph arises only from the Perfect Man Who as part of His visitation to man became "a little lower than the angels" in incarnation that He might taste death for us.

Psalm 8 gives us a glimpse into the millennium when the animal world will once more be in subjection to men as was the case in Eden's garden. This answers to Isaiah's literal prophecy of Isaiah 11:6-9.

Isaiah 11:6-9
> 6 "The wolf also shall dwell with the lamb, and the leopard shall lie down with the kid; and the calf and the young lion and the fatling together; and a little child shall lead them.
> 7 And the cow and the bear shall feed; their young ones shall lie down together: and the lion shall eat straw like the ox.
> 8 And the sucking child shall play on the hole of the asp, and the weaned child shall put his hand on the cockatrice' den.
> 9 They shall not hurt nor destroy in all My holy mountain: for the earth shall be full of the knowledge of the Lord, as the waters cover the sea."

However, 1 Corinthians 15:27 shows us that Psalm 8 sees beyond the millennium to the eternal state when death and its cause (sin) will be among the "all things" which He has put "under His feet". Note 3

Later in this book, Psalms 89 and 102 give us a further glimpse into the eternal state when the third heaven, i.e. the eternal and uncreated abode of God comes down to tabernacle on the New Earth.

Revelation 21:2-4
> 2 "And I John saw the holy city, new Jerusalem, coming down from God out of heaven, prepared as a Bride adorned for her Husband.
> 3 And I heard a great voice out of heaven saying, Behold, the tabernacle of God *is* with men, and He will dwell with them, and they shall be His people, and God Himself shall be with them, *and be* their God.
> 4 And God shall wipe away all tears from their eyes; and there shall be no more death, neither sorrow, nor crying, neither shall there be any more pain: for the former things are passed away."

Even then the distinction between the celestial redeemed people of the Church (who will enjoy unending residence of the eternal celestial temple city now on earth) and the terrestrial redeemed people who will inhabit the New Earth will be retained. However, at the eternally open gates (Revelation 21:25) of the heavenly city now on earth there will be free communication of the saints of the Church era (the celestial ones) and all the other redeemed ones of every age (the terrestrial ones) forever and ever (Revelation 21:24). What a day of glory that is going to be! Note 4

Conclusion

Christ, the Immortal One, had come to make a visitation of blessing to "frail mortal man" (*enosh*). To do so, He veiled His glory (*hadar*) and by death defeated death. Now, in resurrection He stands the Head of a new creation in all His *hadar* which, according to 1 Corinthians 15, will eventually culminate in the eternal state, free from sin and death "with all things under His feet". With this Glorified Man in a death-free universe we will reign in glory with bodies like unto His, characterised by "glory and honour (*hadar*)". In the New Earth there will be no dissenting voices to the grand chorus:

Psalm 8:9

"O Lord our Lord, How excellent is Thy Name in all the earth!"

1. In verses 5-8 the Psalmist is referring to man in general who in future glory will enjoy Eden garden type privileges of dominion over creation. Hence in Psalm 8:5-8, occurrences of "him" (verses 5 and 6) and "his" (verse 6) are in lower case. However, when this passage is expounded in Hebrews 2 it is seen there that the Lord Jesus, is the first Man in Whom these verses are fulfilled. This all flows from His visitation to humanity as the perfect and ideal Man Who defeated death and Satan and thus re-established all that which was lost by the fall in Eden's garden and much more besides. If the verses are read with that particular meaning, then the pronouns "him" and "his" in verses 5-6 should be read as "Him" and "His". It is worth reminding ourselves that in the original Hebrew text there was no distinction between upper and lower case. Since the passage refers to redeemed humanity in general who will benefit from the Lord's victory, and the Lord Jesus in particular Who brings about the victory, it is legitimate to read Psalm 8:5-6 with both meanings in mind as both are contextually accurate. This is discussed in the text.

2. "lower than the angels" is sometimes translated "lower than God". This is because the word for "angels" here is *elohim* in Hebrew, which usually is translated as "God". However, there are specific occasions when *elohim* does not mean God and this is discussed in Psalm 82. This is such an example, and the New Testament translation of Psalm 8:5 as "lower than angels" in Hebrews 2:9 is quite correct, and removes any doubt as to how the verse is to be understood in the Old Testament.

3. Not only will redeemed mankind in that coming day enjoy being "crowned with glory and honour", but Romans 16:20 foresees the day when "The God of peace will bruise Satan **under your feet shortly**" which is no doubt included in the prophetic description of redeemed man having "all things under his feet" (Psalm 8:6). However, redeemed mankind can only **fully** enter into the victory prophesied in Psalm 8:5-6 when the Ideal Man, the Lord Jesus Christ, first has had all things put under **His nail pierced feet** and this includes Satan and death itself.

4. Today, all mankind are 'earthy ones', like the 'earthy one' who is Adam (1 Corinthians 15:48). After the rapture for the Church, 'celestial ones' ('they also that are heavenly') make up the Church (1 Corinthians 15:48) and are then like Christ, 'the Celestial One'. In contrast to the 'celestial ones' are the 'terrestrial ones' (1 Corinthians 15:40), who have an earthly (terrestrial) inheritance. These are believers who died in the Old Testament and tribulation eras and who rise from the dead on the return of the Lord Jesus to the earth at the end of the tribulation.

3

PSALM 16

Michtam of David.
1 "Preserve Me, O God: for in Thee do I put My trust.
2 O My soul, Thou hast said unto the Lord, Thou art My Lord: My goodness extendeth not to Thee;
3 But to the saints that are in the earth, and to the excellent, in whom is all My delight.
4 Their sorrows shall be multiplied that hasten after another god: their drink offerings of blood will I not offer, nor take up their names into My lips.
5 The Lord is the portion of Mine inheritance and of My cup: Thou maintainest My lot.
6 The lines are fallen unto Me in pleasant places; yea, I have a goodly heritage.
7 I will bless the Lord, Who hath given Me counsel: My reins also instruct Me in the night seasons.
8 I have set the Lord always before Me: because He is at My right hand, I shall not be moved.
9 Therefore My heart is glad, and My glory rejoiceth: My flesh also shall rest in hope.
10 For Thou wilt not leave My soul in hell; neither wilt Thou suffer Thine Holy One to see corruption.
11 Thou wilt shew Me the path of life: in Thy presence is fullness of joy; at Thy right hand there are pleasures for evermore."

Background

In Psalm 2 we saw that the eternal Sonship of Christ is proven by His resurrection from the dead. In Psalm 16, His resurrection from the dead is presented as evidence for His Holy character. In other words, in Psalm 2, His resurrection testifies to His Person, namely Who He is – the Son ("Thou art My Son"). In Psalm 16, His resurrection testifies as to His Character, namely He is Holy ("Thine Holy One"). The particular aspect of His holy character being revealed here is His ministry as the Great High Priest, which demonstrates the "Goodness" of God.

The revelation of God to men

Psalm 16:1-3
> 1 "Preserve Me, O God: for in Thee do I put My trust.
> 2 *O My soul*, Thou hast said unto the Lord, Thou *art* My Lord: My goodness *extendeth* not to Thee;
> 3 *But* to the saints that *are* in the earth, and *to* the excellent, in whom *is* all My delight."

How could God reveal to men His divine character and His Goodness? Moses desired such a revelation, and God granted him his desire in a limited way. As Moses stood in the "clift of the rock" (Exodus 33:22), God caused His divine Goodness to pass before him. However, it was only the hinder aspect of this awesome revelation of the divine presence that he was permitted to glimpse, as God safely sheltered him with His hand.

Exodus 33:17-23
> 17 "And the Lord said unto Moses, I will do this thing also that thou hast spoken: for thou hast found grace in My sight, and I know thee by name.
> 18 And he said, I beseech Thee, shew me Thy glory.
> 19 And He said, I will make **all My goodness** pass before thee, and I will proclaim the Name of the Lord before thee; and will be gracious to whom I will be gracious, and will shew mercy on whom I will shew mercy.
> 20 And He said, Thou canst not see My face: for there shall no man see Me, and live.
> 21 And the Lord said, Behold, *there is* a place by Me, and thou shalt stand upon a rock:
> 22 And it shall come to pass, while My glory passeth by, that I will put thee in a clift of the rock, and will cover thee with My hand while I pass by:
> 23 And I will take away Mine hand, and thou shalt see My back parts: but My face shall not be seen."

In this Psalm, we learn that God has a program whereby His Goodness should be revealed to men. This revelation of the Goodness of God to men could only come through the advent to earth of One Who is Holy and yet Who displays the characteristics of a perfect and dependent Man. This stands in complete contrast to Adam when he fell, and subsequently to the entire human family, which by nature acts independently of God.

Accordingly, therefore, the Psalm begins with the Lord Jesus speaking in all the beauty and perfection of dependent manhood:

Psalm 16:1
> "Preserve Me, O God: for in Thee do I put My trust."

Sadly, in this matter of dependence on God, so many Old Testament worthies of faith at times faltered. Well known examples of this include Abraham going down to Egypt in time of famine, Moses striking the rock instead of speaking to it, and the sad occasion of David numbering the people. In contrast, the Lord Jesus, as God manifest in flesh, at all times was seen in absolute dependence on His Father. He never stepped outside this sublime relationship. This would have been impossible. We are privileged by the Psalmist to eavesdrop into a conversation between the Son and the Father.

Psalm16:2-3

2 "*O My soul*, Thou hast said unto the Lord, Thou *art* My Lord: My goodness *extendeth* not to Thee;
3 *But* to the saints that *are* in the earth, and *to* the excellent, in whom *is* all My delight."

The Lord Jesus speaks to the Father: "Thou art My Lord!" This is the language of the dependent and obedient One. It follows from this that there is no questioning as to His going on the mission of revealing God's heart to men.

In this conversation between the Son and the Father, the Son expresses the movement of His Person: it is to move outward to men in order that God's character, i.e. His divine Goodness, should be revealed to men. "My Goodness extendeth not (only) to Thee; but to the saints which are upon the earth…." How grateful we should be that God has been fully revealed to men in the Person of His Eternal Son, Who is "the brightness of *His* glory, and the express image of His person" (Hebrews 1:3). Let us not forget that it was in the guise of this lovely dependent Man, moving on earth, that the Goodness of God was fully revealed to men, having been only partially unveiled to Moses.

However, the Psalm shows us that this wondrous revelation of His character would not be appreciated by all. The "saints that are in the earth" would appreciate it, as well as the "excellent (ones) in whom is all My delight". Throughout time, there has always been a faithful remnant of "saints", i.e. believers who longed for the coming of Christ, and since His manifestation 2000 years ago there still are "saints" who continue to rejoice in this. The affection in which the Saviour holds His saints throughout the centuries is clear. In the eyes of the world, the saints may be insignificant, but in the eyes of the risen Christ, they are "excellent" or "noble" and the object of His delight. The phrase, "in whom is My delight", in Hebrew is *chephtsi-v-am* (literally: My pleasure is in them). One is reminded of similar language used to describe Jerusalem in millennial glory, when He refers to the city as *chephtsi-v-ah* (literally: My pleasure is in her (Hephzibah)) (Isaiah 62:4). The word "excellent" also carries the idea of "famous" or "well known" (Psalm 136:18). The phrase is teaching us that in the eyes of heaven, the saints are by no means strangers. They are "well known", and no doubt this shall be in evidence in a coming day when He will not be ashamed of His saints in coming glory! Thus, in these verses we learn that it is Christ's desire that the full character of God should in Himself be revealed to the saints and, as the grateful recipients of such divine illumination, His saints have become the objects of divine pleasure. Breathtaking words!

Psalm 16:4

"Their sorrows shall be multiplied *that* hasten *after* another *god:* their drink offerings of blood will I not offer, nor take up their names into My lips."

Amazingly, though, not all will be appreciative of such divine favours. In self-willed rejection of the revealed One, "their sorrows shall be multiplied who hasten after another!" Why should man not only reject the revealed Saviour of 2000 years ago but then hasten after another? The Psalm does not suggest an answer, but the next phrase implies that part of the problem lies in the age-old human tendency to reject the divine requirement for unswerving obedience, submission and faith and, conversely, to follow idolatrous religious pursuit: "Their drink offerings of blood…" Throughout the pre-Babylonish history of Israel, many within that privileged nation were constantly seduced into idolatry. This happened despite the wonderful revelations of God in His Word through His servants, the prophets. The result lay only in multiplied sorrow for all those involved. ("Their sorrows shall be multiplied that hasten after another…"). One day, the Lord Jesus, having publicly declared to the nation His claim to be Messiah, went on to reveal that "if another shall come in his own name, him ye will receive" (John 5:43). These words are yet to be fulfilled, when, in a day still future, many in the beleaguered nation of Israel will be conned into accepting a false messiah – "another" who will "come in his own name".

Alas, for such who reject Him, hasten after another and engage in the idolatrous worship which this entails, there shall be the dreadful prospect of Him, in turn, rejecting them. He will not "take up their names" into His lips. What a tragedy to hear Him say,

Matthew 7:23

"I never knew you: depart from Me, ye that work iniquity."

It is clear that the revelation of Christ and His Goodness to men has two results. Either He is accepted by the "saints" whom He tenderly describes as the "excellent ones in whom is all My delight", or He is rejected by those "who hasten after another", multiplying to themselves sorrows in the process and eventually being rejected by the Saviour Himself.

The cost to Christ of revealing God's Goodness to men

Psalm 16:5-6

5 "The Lord *is* the portion of Mine inheritance and of My cup: Thou maintainest My lot.
6 The lines are fallen unto Me in pleasant *places;* yea, I have a goodly heritage."

Christ revealed God's Goodness to mankind by becoming a Priest. The realisation of this office required His death, burial, resurrection **and** ascension to God's right hand. Psalm 16 describes all of these events in the Lord's journey from the Father's side to this earth and then back to the Father at God's right hand. It was all necessary for Him to become our Great High Priest. This truth is discussed in further detail in our meditations of Psalms 40 and 110 but is being gently introduced to us in this Psalm.

In verse 5, He takes upon His lips, what the Lord had said to Aaron many years earlier, when He detailed to him the nature of his inheritance. The rest of the nation of Israel was allocated land in the Promised Land in Numbers 18, but to Aaron and his sons the inheritance was quite different.

Numbers 18:19-20

> 19 "All the heave offerings of the holy things, which the children of Israel offer unto the Lord, have I given thee, and thy sons and thy daughters with thee, by a statute for ever: it *is* a covenant of salt for ever before the Lord unto thee and to thy seed with thee.
> 20 And the Lord spake unto Aaron, Thou shalt have no inheritance in their land, neither shalt thou have any part among them: **I** *am* **thy part and thine inheritance** among the children of Israel."

The Lord was the portion of Aaron's inheritance. In practice, this meant that as Aaron presented the sacrifices of the people to God at the altar, he was granted a portion of the sacrifice for himself and his family. In other words, as Aaron presented the worship of the people to God, Aaron received his portion; in fact it could be said of Aaron that the Lord was the portion of his inheritance.

Why then should the Lord Jesus Christ use such graphic language at this point in the Psalm? In the previous statement, He is, of course, speaking of Himself as a Priest, refusing to offer certain sacrifices of the people because they were idolatrous ("Their drink offerings of blood will I not offer" (Psalm 16:4)). However, now, by way of a happy contrast, He is speaking of His role in presenting worship which is acceptable to God. Like Aaron, He Himself receives His portion for He says: "The Lord *is* the portion of Mine inheritance and of My cup".

Let us never forget, that as we pray to the Father in the Name of the Lord Jesus Christ, He, as our Great High Priest, presents our worship and praise to the Father. In so doing, He receives the portion which is His by right. By praying to the Father through Him, as we are instructed to do at all times in Ephesians 5:20 and Colossians 3:17, we do not rob Him of glory; rather we ascribe to Him the glory which is rightly His.

Now we are beginning to observe the symmetry of the thought-flow of Psalm 16. Verses 2-3 tell us of the Lord Jesus in His role, extending the revelation of His Goodness to men, and then in verses 5-6 we see Him presenting the worship of the saints to God and receiving His portion from it. In this sense, we see Him acting in priestly capacity, representing God to men and representing the saints to God.

Once again, this sacred office of Priest is something which God has reserved for Him irrespective of the rejection of men. Consequently, the Saviour says, "Thou maintainest My lot". The word "to maintain", means to hold on to and support. In other words, the rebellion of this world and the subsequent rejection of the Son shall not deflect the divine objective of the Lord Jesus from presenting His people's praise to the Father eternally. Moreover this inheritance of worship is pleasant to the Lord

Psalm 16:6

"The lines are fallen unto Me in pleasant *places;* yea, I have a goodly heritage."

In Psalm 2 we saw how that His inheritance was the "heathen" and "the uttermost parts of the earth" were His "possession". This is an inheritance fit for a King and will be particularly seen in the coming Kingdom. In Psalm 16:5, the phrase "The Lord *is* the portion of Mine inheritance and of My cup" clearly refers to His priestly ministry which was effective from the moment of His ascension to God's right hand. How delightful it is for us today to remember that as He presents to His Father the praises of His people, He receives His portion. This is an inheritance fit for the Great High Priest. Sublimely, as the Lord Jesus lingers on **this theme**, there arises, from His lips, worship to the Father.

Psalm 16:7

"I will bless the Lord, Who hath given Me counsel: My reins also instruct Me in the night seasons."

One cannot but reflect here on those night seasons when the Saviour continued in prayer with His Father. The "reins" (kidneys) in Scripture are used figuratively of the seat of the emotions (Proverbs 23:16; Job 19:27; Psalm 73:21). In Hebrews 2:18 and 4:15 we are reminded of the feelings of Christ.

Hebrews 2:17-18

17 "Wherefore in all things it behoved Him to be made like unto *His* brethren, that He might be a merciful and faithful High Priest in things *pertaining* to God, to make reconciliation for the sins of the people.
18 For in that **He Himself hath suffered being tempted**, He is able to succour them that are tempted."

Hebrews 4:15

"For we have not an High Priest **Which cannot be touched with the feeling** of our infirmities;"

The Lord Jesus' priestly ministry is the outworking of the eternal counsels of God (Psalm 16:7). Moreover, through His priestly ministry we experience the display of the feelings of kindness (reins) of the Lord Jesus towards us every step of our lives. When we read of the Lord giving Him "counsel", this does not suggest that the Lord Jesus lacked omniscience. Note 1 The "counsel" referred to in verse 7 is the ongoing continuation of the eternal counsels of God in eternity past, and the display of these counsels is the program of redemption, especially the Lord Jesus becoming our High Priest. Psalm 16:8 shows us that the counsel referred to in verse 7, was on the basis of **equality** between the Lord Jesus and the Father.

Psalm 16:8

"I have set (*shivviti*) the Lord always before Me: because *He is* at My right hand, I shall not be moved."

The verb "I have set"(*shivviti*) (in the *Piel* form of the root *shavah*) literally means "to set as an equal". In Isaiah 28:25, the prophet uses the same grammatical form of the same verb *shavah* to describe the ploughman preparing the land for seed and **levelling** the ground. He tells us that the ploughman working the ground "hath made plain (*shivvah*) (made level) the face thereof". In the causative active (*Hiphil*) form of the same verb it is translated "equal" in Lamentations 2:13, "…What shall I liken to thee O daughter of Jerusalem? What shall I **equal** to thee (root = *shavah*), that I may comfort thee, O virgin daughter of Zion?"

Accordingly, the phrase, "I have set (*shivviti*) (as an equal) the Lord always before My face", is a powerful statement of the equality of the Son with the Father. Since this passage brings before us the counsels of God, it is touching that the One Who is **always** on equality with the Father should now, as the perfect dependent Man, speak prophetically of His impending death and resurrection. There is no doubt that Philippians 2:5-11 expresses in New Testament language this same truth and Psalm 16 may have been in the mind of the apostle Paul as he wrote concerning Christ that He "thought it not robbery to be equal with God".

Philippians 2:5-11

5 "Let this mind be in you, which was also in Christ Jesus:

6 Who, being in the form of God, thought it not robbery to be equal with God:

7 But made Himself of no reputation, and took upon Him the form of a servant, and was made in the likeness of men:

8 And being found in fashion as a man, He humbled Himself, and became obedient unto death, even the death of the cross.

9 Wherefore God also hath highly exalted Him, and given Him a Name which is above every name:

10 That at the Name of Jesus every knee should bow, of *things* in heaven, and *things* in earth, and *things* under the earth;

11 And *that* every tongue should confess that Jesus Christ *is* Lord, to the glory of God the Father."

God's thoughts and counsels had in mind the revelation of the Person of Christ as being **always** on equality with God and yet coming to live a perfect life on earth as a dependent Man, so as to take on as Priest the great honour of being the revealer of God's Goodness to men and the presenter of men's worship to God. The outworking of these counsels required His death, **resurrection** from the dead and ascension to God's right hand as is further developed in Psalms 40 and 110.

Psalm 16:9

"Therefore My heart is glad, and My glory rejoiceth: My flesh also shall rest in hope."

This is ground so holy that commenting on such a verse seems to detract from the language. We are permitted to hear the Lord Jesus, prior to His death and resurrection, communing with His Father with intense joy over the impending victory of His death and resurrection triumph. These are the words of "Thine Holy One" and His innermost feelings and joys are opened to us here. This calls forth worship in His presence.

The triumph of His resurrection

Psalm 16:10

"For Thou wilt not leave My soul in hell (*Sheol*); neither wilt Thou suffer Thine Holy One to see corruption."

Where and what is Sheol?

The word *Sheol* occurs 66 times in the Old Testament. Sometimes it is translated "hell", other times as "the grave". A careful study of the contextual use of the word would prevent us from translating *Sheol* as "the grave" in Psalm 16. For example, in Genesis 37:33, Jacob is in deep mourning believing that "an evil beast" had devoured Joseph his son.

Genesis 37:35

"And all his sons and all his daughters rose up to comfort him; but he refused to be comforted; and he said, For I will go down into the grave (*Sheol*) unto my son mourning. Thus his father wept for him."

Clearly, it is inappropriate to consider *Sheol* here as referring to the grave. As far as Jacob was concerned, Joseph's supposed grave was the inside of a wild animal. When Jacob said that he would go down into *Sheol* unto his son, he did not expect to end his life in the stomach of the same wild animal. Rather he was referring to *Sheol* as the abode of the departed Spirits. If *Sheol* is translated as "hell" on so many occasions, why is it that Old Testament saints speak of themselves going to *Sheol*? For example, in Genesis 37:35 Jacob clearly knew he would go to *Sheol*. Hezekiah in Isaiah 38:10, likewise was clear on this. During his illness he said:

Isaiah 38:10

"I said in the cutting off of my days, I shall go to the gates of the grave (*Sheol*): I am deprived of the residue of my years."

The answer to this lies in the very clear distinction which Scripture makes between *"Sheol* beneath*"* and *Sheol*. In fact, wherever we read of *Sheol* accompanied by an expression regarding its **depth**, we are speaking of the abode of **the lost** in the Old Testament. There are several examples:

1 Concerning the wicked king of Babylon, it is said:

Isaiah 14:9
"Hell **from beneath** is moved for thee to meet *thee* at thy coming."

2 Solomon speaks of the destiny of those who lead immoral lives:

Proverbs 9:17-18
17 "Stolen waters are sweet, and bread *eaten* in secret is pleasant.
18 But he knoweth not that the dead *are* there; *and that* her guests *are* in the **depths** of hell (*Sheol*)."

3 In Deuteronomy 32:22 we read,
"For a fire is kindled in Mine anger, and shall burn unto the **lowest hell** (*Sheol*)…"

This indicates that the "lowest" *Sheol* is a place of divine judgment and burning fire.

4 Moreover, although David, like Jacob and Hezekiah, knew that one day he would be in Sheol, he was thankful that he would never be in the lowest Sheol:

Psalm 86:13
"For great *is* Thy mercy toward me: and Thou hast delivered my soul from the **lowest hell** (*Sheol*)."

5 Similarly, Solomon warns his readers to be wise regarding their eternal destiny:

Proverbs 15:24
"The way of life *is* **above** to the wise, that he may depart from hell (*Sheol*) **beneath**."

The terms *"Sheol* beneath*"*, the "lowest *Sheol*", and the "depths of *Sheol*" collectively described the abode of the lost. Although the term "upper *Sheol*" is not used in Scripture, this term is helpful when we describe the compartment of *Sheol* where the departed Old Testament saints rested. Note that the direction of travel to the abode of the saved was still downwards. Jacob spake of going down to *Sheol*. This is important, since some teach that Old Testament saints went directly up to heaven and that *Sheol*, in their case, referred to a heavenly abode for them. This cannot be so, since Old Testament saints spoke of going down to *Sheol*. Taking all of these Scriptures together, it is clear that the unsaved in the Old Testament went to the lowest *Sheol*, a place of burning and punishment. However, the saved went to upper *Sheol*. In Luke 16, the rich man is in a place of flame and torment which is beneath the abode of Abraham and Lazarus. Note that the rich man "lifted up his eyes" to behold Abraham and Lazarus afar off. This language is not parabolic. It is describing exactly the depths of *Sheol* and its terrors in comparison with the upper region of *Sheol* which was characterised by comfort and rest.

A particular mention has to be given to the occurrences of the word *Sheol* in Psalm 49:14 where its contextual use in that passage has led some to suggest that, in that verse at least, *Sheol* must mean the grave and not the abode of the departed spirits.

Psalm 49:14
"Like sheep (Hebrew: a flock) they are laid in the grave (Hebrew: *Sheol*); death shall feed on (Hebrew: shepherd) them; and the upright shall have dominion over them in the morning; and their beauty (Hebrew: form or image) shall consume in the grave (Hebrew: *Sheol*) from their dwelling."

The argument is as follows. Sheep are animals and their souls certainly do not go to the abode of departed spirits on death. Therefore, if on death the Psalm indicates that sheep go to *Sheol*, then *Sheol* must mean the grave and not the abode of the departed spirits. Moreover, the argument goes, in the grave death "feeds" on the body as it turns to corruption.

Any who follow this suggestion should consider the following. The word for sheep here is flock, where a shepherd is in charge. A shepherd does not herd his sheep to the grave. These creatures are shepherded carefully for eventual slaughter to be eaten by men and not for an entire flock to go to the grave. Mass eradication and burial of entire flocks of sheep formed no part of agricultural practice in the ancient world. When we read "like a flock they are laid in *Sheol*…" the Psalmist is using the word "flock" to describe the unthinking group-behaviour of men who are willingly directed to hell by the shepherd of death who feeds them (shepherds them) with entertainment right until the end.

The simile "like a flock" is describing the collective, unthinking character of mankind who, led on by the shepherd called "death", namely the devil, go, oblivious of their individual responsibility to God, into eternal damnation. Psalm 49:14 depicts the sad end of the journey of the unthinking human "flock", who start out on their wanderings in Isaiah 53:6.

Isaiah 53:6
"All we like sheep (Hebrew: a flock) have gone astray; we have turned every one to his own way; and the LORD hath laid on Him the iniquity of us all."

The literal translation is as follows: "All we like a flock (singular) have gone astray (plural verb)…" Clearly, in Isaiah 53:6 it is not a flock going astray which is the concern of the prophet but rather men, who are likened to a flock in their thoughtless wanderings from God. The end of the journey is *Sheol*, the abode of the lost which, in the context of Psalm 49:14, is not upper *Sheol* because those who find themselves there are being consumed and are depicted in stark contrast to the "upright". Moreover, these unrighteous ones have the dreadful prospect that "their beauty (Hebrew: image or form) shall consume in *Sheol*". Those who believe that *Sheol* is the grave and that the phrase "their beauty shall consume in *Sheol*" refers to the decomposition of the human body in the grave have to explain how it is that the verse does not envisage the "upright" having the experience of "their beauty consuming in the grave" but only the ungodly. The sad fact is that as far as the grave is concerned both righteous and unrighteous who die will experience bodily corruption. Accordingly, the word *Sheol* in the verse cannot mean the grave since both righteous and unrighteous will be laid in the grave. However, only the unrighteous will experience their "form" or "image" being consumed in the Spirit world of *Sheol*. It is a solemn fact that man was made **in the image of God**. As will be considered in detail in Psalms 69 and 110, this means that man was created as a unique being who loved God since he is made in God's image. How sad it is that such a being should live life denying God the true purpose of human creation, namely loving God! How tragic it is that, if not delivered from this state in time, man will enter into eternal death as a creature who in life remained estranged from God without experiencing what it means to be in God's image, i.e. loving God, but rather undergoing relentless, moral degradation referred to as "their image shall consume in *Sheol*". In other words, they will continue to increasingly hate God forever. We know from Luke 16 that this is accompanied by horrendous and eternal torments. How tragic and troubling to even contemplate!

Let us discover the characteristics of *Sheol* when it refers to the abode of the saved in the Old Testament.

1 As seen in Luke 16:25 it is a **place of comfort for both Abraham and Lazarus**:

"He is comforted."

2 Daniel was reassured that that he would "rest" when he would go his way, i.e. die. **It is a place of rest**.

Daniel 12:13

"But go thou thy way till the end *be:* for thou shalt **rest**, and stand in thy lot at the end of the days."

3 Job exclaims in **Job 14:13**

"O that Thou wouldest **hide me in the grave** (*Sheol*), that Thou wouldest keep me secret, **until** Thy wrath be past, that Thou wouldest appoint me a set time, and remember me!"

Here we discover that upper *Sheol* was **a place of hiding until** the wrath would be past. What does this mean? In the Old Testament, sins could only be covered (Psalm 32:1) and passed over. In Romans 3, Paul tells us that God was righteous in this. We read in Romans 3:25 of the righteousness of God in the remission, (Greek = passing over) of the sins that were past through the forbearance of God.

Romans 3:24-26
> 24 "Being justified freely by His grace through the redemption that is in Christ Jesus:
> 25 Whom God hath set forth *to be* a propitiation through faith in His blood, **to declare His righteousness for the remission (literally = passing over or overlooking) of sins that are past, through the forbearance of God;**
> 26 To declare, *I say,* at this time His righteousness: that He might be just, and the justifier of him which believeth in Jesus."

In other words, God has been perfectly righteous in covering and passing over the sins of Old Testament believers who put their trust in the coming Messiah. (We will consider this later in Psalm 22.) However, until the sins were dealt with and consequently put away, the wrath was not over. That would require the coming of the Lord Jesus Christ and His bearing the judgment at Calvary. On the triumph of His resurrection, the **hiding place** of *Sheol* was no longer needed. Upper *Sheol* **was temporary.** Old Testament believers believed that they would be redeemed and ransomed from *Sheol* **and** death. These are not synonymous concepts as some may suppose and the important Biblical distinction between redemption from *Sheol* and death will be later considered in greater detail in Psalm 69:18. It will be sufficient at this stage to note the Old Testament references to redemption from *Sheol* and death:

Psalm 49:15
> "But God will **redeem** my soul from the power of (hand of) the grave (*Sheol*): for He shall receive me. Selah."

Hosea 13:14
> Jehovah says, "I will **ransom** them from the power of the grave (from the hand of *Sheol*); I will **redeem** them from death: O death, I will be thy plagues; O grave, I will be thy destruction: repentance shall be hid from Mine eyes."

This verse in Hosea is interesting. It draws a distinction between the deliverance from *Sheol* and from death. This too is consistent with New Testament revelation, where we read:

1 Corinthians 15:55-56
> 55 "O death, where *is* thy sting? O grave (Hades), where *is* thy victory?
> 56 The sting of death *is* sin; and the strength of sin *is* the Law."

The victory over *Sheol* has already been accomplished and the risen One carries the keys (Revelation 1:18). The victory over death has yet to be demonstrated. Hence Paul says,

1 Corinthians 15:26
"The last enemy *that* shall be destroyed *is* death."

Nevertheless, the prospect of the destruction of *Sheol*, the abode of the Old Testament saved ones, was a cause for joyful anticipation for Old Testament believers. In Hosea 13:14, God affirms to His people, "O death, I will be thy plagues; O grave (*Sheol*), I will be thy destruction: repentance shall be hid from Mine eyes." A helpful illustration would be to consider a bitter conflict between two armies. Until the final battle and victory, a refugee camp has to be set up. It is a place of comfort, hiding and rest. Yet it is clearly only temporary and can be dismantled once the final victory is won and the citizens are then clear to go to their rightful homes.

However, *Sheol* is also described in language indicating a place of captivity. Hezekiah speaks of the "**gates of *Sheol***":

Isaiah 38:10
"I shall go to the gates of the grave (*Sheol*)."

The Psalmist, David, speaks of "**the cords of *Sheol***" compassing him about:

Psalm 18:5
"The sorrows (**cords**) of hell (*Sheol*) compassed me about: the snares of death prevented me."

Job mentions the "**bars** of *Sheol*".

Job 17:16
"They shall go down to the **bars** of the pit (*Sheol*), when *our* rest together *is* in the dust."

When we see *Sheol* described as a place with **gates, cords** and **bars**, we begin to see how Old Testament saints regarded it as a place of temporary captivity, albeit a place of comfort and rest.

It is interesting to note that *Sheol* was not a place of praise.
Hezekiah says:

Isaiah 38:18
"For the grave (*Sheol*) cannot praise Thee, death can *not* celebrate Thee…"

David says:

Psalm 6:6
"In the grave (*Sheol*) who shall give Thee thanks?"

It is apparent that upper *Sheol* was a necessary holding centre for Old Testament believers, but they were longing for a deliverance from it.

Perhaps, this is what is meant in Hebrews 2:15, when the writer speaks of the deliverance for those "who through fear of death were all their lifetime subject to bondage". Today, in this Church age, we are no longer subject to the bondage of this fear of death. In fact, the Lord Jesus tells us that the gates of *Sheol* will never prevail over anyone in His Church:

Matthew 16:18
"And I say also unto thee, That thou art Peter, and upon this Rock I will build My Church; and the gates of hell shall not prevail against it."

This was a tremendous statement for the disciples to hear. Although we may die and be put in the grave, no departed saints in this Church age will find themselves, like Hezekiah or his friends, behind the gates of *Sheol*. Those gates will never prevail against us! Such has been the victory of the risen One.

Psalm 16:10
"For Thou wilt not leave My soul in hell (*Sheol*); neither wilt Thou suffer Thine Holy One to see corruption."

The phrase, "Thou wilt not leave", (*lo taazov*) means "Thou wilt not abandon My soul to *Sheol*".

There are two interpretations of this verse.

One view is that "Thou wilt not abandon", indicates that immediately on dying His soul went to His Father in heaven. If this interpretation is correct then the verse is referring **to the moment of His death** and implies that immediately on dying, His soul was not abandoned to *Sheol*.

The other view is that the phrase, "Thou wilt not abandon", indicates that although He did go to *Sheol*, He was not "abandoned" or "forsaken" there. In other words, His sojourn in *Sheol* was only temporary. If this interpretation is correct, then the verse does not refer to the moment of His death. It refers to **the moment of His resurrection** when His sojourn in *Sheol* ended, indicating that He had not been abandoned there.

Determining which of the two interpretations has scriptural support will depend on elucidating whether the verse refers to **His death** or **His resurrection**. Thankfully, we are not left in the dark as to the meaning of the verse because, as always, the Scripture itself is its own interpreter. In Acts 2:25-32, we discover whether first century A.D. Christians understood the verse to refer to the moment of His death (i.e. He did not go there at all) or the moment of His resurrection (i.e. He went there but was not abandoned there).

Acts 2:24-31
24 "Whom God hath raised up, having loosed the pains of death: because it was not possible that He should be holden of it.
25 For David speaketh concerning Him, I foresaw the Lord always before My face, for He is on My right hand, that I should not be moved:
26 Therefore did My heart rejoice, and My tongue was glad; moreover also

My flesh shall rest in hope:

27 Because Thou wilt not leave My soul in hell, neither wilt Thou suffer Thine Holy One to see corruption.

28 Thou hast made known to Me the ways of life; Thou shalt make Me full of joy with Thy countenance.

29 Men *and* brethren, let me freely speak unto you of the patriarch David, that he is both dead and buried, and his sepulchre is with us unto this day.

30 Therefore being a prophet, and knowing that God had sworn with an oath to him, that of the fruit of his loins, according to the flesh, He would raise up Christ to sit on his throne;

31 He seeing this before **spake of the resurrection of Christ, that His soul was not left in hell, neither His flesh did see corruption**."Note 2

From Acts 2:31, it is clear that Psalm 16:10 refers to His resurrection. The meaning is unambiguous. He did go to *Sheol* but was not abandoned there. His resurrection is the proof of this. There are other passages, however, which raise questions in the minds of some. **For example,** what is meant by the Lord's statement, "Father, into Thy hands I commend My Spirit (Luke 23:46)"? Note 2 Does not this indicate that He went into heaven on the moment of His death? The answer is that although His death was unique, it was real. We discover from Ecclesiastes 12:7, that for each person, a feature of death is that the spirit returns to "God Who gave it".

Ecclesiastes 12:7
"Then shall the dust return to the earth as it was: and the spirit shall return unto God Who gave it."

This was the experience of all the Old Testament saints, but when their spirit returned to God Who gave it, they were hidden in the security and comfort of the hiding place of *Sheol*. Similarly, the spirits of the unsaved dead in the Old Testament returned "to God Who gave it", and were then consigned to the **lowest** *Sheol*. The phrase, "into Thy hands I commend My Spirit", does not indicate that He did not go to *Sheol*, any more than the phrase, "the spirit shall return to God Who gave it", suggests that Old Testament saints did not go to *Sheol*.

What is meant by the words of the Lord to the dying thief?

Luke 23:43
"And Jesus said unto him, Verily I say unto thee, Today shalt thou be with Me in paradise."

The Hebrew word for paradise (*pardes*) occurs in:

1 Song of Solomon 4:13
"Thy plants *are* an orchard (*pardes*) of pomegranates, with pleasant fruits; camphire, with spikenard."

2 Ecclesiastes 2:5
"I made me gardens and orchards (*pardes*), and I planted trees in them of

all *kind of* fruits."

3 **Nehemiah 2:8**

"And a letter unto Asaph the keeper of the king's forest (*pardes*), that he may give me timber to make beams for the gates of the palace which *appertained* to the house, and for the wall of the city, and for the house that I shall enter into. And the king granted me, according to the good hand of my God upon me."

In none of these passages does it refer to heaven directly, although the "paradise" or "orchard" in the Song of Solomon 4:13 is surely pictorial of the beauty of purity and loving devotion of the Bride to her Bridegroom, something which will really only first be seen by the Bridegroom Himself in the heavenly paradise following the arrival there of His Bride (see Psalm 45). These Old Testament references show that the underlying meaning is of a walled garden. The picture is of protected tranquility, fruitfulness, purity and pleasure.

In the ancient Greek translation of the Hebrew Old Testament the Garden of Eden is described in Genesis 2:8 as paradise (*paradeisos*), so the word is used to describe the sin-free environment of Eden's garden **before** man fell. In the Greek New Testament, the "overcomers" in the Church at Ephesus were promised the prospect of eating of the tree of life in the midst of the "paradise of God". This is another interesting detail about the heavenly home of a believer today, that in addition to the Father's house of John 14 there is a garden reminiscent of Eden's garden before the fall which is called the "paradise of God".

Revelation 2:7

"He that hath an ear, let him hear what the Spirit saith unto the Churches; To him that overcometh will I give to eat of the tree of life, which is in the midst of the paradise of God."

It is of this amazing place that Paul had a preview.

2 Corinthians 12:2-4

2 "I knew a man in Christ above fourteen years ago, (whether in the body, I cannot tell; or whether out of the body, I cannot tell: God knoweth;) such an one **caught up to the third heaven** (literally: as far as the third heaven). 3 And I knew such a man, (whether in the body, or out of the body, I cannot tell: God knoweth;)
4 How that he was **caught up into paradise**, and heard unspeakable words, which it is not lawful for a man to utter."

Paul's journey to paradise was in two stages. He was caught up as far as the third heaven (2 Corinthians 12:2) and then was caught up **into** paradise. This would suggest to us that "paradise" is not a general term to describe the third heaven but rather is a location within the third heaven. Since we already know that within the third heaven is "the Father's house", one cannot but wonder if the Father's house is within the garden of paradise. Indeed, one cannot help but contemplate if such was Paul's ecstatic experience in the "garden" what will it be like in the "Father's house" and in the special "abiding place" that He has gone to prepare for His Church?

In 2 Corinthians 12 "paradise" is a location in the "third heaven". However, when we review all the uses of the word "paradise" in Scripture both in the Hebrew Old Testament and the Septuagint, we discover that this word can refer to different places:

1 an orchard or garden on this earth

2 Eden's Garden before the fall of man

3 the heavenly garden, containing the tree of life within the third heaven.

This means that the **context** of the passage must be considered in each use of the word to determine which of these meanings is intended. However, whatever the context, the meaning **always** is of a place of peace, tranquility, beauty and rest. When the Lord said to the dying thief, "Today shalt thou be with Me in paradise", the literal translation is "With Me shalt thou be today in paradise". The Lord's emphasis was that the man would firstly be "with Christ" and secondly the use of the word paradise indicated that this would be an experience of Garden of Eden-type bliss. To determine whether the phrase "in paradise" refers to heaven or to *Sheol,* we must first determine from other passages where the Lord went immediately on His death and what is meant by "with Me".

As we have noted in Psalm 16:8, immediately on His death The Lord's soul moved to *Sheol*. This was clearly Peter's understanding of the events (Acts 2). This shows us that the phrase, "in paradise", describes the character of the upper *Sheol* to which the Lord, and later the thief, went that day. It was a place of peace, tranquility, beauty and rest. Prior to the Lord speaking these words at the cross, there is no occurrence of the word either in the Hebrew Bible or Septuagint as referring specifically to heaven. This had to await New Testament revelation subsequent to the resurrection and ascension of the Lord Jesus. Thus, when the Lord explained to the thief that shortly he would be with the Lord Jesus in paradise, there was nothing in the context of the Lord's words to indicate that by "paradise" He was referring to a location other than upper *Sheol*, also known as Abraham's bosom (Luke 16) where he would be comforted. Moreover, the dying thief would only have known of an earthly inheritance for the saved subsequent to resurrection. He even indicated this by saying, "Lord, remember me when Thou comest into Thy Kingdom"

Luke 23:42

"And he said unto Jesus, Lord, remember me when Thou comest into Thy Kingdom."

Why then did the Lord use the word paradise to describe upper *Sheol* to the thief? Our Lord's use of the word "paradise" shows His kindness in speaking to this suffering malefactor, albeit now believing and forgiven.

By characterising upper *Sheol* as "paradise", He was strongly comforting this very new believer that in just a very few hours he would exchange the excruciating pains of a Roman cross for upper *Sheol* with all its unparalleled comfort and peace. Above all, the thief in his dying moments had the prospect of being in the presence of the Soul of the Person of Christ in *Sheol* and would have consciously experienced the joy of His triumph over *Sheol* when in a brief three days, He arose from the dead guaranteeing the ultimate resurrection of the thief.

When the Lord Jesus told the thief in **Luke 23:43** "Verily I say unto thee, Today shalt thou be **with** (*meta*) me in paradise" the preposition "with" is *meta* in contrast to the other Greek preposition for "with" which is *sun*. As discussed in detail in Psalm 68 and in **Appendix 4**, *meta* can often mean "with" in a spiritual sense and is used here because the Lord's physical body was in the tomb. In other words the thief in his disembodied soul would be in the abode of the redeemed souls in upper *Sheol* consciously with (*meta*) the soul of the Lord Jesus Whose soul according to Psalm 16:10 was in upper *Sheol* but not abandoned there.

Psalm 16:10

"For Thou wilt not leave (abandon) My soul in hell (*Sheol*); neither wilt Thou suffer Thine Holy One to see corruption."

Now we have seen how that in Psalm 2, resurrection proves Who He is – God's Son. Here, in Psalm 16, we learn that resurrection proves of what character He is – Holy. Interestingly, Paul, when preaching the gospel in Acts 13, uses Psalm 2 and Psalm 16 to prove to his hearers Who Jesus is: the Son, as confirmed at resurrection in Psalm 2, and of what character He is: Holy – again proved by resurrection in Psalm 16. Both the doctrines of Who He is, and of what character He is, are vital in the gospel presentation. It is in light of this that Paul says:

Acts 13:38

"Be it known unto you **therefore**, men *and* brethren, that through this Man is preached unto you the forgiveness of sins."

How important is this word "therefore"! It highlights for us that because resurrection has established beyond question that He is God's eternal Son, and that He is Holy, His death must of necessity have made propitiation for sin. In other words, resurrection shows that it certainly could not have been for sins of His own that He died, since the Psalm shows that He was absolutely holy and impeccable. On the basis alone of His death for sin and triumphant resurrection can forgiveness of sins be offered to mankind.

However, why should the Psalm, which presents Christ to us as the Priest, emphasise His resurrection and Holy character? Unlike Aaron, whom death conquered, our Great High Priest has conquered death and can never die. Unlike Aaron, who had to offer for his own sins, our Great High Priest has been proven by **resurrection** to be Jehovah's Holy One. It is in the context of Christ as our Advocate **in heaven** that John speaks of Him as "Jesus Christ the Righteous" (1 John 2:1). Today, the risen One is at God's right hand. The Psalm attests to this vital doctrinal attribute of our Great High Priest in the final verse:

Psalm 16:11

"Thou wilt shew Me the path of life: in Thy presence *is* fullness of joy; at Thy right hand *there are* pleasures for evermore."

The doctrinal significance of these considerations.

As is discussed in Psalms 22, 40 and 110 the Lord Jesus became a "Priest forever after the order of Melchisedec" **subsequent** to His death, resurrection and ascension to God's right hand. Prior to this, all Old Testament believers in their lifetimes, including Aaron and his sons, could not function as priests in the **heavenly sanctuary** (Psalms 40 and 69) in contrast to believers living in this New Testament era. Furthermore, immediately following their deaths, souls of Old Testament believers could not be admitted to the heavenly sanctuary to function as priests, since their consecration to priesthood had to await the consecration of the Lord Jesus to be Priest, first of all (Psalms 40, 69 and 110). Until this time, souls of departed Old Testament believers remained in the safety and comfort of upper *Sheol* (Psalm 16). The death of the Lord Jesus, the shedding of His precious blood and his resurrection were necessary before Old Testament believers who had already died could be made priests around the throne in heaven singing the New Song (Psalm 40). In other words, they could not become priests **before** the Lord Jesus **first of all** became our Great High Priest. Any suggestion that Old Testament believers, on death, passed immediately to heaven even before the death of the Lord Jesus, arises from a misunderstanding of the sanctuary nature of heaven and the requirement for all mankind who are admitted there to be able to function within those sacred precincts as priests. The Lord Jesus must always have the preeminence. Accordingly, it would be incongruous for Old Testament believers to be able to function before the throne of God in heaven either in life or subsequent to their deaths, as priests, if the Lord Jesus was not yet first consecrated as a Priest by His own death, after which in resurrection He entered in by virtue of His own blood as a Priest forever. Just as the earthly tabernacle and temple sanctuaries required all who entered into them to be priests (as Uzziah discovered too late in 2 Chronicles 26:18), similarly the heavenly sanctuary, of which the earthly sanctuary was but a picture (Hebrews 8:5, 9:23) can only admit those who have been firstly consecrated as priests (Psalms 22, 40, 69 and 110). This is the case with New Testament believers today, from the moment of conversion. This became the experience of Old Testament believers after the Lord ascended to heaven when their temporary abode in upper *Sheol* was exchanged for heaven which they entered as priests as explained in Psalm 40.

In conclusion, Psalm 16 presents to us the Lord Jesus Christ as the One fully qualified to be our High Priest. He is the perfect dependent Man yet **always** on equality with God. He represents God to men and men to God. In accordance with God's eternal counsels He has died, risen and ascended to God's right hand where His high priestly ministry became effective never to come to an end. All of these truths are taken up again in Psalms 22, 40, 69 and 110 where we learn further how that His high priestly ministry brings all believers of all ages and dispensations into the privileged position of priests before God.

1. There is a teaching by some, that the Lord Jesus, in order to be a perfect dependent man voluntarily and temporarily divested Himself of omniscience. Those who hold this view quote Mark 14:32 to suggest that at least in the matter of His second coming the Lord Jesus did not have full omniscience while on earth.

> *Mark 14:32*
>
> *"But of (Greek: peri meaning "concerning") that day and that hour knoweth (Greek: oiden) no man,*
> *no, not the angels which are in heaven, neither the Son, but the Father."*

The verb "knoweth" (*oiden*) is an irregular Greek verb. Some remarks are needed to elucidate its meaning.

The present tense of *oiden* is *ido* (I see) which is an unused root in ancient Greek and a different verb *horao* (I see) is used in ancient Greek to express "I see". The **aorist** (simple past) tense of the unused Greek word *ido* "I see" is *eidon*. The word *eidon* is normally translated "I saw". The infinitive form for *eidon* is *idein* which is sometimes translated " to see or to know". The **perfect tense** of the unused *ido*, is *oida* which literally means "I have seen". However, although the verb is morphologically in a perfect past form, it normally means "I know" in a **present** sense. This is understandable when we remember that the underlying concept for "I know" in Greek is based on the fact that "I have seen". Similarly if in ancient Greek there is a need to say "I have known" **the pluperfect** of the unused *ido* is employed (*eidea*) meaning literally "I **had** seen". You may notice a similarity with our English word "idea".

Normally when the verb *oida* (I have seen or I know) is followed by an object in the accusative case, the meaning is "I know (about) the object". An example is Matthew 25:13.

> *Matthew 25:13*
>
> *"Watch therefore, for ye **know** neither the day nor the hour wherein the Son of man cometh".*
> *However, this is not the construction used in Mark 14:32. Here the verb oida is linked with the*
> *preposition peri meaning "about or concerning."*

A useful New Testament example of the infinitive form of *idein* linked with *peri* illustrates this. Acts 15:6 "And the apostles and elders came together for to consider (*idein*) of (*peri*) this matter". The sense is that the apostles and elders had come together to "see to or concerning this matter". It is not correct to suggest that the Lord Jesus while on earth was limited with regard to the divine attribute of omniscience. The verb "to know" (*oida*) when linked to the preposition *peri* is a rare construction but it does not carry the sense of knowledge of facts. Rather the idea is of "seeing to" a matter or issue in the sense of managing or attending to it. It is not that the Lord Jesus while on earth had incomplete knowledge about the day of His second coming. The verse is showing us that "seeing to" or "seeing concerning" this great future day is the role of the Father. The author understands that aspects of this helpful explanation of Mark 14:32 were taught in ministry by the late Mr E.W. Rogers in Armagh Gospel Hall, in Northern Ireland *circa* 1970.

2. In Psalm 31:5 David says "into Thine hand I commit my spirit".
Psalm 31:5 "Into Thine hand I commit my spirit: Thou hast redeemed me, O Lord God of truth."
As will be discussed later in Psalms 40 and 69, the word used for redemption in this verse (*padah*) is in the context of Old Testament believers' souls being freed from *Sheol* to be fitted for the heavenly sanctuary subsequent to the resurrection and ascension of the Lord Jesus. In Psalm 31:5 David is speaking of his death and his unshakeable belief that he would be redeemed from *Sheol* to be fitted to sing the New Song around the throne in heaven (see Psalm 40). When the Lord Jesus said similar words at the cross "Father into Thy hands I commend My Spirit" He was indicating that just as David's death was real, so His own death was real. The difference, however, was that David needed to be redeemed (*padah*) from *Sheol* as will be discussed in Psalms 40 and 69. In contrast the Lord Jesus came forth in resurrection victory out of *Sheol* as the Redeemer.

3. Readers who wish to read more on *Sheol* would benefit from reading a helpful monograph on the subject by John Brown, of Scotland published in 1930 called
"'Hell', 'Sheol-Hades', 'Gehenna', 'Tartarus', 'the Lake of Fire': An exposition thereof." by John Brown of Edinburgh Scotland, January 1930 published by WM Ross, 132 Seagate, Dundee.

4

PSALM 18

To the chief Musician, A Psalm of David, the servant of the Lord, who spake unto the Lord the words of this song in the day that the Lord delivered him from the hand of all his enemies, and from the hand of Saul: And he said,

1 I will love Thee, O Lord, my strength.

2 The Lord is my Rock, and my fortress, and my deliverer; my God, my strength, in Whom I will trust; my buckler, and the horn of my salvation, and my high tower.

3 I will call upon the Lord, Who is worthy to be praised: so shall I be saved from mine enemies.

4 The sorrows of death compassed me, and the floods of ungodly men (floods of Belial) made me afraid.

5 The sorrows of hell compassed me about: the snares of death prevented me.

6 In my distress I called upon the Lord, and cried unto my God: He heard my voice out of His temple, and my cry came before Him, even into His ears.

7 Then the earth shook and trembled; the foundations also of the hills moved and were shaken, because He was wroth.

8 There went up a smoke out of His nostrils, and fire out of His mouth devoured: coals were kindled by it.

9 He bowed the heavens also, and came down: and darkness was under His feet.

10 And He rode upon a cherub, and did fly: yea, He did fly upon the wings of the wind.

11 He made darkness His secret place; His pavilion round about Him were dark waters and thick clouds of the skies.

12 At the brightness that was before Him His thick clouds passed, hail stones and coals of fire.

13 The Lord also thundered in the heavens, and the Highest gave His voice; hail stones and coals of fire.

14 Yea, He sent out His arrows, and scattered them; and He shot out lightnings, and discomfited them.

15 Then the channels of waters were seen, and the foundations of the world were discovered at Thy rebuke, O Lord, at the blast of the breath of Thy nostrils.

16 He sent from above, He took me, He drew me out of many waters.

17 He delivered me from my strong enemy, and from them which hated me: for they were too strong for me.

18 They prevented me in the day of my calamity: but the Lord was my stay.

19 He brought me forth also into a large place; He delivered me, because He delighted in me.

20 The Lord rewarded me according to my righteousness; according to the cleanness of my hands hath He recompensed me.

21 For I have kept the ways of the Lord, and have not wickedly departed from my God.

22 For all His judgments were before me, and I did not put away His statutes from me.

23 I was also upright before Him, and I kept myself from mine iniquity.

24 Therefore hath the Lord recompensed me according to my righteousness, according to the cleanness of my hands in His eyesight.

25 With the merciful Thou wilt shew Thyself merciful; with an upright man Thou wilt shew Thyself upright;

26 With the pure Thou wilt shew Thyself pure; and with the froward Thou wilt shew Thyself froward.

27 For Thou wilt save the afflicted people; but wilt bring down high looks.

28 For Thou wilt light my candle: the Lord my God will enlighten my darkness.

29 For by Thee I have run through a troop; and by my God have I leaped over a wall.

30 As for God, His way is perfect: the Word of the Lord is tried: He is a buckler to all those that trust in Him.

31 For who is God save the Lord? or who is a rock save our God?

32 It is God that girdeth me with strength, and maketh my way perfect.

33 He maketh my feet like hinds' feet, and setteth me upon my high places.

34 He teacheth my hands to war, so that a bow of steel is broken by mine arms.

35 Thou hast also given me the shield of Thy salvation: and Thy right hand hath holden me up, and Thy gentleness hath made me great.

36 Thou hast enlarged my steps under me, that my feet did not slip.

37 I have pursued mine enemies, and overtaken them: neither did I turn again till they were consumed.

38 I have wounded them that they were not able to rise: they are fallen under my feet.

39 For Thou hast girded me with strength unto the battle: Thou hast subdued under me those that rose up against me.

40 Thou hast also given me the necks of mine enemies; that I might destroy them that hate me.

41 They cried, but there was none to save them: even unto the Lord, but He answered them not.

42 Then did I beat them small as the dust before the wind: I did cast them out as the dirt in the streets.

43 Thou hast delivered me from the strivings of the people; and Thou hast made me the head of the heathen: a people whom I have not known shall serve me.

44 As soon as they hear of me, they shall obey me: the strangers shall submit themselves unto me.

45 The strangers shall fade away, and be afraid out of their close places.

46 The Lord liveth; and blessed be my Rock; and let the God of my salvation be exalted.
47 It is God that avengeth me, and subdueth the people under me.
48 He delivereth me from mine enemies: yea, Thou liftest me up above those that rise up against me: Thou hast delivered me from the violent man.
49 Therefore will I give thanks unto Thee, O Lord, among the heathen, and sing praises unto Thy Name.
50 Great deliverance giveth He to His king; and sheweth mercy to His anointed, to David, and to his seed for evermore.

The context of this Psalm

Psalm 18 is quoted in its entirety in 2 Samuel 22 where it immediately precedes what are recorded in 2 Samuel 23:1 as "the last words of David". In this Psalm, David is at the very end of life and is facing death. A detailed study of the Psalm will show that it considers the matter of David's death, the return to the earth of the Lord Jesus resulting in David's ultimate resurrection from the dead, the review of his life by the Lord Jesus and then his reward and position in the coming earthly Kingdom. Immediately following such a wonderful chapter depicting the Lord's return in manifested glory and the raising from the dead of the Old Testament saints, it should not surprise us that the subject matter in the next section in 2 Samuel 23 is of the Lord Jesus in His coming Kingdom being described as "the light of the morning, when the sun riseth, even a morning without clouds".

2 Samuel 23:2-4

2 "The Spirit of the Lord spake by me, and His word *was* in my tongue.
3 The God of Israel said, the Rock of Israel spake to me, He that ruleth over men *must be* just, ruling in the fear of God.
4 And *He shall be* as the light of the morning, **when the sun riseth**, *even* a morning without clouds; *as* the tender grass *springing* out of the earth by clear shining after rain."

Moreover, the rest of 2 Samuel 23 is dealing with David's mighty men being honoured for their faithful service in their lifetimes. The context, then, of Psalm 18 is of the Lord's second coming and His rewarding the Old Testament saints for faithfulness to Him in their lifetimes. Just as 2 Samuel 23:4 depicts the Lord Jesus in His coming Kingdom by the metaphorical picture of the "light of the morning, when the sun riseth, even a morning without clouds" it should be noted that in the parallel passage of Psalm 19, which immediately follows Psalm 18 in the Psalter, there is reference again made of the sun "as a Bridegroom coming out of His chamber, and rejoiceth as a strong Man to run a race".

Psalm 19:1-7

To the chief Musician, A Psalm of David.
1 "The heavens declare the glory of God; and the firmament sheweth His handywork.

2 Day unto day uttereth speech, and night unto night sheweth knowledge.

3 *There is* no speech nor language, *where* their voice is not heard.

4 Their line is gone out through all the earth, and their words to the end of the world. **In them hath He set a tabernacle for the sun,**

5 **Which** *is* **as a Bridegroom coming out of His chamber,** *and* **rejoiceth as a strong Man to run a race.**

6 **His going forth** *is* **from the end of the heaven, and His circuit unto the ends of it: and there is nothing hid from the heat thereof.**

7 The Law of the Lord *is* perfect, converting the soul: the testimony of the Lord *is* sure, making wise the simple".

Immediately following the quotation of Psalm 18 in 2 Samuel 22, the Lord Jesus in coming glory is described as "the sun", so we see a deeper significance to Psalm 19:5 in the description of the sun as a "Bridegroom coming out of His chamber". Ordinarily, the description of the sun "as a bridegroom coming out of his chamber" might strike us as unusual language. However, we should understand that Scripture is not just written for its literary beauty. There is a spiritual significance to every phrase and metaphor. In fact, the significance is apparent now to us in this New Testament era when the Lord Jesus is revealed to us as the Bridegroom. During the millennium, the Church will be in the heavenly city orbiting the earth and this is what is meant as "a tabernacle for the sun", where the "tabernacle" is the Church and the "Sun" is the heavenly Bridegroom. This is perfectly consistent with New Testament metaphorical language where the Church is seen as "an habitation of God through the Spirit".

Ephesians 2:21-22

21 "In Whom all the building fitly framed together groweth unto an holy temple in the Lord:

22 In Whom ye also are builded together for **an habitation of God through the Spirit**."

The light of this heavenly city, namely the Church where the Lord Jesus will be present, will floodlight the earth beneath, and in that coming day the inhabitants of the millennial earth will understand the words of Psalm 19:6 **"His going forth** *is* **from the end of the heaven, and His circuit unto the ends of it: and there is nothing hid from the heat thereof."**

In that day, the heavens will indeed declare the glory of God – not merely the glory of God in creation which they eloquently do today but, in addition, the glory of God in redemption, when from our home in the heavenly inheritance (1 Peter 1:4) and our fulfilled hope, which is in the heavens (Colossians 1:5), we shall be involved in the administration of His earthly Kingdom. In that day the will of God will be done on earth as it is in heaven in fulfilment of the "Lord's Prayer" (Luke 11) and there will be universal recognition of the perfection of the Law of the Lord and the righteousness of His statutes.

Psalm 19:7-9
> 7 "The Law of the Lord *is* perfect, converting the soul: the testimony of the Lord *is* sure, making wise the simple.
> 8 The statutes of the Lord *are* right, rejoicing the heart: the commandment of the Lord *is* pure, enlightening the eyes.
> 9 The fear of the Lord *is* clean, enduring for ever: the judgments of the Lord *are* true *and* righteous altogether."

Since the heaven and heavens will be discussed in detail in later Psalms, especially Psalms 89 and 102, it is appropriate to consider an introduction to the Biblical teaching of heaven and heavens at this point.

Heaven and heavens

In the Old Testament, we read of the **created** heavens (Genesis 1:1) (Hebrew: *shamayim* (dual)) and also of the **uncreated and eternal abode of God,** which is beyond the created universe (Psalm 8:1). The **uncreated and eternal abode of God** is described as the "heavens of heavens (*shmey hashshamayim*)" (2 Chronicles 2:6).

In Hebrew nouns are either in the singular, dual (two) or plural (three or more). A word which is in the dual form ends in "…*ayim*". Since the word heavens (*shamayim*) ends in "…*ayim*" this shows that in the Old Testament the **created** heavens are considered as having two distinct aspects. However, the Old Testament does not define what these two aspects are. In Psalm 8:8 we read of the "birds of the heavens (*shamayim*)" and in Genesis 26:4 of "the stars of the heavens (*shamayim*)". In Old Testament times believers understood that the created heavens **included** an atmospheric component where the birds fly and a region beyond this where the stars are found. Nevertheless the Old Testament does not specifically define what makes up each of the two aspects of the created heavens. This is clarified in the New Testament where we read of heavens (*ouranoi*) (plural) and of heaven singular (*ouranos*). A study of the occurrences of heaven (singular) in the New Testament shows that the atmospheric heaven (*ouranos*) (singular) is distinguished from the stellar heaven (*ouranos*) (singular). When both aspects are to be understood, the New Testament speaks of heavens (*ouranoi*) (plural) which include both the atmospheric and stellar heavens.

These distinctions are clear in the following examples. The New Testament speaks of the "birds of the air (*ouranos*: heaven (singular)) (Matthew 6:26)" and "the stars of heaven (*ouranos*: heaven (singular)) (Revelation 6:13)". Together the atmospheric heaven (*ouranos*) and the stellar heaven (*ouranos*) make up the heavens (plural) (*ouranoi*). These matters are clearly illustrated in the Scriptures describing the ascent of the Lord Jesus from earth to heaven in Hebrews.

First He passed **into** the created heavens.
> **Hebrews 4:14** "Seeing then that we have a Great High Priest, that is passed **into the heavens (ouranoi) (plural)**, Jesus the Son of God, let us hold fast *our* profession".

Then He ascended **higher than** the heavens.

Hebrews 7:26 "For such an High Priest became us, Who is holy, harmless, undefiled, separate from sinners, and made **higher than the heavens (*ouranoi*)(plural);**"

Lastly He moves **into heaven itself (singular)**, the eternal and uncreated abode of God which is higher than the created heavens.

Hebrews 9:24 "For Christ is not entered into the holy places made with hands, *which are* the figures of the true; but into **heaven (*ouranos*) (singular) itself**, now to appear in the presence of God for us."

"Heaven itself" is the same as the "third heaven" which lies above the two regions of the created heavens, namely the atmospheric and stellar heavens. It is the uncreated abode of God.

2 Corinthians 12:2 "I knew a man in Christ above fourteen years ago, (whether in the body, I cannot tell; or whether out of the body, I cannot tell: God knoweth;) such an one caught up **to the third heaven** (*ouranos*) (singular)".

The Bible shows that the created heavens (plural) will pass away (2 Peter 3:10) together with the created earth. This will give way to a new heavens (plural) and a new earth in the eternal state.

2 Peter 3:13

"Nevertheless we, according to His promise, look for **new heavens** and a new earth, wherein dwelleth righteousness."

This suggests that the "new heavens" will involve atmospheric and stellar components infinitely more beautiful and wonderful than what we know today.

It is significant that John does not see in his vision "new heavens" in the eternal state but a "new heaven" (singular) and "a new earth".

Revelation 21:1

"And I saw a new heaven (singular) and a new earth: for the first heaven (singular) and the first earth were passed away; and there was no more sea."

John is here focusing only on one aspect of the "new heavens" namely the atmospheric heaven which immediately surrounds the new earth. He is interested in it because it is to here that the tabernacle of God has descended to be on the new earth. In other words, the third heaven, the uncreated and eternal abode of God is now upon the New Earth. God is now dwelling among men in the city four-square on the New Earth. In the eternal state it will be literally "heaven on earth". These matters will be considered later in Psalm 89 and Psalm 102.

In the eternal state redeemed ones of all dispensations of time will be able to stand on the new earth and look up into the new heavens conscious of this wonderful thing that the third heaven is now on earth itself where now God will dwell forever.

The New Testament indicates that during the millennial reign of the Lord Jesus the Church will be in the heavens above the earth where the Old Testament believers and tribulations believers will be present. This is the period envisaged in Psalm 19. This understanding is based on clear statements that our inheritance (1 Peter 1:4), our hope (Colossians 1:5), our city (Hebrews 12:22-23) and our reward are in the heavens (Matthew 5:12). In contrast the Old Testament and tribulation believers will inherit the earth (Matthew 5:5). The exact place in the heavens is not specified where the Church's inheritance is found during the millennium. However, Psalm 19 would suggest that it is in the stellar heavens since the sun is compared to the orbiting Bridegroom in His marriage tent. This will be considered in more detail in Psalms 89, 102 and 110 where the distinctive positions of Israel and the Church in the millennium and the eternal state will be reviewed. In particular in Psalm 110 it will be considered in detail how that after establishing His Kingdom on earth the Lord returns to govern His millennial Kingdom from the heavens in the company of His Bride the heavenly people.

The New Testament use of Psalm 18

This Psalm is regarded as a Messianic Psalm because the phrase in verse 2, "My God ...., in Whom I will trust..." is quoted in Hebrews 2:13 and attributed to the Lord Jesus.

Hebrews 2:13
> "And again, I will put My trust in Him. And again, Behold I and the children which God hath given Me."

Furthermore, verse 49 is quoted in Romans 15:9, the significance of which will be considered at the end of this chapter.

Romans 15:9
> "And that the Gentiles might glorify God for *His* mercy; as it is written, For this cause I will confess to Thee among the Gentiles, and sing unto Thy Name."

The significance of the Hebrews 2 quotation

In Hebrews 2, the phrase "I will put My trust in Him" is taken from a cluster of three quotations (Psalm 22:22, Psalm 18:2, Isaiah 8 :18).

Hebrews 2:11-13
> 11 "For both He that sanctifieth and they who are sanctified *are* all of one: for which cause He is not ashamed to call them brethren,
> 12 Saying, **I will declare Thy Name unto My brethren, in the midst of the Church will I sing praise unto Thee** (from Psalm 22:22).
> 13 And again, **I will put My trust in Him** (from Psalm 18:2). And again, **Behold I and the children which God hath given Me**" (from Isaiah 8:18)."

These three Old Testament quotations are linked together in Hebrews 2 in that they consider the three great offices of the Lord Jesus as Priest (Psalm 22:22), King (Psalm 18:2) and Prophet (Isaiah 8:18).

His future priestly ministry

In the first of these 3 references taken from Psalm 22:22, He is presented as Priest: "in the midst of the Church will I sing praise unto Thee". The significance of this quotation is considered in more detail in Psalm 22. One reason why this is stated in Hebrews 2 is that the greatness of His Priesthood is being presented against the background of concerns regarding the apparent delay in His future manifestation as King. For example, in Hebrews 2:8 we read of this implied delay in the words "not yet" within the phrase "now we see **not yet** all things put under Him".

Hebrews 2:8

"Thou hast put all things in subjection under His feet. For in that He put all in subjection under Him, He left nothing *that is* not put under Him. But now we see **not yet** all things put under Him."

Furthermore, there is an implied delay in the "until" of Hebrews 1:13.

Hebrews 1:13

"But to which of the angels said He at any time, Sit on My right hand, **until** I make Thine enemies Thy footstool?"

In other words, if His word cannot be depended upon for Him to return in manifested Kingly glory in a coming day, how can He be depended upon to be our Great High Priest today? This seems to be the underlying insinuation of the "divers and strange doctrines" alluded to in Hebrews 13:9. The writer of Hebrews draws from multiple Old Testament passages, showing that there is an acknowledged delay between His first coming and His return to reign (see Psalms 8 and 110). During this period of delay, we come to know and prove Him as our High Priest in the experiences of life.

However, in Hebrews 2:12 it is apparent that the Lord Jesus, in a coming day, will be in the midst of the Church and will quote from Psalm 22:22 as He engages in direct praise to His Father. This is not just His being present in the midst of His Church in a mystical way, in the sense in which He is present in the midst of the public gatherings of His people today (Matthew 18:20). The sense, in Hebrews 2:12, is His being bodily present in the midst of the Church, where each member of His Church is gathered around Him and He is in the midst. This must surely be subsequent to the rapture of the Church when every redeemed one of this era will be part of what Paul refers to as "our gathering together unto Him" (2 Thessalonians 2:1).

One reason in support of this understanding of the passage is that there is a unity which characterises this great gathering described as "all of one" (Hebrews 2:11). Sadly, there are many divisions among those who make up His Church on earth today, but in the occasion envisaged in Hebrews 2:12

such divisions are gone forever. As He stands in the midst of His unified Church, He leads the praise and declares the Father's Name unto His own. He will be involved in praise to the Father and in teaching His own. This is a wonderful verse which shows us that the activity of heaven will be entirely centred around the Lord Jesus Christ. As we listen to Him praising the Father and, in turn, declaring the Name of the Father unto us in the infinite revelation which eternity will entail, we will just begin to see the wonder of our Lord Jesus Christ in His office as our Great High Priest.

However, in this unique passage of Hebrews 2:12 we are given additional insights into the teaching ministry of our Lord Jesus Christ in heaven. He turns the attention of His redeemed ones to two Old Testament passages from which He makes quotation. They are Psalm 18:2 and Isaiah 8:13-18. Although the Hebrews' writer mainly quotes excerpts from these two Old Testament passages, it is likely that these "excerpts" are simply abbreviations or headings for what will be an amazing exposition of these two passages which awaits us in heaven. We should note that as the Lord quotes from these two sections, in that coming day, He is providing a divine exposition of Psalm 18 and Isaiah 8. He will undoubtedly show us how that Psalm 18:2 is a statement of faith by David regarding his trust in the coming King. Furthermore, He will show us how that Isaiah 8:18 is a statement of faith by Isaiah of his role as a silent witness to the coming Prophet i.e. Christ Who will, on His next intervention upon earth, deal with all doctrinal opposition to His claim to be the True One sent of God.

Why then will the Lord Jesus in that coming day, when we are all around Him in heaven, quote from what today many of us may regard as enigmatic and quite difficult to be understood passages? Certainly, He is not doing this to confuse us! What a day it will be when His redeemed ones will be privileged to listen to the Prince of teachers as He lifts out passages from the Old Testament, which many of us have struggled to understand, and will then expound them to us in clarity.

Evidently, as He unveils the Father's Name to His own in the Church He will want to tell them about His imminent plan to return to this earth to raise from the dead the Old Testament and tribulation believers and give them the rewards due to them and institute His earthly Kingdom over which He will reign with His Church which will, in that day, be involved in the administration over His Kingdom.

As we are about to see in our study of Psalm 18, this passage is dealing with such an impending event and speaks of our Lord Jesus returning to reign, raising from the dead the Old Testament believers, reviewing their lives and giving them their rewards and setting up the Kingdom, with them involved in positions of responsibility therein. By quoting from this preliminary section in Psalm 18 to His Church in heaven, it is apparent that the Lord Jesus is instructing His own regarding the events which are about to unfold and which they will witness from their vantage point of the heavenly city. In this the Lord Jesus will be teaching His own regarding **His office as King**.

Furthermore by quoting from Isaiah 8:18 He is showing them that, **as the Prophet** Whose words on earth were rejected, He will return to deal with all who refused to believe in Him and by so doing will vindicate the "children" who bore testimony to Him in the era of His rejection. Let us look now in more detail at these twin truths of the revelation of Him as undisputed King and Prophet.

His future role as King

Having shown from Psalm 22 that He is Priest, the Hebrews' writer is quick to reaffirm that He is also the coming King in Psalm 18. In this Psalm, we are reminded of David's confidence in his future personal vindication on the occasion of the future manifestation in glory of the Lord Jesus. In Psalm 18, David's confession, "I will put my trust in Him" is a statement of his faith in the coming King and His righteous Kingdom. Hence, this is the Psalm of the King. The application is clear: David did not doubt in Psalm 22 that His Messiah Son would one day act as Priest. Similarly, He has not the shadow of doubt in His future Kingly office. This was the message for the Hebrew Jewish Christians who appeared to be assailed on this truth.

His future ministry as the returned Prophet

Finally, we have a reference to the Lord Jesus as Prophet. In Isaiah 8, the prophet declares, "Behold I and the children whom God hath given me are for signs and for wonders in Israel". This is an allusion to the prophetic ministry of the Lord Jesus.

Isaiah 8:13-18

13 "Sanctify the Lord of hosts Himself; and *let* Him *be* your fear, and *let* Him *be* your dread.

14 And He shall be for a **Sanctuary**; but for a Stone of stumbling and for a Rock of offence to both the houses of Israel, for a gin and for a snare to the inhabitants of Jerusalem.

15 And many among them shall stumble, and fall, and be broken, and be snared, and be taken.

16 Bind up the testimony, seal the Law among My disciples.

17 And I will wait upon the Lord, that hideth His face from the house of Jacob, and I will look for Him.

18 Behold, **I and the children whom the Lord hath given me** *are* **for signs and for wonders** in Israel from the Lord of hosts, which dwelleth in mount Zion."

It is truly something for every believer of this era to look forward to, when, in the glory of heaven, our glorified Lord and Saviour takes this passage and expounds it to us in fullness, as Hebrews 2 anticipates. Some elements of that future exposition can be gleaned from reading Isaiah 8:13-18. These are considered below but the full exposition will await that great day of heavenly revelation above.

In this section, Isaiah prophecies that the Lord Himself shall be a "Sanctuary", i.e. a Holy Temple, referring to the incarnation of the Lord

Jesus. The Lord Jesus Himself spoke of the "Temple of His Body" (John 2:21) and Paul tells us that "in Him dwelleth all the fullness of the Godhead bodily" (Colossians 2:9). By presenting this truth again, Isaiah is reinforcing his teachings of Isaiah 7:14 regarding Immanuel, "God with us".

In this section, the prophet goes on to show that, remarkably, this divine Person shall be rejected of His own nation in a general way. In light of this, the Lord declares, "Bind up the testimony and **seal** the Law among My disciples". In response Isaiah exclaims "and I will wait upon the Lord…" (Isaiah 8:16-17). It is a prophet's responsibility to teach the Law and not to seal it. However, Isaiah seals up the scroll of the Law before the watching Jews to indicate that it will become a closed book to them **after** they reject the coming One, i.e. Immanuel, "God with us".

The Lord Jesus in Luke 4:20 closed the book rather than present the "day of vengeance of our God". When Isaiah seals up the book, he says, "I will wait upon the Lord that hideth His face from the house of Jacob and I will look for Him". The implication is that if the nation rejected Isaiah's message of the One Who is "the Sanctuary", i.e. God dwelling in Manhood, Isaiah had nothing more to say to them as the nation's prophet. Symbolically, he would step aside from his role and "wait upon the Lord". In other words, He would leave the next and final word to the Lord Himself. The unspoken implication in the Hebrew poem is that it is the **Lord** Who will assume the role of the Prophet, Who will deal with those who reject Him and Who will have the undisputed last word. People may dispute Isaiah's prophecies but they will not argue with the Lord when He comes the second time, following His first advent as Immanuel.

Isaiah then says, "Behold I and the children which God hath given me". As Isaiah closed the scroll and fell silent, he was pictorially demonstrating (i.e. acting as a sign) the silence which God would in a future day show to his nation in a general way when they would reject their Messiah, Who is God's only revelation to the nation and the world. However, this passage shows that God will always have a remnant in Israel, even if the general trend within this nation for many years would be to say no to their Messiah. Isaiah and his two boys were a picture of the remnant Jews who would, in the long era of their Messiah's rejection, long for the arrival of the Messiah in manifestation. (The boys are called, Shear-jashub meaning a "remnant shall return", and Maher-shalal-hash-baz meaning, "in making haste to the prey he divides the spoil"). Both little boys' names bore testimony to the coming restoration of the nation and the judgment on the "prey" (i.e. the enemies of God). Isaiah is showing that if he, the prophet, has closed the book to wait upon the Lord, then he (that is Isaiah) is leaving the prophetic response to the nation's rejection to the rejected One Himself, i.e. the Lord Who, just like Isaiah, is "hiding His face from Jacob" in this the day of His rejection. It will be Christ's prerogative to reopen the book which Isaiah had pictorially closed. He will reopen the sealed book and pour out, this time, its prophetic judgments in a coming day (Revelation 5:9). Isaiah 8, therefore, presents the Lord Jesus as the Prophet Who will do just that.

In summary then, the significance of these three references in Hebrews chapter 2 to Christ's three-fold offices are as follows.

His Priestly Office (Psalm 22)

As we discuss in detail in Psalm 110, while our Lord was on earth, He was not our Great High Priest.

This ministry is subsequent to His death, resurrection and ascension and is vital for us **now**. The writer of Hebrews is teaching us that now that He is in heaven, He is there as our High Priest.

His Kingly Office (Psalm 18)

While on earth He was the King in waiting but not in manifestation. That is why there is unfairness in this world and corruption on every hand. When He reigns in manifestation (Psalm 24) there will be dignity in government (see later). Luke brings us this distinction in Luke 19:12 as He shows us that He left this world as a Nobleman but returns as King to reward His servants. As we will consider shortly in Psalm 18 it is the returned King Who rewards His servants who have been faithful to Him.

His prophetic office (Isaiah 8)

While on earth He was Prophet in fulfilment of Moses' prophecy, "A Prophet shall the Lord your God raise up ... like unto me" (Deuteronomy 18:18-19; Acts 3:22). It was a prophet's role to expound the Law. Prophets pointed out that the Law was broken, and then pointed to the future consequences of this: certain judgment on the lawbreakers, but, as well, they spoke of divine mercy on the lawbreaker which is introduced to us on Moses' second descent from Mount Sinai:

Exodus 34:6
"The Lord God (Jehovah), merciful and gracious. "

Grace and Mercy are seen only in Christ Who becomes the object and fulfilment of all prophecy. The Lord Jesus as the Prophet not only expounded the Law, He uniquely went further: He fulfilled it in both His life and His death. At His first advent He exhibited only the blessing miracles of the prophets Elijah and Elisha e.g. resurrection (1 Kings 17:22), multiplication of the loaves (2 Kings 4:43), and cleansing from leprosy (2 Kings 5:14). At His second advent, the world will see this Prophet display the judgment miracles of Elijah such as fire from heaven (2 Kings 1:12).

Let us remember that on His return He will be Prophet (Isaiah 8), Priest (Psalm 110) **and** King (Psalm 18).

Let us now return to Psalm 18 and remind ourselves that the reason why the writer of Hebrews quotes from Psalm 18 is that He wants to affirm to his Jewish Christian audience the absolute certainty that there **must be** a coming Kingdom, literally on earth, because reneging on this would be to betray the aspirations of David expressed in Psalm 18.

Title of the psalm

"To the chief musician, *A Psalm* of David, the servant of the Lord, who spake unto the Lord the words of this song in the day *that* the Lord delivered him from the hand of all his enemies, and from the hand of Saul."

This title of the Psalm tells us that the Lord delivered David, the servant of the Lord, "from the hand of all his enemies, and from the hand of Saul". This Psalm can be profitably studied by linking phrases within it to crises in David's life from which he was delivered. For example, he speaks of being **rewarded** according to his **righteousness** in verse 20, reminding us of the occasion when he spared Saul's life and David exclaimed to Saul:

1 Samuel 26:23
> "The Lord **render** to every man his **righteousness** and his faithfulness: for the Lord delivered thee into *my* hand today, but I would not stretch forth mine hand against the Lord's anointed."

Again, we read of **the sorrows of death** (verse 4) and **the snares of death** (verse 5) targeting David and we may think of the many occasions when David's life was in danger, particularly at the hand of Saul. We read of the floods of ungodly men (floods of Belial) (verse 4) terrifying him and we may wonder if this is a reference to the time that Satan tempted David and he numbered the people (1 Chronicles 21:1), following which we read that David was "terrified" to go up to the house of the Lord (1 Chronicles 21:30). However, these experiences in David's life do not adequately reflect the circumstances depicted by the language used in the Psalm.

There are a number of features of this Psalm which suggest that the Psalm carries a prophetic significance stretching out to the future millennial age when David will be raised from the dead and will have entered into the earthly Kingdom:

1 The description of death (in verses 4-5) uses language which goes beyond being under death's threat or even surviving a near-death experience. It is difficult to read the language used and not conclude that it is written to describe the experience of someone for whom death is now a distant memory and from which they have been delivered by resurrection.

2 He speaks of being rewarded according to his righteousness (verse 20) but says nothing of his sin and failures. This would suggest that this Psalm is projecting forward to the other side of resurrection when our sins and iniquities are beyond memory.

3 He speaks of a people that he did not know serving him (verse 43). This is very clearly prophetic and refers to the future Kingdom when David shall be in a position of responsibility in the Messiah's earthly administration.

As we read the Psalm, we will endeavour to consider it from the perspective of David, in a coming day, looking back to his earthly pilgrimage, terminating in his death, and describing the second coming of the Lord Jesus to earth to shake it and raise from the dead the Old Testament and tribulation saints.

Psalm 18:1-3

1 "I will love Thee, O Lord, my strength.
2 The Lord *is* my rock (*Sela* = Crag-Rock), and my fortress, and my deliverer; my God, my strength (*Tsur* = Bed-Rock), in Whom I will trust; my buckler, and the horn of my salvation, *and* my high tower.
3 I will call upon the Lord, *Who is worthy* to be praised: so shall I be saved from mine enemies."

David's confidence in the Lord is based on firm doctrine. In contrast, the nation's unbelief was expressed at Massah and Meribah:

Psalm 95:8

"Harden not your heart as in the provocation (*Meribah)* and as in the day of temptation (*Massah*) in the wilderness."

At Massah, the Lord is presented as the "Bed-Rock" (*Tsur),* smitten so that blessing may emerge and later as the "Crag-Rock" *(Sela),* spoken to, so that blessing may flow. The former speaks of Christ in humiliation as the smitten One, whereas the Crag-Rock presents Him as the glorified One.

David's faith in the coming King is based on the "Crag-Rock" truth of His exaltation as well as the "Bed-Rock" of His humiliation. Both demand His public manifestation as King. At this point, David says, "I will call upon the Lord, Who is worthy to be praised: so shall I be saved from mine enemies".

When we remember that the title of the Psalm is considering a time period when David can declare confidently that "the Lord **delivered** him from the hand of all his enemies," the question arises as to why in verse 3 David says, "I **will** call upon the Lord ....so **shall** I be saved from mine enemies". In other words, if David has been already delivered from his enemies why does he call upon the Lord to yet save him from his enemies? This apparent difficulty in our English translation can be explained when we note that the cluster of verbs in verses 1-3 is in the long tense, carrying the idea of a present action leading on into the future. Therefore, when he says, "I will love Thee", "I will trust", "I will call" and "I shall be saved", the meaning is not that his love for the Lord, his trust in the Lord, his calling upon the Lord and his being saved by the Lord are phenomena only to be experienced in the future. Rather, these verbs describe David's experience at the time of writing and carry the knowledge that they will operate into the future. In other words, the verse could be translated: "I am calling and will call upon the Lord, worthy of praise, and I am saved and will be saved from my enemies". His salvation is one which is presently enjoyed but will have a future aspect and, as the tense suggests, an unending salvation. Although David enjoyed being saved, there was still a future aspect of salvation from his enemies to which he alludes. This Psalm is largely devoted to the salvation from his last great enemy. That last great enemy is death, as the New Testament tells us,

1 Corinithans 15:26
"The last enemy *that* shall be destroyed *is* death."

David, though still very much alive, contemplates death, his last enemy and uses prophetic language which is projected away beyond death to the great future when death shall only be a memory to those who have risen again.

Psalm 18:4-6

4 "The sorrows of death compassed me, and the floods of ungodly men (floods of Belial) made me afraid.
5 The sorrows of hell compassed me about: the snares of death prevented me.
6 In my distress I called upon the Lord, and cried unto my God: He heard my voice out of His temple, and my cry came before Him, *even* into His ears."

Verses 4-6 are the experience of someone who has already died. Since David had not died at the time of writing, he is using a literary technique frequently used in prophecy when speaking of a future event i.e. his death and resurrection as if they had already occurred.

Sorrows compassed him, floods of Belial terrified him, sorrows of hell (*Sheol*: please see Psalm 16) surrounded him and the snares of death "prevented" him. To "prevent" someone means "to get there before" that person. The floods poured out by "Belial" had "got there first" in David's experience. In other words, there were experiences which David would not enter into in this life simply because "death" and the "waters of Belial" would cut him off. When we reach the New Testament, we discover that Old Testament saints "through fear of death were all their lifetimes subject to bondage" (Hebrews 2:15). David is an example of an Old Testament believer who expressed his fears of "the last great enemy", death itself. This is depicted as a torrential river issuing forth from "Belial" or Satan himself. The ensuing verses depict the Lord's response to death and its effects on His own people

Psalm 18:7-8

7 "Then the earth shook and trembled; the foundations also of the hills moved and were shaken, because He was wroth.
8 There went up a smoke out of His nostrils, and fire out of His mouth devoured: coals were kindled by it."

Why should death and its effects cause the Lord to be "wroth"? Some may argue that it is with ungodly men that the Lord is angry. Whilst this is the case in other passages of Scripture, this does not seem to be the factor leading to the Lord being wrathful here. The context points to death as being the cause of the Lord's anger. Interestingly, when we see the Lord standing at the tomb of Lazarus we read that "He groaned in spirit" (John 11:33 and 38). The verb translated "groaned" means to "be angry or indignant". Here we see the response of the Lord to the effects of death on one of His own – and it is a comforting thought that, doubtless, in a general sense He retains this emotion as He witnesses the effects of death on all His saints from all ages until such times as He accomplishes their resurrection.

Psalm 18:9-19: The descent of the Lord

9 "He bowed the heavens also, and came down: and darkness *was* under His feet.

10 And He rode upon a cherub, and did fly: yea, He did fly upon the wings of the wind.

11 He made darkness His secret place; His pavilion round about Him *were* dark waters *and* thick clouds of the skies.

12 At the brightness *that was* before Him His thick clouds passed, hail *stones* and coals of fire.

13 The Lord also thundered in the heavens, and the Highest gave His voice; hail *stones* and coals of fire.

14 Yea, He sent out His arrows, and scattered them; and He shot out lightnings, and discomfited them.

15 Then the channels of waters were seen, and the foundations of the world were discovered at Thy rebuke, O Lord, at the blast of the breath of Thy nostrils.

16 He sent from above, He took me, He drew me out of many waters.

17 He delivered me from my strong enemy, and from them which hated me: for they were too strong for me.

18 They prevented me in the day of my calamity: but the Lord was my stay.

19 He brought me forth also into a large place; He delivered me, because He delighted in me."

In verse 4, death is depicted as a torrential river which claims its victims with seeming impunity but in verse 16, we see it having to give up its captives.

Psalm 18:16

"He sent from above, He took me, He drew me out of many waters."

For this to be effected the Lord has to descend.

Psalm 18:9

"He bowed the heavens also and came down and darkness was under His feet."

As the returning King re-enters the atmospheric heavens, the description is that of a storm with low-lying and descending clouds. This is fulfilled when the Lord "cometh with clouds" and "every eye shall see Him" (Revelation 1:7).

In Matthew 17, the Lord reminds his hearers of that prophetic morning of foul weather when the "sky shall be red and lowering", a clear reference to

His second coming in judgment.

Matthew 17:1-3
> 1 "The Pharisees also with the Sadducees came, and tempting desired Him that He would shew them a sign from heaven.
> 2 He answered and said unto them, When it is evening, ye say, *It will be* fair weather: for the sky is red.
> 3 And in the morning, *It will be* foul weather to day: for the sky is red and lowring. O *ye* hypocrites, ye can discern the face of the sky; but can ye not *discern* the signs of the times?"

Psalm 18:10
> "He rode upon a cherub."

When He came the first time, it was alone as the Kinsman Redeemer. When He comes in manifestation, it will be in glory riding upon the cherub. We know these winged creatures are celestial servants of the Lord. When He comes back to reign, Revelation 20 sees Him riding on a white horse.

Revelation 20:11
> "And I saw heaven opened, and behold a white horse; and He that sat upon him *was* called Faithful and True, and in righteousness He doth judge and make war."

Is this white horse the same creature as the winged cherub of Psalm 18:10? What a dramatic sight will emerge from the dark cloud which hides Him on His approach to planet earth! Just as a cloud "received Him out of their sight" on His ascension, on His return the converse will happen. The dark cloud will pass as He steps out of it, riding upon His cherub. Thunderings, lightenings and arrows will shoot forth from this august Person and "discomfit" them. The people who will be discomfited in verse 14 are not defined until later in verse 17, where we discover that they are those who hated David "for they were too strong for me". We will see in Psalm 69 that those who hated David are motivated, in effect, by hatred of David's Messiah – "the reproaches of them that reproached Thee fell upon me" (Psalm 69:9).

Accordingly then, the return of the Lord Jesus will mean judgment against those who rebel against the Son of David, Who is to reign as King in that coming day. Just as David had to rely on his son Solomon to deal with his enemies, in a greater sense God relies, in that coming day, on the Son of David to deal with those who hate Him or, more precisely, hate His Son, the Son of David. Clearly, the problem of death must be dealt with before David's claim to be in the lineage of the future King can be publicly vindicated. Whether it is a watery grave or an earthly grave, there is no place from where anyone who has died cannot be delivered. Planet earth is shaken by this display of divine majesty. "The earth shook and trembled" (verse 7). This is consistent with the events described in Revelation 11:13-18.

Revelation 11:13-18

13 "And the same hour was there a great earthquake, and the tenth part of the city fell, and in the earthquake were slain of men seven thousand: and the remnant were affrighted, and gave glory to the God of heaven.

14 The second woe is past; *and,* behold, the third woe cometh quickly.

15 And the seventh angel sounded; and there were great voices in heaven, saying, The kingdoms of this world are become *the kingdoms* of our Lord, and of His Christ; and He shall reign for ever and ever.

16 And the four and twenty elders, which sat before God on their seats, fell upon their faces, and worshipped God,

17 Saying, We give Thee thanks, O Lord God Almighty, Which art, and wast, and art to come; because Thou hast taken to Thee Thy great power, and hast reigned.

18 And the nations were angry, and Thy wrath is come, and the time of the dead, that they should be judged, and that Thou shouldest give reward unto **Thy servants the prophets**, and to **the saints**, and **them that fear Thy Name**, small and great; and shouldest destroy them which destroy the earth."

Note in this passage that it is on the occasion of "His wrath" that the dead should be judged. Clearly, "the dead" in this section are the righteous dead at the end of the tribulation because they are described as "Thy servants the prophets" and " the saints" and "them that fear Thy Name both small and great". They will be raised from the dead and will be judged. It is not judgment against sin that is in question, but rather an assessment of their lives on earth so that they might receive reward.

Psalm 18:16-19: The reward

16 "He sent from above, He took me, He drew me out of many waters.

17 He delivered me from my strong enemy, and from them which hated me: for they were too strong for me.

18 They prevented me in the day of my calamity: but the Lord was my stay.

19 He brought me forth also into a large place; He delivered me, because He delighted in me."

Just as in Revelation 11, resurrection from the dead leads to the divine judgment of the Old Testament and tribulation saints and their being rewarded for fidelity to the Lord during their lifetimes, similarly in this Psalm, David tells us how that he foresees a day when he can say with joy, "He sent from above, He took me, He drew me out of many waters" (verse 16). This is an allusion to deliverance from the river of death referred to earlier in the Poem.

In the ensuing section, we learn solemn principles of the Judgment of the Just – i.e. Old Testament and tribulation saints. This same principle, no doubt, applies to the saints of this Church era who will have a separate judgment at the *Bema*, the Judgment Seat of Christ (2 Corinthians 5:10). In that coming day, there is no reference to sin or failure or defeat. It is as if these have been removed completely from the assessment. Only that which is righteous is dealt with. All memory of sin appears to have been expunged in this remarkable passage.

Psalm 18:20-24: The assessment of righteousness

20 "The Lord rewarded me according to my righteousness; according to the cleanness of my hands hath He recompensed me.
21 For I have kept the ways of the Lord, and have not wickedly departed from my God.
22 For all His judgments *were* before me, and I did not put away His statutes from me.
23 I was also upright before Him, and I kept myself from mine iniquity.
24 Therefore hath the Lord recompensed me according to my righteousness, according to the cleanness of my hands in His eyesight."

In David's lifetime he acknowledges much failure and sin (see Psalm 69 especially). However, in this Psalm this seems to have been removed completely. "Their sins and iniquities will I remember no more forever" (Hebrews 10:17) applies even here at the judgment seat. This does not, of course, mean that the judgment of the just in any way lacks solemnity. The Lord searches our lives for reasons to recompense us. He looks for

1. Righteousness (verse 20)
2. Cleanness of hands (verse 20)
3. Keeping the ways of the Lord (verse 21)
4. Not wickedly departing from my God (verse 21)
5. Being upright (verse 23)
6. Keeping myself from mine iniquity (verse 23)

"Therefore hath the Lord recompensed me" will be the verdict of every saint in that coming day. The matter of sin is not called into question. He has borne the penalty of that Himself upon the tree. However, now He is looking for the fruit of righteousness in our lives.

Psalm 18:25-28

25 "With the merciful Thou wilt shew Thyself merciful; with an upright man Thou wilt shew Thyself upright;
26 With the pure Thou wilt shew Thyself pure; and with the froward Thou wilt shew Thyself froward.
27 For Thou wilt save the afflicted people; but wilt bring down high looks.
28 For Thou wilt light my candle: the Lord my God will enlighten my darkness."

Every act of mercy and uprightness will be rewarded. Every action to preserve ones purity will be recognised. There is a hint of loss, however, which will be brought to the attention of the believer in that day.

Psalm 18:26-27

26 "With the froward Thou wilt shew Thyself froward.
27 For Thou wilt save the afflicted people; but wilt bring down high looks."

Stubbornness to obey Him (being froward) will be met with a suitable response. Thinking too highly of oneself will be rectified: He will "bring down high looks". There will be no place for stubbornness or pride as we stand before the Judge.

Victories remembered.

We will be reminded of our victories such, as they were. However, even they will not give any room for "high looks". He will explain to us that our victories were entirely attributable to Him alone.

Psalm 18:29

"For by Thee I have run through a troop; and by my God have I leaped over a wall."

How helpful it is for us to recognise that only He gives us future victory and only He is to be praised for past victories. We will acknowledge this in His presence in that future solemn day of review.

Psalm 18:30

"*As for* God, His way *is* perfect: the Word of the Lord is tried: He *is* a buckler to all those that trust in Him."

As believers get their reward, whether it is at the Judgment Seat in heaven for the Church or, as in this case, at the Judgment of the Old Testament and tribulation saints prior to the millennium, the response will be the same: "As for God, His way is perfect".

We all will recognise God's way in our lives! It was truly perfect. In the measure in which we put His Word to the test and step out in dependence upon Him, we will realise His perfect way. We may well ask ourselves today, how can we find God's perfect way in our lives? The remaining verses makes this clear.

Verse 31 emphasises the importance of depending on Him in life to enjoy the victory:

Psalm 18:31

"For who *is* God save the Lord? or who *is* a Bed-Rock save our God?"

This is the same as Isaiah's message in Isaiah 26:4, "Trust ye in the Lord for ever: for in the Lord JEHOVAH *is* everlasting strength ((Bed)Rock of the ages)."

Psalm 18:32

"*It is* God that girdeth me with strength, and maketh my way perfect."

Oh, that we could know this strength in our lives today and realise God's perfect way in our day-to-day lives.

Numerous victories are catalogued in verses 33-43, each of which David carefully attributes to the Lord.

David had high spiritual experiences: God "setteth me upon my high places".

In the conflict it was God Who taught him what to do, so that seemingly impossible acts were performed. It was God Who upheld him, prevented his feet from slipping and strengthened him.

In that coming day of review, victories which we thought we had won ourselves, we will discover were the Lord's victories, in which we were graciously allowed to participate. This will, in itself, bring forth worship to Him in that great day of review.

Psalm 18:33-43

33 "He maketh my feet like hinds' *feet*, and setteth me upon my high places.
34 He teacheth my hands to war, so that a bow of steel is broken by mine arms.
35 Thou hast also given me the shield of Thy salvation: and Thy right hand hath holden me up, and Thy gentleness hath made me great.
36 Thou hast enlarged my steps under me, that my feet did not slip.
37 I have pursued mine enemies, and overtaken them: neither did I turn again till they were consumed.
38 I have wounded them that they were not able to rise: they are fallen under my feet.
39 For Thou hast girded me with strength unto the battle: Thou hast subdued under me those that rose up against me.
40 Thou hast also given me the necks of mine enemies; that I might destroy them that hate me.
41 They cried, but *there was* none to save *them: even* unto the Lord, but He answered them not.
42 Then did I beat them small as the dust before the wind: I did cast them out as the dirt in the streets.
43 Thou hast delivered me from the strivings of the people;"

David's role in the Kingdom based on his reward.

Psalm 18:43b-46

43b "*and* Thou hast made me the head of the heathen: a people *whom* I have not known shall serve me.
44 As soon as they hear of me, they shall obey me: the strangers shall submit themselves unto me.
45 The strangers shall fade away, and be afraid out of their close places.
46 The Lord liveth; and blessed *be* my Rock; and let the God of my salvation be exalted."

This end of verse 43 confirms that this Psalm is prophetic: "A people whom I have not known shall serve me". No doubt, David is looking forward to that coming day of service when, in the Millennial Kingdom, he will enjoy a position of authority in the Name of the Messiah where he will have an important role in the earthly administration of that Kingdom.

Psalm 18:47-48

47 "*It is* God that avengeth me, and subdueth the people under me.
48 He delivereth me from mine enemies: yea, Thou liftest me up above

those that rise up against me: Thou hast delivered me from the violent man."

In that day David will look upon the Lord Jesus not just as his Kinsman Redeemer but as his Kinsman Avenger. All the reproach which David ever sustained in life, by being linked with the Messianic promise (see Psalm 69), shall be compensated in that coming day of glory. For us, in this Church era, it will be the same.

David's response

David will then know the reason why he experienced trials. He will have assented to God's analysis of his life. He will have attributed all the glory to the One Who redeemed Him. He will be overwhelmed by His Grace and His kindness to Him. He will leave the judgment seat with a heart welling up in worship.

Psalm 18:49

"Therefore will I give thanks unto Thee, O Lord, among the heathen, and sing praises unto Thy Name."

When we come to Romans 15:9, this verse is quoted again, where we discover that the "heathen" are those who were saved during the Church era.

Romans 15:9

"And that the **Gentiles** might glorify God for *His* mercy; as it is written, For this cause I will confess to Thee among the Gentiles, and sing unto Thy Name."

Despite not being in the Church, David's praise will be mingled with that of the praise of the "heathen" – (the nations saved from this era) – as together we praise the One Who has wrought this great work of glory. The details of David's song, the "New Song" are considered in our later meditations of Psalms 40, 96, 97, 98 and 99.

In that day it can be truly said:

Psalm 18:50

"Great deliverance giveth He to His king; and sheweth mercy to His anointed, to David, and to his seed for evermore."

5

PSALM 22

To the chief Musician upon Aijeleth Shahar, A Psalm of David.

1 My God, My God, why hast Thou forsaken Me? why art Thou so far from helping Me, and from the words of My roaring?

2 O My God, I cry in the daytime, but Thou hearest not; and in the night season, and am not silent.

3 But Thou art holy, O Thou that inhabitest the praises of Israel.

4 Our fathers trusted in Thee: they trusted, and Thou didst deliver them.

5 They cried unto Thee, and were delivered: they trusted in Thee, and were not confounded.

6 But I am a worm, and no man; a reproach of men, and despised of the people.

7 All they that see Me laugh Me to scorn: they shoot out the lip, they shake the head, saying,

8 He trusted on the Lord that He would deliver Him: let Him deliver Him, seeing He delighted in Him.

9 But Thou art He that took Me out of the womb: Thou didst make Me hope when I was upon My mother's breasts.

10 I was cast upon Thee from the womb: Thou art My God from My mother's belly.

11 Be not far from Me; for trouble is near; for there is none to help.

12 Many bulls have compassed Me: strong bulls of Bashan have beset Me round.

13 They gaped upon Me with their mouths, as a ravening and a roaring lion.

14 I am poured out like water, and all My bones are out of joint: My heart is like wax; it is melted in the midst of My bowels.

15 My strength is dried up like a potsherd; and My tongue cleaveth to My jaws; and Thou hast brought Me into the dust of death.

16 For dogs have compassed Me: the assembly of the wicked have inclosed Me: they pierced My hands and My feet.

17 I may tell all My bones: they look and stare upon Me.

18 They part My garments among them, and cast lots upon My vesture.

19 But be not Thou far from Me, O Lord: O My strength, haste Thee to help Me.

20 Deliver My soul from the sword; My darling from the power of the dog.

21 Save Me from the lion's mouth: for Thou hast heard Me from the horns of the unicorns.

22 I will declare Thy Name unto My brethren: in the midst of the congregation will I praise Thee.

23 Ye that fear the Lord, praise Him; all ye the seed of Jacob, glorify Him; and fear Him, all ye the seed of Israel.

24 For He hath not despised nor abhorred the affliction of the Afflicted; neither hath He hid his face from Him; but when He cried unto Him, He heard.

25 My praise shall be of Thee in the great congregation: I will pay My vows before them that fear Him.

26 The meek shall eat and be satisfied: they shall praise the Lord that seek Him: your heart shall live for ever.

27 All the ends of the world shall remember and turn unto the Lord: and all the kindreds of the nations shall worship before Thee.

28 For the Kingdom is the Lord's: and He is the governor among the nations.

29 All they that be fat upon earth shall eat and worship: all they that go down to the dust shall bow before Him: and none can keep alive his own soul.

30 A seed shall serve Him; it shall be accounted to the Lord for a generation.

31 They shall come, and shall declare His righteousness unto a people that shall be born, that He hath done this.

Introduction

Psalm 22 brings us into the sacred ground of how a believer is forgiven through the death of the Lord Jesus Christ. It brings before us the doctrines of atonement, expiation, propitiation and forgiveness. It raises the question of how Old Testament believers were saved, and if there are any differences in the privileges they enjoyed subsequent to their salvation and the privileges a New Testament believer enjoys today. Before considering the details of the Psalm, we will consider how Old Testament believers were saved and if there are differences in the privileges they enjoyed compared to a New Testament believer. Then we will look at the reason why there was a tabernacle/temple system in the Old Testament and its significance. Then, briefly, we will consider the definitions of atonement, expiation and propitiation before looking at the details of the Psalm which focuses our attention so wonderfully on the great work of the Lord Jesus at Calvary when He made propitiation for our sins.

How were Old Testament believers saved?

There are several views which we will evaluate in light of Scripture.

1 Provisional salvation on the basis of animal sacrifices

It is supposed by some that until the death of the Lord Jesus Christ which made propitiation for sin, Old Testament believers were saved provisionally by the blood of the animal sacrifices which they offered. Those who hold this view believe that it was the blood of the animal sacrifice in the Old

Testament which provided a covering or atonement (*cippur*) for their sins to allow God to provisionally forgive them in light of the death of the Lord Jesus Christ, which had yet to be fulfilled.

There are fundamental difficulties with this view. In lands where there was no temple how could people be saved? For example, during the captivity in Babylon when there was no opportunity to go to the temple to offer sacrifices, how could people be saved? Clearly, during the 70 years of the captivity there were many believers who were not depending on animal sacrifices.

Furthermore, if one were to offer an animal sacrifice for one or more sins and died after inadvertently sinning thereafter, would that have meant that such an individual could not experience salvation? Clearly this cannot be the case. Eternal salvation in the Old Testament was not based on the blood of an animal sacrifice. It is true that in the Old Testament, as far as eternal salvation was concerned, believers enjoyed an atonement (covering) of all their sins which was **provided by God** and not Aaron.

Ezekiel 16:62-63
"And I will establish My covenant with thee; and thou shalt know that I am the Lord: that thou mayest remember, and be confounded, and never open thy mouth any more because of thy shame, **when I am pacified toward thee (I have made an atonement for thee)** for all that thou hast done, saith the Lord God."

This atonement or covering for sin (*cippur*) lasted until the death of the Lord Jesus when their sins were no longer covered over (atoned for), but rather put away forever, blotted out and remembered no more.

Isaiah 43:25
"I, even I, am He that blotteth out thy transgressions for Mine own sake, and will not remember thy sins."

The basis of this atonement provided by God and not Aaron was **not on the basis of an animal sacrifice**, but rather on the basis of the anticipated death of the Lord Jesus Christ. The death of the Lord Jesus Christ made an end of the era when God covered over (made atonement for) the sins of the Old Testament believers. Subsequent to the death of the Lord Jesus Christ, God blotted out their transgressions and remembered them no more. This is much much more than merely covering them over. It is in this context that Romans 3:24-25 describes the righteousness of God in "passing over" the sins of the Old Testament believers, referred to as "the sins that are past", before the Lord Jesus made the propitiation at Calvary.

Romans 3:24-25
24 "Being justified freely by His grace through the redemption that is in Christ Jesus:
25 Whom God hath set forth to be a propitiation through faith in His blood, to declare His righteousness for the remission (passing over) of sins that

are past, through the forbearance of God;"

Similarly, in Hebrews 9:15 the writer speaks of the "redemption of the transgressions that were under the first covenant". It was on the basis of the death of Christ that the transgressions which were under the first covenant were redeemed forever.

Hebrews 9:15
"And for this cause He is the Mediator of the new testament, that by means of death, for the redemption of the transgressions that were under the first testament, they which are called might receive the promise of eternal inheritance."

These considerations show that Old Testament believers were not relying on animal sacrifices for their eternal salvation.

2 The timing of the death of Christ did not matter
Another view is that the actual timing of the death of the Lord Jesus did not matter and that even before He died and rose, Old Testament believers could be saved by faith enjoying the same privileges as New Testament believers. This statement is partially true in as far as forgiveness and justification could be granted to an Old Testament believer on the basis of the anticipated death of the Lord Jesus Christ. However, it is not true that all the blessings of salvation could be enjoyed immediately. Some of these blessings were deferred until after the death of the Lord Jesus. What privileges did they enjoy as part of their salvation? Here are some of them:

Firstly they could say that "their sins had been moved at a distance from them".

Psalm 103:12
"As far as the east is from the west, so far hath He removed (distanced) our transgressions from us."

In other words, as far as they were concerned their sins had been uncoupled from them and moved elsewhere.

Secondly, their sins were "cast into the depth of the sea."

Micah 7:19
"He will turn again, He will have compassion upon us; He will subdue our iniquities; and Thou wilt cast all their sins into the depths of the sea."

Thirdly, they could say that their sins were "covered".

Psalm 32:1
"Blessed is he whose transgression is forgiven, whose sin is covered."

Fourthly they could say that their sins were atoned for (covered over).

Psalm 78:38
> "But He, *being* full of compassion, forgave (covered over; **atoned for**: same root as *cippur*) *their* iniquity, and destroyed *them* not; yea, many a time turned He His anger away, and did not stir up all His wrath."

Fifthly, they could say that the Lord had cast all their sins behind His back.

Isaiah 38:17
> "Behold, for peace I had great bitterness: but Thou hast in love to my soul *delivered it* from the pit of corruption: for Thou hast cast all my sins behind Thy back."

However, there were at least three blessings linked to their salvation which were assured to them in the future but deferred to them until the death and resurrection of the Lord Jesus. These three guaranteed, albeit "deferred" blessings, were as follows:

A The Remembrance of sin no more forever
Although their sins were forgiven, they could not say that they were forgotten. This is because that so long as there was a Day of Atonement on the 10th day of the 7th month, there was a remembrance made of sin every year (Hebrews 10:3). Nevertheless, they had an assurance that their sins would be forgotten and remembered no more forever (Jeremiah 31:34).

Jeremiah 31:33-34
> 33 "But this shall be the covenant that I will make with the house of Israel; After those days, saith the Lord, I will put My Law in their inward parts, and write it in their hearts; and will be their God, and they shall be My people. 34 And they shall teach no more every man his neighbour, and every man his brother, saying, Know the Lord: for they shall all know Me, from the least of them unto the greatest of them, saith the Lord; **for I will forgive their iniquity, and I will remember their sin no more.**"

This remembering no more forever of sin would require the once-and-for-all death of the Covenant Victim, the Lord Jesus Christ, to make propitiation for sin.

B The blotting out of sin
For the same reason, they could not say their sins had been blotted out. The blotting out of their sins was linked with the same event as when they would be remembered no more (Isaiah 43:25) which as we know from Jermiah 31:33-34 was future.

Isaiah 43:25
> "I, even I, am He that blotteth out thy transgressions for Mine own sake, and will not remember thy sins."

When the two passages which speak of sins being remembered no more forever are compared (Isaiah 43:25 and Jeremiah 31:33-34), we discover that "the blotting out" and "remembering of sin no more" are different aspects of the same event. Moreover, these blessings arise as a result of the shedding of the blood of the Victim of the New Covenant Whom the Lord Jesus declared in the upper room to be Himself (Luke 22:20). Old Testament believers enjoyed a present peace with respect to their sins being removed from them. However, they looked forward with glad anticipation to the Covenant Victim through Whom sins would be not merely covered (same root as *cippur*), but rather put away, blotted out and remembered no more forever. It is worth bearing in mind that in this present Church era subsequent to the death and resurrection of the Lord Jesus it is not, strictly speaking, accurate to thank the Lord for "removing our sins from us" or "casting our sins behind His back" or "casting our sins in the bottom of the sea". This language is never used in the New Testament. The reason is quite simply because the Lord Jesus at Calvary has not merely removed our sins from us, nor indeed cast them at the bottom of the sea. He has borne them away and blotted them out such that they can be remembered no more forever. Note 1

Those who have difficulty in grasping this should remember that on the cross the burden of sin was "exacted by God" as a conscious, infinite and divine act. This included a remembrance **by God at Calvary** of all the Old Testament saints' sins, which for many years had been covered (root *cippur*), as well as divine foreknowledge of all those who would ever sin subsequent to His death to make propitiation for sin. This is what is meant by Isaiah 53:6, where we read, "the Lord hath laid on Him the iniquity of us all".

Isaiah 53:6
> 6 "All we like sheep have gone astray; we have turned every one to his own way; and the Lord hath laid on Him the iniquity of us all".

Subsequent to Calvary, all who are saved, both in Old and New Testaments, can rejoice in the glorious fact that "our sins and iniquities will He remember no more forever".

These considerations help us understand Isaiah 6:5-7 where we have the essential elements of an Old Testament conversion described in detail. On that occasion, Isaiah describes how he obtained forgiveness of sins and call to divine service. In Isaiah 6:7, he recounts how in his vision of the holiness of God he became aware of his own sinfulness. His relief from guilt came when the seraph flew to him, bringing a live coal from the altar in heaven which touched his lips. He heard these words, "Lo, this hath touched thy lips; and thine iniquity is taken away, and thy sin purged" (Isaiah 6:7). The literal translation is, "Lo this hath touched thy lips; and thine iniquity has departed, and thy sin been covered (same root as *cippur*)."

Isaiah's personal forgiveness and deliverance from sin did not come from ceremony in the temple or any earthly altar. Rather it was from the **heavenly altar** that the live coal came, indicating that the covering (*cippur*) of his sin was a divine act and not an activity of an Aaronic priest. Moreover, when we read, "thine iniquity is taken away" or perhaps more literally, "thine iniquity has departed", it is clear that the guilt of his sin was uncoupled from him. He no longer bore it. It would of course be on a later occasion that this sin would be "blotted out" and "remembered no more" (Isaiah 43:25) i.e. when the Lord Jesus would bear it away as prophesied in Isaiah 53. Following the triumph of our Lord Jesus at Calvary, all believers of every age can rejoice that their sins have been blotted out and remembered no more, something which is infinitely greater than sins "departing" and "being covered".

Let us be ever thankful for the "so great salvation" (Hebrews 2:3) the Lord Jesus has accomplished for us.

C Being made priests

Old Testament believers could not be priests in the presence of God such as New Testament believers today. This privilege could only happen to them and to us after the Lord Jesus Christ was consecrated as a Priest as a result of His death at Calvary and subsequent resurrection and ascension (see Psalms 2, 16, 40, 69 and 110). Old Testament believers looked forward to a day when they could enjoy priestly access to the throne of God subsequent to the once-and-for-all Sacrifice of the Lord Jesus by which their sins would be blotted out and remembered no more. Until that moment they must be kept in the safety and comfort of upper *Sheol* before the risen and seated Christ could grant them priestly access to the throne in heaven. This is considered in detail in Psalms 40 and 110.

These meditations show that the timing of the death of the Lord Jesus Christ did matter in regard to the blessings enjoyed by the people of God. Spiritual blessings which believers enjoy subsequent to the resurrection and ascension of the Lord Jesus are unlimited. This is why in Ephesians we read that we are not blessed with "some blessings" but rather with "**all spiritual blessings** in Christ Jesus".

Ephesians 1:3
> "Blessed *be* the God and Father of our Lord Jesus Christ, Who hath blessed
> us with all spiritual blessings in heavenly *places* in Christ".

May the Lord touch the hearts of those of us who are believers in our Lord Jesus Chirst to be forever thankful to Him for these superlative blessings.

3 Saved by faith

We have seen how Old Testament believers were not saved by animal sacrifices and that when they did get saved their blessings and privileges in their lifetimes were more limited than what we enjoy today. How then were they saved? The answer is in Genesis 15:6 and Romans 4:3 where we read, "Abraham believed God and it was counted unto him for righteousness." This was a declaration of righteousness i.e. justification. And it was not on the basis of an animal sacrifice. It was alone through faith in the Lamb of God's providing (see Psalm 24) that Old Testament believers obtained salvation and the promise of eternal security. **This alone** was how all Old Testament believers were saved. It is still also how we get saved today!

What then was the role of the animal sacrifices in general and the tabernacle/temple system of worship in particular if it lacked eternal saving power?

The tabernacle - and later the temple - was an earthly sanctuary where God was spiritually present. It therefore was first and foremost a place where the people went to centrally meet and have fellowship with God and with one another. The ceremonies within it were designed to remove any possibility of mistaking that tabernacle/temple rituals were of any value as far as securing eternal destiny is concerned and propitiating God's throne in heaven. For example, the sins it dealt with were ceremonial sins such as touching a dead body, contracting ceremonial defilement etc. If there were presumptuous sins, such as blaspheming or rebellion (e.g. gathering sticks on the Sabbath (Numbers 15:30-36)) there was no sacrifice for sin - only death by stoning. Moreover, the tabernacle/temple system had no remedy for sins of the heart such as covetousness etc. As far as eternal deliverance from the guilt of such sins (including adultery) was concerned, the tabernacle/temple sacrificial system had no remedy (Psalm 51:1-17).

One could summarise the ceremonial law as based on four **temporary** things.

There was (1) a temporary **inheritance** (the land of Israel), acquired through (2) a temporary **redemption** (from Egypt), on the terms of (3) a temporary **covenant** (the Mosaic covenant) administered and guaranteed by (4) a temporary **priesthood**. The conceptual link between the temporary inheritance acquired through the temporary redemption from Egypt will be considered in detail later in Psalm 69. The conceptual link between the temporary covenant and the temporary priesthood will be considered in detail in Psalm 110. Interestingly, these four temporary things have within the covers of the Old Testament a **permanent** counterpart which is regarded as eternal, and it was this eternal goal which the Old Testament saints longed for. For example, (1) in Isaiah 60:21 the prophet speaks of an **eternal inheritance** for the nation. This will become theirs when the Messiah reigns supreme. Regarding (2) **an eternal redemption**, Psalm 49:8 tells us that "the redemption of their soul is precious, and it ceaseth for ever". Jeremiah 31:33-34 and Psalm 111:9 speak of an (3) **everlasting covenant** and we read in Psalm 110:4 (4) of a **forever and eternal priesthood**. This shows us that the Old Testament distinguished between the temporary illustrative tabernacle system and the eternal verities of which the tabernacle system was a divinely given learning tool. In fact, the revelation of the tabernacle system was called a "pattern" in Exodus 25:40. However, what Moses was shown in Exodus 25:40 was not just a "pattern" of the details of the earthly tabernacle.

Exodus 25:40
> "And look that thou make *them* after their **pattern**, which was shewed thee in the mount."

According to Hebrews 8:5, it was a pattern of something greater. It was a pattern of the heavenly sanctuary and **how to gain access there as a priestly people**.

Hebrews 8:5
> 4 "For if He were on earth, He should not be a Priest, seeing **that there are priests that offer gifts according to the Law:**
> 5 **Who serve unto the example and shadow of heavenly things,** as Moses was admonished of God when he was about to make the tabernacle: for, See, saith he, *that* thou make all things **according to the pattern shewed to thee in the mount.**"

It follows, therefore, that the entire tabernacle/temple worship system, by virtue of its temporary nature, was not to fit a soul for eternity but rather to **teach principles** as to how men can be redeemed to be priests with access to the throne of God in heaven. This subject is discussed in detail in the consideration of redemption unto priesthood in Psalms 40 and 69. The other great significance of the tabernacle/temple system was that in Old Testament times it was **the place** where Jehovah had placed His Name. Accordingly, all who were saved by faith in the Old Testament loved the tabernacle because it was where they went to have fellowship with their God. A New Testament believer will find an analogy in New Testament assembly gatherings. We attend the gatherings not in order to obtain salvation but rather because we have already obtained it. Attending the tabernacle and temple was on exactly the same principle. Moreover, we attend the New Testament assembly because we learn there many principles regarding the Lord. He is there. He has promised to be in the midst. We also recognise that the assembly is temporary and reflects the permanent thing, namely the Church which is His body. This does not mean that we regard the assembly with carelessness. Far from it! Because the Lord is there we must be most careful how we act. Similarly, in the tabernacle/temple system the worshippers did not act carelessly in the presence of the Lord. Nadab and Abihu learned this too late (Leviticus 10:1) as did King Uzziah (2 Chronicles 28:18).

Because it was important in one's day-to-day life in the Old Testament to enjoy fellowship with God, the ceremonial Law with all its details was important. Carelessness in this could lead to a premature end to one's life. This did not mean that the person who so transgressed would face eternal punishment. It was just that they came under the disciplinary hand of God which was so solemn. Similarly, in the New Testament the assembly is not a place to cast aside the godly order given in the New Testament as to how gatherings should be conducted. Paul lovingly warned the Corinthian believers to be careful in this matter. The tabernacle was temporary and so is the assembly. The tabernacle/temple system will one day give way to the earthly temple in the future millennial Kingdom. The assembly will one day give way to the great congregation in the sky. Those who benefited from the Lord's presence in their lifetimes in both these divinely ordained places will one day look back with fond memories to the provision which was provided along life's wilderness journey within these meeting places. Should there be a believer reading these words who is not yet in assembly fellowship it is the Lord's will that you should be found there.

In summary then, it can be said that the Old Testament earthly system of worship involved a temporary **redemption** (1), unto a temporary **inheritance** (2), serviced by a temporary **priesthood** (3) and legitimised by a temporary **covenant** (4). However, the Old Testament recognised that there was an eternal redemption (Psalm 49:8) to an eternal inheritance (Isaiah 60:21), serviced by an eternal Priest (Psalm 110), legitimized by an eternal covenant (Jeremiah 31:33-34). Accordingly, it should not surprise us that the epistle to the Hebrews confirms this by again speaking of an **eternal redemption** (Hebrews 9:12) to an **eternal inheritance** (Hebrews 9:15), serviced by an **eternal Priest** (Hebrews 7:24-25), legitimized by an **eternal covenant** (Hebrews 13:20-21). These four aspects of eternal truth are quoted below:

(1) The eternal redemption in Hebrews

Hebrews 9:12
"Neither by the blood of goats and calves, but by His own blood He entered in once into the holy place, having obtained **eternal redemption** *for us*."

(2) The eternal inheritance in Hebrews

Hebrews 9:15
"And for this cause He is the Mediator of the New Testament, that by means of death, for the redemption of the transgressions *that were* under the first testament, they which are called might receive the promise of **eternal inheritance.**"

(3) The eternal Priest in Hebrews

Hebrews 7:24-25
24 "But this *Man*, because He **continueth ever**, hath an unchangeable priesthood.
25 Wherefore He is able also to save them to the uttermost that come unto God by Him, seeing He **ever liveth** to make intercession for them."

(4) The eternal covenant in Hebrews.

Hebrews 13:20-21
20 "Now the God of peace, that brought again from the dead our Lord Jesus, that great Shepherd of the sheep, through the blood of **the everlasting covenant**,
21 Make you perfect in every good work to do His will, working in you that which is well pleasing in His sight, through Jesus Christ; to Whom *be* glory for ever and ever. Amen."

The distinctions between the temporary and eternal aspects of "redemption", "inheritance", "priesthood" and "covenant" were **already** made in the Old Testament. What the writer to the Hebrews is doing is **emphasisng and confirming** the significance of these distinctions. The importance of this is to emphasise that New Testament teaching does not contradict Old Testament teaching. Rather New Testament truth emphasizes and confirms Old Testament doctrine. This is consistent with the divine pattern of God communicating His truth twice (Job 33:14).

Job 33:14
> "For God speaketh once, **yea twice,** *yet man* perceiveth it not."

Those who see a conflict between the doctrines of the Old and New Testaments have misunderstood both. Those who by faith have come to grasp the unity of Old and New Testaments can begin the eternal occupation of worshipping the Divine Author Who has revealed His innermost counsels within the sacred volumes of Old and New Testaments.

A brief definition of atonement, expiation and propitiation

Atonement (Hebrew *cippur*) is an Old Testament concept and it means to "make a covering". As we have considered above, it was used in the tabernacle/temple system to make **a covering for the sins of the people** within the limitations of that system. However, this aspect of atonement within the tabernacle was a picture of how God in Old Testament times **covered over the sins of Old Testament believers** (Isaiah 6:7) **until** the death of the Lord Jesus Christ when sins would no longer be covered over (atoned for) but put away forever and blotted out (Isaiah 43:25).

It should be noted that there were other aspects of atonement in the tabernacle which involved covering of **persons** rather than the idea of covering of **sin** mentioned above. Because covering of sin was not in question, the sin offering was not involved. An example was the **covering before God** enjoyed by those persons who offered a burnt offering. We should consider this as the **covering of the worshipper**.

Leviticus 1:3-4
> 3 "If his offering *be* a burnt sacrifice of the herd, let him offer a male without blemish: he shall offer it of his own voluntary will at the door of the tabernacle of the congregation before the Lord.
> 4 And he shall put his hand upon the head of the burnt offering; and it shall be accepted for him to **make atonement (covering)** for him".

Again it can be emphasised that sin was not being considered because the burnt offering did not deal with sin. Within the tabernacle, the offering of the burnt offering only happened **after** any necessary sin offerings dealing with sin had been offered. The burnt offering was all for God and illustrates all that God saw in the Person and work of Christ, away beyond His work of putting away of sin. The offerer of the burnt offering in the tabernacle already had his sin and guilt dealt with by the sin offering and covered over. Now as he offered his burnt offering he stood before God as a **person** "covered" (atoned for) by **the burnt offering**. It was as if God looked upon the worshipping Israelite in all the value of the burnt offering and not on his own merit. The offerer of the burnt offering could say that the burnt offering was accepted for him (by God) to provide him with a covering (Leviticus 1:4) and thus a standing in God's presence. He was assured of this when the divine fire consumed that burnt offering. In the Old Testament, the burnt offering was **accepted by God** for the Israelite and provided a **covering** for that Israelite in the sight of God. When we come to the New Testament, the fulfilment of this Tabernacle illustration is even more sweet. Here we discover that now that our sin is put away (Ephesians 1:7), we are accepted "in the Beloved" (Ephesians 1:6).

Ephesians 1:5-6
> 5 "Having predestinated us unto the adoption of children by Jesus Christ to Himself, according to the good pleasure of His will,
> 6 To the praise of the glory of His grace, wherein He hath made us **accepted in the Beloved.**
> 7 In Whom we have redemption through His blood, the forgiveness of sins, according to the riches of His grace".

Just as the Israelite stood in all the acceptability of the burnt offering in the presence of God, now we stand before God accepted in all the immeasurable fullness of the belovedness of Christ to God His Father.

The **worshipping Israelite** in Leviticus 1 had not come to present his own merits to God. He was very happy to be seen by God only in the merit of the burnt offering he brought. How glad we are that as redeemed and forgiven worshippers today, in the Lord's presence we are not seen in all our imperfections and weaknesses but in the acceptability of Christ alone! Worship is not the presentation of one's own merits to God. This is the way of Cain (Jude 1:11). Worship is the presentation of Christ to God by a grateful redeemed soul.

The second aspect of the covering (atonement) of persons in the sight of God is the covering of the **servant of God**. Just as the **worshipper of God** does not present his own merits to God and has nothing in himself to boast of, similarly, the **servant of God** moves in God's service not in his own merit but alone in the acceptability of Christ. He longs that he should not be the one who is seen in the Lord's service but that only Christ is seen as he labours for the Master. The moment the Lord's servant wishes to exult in his own abilities or prominence or longs for promotion of self in Christian service, he instantly exits usefulness for God. He may continue to serve the Lord but thereafter does so only ineffectively until restored to the Lord again. This becomes clear in the covering (atonement) of the Israelite for service (Exodus 30:11-15). Here again, sin is not in question so the sin offering is not involved. The Israelites were being numbered as a serving people and the twenty gerahs which were paid for the atonement money were a covering for that service. In other words, the value of the service of the Israelite was paid **in advance of their life of public service** and acted as a **covering (atonement)** for that life of service, however long or short, and however humble or prominent.

Exodus 30:11-15
> 11 "And the Lord spake unto Moses, saying,
> 12 When thou takest the sum of the children of Israel after their number, then shall they give every man a ransom for his soul unto the Lord, when thou numberest them; that there be no plague among them, when *thou* numberest them.
> 13 This they shall give, every one that passeth among them that are numbered, half a shekel after the shekel of the sanctuary: (a shekel *is* twenty gerahs:) an half shekel *shall be* the offering of the Lord.
> 14 Every one that passeth among them that are numbered, from twenty years old and above, shall give an offering unto the Lord.
> 15 The rich shall not give more, and the poor shall not give less than half a shekel, when *they* give an offering unto the Lord, to **make an atonement** for your souls.
> 16 And thou shalt take the **atonement money** of the children of Israel, and shalt appoint it **for the service of the tabernacle of the congregation**; that it may be a memorial unto the children of Israel before the Lord, **to make an atonement** (same root as *cippur*) for your souls".

Failure to remember this truth leads to a plague among the people of God (Exodus 30:12). Today in Christian service, operating in our own merits or abilities will hinder rather than help in the Lord's service and ultimately be injurious to the Lord's servant. May all of us who seek to serve the Lord be ever before Him in exercised prayer that He alone may be seen in our lives and service. In other words, in our service we have the divine covering (atonement) of Christ. Paul lived out this truth in his Christian service as indicated by his desire to be "found **in Him** not having mine own righteousness" (Phillipians 3:7-12).

Phillipians 3:7-12
> 7 "But what things were gain to me, those I counted loss for Christ.
> 8 Yea doubtless, and I count all things *but* loss for the excellency of the knowledge of Christ Jesus my Lord: for Whom I have suffered the loss of all things, and do count them *but* dung, that I may win Christ,
> 9 **And be found in Him, not having mine own righteousness**, which is of the Law, but that which is through the faith of Christ, the righteousness which is of God by faith:
> 10 That I may know Him, and the power of His resurrection, and the fellowship of His sufferings, being made conformable unto His death;
> 11 If by any means I might attain unto the resurrection of the dead.
> 12 Not as though I had already attained, either were already perfect: but I follow after, if that I may apprehend that for which also I am apprehended of Christ Jesus."

Expiation is the act of putting away sin. This is what the Lord Jesus did at

Calvary when He "put away sin by the Sacrifice of Himself" (Hebrews 9:26).

Propitiation is derived from the Latin word *propitiatio* meaning "appeasement" which was used in the Ancient Latin Vulgate translation to translate the related Greek words *hilasterion* and *hilasmos* which occur in the New Testament.

Romans 3:24-25
> 24 "Being justified freely by His grace through the redemption that is in Christ Jesus:
> 25 Whom God hath set forth *to be* a **propitiation** (*hilasterion*) through faith in His blood, to declare His righteousness for the remission of sins that are past, through the forbearance of God".

John 2:1-2
> 1 "My little children, these things write I unto you, that ye sin not. And if any man sin, we have an Advocate with the Father, Jesus Christ the righteous:
> 2 And He is the **propitiation** (*hilasmos*) for our sins: and not for ours only, but also for *the sins of* the whole world".

What then is the meaning of *hilasterion* and does the Latin rendering *propitiatio* which has come into our English Bibles as "propitiation (appeasement)" fully encompass its significance? The exact meaning of *hilasterion* has been a matter of much debate among scholars. However, there can be no debate as to its meaning in Hebrews 9:5 where the word clearly refers to the covering of the ark of the covenant otherwise known as the "mercy seat" in the tabernacle.

Hebrews 9:2-5
> 2 "For there was a tabernacle made; the first, wherein *was* the candlestick, and the table, and the shewbread; which is called the sanctuary.
> 3 And after the second veil, the tabernacle which is called the Holiest of All;
> 4 Which had the golden censer, and the ark of the covenant overlaid round about with gold, wherein *was* the golden pot that had manna, and Aaron's rod that budded, and the tables of the covenant;
> 5 And over it the cherubims of glory shadowing the mercyseat (*hilasterion*); of which we cannot now speak particularly."

The word *hilasterion* is used in Hebrews 9:5 to describe the mercy seat in the tabernacle. The fact that the Lord Jesus is also referred to as the *hilasterion* in Romans 3:25 shows that He is the fulfilment of that of which the mercy seat in the ancient tabernacle was a picture. It is highly significant that in Hebrews 9:5 the mercy seat is being described on the Day of Atonement since the golden censer in Hebrews 9:4 is described as also being present in the Holiest of All, something that only happened on the Day of Atonement, when the cloud of incense emerging from it shielded Aaron from the presence of God on that occasion. This means that the *hilasterion* (mercy seat) of Hebrews 9:5 **had blood upon it**, since the occasion being considered is the Day of Atonement, the one day of the year when this was the case.

Since the *hilasterion* was the place where the blood was placed on the Day of Atonement exclusively for **the eyes of God** so that the sins of the people could be forgiven, it follows that the Biblical use of the word *hilasterion* emphasises **what God sees** in the infinite value of the precious shed blood of the Lord Jesus Christ. No wonder scholars have been limited as to defining the meaning of this wonderful word. This is because the definition of *hilasterion* is found alone in the indefinable, infinite person of Christ and God's measureless pleasure in Him and the value of His precious shed blood. The ancient Latin translation of *hilasterion* as *propitiatio,* meaning "appeasement", was an attempt to define God's thoughts of the precious blood of the Lord Jesus. The word "appeasement" calls our attention to God's righteous anger in the matter of sin and how this has been fully satisfied in the shed blood and death of the Lord Jesus. While this is no doubt included in the meaing of *hilasterion,* the word carries a significance far beyond the idea of appeasement. Appeasement applies only to the cessation of wrath. God's thoughts of the preciousness of the blood of Christ go far beyond this. Through His blood God can redeem us (1 Peter 1:19), which is **much much more** than appeasing His abiding wrath against us in our persistent unbelief (John 3: 36). A little of the wonder of redemption by the blood of Christ is considered in Psalms 40 and 69 and there we will find that redemption by the blood of Christ far exceeds the rather negative concept of appeasement of an angry God, which is what the Latin word *propitiatio* and its English derivative *propitiation* mean. In fact, in 1 John 4:10, John shows that propitiation (*hilasmos*) is a key element of divine *agape* love which is very positive and measureless.

I John 4:10
   "Herein is **love (agape),** not that we loved God, but that He loved us, and
   sent His Son *to be* the propitiation (*hilasmos*) for our sins".

It follows, therefore, that the Biblical definition of *hilasterion* and *hilasmos,* which are rendered *propitiatio* in Latin and *propitiation* in English, goes far beyond the idea of appeasement and assuaging of divine wrath which is the literal meaning of propitiation. It is true that propitiation involves the assuaging of divine wrath through the blood of Christ. However, **the Biblical use** of the word demonstrates a wider sigificance which includes an **infinite outpouring of divine agape love** (1 John 4:10) and **mercy** (Luke 18:13).

The words atonement, expiation and propitiation words will occur again and again in our consideration of Psalm 22 and in many other passages considered in this book.

The Hind of the Dawn
In Psalm 16, the dependent manhood of Christ is brought before us as vital truth in the divine programme of God revealing His Goodness to men. This aspect of doctrine is further portrayed to us in the introduction to Psalm 22

where, in the title, we read, "To the chief Musician upon Aijeleth Shahar, A Psalm of David". *Aijeleth Shahar* is pronounced *Ayyelet haShshachar* and means "the Hind of the Dawn". The scene depicted for us is that of nocturnal darkness abating and the rays of dawn arising, when the entire focus is on a central object of gentleness, beauty and dependence: a lone hind, a symbol of none other than the Saviour Himself. The dreadful final three hours of darkness upon the cross have almost passed and the light is dawning, as His cry in Aramaic arises heavenward: *"Eli Eli lemah shevaktani?"* meaning, "My God, My God, why hast Thou forsaken Me?" These words, quoted by our Lord Jesus on the cross were, in fact, the exact Aramaic equivalent of the Hebrew in the Psalm: *"Eli, Eli, lamah azavtani!"* The phrase, "didst Thou forsake Me" (all one word in Hebrew: *azavtani*), is particularly strong. It carries the idea of, "Why didst Thou abandon Me?".

The Psalmist David must have found the words, which the Holy Spirit inspired him to write, particularly difficult to understand. Why would such a One be called upon to experience such loneliness?

The nature of this abandonment is further described: "so far from helping Me (from My salvation); the words of My roaring."

Psalm 22:1

"Why art Thou so far from helping Me, and from the words of My roaring?"

This phrase is most interesting. Who ever heard a hind roaring? This word, "My roaring (*shaagati*)", is characteristic of a lion with the prey incontrovertibly within its grasp. Far from a cry of weakness, *shaagati* denotes great strength. Once again, we look on the sinless Sufferer upon the cross and are here reminded that, although seen hanging there in apparent weakness, as some may have thought, He was at all times the Almighty One, Who uniquely was able to bear the judgment which should have been ours.

The significance of the answer in the night season (darkness) and of being forsaken

Psalm 22:2

"O My God, I cry in the daytime, but Thou hearest not; and in the night season, and am not silent."

This verse calls our attention to the "daytime" and the "night season". It was in the "day time" that we learn, "Thou hearest not!" This is not contradicted by the later statement in verse 24 "when He (the Lord Jesus) cried unto Him (God), He heard"

Psalm 22:24

"For He hath not despised nor abhorred the affliction of the Afflicted; neither hath He hid his face from Him; but when He Cried unto Him, He heard."

This is because the phrase, "Thou hearest not", should more accurately be rendered, "Thou answerest not" (lo- taaneh). There never was a time when God did not hear the Lord Jesus. In fact, it was at the tomb of Lazarus that He said,

John 11:41-42
41 "... Father, I thank Thee that Thou hast heard Me.
42 And I knew that Thou hearest Me always."

The fact that the Father always hears Him was no less true at the cross. If the phrase translated in the Authorized Version, "Thou hearest not", really means, "Thou answerest not", we must ask ourselves the question, why was He not answered in the day time and what was the significance of this lack of an answer?

The key to understanding this phrase, "Thou answerest not," requires us to recognise that the issue in question here is not, as one may superficially suppose, God's lack of verbal response to a request for communication from His own Son. We must remember that we are reading now about a sacrificial death. Divine acceptance of the sacrifice must be of vital importance. It is here where the Hebrew word *anah* (to answer) is so important, since it was by answering the sacrifice that God indicated His acceptance of it. The following passages illustrate this foundational truth. We will now consider three uses of the word *anah* in the context of the Lord "answering" the slain sacrifice by divine fire.

1 God answered (*anah*) David by fire (1 Chronicles 21:26)

David would always recall the occasion when he numbered the people and, sadly, sinned before God, thus incurring His judgment. Ornan, the Jebusite, furnished him with a sacrifice to offer on his threshing floor which, very significantly, happened to be Mount Moriah. As David placed the sacrifice upon the hastily erected altar, the question uppermost in his mind was whether or not God would be pleased to accept the sacrifice on his behalf. David did not have long to wait in fear. The Scripture tells us that "God answered (*anah*) David by fire upon the altar".

1 Chronicles 21:26
"And David built there an altar unto the Lord, and offered burnt offerings and peace offerings, and called upon the Lord; and He answered him (*anah*) from heaven by fire upon the altar of burnt offering."

2 God answered (*anah*) Elijah but not the prophets of Baal (1 Kings 18:24)

Once again, we meet this important issue in the confrontation between Elijah and the prophets of Baal in Mount Carmel. Elijah stood before the altar of Jehovah with a slain sacrifice upon it while, some distance away, the prophets of Baal stood before the altar of Baal with their sacrifice. The question was, "Who was the true God? Baal or Jehovah? How would the true God reveal Himself?" Elijah's suggestion was clear: "The God Who answers by fire, let Him be God!" Once more, the word "answer" here is *anah*.

1 Kings 18:24
"And call ye on the name of your gods, and I will call on the Name of the Lord: and the God that **answereth** (*anah*) by fire, let Him be God. And all the people answered and said, It is well spoken."
Then in verse 37, Elijah called on the Lord to "answer him".

1 Kings 18:37-38
37 "Hear me (*anah* = answer me), O Lord, hear me (*anah* = answer me), that this people may know that Thou *art* the Lord God, and *that* Thou hast turned their heart back again.
38 Then the fire of the Lord fell, and consumed the burnt sacrifice, and the wood, and the stones, and the dust, and licked up the water that *was* in the trench."

When the divine fire descended and consumed the sacrifice upon the altar of Jehovah, it was apparent that God indeed had answered His servant, and the sacrifice had been accepted by Him. The prophets of Baal, in all their idolatrous rituals, were confounded.

3 God answering His anointed by fire on the altar
In Psalm 20, David by divine inspiration composes a pattern prayer for the people to intercede on behalf of the Lord's anointed in time of trouble i.e. godly kings who would come after him. His prayer is that the Lord should answer such a king (*anah*) through accepting his offerings and burnt sacrifice by divine fire upon the altar and turning them to ashes.

Psalm 20:1-4
1 "The Lord hear thee (*anah:* answer thee) in the day of trouble; the Name of the God of Jacob defend thee;
2 Send thee help from the sanctuary, and strengthen thee out of Zion;
3 Remember all thy offerings, and accept (turn to ashes) thy burnt sacrifice; Selah.
4 Grant thee according to thine own heart, and fulfill all thy counsel."

Some may hold that Psalm 20:1-4 is a prayer that the Offering of the Lord Jesus of Himself on the cross would be accepted (turned to ashes). This cannot be the meaning of Psalm 20:1-4 as our Lord Jesus was not turned to ashes as He bore divine judgment for us at Calvary. Rather, as has often been said, "the Sacrifice consumed the fire" when God answered Him that day.

Although there are several Hebrew words which could be equally well translated "to answer", it is the word *anah* which is employed on those three key occasions described above, when the critical importance of the divine fire answering the sacrifice is being emphasised. However, on every occasion of sacrifice it was important to each godly Jew for his sacrifice to be accepted. Lack of acceptance was apparent if the sacrifice was marked by "no answer". Consequently, the language employed here by the Psalmist would have been readily understood by believing Jews who appreciated the spiritual significance of the altar.

Let us return to Psalm 22. In verse 2 we are told that the Lord Jesus was not answered during the hours of light (daytime). However, later in verse 21 He was answered.

Psalm 22:21

"Save Me from the lion's mouth: for Thou hast heard Me (*anah* answered Me) from the horns of the unicorns (the exalted ones)."

Clearly then, the daytime was a period when there was no answer from heaven. When did the answer come? If it is revealed that the answer was not given in the daytime, but that it did eventually come (verse 21), it is very clear that it was in the hours of the night season (the darkness) that the divine answer was given to Him.

The Hebrew word *anah* carries a second quite distinct meaning often translated "to afflict". For this reason, in most Biblical Hebrew dictionaries *anah* is presented as two identical but quite distinct verbs, where one is translated "to answer" and the other "to afflict". Consequently, because *anah* meaning "to answer" and *anah* meaning "to afflict" are, in Hebrew, identical words, it can only be determined from the context whether the meaning of this word should be translated "to answer" or "to afflict". Accordingly, when the translators of the Authorised Version came upon *anah* in Isaiah 53:7 they translated it as follows:

Isaiah 53:7

"He was oppressed (*or* it was exacted), and He was afflicted (*anah*), yet He opened not His mouth: He is brought as a lamb to the slaughter, and as a sheep before her shearers is dumb, so He openeth not His mouth."

In the Newberry Bible, an alternative reading for the beginning of Isaiah 53:7 is given: "It was exacted and He becometh answerable". Evidently, Mr Newberry had accurately observed that the word "afflicted" is the passive form of *anah* and thus could also legitimately and grammatically carry a passive meaning of the other use of the verb *anah* "to answer". The passive meaning rendered by Mr Newberry was "becometh answerable". Mr Newberry's rendering has been very helpful to Gospel preachers who have used this alternative translation to explain the meaning of Calvary, namely that the debt of sin was exacted and the Person of Christ became answerable to God. However, a careful study of the word *anah* in Isaiah 53:7 would suggest that if we, like Mr Newberry, take the root meaning of *anah* here to be "to answer", the fact that its grammatical form in this verse is in the *Niphal* passive would tell us that the most literal rendering of all would be "it was exacted and **He was answered**".

These observations do not mean that the rendering, "He was oppressed and He was afflicted", is inaccurate. Rather, what we are observing is an example where several equally correct translations can be made from a single Hebrew phrase. Already we have observed that several Hebrew words require many more English words to convey the meaning. Now we see that a Hebrew phrase may require more than one translation, each of which is accurate. Such is the wisdom of God, that an economy of words is employed to convey an eternity of meaning!

The fact on which all believers can rest their souls securely for eternity is simply this: He **was** answered by God that day at Calvary. This is how we know, beyond the shadow of doubt, that His sacrificial death made propitiation for sin and was acceptable to God. God's acceptance of every sacrifice was seen in the "answer", i.e. the fire from heaven; and His Sacrifice is no exception. However, the Scripture is careful to indicate to us that it was not in the daytime that this answer came. That's why it should evoke thanksgiving in the heart of every believer that the Psalmist speaks immediately of the night season. It is also why a believer should well rejoice in the careful record by Matthew, Mark and Luke of the crucifixion describing the three hours of darkness over all the land (Matthew 27:45; Mark 15:33; Luke 23:44). According to Psalm 22, that was when **God answered His Son with divine judgment indicating that the Sacrifice was accepted by God and thus of such value as to make propitiation for our sin.**

In summary, the two passages which present to us the significance of the answer in the night season and of being forsaken are **Isaiah 53** and the story of the scapegoat in **Leviticus 16**. It was in the darkness that He experienced being cut off from God and men and all that spoke of life. This is the fulfilment of the picture provided for us of the suffering Saviour in Leviticus 16 when, on the Day of Atonement (*Yom Cippur*), the scapegoat was led out to the wilderness bearing the iniquities of the people. There it was left to die alone and was cut off in the land "not inhabited" (Hebrew = "land cut off").

The Day of Atonement

When an Israelite committed a trespass, if he did not bring his trespass offering then he "bore his iniquity".

Leviticus 5:1
  "And if a soul sin, and hear the voice of swearing, and *is* a witness, whether he hath seen or known *of it*; if he do not utter *it*, then **he shall bear his iniquity**."

Leviticus 5:17
  "And if a soul sin, and commit any of these things which are forbidden to be done by the commandments of the Lord, though he wist it not, yet he is guilty, and **shall bear his iniquity**."

If not relieved from "bearing iniquity", the inevitable outcome was death, as illustrated in the section regulating garments of the priests, when priests, not clad according to the appropriate standard of "covering the flesh," were defined as "bearing iniquity", and they died as a result.

Exodus 28:42-43

> 42 "And thou shalt make them linen breeches to cover their nakedness; from the loins even unto the thighs they shall reach:
> 43 And they shall be upon Aaron, and upon his sons, when they come in unto the tabernacle of the congregation, or when they come near unto the altar to minister in the Holy Place; **that they bear not iniquity, and die**: *it shall be* a statute for ever unto him and his seed after him."

God had graciously made a provision to relieve an Israelite of this "bearing of iniquity" and the premature death that this would involve. If an Israelite in this position wanted to be released from this burden of "bearing his iniquity" and the ensuing death this would entail, he brought his sin or trespass offering to the door of the tabernacle of the congregation where it was slain. After this, the priest ate of the trespass or sin offering. According to Leviticus 10:16-18 this act meant that, from that moment forward, the priest "bore the iniquity" on behalf of the Israelite.

Leviticus 10:16-18

> 16 "And Moses diligently sought the goat of the sin offering, and, behold, it was burnt: and he was angry with Eleazar and Ithamar, the sons of Aaron *which were* left *alive*, saying,
> 17 Wherefore have ye not eaten the sin offering in the holy place, seeing it *is* most holy, **and God hath given it you to bear the iniquity of the congregation, to make atonement for them before the Lord?**
> 18 Behold, the blood of it was not brought in within the holy *place*: ye should indeed have eaten it in the holy *place*, as I commanded."

The dual significance of the priest eating and not eating the sin offering

It is sometimes suggested that the priest, by eating of the sin offering of a non-priestly Israelite, was somehow internalizing the reality of the Israelite's transgression so as to be able to intercede for this person in the presence of God. A study of the passages dealing with the priest eating of the sin offering indicates that the signifiance of this act was much deeper than mere intercession. The priest by eating the sin offering of a **non-priestly** Israelite was carrying out a **vicarious act** on behalf of this **non-priestly** individual (Leviticus 10:17). The priest bore the iniquity of **another** person so that that individual could go out free. The eating of the sin offering must be clearly distinguished from eating the peace offering. Eating the peace offering was a privilege shared by the officiating priest **as well as** the Israelite who brought the peace offering (Leviticus 3). This was not a vicarious act. Eating of the peace offering was an act of worship to God and fellowship with God and other participating believers.

To further emphasise that the priest's eating of the sin offering was a vicarious act, it should be noted that the priest only ate the sin offering which was offered on behalf of another i.e. a **non-priest**. If the priest himself sinned either as an individual (Leviticus 4:3-12) or collectively with his own congregation (Leviticus 4:13-21) he did not eat of his own sin offering. This becomes apparent when it is understood that because the blood of a **priest's sin offering** must be brought into the tabernacle (Leviticus 4:1-

22), it could not be eaten of by the priest as decreed in Leviticus 6:30. This was to teach the Old Testament believers that the priest could not carry out a vicarious act on his own behalf in the matter of a sin in which he had personal involvement. Moreover, if he was numbered with the rest of the congregation in a particular sin, which is the scenario of Leviticus 4:13-21, he could not eat of that sin offering either (see Appendix 3 where the phrase "numbered with transgressors" is discussed in more detail). The lesson for all humanity is that no human being is allowed to participate in his own atonement. In contrast, however, the blood of the sin offering of non-priests on every day of the year except the Day of Atonement was **not brought** into the tabernacle (Leviticus 4:22-35) which meant that the priest could and **must** eat of it (Leviticus 6:30; Leviticus 10:17) in order for that sin offering to have atoning value. The next section considers how the act of the priest eating from the sin offering of the non-priestly Israelite allowed later validation of that sin offering on the Day of Atonement as being of sin atoning value.

To summarise, then, with regard to every sin offering for a priest's sin, the blood was brought in and the offering was not at all permitted to be eaten of by the priest and what remained of the body (the skin, flesh, head, legs, inwards and dung) was carried outside the camp and burned. It is also true that in every sin offering for **non-priests** the blood was **not brought in** and the flesh of the sin offering was eaten of by the officiating priest. There is a particular sin offering which lies between these two categories. It is the sin offering which was offered on the occasion of the **consecration of the priest** where the priest was not yet fully consecrated and where Moses was the officiating officer (Exodus 29:10-14). On that occasion, Aaron was **not yet** a functioning priest even though he was wearing the official priestly garments. He had not fulfilled the unique right of a consecrated priest, which was to enter into the tabernacle, so there was no possibility of him defiling the tabernacle. Therefore, the blood was not brought in as was the case of sin offerings for non-priests. It is appropriate to indicate at this point that in the Old Testament both priests and non-priests could offer sacrifice. Only a priest **could enter into the sanctuary**. The doctrinal implications of this important distinction are considered in Psalm 40. In Exodus 29, Aaron was not yet able to enter in and exercise the privilege of a consecrated priest. However, because the bullock of Exodus 29:10-14 was for the priest's own sin it was not eaten by a priest (because the priest cannot participate in his own atonement) and, secondly, the priest was not yet fully consecrated anyhow. In other words, there was no one available to eat of the sin offering for the priest and to bear his guilt. No wonder, in this particular sin offering, on the occasion of Aaron being consecrated to the priesthood, as considered in Psalm 40, the Lord **did not have full delight**. This deficiency must have already been apparent to Old Testament believers familiar with the significance of the priest eating the sin offering of the non-priest. However, in common with the sin offering for an officiating priest in Leviticus 4:1-22 the body of the entire animal was taken outside the camp and burned.

A summary of these truths might be appropriate at this point. The prohibition against eating the sin offering, whose blood was brought into the tabernacle, applied to **every sin offering for a priest** who sinned either as an individual or in common with others. This was to remind the Israelites that vicarious bearing of sin, which was the role of the priest, was forbidden to any priest who in the eyes of the Law was not sin-free. Thus if a priest was ceremonially unclean he could not eat of his own sin offering. Only a priest who was ceremonially clean was allowed to perform the vicarious act of eating the sin offering on behalf of another. Sometimes the priest was by his own sin unable to perform the vicarious act of eating the sin offering of another (Leviticus 10:19). He would have to offer for himself **first** before he could resume the role of eating the sin offering on behalf of others. This shows us that the One Who bare our iniquity must be pure and clean. Unlike the Aaronic priests, our Lord Jesus Christ was sinless and could never be disqualified from vicariously bearing our sin at Calvary! Note 2

Evidently, the task of dealing with the many sin and trespass offerings in Israel was so big that Aaron needed the help of his sons to assist in this. This is why the word "you" (plural) is used in Leviticus 10:17, indicating that in the matter of bearing the sins of the people, subsequent to their offering of a sin or trespass offering, the whole priestly family was involved i.e. Aaron and all his officiating sons. We are told that they did this with a view to the Day of Atonement (*Yom Cippur*) "to make atonement for them (the people) before the Lord".

Notice the words, "God hath given it (the sin offering) to you (plural) to **bear the iniquity** of the congregation, to make atonement for them before the Lord". By so doing, the priest not only was bearing the iniquity but, in the eyes of the Law, he was destined to die for that iniquity he was bearing, unless someone could be found to whom the priest could pass all that burden of iniquity.

As the year drew on towards *Yom Cippur*, and as each day went past with more and more sin and trespass offerings being offered, the burden upon the priest became heavier and heavier. Each time he ate of the sin or trespass offering of non-priests he added to the long list of sins he was consciously bearing. He bore these sins, not in the sense of bearing sin's penalty (the pain, suffering, abandonment and death), but rather bearing **sin's guilt and responsibility**. Death was the ultimate penalty which "sin-bearing" demanded. However, God only asked the priest to carry **the guilt of sin** on behalf of the Israelite. The **penalty of suffering and death,** which that "sin-bearing" demanded, would be deferred for the priest until the Day of Atonement when another sin-bearer, the scapegoat, would step in to bear not just the guilt and responsibility but also the penalty of death so dreadful that it was abandoned, cut off and forsaken in the land "cut off".

However, until that dreaded day of *Yom Cippur*, the priest's role in bearing sin's guilt and responsibility for a non-priest was a solemn duty which must have weighed heavily on the priest's mind. As far as the Israelite was concerned, he could go down to his tent from the door of the tabernacle of the congregation secure in the knowledge that the guilt and responsibility of his sin was now borne by the priest, who had eaten his sin offering, and that ultimately the **penalty** would be borne on the coming *Yom Cippur*. Effectively, by coming to the door of the congregation the Israelite had put in his claim for forgiveness for that sin he had committed.

The Day of Atonement and the sin offerings of the previous year

The priest must have looked forward with anticipation to the morning when *Yom Cippur* dawned, because on that day the priest was forbidden to eat of the sin offering for the people. This meant that **no more** sins of that year were given to **him** to bear.

Leviticus 6:30
> "And **no sin offering**, whereof *any* of the blood is brought into the tabernacle of the congregation to reconcile *withal* in the holy *place*, **shall be eaten**: it shall be burnt in the fire."

As we have already seen, the prohibition against eating of the sin offering in Leviticus 6:30 referred to any sin offering offered for a priest's sin or a sin of the entire congregation including the priests (Leviticus 4:1-22). In this context of the priest being defiled by personal sin, eating of the sin offering and carrying out a vicarious act on the behalf of others was clearly forbidden. However, the other occasion when the priest could not eat of the sin offering is *Yom Cippur* when the blood of the sin offerings for the priest as well as the people was brought into the tabernacle, in fact into the Holiest of All. This had to be the case because on that one day of the year, on the Day of Atonement, the priest **no longer** bore the iniquity on behalf of others which he had done so regularly throughout the year.

This also meant an end to an opportunity for anyone else in the congregation to come to the door bringing a sin offering, relevant to a sin of the past year, and the guilt thereof being transferred to the officiating priest. This was very solemn, as it meant that any Israelite who had waited too long to have their sin dealt with in the proper way had no other means of finding relief. He would from that day forth "bear his iniquity" alone and would have to face the premature death such a penalty entailed. For that reason *Yom Cippur* was solemn for the Israelite because it meant the end of further opportunity to have ceremonial sins dealt with for that year. It also was a tremendous relief to the priest, because on that day he was not allowed to eat of the sin offering, and as he looked back over the year and remembered the sin offerings at which he had officiated over the previous months, he was now allowed to be relieved of the heavy load of guilt he had borne. This was possible because on that day another "sin bearer" was found. This was not the priest. It was the "scapegoat" – one of two goats which together acted as one sin offering.

On the Day of Atonement, these two goats were taken before the Lord.

Although these were two animals, they acted together to form **one sin offering** for the people (Leviticus 16:5). Lots were cast upon each goat with one lot "for the Lord" and the other "for the scapegoat". The goat upon whom the Lord's lot fell was offered for a sin offering, whereas the other animal, the scapegoat, was presented alive before the Lord (Leviticus 16:7-10). When the goat "for the Lord" was slain, the priest, shielded by a cloud of incense, brought its blood into the Holiest of All where it was sprinkled once **upon** the mercy seat and then seven times **before** the mercy seat.

The significance of the goat "for the Lord"

We are left in no doubt that the blood of the goat which was slain and which was placed upon and before the mercy seat made an atonement for "all the congregation of Israel" (Leviticus 16:17). This teaches us that there is enough in the death of Christ to meet the need of all, as far as the Lord is concerned. This shows that there is no such thing as a "limited atonement". However, just because the blood of the goat "for the Lord" was sprinkled on and before the mercy seat, this did not mean that automatically every Israelite came into the good of this. There had to be an acceptance by each Israelite of the divine provision of atonement. It is here where the second goat, known as the scapegoat, comes in.

The significance of the scapegoat

Leviticus 16:21-22

> 21 "And Aaron shall lay both his hands upon the head of the live goat, and confess over him all the iniquities of the children of Israel, and all their transgressions in all their sins, putting them upon the head of the goat, and shall send *him* away by the hand of a fit man into the wilderness:
> 22 And the goat shall bear upon him all their iniquities unto a land not inhabited: and he shall let go the goat in the wilderness."

The second goat, the scapegoat, was brought before Aaron and he confessed upon it "all the iniquities of the children of Israel, and all their transgressions in all their sins, putting them upon the head of the goat" (Leviticus 16:21). The word "to confess" is in the *hithpael* or reflexive form of the verb *yadah* meaning "to throw, to cast" and means literally "to point out **oneself** as guilty" in the sense of "to cast in one's (own) teeth" (Gesenius' Hebrew and Chaldee Lexicon). This shows us that, in what must have been a very solemn ceremony, Aaron publicly and before God accused **himself** of the sins and iniquities of the people. This is what is meant by the words of Leviticus 16:21 regarding Aaron's confession. This could not have been a light thing in Aaron's experience as, in an intensely personal way, he took responsibility for the guilt of the people before God. It is worth emphasisng, though, that in the eyes of the Law, Aaron was ceremonially clean immediately before he pointed out himself as the guilty one that day in the stead of the people. This is because he had immediately before this just finished offering up the sin offering for his own sin, and was thus clean in the eyes of the Law. The sin offering for Aaron's own sin before he dealt with the sins of the people was to show, by way of contrast, that the One Who would ultimately bear the guilt of the people must be free from guilt Himself (Hebrews 7:27) and thus have no need to offer for His own sin since He had none. This is the Lord Jesus.

A four-fold meaning of the picture

1 An illustration of the willingness of the Lord Jesus to bear our sin at Calvary

It is most touching to consider the fulfilment of this in the experience of the Lord Jesus. Aaron's act of "accusing himself" before God of the sins of the people, which he personally **did not commit,** is a beautiful picture of what the Lord Jesus did as He knowingly took to Himself our sins upon the tree.

2 An illustration of how Old Testament believers were saved even before the Lord had come to bear away their sins

Coming to the door of the tabernacle of the congregation was a lovely illustration of salvation in Old Testament times. Just as the Old Testament person who was guilty of a ceremonial sin could experience immediate relief of personal guilt by coming to the door of the tabernacle, knowing that this act would be validated by the future death of the scapegoat, similarly, in the matter of their soul's eternal salvation, an Old Testament believer received forgiveness of sins through faith in the Lamb of God's providing many years before He came, in the knowledge that this faith would be validated by the future vicarious death of the Messiah. They were depending on the Lamb of God's providing (see Psalm 24), Who would be revealed in a coming day to bear sin's penalty long after their death, yet they could enter into the present enjoyment of sins forgiven in anticipation of the final sin-bearing One Himself.

Only on the Day of Atonement was every sin offering of the previous year validated as being of sin-atoning value. If the Day of Atonement did not take place, then none of the sin offerings of the previous year had any sin-atoning value. The absence of the Day of Atonement in the temple of Ezekiel shows us that the sin offerings of Ezekiel's temple in the millennium are not of sin-atoning value since there is no *Yom Cippur* to "validate them". This means that the sin offerings of Ezekiel's future millennial temple must be of commemorative value only, rather like the remembrance feast of today (see Psalm 118).

Indeed this is made clear in Ezekiel 16

Ezekiel 16:62-63

62 "And I will establish My covenant with thee; and thou shalt know that I *am* the Lord:
63 That thou mayest **remember**, and be confounded, and never open thy mouth any more because of thy shame, **when I am pacified toward thee** for all that thou hast done, saith the Lord God".

The phrase, "when I am pacified toward thee", means literally, "when I **have made an atonement** for thee". This is a remarkable verse, because under the Law of Moses it was Aaron the priest and the priests who succeeded him who "made atonement" on *Yom Cippur*. In this section, the prophet envisages a future day when God's covenant will have been established with the nation and the Day of Atonement will be remembered as an event in the past, when on **one** unique day the Lord GOD Himself made an end of the atonement, in contrast to the many days when priest after priest made the atonement on successive annual *Yom Cippur* occasions. Ezekiel 16:63 looks forward to the day when the redeemed people of Israel will look back to the Day when the Lord Jesus fulfilled the picture of the scapegoat bearing away the guilt and penalty of sin into the land cut off. What a day that is going to be!

The picture is clear for the Old Testament believers. Until the Lord Jesus died at Calvary, the penalty of their sins had not yet been borne. Nevertheless, these believers could die in faith in the assurance that the Messiah would take care of it all when He came to effect redemption. Until Calvary, their sins, referred to in Hebrews 9:15 as "the transgressions that were under the first testament", had merely been "passed over" (Romans 3:25). Now "the transgressions that were under the first testament" have been put away forever.

Hebrews 9:15-16
> 15 "And for this cause He is the Mediator of the new testament, that by means of death, for the redemption of **the transgressions** *that were* **under the first testament**, they which are called might receive the promise of eternal inheritance.
> 16 For where a testament *is*, there must also of necessity be the death of the testator."

3 An illustration of the responsibility of a sinner today to come to Christ

The events of *Yom Cippur* provide a gospel lesson for us also today. When a sinner comes to Christ for salvation, he is putting in his claim for salvation by personal faith in the Lord Jesus Christ. Just as the Israelite must come to **the door** of the tabernacle with his sin offering to benefit from the atonement later provided at *Yom Cippur*, similarly each sinner who wants forgiveness must come to Christ to receive this blessing.

Aaron, **throughout the year**, was not bearing the guilt of those people who had sinned in the congregation of Israel and who **had not come** to the door of the tabernacle confessing their sin and offering their sin offering. These individuals had, by their negligence or reckless pride, doomed themselves to "bear their iniquity" (Leviticus 5:1). They could not **personally benefit** from the work of the scapegoat, who bore not just sin's guilt but its penalty i.e. death. It was too late then. Aaron has, in his confession and in his "remembrance made" (Hebrews 10) of all those sin offerings throughout the year, placed all that guilt and all those iniquities, with which he was by now so familiar, on the head of the scapegoat.

Leviticus 16:21
> "...putting them upon the head of the goat, and shall send *him* away by the hand of a fit man into the wilderness."

Now the priest no longer bore the guilt. He had off-loaded it all onto the head of the scapegoat and it "shall bear upon him all their iniquities unto a land not inhabited: and he shall let go the goat in the wilderness" (Leviticus 16:22). It was the responsibility of each Israelite to make this provision their own by a personal act of faith at the door of the tabernacle of the congregation by bringing their sin offering there.

4 An illustration of the scope Godward and manward of the death of Christ

As we consider the events until now, the question could be asked by some: did the scapegoat only suffer for the sins of those who had brought their sin offering to the door of the tabernacle in the previous year? The question also has often been asked: did the Lord Jesus only suffer for those who would be saved? Such a question arises only out of a very limited estimation of the greatness of the work of the Lord Jesus at Calvary. We will, nevertheless, consider an answer, only with a view to showing the **infinite** greatness of the death of our Lord Jesus Christ.

It is clear that up until *Yom Cippur,* Aaron only bore the guilt of those who had availed themselves of the provision of the sin offering at the door of the tabernacle. However, on *Yom Cippur* the burden placed on Aaron was **much greater** than merely the sins of those who had specifically come to the door of the tabernacle requesting forgiveness. Similarly, we should remember that the death and work of Christ on the cross is much bigger than the matter of putting away the sins of those who would be saved.

A study of the word "confess"

A study of the word "confess" will help in this matter. It will show that it is used of general confession in Nehemiah 1:6 and 2 Chronicles 30:22.

Nehemiah 1:6
> "I **confess** the sins of the children of Israel, which we have sinned against Thee."

2 Chronicles 30:22
> "… making **confession** to the Lord God of their fathers."

However, it is clear that in these passages, specific confession is not in view since a specific "sin" is not in the context. There are some passages however where this word "confess" is used of specific and predefined sins such as in Numbers 5:7 and Leviticus 5:5

Numbers 5:7
> "Then they shall **confess** their sin which they have done."

Leviticus 5:5

"And it shall be, when he shall be guilty in one of these *things*, that he shall **confess** that he hath sinned in that *thing*."

The word "confess" in Leviticus 16:21 (quoted earlier) is, therefore, wide enough in its meaning to allow for **general** as well as **specific** confession. Can the context of Leviticus 16:21 show us if the confession of the priest was for specific, known sins or for all sins in Israel, whether known or unknown to him? The use of the word "all" in Leviticus 16:21 in "**all** the iniquities of the children of Israel" and "**all** their transgressions in **all** their sins" would suggest the latter view is correct: that Aaron's confession included not just the specific sins of which he had prior knowledge, and of which he had borne the guilt before *Yom Cippur*, but also unconfessed sins committed by Israelites which had not been dealt with earlier in the year by offering a sin or trespass offering.

Clearly, Aaron only intelligently knew about the sins of people who had made confession throughout the year by bringing their sin offering to the tabernacle door and of whose sin offerings he and his sons had partaken. There is no doubt that these specific sins and trespasses were **specifically** involved in Aaron's great confession that day. This is clear from the helpful comment in Hebrews 10 of the "**remembrance** made of sin every year" on the Day of Atonement. However, we have seen that the word "confess" used here carries also the idea of **general** confession – even going beyond sins which had escaped finite human memory but which were remembered by God. This is also strongly suggested by the word "all" in the phrase "all the iniquities" and "all their transgressions". The word "all" suggests sins, iniquities and transgressions which went beyond Aaron's finite knowledge but which were known to God, **yet which he also took to himself that day for the very first time.**

This shows us that there were **two** aspects to Aaron's confession.

1 Firstly, throughout the year Aaron, by eating of the many sin offerings, carried the guilt of specific sins of specific Israelites until the Day of Atonement when the scapegoat would carry the load of sin.

2 However, there was an even wider aspect of Aaron's confession that day. On *Yom Cippur*, he took to himself and cast in his own teeth (confessed) **all** the iniquity, transgression and sin of the people whether or not they had come to the door of the tabernacle requesting forgiveness. Aaron took to himself the load of guilt which had not been declared by guilty Israelites at the door of the tabernacle and cast that guilt in his own teeth in a general way. Moreover, that heavy load was also transmitted to the head of the scapegoat. Aaron did this even though he knew that this act would not in any way benefit the Israelite who had failed to bring his sin offering to the door of the tabernacle of the congregation to be slain and eaten by Aaron. As the scapegoat bore away this unconfessed sin to the "land cut off" and suffered underneath its heavy burden, somewhere in the camp of Israel

there were sinners who would never benefit from the forgiveness which that suffering scapegoat could have brought to them, all because they never had come to the door of the tabernacle of the congregation to put in their claim for mercy.

Why then should the scapegoat be asked to bear sins away which would not lead to forgiveness of those who committed those sins due to their rebellious refusal of God's provision? Why did God not limit the suffering and sin-bearing of the Lord Jesus only to the sins of those who would believe on Him and be saved?

All sin arising from Adam's fall must be put away from the eye of God for man to be brought back into a status of pre-fall dignity befitting those who are to become the Bride of Christ, the friends of the Bridegroom and the Virgins, the companions of the Bride (see Psalm 45). How could a redeemed Adam and Eve be comfortable in the New Heavens and New Earth if God had not devised a means to entirely cleanse away the cascade of **sin** arising from their personal fall in Eden's Garden and amplified by millions of sinning sons of Adam all down the millennia? If this amazing goal of reestablishing pre-fall dignity to fallen man was ever to be achieved, sin's defilement and the resulting affront caused to God's holy character must be dealt with **in full**. This has already been considered in Psalm 8, where it was seen how the Lord Jesus will one day forever remove the "sting of death", which is sin itself so that the New Heaven and New Earth can never be sullied by sin eternally. This is as a result of His sacrifice at Calvary.

Some may argue that banishing a lost sinner to hell and the lake of fire forever is enough in God's sight to deal with the sins committed by those who never believe. Such an erroneous idea arises from a failure to understand that punishing a Christ-rejecting sinner in hell and the lake of fire will **not in any way** do away with the sins committed by that person, contrary to what some elements of Christendom hold. This is because a flawed and imperfect victim, namely a lost sinner, cannot by his torment in hell and the lake of fire ever propitiate or appease God's throne for those sins committed. It is because the Lord Himself has "been made sin for us" and paid the price at Calvary for sin in its widest aspect (including the sins of those who would never believe in Him) that the problem of the debt of human sin has been fully solved before God. This is because, as far as God is concerned, no debt remains and an offer of forgiveness and eternal salvation can be made to all mankind who simply have to accept this provision by faith alone .

The purpose of hell and the lake of fire was never to make expiation for human sin and guilt. It **cannot do this**. Hell and the lake of fire were made for the devil and his angels – not human beings. Lost souls in hell and the lake of fire will be no less guilty at the end of **one billion billion years** of punishment than they were at the start of eternity. This is a mind-shattering, troubling and deeply moving fact. Moreover, because hell and the lake of fire were never made for the purpose of expiating sin, the punishment there experienced by lost sinners is eternal – because it can never be exhausted and would never satisfy God in the matter of sin.

However, the death of Christ and the value of His precious, shed blood have dealt with the matter of all sin in its entirety. In particular, the debt incurred by Adam and his fallen posterity has been paid in full. This means that, as we considered in Psalm 8, human sin in all its effects can be obliterated from the universe completely and cannot raise its ugly head in the future blessed eternal state. **The Lord Jesus has brought closure to God for ever, in the matter of sin in its widest aspects.**

This wonderful fact is foreshadowed in the confession of Aaron being **much wider** than the specific sins whose guilt he carried on behalf of the Israelites up to the Day of Atonement. Granted, it is only those individuals who came to the door of the tabernacle who benefited from their guilt being taken away for them personally. However, as for those who did not come to the tabernacle, due to their rejection of the provision, they will have to bear their iniquity personally in terms of divine punishment, even though the scapegoat bore it away from God's sight. Our Lord Jesus Christ has not only suffered for the sins of those who have trusted in Him and also of those who will be saved, He has vicariously suffered for the very principle of sin itself in all its heinous implications so that God can, one day, provide a sin-free new heaven and earth into which sin can never enter. However, outside of this new heaven and earth, in the lake which burns with fire and brimstone, will be those who refused the provision of the suffering and death of the Lord Jesus.

This consideration is most solemn. The suffering of the scapegoat brought forgiveness and relief to all those who had come to the door of the tabernacle of the congregation and put in their claim for forgiveness. It did not bring forgiveness to those who had not put in their claim, even though the scapegoat had suffered for those very sins. This shows us that at the final Great White Throne judgment when each unbeliever, with sins unforgiven, shall meet the Throne Sitter and Judge, Christ Himself, he/she will look into the face of the One Who bore their sins in all the agony of Calvary but because of unbelief on their part they will have to bear the guilt and suffering themselves again eternally. How needless and futile shall this be?

Hebrews 10:29
"Of how much sorer punishment, suppose ye, shall he be thought worthy, who hath trodden under foot the Son of God, and hath counted the blood of the covenant, wherewith he was sanctified, an unholy thing, and hath done despite unto the Spirit of grace?"

Truly, there is a special punishment for those who have rejected the value of the Victim of Calvary.

These considerations show that the suffering of the Lord Jesus was not limited to the sins of those who would be saved (the elect). Any who hold this erroneous idea must teach that those who did not get saved have sins which never were dealt with by the suffering and death of Christ.

They must also erroneously hold that the only way a righteous God can find satisfaction in these sins being dealt with, is in the sinner concerned suffering eternal punishment in hell and the lake of fire. This presupposes (wrongly of course) that the suffering of a lost sinner in hell and the lake of fire is of sin expiating value. As we have already considered, hell and the lake of fire never were designed to bring satisfaction to God in the matter of sin. They cannot do this. A poor sinner can never by his own suffering for his own sins expiate one sin before God whether in time or in eternity. Only the infinite Person of Christ "once suffered for sins the Just for the unjust that He might bring us to God (1 Peter 3:18)."

Isaiah 53 as fulfilment of *Yom Cippur*

All those sins, iniquities and transgressions, in all their awful shamefulness, Aaron took to himself and "cast them in his own teeth". This surely reminds us of the phrase we already considered in Isaiah 53:7: "It was exacted". In Aaron's experience "it was exacted" and on the Day of Atonement he knowingly and intelligently took responsibility for all that guilt in the presence of God.

Isaiah 53:7

> "He was oppressed (*or* it was exacted), and He was afflicted *(anah)*, yet He opened not His mouth: He is brought as a lamb to the slaughter, and as a sheep before her shearers is dumb, so He openeth not His mouth."

Aaron's actions on the Day of Atonement, with respect to the scapegoat, were threefold.

Firstly, Aaron confessed the iniquities, i.e. he personally cast the guilt of all of this in his own teeth. This answers to the idea in Isaiah 53:7 of it being "exacted". However, **Aaron only bore the guilt that day. He did not bear the penalty**, namely the suffering of the abandonment of the land "cut off", which the little scapegoat was about to endure.

Secondly, Aaron "put" all these iniquities upon the head of the goat. **He transferred all of that guilt,** which he had personally taken to himself in its entirety, **upon the head of the scapegoat**. In this sense "it was exacted" upon Aaron's head first of all but then transferred to the head of the scapegoat. It was ultimately upon the scapegoat's head that the debt was exacted. The picture of the debt being exacted required Aaron as well as the goat because the goat could not have understood the sins it was bearing, since it was only an animal. However, Aaron with his hands upon the goat, and by so doing identifying himself with the goat, provides, in combination with the goat, a picture of the perfect Sacrifice of the Lord Jesus upon Whose head the great debt of sin was exacted, but Who, unlike Aaron, was able to be answerable to God for that guilt by suffering (i.e. being answered by) the divine judgment which that guilt and sin deserved, namely the abandonment and suffering of the land "cut off".

Thirdly, as the goat was 'sent away' (verse 21) to the land "not inhabited (Hebrew: cut off)", we see the awfulness of the suffering borne by the Lord

Jesus in the "cut off" place when, in the abandonment of the darkness, He was "answered" by the divine judgment.

It is apparent then that the goat "for the Lord", which was slain and whose blood was brought into the Holy Place, teaches us about the all-sufficiency of the death of the Lord Jesus, with respect to the need of every sinner without exception. However, the scapegoat teaches us that to come into the blessing of sins forgiven there must be a time of coming to the "door" by faith and putting in one's claim, through confessing that sin and claiming the cleansing power of the sin offering.

The goat "for the Lord" teaches us that the death of the Lord Jesus is on "behalf of all". Every time in the New Testament we read of the death of Christ being "for **all**" the Greek preposition "for" is *huper* meaning "on behalf of". However, every time we read of the death of the Lord Jesus Christ being "for **many**" the Greek preposition "for" is *anti* meaning "instead of", i.e. a substitutionary death.

The goat "for the Lord" teaches us that there is enough in the death of Christ to meet the need of absolutely every soul but that, sadly, all will not be saved. The "scapegoat" teaches us that all who come to the "door", i.e. who come by faith to Christ, can rejoice in His death which was "instead of me". This is the truth of substitution which can be enjoyed by every sin-sick soul who comes by faith to the Person of Christ for salvation.

In the Old Testament, they understood that the scapegoat was a picture of the promised Sin-Bearer. The Lord revealed Himself to Moses as the One "forgiving iniquity and transgression and sin" (Exodus 34:7). The word used here for "forgive" (*nasa*) is the same word as is used in Leviticus 16:22 for the scapegoat bearing away the iniquity, transgression and sin.

Leviticus 16:22
> "And the goat shall bear (*nasa*) upon him all their iniquities unto a land not inhabited (Hebrew: cut off) : and he shall let go the goat in the wilderness."

It was apparent, therefore, to Old Testament believers that a **Divine Sin-Bearer** would be revealed. What a moment it was when John the Baptist pointed Him out:

John 1:29
> ".. Behold the Lamb of God, Which taketh away the sin of the world."

John's gospel makes it clear, however, that the blessings of sins forgiven can only be experienced by coming to Him by faith.

More details of the land "not inhabited (cut off)" to which the scapegoat was sent on the Day of Atonement are further expounded by Isaiah.

Isaiah 53:8
> "He was taken from prison and from judgment: and who shall declare His generation? for **He was cut off** out of the land of the living: for the transgression of my people was He stricken."

The word "cut off" is the same root word as the "land cut off" to which the scapegoat was sent to die. The death of the scapegoat, as it bore away the iniquities, was clearly a picture of the Lord Jesus Christ in all the loneliness of Golgotha. The "land cut off" was a picture of the Lord Jesus being "cut off from the land of the living" (literally in Hebrew: "land of life"). This suggests that during this time there was no communication with men. In the first three hours men reviled Him and He was able to converse with the dying thief. The "cutting off" occurred in the darkness. It was to the darkness He was referring when at the end of the three hours of darkness He cried, "*Eli Eli lama sabachthani!*"

What did Peter mean when he said of our Lord, that "His own self bare our sins in His own body on the tree"?

1 Peter 2:24
> "Who His own self bare our sins in His own body on the tree, that we, being dead to sins, should live unto righteousness: by Whose stripes ye were healed."

Does this mean that since the Lord Jesus was on the tree for six hours that He was bearing the iniquity during the full six hours that He was on the tree? To answer this question we must recall that there are **two aspects** to sin-bearing distinguished in the Old Testament, as we have just described.

1 The bearing of the guilt of the sin

The Priest who ate of the Israelite's sin offering, for many months bore the iniquity in the sense of bearing its guilt and its responsibility **but at no time** did he bear its penalty. During this time, Aaron remained in full fellowship with God and could eat of the peace offering. This situation pertained until the morning of *Yom Cippur*.

2 The bearing of the penalty of the sin

On *Yom Cippur* it was the scapegoat who bore all – the guilt, responsibility **and** penalty. The Bible makes it clear that the Divine penalty in the form of the "answer", i.e. the Divine Judgment, only came in the darkness when He was "cut off" like the scapegoat. This was when He bore sin's penalty, which required the loneliness of being "forsaken". However, before this, He must bear sin's guilt and its responsibility.

Sin-bearing in the Old Testament required **Aaron and the scapegoat together** to provide the illustration of **both** aspects of sin-bearing, which would find its fulfilment in the Lord Jesus Who fulfilled both aspects of sin-bearing without help from anyone else. Hence Peter's comment:

1 Peter 1:24
> "**Who His own self** (i.e. without the help of the scapegoat) bare our sins in His own body on the tree."

When Peter refers to our Lord Jesus bearing our sins in His own body on the tree, he is referring to sin-bearing in **both aspects** mentioned above. Like Aaron of old who waited until the day of *Yom Cippur* when the weight of the guilt of sin could be passed to the scapegoat, so the Lord Jesus cried "in the daytime" for the divine answer which would be the payment of sin's dreadful penalty. During that time He was not "cut off" from men or God nor forsaken by His Father. That "answer" came in the night season and involved Him being "cut off from the land of the living".

During the first three hours, as One Who was hanged upon a tree, He became subject to the curse of the Law:

Galatians 3:13
"Christ hath redeemed us from the curse of the Law, being made a curse for us: for it is written, **Cursed** *is* **every one that hangeth on a tree.**"

This is a quotation from Deuteronomy:

Deuteronomy 21:22-23
22 "And if a man have committed a sin worthy of death, and he be to be put to death, and thou hang him on a tree:
23 His body shall not remain all night upon the tree, but thou shalt in any wise bury him that day; (**for he that is hanged** *is* **accursed of God**;) that thy land be not defiled, which the Lord thy God giveth thee *for* an inheritance."

However, just as we have seen how Scripture distinguishes between bearing sin's guilt and bearing sin's penalty, similarly we must distinguish between a curse exacted and a curse executed. Every unsaved person is under the curse of a broken Law but, thankfully, not under the penalty of that curse until they die, if they never are saved. In other words, as far as each unbeliever is concerned the curse of sin is exacted but not yet executed. For the first three hours, the Lord Jesus, when hanging on the tree, came under the curse of the Law in Deuteronomy 21:22, but "the answer" to that curse, namely its penalty, came only in that "divine answer" which the Psalm shows us happened in the second three hours during the abandonment and darkness of Calvary.

We can never, this side of heaven, with our finite and sin-defiled minds fathom or enter into what it meant to the sinless Sufferer, Who Himself had never sinned, to so publicly take to Himself and bear in the first three hours all our guilt and curse with all the ignominy and shame of this and then, in the latter three hours, bear its dreadful penalty alone. Aaron, throughout the year and later as he made the great confession on the Day of Atonement, was bearing the guilt of the people but not its penalty. In this he was only a partial picture of the Lord Jesus Who took to Himself the guilt of an ungodly world. On that dreadful morning of *Yom Cippur*, Aaron took all that guilt and cast it in his own teeth before God. How heavy must that burden of guilt have felt upon his bowed and guilty head! Aaron was unable to bear away the guilt because he could not bear its penalty. That's where the scapegoat came in, because Aaron alone could not fulfill the picture of the ultimate Sin-Bearer. Aaron and the scapegoat together were needed to foreshadow the Lord Jesus at Calvary bearing "our sins in His own body on the tree".

The **six hours** were required to fulfill **both aspects** of sin-bearing.

We read that it was during the hours of light that the Lord Jesus cried, "I cry unto Thee in the day time!" It is clear that this was not a cry of protest or a request for relief. This was a cry for the "answer". Once again, our finite minds cannot fathom what this meant to Him. This is holy ground and we bow our heads in worship. There was only one answer for the weight of curse and human guilt which He had taken to Himself. It was the divine answer and for this He cried. As divine and as One Who hated sin, He longed for the judgment to fall to deal with this. Only He knew what this would mean and yet He cried to God for the answer. The answer came in the darkness when "He was answered". This was God's answer and it remains God's answer to the problem of human guilt.

Did the abuse, which men heaped upon Him at His crucifixion, contribute to our redemption? It should be clear to even the youngest believer that men cannot contribute to their own redemption just as the priest was not allowed to eat of his own sin offering. To suggest that a contribution to the propitiation was made by cruel men is to question the completeness and all-sufficiency of His suffering at the hand of God when He made propitiation for our sin. Only a divine Person could exact sin's penalty and bring about the suffering required for the propitiation, and only a divine Person could endure such propitiating suffering. This is because only a Holy and infinitely all-knowing divine Person could know the debt of sin to be able to exact its punishment and only a divine Person Who hates sin could have suffered in the matter of bearing sin in all of its aspects. The fact that Aaron "confessed" the iniquity intelligently and cast it in his own teeth before "putting it" upon the head of the scapegoat shows that the matter of the propitiation was intelligently and reverently accomplished by an infinite and all-knowing God. To attribute a part in the bringing about of sin-expiating suffering to cruel and sinful soldiers, whose seared consciences had no intelligent understanding of the awfulness of sin in God's sight, cannot be right. Every Israelite understood that only the divine fire from God upon the sacrifice showed its acceptability to God. It would have been unthinkable for someone to approach the altar where the divine fire was consuming the sacrifice with "man-made fire" to assist in the sacrifice. We know from Hebrews 13:11-12 that the burning of the victim was a picture of the suffering of Christ. Since the fire which consumed the sacrifice was always divine fire, we are reminded that it is divinely meted-out suffering which He bore in the matter of putting away our sin. Nadab and Abihu did not appreciate this solemn truth and thought that they could approach the presence of God with strange fire i.e. man-made fire. Their error in this solemn truth led to their tragic and untimely end because it was so very grieving to the Lord. All who love the Lord and who hold Him in godly fear will solemnly take this lesson to heart with a prayerful longing for preservation and divinely imparted grace and enablement to rightly divide these sacred and solemn truths.

Some who hold that sufferings induced by men contribute to the propitiation, base their argument, at least in part, on what Peter said to the nation concerning the Lord Jesus: "Whom ye slew and hanged upon a tree" (Acts 5:30).

Peter is speaking legally and forensically by saying that they slew Him and hanged Him on the tree. By this, Peter means that they stand charged with His manslaughter before God. However, men did not bring about His death as the Lord Himself taught:

John 10:17-18
> 17 "Therefore doth My Father love Me, because I lay down My life, that I might take it again.
> 18 **No man taketh it from Me, but I lay it down of Myself**. I have power to lay it down, and I have power to take it again. This commandment have I received of My Father."

In parallel with this declaration, Pilate was forced to marvel that He died as soon as He did. Some may argue that in nailing Him to the tree, men effected the curse upon Him which He bore for us. We should notice that the curse of Deuteronomy 21 was not on a person who was nailed to a tree but on one who was "hanging upon a tree". Men nailed Him to a tree in crucifixion and hanged Him there but they had no power at all against Him to **keep Him** hanging there, just as they had no power to end His life. Perhaps they thought they had the power to keep Him hanging there when they called on Him to "come down" and He did not. However, in this they were so mistaken. They did not understand that it was love which held Him hanging there of His own will – love to us who were cursed by the broken Law. Men did not make Him accursed for us. They did not have that power. The curse came from God and He willingly took it to Himself for our sakes.

Man cannot contribute to his own propitiation. The scapegoat was utterly alone in the land cut off. The cruel abuse experienced by the Lord Jesus heaped condemnation on man and demonstrated man's wickedness. This is the "preaching of the cross" (1 Corinthians 1:18) and the "offence of the cross" (Galatians 5:11). However, all of this guilt which men had heaped upon themselves in their cruel treatment of Christ at Calvary was taken by God Himself and "made to meet upon Him" in the divine stroke which fell upon Him at Calvary.

Suffering and sufferings

In the New Testament, we read of both the "sufferings"(plural) and the "suffering" (singular) of the Lord Jesus. In 1 Peter 4:13, we learn that His sufferings are those in which we, as believers, are called upon to share even after He has ascended to heaven.

1 Peter 4:13
> "But rejoice, inasmuch as ye are partakers of Christ's **sufferings**; that, when His glory shall be revealed, ye may be glad also with exceeding joy."

In the Gospels, the Lord Jesus said, "The Son of Man must suffer **many things**..."

Luke 9:22
> "Saying, the Son of man must suffer many things, and be rejected of the elders and chief priests and scribes, and be slain, and be raised the third day."

In suffering "many things" He made it very clear that He was speaking in the context of what He would endure at the hands of men. This was something which Peter struggled with.

Matthew 16:21-23
> 21 "From that time forth began Jesus to shew unto His disciples, how that He must go unto Jerusalem, and suffer many things of the elders and chief priests and scribes, and be killed, and be raised again the third day.
> 22 Then Peter took Him, and began to rebuke Him, saying, Be it far from Thee, Lord: this shall not be unto Thee.
> 23 But He turned, and said unto Peter, Get thee behind Me, Satan: thou art an offence unto Me: for thou savourest not the things that be of God, but those that be of men".

Peter never rebuked the Lord Jesus on the many occasions that He spoke of His death. He only rebuked Him when He spoke of His humiliation and shame at the hands of men. These are "the sufferings" of Christ and in Peter's epistles we learn that this is something which Christians are called upon to share. These cannot be sin-expiating "sufferings" since we cannot contribute to our own redemption by any suffering on our part, contrary to what some elements of Christendom still teach today. When it is sin-expiating suffering, i.e. suffering which puts away sin and satisfies the throne of God, i.e. brings about the propitiation, it is always singular:

Hebrews 2:9
> "But we see Jesus, Who was made a little lower than the angels for the **suffering** of death, crowned with glory and honour; that He by the grace of God should taste death for every man."

Isaiah 53:5
> "By His stripe (singular) we are healed."

This is quoted again in 1 Peter 2:24. It was one divine stripe which effected our redemption.

1 Peter 3:18
> " For Christ also hath **once** suffered for sins, the just for the unjust, that He might bring us to God, being put to death in the flesh, but quickened by the Spirit."

His sin-expiating suffering at the hand of God is singular because **once** was enough. His sufferings at the hands of men are plural "sufferings" because men were never satisfied with the cruel treatment they meted out to Him at Calvary, and they express this in their continued persecution of believers in our Lord Jesus Christ who, in their sufferings for His sake, are "partakers of His sufferings".

The implications of these considerations of Psalm 22:2

The above detailed considerations should not be disregarded as an intellectual analysis of that which is sacred. Rather, these meditations are a restatement of doctrinal verities which, if missed, could have disastrous spiritual consequences and lead to eternal loss. Important implications arising from this are here presented with a heartfelt plea from the author for careful attention.

1 Individual faith in the Lord Jesus Christ is vital and, although He died on behalf of (for) all, all will, sadly, not be saved due to individual unbelief.

Application: each individual must have a moment of personal faith in the Lord Jesus Christ for salvation.

2 Man cannot contribute to his own redemption neither by exacting sin-expiating punishment nor by enduring it. Sinful man, i.e. Roman soldiers, could not exact the sinner's debt. This was a divine act.

Application: The hope of some who endure or inflict upon themselves penance, in the hope that this, somehow, can relieve human guilt, is contrary to the scriptural principle that it was **only** Christ Who "once suffered for sins". Moreover, officers of religion who prescribe sin-expiating suffering, i.e. penance to guilty souls, have no authority to do so. The debt has already been paid. Christians can participate in the "sufferings" of Christ (1 Peter 3) but this is not sin-expiating nor does it propitiate God's throne.

3 Only the suffering and death upon the cross of the Lord Jesus Christ were sin-expiating and propitiated God's throne. The eternal punishment of hell and the lake of fire can never make propitiation for sin.

Application: It is too late on the other side of death to have guilt put away. Suffering on the other side of death cannot purge the soul from guilt. Now is the time while yet alive.

Comparisons and contrasts between Day of Atonement (Leviticus 16) and the Sacrifice of Christ.

Until now we have considered how aspects of the rituals of the Day of Atonement, such as sin being exacted by Aaron and then borne away by the scapegoat, all find fulfilment in the Person and work of Christ at Calvary. Furthermore, the importance of human responsibility in availing of the provision of *Yom Cippur* illustrates how sinners today are responsible to obey the gospel and come into the blessing of salvation by faith. In this we see comparisons between the Day of Atonement and the saving work of Christ. However, the New Testament, especially the Hebrews Epistle, brings before us many **contrasts** between the Day of Atonement and Calvary. Through these contrasts the wonders of the Person and work of Christ are magnified.

Contrasts between Aaron entering into the earthly sanctuary and the Lord Jesus entering into the heavenly sanctuary on His ascension to God's right hand.

Hebrews makes clear that Aaron's entry into the Holiest of All on the Day of Atonement is to be **contrasted** with the entry of the Lord Jesus as a Priest into heaven itself on His ascension to glory.

1 **Aaron's work was not completed**. Aaron was engaged in a work which was never completed and needed to be repeated and thus he never could sit down in the tabernacle. The work of Christ was once and for all, never needing to be repeated, after which He could sit down on the throne in heaven (Hebrews 10:12).

2 **Aaron entered in with blood**. Aaron entered into the earthly sanctuary with blood (not without blood) to engage in a work he could never finish. In contrast, the Lord Jesus entered into the heavenly sanctuary on the basis of a work He **had already completed**, not with blood, but **by virtue of His blood** already shed (Hebrews 9:7-12).

3 Aaron entered in to do his incomplete work in garments of humiliation having earlier divested himself of his garments of glory and beauty. The Lord Jesus entered into heaven itself a **glorified Man** (Hebrews 5:5), His humiliation over forever.

In summary, Aaron entered in as a Priest, who couldn't finish the work, with blood of animals, in garments of humiliation. The Lord Jesus entered in as a Priest Who had earlier finished the work, by virtue of His own blood, in garments of glory. These are contrasts between Aaron and the Lord Jesus.

We have already seen that Aaron, laying the iniquity on the scapegoat on the Day of Atonement, is a picture of the penalty of sin being exacted by God at Calvary. However, we noted that on that **one day of the year** Aaron did not bear the iniquity (both its guilt and its penalty) as that was the one day of the year he wasn't allowed to eat of the sin offering. Now here is the contrast between Aaron and the Lord Jesus. For all days of the entire year except the tenth day of the seventh month (Day of Atonement) Aaron was able to bear the guilt of the Israelite (i.e. eat of his sin offering). However, on one very special day of the year, the Day of Atonement, he was not able to bear it. On that day the sin bearer was not the priest. It was the scapegoat who bore away not just the guilt of sin but its penalty into the land cut off. What a contrast with the Lord Jesus! On **one momentous day** at Calvary, "**once** in the end of the age" He "put away sin by the sacrifice of Himself" (Hebrews 9:26). He bore away our sin "into the land cut off" i.e. the darkness of Golgotha. However, now that He is raised from the dead as a "forever Priest" He no longer bears the guilt and penalty of sin ever again. Aaron bore the guilt of the people on a daily basis but not its penalty. Not so the Lord Jesus. He has put away our sin once and for all. Despite this, some argue that Aaron's dealing with sin on the Day of Atonement was a priestly act, and thus the Lord Jesus must have been consecrated as a Priest prior to His death to put away our sin. While this is dealt with more fully in Psalms 40 and 110, it should be noted that on the Day of Atonement Aaron **did not bear away the sin**. The fact that he was not allowed to eat the sin offering on that day was to emphasise the fact that to a priest of the Aaronic order of priesthood, **the privilege of bearing away sin was not given**. Our Lord Jesus is not of the Aaronic order of priesthood. Aaron bore the guilt of the sins of the people all the days of the year save the tenth day of the seventh month. That was the one day that sin was to be borne away, both its guilt and its penalty, and on that day Aaron was disqualified from a sin bearing role. How glad we are that the Lord Jesus was not subject to such limitations. By His death and precious shed blood He has dealt with sin to God's entire satisfaction. On the basis of His forever finished work He has arisen from the dead and entered in as a glorified Priest to God's right hand, no longer needing to bear sin's guilt on our behalf on a daily basis, in contrast to Aaron. The timing as to when the Lord Jesus was consecrated as a Priest is considered in detail in Psalms 40 and 110, but it is already apparent from these considerations that it was as a risen glorified Man, i.e. in resurrection and ascension that He was consecrated as a Priest forever after the order of Melchisedec, the matter of sin bearing dealt with forever. To conclude, it cannot be said that the putting away of sin in the Old Testament was a priestly act, because on the one day of the year that this was done, Aaron the priest was disqualified from bearing sin. Scripture is so very accurate. The Lord Jesus had already borne away our sin before He was consecrated to be a Priest at His ascension. This accurately harmonises with the typical teaching of the tabernacle where the putting away of sin was beyond Aaron's official priestly duty. In contrast to Aaron, who as a Priest bore sin's guilt but could never bear it away completely on the Day of Atonement, our Lord Jesus is a Priest Who has no more sin to bear because He has already borne it away at Calvary! He had already accomplished this great work before He became Priest.

The righteous character of God

Why should God deal with His Son on the cross and not with an ungodly world of sinners who clearly were rejecting Him? The response is found in the next verse.

Psalm 22:3

"But Thou art Holy, O Thou that inhabitest the praises of Israel."

God's righteous character is unveiled at Calvary in "answering" His Son in judgment and thus providing a means of forgiveness for men. It is this transaction, providing propitiation for sin at Calvary, which constituted the "praises of Israel".

The magnitude of divine grace in dealing with His own Son instead of swiftly judging an ungodly world is made all the more evident as we consider the ensuing verses, where the wickedness and hatred of men towards the suffering Messiah are revealed.

However, first of all we have a touching interlude where the suffering Saviour refers to the trust in God which characterised the "fathers" of Israel. Let us always remember that throughout the centuries of Israel's history, despite much failure and apostasy, there always was a faithful godly remnant within the nation who longed for the coming of the Messiah.

While on the cross, the Saviour's thoughts moved to consider those of this faithful remnant. Many of them had already "died in faith" (Hebrews 11:13) and, as we noted in Psalm 16, like Daniel and Job they were "resting" in *Sheol*, that place of hiding and comfort. These true "fathers" of Israel, such as Abraham, Isaac and Jacob, were heroes of faith. The nature of their trust is unfolded in verses 4 and 5.

Psalm 22:4-5

4 "Our fathers trusted in Thee: they trusted, and Thou didst deliver them.
5 They cried unto Thee, and were delivered: they trusted in Thee, and were not confounded."

The fathers' trust is seen in a two- fold way.

Firstly: "They trusted **and Thou didst deliver them** (*tephalltemo*) (long tense)."

Secondy: "They cried unto Thee **and were delivered** (*nimlatu*) (short tense)."

Let us focus on these two occurrences of the word "deliver". In Hebrew these are 2 distinct words. The first word means to deliver in the sense of "escaping captivity". The second word carries the idea of being delivered from danger. Furthermore, each Hebrew word is in a different verbal form. The first (*tephalltemo*) is in the imperfect or long tense, which could carry the idea of a deliverance in the present stretching into the future. The second, *nimlatu*, is in the perfect or short tense suggesting a deliverance fully completed.

Drawing these strands of evidence together, it is possible that the first phrase, "They trusted and Thou didst deliver them" (*tephalltemo*), could include (if we give full emphasis to the long tense of *tephalltemo*) the deliverance which the fathers experienced from Egypt's bondage and later from the bondage of Babylon. However, when we come to Hebrews 2:15, we discover that "all their lifetime" these saints were, through fear of death, "subject to bondage". Since the word *tephalltemo* means to deliver as from bondage, and the long tense in Hebrew grammatically allows for a future fulfilment, one cannot exclude the possibility that the verse also embraces the hope of the fathers that they would eventually be delivered from the bondage of *Sheol* through the coming Messiah (see Psalm 18).

However, there was a further aspect to their faith highlighted in the second phrase (*nimlatu*). It concerned a deliverance which they experienced the precise moment they "cried unto" God for salvation. It was the deliverance which every believer in the Lord Jesus Christ experienced the moment he or she believed in Him and received the deliverance of present salvation.

"They trusted in Thee and were not confounded (ashamed)"

Whether in present possession of salvation while alive, or in the assurance of future delivery from *Sheol* in death, their trust was in Jehovah Who, in fulfilment of His promise, would send His Son; through "answering" His sacrificial offering at Calvary, He would provide the righteous means whereby the sins that "were past" could not only be "covered" but put away finally. Old Testament saints would no longer reside in *Sheol* but have full rights to rest with Him in heaven until the day of resurrection.

It is important for us to realise that the Psalmist deals first of all with the faithful ones in Israel before he moves on to speak of those of the nation and of the rest of mankind who so cruelly rejected Him. Consequently, there is no room whatever for the nations of nominal Christendom to justify their satanic anti-Semitism by blaming Israel exclusively with the rejection of the Messiah. The whole world stands together condemned with the sin of Christ-rejection as we will now learn in the Psalm.

The Psalm gives us an analysis of the rejection of the Sovereign. It was apparent that the gentle and humble presentation of the Messiah to Israel and the world as the "Hind of the dawn" was misinterpreted by the majority of people.

Psalm 22:6

"But I *am* a worm, and no man; a reproach of men, and despised of the people."

"I am a worm", He says, and this was exactly how He was regarded. The worm is a figure of speech used by Job to describe the humiliation and sorrows to which a human being may potentially descend.

Job 25:6

"How much less man, *that is* a worm? and the son of man, *which is* a worm?"

It is also used by Isaiah to describe the humiliation which the nation of Israel would endure in its long history at the hands of its Gentile persecutors:

Isaiah 41:14

"Fear not, thou worm Jacob!"

However, the next phrase, "and no man" (*ve lo ish*), indicates that the experience of the Lord Jesus at the hands of His persecutors involved depths never plumbed before in human existence. The phrase, "and no man", ironically shows us that He Who is more than human – in fact, God manifested in flesh – is being treated not merely as sub-human but rather as non-human, i.e. as an animal. The phrase, "a reproach of men" (*cherpat-adam*), really means "a reproach of Man" (*adam*). In other words, the entire fallen human race, of which Adam is the federal head, stands charged with the rejection of Christ. It is as if the entire human race decided that He was no longer worthy to remain a member of the human family. This charge is broad-sweeping, and equally encompasses Gentiles and Jews together. The preaching of the cross, consequently, presents to us the condemnation of the entire human race. One may have expected that the privileged nation of Israel would separate itself from the rest of fallen humanity in its verdict that He was "worthy of death". Alas, no! It must have been hard for the Psalmist to add the phrase, "despised of the people". Such a startling statement demands explanation, and it comes in the next verse.

The problem for the contemporary nation was simple. How could a suffering and humiliated Christ be the King of Israel? To the Jew, this was clearly a stumbling block. As for the Greeks and Romans, familiar with the concept of military might, such a spectacle was merely "foolishness". The Psalmist in verse 7 envisaged how all would come together in a rare show of unity.

Psalm 22:7

"All they that see Me laugh Me to scorn: they shoot out the lip, they shake the head…"

However, the issue which prompted this irreverent and united outpouring of raucous rejection was the mistaken opinion that, somehow, His being crucified was the final proof that both Christ and His declared mission to save the world lacked divine pleasure and approval. As the official leaders and teachers of Israel watched the cross being upraised, they felt reassured that it was now beyond question that this Teacher from Galilee, Who claimed to be the Son of God, must have been tragically mistaken. Listen to their words, prophetically outlined, hundreds of years before they were uttered in blasphemy around the uplifted cross!

Psalm 22:8

"He trusted on the Lord *that* He would deliver Him: let Him deliver Him, seeing He delighted in Him."

The phrase, "seeing He delighted in Him" (*ki chaphetz bo*), perhaps reveals the fatal flaw in their reasoning. The word "seeing" (*ki*) means "because" and in this context carries all the sarcasm of a mock statement of faith. They did not for one moment believe that God would deliver Him "**because** He delighted in Him", – but, nevertheless, this was their challenge to God and to Christ to prove the veracity not only of His claim to be pleasing to the Father, but also of the Father's revealed verdict from Heaven: "This is My beloved Son in Whom I am well pleased." The challenge of the mockers to the living God was simple and bold. Let God prove His pleasure in this suffering Victim by bringing about a dramatic rescue from the cross.

Their use of the word "delight" (*chaphetz*) would have been most illuminating for those around the cross had they paused for a just few moments to think of what they had said! It is, in fact, the word used to describe the "desire", "pleasure" or "delight" (*chaphetz*) which God shows in a sacrifice acceptable to Him. For example, in Psalm 40:6, we shall see that this is the word used to describe God's lack of pleasure in the inadequacy of Old Testament sacrifices, particularly on the occasion of Aaron's consecration to priesthood: "Sacrifice and offering Thou didst not desire (*lo-chaphatzta*)". How then would God convince men of His pleasure (*chaphetz*) in the suffering Victim? Fallen men required a dramatic deliverance from the cross: "Let Him deliver Him." However, it is here that the utter foolishness of the wisdom of men is revealed, as the so-called "foolishness of God" which is "wiser than men" is unveiled. For the **pleasure** of God was indeed seen in the suffering One that day when, in the language of the prophet Isaiah, "It pleased the Lord to bruise Him" (*Adonay chaphetz dacco*) (Isaiah 53:10). Note that the word "pleased" in Isaiah 53:10 is the Hebrew word *chaphetz*. In other words, the issue under scrutiny that day was as dramatic and real as it was in the confrontation between Elijah and the prophets of Baal. Would God intervene by **answering** the sacrifice and thus demonstrate His **pleasure**?

Psalm 22:9-10

9 "But Thou *art* He that took Me out of the womb: Thou didst make Me hope *when I was* upon My mother's breasts.
10 I was cast upon Thee from the womb: Thou *art* My God from My mother's belly."

Against the background of the cries of those who blasphemously assert that God has no pleasure in Him, He reaffirms to the Father the very issues which caused the Father to have unbroken delight in His Son. Once again, the theme of His dependent Manhood, so beautifully presented to us in Psalm 16, is underlined. Earlier we noted that He was being treated as non-human – "no-man". Here, however, we see reaffirmed the perfection of His humanity. In fact, far from being non-human or sub-human, we learn here that He was much more than mere man. He was "God manifest in flesh" (1 Timothy 3:16). His birth was unique in the annals of humanity: "**Thou *art* He that took Me out of the womb.**" Furthermore, the babe born was clearly omniscient and, although in Mary's arms, He was engaged in conscious fellowship with the Father. Luke tells us that He "increased in wisdom and stature" (Luke 2:52). This "increase" in wisdom and stature, witnessed by those privileged to visit that Nazareth home, was but the gradual unveiling of the infinite wisdom hidden within Him. Note Paul's careful words to the Colossians, so beset with Gnostic theories, of the Person of Christ:

Colossians 2:3

"In Whom are **hid**, all the treasures of wisdom and knowledge."

The wise men in Matthew 2:11 worshipped the Babe directly. These were men of faith, because they recognised that the One, before Whom they bowed, consciously received their homage and knew their hearts. He was

God manifested in flesh, and He did not temporarily relinquish omniscience at Bethlehem! This was already considered in Psalm 16.

Psalm 22:11-13

11 "Be not far from Me; for trouble is near, for there is none to help.
12 Many bulls have compassed Me: strong bulls of Bashan have beset Me round.
13 They gaped upon Me with their mouths, as a ravening and a roaring lion."

In verses 11-21, the Psalmist outlines for us the treatment of the Lord Jesus by several quite distinct groups of people, each described in beast-like character:

1 The bulls
2 The strong bulls (ones) of Bashan
3 Dogs
4 The assembly of the wicked

The bulls, which were ceremonially clean animals, are described as "gaping with their mouths". This may well refer to the people in Jerusalem who, publicly and loudly, were crying out for His crucifixion. However, it is the responsible leaders of the people at that time, alluded to as the "strong ones of Bashan", who are particularly singled out for attention. They were seen in their behaviour as now acting as "a ravening and a roaring lion". In other words, the clean animal was now seen behaving as an unclean carnivorous beast. What a sad description to describe the rejecters of the gentle Messiah! Nevertheless, the Spirit of God is quick to show us that if these leaders regarded the Lord Jesus as sub-human further up the Psalm, the tragic result was that now they themselves were acting in a sub-human, beastlike manner.

Psalm 22:14-15

14 "I am poured out like water, and all My bones are out of joint: My heart is like wax; it is melted in the midst of My bowels.
15 My strength is dried up like a potsherd; and My tongue cleaveth to My jaws; and Thou hast brought Me into the dust of death."

The language which follows gives us insight into the feelings of the Lord Jesus as He is confronted with such a violent and decisive rejection by the leaders of the people.

"**As water, I am poured out**" and "**all My bones are separated**" (literal translation).

In the Scriptures, "pouring out" indicates devotion. In face of the rejection by His own people, His devotion to His Father is undiminished. Onward He goes. No one or nothing can deflect Him. The picture is one of intensity of devotion. The phrase, "all My bones are separated" (the word "joints" is in italics), occurs only here in the Old Testament. This suggests to us that what is in view is an experience of deep physical sufferings with an intensity uniquely experienced by Himself.

"My heart is like wax; it is melted in the midst of My bowels"

Often in Scripture we read of those whose "hearts melted". Usually this metaphorical phrase is used to describe the feelings of those who are filled with intense fear. However, this is not the case here. The Scripture is careful to add, "it is melted in the midst of My bowels". The "bowels" in Scripture are often used metaphorically of compassion and mercy. In Philippians 2:1, the apostle Paul speaks of "bowels and mercies". The combination of the phrase, describing the "melting of His heart" and "in the midst of His bowels", indicates that His heart was melted, not through fear, but rather through compassion. Viewing the metaphor as a whole, we are seeing, beautifully described for us, the intensity of the Saviour's compassion even for those who hated Him. Such was the intensity of His love and compassion that only metaphorical language could begin to describe it.

"My strength is dried up like a potsherd, and My tongue cleaveth to My jaws"

Some have taken this verse to suggest that the Lord Jesus was characterised by physical weakness under the intense thirst resulting from His sufferings. Let us look at the language carefully. The word translated "potsherd" really means "of clay" (*cheres*). The metaphor here described is certainly not of a fire-cracked earthenware vessel which, on the application of more heat, would be likely to disintegrate. On the contrary, this metaphor depicts clay being dried in the fire, becoming firmer every moment. The metaphor, therefore, calls to our attention a picture of intensity of strength, not of weakness. Finally, the moving phrase, "My tongue cleaveth to My jaws", reminds us of the intensity of thirst which He experienced throughout the events of Calvary. Nevertheless, it was not until the six hours were completed that He cried, "I thirst" (John 19:28), and this was in order that one of the remaining unfulfilled Scriptures regarding the events of His death should be fulfilled.

"Thou hast brought Me into the dust of death"

This Scripture reminds us as to why He was there. It was at His Father's command. Those around him thought that they were orchestrating the events around the cross. Little did they know that the Father's hand was in control and, unknown to them, they were fulfilling Scripture in the finest details, as the ensuing verses indicate.

Psalm 22:16-18

16 "For dogs have compassed Me: the assembly of the wicked have inclosed Me: they pierced My hands and My feet.
17 I may tell all My bones: they look *and* stare upon Me.
18 They part My garments among them, and cast lots upon My vesture."

He now leaves the attention of the "bulls" and is handed over to the "dogs". "Dogs **have compassed Me**", He says, "**the assembly of the wicked have enclosed Me**". It has often been pointed out that the "dogs" speak of the unclean Gentiles. This is especially clear in Matthew 15:26, where, in His conversation with the Syrophoenician Gentile woman, the Lord indicates that the Gentiles are aptly described as "dogs". "It is not meet to take the children's (the Jews') meat and cast it to the dogs", He said. Far from responding in a resentful way to this, the Syrophoenician woman replied, "Yea Lord, but the little dogs eat of the crumbs which fall from the master's table". Alas, now the Gentiles are seen in all their ferocious hatred of Israel's Messiah: "**They pierced My hands and My feet.**"

Even here, divine control is seen. "**I may tell (or count) all My bones**". Perhaps the significance of this is that He could account for each bone. In this the second reference of the Psalm to His bones, we are reminded that He was still in control, and although He was nailed to the cross in crucifixion, no bone of His was broken. The next phrase, "**They look and stare upon Me**", does not mean that "His bones" were looking at him. The word for bone is of feminine gender in Hebrew, whereas the pronoun "they look" is masculine plural. This simply means that those who were around Him were intently looking and staring at Him. This is fulfilled in the Gospel account:

Matthew 27:36
"Sitting down they watched Him there."

This clearly was fulfilled in "the daytime" before the darkness descended. However, a further detail was prophesied: "**They parted My raiment among them, and upon My vesture they cast lots.**" This also was one of the events foretold to occur in the "daytime" and illustrates the callous cruelty and greed of the Roman soldiers.

John 19:23-24
23 "Then the soldiers, when they had crucified Jesus, took His garments, and made four parts, to every soldier a part; and also *His* coat: now the coat was without seam, woven from the top throughout.
24 They said therefore among themselves, Let us not rend it, but cast lots for it, whose it shall be: that the Scripture might be fulfilled, which saith, They parted My raiment among them, and for My vesture they did cast lots. These things therefore the soldiers did."

In John's account of this event he tells us that His coat was without seam, woven from the top throughout with the result that the soldiers said: "Let us cast lots for it whose it shall be." John uses the explanatory comment, "that the Scriptures might be fulfilled", to emphasise that the gambling for His garment was yet another direct fulfilment of Psalm 22.

Psalm 22:19
"But be not Thou far from Me, O Lord: O My strength, haste Thee to help Me."

There now follows a short but intense prayer from the Saviour to the Father: "**Be not far**", He requests. This is a request for the **manifestation of**

the divine presence. This would shortly be seen in the divine answer to the sacrifice.

The next phrase is a request for an immediate **manifestation of divine power**. "**O My strength, haste Thee to help Me!**" Once again, the power of God would be seen in the divine answer to the sacrifice. The word for strength used here occurs nowhere else in our Bibles. How significant! This unique occurrence of the word no doubt emphasises to us the unique display of divine power revealed at Calvary.

Psalm 22:20,21

20 "Deliver My soul from the sword; My darling from the power of the dog.
21 Save Me from the lion's mouth: for Thou hast heard Me from the horns of the unicorns."

Now, He describes for us four matters from which He requests deliverance. While it is difficult to precisely define what each of these four issues involve, at least one thing is clear: it was the answer at the end of verse 21 which marked the deliverance. Let us look briefly at each of these.

1 From the sword – "Deliver My soul from the sword."

In Scripture, the metaphorical picture of the soul being pierced by the sword is used to describe Mary's feelings of sorrow which she would experience when Calvary would bring separation from Christ. In Luke 2, as she would witness the betrayal and death of her Son, she was told, "Yea a sword shall pierce through thy own soul also" (Luke 2:35). However, here His prayer is that His soul should be delivered from the sword. It is language which describes for us His longing desire for deliverance from the weight of sorrow He bore. It was the divine answer (judgment for the sin of humanity) which would bring about this deliverance. "Who for the joy that was set before Him endured the cross… (Hebrews 12:2)."

2 From the power (paw, hand) of the dog

Could this be the unclean Gentile hands which so irreverently manhandled him? His request was, "**Deliver My darling from the paw of the dog.**" The Hebrew here requires a little explanation. The word translated "My darling", means "My unique one". The word is feminine, so it is an adjectival description of a feminine noun used earlier in the sentence. The only feminine noun used earlier in the sentence is the word "My soul". The sentence could be translated as follows: "Deliver My soul from the sword, My unique soul from the paw of the dog." Clearly, the Gentile dog regarded Him only as a common criminal. There was nothing unique about Him in their eyes. However, as we will shortly see, it was the divine answer which would change this! It was the divine judgment, as indicated by the darkness and the events which followed, which caused the centurion to confess that He was indeed unique, "Truly this man was the Son of God" and "Certainly this was a righteous Man" (see Appendix 4).

Mark 15:39

"And when the centurion, which stood over against Him, saw that He so cried out, and gave up the ghost, he said, **Truly this Man was the Son of God.**"

Luke 23:47

"Now when the centurion saw what was done, he glorified God, saying, **Certainly this was a righteous Man.**"

3 From the mouth of the lion

"**Save Me from the lion's mouth**..." Once again, this is metaphorical language. But to whom does the lion refer? Furthermore, is there any significance in the "mouth of the lion" being alluded to here? In the New Testament (1 Peter 5:8), the devil is referred to as "a roaring lion, going about seeking whom he may devour". During the temptation account, the devil sought to question His Deity with the words, "**If** Thou be the Son of God". Furthermore, he questioned His unconditional Kingly rights, "All these (kingdoms) will I give Thee **if**...". At the cross, we do not hear the devil speaking directly, but those who reviled the Lord Jesus Christ articulated the exact same sentiments as the devil expressed three and a half years earlier using similar words: "**If** Thou be the Son of God , come down from the cross!" and again, "**If** Thou be the King of Israel come down...!" How would the mouth of the lion be silenced? In other words, how would God prove that He was indeed the Son of God? Once again it is the divine answer which would silence the lion's blasphemous mouth and prove Who He is eternally.

4 From the horns of the unicorns

The exact meaning of the Hebrew text here is obscure in light of present scholarship. It is unclear if the word *remim* refers to a single-horned beast, now extinct, or to some other kind of horned wild animal. Moreover, there is some evidence to suggest that the word *remim* could be translated "the high ones". Perhaps the fact that the meaning is obscure is quite fitting, as we must recognise that there are many aspects of the Calvary story which we cannot understand. No doubt, one day in heaven we will learn exactly what is meant by the "horns of the high ones".

Thou hast heard (answered) Me.

This is clearly the watershed in the Psalm. It marks the division in the Psalm between suffering and glory. It is the fact that He was answered by His God, which causes the Psalm to burst forth into praise. As we noted earlier, the answer was withheld during the hours of light. During this time, He was the object of the cruel taunting of men. Nevertheless, the descent of the darkness and the proof of the divine hand upon Him as the sinless Sin-Bearer answered every one of the taunts which men directed to Him. The divine answer proved His holiness, the pleasure which God had in Him as the acceptable Sacrifice as well as His uniqueness. "The God that answereth by fire, let Him be God!" (1 Kings 18:24).

Psalm 22:22-23

22 "I will declare Thy Name unto My brethren: in the midst of the congregation will I praise Thee.

23 Ye that fear the Lord, praise Him; all ye the seed of Jacob, glorify Him; and fear Him, all ye the seed of Israel."

"I will declare Thy Name unto My brethren"

If the Lord Jesus can speak of His own as His "brethren" this means that they too can address God as "Father". The placing of this important doctrinal truth just here in the Psalm, after the declaration of the accepted Sacrifice of Christ, shows that one of the great outcomes of the death and resurrection of the Lord Jesus is the declaration of the Father to His own. In fact, this forms the theme of the upper room ministry of John 13-17. Through His Sacrifice which makes propitiation for sins we have come to know the Father. Moreover, we have been brought into relationship with Him. As we have already seen, God the Father was known in the Old Testament.

Malachi 1:6

"A son honoureth *his* father, and a servant his master: if then I *be* a Father, where *is* Mine honour?"

Psalm 89:26

"He shall cry unto Me, Thou *art* my Father, my God, and the Rock of my salvation."

However, we in this Church age are now "sons of God" in a way which Old Testament believers did not experience. For example, the Lord taught His disciples to pray to the Father. This was quite new because there are no recorded prayers in the Old Testament where an Old Testament believer addressed God as "Father". As we shall see in our consideration of Psalm 89, when David addressed God as "My Father" he was speaking prophetically. Addressing God as "Father" must await the outcome of the resurrection and ascension of the Lord Jesus Christ when, by the descent of the Spirit, we would receive the divine nature and thus be sons of God, not merely in title but by virtue of having the divine nature placed within us.

John 20:16-17

16 "Jesus saith unto her, Mary. She turned herself, and saith unto Him, Rabboni; which is to say, Master.

17 Jesus saith unto her, Touch Me not; for I am not yet ascended to My Father: but go to My brethren, and say unto them, **I ascend unto My Father, and your Father**; and *to* My God, and your God."

In Hebrews 2, this father-child relationship is one which brings a setting apart (**sanctification**) of the children of God for divine service within the heavenly sanctuary as priests. This truth is futher elaborated in Psalms 40 and 110. The Lord Jesus is not ashamed to be linked with us in this.

Hebrews 2:11

"For both He that sanctifieth and they who are sanctified *are* all of one: for which cause **He is not ashamed to call them brethren**,"

"In the midst of the congregation" (Psalm 22:22)

We may wonder what the Psalmist means by the phrase, "in the midst of the congregation". Hebrews 2:12, however, leaves us in no doubt that what is referred to here is the Church.

Hebrews 2:12
> "Saying, I will declare Thy Name unto My brethren, **in the midst of the Church will I sing praise unto Thee**."

The truth regarding the Church was a mystery hidden in God's heart from before the foundation of the world, so David could not have clearly understood that the "congregation" he referred to in Psalm 22:22 was a future body of people distinct from the nation of Israel but made up of Jews and Gentiles. That understanding of the verse is revealed in the Epistle to the Hebrews. However, armed with this illumination from Hebrews 2:12 we, in retrospect, can easily see that this interpretation is perfectly consistent with the Psalm since, having just spoken of "the congregation" (the Church) (Psalm 22:22), David in the next verse speaks of "God fearers" praising the Lord, followed then by "all the seed of Jacob" and then "all the seed of Israel".

Psalm 22:23
> "Ye that fear the Lord, praise Him; all ye the seed of Jacob, glorify Him; and fear Him, all ye the seed of Israel."

This verse is showing us how God will act to bring to Himself His own nation, **subsequent to** their rejection of Christ.

Firstly, David calls on the God-fearers to praise Him and then on **all the seed of Jacob** to glorify Him. We know from the New Testament that "God-fearers" was a term used to describe Gentiles who held in reverence God and His Word (Acts 10:22;13:26). Is there a hint here that the blessing of the Gentile "God-fearers", i.e. those of this Church era, would provoke the sons of Jacob to jealousy so that they would come to faith in their estranged Messiah? The title, "Jacob", would remind us of the Jewish nation in its state of estrangement from its Messiah, just as Jacob at Peniel wrestled with the divine Visitor throughout the night and, on his submission to the Angel, his name was changed to Israel – prince with God (Genesis 32:24-32)(see also comment on this in Psalm 24).

God is calling on the seed of Jacob, in all its estrangement and sadness, to recognise His divine ways in bringing blessing to the Gentiles through faith in Christ and likewise to give Him the glory and own Him as Lord. Down through the centuries, there have been individual Jewish people who, like Jacob of old, have wrestled in the darkness with their Messiah – and for them the struggle ended in blessing when they cast themselves into His divine arms for blessing and found forgiveness, pardon and unparalleled blessing through faith in Him. Then and only then can one of the seed of Jacob be said to belong to "the seed of **Israel**" – the prince with God now fully restored to fellowship with Him. Notice that the Psalmist now calls on the **seed of Israel** to fear Him.

These steps in Israel's restoration to the Lord are also outlined in Romans chapter 11 where we learn that the Jews are provoked to jealousy when the Gentiles are blessed:

Romans 11:11
"Through their fall salvation is come unto the Gentiles, for to provoke them to jealousy."

Further down the chapter we read of Israel's salvation:

Romans 11:26
"And so **all Israel shall be saved**: as it is written, There shall come out of Sion the Deliverer, and shall turn away ungodliness **from Jacob**." Note 3

David may well have enquired as to the identity of the "congregation" of Psalm 22:22, since we learn in 1 Peter 1 that Old Testament writers were aware of a future, albeit enigmatic, body of people distinct from themselves, who would enjoy blessings of closeness to God, nearer and more wonderful than theirs.

1 Peter 1:12
"Unto whom it was revealed, **that not unto themselves, but unto us** they did minister the things, which are now reported unto you by them that have preached the gospel unto you with the Holy Ghost sent down from heaven; which things the angels desire to look into."

It is worth noting in passing that the Lord sings praises unto the Father (verse 22). In the New Testament, in the public gatherings of the Lord's people, only collective singing is envisaged.

Ephesians 5:19-20
19 "Speaking to yourselves in psalms and hymns and spiritual songs, singing and making melody in your (plural) heart (singular) to the Lord;
20. Giving thanks always for all things unto God and the Father in the Name of our Lord Jesus Christ;"

Colossians 3:16
"In psalms and hymns and spiritual songs, singing with grace in your hearts to the Lord."

In other words, public singing is a collective, not an individual performance. The reason possibly is simply that some very godly believers just cannot sing very well, whereas some people, who may not even be believers, can sing most movingly. Solo singing is independent of the spiritual calibre of the singer. It attracts attention to the performer for the performance to be successful and may, therefore, appeal to the flesh, hence the exhortations in Ephesians 5:19 and Colossians 3:16 to **collective** public singing in the gatherings of the assembly. However, there is one exception. The Lord Jesus in the midst of the Church in a coming day will sing praise to the Father. Orthodox Jews believe that the ancient music of the Psalms has been lost in the mists of history. There is one exception! The Lord Himself; He will teach us the music of the Psalms!

What is the reason for this blessing to the Church, to the God-fearers, to the seed of Jacob and the seed of Israel? The theme is simple yet profound. It is purely because:

Psalm 22:24

"For He (God) hath not despised nor abhorred the affliction of the Afflicted; neither hath He hid His face from Him; but when He cried unto Him, He heard."

Eternally, our theme of praise will return to the principal fact that God heard the Suffering Saviour on the cross (verse 24), and answered Him (verse 21) so that He became the Sacrifice which has made propitiation for sin. This will be our song eternally.

Psalm 22:25

"My praise *shall be* of Thee in **the great congregation**: I will pay My vows before them that fear Him."

In Hebrew, however, this reads literally, "From Thee, shall be My praise in the great congregation". What we discover here, is that we will eternally witness the Father's praise to the Son! How majestic. How wonderful. Those who witnessed His baptism in Matthew 3:17 got a foretaste of this.

Matthew 3:17

"And lo a voice from heaven, saying, This is My beloved Son, in Whom I am well pleased."

This too will be our experience forever.

However, who are the "**great congregation**" (Psalm 22:25) who will witness this great sight? It cannot be the congregation of Israel in the time of the Psalmist, if we accept the interpretation of the word "congregation" (Psalm 22:22) provided for us in Hebrews 2, which we saw referred to the Church of this age. Evidently, the "great congregation" is a company of people which includes the "congregation" (*kahal*) referred to earlier in verse 22 and revealed to be the Church in Hebrews 2. However, the use of the word "great" suggests that this is a company which, in addition to the Church, includes **many other believers** as well who could be described as those who fear God, and **all** those who are of the seed of Israel, as we have already observed. When we come to Psalm 40:9-10, we discover that the **great congregation** is a great future assembly who will eternally enjoy the personal ministry of the Lord Jesus in revealing divine secrets.

Psalm 40: 9-10

9 " I have preached (as Gospel) righteousness in **the great congregation**: lo,

I have not refrained My lips, O Lord, Thou knowest."
10 "I have not concealed Thy lovingkindness and Thy truth from **the great congregation**."

Clearly, therefore, there is one thing which unites all within the "great congregation". It is the fact that they have been given the **full** revelation of the righteousness of God, His lovingkindness and His truth, as revealed in and through the Lord Jesus Christ. This is a revelation which goes beyond the oral ministry of the Lord Jesus on earth where He hid some things from the disciples and spoke in parables and mysteries. In that coming day, He will reveal all to His own. This analysis of the use of the phrase, "the great congregation", would suggest that it is a very all-encompassing phrase describing all of the redeemed down through the centuries, from Adam right down to the last individual saved at the end of the millennium. This passage also indicates that it is not until the very end of the millennial reign that the "great congregation" will be seen in its entirety, although it will function throughout the millennial reign. It does not tell us anything about the various distinctions which mark the members of the great congregation. For example, it does not distinguish between the heavenly people (the Church) and the earthly people (Israel) as we discover in the New Testament. However, that is not the important issue in the Psalm. The point is that the revelation of the Father's pleasure in His Son will be publicly and continuously displayed before the entire millennial hosts of the redeemed and forwards into the Eternal State. As one reads Hebrews 12:22-23 and the account of the **earthly** participants in the millennial reign ("Mount Zion") and the **heavenly** participants ("the heavenly Jerusalem") together with the innumerable company of angels, one wonders if the term used by the Hebrews writer, "the general assembly", (Hebrews 12:23) is not synonymous with "the great congregation" of Psalm 22, i.e. a general description to describe all those who will be saved in the Kingdom and who enter into the Eternal State. Nevertheless, within this "great congregation" or "general assembly", the Church, spoken of as the "Church of the firstborn ones" (Hebrews 12:23), will retain its distinctiveness eternally.

Hebrews 12:22-23
> 22 "But ye are come unto Mount Zion, and unto the city of the living God, the heavenly Jerusalem, and to an innumerable company of angels,
> 23 To **the general assembly** and Church of the firstborn, which are written in heaven, and to God the Judge of all, and to the spirits of just men made perfect."

It is here, in the "great congregation", that we learn that He will pay His vows before them that fear Him.

Psalm 22: 25
> "…I will pay My vows before them that fear Him."

This is no doubt a reference to the Nazarite who, on completion of his vow, made an offering to the Lord, and the sodden shoulder with unleavened cake and wafer was placed in his hands and displayed before the Lord.

Numbers 6:19-20
> 19 "And the priest shall take the sodden shoulder of the ram, and one unleavened cake out of the basket, and one unleavened wafer, and shall put *them* upon the hands of the Nazarite, after *the hair of* his separation is shaven:
> 20 And the priest shall wave them *for* a wave offering before the Lord: this *is* holy for the priest, with the wave breast and heave shoulder: and after that the Nazarite may drink wine."

Psalm 22:25 shows that eternally we will be reminded that He alone finished the work and fulfilled His vow.

Morally, throughout His life, He was a Nazarite. However, in the upper room He said:

Matthew 26:29
> "But I say unto you, I will not drink henceforth of this fruit of the vine, until that day when I drink it new with you in My Father's Kingdom."

Here it could be said that He had become ceremonially a Nazarite. Interestingly, in this connection, at the cross when offered wine with myrrh, He "received it not".

Mark 15:23
> "And they gave Him to drink wine mingled with myrrh: but He received *it* not."

Nowhere in the Old Testament do we read of a Nazarite completing his vow and placing his hair upon the altar. This was a most unusual request because God only received on His altar that which was perfect. Certainly, no Nazarite could claim to be perfect. In contrast, the Lord Jesus Christ, the heavenly Nazarite, placed not just His hair upon the altar – He placed His **all** upon the altar. He alone finished the work. Just as the Nazarite could partake of the fruit of the vine after the completion of his vow, so the Lord told His disciples He would partake of the new wine (this is a non-alcoholic grape juice) in His Father's Kingdom (Matthew 26:29). Thus the Psalm describes the Lord's joy in that coming day of glory when all will rejoice in the fulfilled vow and the finished work of Calvary.

Psalm 22:26
> "The meek shall eat and be satisfied: they shall praise the Lord that seek Him: your heart shall live for ever."

This verse indicates to us that there is going to be a feast within the "great congregation". The subject matter of the celebration is not indicated to us. However, when we turn to Isaiah 25:6-8, we discover that the Lord shall make a feast on Mount Zion. This feast will follow death being swallowed up in victory (Isaiah 25:8), and the resurrection from the dead of the tribulation saints who will be enjoying this feast. Moreover, Isaiah expected to arise at the same time.

Isaiah 26:19
"Thy dead *men* shall live, *together with* my dead body shall they arise. wake and sing, ye that dwell in dust: for Thy dew *is as* the dew of herbs, and the earth shall cast out the dead."

However, neither Isaiah nor the Psalmist had any idea as to the subject of celebration. We must await the revelation in the New Testament to discover that it is the marriage feast of the King, otherwise known as the marriage supper of the Lamb. As for the guests:

Psalm 22:26
"The meek shall eat and be satisfied: They shall praise the Lord that seek Him: your heart shall live for ever."

But what about the living saints at the end of the tribulation who enter into this wonderful joy? Is it possible for them to die during the millennial reign? What a sad disappointment this would be, were this to be the case! Nevertheless, this cannot be so. Notice the reassuring words in the Psalm.

"Your heart shall live for ever"
The word "for ever" ("*la ad* ") is beautiful. It means your heart will live unto eternity. The promise is clear. God has promised them that they will not die but they will indeed be fitted to enter right into "eternity" or, as we say, "the Eternal State". This was already considered in Psalm 8. It is worth remembering that when the Lord Jesus came to raise Lazarus (John 11:28), Martha's words to Mary were: "The Master is come." The phrase "is come" is the verbal form of the word *parousia* used to describe the Lord's eventual coming to the earth. The entire Lazarus incident was a little preview of the events when the Lord Jesus Christ shall return to the Mount of Olives, revealed in Zechariah 14:4, when His feet shall touch it. The spot, to which He will return, is the very place from which He departed 2000 years ago – Bethany (Luke 24:50; Acts 1:11). Hence, the significance of the miracle: Lazarus was raised from the dead. But notice His words to Martha:

John 11:26
"And whosoever liveth and believeth on Me shall never die."

In other words, those who are alive and are saved when He comes to the earth shall enter into His Kingdom with bodies which can **never** die.

Psalm 22:27-28
27 "All the ends of the world **shall remember** and turn unto the Lord: and all the kindreds of the nations shall worship before Thee.

28 For the Kingdom *is* the Lord's: and He *is* the Governor among the nations."

We have already seen from Ezekiel 16 that the fulfilment of *Yom Cippur* in the death of the Lord Jesus shall be the great basis of **remembrance** in the worship of the coming Kingdom. Moreover, as considered earlier in this chapter, all the sin offerings of Ezekiel's future temple will be of a commemorative nature. This will be considered in detail at the end of Psalm 118. We are reminded of this again in Psalm 22:27, when, in the context of worshipping the Lord, "all the ends of the world **shall remember**". Israel shall be the head of the nations and not the tail. "All the ends of the world" (earth) and all the families of the redeemed nations shall return and worship. This, according to Zechariah 14:16, Isaiah 2:3 and Micah 4:2, shall take place at the Mountain of Jehovah in Jerusalem, which we will learn about in Psalm 24. Why will they worship? Simply because the Kingdom is Jehovah's and "He is the Governor (Ruler) among the nations".

Psalm 22:29
"All *they that be* fat upon earth shall eat and worship: all they that go down to the dust shall bow before Him: and none can keep alive his own soul."

But what of those who will be born during the millennium? They must come to a personal saving faith in the Lord Jesus Christ as will be discussed later in Psalm 72. Of course, many will believe. However, some will not. This will be the case even though we learn in Revelation that Satan, the deceiver of souls, will be bound for 1000 years (Revelation 20:2). Psalm 22:29 reveals what will happen to these unbelievers during the millennium.

Psalm 22:29
"All they that go down to the dust shall bow before Him."

Clearly, prior to their judicial death, they will bow in submission before the King. The next phrase, "**None can keep alive his own soul**", seems like a fairly unremarkable statement. However, when we consider the literal translation, we discover that this phrase is telling us precisely why these individuals have to die. The phrase, "none can keep alive his own soul", literally means "and his soul, He quickened it not". The question to the reader is, who is the "He" who "quickened it not"? Most take the "he" to refer to the people who are going down to the dust who find that they cannot keep themselves alive. However, the literal rendering given above allows the alternative understanding of the verse, namely that it is the **Lord** Who "quickens not his soul", i.e. the soul of the one going down to the dust. In other words, these unbelievers who experience the death penalty during the millennium have done so because their souls never were quickened by the divine life that alone comes through faith in the risen Lord Jesus Christ.

Psalm 22:30

"A seed shall serve Him; it shall be accounted to the Lord for a generation."

Verse 30 is all about service. The order here is significant. The earlier verses are all about worship. Now we come to service: "A seed shall serve Him". Worship should always precede service. This principle applies now and will apply in millennial glory.

Psalm 22:31

"They shall come, and shall declare His righteousness unto a people that shall be born, that He hath done *this*."

Who are the people that shall be born? Isaiah tells us that the nation of Israel shall be reborn. The barren women (Israel) shall bear children (Isaiah 54:1-4), and a nation will be born in a day (Isaiah 66:8) (see Appendix 3).

Isaiah 66:8

"Who hath heard such a thing? who hath seen such things? Shall the earth be made to bring forth in one day? *or* shall a nation be born at once? for as soon as Zion travailed, she brought forth her children."

This is metaphorical language to describe what will happen before the onset of the tribulation when a remnant of the nation will turn to their Messiah and believe. This is considered in detail in Appendix 3. It is they who will later welcome the Messiah on His return to the Mount of Olives.

"He hath done *this* (righteously)"

The Psalm ends with the words, "He has done *this*". In the Authorised Version "*this*" is in italics because it is not in the original Hebrew. What then has He done? If left with a verb such as "done" without the object expressed after it, it is appropriate to back-track along the verse to find the subject matter which is the unwritten, albeit understood, object to the verb "He has done". There is one word in the verse which fulfils this role. It is the word "righteousness". If in Hebrew you want to say that someone had done righteously you would say, "He did righteousness". Now we see what our verse means.

"They shall come and declare His righteousness to a nation that shall be born that He has done **righteously** (literally: righteousness)."

The hymn writer, Samuel Medley, expressed these sentiments beautifully in his hymn:

Now, in a song of grateful praise,
To my dear Lord my voice I'll raise;
With all His saints I'll join to tell—
My Jesus has done all things well.

In that future day of glory, the saints will look back over the ages and consider God's wonderful plan of redemption worked out in His Son, leading eventually to His reign in glory where He will be surrounded by the faithful seed of Israel and the God-fearing ones of the nations, while the Church, His Bride, will be by His side. Then, the righteousness of God shall be seen in all its fullness as *Jehovah Tsidkenu* (The Lord our Righteousness) reigns supreme.

1. Quoting from Psalm 32:1-2, Paul in Romans 4:6-7 writes: "David also describeth the blessedness of the man, unto whom God imputeth righteousness without works, Saying, Blessed are they whose iniquities are forgiven, and whose sins are covered." Paul is showing how Old Testament believers whose sins were covered over at conversion, enjoyed the full enjoyment of justification and forgiveness and eternal security **even despite personal failure and backsliding**, such as David encountered in his own life subsequent to his salvation, especially in the matter of Uriah the Hittite.

2. It was the solemn occasion of a priest sinning which is considered in Hebrews 12:10-12. The scenario depicted is the occasion when the priest was not allowed to eat of the sin offering because the blood was carried into the sanctuary. This was when the priest had sinned and thus was debarred from priestly service until his cleansing.

Hebrews 12:10-12

10 "We have an altar, whereof they have no right to eat which serve the tabernacle.

11 For the bodies of those beasts, whose blood is brought into the sanctuary by the high priest for sin, are burned without the camp.

12 Wherefore Jesus also, that He might sanctify the people with His own blood, suffered without the gate."

The significance of Hebrews 12:10-12 is that in contrast to the Old Testament Tabernacle priest, who was temporarily suspended from his priestly duties because of his sin, there is no such constraint on a New Testament priest of the heavenly sanctuary. How sad it would be if due to our sins and failure we were, even for a short time, not permitted to enter the heavenly sanctuary! To be reinstated in his priestly tabernacle ministry, the blood of the sin offering for the Old Testament priest had to be brought into the sanctuary to make remedy for the defilement caused by the priest who daily officiated there. Our situation as New Testament priests of the heavenly sanctuary is so different. Such is the eternal value of the precious blood of Christ that He has provided a cleansing for us which is forever and which we first enjoyed when we got saved. However, His blood provides cleansing to the heavenly sanctuary from any defilement caused by us entering its sacred precincts in our daily priestly ministry there (Hebrews 9:23). Indeed, Hebrews 12:10-12 shows that the blood of Christ not only avails to put away our sins when we got saved, i.e. when we were consecrated as priests, but also cleanses away any sins committed subsequent to becoming priests, so that there is no interruption in our accessing the heavenly sanctuary.

3. Isaiah 59:20 is the verse cited in Romans 11:26. There is an important difference. In Isaiah 59:20 "the Redeemer shall come to Zion, and unto them who turn from transgression in Jacob" whereas in Romans 11:26 the Redeemer is moving out of Zion subsequent to His second advent. Please note that He comes to Zion (Isaiah 59:20) to those who already turn away from transgression in

Jacob, i.e. the already saved remnant (Appendix 3). Those who are not saved will be judged. However, as He moves out from Zion (Romans 11:26) as the Deliverer, He pledges to bring future salvation to the entire nation. Since the remnant is already saved (Isaiah 59:20), the Deliverer, turning "ungodliness from Jacob", (Romans 11:26), can only refer to babies and future unborn generations who will be saved during the millennium and turned from their iniquities (Acts 3:26).

6

PSALM 24

A Psalm of David.
1 The earth is the Lord's, and the fullness thereof; the world, and they that dwell therein.
2 For He hath founded it upon the seas, and established it upon the floods.
3 Who shall ascend into the Hill of the Lord? or Who shall stand in His holy place?
4 He that hath clean hands, and a pure heart; Who hath not lifted up His soul unto vanity, nor sworn deceitfully.
5 He shall receive the blessing from the Lord, and righteousness from the God of His salvation.
6 This is the generation of them that seek Him, that seek Thy face, O Jacob. Selah.
7 Lift up your heads, O ye gates; and be ye lift up, ye everlasting doors; and the King of Glory shall come in.
8 Who is this King of Glory? The Lord strong and mighty, the Lord mighty in battle.
9 Lift up your heads, O ye gates; even lift them up, ye everlasting doors; and the King of Glory shall come in.
10 Who is this King of Glory? The Lord of hosts, He is the King of glory. Selah.

Introduction

This Psalm deals with the Lord's rights to ownership of this world.
It considers:
1 **The fact of ownership (Psalm 24:1):** the earth is His and its population
2 **The basis of ownership (Psalm 24:2):** creation
3 **The proclamation of ownership (Psalm 24:3-10):** two ancient prophecies of the Hill of the Lord

1 The fact of ownership: the earth is His and its population - "The earth is the Lord's."
However, God has rights not just to an empty planet. He also has ownership rights to all its inhabitants:

Psalm 1:1
"............and the fullness thereof; the world, and they that dwell therein."

The "fullness thereof" reminds us of Adam's descendants, for God commanded our first parents to "be fruitful and multiply and **fill up** (*milu*) the earth".

Genesis 1:28
"And God blessed them, and God said unto them, Be fruitful, and multiply, and **replenish** the earth (Hebrew "*milu*"= fill up the earth), and subdue it: and have dominion over the fish of the sea, and over the fowl of the air, and over every living thing that moveth upon the earth."

The Authorised Version translation of *milu* "fill up" is "replenish", which has led some to believe that there was a pre-adamic civilisation that had been destroyed in a catastrophe. This cannot be supported by the use of the word *milu* which simply means "to fill up". God did not create this world with the intention that it should be empty (without form and void). It was ever His intention that it be full of people who happily belonged to Him.

Sadly, this ownership has been contested by Satan as becomes apparent in the temptation in the wilderness:

Luke 4:6
"And the devil said unto Him, All this power will I give Thee, and the glory of them: for that is delivered unto me; and to whomsoever I will I give it."

Men too have denied God's rights to possess His creation in rejecting His Son:

Matthew 21:38
"But when the husbandmen saw the Son, they said among themselves, This is the Heir; come, let us kill Him, and let us seize on His inheritance."

Nevertheless, the Psalm boldly asserts God's rights of ownership to this world and its human inhabitants, who are "the fullness thereof".

The statement of divine ownership of this world is in direct contradiction to heathen idolatrous worship, particularly when it is understood that the Hebrew word *baal* means owner or husband. When this verse from Psalm 24 is quoted in the New Testament, it is not surprising that it is in the context of victory over idolatrous worship (1 Corinthians 10:26).

2 The basis of ownership: creation
The Psalmist shows that God is the rightful owner because He is the creator.

Psalm 24:2
"For He hath founded it upon the seas, and established it upon the floods."

He made it all. Therefore, He has a right to possession. This is being contested in the western world today. Irrespective of whether or not men believe in the Biblical account of creation, all must confess that denial of the creation story fundamentally challenges the Lord's right to ownership of this world and of all those who dwell therein. Moreover, none can deny that in recent years, failure to recognise the rightful claims of the owner of this universe has already resulted in a moral vacuum in the hearts of many, with erosion of the moral fabric of society and outbreaks of violence and anarchy – as predicted in Romans 1:28-32. The primary reason why God is the rightful owner of this world is Creation. This has been largely set aside today.

If God is the rightful owner, He has the right to determine who has tenancy rights to His land and can expect certain levels of responsibility from His tenants. One reason why God intervened in Sinai to give the Law was simply to remind forgetful mankind that He was the rightful owner of this world and its inhabitants. Consequently, in Exodus 19:5 and Leviticus 25:23 we read "the earth is Mine!"

Exodus 19:5
"Now therefore, if ye will obey My voice indeed, and keep My covenant, then ye shall be a peculiar treasure unto Me above all people: **for all the earth *is* Mine.**"

Leviticus 25:23
"The land shall not be sold for ever: **for the land (earth) *is* Mine**; for ye *are* strangers and sojourners with Me."

The laws relating to Jubilee specifically emphasised this doctrine. When God gave the Law, He issued strict instructions regarding the possessing, purchasing and selling of land. The Israelite was given the land for the purpose of bringing forth fruit. If he fell into debt, he could sell the land, but in the Year of Jubilee, every 50 years, the land reverted to him, because **"the earth is the Lord's"**. The Lord was the owner, and, in a sense, the Israelite was merely a tenant, with a responsibility to bring forth fruit for the pleasure of the Lord and the upbuilding and feeding of His people. Each time an Israelite read Leviticus 25, he was reminded that "the earth was the Lord's". This was particularly apparent in the Year of Jubilee.

Alas, Israel often forgot Who the true owner was and began to disregard the claims of their divine Landowner and acted in rebellion against Him. The result was captivity, and they were driven off the Land because "the earth was the Lord's". As they had failed to keep the Law of the Landowner, God Himself invoked the curses of that Law, leading to their eventual expulsion from the Land. At times, the nation of Israel succeeded, but so often they failed and were sent away into captivity – because the "earth was the Lord's". Thus, the Law of Moses, as applied to the nation of Israel, provided an international demonstration of the principle that the "earth was the Lord's". However, God said that if they fulfilled His Law then He would "command the blessing" upon them:

Deuteronomy 28:8
> "The Lord shall command the blessing upon thee in thy storehouses, and
> in all that thou settest thine hand unto; and He shall bless thee in the land
> which the Lord thy God giveth thee."

Alas, this was so rarely the case. Due to the curse of a broken Law, God could not command the blessing upon them and this was His right because "all the earth is Mine". Nevertheless, Deuteronomy 28:8 shows us, by the use of "thou" and "thee"etc., that if there was even One Who could fulfill the conditions of the divine Landowner, as laid out in God's covenant with the nation, then there was a divine pledge of blessings to be poured out upon Him. This brings us to the next section where we meet the One Who brings blessing to men.

3The proclamation of ownership: two ancient prophecies regarding the Hill of the Lord

Psalm 24:3
> "Who shall ascend into the Hill (Mount) of the Lord? or Who shall stand
> in His holy place?"

The Psalm shows that a proclamation of the rightful owner of this world (the King of Glory) would be made on "the Hill of the Lord".

This reference to the "Hill (Mount) of the Lord" brings the reader back to Genesis 22, which is the first reference to the "Hill (Mount) of the Lord" in the Bible. In fact, Psalm 24 forms a detailed spiritual commentary of the events of Genesis 22.

The Hill of the Lord in Genesis 22

It was at the **Hill of the Lord** that God asked Abraham to offer up Isaac "on a mountain that He would tell him of". Abraham called the name of the place "*Jehovah yireh*", meaning "In the **Hill of the Lord (Mount of the LORD)** it shall be seen" (or equally, "in the Hill of the Lord it shall be provided").

Genesis 22:14
> "And Abraham called the name of that place Jehovah-jireh: as it is said *to*
> this day, In the **Mount (Hill) of the Lord** it shall be seen."

The Hill of the Lord as a place of sacrifice

It was clear that the promised seed was destined for the altar. Abraham must truly have wondered how this was possible. Clearly, God only accepted on His altar that which was perfect and without blemish. Isaac certainly was not sinless. How then could God accept him on His altar? As Abraham ascended the mountain he was sure of one thing, that whatever the outcome, he would return again with Isaac alive. "We will come again to you", he said to his servants.

Genesis 22:5
> "And Abraham said unto his young men, Abide ye here with the ass; and I
> and the lad will go yonder and worship, and come again to you."

In answer to Isaac's question: "Behold the fire and the wood but where is the lamb for the burnt offering?" Abraham replied, "God shall provide Himself a Lamb for a burnt offering." This phrase is important and deserves careful attention.

Genesis 22:7-8

7 "And Isaac spake unto Abraham his father, and said, My father: and he said, Here *am* I, my son. And he said, Behold the fire and the wood: but where *is* the lamb for a burnt offering?

8 And Abraham said, My son, **God will provide himself a Lamb (Hebrew: the Lamb) for a burnt offering**: so they went both of them together."

The literal meaning of the phrase highlighted in verse 8 is twofold. Both meanings are equally correct. We noted earlier that God in His Word uses an economy of words to convey an eternity of meaning. Here are the two meanings:

1 "God shall see for Himself **the** Lamb for burnt offering."

2 "God shall provide for Himself **the** Lamb for burnt offering."

The phrase *yireh* means "shall see" or "shall provide".

It is apparent that Abraham had his mind focused on **one** particular Lamb. Notice the definite article in Hebrew, "**the** Lamb".

This was a special Lamb. Not a Lamb which man could see, but One Which God could see. Moreover, it was not a Lamb Which man would provide. God would provide Him.

Here is an important gospel lesson! The Sacrifice would be of God's providing. Mankind cannot by his own merits achieve redemption. God here promised that He would provide **the** Lamb.

As Abraham ascended the mountain he could not see this Lamb. Nevertheless, he states that he would "go yonder and worship" on the Hill of the Lord. In passing, here we learn an important lesson on the subject of worship. Abraham was by faith entering into God's thoughts of the Lamb. This was the Lamb Which God could constantly look upon and one day would provide – Christ.

An individual is saved on the basis of what God sees in Christ. God told the Israelites in Egypt, "When I see the blood, I will pass over you!" (Exodus 12:13).

It was what God saw in the blood which brought deliverance to the Israelite. Here we see an indication of the nature of Abraham's faith. Abraham was not relying on what he saw in the Lamb. He was relying on what God saw in the Lamb Which He would provide. This is saving faith. This is what leads to worship – meditating on what God's thoughts are of the Lamb.

We all are familiar with the account of how God intervened before Abraham could slay his son Isaac and drew his attention to "a ram caught in a thicket by his horns" (Genesis 22:13). It is important for us to notice that it was not a "**lamb** caught in a thicket". Rather it was a ram. This indicates to us that the ram trapped in the thicket was not the fulfilment of Abraham's prophetic utterance: "God will provide (or God will see for Himself) **the** Lamb for a burnt offering!" The Lamb Which God would provide was none other than the Lamb of God, pointed out by John the Baptist on the banks of the Jordan as "the Lamb of God , Which taketh away the sin of the world" (John 1:29).

As the ram was taken, slain and offered to the Lord on that altar on the Hill of the Lord, Abraham and Isaac knew that this was a picture of **the** Lamb Who would be provided by God in the future. Unlike Isaac, who was unfit for the altar, the Lamb of God would indeed be fit to be offered as a Sacrifice well-pleasing to Him.

However, where would **the** Lamb be provided? Where could He be seen? The answer is beautiful. Abraham called the name of the place *Jehovah yireh*, meaning, "In the Hill of the Lord it shall be seen" (or equally, "in the Hill of the Lord it shall be provided"). In this continuation of Abraham's earlier prophetic utterance regarding the fact that God would see and provide **the** Lamb, Abraham now adds the important detail of the location where this would be fulfilled. It would be fulfilled on "the Hill of the Lord!" Where is the Hill of the Lord? Can it be identified today? Isaiah 2:2-5 and Micah 4:1-4 (a quotation from Isaiah 2:2-5) indicate to us that the Temple Mount in Jerusalem is certainly included in the area known as "the Hill of the Lord".

Isaiah 2:2-5

2 "And it shall come to pass in the last days, *that* the mountain of the Lord's house shall be established in the top of the mountains, and shall be exalted above the hills; and all nations shall flow unto it.

3 And many people shall go and say, Come ye, and **let us go up to the Mountain (Hill) of the Lord**, to the house of the God of Jacob; and He will teach us of His ways, and we will walk in His paths: for out of Zion shall go forth the Law, and the Word of the Lord from Jerusalem.

4 And He shall judge among the nations, and shall rebuke many people: and they shall beat their swords into plowshares, and their spears into pruninghooks: nation shall not lift up sword against nation, neither shall they learn war any more.

5 O house of Jacob, come ye, and let us walk in the light of the Lord."

In 2 Chronicles 3, the Temple Mount is referred to as Mount Moriah or (literally) "the Hill of Moriah".

2 Chronicles 3:1-2

1 "Then Solomon began to build the house of the Lord at Jerusalem in Mount Moriah, where *the Lord* appeared unto David his father, in the place that David had prepared in the threshingfloor of Ornan the Jebusite.

2 And he began to build in the second *day* of the second month, in the fourth year of his reign."

Taking these passages together, it seems that the area known as "the Hill of the Lord" must at least encompass the spot where Abraham offered up Isaac as well as the site of the Lord's house – the temple of Solomon.

Whether or not the temple was built on the same spot as Isaac was laid on the altar we are not told, but one thing is clear: the phrase, "Hill of the Lord", includes both the Temple Mount and the place where Abraham offered up Isaac. However, we must note that the phrase, "Hill of the Lord", does not merely refer to what we may regard as the temple precincts. Several passages suggest that it encompassed a wider area. On occasions, the Lord spoke of "My holy Hill". Since it is the Lord Who is speaking, it follows that the phrase, "My Hill", must be synonymous with "the Hill of the Lord". An examination of the "My Hill" passages suggests that the phrase is not restricted to the temple precincts but included immediately adjoining areas in Jerusalem. For example, in Isaiah 66, the Lord speaks of "My holy Mountain, Jerusalem".

Isaiah 66:20
> "And they shall bring all your brethren *for* an offering unto the Lord out of all nations upon horses, and in chariots, and in litters, and upon mules, and upon swift beasts, **to My holy Mountain (Hill) Jerusalem**, saith the Lord, as the children of Israel bring an offering in a clean vessel into the house of the Lord."

It was here that **the** Lamb would be seen. Of course, down through the centuries many lambs were slain on the altar at the temple on Mount Moriah. However, all of these lambs were brought by Jewish worshippers. In contrast, Abraham foresaw the day when **the** unique Lamb would be seen on the Hill of the Lord, Who would be provided by God Himself. This Lamb, for Whom Israel patiently waited for centuries, would be the promised Seed of Abraham, in Whom "all nations of the earth would be blessed". As a consequence, Israel's expectation throughout the Old Testament period was for the eventual revelation of this Lamb that God would provide.

There was no doubting as to where the Lamb would be revealed. It would be on the Hill of the Lord at Jerusalem. Abraham had made this clear. The question was: Who would He be and what would characterise Him? It is this very question which David addresses in Psalm 24.

Psalm 24:3
> "Who shall ascend into the Hill of the Lord? Or Who shall stand in His Holy place?

The fact that there are two questions suggests to us that the ascent into "the Hill of the Lord" is **distinct** from standing "in His Holy place".

Secondly, the sequence of the two questions may suggest that ascending the Hill of the Lord was a **prerequisite** to standing in the Holy Place.

The first question was answered when the Lord Jesus, as the promised Son of Abraham, ascended the Hill of the Lord as the Lamb of God. He had come, unlike Isaac, to die. Isaac came off the altar as a picture of resurrection.

Hebrews 11:17-19
> 17 "By faith Abraham, when he was tried, offered up Isaac: and he that had

received the promises offered up his only begotten *son,*
18 Of whom it was said, That in Isaac shall thy Seed be called:
19 Accounting that God *was* able to raise *him* up, even from the dead; **from whence also he received him in a figure.**"

Isaac arose from the altar that day in a "figure" or type of resurrection. In contrast, the Lord Jesus arose the third day in literal resurrection.

For any who contend that Abraham did not understand his utterances regarding the Lamb of God's providing, as referring to the coming Messiah, it is worth reflecting what the Lord Jesus said in John 8:56.

John 8:56
"Your father Abraham rejoiced to see My day: and he saw *it,* and was glad."

If the Lamb of God died and rose on the Hill of the Lord in fulfilment of the promise to Abraham, when did He enter the Holy Place to stand there as indicated in the second question?

The New Testament answer comes primarily in the vision of the **Lamb** in Revelation, where John sees a Lamb "standing" as freshly slain. He is not standing before the throne on earth (i.e. the Ark of the Covenant) as was Aaron on the Day of Atonement. He is **"in the midst of the throne"** in heaven.

Revelation 5:6
"And I beheld, and, lo, in the midst of the throne and of the four beasts, and in the midst of the elders, **stood** a Lamb as It had been slain, having seven horns and seven eyes, which are the seven Spirits of God sent forth into all the earth."

John describes for us the Lamb, provided by God, **now** in heaven. He is standing because He is alive in the freshness of resurrection. What a triumph! However, the memory of His death is ever present, hence He is described as "freshly slain". This is the New Testament answer to the question, "Who shall stand in His Holy place?" Interestingly, in the New Testament we read that our Lord Jesus "sat down" at God's right hand when He entered heaven (Hebrews 10:12). In Revelation 5:6, He is seen as the Lamb **standing** in the midst of the throne. Clearly, in Revelation 5:6 He has moved from His seated position because He is about to return in judgment to this world.

A second New Testament answer to the question, "Who shall stand in My Holy Place?" comes in Hebrews.

Hebrews 9:24
"For Christ is not entered into the holy places made with hands, *which are* the figures of the true; but into heaven itself, now to appear in the presence of God for us."

The Lord Jesus never entered into the Holy Place in Herod's temple. He entered into the Holy Place in heaven. That's why the word "stand" in verse

3 also means "arise". He entered the Holy Place in heaven in the value of His Sacrifice on the Hill of the Lord.

In other words, He ascended the Hill of the Lord to die a sacrificial death to be consecrated as Priest. In resurrection and ascension He arose into the Holy Place in Heaven as a consecrated Priest (see Psalm 110). This order was very familiar to the Hebrew believers in first century AD, who understood the pattern of events in the earthly priesthood where, outside the tabernacle (i.e. at the door of the tabernacle (Exodus 29:4)), Aaron was first consecrated by sacrifice before he was allowed to enter the Holy Place **within the tabernacle before the Ark of the Covenant, which was the symbol of the throne of God**.

The picture of (1) ascending the Hill of the Lord and then (2) entering the Holy Place in Heaven brings before us at least two aspects of the Lord's character.

Firstly, we are reminded of our Lord as the **Lamb Which God provided** as the Sacrifice at Calvary Who now is the Lamb in the midst of the throne.

Secondly, we are reminded of His **consecration as Priest** because of Calvary and then His entering into the Holy Place in heaven in resurrection and ascension.

Down through the centuries, godly Jews wondered when would the Lamb of God be revealed on the Hill of the Lord. Two thousand years ago, the prophecy to Abraham was fulfilled when the Lamb Which God provided died and rose on Mount Moriah on the Hill of the Lord.

The characteristics of the Risen Lamb

1 He must be perfect

This Man Who would firstly ascend the Hill of the Lord and then stand in priestly capacity before the Lord must be morally without blemish. Let us look at the divine standard – a standard so high that David and the very best of his followers were excluded. Even the greatest priests were excluded and could only enter the Holy Place on the basis of sacrifice. As for the One Who is referred to here, absolute moral perfection would characterise Him.

Psalm 24:4

"He that hath clean hands, and a pure heart; Who hath not lifted up His soul unto vanity, nor sworn deceitfully."

2 He shall bear the blessing and dispense it to others

Psalm 24:5

"He shall receive (bear) the blessing from the Lord, and righteousness from the God of His salvation."

Once He came as the Lamb to bear the sin of the world. Now in heaven He "bears the blessing". That means He is the sole means of conveying divine blessing to men. There is One in the Holy Place in heaven Who is the channel of divine blessing to men. This is a priestly role, just as Aaron in the earthly tabernacle blessed the people with his hands upheld in blessing.

3 He shall be sought after by the sons of Jacob

Psalm 24:6

"This *is* the generation of them that seek Him, that seek Thy face, O Jacob.
Selah."

This is at first glance a difficult verse to understand as the questions arise:
Who is "the generation?"

Whose "face" is referred to? Is it the face of God or the face of Jacob?

The ancient Jewish translators of the Septuagint, who translated the
Hebrew Bible into Greek, translated the verse as: "This is the generation
of them that seek Him, that seek Thy face, O God of Jacob. Selah". They
understood that the "seekers" in the verse were seeking after the face of
God.

However, there is no escaping the literal translation of the Hebrew text
which is as follows: "This is the generation of his seekers, even the seekers
of Thy face – even Jacob." The word "Jacob" is being used as a collective
noun to describe those elements within the remnant nation ("his seekers")
in a coming day who will seek the face of Christ, just as Isaiah addresses
the remnant nation as "Jacob" in Isaiah 41. The "generation of his (Jacob's)
seekers" are the seekers of "Thy face" i.e. the face of God. It is not that these
seekers are seeking after the face of Jacob. Jacob has long been gone from
this scene. However, the "seekers" after "Thy face", i.e. the face of God, are
addressed as "Jacob". Surely, this is an allusion to *Peniel* (meaning in Hebrew
"face of God") when a troubled Jacob struggled with his Heavenly Visitor
for a long night and then said, "I will not let Thee go, except Thou bless
me" (Genesis 32:26). The Heavenly Visitor was the "bearer" of the blessing
to Jacob. Jacob saw the face of God at *Peniel* and lived (Genesis 32:30). It
was a life-transforming moment and is pictorial of a future encounter which
the remnant nation of Israel, still in "Jacob standing", will have with her
Messiah when, after 2000 years of struggling with Him throughout this
Church era, following the rapture of the Church they will accept Him and
receive the blessing. (This is considered further in Appendix 3). Even today,
all those who seek Him will not be disappointed.

The revelation of the owner

When Abraham foretold that "in the Hill of the Lord it would be seen",
his prophecy not only included the revelation of the sacrificial Lamb, it **also**
looked forward to the day when He "would inherit the gate of His enemies".
This is what the second part of Psalm 24 is about. Just as the Hill of the Lord
once saw Him in humiliation and shame, in a coming day He will return to
the Hill of the Lord in Jerusalem, in unrivalled glory. In that coming day, it
can once more be said, "In the Hill of the Lord it shall be seen".

Some have taken this second part of the Psalm to refer to His ascension
into heavenly glory as the Victor of Calvary. Firstly, the phrase, "Who

shall stand in His Holy Place?", refers to where He is just now – in heaven, the Holy Place not made with hands. Secondly, in the phrase, "The King of Glory shall come *in*", it is important to note that "in" is in italics. It is not in the original. The phrase simply is, "The King of Glory shall come!" The King of Glory is seen as the Victor of the battle and referred to as "the Lord of Hosts". When the Lord Jesus ascended to heaven, He was Victor of Calvary, but there is a further battle to fight – the battle of Armageddon and the destruction of the wicked nations before He takes up His Kingdom and reigns from Jerusalem. However, in this portion of the Psalm, even this battle is behind Him. He is referred to as the One Who has completed the battle, the mighty Man of the battle. The Psalm is speaking of that time when there will be no one left who would dare raise a finger in objection to His right to reign. This is the return to Jerusalem of the Conqueror, unrivalled in His glory. The Creator and owner has arrived to take possession of what is rightly His.

Psalm 24:7-8

> 7 "Lift up your heads, O ye gates; and be ye lift up, ye everlasting doors; and the King of Glory shall come in.
> 8 Who *is* this King of Glory? The Lord strong and mighty, the Lord mighty in battle."

"Lift up your heads O ye gates!" It is perhaps a little daunting initially to determine what this phrase really means, but we must at least acknowledge that the language is metaphorical. Evidently, gates are inanimate objects and cannot heed an exhortation to lift up their heads! However, the phrase includes two ideas which have metaphorical meaning in Hebrew.

1 The lifting up of the head in Hebrew refers to the restoration of dignity (compare Psalm 110:7, "He shall drink of the brook in the way: therefore shall He lift up the head...").

2 The city gate in Hebrew is the place of administration and authority.

Taking these two ideas together we learn that whatever else this phrase means, it at least suggests that before the return of the Messiah in glory, the place of administration in Jerusalem will be lying in shame and dishonour.

However, now that the rightful King is returning, this will change. The gates can indeed lift up their heads. Dignity is once again going to return to the place of administration in Jerusalem and consequently in this whole world. Notice the phrase, "Ye everlasting doors". A study of this phrase suggests that a future scene is being envisaged here rather than a reference to the ancient character of the city of Jerusalem. This is disucsssed in the footnote. Note 1

To summarize, "Ye everlasting doors", or literally "ye doors of the age" (*olam*), refer to the millennial gates of Jerusalem, which shall firstly welcome the victorious divine Conqueror and then disseminate His will to the uttermost parts of the millennial earth.

However, Who is this King of Glory? Look, He is the Lord of Hosts! When

He presented Himself at the Mountain of the Lord 2000 years ago, He came alone and in humiliation. Now, on His return, He is to be followed by the myriads of angelic armies. Truly He will be seen as "the Lord of Hosts". However, when we look again we see a beautiful thing: the King of Glory is a glorified Man.

Psalm 24:8

"Who *is* this King of Glory? The Lord strong and mighty (*gibbor* mighty Man), the Lord mighty (*gibbor* mighty Man) in battle."

He is referred to as "the Lord, strong (*izzuz*) and mighty (*gibbor*)." We are going to meet this word "*gibbor*" in subsequent Psalms. It literally means the "Mighty **Man**" as is used of Boaz in Ruth 2:1. Herein lies a uniform principle in Scripture. Everywhere that the Messiah's humanity is brought before us, as here, the Spirit of God will **always** emphasise His deity. He is the Lord of Hosts, but He is also "*gibbor*" the Mighty Man! How wonderful that the One Who ascended the Hill of the Lord 2000 years ago in rejection, and Who as the risen Man functions for us as Priest in the "Holy Place" in heaven, will return as the Lord, the Mighty Man! He will be seen in that day as "God manifest in flesh", the King of Glory! Once more, the call is made for the gates to lift up their heads and for the King of Glory to enter. Who is He? He is the Lord, the Mighty Man in battle. Note the word "Mighty (Man)" is also "the Lord, the Mighty Man (*gibbor*) of battle!" Clearly, the Spirit of God is quick to remind us again and again that the One Who returns is verily the Lord of Hosts, yet truly the Mighty Man of the battle. What a delightful proof within the Old Testament that the Messiah must be "God manifest in flesh"!

This One is the rightful possessor of the world. It is for His return that this world now awaits.

The practical implications of this Psalm

The phrase from the Psalm, "The earth is the Lord's and the fullness thereof", is twice quoted in 1 Corinthians 10:23-32.

1 Corinthians 10:23-32

23 "All things are lawful for me, but all things are not expedient: all things are lawful for me, but all things edify not.

24 Let no man seek his own, but every man another's *wealth*.

25 Whatsoever is sold in the shambles, *that* eat, asking no question for conscience sake:

26 For the earth *is* the Lord's, and the fullness thereof.

27 If any of them that believe not bid you *to a feast*, and ye be disposed to go; whatsoever is set before you, eat, asking no question for conscience sake.

28 But if any man say unto you, This is offered in sacrifice unto idols, eat not for his sake that shewed it, and for conscience sake: **for the earth *is* the Lord's, and the fullness thereof:**

29 Conscience, I say, not thine own, but of the other: for why is my liberty

judged of another *man's* conscience?
30 For if I by grace be a partaker, why am I evil spoken of for that for which I give thanks?
31 Whether therefore ye eat, or drink, or whatsoever ye do, do all to the glory of God.
32 Give none offence, neither to the Jews, nor to the Gentiles, nor to the Church of God."

The context is of a believer eating meat offered to idols. A believer who understands the teaching of Psalm 24 will be clear that the Lord is the rightful owner to this world and will not be discouraged by any attempt by Satan or his emissaries to usurp this ownership in their idolatrous rituals, such as eating meat offered to the idol. In the Old Testament, Baal meant "husband" and "**owner**" or "**possessor**". Knowledge of the rightful ownership of the Lord Jesus of this world should truly liberate believers who, before conversion, served idols and should lead them to acknowledge that now **they belong** to Christ. This is a joyful truth for any young believer now saved from idolatrous bondage and who may even have once been "**possessed**" by demonic power. However, knowledge of the Psalm leads a modern day believer to conclude that even though there is no possibility of Satan successfully challenging the Lord Jesus' right to ownership and possession of a redeemed soul, the "freedom" which such knowledge affords (1 Corinthians 10:26) should not render us insensitive to the tender conscience of less well-taught believers who struggled to eat such meat (1 Corinthians 10:28). The fact is that these believers who refused to eat such meat for conscience sake **also** belong to the Lord Jesus – not just on the basis of creation but also by redemption. That should be an adequate reason alone to cause us to be careful not to stumble another believer by taking liberties which the latter may find discouraging.

In summary, this Psalm not only teaches us the fact of divine ownership of this world but it gives us the reasons for this ownership. The Lord Jesus Christ is the rightful owner as Creator **and also** as Redeemer. However, one day this ownership will be universally acknowledged on the Hill of the Lord when He will "**possess**" the gate of His enemies (Genesis 22:17). In the meantime, all who acknowledge His Lordship belong to (are owned or possessed by) Him and, therefore, all believers must treat fellow-believers with all the dignity befitting those who are His.

---

1. Some have thought "Ye everlasting doors" means "ancient doors" and accordingly this would mean the ancient gates of the city of Jerusalem are what is being referred to here. If that were the case, there is an expositional difficulty as the ancient gates of Jerusalem are no longer in use today. Only the archeological remains are visible. As is so often the case in these questions, an investigation of the literal meaning of the phrase is helpful. The phrase, "Ye everlasting doors", literally means, "Ye gates of the age (*olam*)". This word *olam* is important. Depending on the context it is sometimes translated "everlasting", "perpetual","of old" etc. Hence, it is understandable

how some have rendered this phrase, "ye ancient gates". However, the underlying meaning is "the age". When this is kept in mind, the seeming difficulties in consistently translating this word disappear, particularly once it is appreciated that the Bible distinguishes **different** ages in Biblical history, past, present and future, some which are in time and thus of finite duration, and others in eternity both past and future where time is infinite. The Scripture is always clear to give a context to allow clear understanding of which of these ages is meant.

Examples of *olam* referring to an age of limited duration

Olam refers to an age which is limited and defined as to its duration.

1 The limited era of the desolations of Jerusalem

Jeremiah 25:8-11

8 "Therefore thus saith the Lord of Hosts; Because ye have not heard My words,

9 Behold, I will send and take all the families of the north, saith the Lord, and Nebuchadrezzar the king of Babylon, My servant, and will bring them against this land, and against the inhabitants thereof, and against all these nations round about, and will utterly destroy them, and make them an astonishment, and an hissing, and **perpetual desolations** (desolations of the age *charvoth-olam*).

10 Moreover I will take from them the voice of mirth, and the voice of gladness, the voice of the bridegroom, and the voice of the bride, the sound of the millstones, and the light of the candle.

11 And this whole land shall be a desolation, and an astonishment; and these nations shall serve the king of Babylon seventy years."

In the section of Jeremiah 25:8-11, the "age" of the "desolations" of this prophecy is clearly limited to an era of seventy years, after which the restoration could begin, as also understood by Daniel the prophet in Daniel 9.

2 The limited era of a functional Levitical priesthood

A further example is the Levitical priesthood which is described as "an everlasting priesthood" (*cehonat-olam*).

Exodus 40:15b

"…an everlasting priesthood throughout their generations."

In Hebrew, "priesthood of" is *cehonat* and "the age" is *olam*, the full phrase meaning, "priesthood of the age". Lest there be any ambiguity, "the age" in question is immediately clarified as "throughout their generations", indicating that it is not eternal. This is, of course, in contrast to the Melchisedec priesthood of the Lord Jesus Christ which is described in Psalm 110 as *leolam* or *le* (to) *olam* ("the age"), where the age in question is eternity.

Olam referring to eternity (past and future)

There are occasions when it refers to the future endless age of eternity and to the endless expanses of eternity past. The context in each occasion is always unambiguous as to which meaning is intended such as in Psalm 90:2.

Psalm 90:2

"Before the mountains were brought forth, or ever Thou hadst formed the earth and the world, even from everlasting (*me-olam*) to everlasting (*ad-olam*), Thou art God."

In fact, in each passage where the word *olam* is found, the context must determine **when** "the age" is and if it is past or future. If the phrase is "**from** the age" (*me-olam*, Psalm 90:2) or "**from** the days of the age" (Micah 5:1), it is clearly a past age or era that is intended. If the phrase, "to the age", given by two Hebrew phrases: *ad–olam* or *le-olam*, is used in reference to the Lord Himself, then a future eternal age is always clearly intended and understood from the context. Examples are the Lord as a "Priest forever (*le-olam*)" (Psalm 110:4), the divine Title "I AM" lasting "forever (*le-olam*)" (Exodus 3:15), the "truth of the Lord" lasting "forever (*le-olam*)" (Psalm 117:2), and the Lord enduring "to everlasting (*ad-olam*)" (Psalm 90: 2).

Therefore, can the phrase "ye everlasting doors", meaning literally "ye gates (doors) of the age", be taken to refer to future gates of the future millennial city of Jerusalem?

The word "desolations" in Jeremiah 25:9 is in the Hebrew construct state, meaning "desolations of". This is then followed by *olam* meaning "age or era". The resulting phrase, "desolations of the age" is of a similar grammatical construction to the phrase, "gates of the age" in Psalm 24 where "gates of" is in the construct state followed by *olam* meaning "gates of the age". This comparison is helpful to determine if the phrase, "gates of the age", means "ancient doors", i.e. gates of a bygone era (as some translations have rendered it), or, in contrast, gates of a future age. Since the phrase, "desolations of the age", referred to **a future** age at the time of Jeremiah's prophecy (i.e. not desolations of an ancient or previous era), it follows that the phrase, "gates of the age", in Psalm 24 also refers to a future era and describes the gates of the city of Jerusalem when the Lord will return to reign in the millennium. This consideration is helpful to clarify that the events described by the phrase, "lift up your heads O ye gates", are yet future and will involve the actual future gates of the city of Jerusalem on the occasion of our Lord's return to reign.

In the New Testament, these distinctions are further explained for us. The New Testament speaks of "this age". This is the age of His rejection. Thus we read of the devil as the "god of this age" (2 Corinthians 4:4). The disciples wondered how long their Lord would remain in rejection and they said, "What shall be the sign of Thy coming and of the end of the age?" (Matthew 24:3). Clearly they were longing to know when this, the age of His rejection, would come to a close. However, the Scripture tells us about the "age to come". Sometimes it is translated as "the world to come", but it really means the "age to come" (Hebrews 6:5). In contrast to this present age, which is the age of His rejection, the "age to come" is the age when He will reign supreme in millennial glory. However, the "age to come" is going to merge into what the New Testament speaks of as the "ages to come", an unending era we sometimes refer to as "the eternal state" (Ephesians 2:7). Similarly, in the Old Testament, an unending period called the "ages of the age" is foreseen (Isaiah 45:17) which answers to the "ages to come" of the New Testament or "the eternal state".

7

PSALM 40

To the chief Musician, A Psalm of David.
I waited patiently for the Lord; and He inclined unto me, and heard my cry.
2 He brought me up also out of an horrible pit, out of the miry clay, and set my feet upon a rock, and established my goings.
3 And He hath put a New Song in my mouth, even praise unto our God: many shall see it, and fear, and shall trust in the Lord.
4 Blessed is that man that maketh the Lord his trust, and respecteth not the proud, nor such as turn aside to lies.
5 Many, O Lord my God, are Thy wonderful works which Thou hast done, and Thy thoughts which are to us-ward: they cannot be reckoned up in order unto Thee: if I would declare and speak of them, they are more than can be numbered.
6 Sacrifice and offering Thou didst not desire; Mine ears hast Thou opened: burnt offering and sin offering hast Thou not required.
7 Then said I, Lo, I come: in the volume of the book it is written of Me,
8 I delight to do Thy will, O My God: yea, Thy Law is within My heart.
9 I have preached righteousness in the great congregation: lo, I have not refrained My lips, O Lord, Thou knowest.
10 I have not hid Thy righteousness within My heart; I have declared Thy faithfulness and Thy salvation: I have not concealed Thy lovingkindness and Thy truth from the great congregation.
11 Withhold not Thou Thy tender mercies from me, O Lord: let Thy lovingkindness and Thy truth continually preserve me.
12 For innumerable evils have compassed me about: mine iniquities have taken hold upon me, so that I am not able to look up; they are more than the hairs of mine head: therefore my heart faileth me.
13 Be pleased, O Lord, to deliver me: O Lord, make haste to help me.
14 Let them be ashamed and confounded together that seek after my soul to destroy it; let them be driven backward and put to shame that wish me evil.
15 Let them be desolate for a reward of their shame that say unto me, Aha, aha.
16 Let all those that seek Thee rejoice and be glad in Thee: let such as love Thy Salvation say continually, The Lord be magnified.
17 But I am poor and needy; yet the Lord thinketh upon me: Thou art my help and my Deliverer; make no tarrying, O my God.

Introduction

Psalm 40 charts for us increasing degrees of devotion in a believer's relationship with God. The writer commences by recalling a time when he was in the outside place without knowing God and progresses to a state of complete childlike dependence on the Lord.

1 Talking about the Lord (Psalm 40:1-4)

This Psalm begins with the Psalmist talking about the Lord and how he came to trust in Him (verses 1-3). He mirrors this with a warning of those who trust in falsehood (verse 4). This section is about the Psalmist's **conversion.**

2 Talking to the Lord (Psalm 40:5)

In verse 5, the Psalmist ceases to talk about the Lord. He now speaks to the Lord with words of worship and adoration as he enters into God's thoughts towards us. Speaking to the Lord in worship is a higher level of devotion than merely speaking about the Lord. This attitude of worship arises from a realisation of the impossibility of fully **counting his blessings.**

3 Listening to the Lord (Psalm 40:6-10)

In verses 6-10, the Psalmist ceases to talk both about and to the Lord. He falls silent and now listens to the Lord speaking in heaven about His thoughts towards us. He hears a conversation between the Son of God (as yet unrevealed) in heaven and His Father regarding His future incarnation and sacrificial death. As the Psalmist, by divine inspiration, records this momentous conversation taking place within the celestial courts, he attains a pinnacle of revelation reminiscent of Isaiah in Isaiah 6:1 when he "saw the Lord high and lifted up". He listens to the Lord speaking about His first **coming** and the resulting fruit – the future **congregation of the redeemed** in the Kingdom.

4 Pleading with the Lord (Psalm 40:11-17)

Finally, at the end of the Psalm, David is greatly affected practically by this revelation of the Son speaking to the Father. Just as Isaiah felt a sense of his own unworthiness in Isaiah 6:5 when he witnessed the revelation of the Lord seated in His heavenly temple, similarly David now becomes acutely aware of his failures and sin. All true worship has this effect and leads to confession of sin in His presence and casting oneself in complete dependence on the Lord, in Whom we have come to trust. So, the Psalmist in this section is now praying to the Lord for his **continuation.** This is the practical lesson of the Psalm and should lead a true believer to increased godliness.

David talks about the Lord

Psalm 40:1

"I waited patiently for the Lord; and He inclined unto me, and heard my cry."

"I waited patiently" could be translated, "I surely hoped (emphatic) in the Lord". David goes back in his experience to a specific moment in his life when he hoped (trusted) in the Lord. The context, involving the later reference to "the New Song", would suggest that this was the moment of his salvation. David recalls that the Lord "inclined unto him". This shows us that the Lord, listening to David's cry, did not do so uncaringly, but, as it were, leaned over to hear David's confession of trust in Him. What a lovely picture the Psalmist describes for us here as he tells us of the God of heaven leaning over, waiting and longing to hear that feeble confession of trust in Him which brings so much blessing to the soul sinking in the pit of sin!

Psalm 40:2

"He brought me up also out of an horrible pit (pit of noise), out of the miry clay, and set my feet upon a rock, *and* established my goings."

David could gladly recall the time when he trusted in the Lord. He was lifted up from the "pit of noise" and from the "miry clay". His feet were set upon the "rock". The word "rock" (*sela*) means "crag rock". When the people were thirsty, Moses smote the rock. That was "the bed rock" (*tsur*).

Exodus 17:6

"Behold, I will stand before thee there upon the rock (bedrock) (*tsur*) in Horeb; and thou shalt smite the rock (bedrock) (*tsur*), and there shall come water out of it, that the people may drink. And Moses did so in the sight of the elders of Israel."

However, on a further occasion when the people were thirsty, God instructed Moses to merely speak to the rock. On this second occasion, however, it was to a "crag rock" (*sela*) that Moses was asked to speak.

Numbers 20: 7-12

7 " And the Lord spake unto Moses, saying,

8 Take the rod, and gather thou the assembly together, thou, and Aaron thy brother, and speak ye unto the **rock (crag rock)** before their eyes; and it shall give forth his water, and thou shalt bring forth to them water out of the **rock (crag rock)**: so thou shalt give the congregation and their beasts drink.

9 And Moses took the rod from before the Lord, as He commanded him.

10 And Moses and Aaron gathered the congregation together before the **rock (crag rock),** and he said unto them, Hear now, ye rebels; must we fetch you water out of this **rock (crag rock)**?

11 And Moses lifted up his hand, and with his rod he smote the **rock (crag rock)** twice: and the water came out abundantly, and the congregation drank, and their beasts *also*.

12 And the Lord spake unto Moses and Aaron, Because ye believed Me not, to sanctify Me in the eyes of the children of Israel, therefore ye shall not bring this congregation into the land which I have given them."

It has often been rightly pointed out that the bedrock (*tsur*) speaks of Christ in humiliation, bearing the rod of divine judgment for sin. In contrast, the crag rock (*sela*) speaks of our Lord Jesus Christ exalted in glory as in Isaiah 32:1-2.

Isaiah 32:1-2
> 1 "Behold, a King shall reign in righteousness, and princes shall rule in judgment.
> 2 And a Man shall be as an hiding place from the wind, and a covert from the tempest; as rivers of water in a dry place, as the shadow of a great rock ("*sela-caved*" meaning "huge crag rock") in a weary land."

Interestingly, the adjective *caved*, meaning "great" or "huge", used in Isaiah 31:2 shares the same root as *cavod*, meaning "glory".

The Psalmist did not say that his feet were set on the edge of the pit and that he was at risk of falling into it again. In contrast to this, David tells us that his feet have been set on the "Crag Rock" well away from that horrible pit. What a contrast it is for a believer, once sinking deep in sin, now to know the absolute security of faith in the exalted One Who once was smitten for us! Doubting now was over for him. David tells us that the Lord "established my goings" (directed my steps). He was saved, not to stand shivering at the side of that pit, but to stand on the secure foundation of the Crag Rock with new direction to his life. Perhaps, more than most, the direction of his life was quite unique. He was in the royal line of the Messiah, and his mission was to keep the message of the coming Messiah before his fellow men. Similarly, it should be the mission of everyone delivered from the pit of sin today to tell of the Messiah's saving power.

Psalm 40:3
> "And He hath put a New Song in my mouth, *even* praise unto our God: many shall see *it*, and fear, and shall trust in the Lord."

The Lord had put a New Song in David's mouth. The exact words which make up the New Song are not given to us in this Psalm. We are just told that it is "praise unto our God". Some clues as to the **context** of the song are given in the other Old Testament references to the New Song. However, it is the New Testament which gives us the **content** of the song.

The context of the song as given in the Old Testament

1 With what is this song sung?
It is sung with the harp.

Psalm 33
> 1 "Rejoice in the Lord, O ye righteous: *for* praise is comely for the upright.
> 2 Praise the Lord **with harp**: sing unto Him with the psaltery *and* an instrument of ten strings.
> **3 Sing unto Him a New Song**; play skilfully with a loud noise.
> 4 For the Word of the Lord *is* right; and all His works *are done* in truth.
> 5 He loveth righteousness and judgment: the earth is full of the goodness of the Lord."

Here we learn that the New Song is sung to the accompaniment of the harp. Skill is required (Psalm 33:3). Its performance will be one of the greatest musical masterpieces this universe has ever seen. We see this again in Revelation 5. We are also given at least one good reason for singing the song in Psalm 33:4: "for (or because) **the Word** of the Lord is right…" and this is compatible with **His works.** In other words, what God says He carries out. His Word is dependable. That is worth singing about!

2 From where has the song originated?
It originated from God Himself.

The song is not composed by men for men. It was composed by God and then given to men. Their role is simply to sing it – "He (the Lord) hath put a New Song in my mouth."

3 Who sings the song?
It is sung by those who are saved from the earth. This is illustrated in Psalm 96 and later in Psalm 98.

Psalm 96
1 **"O sing unto the Lord a New Song:** sing unto the Lord, **all the earth.**
2 Sing unto the Lord, bless His Name; shew forth His salvation from day to day."

The significance of the mention of the New Song in Psalm 96 will be considered in more detail in our later meditations of Psalm 97. Suffice to say at this stage that Psalm 96 refers to the events leading up to our Lord's coming in manifestation and thus relates to the future tribulation period. This shows us that the saints of the seven-year tribulation period will be singing the New Song. Psalm 97 describes the actual events of the Lord's return to the earth to reign. Psalms 98 and 99 describe the events **after** the Lord's return in manifested glory to reign.

It is the Lord's will that the song should have a global impact and be sung by the nations all over the earth. Psalm 98 envisages a coming day on earth when the Lord Jesus reigns supreme and it will be sung globally by all nations. The song is clearly for redeemed men and women who know "His Salvation" and, therefore, it is not for angels. This is seen again in Revelation 5 when the singers of the song are "redeemed from every kindred, tongue and people and nation". (The special doctrinal significance of the New Song, as mentioned in Psalms 96 and 98, is discussed in great detail in the chapter on Psalms 69 and 97).

Gentiles sing the song

Isaiah 42
9 "Behold, the former things are come to pass, and new things do I declare: before they spring forth I tell you of them.
10 **Sing unto the Lord a New Song,** *and* His praise from the end of the earth, ye that go down to the sea, and all that is therein; the isles, and the inhabitants thereof."

This section shows that the Gentile nations in general and Arab nations in particular, namely the dwellers of the tents of Kedar (sons of Esau) and the inhabitants of the rock, will sing the song in a coming day and the Lord will use this to provoke the Jews to jealousy so that they will want to learn the song also. This is consistent with the reference to the New Song in Revelation: "**Thou hast redeemed us to God by Thy blood out of every kindred, and tongue, and people, and nation**" (Revelation 5:9).

4 Why is the song sung?

Firstly, it is a song of victory.

Psalm 98:1, 2,7-9

1 "O sing unto the Lord a New Song; for He hath done marvellous things: **His right hand, and His holy Arm, hath gotten Him the victory.**
2 The Lord hath made known His Salvation: His righteousness hath He openly shewed in the sight of the heathen...
7 Let the sea roar, and the fullness thereof; the world, and they that dwell therein.
8 Let the floods clap *their* hands: let the hills be joyful together
9 Before the Lord; for He cometh to judge the earth: with righteousness shall He judge the world, and the people with equity."

A further reason to sing the song is because the Lord will return as the victorious One to judge the world. This becomes particularly important as we listen to the singing of the New Song in Revelation 5.

5 For how long will the song be sung?

It will be sung on the other side of death and resurrection – sung by redeemed ones as expression of their individual praise: "I will sing a New Song unto Thee."

Psalm 144

7 "Send Thine hand from above; rid me, and deliver me out of great waters, from the hand of strange children;
8 Whose mouth speaketh vanity, and their right hand *is* a right hand of falsehood.
9 **I will sing a New Song unto Thee, O God:** upon a psaltery *and* an instrument of ten strings will I sing praises unto Thee."

Psalm 144 quotes from Psalm 18 where we have already seen that the Lord's return to earth and the resurrection of the Old Testament saints (including David) from the dead are events which are immediately followed by the assessment of the lives of these believers. Psalm 144 similarly describes the return of the Lord Jesus to the earth and the delivery of the saints from the river of death ("great waters"), i.e. their resurrection from the dead. In our meditation of Psalm 18, we saw at this point the Lord's assessment of the individual personal life of the Old Testament believer. Psalm 144 looks at a slightly different aspect of the assessment on that day. It assesses the **fruit that remains** of one's personal life of service for the Lord. That is why the analysis in Psalm 144 is of whether the children, once thought to be genuine, **are real or otherwise**. In other words, it is the impact of a believer's life on the spiritual wellbeing and godliness of others which is evaluated. As the Psalmist David walks away from the evaluation of his life of service he will still be singing the New Song in that coming day.

7 How is the song sung?

It is sung collectively "in the congregation of the saints".

Psalm 149

1 "Praise ye the Lord. **Sing unto the Lord a New Song**, *and* His praise **in the congregation of saints.**

2 Let Israel rejoice in Him that made him: let the children of Zion be joyful in their King…

4 For the Lord taketh pleasure in His people: He will beautify the meek with salvation."

Psalm 149 shows us that those who sing the song in Psalm 144 are doing so collectively just as they do in Revelation 5 when the twenty-four elders sing the song together.

All of these seven Old Testament references to the New Song have a prophetical significance and anticipate the time when Israel's Messiah will reign as King over all the earth. However, these seven references are about the **context** of the song, not its **content**.

The content of the song

The actual **content** of the New Song must await John's description of it in the prophecy of Revelation. There we discover that its subject matter is of personal redemption, being made kings and priests and one day reigning upon the earth.

The first group to sing the song in Revelation 5:9-10 are the "four and twenty elders" seated in thrones around the throne of God in heaven.

Revelation 5:6-10

6 "And I beheld, and, lo, in the midst of the throne and of the four beasts, and in the midst of the elders, stood a Lamb as It had been slain, having seven horns and seven eyes, which are the seven Spirits of God sent forth into all the earth.

7 And He came and took the book out of the right hand of Him that sat upon the throne.

8 And when He had taken the book, the four beasts (**neuter gender**) and **four *and* twenty elders** (**masculine gender**) fell down before the Lamb, having every one (Greek: *hecastos* each one (**masculine gender**)) of them harps, and golden vials full of odours, which are the prayers of saints.

9 **And they sung a New Song, saying, Thou art worthy to take the book, and to open the seals thereof: for Thou wast slain, and hast redeemed us to God by Thy blood out of every kindred, and tongue, and people, and nation;**

10. **And hast made us unto our God kings and priests: and we shall reign on the earth.**"

Who are the four beasts (living creatures)? They are angelic beings ministering at the throne of God. They are in the company of the twenty-four elders, but only the elders sing the New Song of Revelation 5:9. This becomes apparent once it is noted that while beasts and elders together fall before the Lamb, it is only the group of elders (masculine gender) which make up the individuals within the phrase: "every one of them (also masculine gender) having golden vials etc...". This is the song of "the saints" of Revelation 5:8 and not of the angels. Who then are these twenty-four elders who sing the song? Bible teachers have differed much as to their identity. Are they angels, the Church or Old Testament believers?

Are the twenty-four elders angels?

If we follow the Revised Version rendering of Revelation 5:9-10, the song is not a song of personal redemption, but rather a song about the redemption of others.

Revelation 5:9-10 (Revised Version)

9 "...for Thou wast slain, and hast redeemed to God with Thy blood out of every tribe, and tongue, and people, and nation;
10 And madest **them** to be unto our God a Kingdom and priests: and **they** shall reign upon the earth."

Those who follow this rendering hold that the twenty-four elders are angelic beings around the throne singing about the redemption of men. However, the present author is happy with the Authorized Version text:

Revelation 5:9-10 (Authorised Version)

9 "…….for Thou wast slain, and hast redeemed us to God by Thy blood out of every kindred, and tongue, and people, and nation;
10 And hast made **us** unto our God kings and priests: and **we** shall reign on the earth."

It seems inconceivable that the New Song is a song about the redemption of others and not personal redemption. Certainly, when David had experienced the deliverance from the pit, his song was of personal redemption and deliverance. This alone suggests that the twenty-four elders cannot be angels.

Are the twenty-four elders the Church or Old Testament saints?

Once we accept that the New Song is of personal redemption, then it is apparent that the twenty-four elders are believers, who are in heaven by virtue of saving faith in the Lamb. However, the next question is: Are they representative of believers from the Old Testament era or the Church era or both?

The answer comes from the observation that they "shall reign on (upon) the earth" (Revelation 5:10). It is clear that these twenty-four elders have a destiny, which is yet future, of reigning upon the earth, even though at the time of John's vision in heaven they are seen around the throne. This suggests that these believers are in heaven in their spirit form awaiting resurrection and their return to reign on the earth. This identifies them as being distinct from the Church, which has a heavenly destiny and hope, and places them as notable individuals among the congregation of Old Testament believers, who have an earthly destiny and hope, following their resurrection from the dead (Psalms 18, 71, 72 and 89). It is worth noting that the only other time that we find twenty-four people in Scripture is in 1 Chronicles 24:1-18 when there were twenty-four divisions of priests who served before the Lord in His House.

It is apparent in Revelation 5 that the twenty-four elders are similarly functioning as priests before the throne. However, it is clear that they are not merely Jews. This group is made up of saints from every tribe and people and nation. This leads to another question. None of the Aaronic order of priests could claim to be a **Kingdom** of priests. Combining the offices of Kingship and Priesthood in one person or more was forbidden in the Old Testament. Remarkably, however, the twenty-four elders are singing of having been made kings **and** priests by the Lamb of God. If the twenty-four elders are Old Testament believers, when did they become priests? Clearly, this did not happen in their lifetimes. This has happened subsequent to the shedding of the Blood of the Lamb Who has made them "kings and priests".

In Psalm 69, the doctrine of redemption will be considered in detail. Briefly, at this stage it can be said that an important part of the Biblical teaching on redemption is that **all believers of all dispensations** should be ultimately consecrated as priests who are able to function before the throne of God in heaven. Today, all believers in the Church era already enjoy this priestly privilege and have access to the throne of God in their lifetimes. However, this was not the case for Old Testament believers when on earth. They were not priests in the heavenly sanctuary. Their first access to the throne of God as priests was after the ascension of the Lord Jesus to heaven. In their lifetimes they prayed to God on earth and God **came out** to them and communed with them on earth. In death they rested in *Sheol* and were not yet admitted to the heavenly sanctuary. Now their souls are before God in the heavenly sanctuary where they function as priests fitted to sing the New Song of redemption. We New Testament believers, in our lifetimes, already **come in** to the presence of God before the throne of grace as New Testament priests each time we come before Him in prayer and worship. On our death we, in this Church era, are instantly admitted to heaven's sanctuary to continue this priestly ministry there. This great blessing is what is meant by "the redemption of the soul" (Psalm 49:8) and will be discussed in detail in Psalm 69, but is mentioned here as it constitutes an intrinsic aspect of the New Song.

Does the crown of gold identify them as being saints of the raptured Church who have received their reward after the judgment seat of Christ?

It is true that the twenty-four elders bear in heaven the insignia of royalty. This is clear because they sit upon thrones (*thronoi*) and on their heads are crowns (*stephanos*) of gold.

Revelation 4:4
> "And round about the throne *were* four and twenty seats (thrones): and upon the seats (thrones) I saw four and twenty elders sitting, clothed in white raiment; and they had on their heads crowns of gold."

This has led some to look upon the twenty-four elders in this passage as being the raptured Church, subsequent to the judgment seat of Christ at which the rewards of crowns will have been given by the Lord Jesus Christ. As a result, those in the Church are preparing to reign with Christ and hence are seen sitting upon thrones.

There are some significant problems with this view.

Firstly, the twenty-four elders anticipate an **earthly destiny**, of reigning upon the millennial earth. This excludes them from being in the Church, who will reign **over** the earth in the millennium, not **upon** it. Secondly, the New Testament does not describe the victor's crown (*stephanos*), given to believers of this Church era at the judgment seat of Christ, as being made of **gold, as is the case here with the twenty four elders**. Rather, the *stephanos* crown, in the context of the judgment seat of Christ, is described as a crown of life (James 1:12), glory (I Peter 5:4) and righteousness (2 Timothy 4:8). This crown, by reason of being "incorruptible", stands in contrast to the fading, corruptible garlands of earth's games (1 Corinthians 9:25). At the judgment seat of Christ, believers of this Church era will receive **incorruptible** crowns of life, glory and righteousness, but **it does not say** that crowns of gold are given out to those in the Church.

In contrast, David spoke of the Lord establishing him in His Kingdom by setting "a **crown of pure gold on his head**" (Psalm 21:3). In the next verse, in Psalm 21:4, David tells us that when he "asked life of Thee" (the Lord), "Thou (the Lord) gavest it him, even length of days for ever and ever". This answer to David's request clearly goes beyond longevity and stretches out into an eternal existence on the other side of death, "for ever and ever". Of note to this present discussion of a personal New Song of redemption is David's exclamation that his eternal existence, where he would be made "exceeding glad with Thy countenance (i.e. God's immediate presence)" (Psalm 21:6), all flows out from "Thy Salvation" (Psalm 21:1).

Psalm 21:1-7
> 1 "The king shall joy in Thy strength, O Lord; and in Thy salvation how greatly shall he rejoice!
> 2 Thou hast given him his heart's desire, and hast not withholden the request of his lips. Selah.
> 3 For Thou preventest him with the blessings of goodness: **Thou settest a crown of pure gold on his head.**
> 4 He asked life of Thee, *and* Thou gavest *it* him, *even* **length of days for ever and ever.**
> 5 His glory *is* great in Thy salvation: honour and majesty hast Thou laid upon him.

6 For **Thou hast made him most blessed for ever: Thou hast made him
exceeding glad with Thy countenance.**
7 For the king trusteth in the Lord, and through the mercy of the most High
he shall not be moved."

This passage shows that David's golden crown was given to him eternally
and would be worn in the Lord's immediate presence. This is most
supportive of the idea that David is among the twenty-four elders, who are
wearing golden crowns and sitting around the throne of God in heaven in
the immediate presence of God.

In the Old Testament Septuagint translation, the **crown** of gold is taken
as the insignia of regal office (2 Samuel 12:30) either of the king himself or
of someone in high position of authority within the kingdom, eg Mordecai
(Esther 8:15,10:3). The fact that the twenty-four elders are prepared to step
off their thrones and cast their **crowns of gold** before the Lord Jesus shows
that these Old Testament believers, irrespective of whatever honoured role
they may have filled in their lifetimes, are happy to hand over any dominion
which had been theirs to the King of kings and Lord of lords.

A further clue as to the identity of the twenty-four elders comes at the end
of Revelation 11, which describes the events just prior to the Lord raising
from the dead and rewarding the Old Testament believers.

Revelation 11:18
"the time of the dead that they should be judged and that Thou shouldest
give reward unto Thy servants…"

In anticipation of this occasion, we find the twenty-four elders rejoicing in
heaven at the prospect of the Lord's return to the earth.

Revelation 11:16-17
16 "And the four and twenty elders, which sat before God on their seats,
fell upon their faces, and worshipped God,
17 Saying, **We give Thee thanks, O Lord God Almighty, Which art, and
wast, and art to come; because Thou hast taken to Thee Thy great power,
and hast reigned.**"

No doubt, this is because their service to Him among those who "shall
reign on the earth" is just about to begin.

These considerations show that the twenty-four elders cannot be angels
(because they sing of personal redemption) and they cannot be the Church
(because they look forward to reigning upon the earth, whereas the
Church has a heavenly destiny). However, their wearing a crown of gold is
consistent with being Old Testament believers with David the king amongst
their number.

"As it were a New Song": a song very similar to the New Song
Later, in Revelation 14, a song similar to the New Song is also sung in
heaven by another group of people described as "harpers harping with their

harps". They sing "**as it were** a New Song". This group is seen in Revelation 14:2 as distinct from the twenty-four elders in as far as they sing the song "before the throne" and "before the four and twenty elders".

Revelation 14:1-4
1 "And I looked, and, lo, a Lamb stood on the mount Sion, and with Him an hundred forty *and* four thousand, having His Father's Name written in their foreheads.
2 And I heard a voice from heaven, as the voice of many waters, and as the voice of a great thunder: and I heard the voice of harpers harping with their harps:
3 **And they sung as it were a New Song before the throne, and before the four beasts, and the elders: and no man could learn that song but the hundred *and* forty *and* four thousand, which were redeemed from the earth.**
4 These are they which were not defiled with women; for they are virgins. These are they which follow the Lamb whithersoever He goeth. These were redeemed from among men, *being* the firstfruits unto God and to the Lamb".

The "harpers harping with their harps" in heaven are also distinct from tribulation believers, since we learn from Revelation 7:1-8 that the first tribulation believers after the rapture of the Church will be the 144,000 who are described as the "first-fruits unto God and to the Lamb" (Revelation 14:4), i.e. the first people to get saved before the tribulation. If the "harpers harping with their harps" are distinct from the twenty-four elders, who represent Old Testament believers, and in addition are distinct from the 144,000, who are the firstfruits of the tribulation believers and thus might be taken as representative of all tribulation believers, it follows that the company of "harpers harping with their harps" can be seen as being the Church of this dispensation, now raptured and in heaven.

However, how could the New Song, which in Revelation 5:10 states that "we shall reign on the earth", be suitable for the congregation of Church believers in heaven who, in contrast to Israel, have a hope and inheritance which are heavenly? Perhaps the answer lies in the New Song in Revelation 14:3 where it is described as "**as it were** a New Song". This would suggest to us that the song of Revelation 14:3 is **like** the New Song of Revelation 5:9-10 but not quite identical to it. John in Revelation 14 does not elaborate on what difference, if any, there is between the New Song of Revelation 5 and the "**as it were**" New Song of Revelation 14. For John it is sufficient to indicate that the New Song in Revelation 14 is "as it were", i.e. similar to the "New Song" of Revelation 5. It is perfectly right for Old Testament Israel (i.e. the twenty-four elders) and the Church to sing the first part of the New Song together.

Revelation 5:9-10
9 "Thou art worthy to take the book, and to open the seals thereof: for Thou wast slain, and hast redeemed us to God by Thy blood out of every

kindred, and tongue, and people, and nation;
10 And hast made us unto our God kings and priests."

It is only the very end of the New Song which has to be sung differently by Old Testament believers and the Church. Israel, with its earthly destiny, can sing truthfully the end of the New Song: "and we shall reign on the earth" (Revelation 5:10). The Church would have to sing: "We shall reign over the earth".

The fact that the Church, safely raptured to heaven before the tribulation, can sing (as it were) the New Song in the presence of the twenty-four elders shows that there is communication in heaven between the Old Testament believers and Church believers. Moreover, the fact that John (as a representative of a Church believer caught up into heaven) can have a conversation with one of the twenty-four elders further indicates that there will be opportunity for conversation in heaven between Old Testament heroes of faith and members of the raptured Church. What a thought! Not only will we meet the Lord Who redeemed us but we will be able to engage in conversation with the elders of the Old Testament era.

Those who will learn (study) the "as-it-were" New Song
The song of the "harpers harping with their harps" in heaven is described as "as-it-were a New Song". It is similar to the New Song but not identical to it. It will be learned (studied) **on earth** by the 144,000 tribulation saints. It does not say that the tribulation saints will sing that song, i.e. the "as it were" New Song. This is because the "as-it-were" New Song is only for the Church believers to sing. Isaiah 42 and Psalm 96 show that the song which tribulation believers will sing in the tribulation period is the New Song. However, tribulation believers will **learn and study the "as-it-were" New Song of the Church**. It will be instructive to them that the Bride will be reigning over the earth in a coming day. The 144,000 will be aware of the Bride and will study the Church epistles in the New Testament with interest, just as today we read of the histories of the Old Testament believers and learn lessons from them. The tribulation saints are spoken of as virgins (Matthew 25). Interestingly, we will find in Psalm 45 that the virgins are the companions of the Bride at the wedding feast. However, after them there will be millions more who will get saved in the millennium who will learn the New Song on earth.

In summary, then, the New Song is a song of thanksgiving for redemption and for being made priests, able to function in the presence of God before the throne. It includes the prospect of reigning upon the earth and thus is sung by non-Church believers, i.e. believers of the Old Testament, tribulation and millennium. Church believers sing "as-it-were a New Song" and this distinction is because they will not reign upon the earth. They will reign over the earth. The important doctrinal link between redemption of the soul and being consecrated a priest is discussed in Psalm 69.

There was a special sense in which David's call had an impact on others in a way which few could experience. The point was that David was a vital link in the Messianic line. The throne of David was the subject of divine promise. Thus David was acutely aware that as men looked upon him, "many shall see it and fear and shall trust in the Lord" (Psalm 40:3). David's testimony was not only regarding what God had done in him, it also concerned God's promises of the Seed of David. Hence the testimony of David would lead those who feared God to trust in the Lord. Of course, even in David's day there were many who could detract from this revealed truth. Such individuals would be characterised by pride and falsehood. However, those who genuinely loved the Lord would not be influenced by such people. Thus David exclaims:

Psalm 40:4
"Blessed *is* (Oh the happinesses of) that man (*haggever*) that maketh the Lord his trust, and respecteth not the proud, nor such as turn aside to lies."

The word *haggever* means "the strong man" and shows that true human strength lies not in depending on one's self but rather in complete dependence and trust in God. Such a person will not be sidetracked by the "proud". The phrase, "respecteth not", means "to not turn aside to the proud ones". In other words, those who feared God and trusted in God's plan of redemption through the house of David would not be deflected from their trust in Jehovah, even by the flawed reasonings of proud men. In God's sight such a believer is a *gever* or a "strong man". In other words, the man of faith in God's sight is "strong", although in the eyes of the world he may seem quite insignificant. God's plan of redemption cuts across human pride. There was but one way of redemption and that was through the promised Messiah, Who would emerge through the lineage of David. This would completely cut across the flawed and lying thoughts of proud men. This coming Messiah formed the centre of God's programme from beginning to end. And as David thought of this, it caused him to burst forth in doxology.

David talks to the Lord

Psalm 40:5
"Many, O Lord my God, *are* Thy wonderful works *which* Thou hast done, and Thy thoughts *which are* to us-ward: they cannot be reckoned up in order unto Thee: *if* I would declare and speak *of them*, they are more than can be numbered."

God's many wonderful works
Alas, so blind are the "proud," referred to in this Psalm, that the "wonderful works" of God are meaningless to them. The word "many" (*rabot*) occurs at the beginning of the verse in the Hebrew text, and the Authorised Version translation conveys not just the meaning of the verse but it also replicates the structure of the underlying Hebrew Poem. The word *rabot* is in the feminine plural to agree grammatically with the word at the very end of the phrase

– "Thy wonderful works" (*niphlotecha*). In the very centre of the phrase in the Hebrew text we have a precious delightful title of God Himself, "Thou, Jehovah, my God!" David recognises in his worship here that God is to be seen at the very centre of His wonderful works. It is clear that any meditation of those wonderful works will point the worshipper to God Himself. There is, however, a special sweetness in the Psalmist's reference to "my God", telling us simply that he has come to know this wonderful God in a very personal and interactive way. This reflects the personal nature of the "New Song" – a song of personal redemption.

The word *niphlot,* meaning "wonderful works of the Lord", is used on occasions to describe the bringing of Israel out of Egypt (Exodus 3:20 – "all My wonders"). That was unquestionably God's work. Israel had to watch on helplessly as God intervened to deliver them. Similarly, just as God intervened nationally to deliver Israel from Egypt's bondage through wonderful works, this same God has intervened to deliver David personally from the bondage of sin and set his feet on the rock. However, as David begins to contemplate the living God, Who is at the centre of His own works, he rises to a higher plane of revelation to contemplate the very thoughts of God Himself in planning the blessings for His own. It is always in God's purpose to share His thoughts with men and, in this Psalm, David is allowed to have a glimpse into the wonderful plans of God in redemption. It is to the man who is worshipping in the Lord's presence that this experience is granted.

"Thy thoughts *which are* to-usward"

These "thoughts", like the "wonderful works", are described as many in number. However, as the Psalmist considers placing God's thoughts in some kind of "order" or arrangement so as to render them comprehensible to the human mind, he is sharply reminded that such a thing is completely impossible. "They (God's thoughts) cannot be reckoned up in order unto Thee…". It is good to grasp that the thoughts of God are completely beyond our finite grasp and defy human analysis. The idea that it is not possible "to reckon up in (chronological) order" God's thoughts, strongly implies the eternal nature of God's purposes. In other words, His first thoughts cannot be distinguished from His last thoughts. God is never taken by surprise. He is eternal and all-knowing. Remarkably, at the very centre of His eternal counsels, we are the unworthy objects of His plans for blessing!

"If I would declare and speak of them, they are more (root: *atsam*) than can be numbered"

The words "*if*" and "*of them*" are in italics. It is not that the Psalmist is entertaining the possibility of declaring and speaking forth God's thoughts. He has already indicated to us that this is not possible. Rather, he is declaring and speaking forth a staggering truth. "They (God's thoughts) are more than can be numbered". Alternatively, and equally accurately, this could be translated, "they are more mighty than to recount them". An example of *atsam* translated as "being powerful or mighty" is Genesis 26:16.

In other words, as to their number, God's thoughts are infinite. However, they are mighty thoughts, in that God has the power and the will to execute His thoughts in a way which defies human expression. God's thoughts of blessing towards us are accompanied by infinite power to bring those thoughts to fulfilment in our individual experience.

Worship is so often a silent expression of awe in the presence of God. As we saw in Psalm 24, when Abraham climbed the Hill of the Lord in Genesis 22 to worship, he was entering into God's **thoughts of the Lamb**. Here in this section, as David worships he is entering into God's **thoughts about us**. It is perhaps comprehensible why God's thoughts of the Lamb, which Abraham mused upon in Genesis 22, should be so wonderful. However, it is incomprehensible that God should have such infinitely mighty thoughts of blessing bestowed on such undeserving objects as those who once sank in the mire and who now sing the New Song!

It is interesting that the Psalmist uses the three major Hebrew words for speech:

aggidah – "I will declare"

adabberah – "I will speak"

missapper – "to speak forth *or* number"

It is almost as if the Psalmist is ransacking the Hebrew language to find vocabulary to convey the wondrous thoughts of God, but he is defeated. David falls silent. This is true worship in the Lord's presence. However, it is delightful to notice that what language could not convey, God has conveyed in a Person by sending His own Son. He is **the expression of God's thoughts**. True worship is a response to this and is our presentation of the infinite and all-worthy Person of Christ to God for His delight in recognition that our understanding and vocabulary are simply inadequate. Of the many beneficent thoughts of God toward us, the next section lifts out perhaps the most wonderful of all, **namely that all of God's people should be consecrated as priests in His presence** — in other words, fitted to sing either the New Song or "as-it-were the New Song". Now please read on to see how the next section of the Psalm shows how men are fitted to become priests in the presence of the Lord! This truth is at the very centre of God's infinite thoughts of blessing towards us.

David listens to the Lord

David listens to the Lord speaking prophetically of His **first coming** (verses 6-8) and of the **future congregation** (verses 9-10). Before looking at the details of both sections, it is important to notice that just because in the English translation these two sections are in the past tense, this does not alter the prophetic import of their content. It is a common technique in the Old Testament to describe future events in the past (short) tense. This indicates that in the eyes of eternity these events are as real as if they have already happened. This form of presenting prophecy in the Hebrew Bible emphasizes the certainty of events not yet experienced by humans but certain to occur in the mind of God.

A Prophecy of His first coming

Psalm 40:6-8

> 6 "Sacrifice and offering Thou didst not desire; Mine ears hast Thou
> opened: burnt offering and sin offering hast Thou not required.
> 7 Then said I, Lo, I come: in the volume of the book *it is* written of Me,
> 8 I delight to do Thy will, O My God: yea, Thy Law *is* within My heart."

The first two sections of the Psalm (verses 1-5) tell us how David began
to sing the New Song. With New Testament insight from Revelation 5 we
discover that this song is looking to the day when even Old Testament
believers will be **priests and reign** on the earth. This New Testament
illumination of the content of the New Song is the key to unlock the meaning
of the rest of the Psalm. In fact, it is about how the Lord Jesus will bring about
the fulfilment of the New Song by being consecrated Himself as a Priest
in order that all believers, from whatever era of Biblical history (including
Old Testament believers), would one day be consecrated as priests in God's
presence.

Consecration to priesthood

Verses 6-10 of Psalm 40 are quoted in Hebrews, confirming that this a
Messianic Psalm.

Hebrews 10:5-10

> 5 "Wherefore when He cometh into the world, He saith, Sacrifice and
> offering Thou wouldest not, but a body hast Thou prepared Me:
> 6 In burnt offerings and *sacrifices* for sin Thou hast had no pleasure.
> 7 Then said I, Lo, I come (in the volume of the book it is written of Me,) to
> do Thy will, O God.
> 8 Above when He said, Sacrifice and offering and burnt offerings and
> *offering* for sin Thou wouldest not, neither hadst pleasure *therein;* which are
> offered by the Law;
> 9 Then said He, Lo, I come to do Thy will, O God. He taketh away the first,
> that He may establish the second.
> 10 By the which will we are sanctified through the offering of the body of
> Jesus Christ once *for all*."

Hebrews 10:5-10 confirms that Psalm 40:6-10 applies only to the Lord
Jesus and not to David. However, to some extent this was clear even before
the New Testament was given. For example:

1 The combination of offerings used in Psalm 40:6 refers specifically to the
occasion of the consecration of a priest (see later), and this could not refer to
David personally, because as king he could never be a priest in the earthly
sanctuary.

2 Only of the Lord Jesus can it be said, "I delight to do Thy will" and "Thy
Law is within My heart". Alas, David could recall valley experiences in life
when the Law of God was not effective in preventing failure in his life. In
glorious contrast, this could never be said of the promised Messiah and this
must have been a great comfort to David.

The failure of Old Testament priestly consecration in contrast with the unfailing nature of the coming Messiah

Psalm 40:6

"Sacrifice and offering Thou didst not desire; Mine ears hast Thou opened: burnt offering and sin offering hast Thou not required."

Let us determine the significance of the bringing together in this verse of:
sacrifice (*zevach*)
offering (*minchah*)
burnt offering (*olah*)
sin offering (*chataah*)

Sacrifice (*zevach*)

Interestingly, the word for sacrifice (*zevach*) is used only of the peace offering (Leviticus 3) and once of the Passover (Exodus 12:27). For example, we never read of a sacrifice of burnt offering, or a sacrifice of sin offering, or a sacrifice of trespass offering. We only read of a sacrifice of peace offering. Accordingly, in the Old Testament, the word sacrifice may be used to describe a peace offering. When the word is used to describe the Passover, it reminds us of the peace offering aspect of the paschal lamb.

Offering (*minchah*)

This word is used to describe the meal offering of Leviticus chapter 2. Normally, this accompanied the daily burnt offering (Exodus 29:41) but also on special occasions when the burnt offering was offered, a meal offering was often presented (Numbers 15:4).

Burnt offering (*olah*)

This was a sweet savour offering which was all for God (Leviticus 1). If offered alone, sin was not in question nor brought to remembrance.

Sin offering (*chataah*).

This is dealing with the question of sin or ceremonial defilement (Leviticus 4,5).

Interestingly, the other offering of Leviticus 1-5, the trespass offering (*asham*), is not mentioned in Psalm 40:6.

It is important to identify the significance of this combination of offerings: peace offering, meal offering, burnt offering and sin offering. Where in the Old Testament do we get these **four offerings grouped together** without a fifth added in or one missing?

The combinations of offerings and their doctrinal significance make for profitable study. Here are some important combinations:

The burnt offering and meal offering

This occurred as part of the daily sacrifice (Exodus 29:41). However, this is not what is in view here since there are, in addition, a peace offering and a sin offering in Psalm 40:6.

The burnt offering and sin offering

This was offered on the occasion of the Day of Atonement (Leviticus 16:3;16:5) and on the occasion of the cleansing of a woman after childbirth (Leviticus 12:6). However, the presence of the meal offering and the peace offering in Psalm 40:6 shows that these occasions are not in view here.

The burnt offering with the trespass offering, sin offering and meal offering

This was on the occasion of the cleansing of the leper (Leviticus 14). However, this cannot be the occasion in view in Psalm 40:6 since in Leviticus 14:12 there is no peace offering and a trespass offering is present.

The burnt offering together with the sin offering, peace offering, meal offering and drink offering

This was offered on the occasion of the completion of the Nazarite vow (Numbers 6). However, there is no mention of the drink offering in Psalm 40:6, suggesting that it is not the completion of the Nazarite vow which is in view.

The burnt offering together with the sin offering, peace offering and meal offering

This was on the occasion of the **consecration of Aaron and his sons to the priesthood** (Exodus 29). It is, therefore, the present author's understanding that this is what is in view in Psalm 40:6.

The bullock was a **sin offering** (Exodus 29:1-14)

Exodus 29:1-3,14
> 1 "And this *is* the thing that thou shalt do unto them to hallow them, to minister unto Me in the priest's office: Take one young bullock, and two rams without blemish,
> 2 And unleavened bread, and cakes unleavened tempered with oil, and wafers unleavened anointed with oil: *of* wheaten flour shalt thou make them.
> 3 And thou shalt put them into one basket, and bring them in the basket, with the bullock and the two rams.
> 14 But the flesh of the bullock, and his skin, and his dung, shalt thou burn with fire without the camp: it *is* a sin **offering**."

The ram was for **burnt offering** (Exodus 29:16-18)

Exodus 29:16-18
> 16 "And thou shalt slay the ram, and thou shalt take his blood, and sprinkle *it* round about upon the altar.

17 And thou shalt cut the ram in pieces, and wash the inwards of him, and his legs, and put *them* unto his pieces, and unto his head.

18 And thou shalt burn the whole ram upon the altar: it *is* a **burnt offering** unto the LORD: it *is* a sweet savour, an **offering** made by fire unto the LORD."

The "other ram" (Exodus 29:19-20), referred to as the ram of consecration, was for a **peace offering,** something which becomes evident in Exodus 29:28.

Exodus 29:19-20

19 "And thou shalt take the other ram; and Aaron and his sons shall put their hands upon the head of the ram.

20 Then shalt thou kill the ram, and take of his blood, and put *it* upon the tip of the right ear of Aaron, and upon the tip of the right ear of his sons, and upon the thumb of their right hand, and upon the great toe of their right foot, and sprinkle the blood upon the altar round about."

From this animal was obtained the "wave breast" and the "heave shoulder" which, we discover in verse 28, constituted this particular sacrifice as a **"peace offering".**

Exodus 29:27-28

27 "And thou shalt sanctify the breast of the wave **offering**, and the shoulder of the heave **offering**, which is waved, and which is heaved up, of the ram of the consecration, *even* of *that* which *is* for Aaron, and of *that* which is for his sons:

28 And it shall be Aaron's and his sons' by a statute for ever from the children of Israel: for it *is* an heave **offering**: and it shall be an heave **offering** from the children of Israel of the **sacrifice of their peace offerings,** *even* their heave **offering** unto the LORD."

It should be noted that the **meal offering** (*minchah*) was presented alongside the fat, the rump, the fat covering the inwards, the caul above the liver, the two kidneys and the right shoulder of the ram of **sacrifice of peace offering,** indicating that the **peace offering and the meal offering** were seen together in Exodus 29:22-24, in contrast to the daily burnt offering where the burnt offering and meal offering are seen together.

Exodus 29:22-24

22 "Also thou shalt take of the ram the fat and the rump, and the fat that covereth the inwards, and the caul *above* the liver, and the two kidneys, and the fat that *is* upon them, and the right shoulder; for it *is* a ram of consecration:

23 And one loaf of bread, and one cake of oiled bread, and one wafer out of the basket of the unleavened bread that *is* before the LORD:

24 And thou shalt put all in the hands of Aaron, and in the hands of his sons; and shalt wave them *for* a wave **offering** before the LORD."

Of note, in Psalm 40:6 the **meal offering** and **peace offering** are seen **together** as *zevach* and *minchah* calling to the reader's attention that it is the consecration of the priest which is in view, as described in Exodus 29:22-24.

These details have been necessary to establish that what the Psalmist has in mind in Psalm 40:6 is the occasion of the **consecration of Aaron and his sons**.

Why should this particular Old Testament ritual form a key element of God's beneficent thoughts towards us?

Clearly, it always was God's intention that His people should move in fellowship with Him. God intended all His ancient people to be a nation of priests (see Psalm 69 in the consideration of aspects of redemption). That was His will. Unfortunately, due to their failure this was not possible so He appointed Aaron and his sons to function in this capacity. Their role was to represent God to men and represent men to God. "The priest's lips should keep knowledge" (Malachi 2:7), and thus teaching God's will and God's Word was an important aspect of priestly work (see Psalm 110).

Doubtless, David had recourse to priestly men for advice and he valued their intercession for him. We know how he received sustenance from Ahimelech the priest in 1 Samuel 21 and how Zadok and Abiathar helped him during the Absalom rebellion (2 Samuel 15:24). Nevertheless, Psalm 40:6 indicates that the consecration of the priests was in itself a flawed process, for God did not have complete satisfaction in the sacrifices offered. Moreover, the priests themselves failed on numerous occasions (see Psalm 22).

Hebrews 10:6
> "In burnt offerings and sacrifices for sin Thou hast had no pleasure (didst not delight in)" .

"Thou didst not delight in" (*lo chaphatzta*) does not mean that God did not accept the sacrifices offered on the occasion of Aaron's consecration. We know that God did accept these sacrifices, because the divine fire consumed the sacrificial victim, indicating divine pleasure in the sacrifice (Leviticus 9:24). However, the phrase *lo chaphatzta* (negative short tense) suggests that God was not **completely** satisfied in the sacrifice. What a contrast to the Sacrifice offered by the Lord Jesus in which He had complete delight!

One of the features of a priest is that "he must be taken from among men" (Hebrews 5:1). David must have been amazed to think that the Son of David, when He would be revealed, would in fact be the unfailing Priest and for that reason must, of necessity, be perfectly human. In contrast to the Old Testament priests, who so often failed to adequately represent God to men, the Lord Jesus, when revealed, would not just teach the Law, He would fulfill it (for it was within His heart). This would involve Him fully loving His Father and loving His neighbour as Himself. We know from Hebrews 8:4 that while on earth He did not function as a Priest, "seeing that there are priests that offer gifts according to the Law".

Hebrews 8:4
> "For if He were on earth, He should not be a priest, seeing that there are priests that offer gifts according to the Law."

However, now that He is in the Holy Place "not made with hands", He functions as a Priest for us today. Nevertheless, His incarnation in Bethlehem and the experiences of His thirty-three and a half years were necessary to equip Him to be our Great High Priest in Heaven. Here we get a little insight into the thoughts of God towards us in His sending the Lord Jesus to be born at Bethlehem.

As far as David was concerned, he would not have known the Lord Jesus in the sense that we do as our Great High Priest. Nevertheless, he must have marvelled that the failing Aaronic priesthood was going to be replaced by the unfailing Priest-King Himself.

Psalm 40:6
> "Sacrifice and offering Thou didst not desire; Mine ears hast Thou opened: burnt offering and sin offering hast Thou not required."

As we have seen, verse 6 brings before us the consecration of the Aaronic order of priests and reminds us that the Lord did not have complete satisfaction in this. We know that for Aaron to be consecrated as priest, sacrifice, offering, burnt offering and offering for sin were necessary first of all. In other words, the deaths of the sacrificial victims were first needed for Aaron to be consecrated as a priest, able to enter into the Holiest of All. For the Lord Jesus Christ to be consecrated as a Priest, not only was sacrifice necessary (Hebrews 8:3), but His **resurrection was also required!**

The Scripture provides us with some striking comparisons and contrasts between the Lord Jesus being consecrated as a Priest and Aaron being consecrated to the Aaronic priesthood.

As Aaron stood at the door of the tabernacle of the congregation to undergo the ceremony of consecration to priesthood, he was already clothed in his garments of glory and beauty even though he was not yet fitted to carry out priestly duties. What a contrast we see in the experience of the Lord Jesus Who, throughout His earthly sojourn (with the exception of the occasion on the mount of transfiguration), voluntarily veiled His glory. In fact, John indicates that prior to His resurrection "Jesus was not yet glorified" (John 7:39). This is especially clear at Calvary, where we see the Lord Jesus being set at naught by man His creature. Here we recognise the truth of Philippians 2:8: "He **humbled Himself**, and became obedient unto death, even the death of the cross." Calvary was not the occasion of His glorification. Unlike Aaron's consecration, our Lord Jesus offered Himself in circumstances of profound humiliation. However, the Scripture is careful to affirm that when the Lord Jesus emerged as a consecrated High Priest, this occurred at the same time as His **glorification**, confirming that He was not a Priest during the period of His humiliation. This is clear in Hebrews

5:5 where the occasion of the Lord Jesus being "made an High Priest" is linked with God **at the same time** glorifying Him.

Hebrews 5:5

> 5 "So also Christ **glorified not Himself** to be **made an High Priest**; but He that said unto Him, Thou art My Son, to day have I begotten Thee."

We have already seen in Psalm 2 that the phrase, "this day have I begotten Thee", refers to His resurrection from the dead and not His incarnation. The point is that our High Priest is not just a Man. He is a risen and glorified Man. Aaron was consecrated as a priest on the basis of sacrificial death. Our Lord Jesus is consecrated as our High Priest on the basis of His victory over death, i.e. His resurrection from the dead.

However, we should notice another important contrast. Having been consecrated as high priest at the entrance to the tabernacle, Aaron still had the task of entering into the Holiest of All on the Day of Atonement with blood to make a covering for sin, a ceremony which was never complete and needed repeated annually. What a striking contrast to our Lord Jesus! When He arose from the dead He had no further work to do to put away sin. He already had completed the putting away of sin by the Sacrifice of Himself. Aaron was a consecrated priest who faced the solemn task of trying to make covering for sin on the dreadful Day of Atonement, and who knew, even as he did this, that his best efforts on the Day of Atonement were only incomplete. The contrast with our Lord Jesus is so beautiful. He comes forth as a risen, glorified eternal High Priest Who has defeated death and Who no longer needs to offer for sin. Aaron was consecrated to deal with sin incompletely. Our Lord Jesus is consecrated as One Who has already completely dealt with the sin question, as attested to by His resurrection from the dead. On the Day of Atonement, Aaron enters in to the Holiest of All "not without blood" (Hebrews 9:7) to address the problem of sin. In striking contrast, the Lord Jesus, Who has already fully and finally addressed the problem of putting away sin, ascends and enters into the Holiest of All in heaven, not with blood, as was the case with Aaron, but rather "by virtue of His own blood".

Hebrews 9:11-12

> 11 "But Christ being come an High Priest of good things to come, by a greater and more perfect tabernacle, not made with hands, that is to say, not of this building;
> 12 Neither by (**virtue of**) the blood of goats and calves, but by (**virtue of**) His Own blood He entered in once into the holy place, having obtained eternal redemption *for us.*"

We again encounter in Psalm 110 the consecration of our Lord Jesus to be our Great High Priest. There we will see that His ascension was important as also emphasised in Hebrews 8:4.

Hebrews 8:4
> 4 "For if He were on earth, He should not be a Priest, seeing that there are priests that offer gifts according to the Law"

Despite these clear Scriptures, some still wonder how the Lord Jesus could offer Himself as a Sacrifice to God at Calvary if He were not already a fully functioning Priest. This idea arises from the incorrect supposition that only an official functioning Aaronic priest could offer sacrifice to God in the Old Testament. This is not the case of course. For example, Abel's sacrifice was acceptable to God, even though he was not Adam's first born son, nor was the Aaronic priesthood instituted as yet. Moreover, David offered to the Lord in 2 Samuel 24:25 even though he was not of the tribe of Levi.

2 Samuel 24:25
> "And David built there an altar unto the LORD, and offered burnt offerings and peace offerings. So the LORD was intreated for the land, and the plague was stayed from Israel"

It is clear that in the Old Testament priests and non-priests could offer sacrifice, but only a priest could enter into the holy place.Note 1 Entering into the holy place was exclusively a priestly privilege as Uzziah discovered (2 Chronicles 26:18). Thus it is fully compatible with Old Testament revelation for the Lord Jesus to offer Himself to God before being made a Priest. By so doing He made an end of our sin. However, as the risen Victor over death, as a fully consecrated, glorified Priest He ascended up and entered into the Holiest of All in heaven. Note 1

However, there are comparisons between the consecration of Aaron and the consecration of the Lord Jesus. Aaron stood at the door of the tabernacle of the congregation, anointed and clothed in his official priestly garments even though he was **not yet** a functioning priest. He was not yet able to enter into the holy place. When the bullock for the sin offering was offered on his behalf on the occasion of his consecration, its blood was not brought into the holy place (Exodus 29:12). We saw in our meditations in Psalm 22 that when a sin offering was being offered on the behalf of **a non-priest**, the blood was not brought into the holy place (Leviticus 4:25). However, when the sin offering was offered on the behalf of an anointed priest then the blood was brought into the holy place (Leviticus 4:5). Why then was the blood of Aaron's sin offering not brought into the holy place on the day of his consecration, even though he was already anointed and clothed in his official priestly garments? The reason is that Aaron was not yet consecrated as a priest, even though he was wearing the priestly garments and was anointed with the holy anointing oil. The significance of this is beautiful. Garments in Scripture signify character. Even though Aaron was not yet consecrated as a priest, he exhibited all the characteristics of the high priest as signified by his priestly attire. This finds fulfilment in the Lord Jesus, Who in the days of His flesh, prior to His resurrection, exhibited all the characteristics of a merciful, caring, loving high Priest in all the priest-like actions He performed prior to Calvary. This is especially seen in His intercessory prayers for His own, recorded in the Gospels (John 17; Luke 22:31-32) and in Hebrews 5:7. All of these priestly characteristics were seen in Him **before** He was consecrated a glorified Priest. Furthermore, by the same reasoning, Aaron was anointed with the holy anointing oil before he functioned as a priest (Exodus 29:7). Again this finds fulfilment in the Lord Jesus. Even before His resurrection and glorification as our High Priest, during the the days of His flesh and His humiliation, Peter tells us that He was "Anointed with the Holy Ghost and with power (Acts 10:38). John also adds: "God giveth not the Spirit by measure unto Him" (John 3:24). However, before we could receive the indwelling Spirit of God and function as New Testament priests, He must first enter into the Holy Place in heaven and send us down the Spirit of God (John 16:7).

John 16:7
> "Nevertheless I tell you the truth; It is expedient for you that I go away: for if I go not away, the Comforter will not come unto you; but if I depart, I will send Him unto you".

There is a further comparison worthy of note. The sacrifices offered on the occasion of Aaron's consecration emphasised that a sacrificial death was needed before Aaron could be declared a priest. However, at the end of the ceremony of Exodus 29, the shoulder was taken from the ram of peace offering and **lifted up** before God before it became Aaron's portion to eat. The lifting up of the heave offering (lifted up offering) at the end of the ceremony of Aaron's consecration reminds us of the risen Lord Jesus ascending up in glory as the Great High Priest.

Exodus 29:26-28
> 26 "And thou shalt take the breast of the ram of Aaron's consecration, and wave it *for* a wave offering before the Lord: and it shall be thy part.
> 27 And thou shalt sanctify the breast of the wave offering, **and the shoulder of the heave offering, which is waved, and which is heaved up, of the ram of the consecration**, *even* of *that* which *is* for Aaron, and of *that* which is for his sons:
> 28 And it shall be Aaron's and his sons' by a statute for ever from the children of Israel: for it *is* an heave offering: and it shall be an heave offering from the children of Israel of the sacrifice of their peace offerings, *even* their heave offering unto the Lord."

These considerations show how the Lord Jesus offered Himself to God as a Sacrifice before He became a Priest. However, in resurrection and ascension He enters into the heavenly temple as a Great High Priest, not with blood, but by virtue of His blood. This Priest, in contrast to Aaron, has defeated death, made an end of sin and never needs to add to His work of propitiation ever again!

"Mine ears Thou hast opened."

The phrase, "Mine ears hast Thou opened (digged)", either in English or in Hebrew is truly difficult if not impossible to explain, particularly as the phrase occurs nowhere else in our Hebrew Bible. This has not hindered many Godly and highly respected expositors from speculating as to its meaning. The generally accepted interpretation of the phrase, "Mine ear Thou hast digged", is to identify this phrase with the boring through of the ear of the Hebrew servant of Exodus 21:1-6, who, because of his love for his master and his wife, refuses to go out free, which is his legal right, and chooses rather to be a servant forever. This decision is permanently displayed by having his ear bored through with an aul.

Exodus 21:1-6

1 "Now these *are* the judgments which thou shalt set before them.

2 If thou buy an Hebrew servant, six years he shall serve: and in the seventh he shall go out free for nothing.

3 If he came in by himself, he shall go out by himself: if he were married, then his wife shall go out with him.

4 If his master have given him a wife, and she have born him sons or daughters; the wife and her children shall be her master's, and he shall go out by himself.

5 And if the servant shall plainly say, I love my master, my wife, and my children; I will not go out free:

6 Then his master shall bring him unto the judges; he shall also bring him to the door, or unto the door post; and his master shall bore his ear through with an aul; and he shall serve him for ever."

There is absolutely no doubt that the Hebrew servant of Exodus 21 is a beautiful picture of the Lord Jesus Christ as the Perfect Servant of Jehovah Who, due to His love for His Bride (the Church) and His love to God, refused to go out free and remains a Servant eternally. Accordingly, it may be appropriate to use the illustration of the Hebrew servant in Exodus 21 as a secondary application to Psalm 40. However, it may not be appropriate to say that Exodus 21 is the primary meaning of Psalm 40. The reason is that the word for "digged" is different from the verb "to bore through" in Exodus 21:6. This immediately alerts us that the boring through of the Hebrew servant's ear is a different entity from the digging of the ear of the Messiah in Psalm 40. Moreover, when this passage is quoted for us in Hebrews 10, the phrase, "Mine ear Thou hast digged", is given as, "a Body hast Thou prepared Me" (Hebrews 10:5). In Hebrews 10:5, there is no mention made of the ear. The reference is to the Body prepared for Him at His incarnation. When we return to the original phrase in Psalm 40, "Mine ear Thou hast digged", it might be best to acknowledge that this is language and expression which defies our finite human understanding, including that of the Psalmist himself.

Now, such a conclusion should not alarm us. After all, in the preceding verses the Psalmist has been acknowledging that God's thoughts go completely beyond human comprehension. Now that the Psalmist has been privileged to enter into God's thoughts, it should not be a surprise to us if we encounter a phrase in the conversation between the Lord Jesus and the Father which defies our finite comprehension. Surely the response the Lord is looking from us is to be like David, in his humble acknowledgement to the Lord, that God's thoughts are higher than our thoughts. Like David, we should accept that there are scriptural truths greater than our intellectual capacity to grasp, because we are finite and God is infinite.

The answer to the meaning of the phrase in Psalm 40, "Mine ear Thou has digged", is given in Hebrews 10, "a Body hast Thou prepared Me". The lesson is clear for us. Hebrews 10 shows us that the phrase, "Mine ear Thou hast digged", describes **the fact** of His incarnation. However, since in Psalm 40 the expression used is enigmatic and impossible for us to understand, we learn that the incarnation, while factual (Hebrews 10), defies human understanding (Psalm 40). This is Holy Ground. We do not go beyond what is revealed in Scripture. There are truths regarding the Person of Christ which Christians accept by faith but do not pry into. The men of Beth Shemesh thought they could lift the lid of the Ark and look in (1 Samuel 6:20). **The equivalent of "looking into the Ark" today is to speculate as to medical details of His incarnation and death.** This passage would warn us that the truths relating to His incarnation and His death are not to be treated as common matters for intellectual or scientific debate. It is best to take off the shoes from off our feet, bow our heads and worship in His presence at the wonder that the eternal Son of God should be "manifest in flesh" in order to become our Great High Priest, consecrated as such by His own sacrificial death.

Psalm 40:7

"Then said I, Lo, I come: in the volume of the book *it is* written of Me..."

The Psalm is showing that Christ, when He comes in incarnation, is the "express image of His Person" (Hebrews 1:3). He comes "in the volume of the book". In other words, all of Old Testament Scripture — the Law, the Prophets and the Writings — attest to Him. As "God manifest in flesh" (1 Timothy 3:16), He is the full expression of the Father. In His Glorious Person we have, reaching into eternity, the complete telling forth of God's righteousness, Law, compassions, truth and lovingkindness (all outlined in verses 6-10). This revelation of Himself causes us to be like David: dumbfounded in His presence and bowing low before Him in worship.

Psalm 40:8

"I delight to do Thy will, O My God: yea, Thy Law *is* within My heart."

The phrase, "Thy Law is within My heart", means literally, "Thy Law is within My bowels". The bowels are used metaphorically in Scripture to describe the seat of the emotions within a person. When we learn that the Law was within His bowels, this would suggest to us that the Law of God in all its solemn inflexibility was completely immersed in the infinite compassions of Christ's innermost being. Hebrews 10:9 quotes from Psalm 40:8 to highlight **the will of God** which the Lord Jesus delighted to do.

Hebrews 10:9-10
> 9 "Then said He, Lo, I come to do Thy will, O God. He taketh away the first, that He may establish the second.
> 10 By the **which will we are sanctified** through the offering of the body of Jesus Christ once *for all*."

The "will of God" in Psalm 40:8 is not defined in detail. However, in Hebrews 10:9 the Spirit of God tells us specifically which aspect of God's **will** is in view in Psalm 40:8. It is that we should be sanctified: "by the which will **we are sanctified**". When we realise that Psalm 40 is about the consecration of the Lord Jesus to be our Great High Priest, we learn in Hebrews 10:10 that Psalm 40:8 speaks of God's will that we should be sanctified as priests also. Sanctification in Exodus 29 is being set apart to function in the Holy Place. This is what God had in mind. It is His will that **all** the redeemed of every era should be fitted to praise Him in the sanctuary as priests. This, then, is the fulfilment of the New Song. It is God's will that it should be brought to pass and only by the death and resurrection of the Lord Jesus could it be made a Song in reality.

In this section we meet the "great congregation"– a wonderful gathering of the redeemed, all of whom are fitted to function as priests before Him. Now there are different "subsets" within the "great congregation".

A prophecy of the future great congregation

Psalm 40:9-10
> 9 "I have preached righteousness in the great congregation: lo, I have not refrained My lips, O Lord, Thou knowest.
> 10 I have not hid Thy righteousness within My heart; I have declared Thy faithfulness and Thy salvation: I have not concealed Thy lovingkindness and Thy truth from the great congregation."

In Psalm 22, we saw that "the congregation" is the Church, whereas the "great congregation" was a body of people which was even greater than the Church. We saw that the "great congregation" is a term used to describe all the redeemed of all ages. The Church differs from the Old Testament believers in that we are priests, already fitted to function in the heavenly sanctuary in our lifetimes. This is because our Great High Priest has already entered into the Holiest in the heavens with the result that we "who are sanctified" (Hebrews 10:10) can likewise enter in today "by His Blood" (Hebrews 10:19). This is a wonderful privilege which Old Testament believers did not have. They could pray, but to enter in as priests was something they were not able to do. Now, however, their souls are around the throne in heaven and they are able to worship as priests there. When they are raised from the dead at the end of the tribulation and enter into the earthly Kingdom, they will then, for the first time in their experience, be priests on earth.

The Lord now declares prophetically that to this great congregation He has:

1 preached (as good news) righteousness

2 declared to them God's faithfulness and God's salvation

Moreover, he indicates that He has not hidden from them God's lovingkindness or truth (verse 10). This comment about not hiding the truth of God from the great congregation shows us that the period of time referred to in the verse cannot be the Old Testament period, when the truth of the New Testament mysteries was entirely hidden in God's heart. Moreover, verses 9-10 cannot be fulfilled in the earthly ministry of the Lord Jesus since there were some truths which He did hide from them as He spoke in parables and in proverbs (Matthew 13:13; John 16:29). It is clear that the verses envisage a day when there shall be no more truth hidden from the people of God, and all shall be revealed by the Lord Jesus Himself. This lets us see that verses 9-10 cannot be this present Church era since it is the Spirit of God Who today teaches the truth to the Lord's people. Since the verse is speaking of the Lord Jesus directly teaching the truth of God to the great congregation, it follows, therefore, that verses 9-10 must be referring to a future period when the Lord will totally reveal His truth to His redeemed ones.

In that day, He will no longer speak in proverbs (John 16:25) nor in mystery (Matthew 13). Nothing will be withheld by "refrained lips" or be hidden or concealed. It is the Lord Jesus Who will personally have the role of expounding to the great congregation, i.e. all the redeemed of all ages, the truth of the **righteousness of God** (Psalm 40:9), His **faithfulness** (Psalm 40:10), **lovingkindness** and **truth** (Psalm 40:10). This gathering must surely stretch out into the eternal state (see Psalms 8 and 102) when, in that sin-and-death-free environment, the Lord Jesus will show us all the wonder of the righteousness of God, as well as His lovingkindness and truth down through the ages, including His dealings with each of us as individuals in our lives on this earth. What a day that will be! As we look back over life's pathway and review the Lord's management of the past ages, we will see the infinite wonder of "God's thoughts" displayed – His thoughts "to us-ward"!

"I have preached" means literally "I have **declared as good news** righteousness in the great congregation" (Psalm 40:9).

To the ungodly world, the righteousness of God comes as news which fills their hearts with dread. If God is righteous, they know that means judgment for them. However, when righteousness is proclaimed as good news it encapsulates for us the story of how God can be righteous in saving lost sinners and offering them forgiveness of sins. What good news is the Gospel of the righteousness of God as fully proclaimed by the Person of Christ! We may marvel that the Lord will expound to us the Gospel again in that heavenly sphere. Just as a believer today loves to hear the Gospel being preached and finds it warms his heart and draws forth worship, so in that coming day the Lord Jesus will expound to us the good news of the Gospel which we believed on the occasion of our escape from the deep pit of despair. We shall never exhaust its wonder. Perhaps, it is only then that those of us who have endeavoured to preach the Gospel will realise how failingly we have represented our Saviour. However, it will be too late then to go forth and proclaim it to the lost.

The Psalmist pleads with the Lord

In verses 11-17, the Psalmist pleads with the Lord for preservation from evils within and without.

Psalm 40:11-17

11 "Withhold not Thou Thy tender mercies from me, O Lord: let Thy lovingkindness and Thy truth continually preserve me.

12 For innumerable evils have compassed me about: mine iniquities have taken hold upon me, so that I am not able to look up; they are more than the hairs of mine head: therefore my heart faileth me.

13 Be pleased, O Lord, to deliver me: O Lord, make haste to help me.

14 Let them be ashamed and confounded together that seek after my soul to destroy it; let them be driven backward and put to shame that wish me evil.

15 Let them be desolate for a reward of their shame that say unto me, Aha, aha.

16 Let all those that seek Thee rejoice and be glad in Thee: let such as love Thy Salvation say continually, The Lord be magnified.

17 But I am poor and needy; yet the Lord thinketh upon me: Thou art my help and my deliverer; make no tarrying, O my God."

In the previous section, the Psalmist was unable to quantify God's beneficent thoughts towards him, especially in the context of the Lord coming to be consecrated as our High Priest to fit us to function in His sanctuary. It was truly a wonderful revelation which David received as he was uniquely privileged to listen in to a divine conversation taking place in heaven. Just as Isaiah in Isaiah chapter 6 saw the Lord in heaven "high and lifted up" and almost immediately felt his own sinfulness, similarly David responds to the revelation he has just received with deep feelings of unworthiness and sinfulness. This does not mean that he is in anyway doubting the reality of his deliverance from the "pit of noise" and the security of being given a standing upon the Rock. Rather, what has happened is that his nearness to the Lord and his entering into the Lord's own thoughts have heightened his own sensitivity to sin around him and within himself. When this section of Psalm 40 is repeated again in Psalm 70 it, similarly, is expressing the Psalmist's unworthiness after the heights of revelation received in Psalm 69 (see later in chapter on Psalm 69).

On the basis of the future accepted Sacrifice, the Psalmist makes a number of requests in his spiritual distress:

1 He requests deliverance from personal failure

Psalm 40:13

"Be pleased, O Lord, to deliver me: O Lord, make haste to help me."

The word "be pleased" literally means "be accepting of...". The occurrences of this word elsewhere in the Old Testament, in the grammatical form in which it is used in Psalm 40:13, involve some kind of definition of that with which the Lord is pleased or of which He is accepting. However, in verse 13 the Psalmist does not specify that of which he wants the Lord to be accepting. He is concentrating on the result of this acceptance – namely the ability of the Lord to deliver the Psalmist on the basis of the acceptance. However, the context of the Psalm shows us that the object of the divine "pleasure" or "acceptance" is no doubt the future Sacrifice of the Lord Jesus Himself, in contrast to the offerings and sacrifices with which the Lord was not fully well pleased, spoken of earlier in the Psalm. This is the key to any episode in a believer's life where evils within and without overwhelm the soul. It is God's acceptance of the Sacrifice of Christ which is the basis of our standing with Him. This is what is meant in Ephesians 1:6 where we are seen as "accepted in the Beloved".

Ephesians 1:6

"... He hath made us accepted in the Beloved."

These thoughts are beautifully summarised in Charitie Lees Smith's hymn.
"When Satan tempts me to despair.
And tells me of the guilt within,
Upward I look and see Him there
Who made an end of all my sin.
Because the sinless Saviour died
My sinful soul is counted free.
For God the Just is satisfied
To look on Him and pardon me."

Let us never lose sight of Him and God's thoughts of Him, because God's thoughts towards us, which are the subject matter of the Psalm, are entirely based on His thoughts towards His own Son.

2 He requests the defeat of his enemies (Psalm 40:14-15)

David links the acceptance of the Sacrifice as not only the basis of his deliverance from personal sin and failure, but also the basis of deliverance from his enemies (Psalm 40:14-15). Interestingly, in Psalm 110:4-7 it is the "Priest forever after the order of Melchisedec", Who by death has defeated death, Who comes out to put down His enemies.

3 He requests that spiritual rejoicing should sustain those who seek the Lord

Psalm 40:16

"Let all those that seek Thee rejoice and be glad in Thee: let such as love
Thy Salvation say continually, The Lord be magnified."

Perhaps, as in Psalm 22:21-23, it is the thought of the acceptance of the
Lord Jesus' Sacrifice forming the basis of eternal praise which is in view
here again.

Finally, the Psalmist returns to God's thoughts about him. He says, "yet
the Lord thinketh upon me". This means that God's plans and mighty
thoughts to bless him, discussed earlier in the Psalm, would all be fulfilled
despite the Psalmist's undoubted failures. This is the wonder of the all-
sufficient Sacrifice of Christ, that through Him God's mighty thoughts of
blessing toward us come to fruition.

Psalm 40:17

"But I *am* poor and needy; *yet* the Lord thinketh upon me: Thou *art* my help
and my deliverer; make no tarrying, O my God."

David could not wait until the triumph of the risen Lord would lead to his
being fitted as a priest to praise the Lord around the throne in heaven, as in
Revelation 5. In the meantime, he felt as one "poor and needy". This aspect
of David's insightful grasp of his own failings is considered in more detail
in Psalm 41. Here in Psalm 40, David considers **God's thoughts** towards
him. In Psalm 41, he is thinking of **men's thoughts towards** him as, despite
his personal failures, he finds himself in the line of the promised Messiah.

The practical import of Psalm 40 to us today

The application for us as believers today is clear. The central objective
of God's thoughts to us is to fit us to be priests, so that we will be able to
engage in priestly ministry before Him, accepted in all the acceptability of
Christ. This is something which God has graciously brought us into in our
lifetimes, unlike Old Testament believers, who have had to wait until the
Lord Jesus entered into heaven on His ascension. If God values so highly
this privilege which He has afforded to us today, we as believers should
be careful to beware against ever taking for granted this holy privilege or
treating it with familiarity.

---

1. In "The Gospel and its Ministry" Sir Robert Anderson makes the point that priesthood is not
essential to the act of sacrifice in the Levitical System.

8

PSALM 41

To the chief Musician, A Psalm of David.
1 Blessed is he that considereth the poor: the Lord will deliver him in time of trouble.
2 The Lord will preserve him, and keep him alive; and he shall be blessed upon the earth: and Thou wilt not deliver him unto the will of his enemies.
3 The Lord will strengthen him upon the bed of languishing: Thou wilt make all his bed in his sickness.
4 I said, Lord, be merciful unto me: heal my soul; for I have sinned against Thee.
5 Mine enemies speak evil of me, When shall he die, and his name perish?
6 And if he come to see me, he speaketh vanity: his heart gathereth iniquity to itself; when he goeth abroad, he telleth it.
7 All that hate me whisper together against me: against me do they devise my hurt.
8 An evil disease, say they, cleaveth fast unto him: and now that he lieth he shall rise up no more.
9 Yea, mine own familiar friend, in whom I trusted, which did eat of my bread, hath lifted up his heel against me.
10 But Thou, O Lord, be merciful unto me, and raise me up, that I may requite them.
11 By this I know that Thou favourest me, because mine enemy doth not triumph over me.
12 And as for me, Thou upholdest me in mine integrity, and settest me before Thy face for ever.
13 Blessed be the Lord God of Israel from everlasting, and to everlasting. Amen, and Amen.

Introduction

The historical background to this Psalm is the betrayal of David by his long time friend and counsellor, Ahithophel on the occasion of Absalom's rebellion.

There are two distinct themes running in parallel through Psalm 41, both of which are presented in John 13 where the Psalm is quoted. The first is

prophetical truth, where the rejected David is seen as a **prophetical picture** of the future rejected Messiah, which is why the Psalm is Messianic. This becomes clear in the upper room where Ahithophel's betrayal of David is prophetic of Judas' betrayal of Christ.

The second theme is **practical truth** where David is seen not as a type of Christ but **as a once backslidden believer** now restored who, because of his links to Christ, should be loved by fellowbelievers. Again, this is clear in the upper room where Peter's denial and restoration were **foretold** by the Lord Jesus, no doubt with a view to his being fully accepted by the other apostles once he was restored by the Lord.

A) The prophetical aspect of the Psalm (David as a type of the rejected future Messiah)

This Psalm (Psalm 41:9) is quoted in the New Testament in the context of Judas Iscariot betraying the Lord Jesus (John 13:18). There the phrase,"that the Scripture may be fulfilled", shows that Psalm 41:9 is a prophecy of Judas' betrayal.

John 13:18
> "I speak not of you all: I know whom I have chosen: but **that the Scripture may be fulfilled, He that eateth bread with Me hath lifted up his heel against Me.**"

Immediately, an apparent difficulty presents itself to some. The background to Psalm 41 is the betrayal of David by Ahithophel (2 Samuel 15:20-23) on the occasion of Absalom's rebellion. How then is this historical episode of rejection and betrayal in David's life prophetical of the betrayal and rejection of the Lord Jesus Christ?

There are several interpretations of this. A widely held view is that in John 13:18 the Lord Jesus lifted out Psalm 41:9 from its immediate context of David's betrayal and then applied it to Himself. The difficulty with this view is that the Lord stipulates "that the Scripture may be fulfilled". This shows that He regarded Psalm 41:9 as a direct prophecy of His Own betrayal which would in detail be fulfilled. The Lord Jesus did not quote the verse out of context. It already directly applied to Him. How can this be?

Until now in *Meditations in the Messianic Psalms,* we have been looking at prophecies regarding the Lord Jesus which have been statements of prophecy. Here we encounter a different method of presenting prophecy which is widespread in the Old Testament. It is the account of historical events which are identified elsewhere in Scripture as having prophetical import. If an historical event has prophetical import this **must be specifically identified elsewhere** in Scripture to allow such an interpretation to be legitimate. In this context it is worth remembering that the Old Testament Scriptures are divided into three scrolls: the scroll of the Law (*Torah*), the scroll of the Prophets (*Neviim*), and the scroll of the Writings (*Ctuvim*). This is discussed again in Psalm 110. The scroll of the Prophets contains the historical prophets as well as the later doctrinal prophets (eg Isaiah, Jeremiah etc). The historical prophets include Joshua, Judges, 1 and 2 Samuel and 1 and 2 Kings. In these books there are many **historical events** which carry prophetical significance. This is one reason why there are major historical books within the scroll of the prophets. One important event is found in Psalms 96-100 where the historical journey of the ark of the covenant from the temple of Dagon to Solomon's temple is identified as of major prophetical significance. As an historical allegory it prophetically charts the "journey" of the Lord Jesus from Calvary right through to His future Kingdom glory, particularly emphasisng His relationship with men throughout the various eras along the way. This will be considered in Psalms 96-99.

An important historical theme which permeates 1 and 2 Samuel, and which is identified in Psalm 69 as having a prophetical import, highlights the many **rejection** episodes in David's life and **the reproach** which was often heaped upon him by his enemies. Since David's claim to be in the line of the promised Messiah was widely known, and was in fact his only claim to legitimacy upon his throne, rebellion against him was anti-messianic in character. Psalm 69 shows how David bore reproach for his claim to be in the line of the promised Messiah, and sometimes this reproach spilled over into open rebellion. Since Psalm 69 is a Messianic Psalm, this matter will be considered in detail later. However, at this stage a summary is appropriate since this will show how the story of David's **rejection** by Ahithophel, and the **reproach** he bore at that time were prophetic of Judas' betrayal of the Lord .

In Psalm 69, David indicates that:

1 He was suffering because of his link with the coming Messiah and not just because of his own failures.

Psalm 69:7

"Because for **Thy sake** I have borne **reproach**; shame hath covered my face."

2 The Messiah would Himself experience at first hand **the reproach** borne by David because of his link with the Messianic promise. In Psalm 69:19, David says, "Thou has known **my reproach**…". Although in the English translation the phrase, "Thou hast known", is in the past tense this phrase could also be translated in the future, "Thou wilt know my reproach…". However, as we will see in our study of Psalm 69, the Lord's knowledge of David's **reproach** in Psalm 69:19 is in the immediate context of Him first becoming "near unto David" as "Kinsman Redeemer (*goel*) (Psalm 69:18). In other words, the Lord would come near as Kinsman Redeemer, i.e. become related to us at Bethlehem by becoming Man and in this guise would know David's reproach **at first hand**. Experiences of reproach which David encountered, specifically arising from his involvement in the lineage of the Messiah, would in turn become the first-hand knowledge of the Lord Himself as seen in Psalm 69:19-21.

Psalm 69:19-21

> 19 "Thou hast known (directly) my reproach, and my shame, and my dishonour: mine adversaries *are* all before thee.
> 20 Reproach hath broken my heart; and I am full of heaviness: and I looked *for some* to take pity, but *there was* none; and for comforters, but I found none.
> 21 They gave me also gall for my meat; and in my thirst they gave me vinegar to drink."

David knew that the **anti-Messianic reproach**, which he was called to bear for Christ's sake, would be known **at first hand** by the Lord Jesus Himself when He would come. Some of these experiences which David endured are cited in Psalm 69:19-21 as examples of what the Lord Jesus would know at first hand Himself when He would personally come. A detailed consideration of this is given in the chapter on Psalm 69.

In Psalm 69:19-21, unspecified occasions in David's life when he endured such **reproach** are described. A specific example of such reproach is given in Psalm 55 which, like Psalm 41, is also a commentary on Ahithophel's betrayal of David.

Psalm 55:12-14

> 12 "For *it was* not an enemy *that* **reproached me**; then I could have borne *it:* neither *was it* he that hated me *that* did magnify *himself* against me; then I would have hid myself from him:
> 13 But *it was* thou, a man mine equal, my guide, and mine acquaintance.
> 14 We took sweet counsel together, *and* walked unto the house of God in company".

This passage is significant as it shows that Ahithophel's betrayal involved **reproach** to David. Psalm 69:19 shows that the Lord Jesus, when He would come, would enter into David's reproaches at first hand. Psalm 69 is careful to show that these reproaches which David endured and which the Messiah would experience did not directly arise from the consequences of sin in David's life. Rather, David tells us that "the reproaches of them that reproached Thee are fallen upon me" (Psalm 69:9). In other words, the reproaches David was enduring were primarily being directed at the unborn Messiah (Thee), but because these enemies of God could not directly harm Him, they directed their rebellion at His servant David. When there was failure in David's life, this provided even further pretext for these enemies of God to reproach him. However, this was not the primary motive behind their actions as the inspired commentary of Psalm 69 shows. It was primarily hatred of David because of his link to the promised Messiah, and any failure in his life was used as leverage against him.

Similarly, it is apparent that Ahithophel's rejection of David was regarded by the Lord in John 13:18 as also being prophetical of His betrayal by Judas. Clearly, this was another reproach of David identified in Psalm 69, which He as Kinsman Redeemer (*goel*) would experience at first hand. Accordingly, the Lord quotes from Psalm 41:9 and says, "That the Scripture may be fulfilled" (John 13:18).

Psalm 41 presents David as one who experienced rejection by Ahithophel and by so doing is a prophetical picture of the Lord Jesus Who would experience betrayal. Some may argue that in this context David is a poor portrayal of the coming Messiah, because that whole historical episode was marked by David's personal failure, something which placed him in contrast to the Messiah rather in comparison to Him. For example, Ahithophel, some may argue, could have had a reasonable grudge against David because of his treatment of his relative, Bathsheba. Furthermore, David should have been more firm in his handling of Absalom before this. However, a wise man like Ahithophel knew very well about David's place in the Messianic line, and thus to reject David in the manner he did was a direct repudiation of the God Who had promised the coming Messiah. Ahithophel rejected a flawed king, even though, as a man of wisdom, he knew David was the forerunner of the perfect King. In this sense his treachery was prophetic of the knowing treachery which Judas directed at the Lord. The Jewish nation in ignorance rejected Christ. Accordingly, the Lord prayed, "Father, forgive them; for they **know not** what they do" (Luke 23:34). Many obtained this very forgiveness in the early days of the Acts of the Apostles. In contrast, Judas in **full knowledge** rejected Him as did Ahithophel in his rejection of David. Neither found forgiveness. How solemn!

Another New Testament example of rejection in David's life being prophetical of the Lord's rejection while on earth is found in Matthew 12:1-8 where the rejected Lord reminded His hearers of David fleeing from Saul.

Matthew 12:1-4
> 1 "At that time Jesus went on the sabbath day through the corn; and His disciples were an hungred, and began to pluck the ears of corn, and to eat.
> 2 But when the Pharisees saw *it*, they said unto Him, Behold, Thy disciples do that which is not lawful to do upon the sabbath day.
> 3 But He said unto them, **Have ye not read what David did**, when he was an hungred, and they that were with him;
> 4 How he entered into the house of God, and did eat the shewbread, which was not lawful for him to eat, neither for them which were with him, but only for the priests?"

Clearly, this rejection episode in David's life in the matter of Doeg the Edomite (also commented upon in Psalm 52) was taken by the Lord Jesus as being pictorial and indeed prophetical of His rejection by His own nation.

B) The practical aspect of the Psalm (David as a picture of a believer encountering personal failure in life)

As we have noted, the background to Psalm 41 is Ahithophel's betrayal of David. There is a sad lead up to this. It is the matter of Bathsheba, who was Ahithophel's granddaughter. Some have speculated that this could have led Ahithophel to have had a grudge against David. However, this sin in David's life was forgiven. Ahithophel should have continued to be loyal to him because of the One to Whom David was linked. He was linked to the coming Messiah. Ahithophel should have had compassion on David and considered him not for who he was but because of Whose he was, i.e. David belonged to Christ. Accordingly, the Scripture does not recognise any justification or excuse for Ahithophel's actions.

Remarkably, when Psalm 41:9 is quoted in the upper room by the Lord Jesus, the context is not only about His imminent betrayal by the New Testament Ahithophel equivalent, i.e. Judas, it is about the imminent denial by His faithful disciple Peter. Peter was about to deny the Lord Jesus and the Lord makes this clear before it happens. Now the Lord, by reminding the disciples of Psalm 41, is in a timely way drawing their attention to the other great message of that chapter, namely that David is a picture of a flawed, albeit restored believer who still should be accepted by those who love the Lord. In other words, just as David should be accepted because of the One to Whom he was linked, similarly Peter should be accepted when he was restored, because of the One to Whom he was linked, namely the Lord Jesus. This is the other great theme running through Psalm 41, where David is seen not so much as a picture of the rejected Messiah, but as an example of a restored believer, grappling with the consequences of failure who should, nevertheless, be accepted by fellow believers, just as a restored Peter was accepted by the early Apostles. We will encounter the important truth of the restoration of a backslidden believer in this Psalm.

Details of the Psalm in the context of John 13

John 13:16-30 describes the moments when the Lord in the upper room tells the disciples that His betrayal by Judas was imminent.

John 13:16-30
16 "Verily, verily, I say unto you, The servant is not greater than his Lord; neither he that is sent greater than He that sent him.
17 If ye know these things, happy are ye if ye do them.
18 I speak not of you all: I know whom I have chosen: but **that the Scripture may be fulfilled, He that eateth bread with Me hath lifted up his heel against Me.**
19 Now I tell you before it come, that, when it is come to pass, ye may believe that I am *He*.
20 Verily, verily, I say unto you, He that receiveth whomsoever I send receiveth Me; and he that receiveth Me receiveth Him that sent Me.
21 When Jesus had thus said, He was troubled in spirit, and testified, and said, Verily, verily, I say unto you, that one of you shall betray Me.
22 Then the disciples looked one on another, doubting of whom He spake.
23 Now there was leaning on Jesus' bosom one of His disciples, whom Jesus loved.
24 Simon Peter therefore beckoned to him, that he should ask who it should be of whom He spake.
25 He then lying on Jesus' breast saith unto Him, Lord, who is it?
26 Jesus answered, 'He it is, to whom I shall give a sop, when I have dipped *it*'. And when He had dipped the sop, He gave *it* to Judas Iscariot, *the son*

of Simon.

27 And after the sop Satan entered into him. Then said Jesus unto him, That thou doest, do quickly.

28 Now no man at the table knew for what intent He spake this unto him.

29 For some *of them* thought, because Judas had the bag, that Jesus had said unto him, Buy *those things* that we have need of against the feast; or, that he should give something to the poor.

30 He then having received the sop went immediately out: and it was night."

How Psalm 41:9 is a prophecy of the rejection of Christ

When Psalm 41:9 is quoted in John 13:18, the phrase, "that the Scripture may be fulfilled", indicates that the record of the historical episode of Ahithophel's betrayal of David forms a prophecy, which was fulfilled when Judas betrayed the Lord Jesus Christ. If that is the case, then why is it that within the confines of Psalm 41 itself there are no direct references to the coming Messiah? The answer lies in verse 5:

Psalm 41:5

"Mine enemies speak evil of me, When shall he die, and **his name perish**?"

The plot was to end forever the name of David and that would have meant an end to the Messianic promise which was linked with that **name**. This heightens the significance of the anti-David sentiments expressed by his enemies to an anti-Messiah (anti-Christ) plan. This phenomenon is met again in Psalm 69 and will be considered in more detail in that chapter.

The divisions of the Psalm

1 The **principle of** blessedness of the one who considers the poor (Psalm 41:1-3)

2 The **past** experience of David's restoration from sin (Psalm 41:4)

3 The **present** experience of David's rejection by enemies (Psalm 41:5-8) and Ahithophel (Psalm 41:9)

4 The **prospect** of David's vindication (Psalm 41:10-13)

The principle of the blessedness of the one who considers the poor

Psalm 41:1-3

1 "Blessed *is* he that considereth the poor (*dal*): the Lord will deliver him in time of trouble (Hebrew: day of evil (*yom raah*)).

2 The Lord will preserve him, and keep him alive; *and* he shall be blessed upon the earth: and Thou wilt not deliver him unto the will of his enemies.

3 The Lord will strengthen him upon the bed of languishing: Thou wilt make all his bed in his sickness."

This section considers two parties: one who is described as "poor" and another who is described as "the considerer of the poor" (*maschil el dal*). The question for the student of Scripture is to determine the significance of these two designations and whether they can be identified as individuals in Scripture.

The poor (dal)

Psalm 40 ends with David declaring, "I am poor (*ani*) and needy". Although the words translated "poor" in Psalm 40 and Psalm 41:1 are different in Hebrew, the ending of Psalm 40, where David is depicted as one "poor and needy", seems to lead directly into Psalm 41:1, where those who consider the "poor" (one) are seen as those who merit divine blessing and preservation. Since the context of Psalm 41 is the occasion of David being betrayed by Ahithophel, his former counsellor and confidant, it is clear that, at that time, David's considerable material possessions in reality had melted from his grasp, as in total poverty he fled from Jerusalem with hardly enough food to meet his own needs and those of his faithful followers (2 Samuel 15:14). Truly, David fully qualified for the description of "poor" (one). Those who "considered (*maschil*) the poor" were those who saw beyond David's difficult circumstances and continued to love and be loyal to him. Their love to David was unconditional and stood in stark contrast to those who hated him in Psalm 41:7.

We have noted above that David, in times of rejection, bears a prophetic witness to the rejection of the Lord Jesus centuries later, not just by Judas (John 13) but also by His own nation in a general way (Matthew 12). However, the Scriptures show that the rejection of the Lord Jesus did not end on the occasion of His departure from this world and His ascension to God's right hand in heaven. The reproach of Christ is still borne by His own both in this age and in the future tribulation period. In fact, those who considered the poor (David) in Psalm 41 prophetically illustrate those who would consider (*maschil*) the Lord Jesus in a coming day subsequent to His ascension in a period known as "the day of evil (*yom raah*)". When is this time period and how is this possible even after the Lord Jesus has departed this world?

When is the evil day?

The evil day, or literally "the day of evil", has prophetic connotations in other passages. For example, in Jeremiah 51:2 it is the era when Babylon will fall finally. We know from the book of Revelation that the prophecies in the Old Testament regarding the destruction of ancient Babylon (e.g. Jeremiah 51) await complete fulfilment in the destruction of future Babylon in the midst of the great tribulation (Revelation 17:5). We thus discover that those who considered David as the poor man in the time of his rejection and showed him kindness are prophetically pictorial of those who will identify with the suffering Jewish remnant of the tribulation in a coming day, and by showing acts of kindness to them they will win the Lord's approval because "inasmuch as ye have done it unto one of the least of these My brethren, ye have done it unto Me" (Matthew 25:40).

Matthew 25:34-40

34 "Then shall the King say unto them on His right hand, Come, ye blessed of My Father, inherit the Kingdom prepared for you from the foundation of the world:

35 For I was an hungred, and ye gave Me meat: I was thirsty, and ye gave
Me drink: I was a stranger, and ye took Me in:
36 Naked, and ye clothed Me: I was sick, and ye visited Me: I was in prison,
and ye came unto Me.
37 Then shall the righteous answer Him, saying, Lord, when saw we Thee
an hungred, and fed *Thee?* or thirsty, and gave *Thee* drink?
38 When saw we Thee a stranger, and took *Thee* in? or naked, and clothed
Thee?
39 Or when saw we Thee sick, or in prison, and came unto Thee?
40 And the King shall answer and say unto them, **Verily I say unto you,
Inasmuch as ye have done *it* unto one of the least of these My brethren,
ye have done *it* unto Me.**"

In David's day, those who were "considerers of the poor" identified with
the rejected King and gave him and his followers food and sustenance (2
Samuel 17:27-29). In the "day of evil" (*yom raah*), or the coming tribulation,
those who consider the persecuted remnant and show them kindness will
be regarded by the Lord as if they showed this act of kindness **directly** to
Him. This is the teaching of the Lord Jesus in Matthew 25.

For those who remained loyal to David (the poor man) in his hour of
rejection, there was the prospect of deliverance and blessing. This is even
more clearly seen in the future "day of evil" when those who consider the
poor will, by that act, have demonstrated the sincerity and veracity of their
faith in Christ and thus are promised divine protection in the midst of that
dreadful period of time, "the day of evil".

Deliverance in the evil day

Psalm 41:1

"The Lord will deliver him **in time** of trouble."

Notice it is not deliverance **from** the evil day, but deliverance **in** the evil
day. When we remember that this Psalm is a prophecy, these words take on
a special significance.

Psalm 41:2

The Lord will preserve him, and keep him alive;"

This is a promise of preservation in the midst of the evil. The promise to
"keep him alive" does not merely include longevity. Doubtless, the Lord will
preserve some believers in Him through the tribulation. However, many
will be martyred for Christ's sake. For such the promise still stands good,
as the phrase "keep him alive" could be also translated "quicken him", i.e.
raise him from the dead (1 Samuel 2:6). What a prospect for the suffering
and persecuted believers of that dreadful tribulation era!

"*and* he shall be blessed upon the earth:"

For the Old Testament saints who were faithful to David in the time of his
rejection, and for the tribulation saints who are faithful to the rejected Son of

David by showing kindness to the "poor", there awaits an **earthly** Kingdom. Hence the reassuring refrain: "He shall be blessed **upon the earth**." This is in contrast to us in the Church era whose blessings **are heavenly**.

"and Thou wilt not deliver him unto the will (soul) of his enemies."

The attacks of the enemies of the King upon His rejected and persecuted followers will be futile. The evil desires of the enemies of God will be extinguished.

Psalm 41:3
"The Lord will strengthen him upon the bed of languishing: Thou wilt make (turn around) all his bed in his sickness."

In the early Church, there were miracles of healing which carried a special doctrinal significance. These and other miracles are spoken of as the "powers of the age to come" (Hebrews 6:5). It is likely that in the tribulation, miraculous healings of believers in the Lord Jesus Christ will again be seen.

Past restoration from sin

Psalm 41:4
"I said, Lord, be merciful (gracious) unto me: heal my soul; for I have sinned against Thee."

This is a reference to an event in David's past when he sought the Lord's mercy (grace) for sin committed, and he obtained divine forgiveness. In the context of the blessings attending the one who "considers the poor", it is very possible that David's sin in question, for which he now has obtained forgiveness, was in fact an act of not considering the poor. This interpretation is wholly consistent with Nathan's charge against David of abusing a poor man, i.e. Uriah the Hittite, in the matter of Bathsheba (2 Samuel 12:1-14). For this sin David has now experienced full forgiveness by divine grace. Sadly though, not everyone accepted the reality of this forgiveness. Ahithophel, the grandfather of Bathsheba, was one such. In John 13, the Lord indicated in advance of Peter's denial that his restoration would take place (John 13:36). Happily, none of the disciples resented Peter for his denial. They clearly accepted his repentance and restoration in John 21 as genuine, and in the early chapters of the Acts of the Apostles he takes the leading role in proclaiming the risen Christ. Those who considered David as the poor man and felt love towards him did so despite his failures. This is the true *agape* love further expounded by the Lord Jesus in the upper room. It is significant that the Lord should draw the disciples' attention to Psalm 41 in the upper room **at the same time** as He predicted Peter's denial **and restoration** (John 13:36-38). Was this to encourage the other disciples to unreservedly accept Peter after he had been restored to the Lord on the other side of His resurrection from the dead?

Present rejection by enemies and his close friend

Psalm 41:5-9

5 "Mine enemies speak evil of me, When shall he die, and his name perish?
6 And if he come to see *me*, he speaketh vanity: his heart gathereth iniquity to itself; *when* he goeth abroad, he telleth *it*.
7 All that hate me whisper together against me: against me do they devise my hurt.
8 An evil disease, *say they*, cleaveth fast unto him: and *now* that he lieth he shall rise up no more.
9 Yea, mine own familiar friend, in whom I trusted, which did eat of my bread, hath lifted up *his* heel against me."

Alas, even in David's day there were those who hated him. When difficult circumstances crossed the king's pathway, his enemies gloated over his problems. The thoughts of these ill-wishers are displayed for us in the next few verses, and they do not make for encouraging reading! Their central hope was, "When shall he die and his name perish?" (Psalm 41:5). It is not merely the name of David that was the object of their hostility, it is the promise of the coming Messiah which was linked with the name of David which they resented. These men who hated David wished him ill, and when they heard of him being sick they hoped that this would be the end. In fact, they even had the hypocrisy to come to see him, and when they left the bedside of the sick man, they whispered gloatingly to their friends regarding what they hoped were David's unlikely chances of recovery. It is clear that such behaviour is the exact opposite to the lofty standards of Christian living set out by the Lord in the upper room, when we are called upon to love one another. Yes, despite the failures of our fellow believers we should truly love them, not for what they are, but **despite what they are**, not for who they are, but **for Whose they are**. This is certainly included in the meaning of the phrase, "considering the poor", at the beginning of the Psalm.

Chief among those who wished David ill were his former dearest friends. Ahithophel, David's former counsellor, who treacherously turned to support the cause of David's apostate son Absalom (2 Samuel 15:20-23), is undoubtedly referred to in the phrase, "My own familiar friend in whom I trusted, who ate of my bread has lifted up his heel against me". The phrase, "My own familiar friend" (*ish shlomi*), in Hebrew means "the man of my peace (or well-being)". This describes the apparent character of the man who seemed to be bound up in the well-being of David. "In whom I trusted", is a sad refrain telling us of the confidence David once placed in him. "Who ate of my bread", is particularly touching as it suggests the many hours of fellowship which David shared with this man. David's bitter feelings of disappointment at the treachery of Ahithophel are used by the Lord Himself in the upper room (in John 13) to illustrate His own feelings on the occasion of the infinitely greater treachery of Judas Iscariot, who betrayed the Lord. Clearly, He was meditating on this Psalm and its **prophetic aspect** as He sat with the twelve disciples in the upper room.

However, we must learn here a careful lesson from the **practical aspect** of the Psalm. Ahithophel exhibited treachery to David by his betrayal of him in his hour of need despite knowing about the One to Whom David was linked. Similarly, in the prophetical fulfilment of this, Judas showed treachery to the Lord Jesus by betraying Him despite knowing Who He was. The **practical** application to all present day believers is that we should regard all fellow believers not for who they are but for **Whose they are**, and this would lead to us fulfilling the principles expounded by the Lord in the upper room to "love one another". This is the antithesis to treachery and betrayal and should characterise all within the family of God. Anyone claiming to be a believer who nurses a long-term grudge against another believer (even if an underlying wrong has been confessed and forgiven) has violated this principle and should carefully verify to themselves the reality of the faith they profess. In contrast, may we as believers actively seek about showing kindness, and genuinely and unconditionally demonstrating true Christian concern and *agape* love for the well-being of our brethren. Then will we begin to taste afresh the blessedness of which this Psalm speaks.

A further application of the principle of "considering the poor" is seen in how the true believers in David's day regarded him even **despite his failures**. They loved him unconditionally. The Lord's quotation from this Psalm in John 13 was a timely reminder to the disciples to remember to "consider the poor" in the specific context of Peter's impending denial. When the Lord later restored Peter it was to serve Him again. John Mark in the New Testament is another example of a backslider obtaining full restoration to service (see Psalm 45). May we be preserved from negligence in the matter of recognising genuine, spiritual restoration in the backslider. Failure to do so is grieving to the Lord.

Prospect of future vindication

Psalm 41:10
"But Thou, O Lord, be merciful (gracious) unto me, and raise me up, that
I may requite them."

David had already experienced the grace of God in Psalm 41:4 when, by God's grace, his sin of adultery was dealt with by God and pardoned. However, now David needs ongoing divine grace to overcome the consequences of that sin.

The appeal to the Lord to "be merciful" (**gracious**) is a call to the Lord to show **grace** unto His servant in dealing with the consequences of his failure. This prayer was fulfilled, at least partially, in the restoration of the kingdom to David after Absalom's rebellion. This is clearly shown in 2 Samuel 15:25 where David tells us what he meant by asking the Lord to show him "**grace**".

2 Samuel 15:25
"And the king said unto Zadok, Carry back the ark of God into the city: if

I shall find favour (**grace** *chen*) in the eyes of the Lord, He will bring me again, and shew me *both* it, and **His habitation.**"

Psalm 41:10 tells us of David's prayer for this "**grace**" to be his. 2 Samuel 15 brings us the historical answer to this prayer when David received the grace of restoration to the habitation of the Lord (the tabernacle). Surely it is **grace** when one, under the disciplinary hand of God, **makes his way back** to the habitation of the Lord!

Psalm 41:11

"By this I know that Thou favourest me (hast pleasure (*chaphetz*) in me), because mine enemy doth not triumph over me."

As David fled from Absalom, he indicated that he would know if the Lord had no pleasure (*chaphetz*) towards him if he was not allowed back into the city and the habitation of the Lord. His attitude was not one of objection but rather of casting himself wholly upon the Lord to do "as seemeth good unto Him" (2 Samuel 15:26). David was a broken man and very accepting of the Lord's hand upon him in this dark experience of his life. There was no murmur of complaint from his lips. Although he was fully forgiven for the Bathsheba incident, the events surrounding the Absalom rebellion and Ahithophel's betrayal can be seen as a consequence of the sad Bathsheba story. Doubtless, David understood this bitter fact. The lesson for us today is really solemn. Sins can be fully forgiven and the believer restored but consequences can still come back to hurt even the restored believer and others. There is but one course of action for such a restored saint of God grappling with the consequences of previous failures in life. It is to say simply as did David:

2 Samuel 15:26

"If He thus say, I have no delight in thee (*chaphetz*); behold, *here am* I, let Him do to me as seemeth good unto Him".

The Psalm ends with David being viewed as God sees him; not as men see him. This is seen in Psalm 41:12-13.

Psalm 41:12-13

12 "And as for me, Thou upholdest me in mine integrity, and settest me before Thy face for ever.
13 Blessed *be* the Lord God of Israel from everlasting, and to everlasting. Amen, and Amen."

What a contrast with the opinions of men expressed earlier on in the Psalm, where David's failure is the subject of their occupation! David tells the Lord: "Thou upholdest me in mine integrity (my perfection)". David was not sinlessly perfect. He knew this all too painfully. However, in Psalm 41:12 he is being seen as one justified by God, i.e. as one who has obtained divine "grace". As far as God is concerned, David's sin is dealt with. Divine forgiveness is complete. On the basis of this, God can set him "before His face forever". What a welcome awaits the backslidden believer who is restored to the Lord again!

If in Psalm 40 we learn of the Lord Jesus' high priestly ministry towards us, in Psalm 41 we learn of how He actively preserves us and restores us to Himself. Psalm 41 illustrates this principle in the experiences of the restoration of David in the Old Testament. Moreover, its quotation by the Lord Jesus in John 13 in the context of Peter's impending denial and restoration emphasises this further. John further develops this ministry regarding the restoration of the backsliding believer in 1 John 2:1 as he speaks of the Lord Jesus as our "Advocate with the Father, Jesus Christ the Righteous" (1 John 2:1). David's restoration brought him back to the "habitation of the Lord", and this is the objective of the ministry of our "Advocate with the Father" that our lives should be characterised by "abiding in Him" (1 John 1-2).

In summary, the weight of teaching in Psalm 41 addresses the restoration of David after his failures, and challenges us with **practical implications** in restoration of backsliding believers today. The challenge is not just to the backslider who is being restored, but also to fellow believers who may be involved in that restoration. The New Testament application of this is illustrated in the denial and restoration of Peter and his acceptance by his fellow apostles thereafter. Less prominent, but no less important, are the **prophetical** aspects of the Psalm. On a **negative** note, David's rejection by Ahithophel is **prophetic** of Judas' betrayal of the Lord Jesus. Moreover, on a **positive** note, those who publicly identified with the "poor man", i.e. David the rejected king, are **prophetic** of those who, in a coming period known as "the evil day" (i.e. the tribulation), will identify with Christ the rejected King through identifying with suffering tribulation saints. Accordingly, to any who do identify with these suffering believers the Lord will say, "Verily I say unto you, Inasmuch as ye have done it unto one of the least of these My brethren, ye have done it unto Me" (Matthew 25:40) .

This Psalm brings to us the contrasts of treacherous betrayal on the one hand, and on the other hand the faithful steadfastness of those who, in loving their suffering fellow believers, are doing it unto the Lord. It is the Lord Who reads the hearts and motives. He has pledged "blessedness" to the one who considers "the poor". May **such sensitivity** characterise believers in this era so that this "blessedness" can be claimed in all our gatherings and lead to enlargement of our coasts in His service.

How fitting then that this Psalm which expresses such spiritual aspirations should end with : "Amen and Amen!"

9

PSALM 45

To the chief Musician upon Shoshannim, for the sons of Korah, Maschil, A Song of loves.

1 My heart is inditing a good matter: I speak of the things which I have made touching the King: my tongue is the pen of a ready writer.

2 Thou art fairer than the children of men: grace is poured into Thy lips: therefore God hath blessed Thee for ever.

3 Gird Thy sword upon Thy thigh, O most Mighty, with Thy glory and Thy majesty.

4 And in Thy majesty ride prosperously because of truth and meekness and righteousness; and Thy right hand shall teach Thee terrible things.

5 Thine arrows are sharp in the heart of the King's enemies; whereby the people fall under Thee.

6 Thy throne, O God, is for ever and ever: the sceptre of Thy Kingdom is a right sceptre.

7 Thou lovest righteousness, and hatest wickedness: therefore God, Thy God, hath anointed Thee with the oil of gladness above Thy fellows.

8 All Thy garments smell of myrrh, and aloes, and cassia, out of the ivory palaces, whereby they have made Thee glad.

9 Kings' daughters were among Thy honourable women: upon Thy right hand did stand the Queen in gold of Ophir.

10 Hearken, O daughter, and consider, and incline thine ear; forget also thine own people, and thy father's house;

11 So shall the King greatly desire thy beauty: for He is thy Lord; and worship thou Him.

12 And the daughter of Tyre shall be there with a gift; even the rich among the people shall intreat thy favour.

13 The King's daughter is all glorious within: her clothing is of wrought gold.

14 She shall be brought unto the King in raiment of needlework: the virgins her companions that follow her shall be brought unto Thee.

15 With gladness and rejoicing shall they be brought: they shall enter into the King's palace.

16 Instead of Thy fathers shall be Thy children, whom Thou mayest make princes in all the earth.

17 I will make Thy Name to be remembered in all generations: therefore shall the people praise Thee for ever and ever.

Introduction

This Psalm is undoubtedly a Messianic Psalm as Psalm 45:6-7 is quoted in Hebrews 1:8-9 as follows:

Hebrews 1:8-9

8 "But unto the Son *He saith*, Thy throne, O God, *is* for ever and ever: a sceptre of righteousness *is* the sceptre of Thy Kingdom.
9 Thou hast loved righteousness, and hated iniquity; therefore God, *even* Thy God, hath anointed Thee with the oil of gladness above Thy fellows."

Here the Hebrews writer confirms to us that in Psalm 45:6-7, it is the Father Who is the Speaker as He addresses His Son on the occasion of His coming back to set up His Kingdom and reign. As will be discussed in detail in Psalms 94 and 95, the background to the Hebrews epistle is disquiet in the heart of New Testament Hebrew believers at an apparent delay in Old Testament promises of the coming Kingdom of Christ on earth being literally fulfilled. This citation in Hebrews 1 of Psalm 45:6-7 is directly relevant to this spiritual need of these early Hebrew believers. In particular, the restatement in Hebrews 1 from Psalm 45 of the Lord reigning in glory with His Bride (the Church) by His side powerfully demolished any idea that the introduction of Church teaching in the New Testament era should abrogate the promises of a literal future earthly Kingdom.

Psalm 45 is dedicated to "the sons of Korah". Let us recall the historical background of these men. Some of the events of the wilderness story of the nation of Israel were prophetic of God's future dealings with them. For example, the smiting of the rock at Massah and Meribah (Exodus 17 and Numbers 20) was prophetic of the rejection by the nation of the Lord Jesus during the time of His first advent (see Psalm 95). In Numbers 14, the rejection at Kadesh of the signs and wonders in Egypt and the wilderness (Numbers 14:22) is pictorial of the rejection by the nation of the offers of divine blessing in the Acts of the Apostles, which were backed up with "signs and wonders and divers miracles" (Hebrews 2:4) (see Psalm 95). However, the apostasy of Korah, Dathan and Abiram in Numbers 16 provides us with a prophetic cameo of the future great apostasy of the nation, when they will accept the religious leadership of a false messiah, the false prophet, otherwise known as the wicked (lawless) one. This man will engage in false worship of the man of sin in the temple in Jerusalem (see Appendix 2). In other words, he will set up and engage in a counterfeit worship system in Jerusalem. In Numbers, when Moses called on the people to get away from the **tabernacle of Korah** (Numbers 16:24,27), this would suggest to us that Korah and his associates had set up a completely counterfeit **tabernacle worship** system with a tabernacle and a **congregation, known as** "the congregation of Korah" (Numbers 16:16).

Despite being joined to the apostate leaders by family relationship, there was a minority, a remnant, from the very family of Korah, who separated themselves from Korah's apostate worship system and identified themselves publicly and courageously with the true worship of Jehovah. These men and their descendants in a special way won divine approval and affection and are thereafter known as "the sons of Korah". Theirs was a privileged role in tabernacle and temple worship in recognition of the courageous stand of their forefathers who stood firmly for the truth in the context of a landslide-apostasy.

It appears, therefore, that Korah and his associates have become a picture of the future false prophet and his evil, false worship in the temple in Jerusalem. Moreover, Korah went alive into the pit (Numbers 16:33) so his end is similar to that of the beast and the false prophet who will be cast into the lake of fire (Revelation 19:20). We now can easily see that the sons of Korah are pictorial of a future remnant of faithful Jewish believers who will separate themselves from their kinsmen who have adopted the apostate temple worship system led by the beast and the false prophet. The Psalms dedicated to the sons of Korah will be special Hebrew hymns suitable for Jewish and non-Jewish tribulation believers.

In Psalm 2, we read the warning to the kings in that coming day: "Be wise now therefore O ye kings". The word "wise" is the same root word as *maschil*, meaning "giving instruction". No doubt these tribulation saints will be pleading with others to "be wise" and accept their Messiah even in face of the overwhelming deception of tribulation days. They will be motivated by intense love of their Lord. Psalm 45 is a hymn of loving praise extolling the wonders and beauties of the Messiah, our Lord Jesus.

A detailed consideration of the Psalm

There are allusions in Psalm 45 to how the Lord Jesus will be presented in the Gospels as King, Perfect Servant, Perfect Man and Son of God.

John's Gospel

Psalm 45:1

"My heart is inditing a good matter (*davar*)."

The word for matter (*davar*) is often translated "word". "Inditing" means "bubbling up". Here we have a spontaneous occupation of the heart with "a good word". We are reminded of the statement of our Lord: "None is good save One that is God" (Luke 18:19). The Psalmist is indeed, as we will shortly see, occupying himself with a divine Person: "Thy throne O God is for ever and ever" (Psalm 45:6). In the "Good Matter" or the "Good Word", we have John's presentation of our Lord Jesus in his Gospel – "The Word was with God and the Word was God" (John 1:1).

Matthew's Gospel

Psalm 45:1

"I speak of the things which I have made touching the King:" .

This may well be an allusion to Matthew's presentation of the Messiah as the King. How the tribulation believers will long for the revelation of the King in His glory! It will mean the end of all their sufferings and spell glory for them.

Mark's Gospel

Psalm 45:1

"My tongue *is* the pen of a ready writer (a swift scribe)."

In Mark's Gospel, the Gospel of the Perfect Servant, we meet the words "anon" and "immediately" repeatedly. This Servant was not tardy in His duties. Mark, the gospel writer, (scribe) was once a failing and unreliable servant who turned back when Paul had directed his ministry to Gentile Asia (Acts 15:38). However, he became "profitable to the ministry" (2 Timothy 4:11) and was taken up by the Spirit of God to tell us of the Perfect Servant Who was never late for His Father that appointed Him. The swift scribe may remind us of the restored scribe, Mark, and his presentation of the Perfect Servant, Who so often acted "immediately" (Mark 1:12; 2:8; 5:30 etc.) and "anon" (Mark 1:30).

Luke's Gospel

Psalm 45:2

"Thou art fairer than the children of men: grace is poured into Thy lips: therefore God hath blessed Thee for ever."

Would this verse remind us of Luke's presentation of Christ as the Perfect Man? We discover in the Psalm that He was fairer than the children of men. How do we understand this verse in light of Isaiah 53, "He hath no form nor comeliness (*hadar*)" (Isaiah 53:2)? We have already met this word in our meditations in Psalm 8. We noted there that the word translated "comeliness" (*hadar*) in Isaiah 53 does not refer to His beauty as our modern understanding of "comeliness" might imply. The word *hadar* means "outward splendour". This shows us that it is an incorrect understanding of Isaiah 53 to infer that our Lord Jesus Christ was not beautiful to look upon. Isaiah is simply telling us that prior to His death He was not characterised by outward splendour. Isaiah goes on to say why: "He hid as it were His face from us" (Isaiah 53:3). The Lord Jesus had veiled His outward splendour (*hadar*). When He returns this will not be veiled. Repeatedly, we find this word (*hadar*) used to describe His glory on the other side of resurrection (see later in this Psalm and in Psalm 110).

The verb, *yaphyaphita*, translated as "Thou art fairer", is from a root word meaning "to be fair or beautiful". Davidson points out that in the particular grammatical form used here it means "to be very beautiful" (Davidson Analytical Hebrew and Chaldee Lexicon: page 435). Interestingly, this form of the verb occurs nowhere else in the Bible. We can conclude that our Lord Jesus was exceedingly beautiful and none can compare with Him.

Commensurate with His resplendent beauty were His words of grace. The phrase, "grace is poured into Thy lips", was fulfilled in Luke chapter 4 when the people in the synagogue marvelled at "gracious words which proceeded out of His mouth" (Luke 4:22). It was truly grace as they watched Him close the scroll after reading and proclaiming from Isaiah 61:1-2 the commencement of the year of Jubilee. To have read on would have instituted "the day of vengeance of our God". However, by closing the scroll He indicated that He had come to save, not to judge. What grace! One might have expected this to have been met with appreciation by His audience that day, but the Lord began to show that this grace would not find general acceptance in Israel. However, despite this, His divine grace would reach out to Gentiles, as illustrated by the blessing in the Old Testament which was received by Naaman the Syrian (2 Kings 5) and the widow of Sarepta through the ministry of Elias (Elijah) and Eliseus (Elisha) the prophets (Luke 4:25-27).

Luke 4:25-27
> 25 "But I tell you of a truth, many widows were in Israel in the days of Elias, when the heaven was shut up three years and six months, when great famine was throughout all the land;
> 26 But unto none of them was Elias sent, save unto Sarepta, *a city* of Sidon, unto a woman *that was* a widow.
> 27 And many lepers were in Israel in the time of Eliseus the prophet; and none of them was cleansed, saving Naaman the Syrian."

We discover from Luke that the grace which was "poured into (or in) His lips" was indiscriminate in its scope. It reached out to Gentiles especially in this day of grace, even despite a generalised apathy to Him on the part of His own nation. "Therefore God hath blessed Thee forever" (Psalm 45:2). We will soon discover that the Bride is the fulfilment of this blessing upon the Lord Jesus. The blessing from His God is "forever", reminding us of the indissoluble bond of marriage. We see grace and blessing linked together in the story of Ruth and Boaz. Ruth said to Boaz, "Why have I found **grace** in thine eyes?" (Ruth 2:10). Here we find a Gentile, Moabitess damsel finding grace in the eyes of Boaz – the unlimited kindness and love of Boaz. In response to this, Naomi said, "Blessed be he (Boaz) of the Lord" (Ruth 2:20). This is but a picture of the blessing of the Father to His Son, in presenting to Him His Bride, the Church. Ephesians tells us of the grace of God reaching out to Gentiles (Ephesians 3:1-6) and of the Bride of Christ (Ephesians 5:22-33).

The preparations for the wedding feast celebrations
Before the celebrations of the wedding can publicly take place and the guests be invited, the enemies of the King must be destroyed and the ground cleared for the safe enjoyment of the wedding feast.

Psalm 45:3
"Gird Thy sword upon *Thy* thigh,"

When David prepared Himself to attack Nabal he girded on his sword. Interestingly, this sequence of events led to his marriage to Abigail.

1 Samuel 25:13
"And David said unto his men, Gird ye on every man his sword. And they girded on every man his sword; and David also girded on his sword: and there went up after David about four hundred men; and two hundred abode by the stuff."

This phrase, "Gird Thy sword upon Thy thigh", is a call to the Lord from the sons of Korah, the tribulation saints, to prepare the way for the wedding feast – the millennial Kingdom. It is an "imprecatory prayer", i.e. a prayer of judgment on the enemies of the Lord. Interestingly, in this Church era imprecatory prayers are not fitting. In this unique Church era the servants of God pray for the repentance, salvation and spiritual blessing of their enemies and the enemies of the Lord.

Psalm 45:3
"O *most* Mighty (Man) (*gibbor*),"

It was a lovely Man of grace Who proclaimed the year of Jubilee and taught the people in the synagogue that He would bring the Gentiles into blessing. Now that the context has changed to the subject of judgment, the Lord is referred to as *gibbor* or "Mighty Man".

The Hebrew word *gibbor* reminds us of the humanity of the Lord Jesus. It was used of Boaz, the "mighty man of wealth" (*ish gibbor chayil*) (Ruth 2:1). It is worth reminding ourselves that the "Man" Who revealed the grace of God to an unbelieving world in the synagogue in Nazareth is the "Mighty Man" Who reveals the truth and righteousness of God to an unbelieving world by wielding the sword of judgment. What is the nature of this sword? The next phrase will tell us.

Psalm 45:3
"with Thy glory and Thy majesty (*hadar*)."

The word "with" should be in italics. The verse could read like this, "Gird Thy sword upon Thy thigh ... even, Thy glory and Thy Majesty". The sword which the Lord wields is, in fact, His glory and His majesty. Prior to His resurrection, the Lord had not wielded the sword of His majesty or splendour (*hadar*), as we saw in Isaiah 53:3. This was because His majesty (*hadar*) was hidden from men. Accordingly, we read in the New Testament, that "He hid himself" (John 8:59). This was not because of fear of men. On the contrary, this was a veiling of His glory in grace lest men be consumed by it. What a contrast we see in His second advent when His *hadar* is unveiled to the extent that it has become a weapon of destruction against His enemies!

In the same context, in Psalm 68:2 we read, "Let the wicked perish at the presence of God". They will be consumed by the brightness of His coming (*parousia*) (see Psalm 68). His unveiled *splendour* and glory will spell destruction to all His enemies.

Psalm 45:4

"And in Thy majesty ride prosperously."

This could be translated, "And, Thy Majesty, ride! Prosper! …"
This is a title of the King –"Thy Majesty!" What a lovely title this is! In modern English we address a monarch, as "Your majesty". In the same way, the respectful title, "Thy Majesty", is used to address the Lord Jesus Christ.

Psalm 45:4

"…because of "the Word of truth and meekness *and* righteousness;"

As He wields the sword, there are two enemies who will be special targets for His judgment. The first is the false (*pseudo*) prophet (Revelation 16:13; 19:20), also known as the "wicked (lawless) one" (2 Thessalonians 2:8), who perpetuates the lie (*pseudos*), and the second is the man of sin who is characterised by evil (2 Thessalonians 2:3). The lie of the false prophet cannot prevail before the "**Word of truth**", nor can the evil of the man of sin stand before the "**righteousness**" of this King. His campaign is guaranteed success. A detailed discussion on the differing identities of "the man of sin" and the "wicked (lawless) one" of 2 Thessalonians 2 is considered in Appendix 2.

His judgments are appropriate and measured

Psalm 45:4

"….and Thy right hand shall teach (*tor-cha*) Thee terrible things."

The word "to teach" used here (*tor-*) is from the root *yarah* from which we get the word for the law (*torah*). The terrible things which He will do in judgment shall be consistent with the teachings (*torah*) of "Thy right hand". The right hand of the Lawgiver is now executing the penalty of a broken Law.

The judgment will be meted out with pin-point precision upon all those who merit it. No one will suffer by mistake, in contrast with what happens so often in modern warfare. This judgment is appropriate and none will escape who deserve it. This is described for us under the picture of arrows hitting their target with instant destructive effect.

Psalm 45:5

"Thine arrows are sharp in the heart of the King's enemies; whereby the people fall under Thee."

The arrows target the "heart" (singular) of the King's enemies. This indicates to us that all the enemies of the Lord will have united as in one heart. Even today, members of the United Nations seldom agree. In that day, former enemies will agree to set aside their differences and unite in their enmity to the Messiah.

At this point, the noise and atmosphere of battle clear away to a peaceful silence. The Kinsman Redeemer, Who came to save in verses 1- 2 and Who has now completed His work as Kinsman Avenger in 3-6, is now found seated on the throne, His work of avenging the adversary having been completed. Now in unopposed glory He wields the sceptre of authority over this world. The One, Who in perfect manhood at His first advent is described as "fairer than the children of men" and Who at His second advent is seen as "the Mighty Man" of conquest, bearing the title "Thy Majesty", is now addressed as "O God". It is a principle of Scripture that every passage which considers the manhood of Christ **always** affirms His deity. This passage is no different. Accordingly, He is addressed as follows:

Psalm 45:6
"Thy throne, O God, *is* for ever and ever: the sceptre of Thy Kingdom *is* a right sceptre."

The sceptre He bears is a righteous sceptre. Righteousness marks His Kingdom and all those who are subjects in it. However, it is because of His love for righteousness that God has anointed Him as the Bridegroom King.

The approval by the Father of His Son
In this section, the wedding feast begins by a public declaration by the Father of His total and incomparable approval of His Son. In the past, God has approved of actions of His servants but never in such an unqualified way as happens here.

The reason for His approval is given so clearly:

Psalm 45:7
"Thou lovest righteousness, and hatest wickedness:"

It is good to understand this in a twofold way, firstly in grace (His first advent in verses 1-2) and secondly in judgment (His second advent in verses 3-6).

In His first advent it was His love of righteousness which led Him to Calvary to die. Nowhere is the righteous mercy of Christ more evident than at His death. This righteousness of Christ in mercy was demonstrated on the occasion of His baptism by John the Baptist. When John remonstrated with Him that he had more need to be baptized by Christ than vice versa, the divine response was, "Thus it becometh Us to fulfill all righteousness" (Matthew 3:15). In other words, since John's baptism was a symbol of the death, which those who underwent this ritual acknowledged that they deserved, it seemed to John inappropriate that the only One Who deserved to live should be baptized by him. The Lord's response, "Thus it becometh Us to fulfill all righteousness", indicated that only through His death (of which His baptism was but a symbol) could all righteousness be fulfilled. So just as at His baptism, when the actions of the Trinity were seen, similarly at His death, of which His baptism was a picture, the actions of the Father, Son and Holy Spirit are seen when "He (Christ) through the Eternal Spirit offered Himself without spot to God" (Hebrews 9:14). Now we understand the divine "Us" when He said to John, "Thus it becometh Us to fulfill all righteousness". Lest there be any misunderstanding as to the significance of the Lord's baptism, God opened the heavens to indicate that this symbolic death was not suggesting that there was anything worthy of death found in Christ, but that rather "This is My Beloved Son, in Whom I am well pleased" (Matthew 3:17). In other words, His death, of which His baptism was but a symbol, was not for any sin on His part. It must therefore be a vicarious death fulfilling all righteousness and providing a righteous means of access to God. Accordingly, God's love of righteousness and hatred of wickedness are primarily seen at Calvary when He provided the righteous means of reconciling men to God.

In His second advent, it is His love of righteousness which is demonstrated in His righteous judgment. This is seen in Psalm 45, when He girds His sword in preparation for judgment and delivers arrows of divine precision destroying only those who oppose Him. Only those who merit the judgment receive it, and none who merit His judgment will escape it. This is because He loves righteousness and hates iniquity.

In summary then, it is His love of righteousness and hatred of iniquity which bring us salvation through His intervention as our Kinsman Redeemer (Luke 4:18-19). Solemnly, in a coming day as Kinsman Avenger (Luke 18:3; 21:22) He will bring in judgment. The Father approves of His Son in both roles and publicly shows this at the marriage feast in the anointing oil!

The Person Who does the anointing

Psalm 45:7

"…..therefore God, Thy God, hath anointed Thee with the oil of gladness above Thy fellows."

It is God Who anoints His Son. However, **the anointing for His burial** was done by Mary (John 12:3) in the home in Bethany. She did this out of appreciation for His raising Lazarus from the dead. The woman in Luke 7:38 "rained tears upon His feet". Note that in Luke 7:38 the literal translation for "wash His feet with tears" is to "rain tears upon His feet", indicating that His feet had no defilement to require the verb "to wash". He was the Holy Son of God, "God manifest in flesh". The woman then wiped His feet with her hair, kissed them and then **anointed them** in appreciation of receiving His forgiveness. The **anointing by God** of the Bridegroom King is also in appreciation of Him – His upholding of righteousness both in mercy (words of grace) and in judgment (ridding the world of rebellion). It is lovely for us to consider just how much the Father appreciates the Son for His grace in righteously saving us, as well as for His righteousness in judging the world.

This passage is another powerful proof of the distinct personalities of the Father and the Son within the Godhead. Here we see God's thoughts of Christ, and Christ's joy in response.

The purpose of the anointing "with the oil of gladness above Thy fellows"

The purpose of the anointing was for the Father to publicly show His pleasure and approval for His Son. The oil of gladness reflects the Father's joy in His Son and we will see how this knowledge of the Father's pleasure in Him rejoices the heart of the Son because it was the oil-saturated garments "out of the ivory palaces" which "have made Thee glad" (verse 8).

The peerlessness of the One anointed "above Thy friends"

The joy attending His anointing with oil of gladness will exceed that of His fellows (Hebrew for "fellows" is literally "friends"). Who are the "friends" and what is the subject of the "gladness"?

In any wedding feast there are two groups of guests. The bridegroom has his friends and the bride, similarly, has her companions. We will firstly try to identify the "friends of the Bridegroom", and later in our Psalm we will discover who are the "companions of the Bride", described as "virgins".

In John 3, we read more about the friends of the Bridegroom (John 3:29) and learn that they are Old Testament believers. They cannot be the friends of the Bride as they never knew the Bride, who was a mystery hidden in God's heart during the entire Old Testament period. However, John the Baptist places himself in this illustrious group of friends of the Bridegroom:

John 3:29
> "He that hath the Bride is the Bridegroom: but the friend of the Bridegroom, which standeth and heareth Him, rejoiceth greatly because of the Bridegroom's voice: this my joy therefore is fulfilled."

Clearly, the reason why the Bridegroom has the oil of gladness above His friends is because "He that hath the Bride is the Bridegroom". His friends may rejoice greatly, as does John the Baptist, but the joy of the Bridegroom is even greater. How is this? It is because to Him is given His wife, the Bride of Christ, the fruit of Calvary. As the Father looks upon the Son with His Bride by His side, the Father shows His approval of His Son, the Bridegroom King, by an anointing which is unique. Upon no other person has such an honour ever been bestowed.

The constituent parts of the oil of gladness

Psalm 45:8
> "All Thy garments *smell* of myrrh, and aloes, *and* cassia, out of the ivory palaces, whereby they have made Thee glad."

The oil of gladness is described for us in the next verse. It contains myrrh, aloes and cassia. Myrrh was bitter to taste (it comes from the root word *mar*, meaning bitter) but was sweet to smell (compare "His lips like lilies dropping **sweet smelling** myrrh" (Song of Songs 5:13)).

Myrrh was linked with His incarnation, i.e. **His coming into this world**: the wise men brought Him gold, frankincense and myrrh (Matthew 2:11). The bitterness lay in His being given the outside place and the sweetness in the appreciation which the Gentile visitors gave Him.

Myrrh was linked with His death, i.e. **His leaving this world**. The bitterness in His dying lay in the mockery which led the soldiers to give Him the wine mingled with myrrh (Mark 15:23). The sweetness is the fact that He refused this beverage lest it dull His pain. This is because the pain and suffering were for our sins and to us this is sweet.

Myrrh was linked with His burial.

John 19:39
"A mixture of myrrh and aloes an hundred pound weight."

The bitterness lay in the sorrow of those who mourned His death. The sweetness is appreciated in that the grave clothes were set aside in resurrection showing His triumph over death.

The **cassia** tells us of compensatory joy. The birth of Job's daughter Kezia (Cassia), (Job 42:14), was to compensate him for the losses and sorrows earlier in his life.

In other words, the myrrh tells us of the sufferings of Christ, whereas the cassia speaks of the glory that should follow. In between we have the aloes.

The **aloes** speak of desire and attractiveness. This is used in a bad sense as well as a good sense. The seductive woman of Proverbs decks her bed with aloes to describe an evil form of attraction (Proverbs 7:17). In contrast, the bride of the Song of Solomon has aloes in her garden, depicting genuine and pure attractiveness to the bridegroom (Song of Songs 4:14). The aloes in the "oil of gladness", described between the myrrh of suffering and the cassia of compensatory glory, tell us simply of the beauty and attractiveness of the One Who suffered and is now glorified. In a coming day in His presence as we witness this event, we will surely exclaim that He is "altogether lovely".

This oil of gladness, with these highly instructive ingredients, is poured upon Him by His Father as a public demonstration of the Father's approval of Him both in His love of righteousness and His hatred of iniquity. This we are told "makes Him glad". In the phrase, "whereby (Hebrew *minni*) they have made Thee glad", the word "they" refers to the garments saturated with the anointing oil. Note 1 This shows us beautifully that the approval of the Father of His finished work at Calvary brings Him joy and gladness. As the Lord Jesus enters into the Father's thoughts of Himself, His heart is rejoiced.

This section of the Psalm is very important as it shows us the thoughts of the Father towards Him and emphasizes that this is centred on His sufferings (the myrrh), the glories that should follow (cassia) and His attractiveness (the aloes).

The more we enter into God's thoughts of Christ (see Psalm 24), the more we can engage in worship. Shortly in the Psalm we will see the Bride being exhorted to worship: "He is thy Lord and worship thou Him" (verse 11). It is worth noticing that it is **after** she has entered into God's thoughts of Him that she is called upon to worship Him.

The quotation of these verses in Hebrews 1:8-9 reminds us that the teaching on worship in Psalm 45, written three thousand years ago, is not remote or irrelevant, but constitutes timeless and vital teaching for all New Testament believers today. May we seek grace to enter into God's thoughts of Christ so as to be able to worship in His presence. Then it could be said of each believer: "My heart is inditing a good matter".

The place of the anointing

The anointing is in the ivory palaces, from which He emerges wearing His garments saturated with the oil of gladness. This cannot refer to the first advent of the Lord Jesus Who walked this earth as "the Man of sorrows". It must refer to His second coming when He comes out from the ivory palaces (i.e. the heavenly abiding places) to rid this world of rebellion and institute the marriage supper of the Lamb (the millennium).

Psalm 45:9

"Kings' daughters *were* among Thy honourable women:"

These "honourable (precious) women" are distinct from "the Bride", "the Queen". They are mentioned before the Bride is introduced and are part of the group who are referred to as the friends of the Bridegroom. However, they are singled out for special mention. They are particularly precious to the King. To determine the spiritual significance of "the honourable (precious) women" it is helpful to consider Proverbs 2 where wisdom is depicted as a woman "more precious (honourable) than rubies" (Proverbs 2:15). In Proverbs 9:10, we discover that the fear of the Lord is the beginning of wisdom. The lesson here is that nearness to the Lord is the fear of the Lord and that holy dread of grieving Him. The word "among" is most instructive. One might have expected that only Kings' daughters (princesses or titled ladies) would have been close to the King. However, the passage does not say, "Kings' daughters *were* Thy honourable women". This situation would pertain in most royal courts on earth. However, it is different here! It says "Kings' daughters *were* **among** Thy honourable women". This teaches us that preciousness and nearness to the Person of Christ is not determined by natural birth. Clearly, there are honourable or "precious" women who were near to the Lord who never were of noble birth. The presence of noble women in this group indicates that although not many mighty are called (1 Corinthians 1:26), it is untrue to say that "not **any** mighty are called". These women of noble birth find themselves in the group of those who are near to the King, lest those of lower estate in this world should despise believers who are of high estate in society. Similarly, the presence of those "among the honourable women" who are of low estate teaches those believers who happen to be of high estate in society not to despise their poorer brethren and sisters in Christ.

Psalm 45:9-11

9 "....upon Thy right hand did stand the Queen in gold of Ophir.
10 Hearken, O daughter, and consider (behold), and incline thine ear; forget also thine own people, and thy father's house;
11 So shall the King greatly desire thy beauty: for He *is* thy Lord; and worship thou Him."

We now meet the Bride, "the Queen". In this Psalm, the sons of Korah must have watched with intelligent interest the word of ministry directed towards the Bride. She is exhorted to hear, behold and incline (stretch out) her ear, i.e. listen intently, to her Lord. The object of the ministry is to lead her to worship her Lord. The sons of Korah distinguished themselves by acting contrary to the ties of nature by separating themselves from the apostate religious system of their father Korah. Now, those illustrious sons of Korah watch as the Bride is similarly called upon to separate herself from her own people and her father's house. Every bridegroom is jealous of his wife's emotions. The more she listens to Christ, looks upon Him and then intently listens to Him, the more she will become detached from the natural ties which bind her to this world. Her affections and loyalties will be exclusively for her heavenly Bridegroom. This heavenly occupation has two effects upon her. She will own Him as her Lord and worship Him (verse 11). We get a little picture of this in Genesis 24 in the moving story of Rebekah's first sight of Isaac her bridegroom.

Genesis 24:63-67

63 "And Isaac went out to meditate in the field at the eventide: and he lifted up his eyes, and saw, and, behold, the camels *were* coming.
64 And Rebekah lifted up her eyes, and when she saw Isaac, **she lighted off the camel**.
65 For she *had* said unto the servant, What man *is* this that walketh in the field to meet us? And the servant *had* said, It *is* my master: therefore she took a vail, and covered herself.
66 And the servant told Isaac all things that he had done.
67 And Isaac brought her into his mother Sarah's tent, and took Rebekah, and she became his wife; and he loved her: and Isaac was comforted after his mother's *death*."

When Rebekah got that first sight of Isaac, she "lighted off the camel". The Hebrew word "lighted off" means that she "fell off" (*naphal*). This shows us that her response was to fall before Isaac, such was the sight which met her eyes. Genesis 24:65-66 are in parenthesis but verse 67 follows on directly from verse 64 and tells us what happened as Rebekah fell off the camel. The Bible does not say that Isaac lifted her up nor is there any indication that she fell to the ground. All we are told is that she fell from the camel and Isaac brought her in. The description given is consistent with Rebekah falling off the camel into the strong and welcoming arms of Isaac who then brought her in.

Worship is being prostrate in His presence. The word is several times translated to bow oneself to the ground, and it happens out of a holy awe and appreciation at the wonder of Christ. However, as we discover in Genesis 22:5, when Abraham said, "I and the lad will go yonder and worship", the high point of that worship is entering into God's thoughts of Christ. When Abraham says, "God will provide Himself a Lamb for a burnt offering" (Genesis 22:8), the verb "to provide" can also be translated, "God will see for Himself the Lamb for the burnt offering". In other words, as Abraham ascended the mountain in worship that day he was entering into God's thoughts of the Lamb. In this Psalm, the Bride is encouraged to hear, look and listen intently. This will lead her to intelligent worship. This will help her to enter into God's thoughts of Christ. In fact, if she listens to God giving His public approval of Him in the oil of gladness, she will be enabled to focus on the beauties of His first advent and worship Him Who is fragrant in myrrh as she thinks of all the bitterness He once endured and all the sweetness which has emerged from His sufferings. As she learns of the cassia within that oil of divine gladness, she will grasp just a little of the joy of God in the compensatory glories which are now Christ's and publicly manifested at His second advent. This will draw out the Bride in further spontaneous worship. However, as she learns of the aloes in that anointing oil and thinks of the attractiveness and loveliness which the Father sees in Him, she will exclaim, "Yea He is altogether lovely".

The sight of the Bride enthralled with Her heavenly Bridegroom will ravish the Heart of the Saviour Himself. The suffering of Calvary will have been worth it:

Hebrews 12:2
  "Who for the joy that was set before Him endured the cross".

Thus we read these touching words: "So shall the King desire thy beauty." Her loyalty to Him is seen in acknowledging His Lordship ("He is thy Lord"). Her love to Him is seen in her worship: ("....and worship thou Him!"). The King's perception of her beauty is linked to her acknowledgement of His Lordship and subsequent worship.

Psalm 45:12
  "And the daughter of Tyre *shall be there* with a gift; *even* the rich among the people shall intreat thy (feminine) favour."

Verse 11 shows us the Bride prostrate in worship and adoration of her beloved Bridegroom. Verse 12 shows us the Bride actively involved in the administration of His Kingdom. Those who are "rich" among the people shall entreat her favour. We will see shortly that positions of authority and responsibility in the millennial Kingdom will be given to Old Testament and tribulation saints in accordance with the Lord's wishes. Some will be "richer" than others in that earthly Kingdom. It is those who are "rich" who intreat the Bride's favour. This position of responsibility and nearness to the King is no doubt a reward for faithfulness to Him in the days of the Old Testament and during the dark days of the tribulation. During the millennial reign, the Church will be involved in the administration of the earthly Kingdom. We will be "able ministers of the New Covenant" (2 Corinthians 3:6). Christ will be the Head of the Church in the heavens. Israel will be the head of the nations on the millennial earth. Headship will prevail as the Bride (the Church) communicates and carries out the will of her Head (Christ) in the administration of this Kingdom. Our responsibility in this seems to follow on directly from our capacity to worship Him in the preceding verse. If we lack the capacity to worship Him we would not have the capacity to administer His Kingdom. If we are not a worshipping people today how can we be entrusted with communicating the will of Christ to "the rich among the people" in that coming day? To know Him today is to worship Him. Those are the persons the Lord will entrust with administering His Kingdom in that future day of glory.

The Glory of the Queen

Psalm 45:13

"The King's daughter is all glorious within: her clothing is of wrought gold."

Earlier we saw that the beauty of the Bride was measured in the eyes of the King by her acknowledging His Lordship and worshipping Him. Verse 13 now moves from the beauty of the Queen to consider her glory. Literally, the verse could be translated, "All the glory of the King's daughter **is inwards**; her clothing is of wrought gold". The glory of the Queen is considered together with her clothing. Although her glory is internal, we learn from Revelation that the Bride has a glory which is divine as to its origin: "Having the glory of God" (Revelation 21:11). Her glory is divine as to its origin and its character. Anything less would not be compatible with her being the eternal companion of Christ. Glory really is the expression of excellence and the Bride has been given such. Interestingly, it is "internal" or "within". Clearly, the picture is of the Bride standing with her glory veiled by her clothing of wrought gold. Moses veiled his glory having received a vision of the grace of God (Exodus 34:33). Moses' glory was a reflected glory; not so the glory of the Bride. Such is God's grace to her that she has been given an internal glory which is her own. She veils this at the wedding by her wonderful garments of wrought gold. Her internal glory is for the eyes of the King alone. It has arisen out of His sufferings at Calvary. Only the glory of Christ shall be publicly seen. The Bride would want nothing less. Her glory has been given to her by God, but she veils it so that all eyes alone are on Christ, Who is the object of her adoring worship. Usually at a wedding all eyes are on the bride. Not so at this wedding. It is the desire of the Bride that all eyes are on the Bridegroom. She has restricted her glory for her Bridegroom's delight alone. There are two applications of this truth:

The truth of headship

Headship shows that only the glory of Christ should be seen, and that which speaks of man's glory can never compete with the glory of Christ, so it must be covered (1 Corinthians 11). This is why sisters' heads are covered in the public gatherings of the Lord's people.

Modesty of dress

There is an application to us today in this world of immodest dress. In today's world in the west, bridal garments so often publicly expose the bride. This is not the case with the Bride of Christ, the Church, who has preserved her God-given glory exclusively for the delight of her heavenly Bridegroom. Such should be the conduct of Godly couples today.

Psalm 45:14

"She shall be brought unto the King in raiment of needlework:"

We now learn two things about her clothing. It is of wrought gold and it is "raiment of needlework". This is effectively the wedding garment which veils her glory so that only the glory of Christ is seen. In Revelation, we learn that the Bride is dressed "in fine linen which is the righteousness of the saints". It has often been pointed out, and rightly so, that faithfulness to the Lord today in living a life pleasing to His righteous standards will be reflected in that fine linen dress of the Bride in that coming day when her works will be publicly seen. However, her glory shall be exclusively for the pleasure of the Lord.

The virgins

Psalm 45:14-15

14 ".....the virgins her companions that follow her shall be brought unto Thee.
15 With gladness and rejoicing shall they be brought: they shall enter into the King's palace."

The virgins follow her. This literally means that they "come after" her. Who are the virgins?
In Revelation, the figure of virgins is used to describe the tribulation saints.

Revelation 14:2-4

2 "And I heard a voice from heaven, as the voice of many waters, and as the voice of a great thunder: and I heard the voice of harpers harping with their harps:
3 And they sung as it were a New Song before the throne, and before the four beasts, and the elders: and no man could learn that song but the hundred *and* forty *and* four thousand, which were redeemed from the earth.

4 **These are they which were not defiled with women; for they are virgins.** These are they which follow the Lamb whithersoever He goeth. These were redeemed from among men, *being* the firstfruits unto God and to the Lamb."

What gladness and rejoicing shall accompany their entrance into the wedding feast! Their tribulations and distresses are over. Now they see the Lord for Whom they suffered so much and for Whom they waited to bring them, the "wise virgins", to the marriage (Matthew 25:1-13).

Now we see the Bride's side of the house at the wedding feast. It would not be appropriate that Old Testament saints should be the companions of the Bride since they never knew her. She was a mystery hidden in God's heart until this dispensation (Ephesians 5:32). In contrast, tribulation saints will know all about the Bride. They will read about her in the prison epistles etc. They will know her unique role in divine purposes. They will know about her mistakes, her trials, her triumphs and her failures. They will know all about her. Moreover, chronologically they will "come after her".

The reward for the Old Testament saints

Psalm 45:16

"Instead of Thy fathers shall be Thy children, whom Thou mayest make princes in all the earth."

Who are "Thy fathers"? Abraham, Isaac, Jacob and David etc. qualify for this description. They are in the royal line of the Messiah. However, now that the Lord is back to reign, these men who are known as "the fathers" shall not be seeking roles superior to the "Son". Although chronologically they came before Him, they are very happy to accept whatever role He is pleased to assign them in His Kingdom. These mighty men of faith will accept their reward, as He will assign to them positions of authority in His Kingdom, "Whom Thou mayest make princes in all the earth".

In this Psalm, we have met Old Testament saints, tribulation saints, millennial saints and, of course, the Church, the Bride of this era. The Psalm now closes with God addressing His Son regarding the saints of these differing epochs of time:

Psalm 45:17

"I will make Thy Name to be remembered in all generations: therefore shall the people praise Thee forever and ever."

All the redeemed from every age shall remember His Name and praise Him for ever and ever. What a day that will be, but central in this choir of praise shall be the Bride whose beauty He will desire forever!

---

1. Some more recent translations take a different view, suggesting that the word "whereby" (*minni*) in "whereby they have made Thee glad" should be translated "stringed instruments".

Scholars who follow this translation argue that it is "stringed instruments" in the "ivory palaces" which gladden Him by their beautiful musical strains. Going against the idea of *minni* meaning "stringed instruments" are the ancient renderings of this passage in the Septuagint, Vulgate and Targum translations which do not render *minni* as "stringed instruments". In particular, the Septuagint translates *minni* as "whereby". It is true that the Hebrew word *minnim* means stringed instruments, and scholars who hold that *minni* also means stringed instruments have to speculate that *minni* is a defective plural, i.e. the last letter "*m*" for some reason is missing- in other words a possible "typo" has entered into the Hebrew textual tradition. This is speculative and it seems safer to concur with the clear exposition of *minni* in Matthew Poole's Commentary as given in this quotation: "Whereby; or, from which; either, 1. From which place or palaces. Or rather, 2. From which thing, i.e. from the sweet smell of Thy garments out of those ivory palaces" (Matthew Poole 1624-1679).

10

PSALM 68

To the chief Musician, A Psalm or Song of David.
1 Let God arise, let His enemies be scattered: let them also that hate Him flee before Him.
2 As smoke is driven away, so drive them away: as wax melteth before the fire, so let the wicked perish at the presence of God.
3 But let the righteous be glad; let them rejoice before God: yea, let them exceedingly rejoice.
4 Sing unto God, sing praises to His Name: extol Him that rideth upon the heavens by His Name JAH, and rejoice before Him.
5 A Father of the fatherless, and a Judge of the widows, is God in His holy habitation.
6 God setteth the solitary in families: He bringeth out those which are bound with chains: but the rebellious dwell in a dry land.
7 O God, when Thou wentest forth before Thy people, when Thou didst march through the wilderness; Selah:
8 The earth shook, the heavens also dropped at the presence of God: even Sinai itself was moved at the presence of God, the God of Israel.
9 Thou, O God, didst send a plentiful rain, whereby Thou didst confirm Thine inheritance, when it was weary.
10 Thy congregation hath dwelt therein: Thou, O God, hast prepared of Thy goodness for the poor.
11 The Lord gave the word: great was the company of those that published it.
12 Kings of armies did flee apace: and she that tarried at home divided the spoil.
13 Though ye have lien among the pots, yet shall ye be as the wings of a dove covered with silver, and her feathers with yellow gold.
14 When the Almighty scattered kings in it, it was white as snow in Salmon.
15 The hill of God is as the hill of Bashan; an high hill as the hill of Bashan.
16 Why leap ye, ye high hills? this is the hill which God desireth to dwell in; yea, the Lord will dwell in it for ever.
17 The chariots of God are twenty thousand, even thousands of angels: the Lord is among them, as in Sinai, in the holy place.
18 Thou hast ascended on high, Thou hast led captivity captive: Thou hast received gifts for men; yea, for the rebellious also, that the Lord God might dwell

among them.

19 Blessed be the Lord, Who daily loadeth us with benefits, even the God of our salvation. Selah.

20 He that is our God is the God of salvation; and unto God the Lord belong the issues from death.

21 But God shall wound the head of His enemies, and the hairy scalp of such an one as goeth on still in his trespasses.

22 The Lord said, I will bring again from Bashan, I will bring My people again from the depths of the sea:

23 That Thy foot may be dipped in the blood of Thine enemies, and the tongue of Thy dogs in the same.

24 They have seen Thy goings, O God; even the goings of my God, my King, in the sanctuary.

25 The singers went before, the players on instruments followed after; among them were the damsels playing with timbrels.

26 Bless ye God in the congregations, even the Lord, from the fountain of Israel.

27 There is little Benjamin with their ruler, the princes of Judah and their council, the princes of Zebulun, and the princes of Naphtali.

28 Thy God hath commanded thy strength: strengthen, O God, that which Thou hast wrought for us.

29 Because of Thy temple at Jerusalem shall kings bring presents unto Thee.

30 Rebuke the company of spearmen, the multitude of the bulls, with the calves of the people, till every one submit himself with pieces of silver: scatter Thou the people that delight in war.

31 Princes shall come out of Egypt; Ethiopia shall soon stretch out her hands unto God.

32 Sing unto God, ye kingdoms of the earth; O sing praises unto the Lord; Selah:

33 To Him that rideth upon the heavens of heavens, which were of old; lo, He doth send out His voice, and that a mighty voice.

34 Ascribe ye strength unto God: His excellency is over Israel, and His strength is in the clouds.

35 O God, Thou art terrible out of Thy holy places: the God of Israel is He that giveth strength and power unto His people. Blessed be God.

Introduction

Psalm 68 is a prayer which will be taken up by the remnant during the tribulation in which they pray for the manifest presence of the Lord on earth and the deliverance this will bring to them in the midst of their trial. Because the Psalm is a prayer for the Lord's manifest presence, it considers the story of God amongst His people past, present and future. There are many solemn lessons for believers today who long for more of His presence in their lives both personally and in assembly gatherings. Where His presence is, there is victory for His own.

The Psalm can be divided into seven sections:

1 Psalm 68:1-6

God's presence on earth will divide humanity in a coming day

There are those who love the presence (face) of Christ and those who are terrified by His presence (face). Accordingly, verses 1-6 consider what the future coming of the Lord to the earth and His presence (revealed face) will mean for those on earth at that time. We find that those who love the Lord Jesus will be attracted to His face in worship and those who never knew Him will recoil in horror.

2 Psalm 68:7-10

God's presence on earth impacted God's earthly people in the past

The next section tells us of the impact on ancient Israel of the Lord's dwelling in their midst. The story starts with Sinai and the earth trembling at the presence of the Lord in the midst of the people as He leads them to their inheritance. This ended in failure and the dispersion due to their inability to keep the Law of Moses. The Lord then confirms His future inheritance for "the poor" even though He tells us of the inheritance being "weary".

3 Psalm 68:11-13

The imminent re-establishment of God's manifest presence on earth will be announced in a divine communiqué

This next section tells of a future communiqué to this world regarding the imminent return of the Lord to set up His Kingdom and dwell in the midst of Zion **forever**.

4 Psalm 68:14

A question from the recipients of the communiqué regarding these good tidings, directed at the Lord Himself

The communiqué of verses 11-13 prompts a question as to how the Lord can dwell amongst His people righteously, given the long history of Israel's estrangement from her God.

5 Psalm 68:15-17

The response of the Lord shows how it is possible for Him to dwell among His people forever with the demands of Moses' Law (the hill of God) satisfied forever

God's answer to any who doubt His ability to bring about the promised Kingdom is to show how the righteous demands of His Law have been met.

6 Psalm 68:18-20

A retrospective look by the future remnant back to this era of grace when the Lord's presence is in the midst of His people in the Church

This section highlights the practical implications of the Divine presence in the lives of believers today. For those who have come by faith to accept God's rescue-plan to prepare them for a future with Him, there are responsibilities. This section deals with these and shows us how a believer can experience spiritual victory in day to day life.

7 *Psalm 68:21-35*

The effects of the Divine presence in the coming Kingdom

There will be judgment on any rebellion against the Lord. There will be Godly order in worship, unity among God's people, and globally the fear of the Lord will prevail. These principles apply today in assembly gatherings where the Lord's presence is already known and experienced.

1 God's presence on earth will divide humanity in a coming day (Psalm 68:1-6)

Psalm 68 begins by looking into the face of Christ in that coming day. Earlier, in Psalm 45, we considered the beauty of the Lord Jesus. In this section of Psalm 68 we consider with awe the majesty of His face.

The Face of Christ

Psalm 68:1-4

1 "Let God arise, let His enemies be scattered: let them also that hate Him flee before Him (**from His face**).
2 As smoke is driven away, *so* drive *them* away: as wax melteth before (**from the face of**) the fire, *so* let the wicked perish at the presence of (**from the face of**) God.
3 But let the righteous be glad; let them rejoice before (**towards the face of**) God: yea, let them exceedingly rejoice.
4 Sing unto God, sing praises to His Name: extol Him that rideth upon the heavens by His Name JAH, and rejoice before (**towards His face**) Him."

The Psalm begins with a quotation from Numbers 33:35. As the congregation in the wilderness moved forward under the leading of the Lord's presence before them, Moses said, "Rise up, Lord, and let Thine enemies be scattered; and let them that hate Thee flee before Thee".

Numbers 10:33-36

33 "And they departed from the mount of the Lord three days' journey: and the Ark of the Covenant of the Lord went before them in the three days' journey, to search out a resting place for them. Note 1
34 And the cloud of the Lord *was* upon them by day, when they went out of the camp.
35 And it came to pass, when the ark set forward, that Moses said, Rise up, Lord, and let Thine enemies be scattered; and let them that hate Thee flee before Thee.
36 And when it rested, he said, Return, O Lord, unto the many thousands of Israel."

These words, quoted by David, remind us of a future day when the Lord will return to establish His presence in glory once more on the earth and this will mean judgment on all who oppose Him.

While Psalm 68 no doubt is referring to His **coming** to the earth, the word "coming" is not used. Rather the Psalmist refers to His **presence** on the earth where the word translated "presence" in verse 2 (*mipne*) means literally "**from the face of**", where *mi* means "from" and *pne* means "the face of".

Notice that the direction is "away from" the Lord. What terror shall fill the hearts of Christ rejecters in that coming day! The exact New Testament equivalent phrase is found in 2 Thessalonians 1:9 where we read of the judgment on those who reject the Lord Jesus at His return:

2 Thessalonians 1:9
"Who shall be punished with everlasting destruction **from the presence of** (Greek: *apo prosopou* meaning literally **from the face of**) the Lord and from the glory of His power."

John tells us in Revelation that when anticipating the imminent return of the Lord, men will cry out:

Revelation 6:16
"Hide us **from the face of** (*apo prosopou*) Him that sitteth on the throne."

Exposure to the face of the Lord Jesus will bring sudden destruction to any who are not believers at that time. This is conveyed in the descriptive language employed to portray the destructive effects of intense heat: "As **smoke** is driven away so drive them away, as wax **melteth before the (from the face of the)** fire so let the wicked perish..." (Psalm 68:2). Similarly, this is consistent with the New Testament description of the same event when the end of the wicked one is described:

2 Thessalonians 2:8
"Whom the Lord shall consume with the Spirit of His mouth and shall destroy with the brightness of His coming."

In contrast with the terror which will fill the hearts of the wicked at His return, the Psalmist describes the deep joy and peace which will fill the hearts of all true believers. Regarding the righteous we read:

Psalm 68:4
"Let them rejoice before **(towards the face of (*liphne*))** God" and "rejoice before Him" **(towards His face (*liphne*))**.

There is a beautiful play on words here in the original text. The word "before" **(*liphne*)** means "**before the face of**" and is a combination of *li* meaning "to" or "towards" and *phne* meaning "face of". It is clear then that there is an enormous contrast between the different reactions of the wicked and the righteous to the face of the returning Messiah. The wicked shall flee **away from His face**, while the righteous shall hasten **towards His face** to behold Him in all His beauty and to rejoice in the wonder of His presence as in Revelation 22:4

Revelation 22:4
"And they shall see His face; and His Name shall be in their foreheads."

In Psalm 68:4, the righteous are exhorted to "extol Him that rideth **upon the heavens** by His Name Jah". The English reader may perhaps think that this is the same idea as is mentioned in verse 33: "to Him *that rideth upon the heaven of* heavens…" However, it should be noted that the word translated "heavens" in Psalm 68:4 literally means "the desolate places" (*aravoth*). Some may wonder why the translators of the Authorised Version called this the "heavens". Possibly they were thinking that the Psalmist was here using the picture of an arid desert as a metaphor for outer space and thus chose the word "heavens" to convey this. However, it is worth noting that this word is used many times to describe desert places on the earth (Numbers 22: 1; Jeremiah 5:6; Jeremiah 39:5). If we simply follow the literal translation, it would read as follows: "extol Him that rideth **in the desert places** by His Name Jah". When will the Lord ride in the desert places? When He returns to this sad earth after seven years of tribulation it shall be both morally and literally a desert-filled scene. He will, of course, change this state of affairs and before long He will cause the desert to blossom as a rose (Isaiah 35:1)! When we understand that the word *aravoth* refers to earth rather than heaven, it strongly confirms that verses 1-6 are referring to the return of the Lord Jesus to planet earth.

The comfort of Christ

Psalm 68:5-6

5 "A Father of the fatherless, and a Judge of the widows, *is* God in His holy habitation.
6 God setteth the solitary in families: He bringeth out those which are bound with chains: but the rebellious dwell in a dry *land*."

The faithful remnant, awaiting His return at the end of the tribulation, will have experienced the effects of bereavement, loneliness and suffering throughout the tribulation period. The Psalmist indicates that on His return the Lord Jesus will correct all this:

He will provide comfort to the fatherless: "a Father of the fatherless".

He will re-establish justice for the oppressed: "a Judge of the widow".

He will provide fellowship for those who have become social outcasts for Christ's sake: "setteth the solitary in families".

He will provide freedom for those in prison for Christ's sake: "bringeth out those which are bound with chains".

Some may argue that coming to know the Lord Jesus as Saviour today brings comfort, justice, fellowship and freedom from the bondage of sin ("deliverance to the captives", Luke 4:18) and that for this reason the verses above cannot carry a literal and future prophetic meaning. Whilst it is true that coming by faith to Christ today brings comfort, fellowship with God and freedom from the bondage of sin, the consideration of justice in the phrase, "a Judge of the widow", points to this verse carrying a future fulfilment on the occasion of the Lord Jesus' return to reign.

Let us focus on the idea of the Lord as "a Judge of the widow". In Luke 18:1-8, in the parable of the unjust judge, a widow, oppressed by an adversary, sought justice from a judge who, because he was unjust, was slow to consider her case and provide the justice she sought for so long. The Lord in this parable was indicating that the Lord's delays in responding to the cries of His suffering people for justice from their persecutors were not, in contrast to the unjust judge of the parable, because the Lord was unjust or insensitive to their predicament. Rather, it was because the Lord was long-suffering and He was waiting for more people on earth to get saved through putting their faith in Him. Thus He concludes the parable of the unjust judge with this lovely statement, "When the Son of Man cometh, shall He find faith on the earth?" (Luke 18:8). The significance of these words is that on His return "to avenge the adversary" as Kinsman Avenger there will be no further opportunity or invitation to trust in Him. The door of opportunity would be closed forever. It is clear from Luke 18 that avenging or providing justice for the widow must await the return of the Lord Jesus as Kinsman Avenger in that coming day. This observation further confirms that verses 1-6 of our Psalm refer to the return of the Lord to this earth, not as Kinsman Redeemer but rather as the Kinsman Avenger.

Verses 1-6 are considering the **future** conditions which will prevail on the occasion of the Lord's second coming to this earth and the **visible presence** of God once more governing on this earth. Above all, these verses emphasize to us that this world's population will be divided into two parts on the occasion of the Lord's return: those who love the Lord Jesus and who are attracted **towards** His face, and those who never trusted Him who will cower **away from** His face. Verses 7-18 present God's masterplan to bring about a means whereby sinful men can be given a fitness to comfortably dwell in the very presence of God. The answer of course is found in the first coming of the Lord Jesus in His death, resurrection and ascension (Psalm 68:18).

2 God's presence on earth impacted God's earthly people in the past (Psalm 68:7-10)

A key element of God's plan for men to dwell forever in His presence is to show men their need of a fitness to dwell in God's presence. To convince humanity of this, God used a multi-generational historical illustration in the long story of how Israel proved unable to keep God's Law, as given by Moses in Sinai, and thus were driven from His presence in the captivity. Accordingly, verses 7-10 consider the past era from Sinai right until the destruction of Solomon's temple by Nebuchadnezzar, when for over 400 years God's **visible presence** was on earth in the midst of His people Israel, a period which came to an end with Zedekiah's captivity, the destruction of the temple and the withdrawal of the *Shechinah* glory as seen by Ezekiel (Ezekiel 11:23).

This entire narrative of history illustrates the principle that men cannot dwell in the presence of God due to their inability to keep His Law. This constant breaking of God's Law leads to a holy God having to deal with His Law-breaking people and driving them from His presence. The historical illustration of this principle begins with the giving of the Law – an event which was characterised by fear on the part of the people. Even Sinai itself shrunk away from the face of (*miphne*) God.

Psalm 68:7-8

7 "O God, when Thou wentest forth before (*liphne*) Thy people, when Thou didst march through the wilderness; Selah:
8 The earth shook, the heavens also dropped at the presence of God: even Sinai itself was moved at the presence (*mipne*) (from the face) of God, the God of Israel."

It was appropriate that the people should shrink from the Lord's face at Sinai, as He had given them a covenant on the basis of which their tenure on the Promised Land (the inheritance) was entirely dependent on their ability to keep Moses' Law. Such a **conditional** covenant, therefore, "gendereth to bondage" (Galatians 4:24). However, it is at this point that the Psalmist reminds us that the Lord had a plan whereby He could dwell with His people **unconditionally** within the inheritance with Sinai's angry demands completely satisfied. This plan would not find its entire fulfilment in Solomon, whose personal failure and that of his descendants would lead to the exile and end of the Davidic monarchy in Jerusalem. There are two references in this section to God's plan.

Psalm 68:9-10

9 "Thou, O God, didst send a plentiful rain, whereby Thou didst confirm Thine inheritance, when it was weary.
10 Thy congregation hath dwelt therein: Thou, O God, hast prepared of Thy goodness for the poor."

Verse 10 speaks of the "poor" in the midst of the inheritance. Poverty was, according to Deuteronomy 28, an indication of the people's failure to keep God's Law, leading to God's judgment upon them, which ultimately ended in the tragic story of the dispersion and the captivity of Babylon. Despite this, God had **confirmed His inheritance** and had **prepared of His goodness** for the poor. What did God "confirm" (verse 9), "prepare" (verse 10) and "desire" (verse 16)? The ensuing verses will reveal that it was a final situation whereby His people could enjoy **unconditional** tenure of the land, with God dwelling forever in Mount Zion ("the hill which God desireth to dwell in" (Psalm 68:16)) and with the Law of Moses satisfied fully. In other words, despite the failure of the people to dwell in the Lord's presence in a bygone era, God had a future programme in redemption whereby men would be able to dwell in His presence forever. This plan is the subject of the communiqué in the next section.

3 The imminent re-establishment of God's visible presence on earth will be announced in a divine communiqué (Psalm 68:11-13)

Psalm 68:11-13

11"The Lord gave the word: great *was* the company of those that published it.

12 Kings of armies did flee apace: and she that tarried at home divided the spoil.

13 Though ye have lien among the pots, *yet shall ye be as* the wings of a dove covered with silver, and her feathers with yellow gold."

This section envisages a day when the Lord would personally proclaim "the word", which would then be presented to a great company (army) to "publish" or perhaps more accurately to "preach as gospel" (*mevassroth*). The context is a proclamation of the imminent return of the Lord Jesus to destroy rebel kings and set up His Kingdom.

It is worth noting that the phrase, "those that published it", is in the feminine gender. Inspired by the Spirit of God to write these words, David may well have remembered how the women celebrated his victory over Goliath with the chant, "Saul hath slain his thousands, and David his ten thousands" (1 Samuel 18:7). However, the occasion in view here goes far beyond David's victory over Goliath, as it is clear that the Lord Himself "gave the word".

Could it be a reference to the news of the victory of the resurrection of the Lord Jesus which was first of all delivered to women in Matthew 28:9-10? This seems unlikely, as in Psalm 68 it is a "great host (army)" of those who "publish it" and it was not a great host of women who met the Lord on the occasion of His resurrection. Moreover, the women in the resurrection story were not speaking of the Lord Jesus returning to reign, as mentioned in Psalm 68:12-14. They were simply rejoicing in the wonderful truth that the One they loved so dearly was alive from the dead.

The significance of the feminine gender being used in the verb, "those that published it" or "those who told the good tidings" (*mevassroth*) (root *bisser*), becomes clear in a consideration of Isaiah 40 where the same verb ("to publish; tell good tidings; preach as gospel" (*bisser*)) is used in the feminine gender to describe the tribulation saints under the collective titles of "Zion" and "Jerusalem", telling forth the good news of the imminent return of the Lord Jesus. In Hebrew both "Zion" and "Jerusalem" are of feminine gender, thus all the verbs in Isaiah 9:9 referring to these tribulation preachers are in the feminine (f) gender as also is the word "cities":

Isaiah 40:9

"O Zion (f), that bringest-good-tidings (f), get-thee-up (f) into the high mountain; O Jerusalem (f), that bringest-good-tidings (f), lift-up (f) thy voice with strength; lift-*it*-up (f), be not afraid (f); say (f) unto the cities (f) of Judah, Behold (f) your God!"

Interestingly, when the gender of the **individual** preacher is considered in Isaiah 52, it is the **male** who is telling forth the glad tidings of the Lord's return.

Isaiah 52:7-8
> 7 "How beautiful upon the mountains are the feet of **him** that bringeth good tidings, that publisheth peace; that bringeth good tidings of good, that publisheth salvation; that saith unto Zion, Thy God reigneth! 8 Thy watchmen shall lift up the voice; with the voice together shall they sing: for they shall see eye to eye, when the Lord shall bring again Zion."

Verses 12-13 are a poetic resumé of this communiqué which the publishers of the divine word would then go on to deliver to their hearers.

The communiqué, arising first from the Lord but broadcast by the gospel preachers (*mevassroth*), announced three things:

(i) The defeat of hostile kings:

"Kings of armies did flee apace" (Psalm 68:12). The Lord, on His return, will triumph over hostile armies, as considered in Psalm 45.

(ii) A home for a beautified Israel:

"she that tarried (*navah*) at home (Hebrew: the beautiful woman (*navah*) of the house) divided the spoil (Psalm 68:12).

The phrase "she that tarried" (*navah*) could also be accurately translated "a beautiful one" (Septuagint and Vulgate) and is also used to describe Zion in Jeremiah 6:2.

Jeremiah 6:2
> "I have likened **the daughter of Zion** to a comely (*navah*) and delicate *woman.*"

Interestingly, Solomon uses the same word to describe Jerusalem and compares his Bride to Jerusalem in Song of Songs:

Song of Songs 6:4
> "Thou *art* beautiful, O my love, as Tirzah, comely (*navah*) **as Jerusalem**, terrible as *an army* with banners."

Although in Psalm 68:12 the person described as *navah* is not identified within the Psalm, the use of the word in Jeremiah 6:2 and Song of Songs 6:4 would suggest that the description is intended to mean the restored nation of Israel in a coming day.

Historically, in ancient battles the conqueror divided the spoils among the female non-combatants, especially his mother, as part of the triumph celebrations (Judges 5:30). How wonderful a day it will be when the restored nation of Israel, under the description of a beautiful women within a stable home environment, will be afforded the unique dignity by the Messiah of dividing the spoils of this world among those who will enter the earthly Kingdom! What a contrast is seen in this final state of the nation of Israel as compared with the 2000 years of wandering when at no time could the wandering Jew truly feel "at home". In Isaiah 53:12, the Lord will "divide the spoil with the strong". It will fall to the restored and beautified nation to distribute the spoil to the other nations of the saved in fellowship with her Lord.

(iii) Restoration of glory to those who were wandering fugitives

Psalm 68:13

"Though ye have lien among the pots, yet shall ye be as the wings of a dove covered with silver, and her feathers with yellow gold."

The phrase, "lien among the pots", (translated "pack saddles" by Gerhard Libowsky in *Konkordanz zum Hebräischen Alten Testament* (1957)) is a metaphor to describe the saddle bags which were placed on the back of a beast of burden. Israel is reminded of times when she "lay amongst the pack saddles". This presents a powerful and pitiful image to us of the wandering Jew, lying down in the vicinity of his pack animal without even a place of security to lay his head for the night. What an accurate depiction of the "wandering Jew" over the past 2000 years. However, the next phrase describes the future conditions of beauty and glory which Israel is destined to enjoy when her Messiah returns: *"yet shall ye be as* the wings of a dove covered with silver, and her feathers with yellow gold".

In Isaiah 60:8, the remnant of Israel being brought back into the Land is depicted under the image of a dove flying home to its "window".

Isaiah 60:8

"Who *are* these *that* fly as a cloud, and as the doves to their windows?"

This verse reminds us of the dove's homing instinct. At last Israel shall have found its home and rest in the security which only her Messiah King can provide.

4 A question from the recipients of the communiqué regarding these good tidings, directed at the Lord Himself (Psalm 68:14)

Psalm 68:14

"When the Almighty scattered (*pares*) kings in it, it was white as snow in Salmon."

The construction of the sentence suggests verse 14 is a response to the communiqué rather than an integral part of the good news. This verse has been much debated by scholars and commentators and consensus is wanting. If we follow a literal translation some illumination is obtainable.

"In the Almighty **spreading abroad** (dispersing) kings in it (the inheritance), **Thou wilt cause it to snow** in Salmon". The literal translation, "**Thou** wilt cause it to snow in Salmon", shows that this verse is different from the communiqué of the previous section. In fact, because in the phrase, "Thou wilt cause it to snow in Salmon", the Lord is being directly addressed and not being spoken about, it becomes clear that Psalm 68:14 is a **response** to the Lord from those who are weighing up "the word" of the communiqué through His gospel preachers in that coming day. This response, while not framed as a question, articulates a quandary in the minds of the recipients of the communiqué and could be regarded as a question from the audience of the tribulation gospel preachers. Admittedly, not all scholars agree. Delitzsch in his commentary on the Psalms argues that the rendering, "Thou wilt cause it to snow", should be understood as "it will snow", since, in the preceding clause, the Almighty is spoken of in the third person: "When the Almighty spread abroad kings", rather than in the second person, "when Thou didst spread abroad kings in it". However, in the Hebrew Bible there is a well known example of a phrase in the second person (thou) being preceded by a phrase in the third person:

Isaiah 53:10
"Yet it pleased the Lord to bruise Him; He hath put *Him* to grief: when Thou shalt make His soul an offering for sin."

"He hath put him to grief" is in the third person whereas "Thou shalt make His soul an offering for sin" is in the second person. This shows that the use of a second person rendering, e.g. "Thou wilt cause it to snow in Salmon", following a preceding phrase in the third person is not unheard of elsewhere in the Hebrew Scriptures. It should now be clear that Psalm 68:14 is a response to the communiqué from those who will hear it. Let us look at this response. It is about the Lord dispersing kings in the inheritance and bringing about a winter in it.

Is the spreading abroad (translated "scattered") here the same as the scattering of the Lord's enemies in Psalm 68:1?

Many expositors look upon this verse and the scattering of the kings as referring to the future judgment on the rebel kings of the earth at the end of the tribulation. However, a careful examination of the verb, "**to spread abroad**" (*pares*), shows that the meaning is not "to destroy" or "to kill". The importance of this distinction is illustrated in Zechariah 2:6, which is the only other time this same verb is used in the *piel* form in the context of scattering of persons. There the context is of the nation **being sent into captivity**.

Zechariah 2:6
"Ho, ho, *come forth*, and flee from the land of the north, saith the LORD: for I have **spread you abroad** (*pares*) as the four winds of the heaven, saith the LORD."

In other words, the Biblical use of the word, "to spread abroad" (*pares*), does not necessarily suggest that this involves the premature death of the persons involved. In fact, the several other Old Testament uses of the verb "*pares*" are to do with the spreading out of the hands in an ordered way, e.g. Psalm 143:6; Isaiah 25:11 etc. Indeed, when Zechariah used *pares* to depict the Lord dispersing the nation from the land, he was showing the reader that the dispersion was entirely subject to divine control. There was nothing haphazard about it. This understanding of the verb *pares* leads us to understand Psalm 68:14 as describing the sending away of Israel and Judah's kings into captivity because of their failure to keep the Law of God. In the case of Judah this is what happened when, in the reign of Zedekiah, the city was captured by the Babylonians, the temple was burnt and the king and the princes sent into captivity. It could then be truly said that the Almighty had dispersed the kings "in it". The little phrase "in it" (*bah*) means literally "in her", and refers to a feminine noun further up the passage. This is "the inheritance" (*nachalah*), a feminine noun referred to in verses 9 and 10.

Psalm 68:9-10

9 "Thou, O God, didst send a plentiful rain, whereby Thou didst confirm Thine inheritance (*nachalah*), when it was weary.
10 Thy congregation hath dwelt therein (in her) (*bah*): Thou, O God, hast prepared of Thy goodness for the poor."

What then is meant by the remainder of the verse 14, "it was white as snow in Salmon"?

Once again many differing suggestions have been made by Bible commentators. However, a review of the literal translation is again helpful.

Psalm 68:14

"In the Almighty spreading forth kings in it (the inheritance), Thou wilt cause it to snow in Salmon."

Note that there is nothing in the original text about the colour of the snow (white is in italics), or about the snow melting or disappearing away. Furthermore, there is no comparison made between the scattering of the kings and the snow as some have suggested, even going as far as to say that the white bones of dead kings on the hillside will look like snow. It is much simpler just to leave the passage as it is: a stark depiction of a winter scene in the land of Israel caused by the direct hand of God: "Thou wilt cause it to snow".

If the meaning of the phrase, as we have just seen, is of the kings of Israel and Judah being scattered from off the inheritance (Israel) through being led into captivity, then it should not surprise us if the inspired poet should append this winter scene to this depiction. He is showing us that indeed as far as Judah is concerned, the words of Jeremiah will have come to pass:

Jeremiah 8:20

"The harvest is past, the summer is ended, and we are not saved."

Psalm 68:14 could be paraphrased as:
"Whenever the Almighty spreads abroad the kings within the inheritance, Thou wilt cause a winter scene."
Israel's captivity was truly a spiritual wintertime for the nation. When the nation broke God's Law, God had to fulfill His promise and drive (disperse)

them (and their kings) off the land, which then commenced a period of spiritual winter.

Now we can understand the reason why the recipients of the communiqué interject in the middle of the announcement of the impending Messiah's victory as proclaimed by the tribulation gospel preachers. The audience, which is largely Jewish, is having to grapple with a message so amazing it sounds almost too good to be true. It is a message of Israel's enemies fleeing, Israel's wanderings being brought to an end and a beautified Israel living in stability in its home i.e. safe in the Land of Israel at last. The hearers in bewilderment remind the gospel preacher that it was the Almighty (*El Shaday*) Who historically dispersed the kings (Israel's own kings) by driving them off their inheritance at the start of the captivity and then, addressing God directly, the questioner protests (in paraphrase): "it was Thou Who didst bring in the winter of Israel's desolations and wanderings". The audience of these tribulation preachers will know that Israel's 2000 year-old wanderings have arisen from God's dealings with His estranged people. How can it be, they ask, that such a God can promise an eternal relationship with Himself?

The next section is the divine response from a loving God to those who are eligible for salvation after the rapture and who are questioning the gospel preachers of the remnant nation as to how this is possible (Appendices 2 and 3.)

5 The response of the Lord shows how it is possible for Him to dwell among His people forever with the demands of Moses' Law (the hill of God) satisfied forever (Psalm 68:15-17)

Psalm 68:15-17
15 "The hill of God *is as* the hill of Bashan; an high hill *as* the hill of Bashan.
16 Why leap ye, ye high hills? *this is* the hill *which* God desireth to dwell in; yea, the Lord will dwell *in it* for ever.
17 The chariots of God *are* twenty thousand, *even* thousands of angels: the Lord *is* among them, *as in* Sinai, in the holy *place*."

We have read of three distinct hills:
• the hill of God (*har – elohim*)
• the hill of Bashan
• the hill which God desires to dwell in (Mount Zion).

A superficial reading of the passage may lead us to suppose that the "hill of God" is the "hill which God desires to dwell in". This, however, is not the case.

The Hill of God
The "hill (or mount) of God" (*har–elohim*) is a term used to describe Sinai, the place where God met with Moses and later gave the Law to the nation and entered into the two-party covenant with them (Exodus 3:1; 24:13). Later, when the nation flagrantly disregarded Moses' Law, Elijah in deep

sadness and discouragement made the long and difficult journey back into the Sinai desert to that same "hill of God".

1 Kings 19:8

"And he arose, and did eat and drink, and went in the strength of that meat forty days and forty nights unto Horeb the **mount (hill) of God**." Note 1

There he told the Lord that the people had broken the ancient covenant made so many years earlier in the time of Moses.

1 Kings 19:10

"And he said, I have been very jealous for the Lord God of hosts: for the children of Israel have forsaken Thy covenant, thrown down Thine altars, and slain Thy prophets with the sword; and I, even I only, am left; and they seek my life, to take it away."

The implications of Elijah's solemn words were that the curses of the broken Law would be meted out upon the nation and their expulsion from the land was unavoidable along with famine, pestilence and sword as promised in Deuteronomy 28:15-68 to the nation if they broke the covenant of Sinai, the hill of God. Therefore, the hill of God had solemn memories of God, Who was revealed as the covenant-keeping God Who must enforce His Law and Who would bring about the expulsion of the nation should they break His commandments. The Psalmist's use of the "hill of God" here powerfully reminds us that the Lord's fulfilment of His expressed desire to dwell forever among His people can be accomplished only through principles which accord with the lofty standards of Sinai. The question of course is how could God in light of the nation's inability to keep the Law of Sinai, find a way to:

- confirm His inheritance (verse 9)?
- prepare of His goodness for the poor (verse 10)?
- dwell in the hill of His desire *forever* (verse 16)?

There was only one way. The Law given at the hill of God must be satisfied and silenced before Israel could ever be the "beautiful women of the house", dwelling in security in her own land into perpetuity. Throughout Israel's history, it was as if the thunderings and lightenings of Mount Sinai continued to pursue the nation. An unsatisfied Law wreaked vengeance on the Law-breaking nation and demanded its expulsion from the land as indicated in Deuteronomy 28. How and when could the hill of God (Horeb), so hostile to Israel's remaining on its inheritance, be satisfied and silenced and become an ordinary hill just like the other hills of Israel?

The Hill of Bashan

In response to the anxious enquiry of Psalm 68:14, the Lord responds with an amazing statement: "The hill of God is as the hill of Bashan". Bashan was just an ordinary hill without any particular spiritual significance attached to it. In fact its ordinariness is highlighted in the quaint description given of it, which becomes apparent in the literal translation where we note that "an high hill... the hill of Bashan" could be literally translated "an hill of humps... the hill of Bashan". Bashan was just an ordinary hill. The Psalmist envisaged the day when even the hill of God would be just an ordinary hill. In other words its significance as a constant principle obstructing the goal of Israel from dwelling securely within its borders would come to an end.

In the next section, this becomes apparent when there is a direct reference to the death, resurrection and ascension of the victorious Christ. In fact, far from obstruction or objection to "the hill of God's desire" (Mount Zion) becoming the permanent abode of His redeemed people, the hill of God (Sinai) and all the other hills in Israel dance (leap) (*ritsed*) in celebration at this wonderful event when the Lord dwells among His people at the end of the tribulation.

There are other prevailing views on this from Bible teachers today which should be acknowledged at this point. Some have taken the "leaping hills" in verse 16 to be hills leaping in consternation and jealously at Mount Zion being singled out for a specially privileged position of authority in the coming Kingdom. Others have gone further and suggested that the verb *ritsed* means "to look jealously at".

These differing views on the meaning of the word arise from the different scholarly approaches to the problem that the verb *ritsed* cannot be determined from other Old Testament passages, since the verb occurs nowhere else in the Old Testament. One approach is to look at the use of similar words in other Semitic languages. In Arabic, there is a word similar to *ritsed* and it means "to look jealously at". Accordingly, some assume that the Hebrew *ritsed* means the same as this similar-sounding Arabic word. However, it is well known that identically or similarly sounding words in different languages can have very differing meanings, e.g. English "deception" and French "déception", where the latter means "disappointment". Hence, it is arguably unsafe to believe that *ritsed* means the same as a similar sounding word in a different, albeit related, language. However, more importantly, there is a doctrinal objection with this view. Any thought that the "hill of God" would be engaged in such a rebellious gesture seems incongruous, which is why the present author understands that the "leaping hills" are leaping out of reverential joy, just as earthquakes and significant earth movements marked the dramatic events of the Lord's **revealed presence** on the occasion of Israel coming out of Egypt as described in Psalm 114:1-7.

Psalm 114:1-7
  1 "When Israel went out of Egypt, the house of Jacob from a people of strange language;
  2 Judah was His sanctuary, *and* Israel His dominion.
  3. The sea saw *it*, and fled: Jordan was driven back.
  4 **The mountains skipped like rams, *and* the little hills like lambs.**
  5 What *ailed* thee, O thou sea, that thou fleddest? thou Jordan, *that* thou wast driven back?

6 Ye mountains, *that* ye skipped like rams; *and* ye little hills, like lambs?
7 Tremble, thou earth, at the presence of the Lord, at the presence of the
God of Jacob;"

How then did the Authorised Version translators determine that this verb
ritsed meant "to leap"? Some light on this question may arise from the entry
by B. Davidson on *ritsed* in his *Analytical Hebrew and Chaldee Lexicon* where
he points out that the ancient Jewish Aramaic Targum translation of this
chapter rendered *ritsed* by the Aramaic *tephaz* meaning "to leap" or "to
spring".

Psalm 68:16

"Why leap ye, ye high hills? *this is* the hill *which* God desireth to dwell in;
yea, the Lord will dwell *in it* for ever."

What a day it will be when the earth will quake in awe as the rightful
King comes to the hill of His desire (Zion) to dwell amongst His people! The
angels of God shall be ascending and descending from earth to the heavenly
city (the Church) in the heavens. This is what is being referred to in Psalm
68:17.

Psalm 68:17

"The chariots of God are twenty thousand, even thousands of angels: the
Lord is among them, as in Sinai, in the holy place."

These verses show us that God will permanently (forever) abide on the hill
of His desire (Zion) but that this will be totally consistent with the principles
of Moses' Law having been met so fully that Sinai is but a memory. It no
longer poses any threat to the stability of the Kingdom by having to demand
judgment on the lawbreakers within it and terminating their tenure on the
land, as stipulated in Deuteronomy 28. The answer to the question of how
God can dwell in the hill of His desire with the demands of a broken Mosaic
Law entirely fulfilled is given in the next section, commencing at verse
18. Here we discover that the Lord Himself is the means of bringing to an
end all such captivity and this includes the bondage of the Law of Sinai.
This alone is the means whereby the divine plan to fit men to dwell in His
presence can be brought to pass.

6 A retrospective look by the future remnant back to this era of grace when the Lord dwells in the midst of His people in the Church (Psalm 69:18)

Psalm 68:18

"Thou hast ascended on high, Thou hast led captivity captive: Thou hast
received gifts for men; yea, *for* the rebellious also, that the LORD God
might dwell *among them*."

The phrase, **"Thou hast ascended on high"**, is addressed to the Lord and no one else. Because David is addressing the Lord, Who is already "high and lifted up" (Isaiah 6:1), it is clear that he presupposes that the Lord must first have descended to earth in order to make valid the statement of His ascent on high. Although David does not actually refer to that descent, his language requires the reader to understand this. In the New Testament, this obvious truth is reinforced in Ephesians 4:8-10.

Ephesians 4:8-10
8 "Wherefore He saith, When He ascended up on high, He led captivity captive, and gave gifts unto men.
9 (Now that He ascended, what is it but that He also descended first into the lower parts of the earth?
10 He that descended is the Same also that ascended up far above all heavens, that He might fill all things.)"

While some have argued that the phrase, "Thou has ascended on high", might just mean that the Ark of the Covenant has been brought up to Jerusalem and right to the Temple Mount, it is worth noting that the phrase "on high" is used elsewhere to describe the Lord's **heavenly** temple.

Isaiah 38:14
"Like a crane or a swallow, so did I chatter: I did mourn as a dove: mine eyes fail with looking upward (on high): O Lord, I am oppressed; undertake for me."

It is this heavenly meaning to the words "on high" which was understood by the New Testament believers, as articulated by the Apostle Paul by divine inspiration in Ephesians 4:8.

Thou hast led captivity captive (shavita shevi)
A very similar construction is found in two other passages. In Numbers 21:1, where Arad the Canaanite was the captor and the Israelites were the captives, we read that he (Arad) "took some of them prisoners" (literally: **"and he led captive captives (*shevi*)"**).

Numbers 21:1
"And *when* king Arad the Canaanite, which dwelt in the south, heard tell that Israel came by the way of the spies; then he fought against Israel, **and took *some* of them prisoners.**"

Similarly, in 2 Chronicles 28:17, we read how Edomites managed "to carry away captives" of Judah. The literal translation is **"and they led captive captives"**.

2 Chronicles 28:17
"For again the Edomites had come and smitten Judah, **and carried away captives.**"

From these examples it is clear that the phrase, "to lead captivity captive", simply means to take prisoners following a battle. In the above two examples,

the pagan armies of Canaan and Edom were the captors and we are not told
what conditions the captives were asked to endure. However, there was
no requirement in the code of pagan nations to treat their captives with
respect. One can only imagine their hardships. There is a New Testament
equivalent to the two Old Testament tragedies of defeat mentioned above,
such as when believers allow themselves to be ensnared in false teaching
and are taken captive in the snare of the devil. Paul speaks of the ministry of
the servant of the Lord in such circumstances, whose actions are such that
"they may recover themselves out of the snare of the devil, who are taken
captive by him at his will" (2 Timothy 2:26).

In contrast, when Israelites took captives in their battles the Law placed
obligations upon them to **look after their captives.**

Deuteronomy 21:10-14
> 10 "When thou goest forth to war against thine enemies, and the LORD
> thy God hath delivered them into thine hands, and thou hast **taken them**
> **captive (led captive his captives)**,
> 11 And seest among the captives a beautiful woman, and hast a desire unto
> her, that thou wouldest have her to thy wife;
> 12 Then thou shalt bring her home to thine house; and she shall shave her
> head, and pare her nails;
> 13 And she shall put the raiment of her captivity from off her, and shall
> remain in thine house, and bewail her father and her mother a full month:
> and after that thou shalt go in unto her, and be her husband, and she shall
> be thy wife.
> 14 And it shall be, if thou have no delight in her, then thou shalt let her go
> whither she will; but thou shalt not sell her at all for money, thou shalt not
> make merchandise of her, because thou hast humbled her."

In this example, "take (them) captive" (Deuteronomy 21:10) means
literally "**thou** has led captive **his** captives". Here the armies of Israel are
the captors and the enemies of God are the captives. However, the captives
are referred to as "his captives", i.e. captives **of the enemy**. This suggests
that the woman captive considered in the passage, in the eyes of the Law of
Moses, had been in captivity in the house of her father and mother before
the Israelite forces captured her and thus, in relation to the enemy, is said to
have been "his captive". This does not mean that this woman was a prisoner
of war in the community of the enemy of Israel, but rather a captive of the
enemy morally, and now that she has been captured by the armies of Israel
she is considered a free woman. In fact, after she mourns her father and
mother, she is married to an Israelite and in this marriage she enjoys the full
freedom of a free, married woman in Israel. As explained in *Modern Trends
in Morality*, under Moses' Law, marriage was freedom and not bondage.
Bondservant wives were not permitted under Law, even though this
practice continued in the community of Israelites in contravention of Moses'
Law (See *Modern Trends in Morality* page 128). This is why in the section
quoted above she was **free** to walk away if subjected to maltreatment by

her husband. Note this is not divorce but rather the proof of her status as a completely free woman under Moses' Law. It is very possible that Rahab the harlot, who was technically a captive of Jericho, came into the full freedoms of blessing including being married into the royal line of the Messiah within the tribe of Judah through the provisions of the passage outlined above in Deuteronomy 21:10.

A further example of captives being treated well is found in 2 Chronicles 28:11 where the forces of the Northern Kingdom defeated the forces of wicked King Ahaz of Judah and took captives. They are referred to as "captives which ye have taken" or more literally **"the captives which ye have taken captive"**.

2 Chronicles 28:11
"Now hear me therefore, and deliver the captives again, **which ye have taken captive** of your brethren: for the fierce wrath of the Lord is upon you."

In this example, disobedient Judah are the captives and backslidden Israel are the captors.

Although the word for "captives" (*shivya*) is slightly different from *shevi* in the earlier examples, the basic root and overall meaning is the same. In this example, the prophet of the Lord intervened to ensure that the captives were well treated, were clothed and fed and carefully brought back to Jericho where they were given their freedom. The point in this illustration was that the prophet of the Lord was reminding the Israelite victors of their responsibility under the Law of Moses to treat their captives well.

When we come to Judges 5:12, we discover that Barak is exhorted to "lead **thy** captivity captive", literally "lead captive **thy** captives!"(Judges 5:12)

Judges 5:12
"Awake, awake, Deborah: awake, awake, utter a song: arise, Barak, **and lead thy captivity captive**, thou son of Abinoam."

In this example, Barak was the captor but who were the captives who are designated by the phrase **"thy captives"**? Clearly, these were people who were once under the sovereignty of Jabin, king of Hazor but who now were the legitimate captives of Barak. In Judges 5, we learn that God had sold the Israelites into the hand of Jabin. That really meant that they were the captives of Jabin. However, in the song of Judges 5, as a result of Barak's wonderful victory they are now the captives of Barak –"thy captives" – and this is the cause of great thanksgiving in Judges 5. What a contrast in living conditions these erstwhile captives of Jabin must have felt, now that they were the willing captives of Barak their saviour!

The pursuit of these occurrences of the phrase, "leading captivity captive", in the Old Testament shows that it means to "take prisoner", but when it is in the context of the armies of the Lord taking the prisoner, it means freedom and privilege for such a person, who could thereafter call themselves a prisoner of the Lord and as such are completely free from the bondage of their former heathen overlords. When we turn to Ephesians 4 we read these words:

Ephesians 4:1-10

1 "I therefore, the **prisoner of the Lord**, beseech you that ye walk worthy of the vocation wherewith ye are called,

2 With all lowliness and meekness, with longsuffering, forbearing one another in love;

3 Endeavouring to keep the unity of the Spirit in the bond of peace.

4 *There is* one body, and one Spirit, even as ye are called in one hope of your calling;

5 One Lord, one faith, one baptism,

6 One God and Father of all, Who *is* above all, and through all, and in you all.

7 But unto every one of us is given grace according to the measure of the gift of Christ.

8 Wherefore He saith, When He ascended up on high, He led captivity **captive**, and gave gifts unto men.

9 (Now that He ascended, what is it but that He also descended first into the lower parts of the earth?

10 He that descended is the same also that ascended up far above all heavens, that He might fill all things.)"

As Paul is writing these verses he is, it appears, a captive of the Roman Empire with his freedom curtailed by all the might of imperial Rome. Not so! Paul tells us that he is a captive – a prisoner of the Lord! How beautiful this is! As a captive of the Lord Jesus Christ he is enjoying the glorious liberty of the children of God. As the chains were dangling from his hands and feet, how good of the Lord to lead him, by divine inspiration, to remind us that when the Lord Jesus ascended on high to heaven He led captivity captive! Just as Barak took the former captives of Jabin and made them the captives of Barak, thus establishing their freedom, so the risen and exalted Lord has captured us from the bondage of sin and Satan and here we are, believers in our Lord Jesus Christ, happy to be called the captives of Christ which, in Paul's case, involved such a commitment to his Lord and Saviour as to lead him to a prison cell for Christ's sake and the gospel's. It is instructive for us to see that it is the believer who reckons himself to be a captive of Christ whom the Lord can turn round and give as a gift to His Church to serve Him and His people. In Paul's case, it was in the role of apostle, prophet and teacher. Today, we don't have apostles and prophets but we do have teachers, evangelists and pastors. Only men of God who consider themselves to be the lawful captives of Christ and are wholly submissive to the Lordship of Christ and His control can function as effective gifts to the Church. May the Lord raise up men of God, submissive to Him, to serve as His captives as evangelists, shepherds and teachers in New Testament Assemblies! May He also raise up women of God to exercise divinely given gifts in the sphere of service their Lord would direct in accordance with His Word.

Thou hast received gifts for men

A helpful literal translation reads as follows: "**Thou hast taken gifts in man, even rebellious ones, that the Lord God might tabernacle among them.**"

The gifts which the risen and ascended Lord gives to men are the captives themselves. As noted above, a true servant of God is one who primarily sees himself as a captive servant of the Lord. He has forfeited all his own rights to the service of his heavenly Lord and risen Head, and in this he finds true freedom and the commensurate divine enabling to carry out the ministry with which God has entrusted him.

However, the risen Lord has looked among His captives and has taken up gifts "in man", i.e. taken up individual persons He has captured and redeemed, and even though they were once avowedly "rebellious" to the throne of God, they are now gifts which He can give to His Church in His service. The objective of this is that "the Lord God might tabernacle among them".

Just as the conditional presence of the Lord in Sinai brought blessing to His own, and fearful judgment to those who transgressed (see verses 7-10), even more so in a future day will the unconditional presence of the Lord bring blessing to His own and terror to those who reject Him (see verses 1-6). However, **in the meantime**, in this era, this same Lord is dwelling (tabernacling) among His captives on earth in the Church, and in the same manner as He had prepared of His "goodness for the poor" in those days, similarly in this day He has prepared of His "goodness for the poor" through the ministry of those gifts He has distributed among men. We know from Ephesians 4 that Psalm 68:18 refers to the risen and exalted Lord captivating unsaved men and then turning round and giving them to His Church in this era. This is clearly, then, the New Testament understanding of Psalm 68:18. This illumination helps us understand the context, for David could not have understood that the people he was writing about in Psalm 68:18 were those of this Church era, as confirmed in Ephesians 4, because the truths about the Church were not revealed to the Old Testament prophets.

The preceding verses of the Psalm (i.e. verses 11-17) bring before us the sequence of events which shall play out in the end of the tribulation when the saved remnant of Israel is just about to welcome back their Messiah to enter into His earthly Kingdom. In that coming day, just before the Lord's return to the earth, the saved remnant of Israel will not be in the dark regarding the identity of the Church, in contrast to David over 3000 years earlier. Rather, they will be in a position to look back over God's dealings with the nation of Israel down through the centuries. A matter of wonder to them will be a realisation of the blessing and salvation God had already brought to the Gentile nations in the preceeding 2000 years of the Church era. In other words, the remnant will understand that the long period of their "winter" was indeed a time of great blessing to the Gentiles when they became the "captives of Christ" and enjoyed the presence of the Lord in their midst in

Church capacity. Psalm 68:18-20, which must have been beyond David's understanding, will then be clear to those tribulation believers. In fact, as they look back over the 2000 years of their nation's spiritual winter they will take upon their lips the words of Psalm 68:18-20, fully understanding that they apply primarily to the Church believers, who have been already raptured to heaven. In the meantime though, these verses are especially instructive to us in this Church era. When the Lord took us as His captives it was with the objective that we should be gifts to His Church.

Psalm 68:19-20

19 "Blessed *be* the Lord, *Who* daily loadeth us *with benefits, even* the God of our salvation. Selah.

20 *He that is* our God *is* the God of salvation; and unto GOD the Lord *belong* the issues from death."

What a wonderful transformation has been effected in the lives of these Church-era believers once described as "rebellious" but who now, as the captives of the Lord, spontaneously and joyfully express their worship for Him with these words: "Blessed be the Lord".

It is worth noting that in the Authorised Version the words, "with benefits", are in italics, which means that this phrase can be left out if we are seeking for the literal meaning of the original text. The passage could then read:

"Blessed be the Lord Who daily loadeth us" or "daily gives us a burden". In his 1844 *Hebrew and English Lexicon of the Old Testament*, William Gesenius translates the phrase as, "even though He impose a burden upon us" (page 805). Although this is a slight paraphrase of the literal meaning of, "Blessed be the Lord Who daily burdens us", it does help us to understand the issue the Psalmist is grappling with here. He recognises that we are the captives of the Lord; willingly and joyously we acquiesce to His will for us. If He gives us as gifts to His Church, that is entirely His will. However, if that is the case, we quickly discover that along with that privilege and responsibility will come a burden which He himself will provide. Such a burden is only intended for our ultimate blessing and to bring out fruitfulness for Him.

For example, how does a New Testament believer recognise his or her gift? Long before a brother is recognised as gifted in shepherding (pastoring) the flock, there is a divinely-begotten burden laid upon him by the risen Lord to feed His lambs. This burden leads to a desire to study the Scriptures and have food wherewith to feed the Lord's people. Similarly, long before a brother is recognised by the Lord's people as a gifted evangelist there will, much earlier, have been a deep burden begotten in His heart by the Holy Spirit to reach the lost with the gospel. Truly, blessed is the Lord Who day by day places such a burden in a believer's heart. In fact, this passage would indicate that true spiritual gift arises from deep burden and exercise of heart. The solemn corollary of this is that display of gift without an underlying, divinely-given burden may only be the arm of the flesh. May each of us have cause to bless the Lord for entrusting to us a burden from Himself!

However, there are other burdens which the Lord may in His gracious wisdom place upon us. Even in this modern western world there are many Christians who have the daily burden of perhaps caring for a disabled child or an elderly and infirm loved one. Others have health burdens such as Paul's "thorn in the flesh". In all of this the believer can say, "Blessed be the Lord". In this the believer stands in complete contrast to the unbeliever who does not have the eternal perspective on our circumstances in life. It is worth noting as well that the burden is not for weeks and months and years. It is only given to us on a day by day basis – "Who daily burdens us". What does this mean? The significance is that He only asks us to bear our burdens one day at a time and to leave the future entirely in His all-sufficient hand. His word to us is:

Psalm 55:22
"Cast thy burden upon the Lord and He shall sustain thee."

In the next few verses, we discover four truths, which will greatly sustain us in this time of burden bearing.

Firstly, we should remember that God is the God of our salvation.

Psalm 68:19
"Blessed *be* the Lord, *Who* daily loadeth us *with benefits, even* the God of our salvation. Selah."

Remembrance of this certainly causes the burdens of life to fade into insignificance. The Hebrew word for salvation is *Yeshuah* from which we have the word "Jesus". It is the remembrance of our Salvation in the Person of the Lord Jesus which firstly causes us to bless God in the burden.

Secondly, we are reminded that God is for us.

Psalm 68:20
"*He that is* our God *is* the God of salvation; and unto God the Lord *belong* the issues from death."

The phrase in verse 20, "He that is our God", means literally in Hebrew, **"God is for us"** (*hael lanu*). Was this in Paul's mind as he wrote Romans 8:31?

Romans 8:31
"What shall we then say to these things? **If God *be* for us**, who *can be* against us?"

No force, either earthly or infernal, can overwhelm the believer who is in the security of the promise: **"God is for us."** Accordingly, it is with this confidence that he declares:

Romans 8:35
"Who shall separate us from the love of Christ? *shall* tribulation, or distress,

or persecution, or famine, or nakedness, or peril, or sword?"

Thirdly, we are reminded that salvation is multifaceted and great.

Verse 20 could be literally translated: "God is for us even the **God of our salvations"** (plural). The phrase, **"the God of our salvations"**, occurs nowhere else in our Old Testament. Moreover, the word "salvations" is uniquely found in this verse. When a word or phrase only occurs once in the whole Hebrew Bible, we are reminded of its unique and superlative nature. If faced with burdens in life, let us remember the greatness of our salvation! However, let us not forget either, that the plural form here emphasises to us that salvation has many aspects. We have present salvation from the power of sin, past salvation from the penalty of sin as well as the certain future prospect of salvation from the presence of sin. Thus we speak of God as the "God of our salvations".

Fourthly, we are reminded that the love of God to us went even to the extent of the death of His Son

Psalm 68:20

"He that is our God is the God of salvation; and unto God the Lord belong the issues from death."

The phrase, "unto God the Lord belong the issues from death", could also, and equally legitimately, be literally translated, "unto God the Lord are **the comings out even unto death"**. Let us consider the evidence for this alternative rendering.

The word "issues" or "comings out" proved difficult for the translators of many versions including the Authorised Version. The problem is that the preposition "from" in the phrase "from death" is "to" in the original Hebrew, giving us the phrase "to death". This seemed difficult for the translators in this context to work out how that "to God the Lord belong issues **unto** death". Then it was noticed that the root word for "issues" in its verbal form *yatsa* means "to go out or come out". Some translators thought perhaps that the phrase means "escapes from death" and there are several translations of the verse which say: "to God the Lord belong the escapes from death". Nevertheless, the problem remains for the translators that the preposition is not "from" but rather "to" death. To get over this difficulty, it has been noted that the preposition "to" sometimes carries the significance "for", which led to the rendering, "to God the Lord belong the escapes for death". Even if we do accept that the word "to" in this case can mean "for", the author still is uncomfortable with *totsaoth* being translated "escapes" because nowhere else in the Old Testament is this word either translated or contextually used in this sense. On the contrary, on many occasions it describes the boundaries of the inheritance in Israel, where the word suggests the passage or movement of the traveller outward from one region to another but not in the idea of an escape.

Joshua 16:3
> "And goeth down westward to the coast of Japhleti, unto the coast of Bethhoron the nether, and to Gezer: and **the goings out** (*totsaoth*) thereof are at the sea."

Of great interest, however, is the observation that the word *totsaoth*, which literally means "comings out", is very similar to the word *motsaoth*, sharing the same root *yatsa* (to go out or to come out) and which also, unquestionably, means "comings out" – this time in the context of the outward movements of the Lord Jesus from eternity past outwards to men. Thus *motsaoth* is a lovely word describing His comings out from eternity past unto Bethlehem Ephratah and then making His way back to the Father.

Micah 5:2
> "But thou, Bethlehem Ephratah, *though* thou be little among the thousands of Judah, *yet* out of thee shall He come forth unto Me *that is* to be Ruler in Israel; Whose **goings forth** (*motsaothav*) *have been* from of old, from everlasting."

These considerations lead to a literal translation of the verse, an understanding of which brings forth worship in the heart of every Christian reader:
> "To God the Lord belong the comings out even to the extent of death."

We can say with Paul:

Romans 8:34-35
> 34 "Who *is* he that condemneth? *It is* Christ that died, yea rather, that is risen again, Who is even at the right hand of God, Who also maketh intercession for us.
> 35 Who shall separate us from the love of Christ? *shall* tribulation, or distress, or persecution, or famine, or nakedness, or peril, or sword?"

When we consider our burden, or as Paul calls it "our light affliction", and weigh it against the enormity of the love of our Lord Jesus Christ, Whose comings out to us have been to the extent even of His own voluntary death for us, we can rest calmly in the assurance of the "exceeding and eternal weight of glory" which will soon be experienced.

2 Corinthians 4:17
> "For our light affliction, which is but for a moment, worketh for us a far more exceeding *and* eternal weight of glory;"

7 The effects of the Divine presence in the coming Kingdom (Psalm 68:21-35)

This final section reminds us that the Lord's enemies, who may burden His people with persecution today, will one day be subjugated.

Psalm 68:21

> "But God shall wound (*yimchats*) (literally meaning "shall pierce through") the head of His enemies, *and* the hairy scalp of such an one as goeth on still

in his trespasses."

God will wound (pierce through) the head of His enemies. Notice that "head" is in the singular, not "heads". This indicates that it is one individual who is in mind who is acting as head over all the enemies of the Lord. He is morally wicked and is described as "going on still in his trespasses". Interestingly, a trespass is something which, when brought to the transgressor's attention, can be dealt with and forgiven. However, persisting in trespass, such as is the situation here, is a matter of iniquity and wickedness and suggests that this person is knowingly sinning against light. He has given himself over wholly to the cause of evil and for someone persisting in that mind-set there can be no forgiveness. The fact that he is described as "the head of the Lord's enemies" suggests that he is the final human figurehead of rebellion against God, and this designation could certainly fit the man of sin in 2 Thessalonians 2 (see Appendix 2).

2 Thessalonians 2:3-4
> 3 "Let no man deceive you by any means: for *that day shall not come*, except there come a falling away first, and that **man of sin be revealed**, the son of perdition;
> 4 Who opposeth and exalteth himself above all that is called God, or that is worshipped; so that he as God sitteth in the temple of God, shewing himself that he is God."

This future world leader behaves in an absolute anti-God fashion and proclaims himself as God. The phrase, "hairy scalp (crown)", means literally "crown (scalp) of hair" and is perhaps a derogatory term graphically reminding us of the beastlike character of this wicked man as is emphasised in Revelation 13.

Psalm 2:4 tells us that "He that sitteth in the heavens shall laugh. The Lord shall have them in derision". Certainly, while the world bows down in reverence to this wicked man, the persecuted believers in the tribulation period will be able to speak of this world leader in a derogatory way as "the man with the hairy scalp".

One cannot fail to notice the parallel with Judges 5:12, when the phrase, "thou hast led captivity captive", is used of Barak's defeat of Sisera, a decisive part of which occurred when a woman named Jael pierced through Sisera's head.

Judges 5:26
> "She put her hand to the nail, and her right hand to the workmen's hammer; and with the hammer she smote Sisera, she smote off his head, when she had pierced and stricken through his temples."

The great return

Psalm 68:22-23

> 22 "The Lord said, I will bring again from Bashan, I will bring *My people* again from the depths of the sea:
> 23 That Thy foot may be dipped in the blood of *Thine* enemies, *and* the

tongue of Thy dogs in the same."

In verse 22, the phrase "My people" in the clause, "I will bring *My people*", is in italics indicating that it is not part of the original text. This has led some to think that what is in mind here is the bringing back of the fleeing enemies of the Lord to Him for judgment. However, a careful study of the phrase, "to bring again", shows that it is used many times to describe the regathering of the nation of Israel on the occasion of the Lord's return (eg Jeremiah 33:11, Ezekiel 34:16). Moreover, the literal meaning of the verb is "to cause to return again; to restore". This implies bringing back to an original location someone or something which had strayed from that location. Those who feel that the verse is speaking of the enemies of the Lord understand the verb "to bring again" to imply that those who are "brought again" had, just prior to the Lord's return to Jerusalem, fled from that city to Bashan or the depths of the sea. There are some difficulties with this view.

Firstly, the "bringing back" from the depths of the sea must surely mean bringing back from death since no one can be alive in the depths of the sea. This seems not unreasonable when we remember that the imagery of drawing out of waters in Psalm 18 was taken to illustrate resurrection. We know from other Scriptures that no **unsaved dead** of any dispensation of time experience resurrection from the dead at the end of the tribulation. All such must await the great white throne judgment at the end of the millennium. This shows that those who are brought again from the depths of the sea, i.e. brought back from death, cannot be ranked among the lost since all unsaved remain dead until the 1000 years have ended. Rather, those who are "brought back" must be dead saints from the Old Testament and tribulation eras.

Secondly, the verb to "bring back; restore; cause to return" implies that the person being "restored" or "caused to return" is being returned to a location which is theirs by right. This cannot be the wicked, who doubtlessly will endeavour to exit Jerusalem as they try to flee away from the face of the Lord on His return.

We may well enquire why Bashan and the depths of the sea are chosen as the two locations from which the remnant will be brought. In fact, by juxtaposing Bashan, the place of hills (verse 14), with the depths of the sea, the Psalmist is describing the entire geographical spectrum from which the Lord will bring His own people to meet Him at His return. Whether it is on land or the most inhospitable part of the sea, all of this world will yield up those who belong to Christ, dead or alive, from the Old Testament and tribulation periods.

In Micah 7, the phrase, "the depths of the sea", is given as the place into which the Lord has cast the sins of the Old Testament believers who enjoyed divine forgiveness.

Micah 7:18-19

18 "Who *is* a God like unto Thee, that pardoneth iniquity, and **passeth by** (passes over) the transgression of the remnant of His heritage? He retaineth not His anger for ever, because He delighteth *in* mercy.

19 He will turn again, He will have compassion upon us; He will subdue our iniquities; and Thou wilt cast all their sins **into the depths of the sea**."

Does the phrase, "the depths of the sea", therefore, mean forgotten forever? Clearly not, since in Psalm 68 we are shown that the Lord's people in the "depths of the sea" will not be forgotten but will be brought to meet their Lord. We should not be alarmed by Micah telling us that the Lord had cast their sins into the depths of the sea, as if this language were to suggest that God's forgiveness lacked permanence. Indeed, Micah has already told us in verse 18 that God "**passed over** the transgressions of the remnant of His heritage". It was in this context that he tells us that God cast their sins into the "depths of the sea".

We also saw in Psalm 22 that the sins of the Old Testament era which belonged to the redeemed of that period had been "passed over" (Romans 3:25) by God but not dealt with.

Romans 3:25
"Whom God hath set forth *to be* a propitiation through faith in His blood, to declare His righteousness for the remission (passing over) of sins that are past through the forbearance of God;"

The sins were "passed over" as far as the Old Testament believer was concerned, but their penalty had not yet been borne. This pertained until the Lord Jesus would come to bear away sin's penalty. All the penalty for the sins of the Old Testament believers, which had long since been forgiven by a merciful God, was remembered by God at Calvary, exacted and laid upon Christ. Even before the Lord came to redeem, as far as those Old Testament believers were concerned, their sins were long since gone and covered; they were at the bottom of the sea. However, only at Calvary did the Lord Jesus bear away the awful penalty of all those sins. There is no danger of even one single sin being discovered.

To return then to the phrase, "I will bring again from the depths of the sea", it is worth noting that the contextual use of the phrase, "the depths of the sea", in Micah suggests a place where things are forgotten from **human living memory**. Thus, by describing the resurrection of the Lord's people of the Old Testament and tribulation periods as being brought again "from the depths of the sea", David is reminding his reader that these people may have been forgotten by men but never by their God. He will bring them from death's domain, whether from land or sea, and bring them to the land where His long promised Kingdom will be centred.

The purpose for this great regathering is given in the next verse.

Psalm 68:23
"That Thy foot may be dipped (*timchatz*) in the blood of *Thine* enemies, *and* the tongue of Thy dogs in the same."

Translation and the resulting exposition of this verse have proved difficult and, accordingly, there are many different translations and interpretations available to the English reader. However, most translations and resulting interpretations could be paraphrased and summarised as describing the foot of the victor being dipped or even washed in the blood of His enemies while the dogs lick up that blood.

There are major doctrinal difficulties with this interpretation.

1 The verb *timchatz* does not mean "to dip" or "to wash". It means "to smite or pierce through". Some have suggested that *timchatz* is a scribal error for what was originally *tirchatz* meaning "that Thou mayest wash (*tirchatz*) Thy foot". However, it is doctrinally impossible that the Lord Jesus should ever "wash" His feet in the blood of His enemies. In fact, while on earth His feet were never recorded as being "washed". When the woman in Luke 7 "washed His feet" (Authorised Version rendering) with her tears, the verb "to wash" means "to rain upon" in Luke 7:38 and Luke 7:44.

Luke 7:36-46
36 "And one of the Pharisees desired Him that He would eat with him. And He went into the Pharisee's house, and sat down to meat.
37 And, behold, a woman in the city, which was a sinner, when she knew that *Jesus* sat at meat in the Pharisee's house, brought an alabaster box of ointment,
38 And stood at His feet behind *Him* weeping, **and began to wash His feet with tears**, and did wipe *them* with the hairs of her head, and kissed His feet, and anointed *them* with the ointment.
39 Now when the Pharisee which had bidden Him saw *it*, he spake within himself, saying, This Man, if He were a prophet, would have known who and what manner of woman *this is* that toucheth Him: for she is a sinner.
40 And Jesus answering said unto him, Simon, I have somewhat to say unto thee. And he saith, Master, say on.
41 There was a certain creditor which had two debtors: the one owed five hundred pence, and the other fifty.
42 And when they had nothing to pay, he frankly forgave them both. Tell Me therefore, which of them will love him most?
43 Simon answered and said, I suppose that *he*, to whom he forgave most. And He said unto him, Thou hast rightly judged.
44 And He turned to the woman, and said unto Simon, Seest thou this woman? I entered into thine house, thou gavest Me no water for My feet: **but she hath washed My feet with tears**, and wiped *them* with the hairs of her head.
45 Thou gavest Me no kiss: but this woman since the time I came in hath not ceased to kiss My feet.
46 My head with oil thou didst not anoint: but this woman hath anointed My feet with ointment."

This teaches us that no defilement adhered to Him, rendering washing unnecessary. This was the miracle of "God manifest in flesh". If this was the case on His first advent how incongruous that He should wash His feet on His return to judge the earth.

2 The second difficulty with the traditional translation is that the word

order of the original text is quite different from the most commonly available translations.

Let us now consider the literal translation of this verse in three parts:

1 That Thy foot may pierce through (*timchatz*)

2 in blood the tongue of Thy dogs

3 His portion from enemies

The verb "to pierce through" or "to smite," does not mean "to dip". In fact, this is the same verb as is used in verse 21, where it is translated "shall wound".

Psalm 68:21

"But God shall wound the head of His enemies."

What does He wound? In verse 21, He wounds the head of His enemies. In verse 23, His foot wounds "the tongue of Thy dogs". However, the tongue of the dog is "in blood". This shows that the dog, on the occasion of its destruction, is in the act of looking for blood. The verse could be paraphrased to reflect these nuances of meaning as follows:

"That Thy foot might pierce through the tongue of Thy blood-thirsty dogs - from enemies His portion."

We saw in Psalm 22 that the dog was a picture of godless Gentiles who pierced the hands and feet of the Lord Jesus. It is, therefore, not inappropriate to consider the dogs referred to here as likewise being ungodly people of Gentile ethnicity or individuals of whatever ethnicity behaving with dog-like brutality. This time, it is the tongue of these wicked and bloodthirsty people which is singled out for specific judgment. It may be asked why these individuals are referred to as "Thy dogs". The final clause of the verse brings the poetic explanation. "Thy dogs" are immediately spoken of as "enemies" from which the Lord receives His portion in allowing the remnant whom they persecuted to witness their judgment. We are familiar with the Lord's enemies being referred to as "Thine enemies". However, it appears that in this verse they are spoken of in the derogatory language of "Thy dogs". The nature of their punishment is that their mouths will be stopped and silenced. This will be witnessed by the remnant of believers who have been "brought again" to meet their Lord on His return. This is their vindication and the punishment of their erstwhile persecutors. This judgment of the living nations, witnessed by the restored remnant, is the Lord's portion from His enemies which the passage here indicates are His dogs.

What a day that will be! Those of the Old Testament and tribulations eras who have died will be raised from the dead to enter into the Kingdom.

They will, joyfully and hurriedly, make their way up to Jerusalem, the city of the Great King, to worship Him. They will form part of the temple procession which is meant by the phrase, "Thy goings O God" (*halichoth*).

As can be see from the illustrative verse given below in Job 6:19, the word *halichoth* describes a procession or train of people.

Job 6:19
> "The troops of Tema looked, the companies (*halichoth*) of Sheba waited for them."

Accordingly, in Psalm 68:24-29 when we read the word "goings" (*halichoth*) we can substitute the word "processions" as follows:

Psalm 68:24-28
> 24 "They have seen Thy processions (*halichoth*), O God; *even* the processions (*halichoth*) of my God, my King, in the sanctuary.
> 25 The singers went before, the players on instruments *followed* after; among *them were* the damsels playing with timbrels.
> 26 Bless ye God in the congregations, *even* the Lord, from the fountain of Israel.
> 27 There *is* little Benjamin *with* their ruler, the princes of Judah *and* their council, the princes of Zebulun, *and* the princes of Naphtali.
> 28 Thy God hath commanded thy strength: strengthen, O God, that which Thou hast wrought for us."

Who will make up the procession? First to be mentioned are the worshippers who are described as singers, players of instruments and damsels (virgins). The purpose will be to bless God, even the Lord (verse 26). Worship is mentioned first, indicating to us that the prime object of the procession is to worship the Lord. The verses which follow show us that one of the key conditions for acceptable worship is unity among the Lord's people. It is thrilling to see in this prophetic vision, the entire redeemed nation of Israel in perfect harmony with each element within itself. No longer is there a division between Benjamin (the tribe of Saul) and Judah (the tribe of David). Nor is there any division between Judah and the Northern Kingdom of Israel (Zebulon and Naphtali). Unity will prevail. Moreover, Godly order will pertain with the counsellors of Judah in full fellowship with the people of Judah and the ruler of Benjamin fully in harmony with the worshippers of his tribe, which stands in contrast to the behaviour of Saul who so often acted in flagrant disregard of the Lord's will and the good of His people. Surely this wonderful prospect must have rejoiced the heart of David who knew all too well about the divisions among the Lord's people in His day.

We know that in that coming day the restored remnant of Israel shall have a pivotal role in the administration of the millennial earth (Isaiah 2). Israel shall be the head of the nations and not the tail. Israel's remnant shall receive its strength and power in the millennial earth by divine decree.

Psalm 68:28
> "Thy God hath commanded thy strength: strengthen, O God, that which Thou hast wrought for us."

There is a sense in which all the saints in the millennium will be characterised by power (strength) as we observed in Psalm 8 ("out of the mouths of babes and sucklings Thou hast ordained strength"). This will be seen in man's dominion over creation which Adam lost in the garden and which will be restored in the millennium. However, there must be a hierarchy of government on the millennial earth, and Israel will hold a special role in the administration of the remaining nations during that period, and divine power will enable them to do this. Moreover, the other nations will gladly and willingly acquiesce to this divine order of administration as the later verses indicate.

Psalm 68:29-32

29 "Because of Thy temple at Jerusalem shall kings bring presents unto Thee.

30 Rebuke the company of spearmen, the multitude of the bulls, with the calves of the people, *till every one* submit himself with pieces of silver: scatter Thou the people *that* delight in war.

31 Princes shall come out of Egypt; Ethiopia shall soon stretch out her hands unto God.

32 Sing unto God, ye kingdoms of the earth; O sing praises unto the Lord; Selah:"

The leaders of the living nations who are saved will bring their gifts up to Jerusalem. This is also stated in Isaiah 2 and Zechariah 14. Of particular interest and wonder to David would be the prospect that the nations of Egypt and Ethiopia would participate in this act of worship to God and submission to His people Israel, since at the time of writing the Psalm, these were two major heathen civilisations in the ancient world.

In verse 30, David interrupts the flow of his millennial description to bring rebuke to a company who are not joining in the procession of worshippers. "Rebuke the company of spearmen", he says. This phrase, "company of spearmen", means literally, "the beast of the reeds", which Gesenius in his Hebrew and English Lexicon of the Old Testament suggests could mean simply "the crocodile". The combination of the picture of a crocodile and the "multitude of the bulls", together with their offspring, "the calves", depicts for us those of the nations during the millennium who are not genuinely saved. This sad phenomenon is discussed in Psalms 22 and 72, where we discover that those born of believing parents in the millennium will themselves need to get saved. For those who do not, they will submit themselves by feigned obedience to the Lord Jesus. They will remain subject to the King even though they do not engage in His worship. Zechariah tells us that they will not come up to Jerusalem to worship, and as a consequence they will not receive rain on their lands.

Zechariah 14:16-19

16 "And it shall come to pass, *that* every one that is left of all the nations which came against Jerusalem shall even go up from year to year to worship the King, the Lord of hosts, and to keep the feast of tabernacles.

17 And it shall be, *that* whoso will not come up of *all* the families of the earth unto Jerusalem to worship the King, the Lord of hosts, **even upon them shall be no rain.**

18 And if the family of Egypt go not up, **and come not, that** *have* **no** *rain;* there shall be the plague, wherewith the Lord will smite the heathen that come not up to keep the feast of tabernacles.
19 This shall be the punishment of Egypt, and the punishment of all nations that come not up to keep the feast of tabernacles."

In fact, this is possibly the meaning of the reference in Psalm 68:6: "the rebellious dwell in a dry *land*". They are not genuine subjects of the King and will send their tribute money to Him in feigned submission, but will themselves gravitate as far away from Jerusalem as they can.

Happily, the Psalm quickly leaves the sad subject of men and women rejecting the Lord Jesus, even in the ideal conditions of His millennial reign, and focuses on inhabitants of planet earth united in their praise unto the Lord. Even though they are Gentiles they will rejoice in their praise of the heavenly One.

Psalm 68:32

"Sing unto God, ye kingdoms of the earth; O sing praises unto the Lord; Selah:"

They will listen to His voice as that of absolute authority and will obey completely.

Psalm 68:33

"To Him that rideth upon the heavens of heavens, *which were* of old; lo, He doth send out His voice, *and that* a mighty voice."

The first part of the Psalm tells us how the Kingdom will be established through the Lord's direct intervention in descending to this earth to ride "upon the wastes" (Psalm 68:4) on the occasion of His return. The end of the Psalm shows us how the ongoing government of His established Kingdom is carried out. This will be from the Heavens where His throne is located (Psalm 68:33) and in "the clouds" (Psalm 68:34). This strongly suggests that after the Lord Jesus has defeated His enemies on the battlefield of earth, He returns to His Bride in the heavens from where His Kingdom is directly administered. This particular truth is further described in Psalm 110 and only partly discussed at this point. These matters may have been difficult for the Psalmist to grasp, but with New Testament revelation we know that throughout the millennial Kingdom the Lord Jesus will be with His Church in the heavens.

It should be acknowledged, however, that where the Lord Jesus and His Bride will be throughout the millennium has been a cause of differing views amongst Bible teachers. Will it be earth or heaven?

One view is that the Lord Jesus will be on earth throughout the entire millennium, and because all acknowledge that the Church will always be **with Him**, the Church must also be with Him on the millennial earth. The difficulty with this view is that the Church anticipates a heavenly inheritance (1 Peter 1:4), a heavenly hope (Colossians 1:5) a heavenly city (Hebrews

12:22) and a heavenly reward (Matthew 5:12). Therefore, it conflicts with many New Testament Scriptures to attribute to the Church an earthly future after the Lord's return to reign. In fact, the above Scriptures, showing the heavenly destiny of the Church, demonstrate that this cannot be the case.

However, an objection to the idea that the Lord Jesus will govern His coming Kingdom from the heavens together with His Bride arises from Revelation 20:4 where it is clearly stated that the Lord will reign **with** the resurrected tribulation saints who will be in the coming Kingdom on earth.

Revelation 20:4

"And I saw thrones, and they sat upon them, and judgment was given unto them: and *I saw* the souls of them that were beheaded for the witness of Jesus, and for the Word of God, and which had not worshipped the beast, neither his image, neither had received *his* mark upon their foreheads, or in their hands; and they lived and reigned **with (Greek: *meta*)** Christ a thousand years."

How is it possible, some may ask, that the Lord Jesus can reign **with** the resurrected tribulation believers, who will be on earth in the millennium, and yet **at the same time** be **with** His Church in the heavens? The answer to this question comes from a study of the following verses which state how the Lord Jesus will be **with** the Church in the heavens. As we look at these verses, it is important to note that in the context of the Lord Jesus being **with** His Church in the heavens, the preposition is no longer *meta,* as is the case of Him being "with" the millennial believers (Revelation 20:4). Rather when the Lord is described as being with His Church in heaven, and Church believers are described as being with Him there, the preposition is *sun* or *sum-* also translated "with".

Philippians 1:23

"For I am in a strait betwixt two, having a desire to depart, and to be with (*sun*) Christ; which is far better."

1 Thessalonians 4:17

"Then we which are alive *and* remain shall be caught up together with (*sun*) them in the clouds, to meet the Lord in the air: and so shall we ever be with (*sun*) the Lord."

2 Timothy 2:12

"If we suffer, we shall also reign with *Him (sum-basileuo* where the word *sum* means "with" and *basileuo* means "to reign"): if we deny *Him,* He also will deny us."

What then is the difference between *sun* and *meta, if* both are translated as "with"?

It is clear that *sun* means "with" in the sense of being in close physical proximity to someone. *Meta* means "with" in a spiritual sense **whether or not** there is close proximity. It is in this sense that we understand the presence of the Lord Jesus as with us today in this Church age as indeed He promised His disciples in Matthew 28:20.

Matthew 28:20
  "...and, lo, I am with (*meta*) you alway, *even* unto the end of the world. Amen."

In the same sense, during the coming, great tribulation, John, in Revelation 14:1, envisages the Lord Jesus standing with (*meta*) the 144,000 sealed remnant believers who will be located on Mount Sion.

Revelation 14:1
  "And I looked, and, lo, a Lamb stood on the mount Sion, and with (*meta*) Him an hundred forty *and* four thousand, having His Father's Name written in their foreheads."

The Lord Jesus is standing with them in the *meta* sense of "with", which suggests that His presence with them is in a spiritual sense. In other words, the Lord Jesus will assure these suffering believers of His presence in exactly the same way as He stood with the remnant of Israel in the dark days of the captivity in Zechariah 1:7-11. Other very instructive occurrences of *sun* and *meta* are discussed in **Appendix 4**.

Now it all becomes clear. Millennial believers on earth can know that the Lord is "with them" (*meta*) in the same sense as believers today can claim His promise, "Lo I am with (*meta*) you always". In contrast, we in the Church era will be with Him (*sun* and *sum*) as in the immediate physical presence of Christ we shall reign with (*sun*) Him. What a joy it is to know that loved ones in Christ who have gone home to heaven are in His immediate physical presence! More details on how the Lord returns to heaven to administer His Kingdom after coming to this earth to establish His authority there are discussed in Psalm 110.

Let us now return to the Psalm. This aspect of teaching described above, as revealed in the New Testament, is entirely consistent with the verses dealing with the order of the millennial government at the end of the Psalm.

The Psalmist tells us that those on the earth will not resent the order of divine authority in that coming Kingdom and the centrality of the role of His people Israel to whom they will happily be subject.

Psalm 68:34
  "Ascribe ye strength unto God: His excellency *is* over Israel, and His strength *is* in the clouds."

Order of headship is seen here. **Strength** belongs to God and is seen in the **clouds**. We saw in Psalms 18 and 19 that the Church will be in the heavens. Christ is the Head of the Church in the heavens. However, Psalm 68:35 shows us that redeemed Israel will be the head of the nations on the earth by divinely imparted power and authority.

Psalm 68:35

"O God, *Thou art* terrible out of Thy holy places: the God of Israel *is* He that giveth strength and power unto *His* people. Blessed *be* God."

This idea of heaven (the Church) and earth (future Israel), united in government and headship, is presented to us in Ephesians 1:10, where we read that "in the dispensation of the fullness of times (the millennium) the Lord will head up together (headship) in one all things in Christ both which are in heaven (the Church) and which are on earth (the millennial saints on the earth) even in Him".

Ephesians 1:10

"That in the dispensation of the fullness of times He might gather together (head up together) in one all things in Christ, both which are in heaven, and which are on earth; *even* in Him:"

Whilst this order of future divine administration in the coming Kingdom is not clearly spelled out in the Psalm, the language of Psalm 68:32-35 is carefully chosen to be entirely consistent with the nation of Israel being on earth, heading the nations of the Kingdom, while the Lord governs His Kingdom from His throne in the heavens, as clearly revealed in the New Testament.

What a day that will be when heaven and earth will enjoy harmony one with the other as our Lord Jesus Christ reigns supreme! When this happens the presence of the Lord, which is the overriding theme of the Psalm, will be the joy of the redeemed ones forever.

---

1. The children of Israel came to Sinai as the 'hill of God' three months after they escaped from Egypt (Exodus 24:13). There they encountered the Law of God and its attendant judgments. Interestingly, when they moved on from that august place, we are told in Numbers 10:33 that they 'departed from the Hill of the Lord' not the 'hill of God'. This is a remarkable change of name, because we know that the 'Hill of the Lord' is the name for Mount Moriah in Jerusalem (Genesis 22:14; Isaiah 2:3; Micah 4:2). As we considered in Psalm 24, this is the place where the Lamb of God's providing would be sacrificially revealed at Golgotha. Why does it say in Numbers 10:32 that when the nation moved on from Sinai they "departed from the Hill of the Lord' rather than "from the hill of God (Sinai)"? Clearly, the wilderness nation had not been to the Hill of the Lord geographically. However, by calling the hill of God, the Hill of the Lord in Numbers 10:33, the Scriptures would have us understand that it was **as if the wilderness people had reached the Hill of the Lord by faith**. At first this may seem a farfetched understanding of Numbers 10:33. However, it becomes very reasonable when we recall that it was at mount Sinai, the hill of God, after the golden calf incident that Moses interceded with God for the people (Exodus 32:11-14) by specifically referring to the oath sworn to Abraham in Genesis 22:16-18 in the Hill of the Lord. This is discussed in Psalm 90. How sweet it is to observe that the recovery of the nation spiritually involved them getting back to the Hill of the Lord by faith. In other words, in language comprehensible to those familiar with gospel preaching, it could be said, "They got by faith to Calvary!" This is the basis of each genuine conversion, and the basis of true restoration of the backslider. It is also the basis of the restoration of the nation in a coming day.

11

PSALM 69

To the chief Musician upon Shoshannim, A Psalm of David

1 Save me, O God; for the waters are come in unto my soul.

2 I sink in deep mire, where there is no standing: I am come into deep waters, where the floods overflow me.

3 I am weary of my crying: my throat is dried: mine eyes fail while I wait for my God.

4 They that hate me without a cause are more than the hairs of mine head: they that would destroy me, being mine enemies wrongfully, are mighty: then I restored that which I took not away.

5 O God, Thou knowest my foolishness; and my sins are not hid from Thee.

6 Let not them that wait on Thee, O Lord God of hosts, be ashamed for my sake: let not those that seek Thee be confounded for my sake, O God of Israel.

7 Because for Thy sake I have borne reproach; shame hath covered my face.

8 I am become a stranger unto my brethren, and an alien unto my mother's children.

9 For the zeal of Thine house hath eaten me up; and the reproaches of them that reproached Thee are fallen upon me.

10 When I wept, and chastened my soul with fasting, that was to my reproach.

11 I made sackcloth also my garment; and I became a proverb to them.

12 They that sit in the gate speak against me; and I was the song of the drunkards.

13 But as for me, my prayer is unto Thee, O Lord, in an acceptable time: O God, in the multitude of Thy mercy hear me, in the truth of Thy salvation.

14 Deliver me out of the mire, and let me not sink: let me be delivered from them that hate me, and out of the deep waters.

15 Let not the waterflood overflow me, neither let the deep swallow me up, and let not the pit shut her mouth upon me.

16 Hear me, O Lord; for Thy lovingkindness is good: turn unto me according to the multitude of Thy tender mercies.

17 And hide not Thy face from Thy servant; for I am in trouble: hear me speedily.

18 Draw nigh unto my soul, and redeem it: deliver me because of mine enemies.

19 Thou hast known my reproach, and my shame, and my dishonour: mine adversaries are all before Thee.

20 Reproach hath broken My heart; and I am full of heaviness: and I looked for some to take pity, but there was none; and for comforters, but I found none.

21 They gave Me also gall for My meat; and in My thirst they gave Me vinegar to drink.

22 Let their table become a snare before them: and that which should have been for their welfare, let it become a trap.

23 Let their eyes be darkened, that they see not; and make their loins continually to shake.

24 Pour out Thine indignation upon them, and let Thy wrathful anger take hold of them.

25 Let their habitation be desolate; and let none dwell in their tents.

26 For they persecute him whom Thou hast smitten; and they talk to the grief of those whom Thou hast wounded.

27 Add iniquity unto their iniquity: and let them not come into Thy righteousness.

28 Let them be blotted out of the book of the living, and not be written with the righteous.

29 But I am poor and sorrowful: let Thy salvation, O God, set me up on high.

30 I will praise the Name of God with a song, and will magnify Him with thanksgiving.

31 This also shall please the Lord better than an ox or bullock that hath horns and hoofs.

32 The humble shall see this, and be glad: and your heart shall live that seek God.

33 For the Lord heareth the poor, and despiseth not His prisoners.

34 Let the heaven and earth praise Him, the seas, and every thing that moveth therein.

35 For God will save Zion, and will build the cities of Judah: that they may dwell there, and have it in possession.

36 The seed also of His servants shall inherit it: and they that love His Name shall dwell therein.

Introduction

This Psalm describes how David bore unjust reproach and criticism for being linked to the Messianic promise of the coming Christ. It shows how this sensitive servant of God felt deeply saddened not only by this but especially by his own intrinsic failures. The answer to David's distress came in a twofold revelation to him: firstly, the Lord in heaven knew in detail all about David's failure and frailty and secondly, even more amazingly, as the coming incarnate Kinsman Redeemer, the Lord would come to know experimentally and at first hand the same hostility and reproach which David experienced in his own lifetime. Accordingly, this Psalm highlights the centrality of the Person of Christ in the divine programme of redemption and shows how this truth should encourage a distressed believer.

1 The Psalmist's distress of soul described (Psalm 69:1-3)

Psalm 69:1-3

1 "Save me, O God; for the waters are come in unto *my* soul.

2 I sink in deep mire, where *there is* no standing: I am come into deep
waters, where the floods overflow me.
3 I am weary of my crying: my throat is dried: mine eyes fail while I wait
for my God."

This Psalm begins with cries of distress from David. His predicament is
likened unto that of a drowning man: "The waters have come in unto my
soul...I am come into deep waters where the floods overflow me."

His helplessness is emphasised by the evocative imagery of his feet trapped
in the deep mire which is inexorably pulling him under the floods (verse 2).
This picture is one of depression and despair – at least from a human point
of view – and expresses an urgent need for deliverance. Obviously, the
language is entirely metaphoric because he tells us the waters have come as
far as his soul.

There are several references to the soul in this Psalm so it is appropriate to
consider what this means. The soul is the aspect of the person which is able
to **hear, see, touch, understand (Leviticus 5:1-5) and love (Deuteronomy
6:4-5).** The soul of man in his unfallen state has the capacity to love God.

Deuteronomy 6:4-5
4 "Hear, O Israel: The Lord our God *is* one Lord:
5 And thou shalt love the Lord thy God with all thine heart, and **with all
thy soul**, and with all thy might."

Man stands alone in all of creation and in contrast to all other created
animate beings the human soul can love God its creator. This is because
man is unique in that he is made **in the image and likeness** of God his
creator; the image of God is shown in Colossians 3 to be characterised by
love. Let us view the Scriptures which substantiate this important truth.

Genesis 1:26
"And God said, Let us make man in **Our image, after Our likeness**:"

What do we understand by the "image of God"? A clue is found in
Colossians 3 where, in the description of the "new man", i.e. the Spirit-
controlled believer, we discover that the characteristics of this newly saved
soul are marked by the "**image** of Him that created him". The features
which make up this divine "image" are mercies, kindness, humbleness of
mind, meekness, longsuffering and forgiveness (Colossians 3:12-13). These
virtues were perfectly shown out in the life of the Lord Jesus Who is "the
image of the invisible God" (Colossians 1:15). However, above all these
characteristics lies one overarching feature – love (Colossians 3:14).

Colossians 3:10-14
10 "And have put on the new *man*, which is renewed in knowledge **after
the image of Him that created him**:
11 Where there is neither Greek nor Jew, circumcision nor uncircumcision,
Barbarian, Scythian, bond *nor* free: but Christ *is* all, and in all.

12 Put on therefore, as the elect of God, holy and beloved, bowels of mercies, kindness, humbleness of mind, meekness, longsuffering;

13 Forbearing one another, and forgiving one another, if any man have a quarrel against any: even as Christ forgave you, so also *do* ye.

14 **And above all these things** *put on* **charity, which is the bond of perfectness.**"

Once we understand that the image of God is characterised by love (charity), as shown in Colossians 3:14, the significance of man being made in the image of God becomes apparent. Humankind is created by God in His image and thus has the capacity to love Him. So an important distinction between the soul of man and the soul of all other created beings is that man has the capacity to love his God with all his heart, **soul** and mind.

Sadly, this was lost by Adam's fall and is only restored to a soul on the occasion of salvation through faith. As far as the unsaved soul is concerned, it is in the pursuit of things to hear, see and touch that the soul so often contracts defilement, causing it to become aware of a feeling of **guilt** (Leviticus 5:1-5).

Leviticus 5:1-5

"And **if a soul sin**, and **hear** the voice of swearing, and *is* a witness, whether he hath **seen** or **known** *of it*; if he do not utter *it*, then he **shall bear his iniquity**.

2 Or if a soul **touch** any unclean thing, whether *it be* a carcase of an unclean beast, or a carcase of unclean cattle, or the carcase of unclean creeping things, and *if* it be hidden from him; he also shall be unclean, and guilty.

3 Or if he **touch** the uncleanness of man, whatsoever uncleanness *it be* that a man shall be defiled withal, and it be hid from him; when he **knoweth** *of it*, then he shall be guilty.

4 Or if a soul swear, pronouncing with *his* lips to do evil, or to do good, whatsoever *it be* that a man shall pronounce with an oath, and it be hid from him; when **he knoweth** *of it*, then he shall be guilty in one of these.

5 And it shall be, when he shall be guilty in one of these *things*, that he shall confess that he hath sinned in that *thing*:"

It is David's **soul** which is overwhelmed by a feeling of failure and sin in his life. He is weary (verse 3) of his crying (or calling out). It seems to him that his calling upon God is not met with a timely answer. Moreover, his soul's vision of God has been impaired under the cloud of depression: "Mine eyes fail while I wait for my God" (verse 3). When the waters of distress come into the soul of a believer, the senses of the soul, which include **seeing, hearing** and **understanding,** may be impaired, including even the awareness of the Lord's presence. This does not mean that such a believer is away from the Lord. It is just that he or she may have a feeling of being distant from their Lord even though in reality the Lord may indeed be very near to them. Under the crucible of distress a believer's soul's vision may be compromised ("mine eyes fail"). The answer to the Psalmist's distress of soul is demonstrated later in the Psalm when David declares his faith that the Near-Kinsman Redeemer would come so near to him as to be able to redeem **his soul (Psalm 69:18)**. The result of this divine intervention in redemption is that not only David but the seed of the Lord's servants shall inherit Zion, namely "they that **love His Name**".

Psalm 69:36
"The seed also of His servants shall inherit it: and they that love His Name shall dwell therein."

David's soul, which was once overwhelmed with distress, shall **eternally love His Name**. It is to this high calling that the human soul was first created in the image of God, and it is as a result of redemption that this goal can be achieved. The centrality of God's programme of redemption in realising this outcome is a major theme of the Psalm.

2 The Psalmist's soul distress explained (Psalm 69:4-12)
The cause of these feelings of despair is threefold:
1 the reproach he had to bear for the sake of the Lord
2 an overwhelming sense of his own failings
3 a dread of causing faithful followers of the Lord to become discouraged.
We will look at all three of these causes in detail and will then consider the secret of how he was delivered from this valley experience.

2.1 Distress through bearing the burden of reproach for Christ's sake

Psalm 69:4
"They that hate me without a cause are more than the hairs of mine head: they that would destroy me, *being* mine enemies wrongfully, are mighty: then I restored *that* which I took not away."

David had many enemies who wanted to destroy him. However, the cause of their hostility to David was based on a lie. This is obvious when we consider a literal translation which could read like this:

Psalm 69:4
"They are mighty, my destroyers, my enemies through a lie: namely that I restore what I did not violently sieze" (author's translation).

The same idea is brought out for us in the New Living Translation:

Psalm 69:4
"Those who hate me without cause are more numerous than the hairs on my head. These enemies who seek to destroy me are doing so without cause. They attack me with lies, demanding that I give back what I didn't steal."

The key to understanding Psalm 69:4 is the observation that the word in the Authorised Version translated "wrongfully" really means "a lie", indicating that the underlying basis of enmity to David was based on a lie. What was the lie? It was the false idea that David had seized by violence the right to the throne of Israel and, therefore, he should forthwith relinquish his claim thereto. This lie completely disregarded the promises by God to David regarding the establishing of David's house (dynasty) and the Messianic promise.

In 2 Samuel 16:7-8, we read of a man called Shimei who, during the Absalom rebellion, felt emboldened to articulate the lie of Psalm 69:4.

2 Samuel 16:7-8

> 7 "And thus said Shimei when he cursed, Come out, come out, thou bloody man, and thou man of Belial:
>
> 8 The Lord hath returned upon thee all the blood of the house of Saul, in whose stead thou hast reigned; and the Lord hath delivered the kingdom into the hand of Absalom thy son: and, behold, thou *art taken* in thy mischief, because thou *art* a bloody man."

On David's triumphant return after the defeat of Absalom, the gravity of Shimei's curses is made clear. He had cursed the Lord's Messiah, i.e. David, who had been anointed to be in the royal line of the Messiah – Christ the Lord.

2 Samuel 19:21

> "But Abishai the son of Zeruiah answered and said, Shall not Shimei be put to death for this, because he cursed the Lord's anointed (Hebrew:**Messiah**)?"

By cursing the Lord's anointed, Shimei had rejected God's promise to David of the coming Messiah Who would arise from the lineage of David.

It is clear that despite the contradictions of his enemies, David's faith was based on God's Word regarding the coming of the Messiah, Who, he clearly understood, would arise from his lineage as we will discover in Psalm 110:1: "The Lord said unto my Lord..." It may seem surprising to us today that the Psalm indicates to us that in David's day there was an element of reproach in keeping this truth before the people.

Let us notice in the following verses the recurrence of the word "reproach".

Psalm 69:7-12; 20

> 7 "Because for Thy sake I have borne **reproach**; shame hath covered my face.
>
> 8 I am become a stranger unto my brethren, and an alien unto my mother's children.
>
> 9 For the zeal of Thine house hath eaten me up; and **the reproaches** of them that **reproached Thee** are fallen upon me.
>
> 10 "When I wept, *and chastened* my soul with fasting, that was to **my reproach**.
>
> 11 I made sackcloth also my garment; and I became a proverb to them.
>
> 12 They that sit in the gate speak against me; and I *was* the song of the drunkards..."
>
> 20 "**Reproach hath broken My heart**; and I am full of heaviness: and I looked *for some* to take pity, but *there was* none; and for comforters, but I found none."

David became the object of the hostility of his enemies – even though they had no legitimate cause for this enmity. Moreover, he found himself isolated by his own family (Psalm 69:8). The only recorded comments of David's brothers, regarding their youngest sibling, are given to us just prior to the occasion of his slaying Goliath.

1 Samuel 17:28-29
> 28 "And Eliab his eldest brother heard when he spake unto the men; and Eliab's anger was kindled against David, and he said, **Why camest thou down hither? and with whom hast thou left those few sheep in the wilderness? I know thy pride, and the naughtiness of thine heart; for thou art come down that thou mightest see the battle.**
> 29 And David said, What have I now done? *Is there* not a cause?"

As the inspired record shows, David's brothers were neither commendatory nor respectful to their brother. This was serious because the Scripture emphasises to us in the preceding chapter that David's brothers had prior knowledge of Samuel's prophecy regarding David's destiny to be king after Saul. In fact, they actually had witnessed Samuel anointing David!

1 Samuel 16:13
> "Then Samuel took the horn of oil, and anointed him **in the midst of his** brethren: and the Spirit of the Lord came upon David from that day forward. So Samuel rose up, and went to Ramah."

How sad, then, that Psalm 69:8 shows us that this initial attitude of David's brothers had persisted long after the Goliath episode and that, sadly, at the time of writing Psalm 69 David still felt ostracised from at least some of his brothers due to his link with the promise of God. The reason for this hostility and isolation was "for Thy sake" (verse 7) because the reproaches of them that reproached the Lord were in fact being targeted at David. This was because he was linked with the Messianic promise which aroused the jealous hostility of those who did not recognise the importance of the coming Christ in the divine programme and, perhaps, most painfully of all, this included some from within his own circle of brothers.

It must have been a matter of much consolation to David to consider that the reproach which he personally was bearing was really directed primarily at the Lord Himself and that he (David) happened to be the one on whom these enemies of the Lord were **indirectly** expending their direct hatred against God. This is what is meant by the statement in Psalm 69:9: "The **reproaches** of them that **reproached Thee** are fallen upon me."

This verse is really the key to understanding the Psalm, as it shows us that the reproaches referred to in the Psalm are primarily aimed at the Messiah, even **before** He was revealed, by those who hated the Messianic promise, who then redirected their unbelieving animosity against king David.

Once we recognise that the Psalm is an analysis of what, in effect, amounted to an anti-Messianic movement in the time of David, we begin to see that the same anti-Messianic movement existed no less actively when the Lord Jesus Himself was on earth.

David, in his longing for the coming Messiah, recognised that the temple which he was planning to have built would one day be graced by the presence of this Coming One. Truly in David's case it could be said: "the zeal of Thine house hath eaten me up" (Psalm 69:9). This was an outstanding feature of one of Israel's greatest kings, and yet for this he clearly suffered reproach by those who did not know the God of Israel. When the true Messiah, the Son of David, arrived at the temple in Jerusalem to purge it from defilement, the disciples were vividly reminded of David's imperfect zeal in Psalm 69:9 as they witnessed the perfect zeal of the Lord Jesus:

John 2:13-17
> 13 "And the Jews' passover was at hand, and Jesus went up to Jerusalem,
> 14 And found in the temple those that sold oxen and sheep and doves, and the changers of money sitting:
> 15 And when He had made a scourge of small cords, He drove them all out of the temple, and the sheep, and the oxen; and poured out the changers' money, and overthrew the tables;
> 16 And said unto them that sold doves, Take these things hence; make not My Father's house an house of merchandise.
> 17 And His disciples remembered that it was written, **"The zeal of Thine house hath eaten Me up." "**

Note that it does not say, "then was fulfilled that which was written, 'the zeal of Thine house hath eaten Me up'", but rather "and His disciples remembered…" No doubt, the disciples remembered not just this verse but also the context – namely the zeal of the well-meaning king David for the Lord's house despite his own intrinsic failures and sin referred to in the Psalm. What a contrast the disciples witnessed that day in the temple as they observed the perfect and holy zeal of the long-promised Messiah, the Lord Jesus, for His Father's house! Unlike David, the zeal of the Person of Christ could never be marred by inconsistency or failure in His altogether sinless life.

By telling us, "the reproaches of them that **reproached Thee** are fallen upon me", David is vividly describing the hatred towards the Messiah hundreds of years before He was revealed. Alas, this hatred had not in any way abated when the Lord Jesus commenced His public ministry, as recorded in John 2:13-17, nor had it diminished after His three and a half years of public teaching which ended in the final rejection at the cross. In this regard, the reproaches which were hurled directly at the Lord in David's day, and then indirectly fell on David, become a very detailed prophetic analysis of the very same anti-Messianic hatred which the Lord would experience when on earth during His public ministry, from the purification of the temple in John 2 to the cross where, in John 19:28-30, we read the account of the detailed fulfilment of the prophecy of Psalm 69: 21 – "in My thirst they gave Me vinegar to drink. "

This understanding shows us that:

1 The **reproach of Christ** which David encountered in his day was

prophetic of the **reproaches** that the Lord would directly bear in the days of His flesh. This means that the verses dealing with David's reproach in this and in other Psalms apply primarily to David but **also** carry a prophetic application to the Person of Christ. When such verses are quoted in *Meditations in the Messianic Psalms* and are applying primarily to David, the pronouns are presented in lower case. When the same verses are considered in their fulfilment in Christ, the pronouns are presented in upper case.

2 When David was speaking of his own failings in the Psalm, they referred only to David and not to the Lord at all.

2.2 David's distress at his sense of failure

Some who are not Christians erroneously accuse New Testament writers of cherry-picking the reproach aspects of the Psalm as applying to the Lord Jesus, while arbitrarily discounting the verses which refer to sin and foolishness as applying to the Messiah. Let us note that David's use of language prevents us from applying any reference of his own foolishness to the Messiah:

There are 2 constructions of the verb "to know":

1 one means "to know about" in the sense of being fully aware of something or somebody

2 the other can carry the significance of knowing at first hand.

The first construction, "to know about", is used to describe David's failure and sin, whereas the second construction, "to know at first hand", is used to describe David's reproach, dishonour and shame which the Lord would enter into at first hand during His life on earth.

Psalm 69:5

"O God, Thou knowest my foolishness; and my sins are not hid from Thee."

It is worth noting that in Hebrew this verse can be literally translated, "O God Thou knowest about (Hebrew preposition *le*) my foolishness…" There is no hint of the Lord ever coming to know David's foolishness in His personal experience. However, He knows about every detail of David's failure including ours as well!

In contrast, later in the Psalm David says:

Psalm 69:19

"Thou hast known my reproach, and my shame, and my dishonour: mine adversaries *are* all before Thee."

This time the verb "to know" is not followed by the preposition *le* meaning "about". This is because the ensuing verses are dealing with experiences of David which would later also affect the Lord Jesus personally when He would come, as the New Testament accounts of His crucifixion so carefully record. A similar construction of the verb "to know" is found in Isaiah 53:3 where the Lord is spoken of as a "Man of sorrows, and acquainted with (knowing) grief". A careful study of the word "grief" shows that it is elsewhere translated "disease" or "sickness". The description in Isaiah 53 is of an intense personal acquaintance with the experience of grief or disease. In what sense did the Lord Jesus know at first hand disease and sickness? Clearly, His body was perfect and flawless and He did not experience sickness in His own body. For that reason, the Scripture is so careful to clarify this point and, therefore, Isaiah in the next verse tells us that it was "**our** griefs" (our sicknesses) that He bore and not His own. Nevertheless, His experience of **our** diseases and griefs was not remote. He was intensely personally affected by them. In fact, the phrase, "He hath borne our griefs", lets us know that He felt at first hand our weight of grief and disease. This becomes apparent when He, by His own hand, touched the leper, took Peter's fevered mother-in-law by the hand and touched the bier of the widow of Nain's dead son. This is to know literally at first hand the grief of His creatures and reaches its climax in the sacred record when we see the Lord weeping at the tomb of Lazarus. How wonderful and touching for us today!

Similarly, in Psalm 69, when it was a question of the Lord personally knowing what David speaks of as "my reproach", it would involve the Lord placing Himself in circumstances where ungodly men could mete out upon Him the same reproach, shame and dishonour as were heaped upon David in his lifetime. This understanding must surely have been a remarkable comfort to David.

At no stage does the Psalm hint that the Lord would personally come to know at first hand failures similar to that experienced by David. Rather, the references in the Psalm to the Lord knowing about "my sins" and "my foolishness" refer to David's awareness of the Lord's all seeing eyes observing and noting his every action. Moreover, when the Psalm indicates that the Lord knows about his failure, the Scripture is emphasisng to us how the Lord must stand distinct from and in contrast to the sin and failure of David.

Later in this Psalm it will be seen how David finds reassurance in restating the principles on which all his sins and guilt have been once and for all dealt with and put away (Psalm 69:18). When going through a valley experience, it is good to be reminded, with all the unmistakable assurance of God's word, that our sins are gone forever and forgiven. A believer with clinical depression may have, as a symptom of that illness, an unremitting emotion of (sometimes irrational) guilt, so it is good to be able to remind him or her of the incontrovertible principle of eternal forgiveness received at conversion. Moreover, we must encourage such a Christian who, like David, may say, "Mine eyes fail while I wait for my God", that irrespective of how he or she feels, it is God's Word which stands unchanging regarding the unshakeable nature of a believer's eternal security.

2.3 Distress lest others should stumble

He was concerned lest his own failings should cause to stumble genuine Old Testament believers who were longing for the coming of the Messiah and looked to David as a key link in the divine promise regarding the coming One. So David says, as he regretfully speaks of his own failings:

Psalm 69:6

"Let not them that wait on Thee, O Lord of God Hosts be ashamed for my sake: let not those that seek Thee be confounded for my sake, O God of Israel."

In this we learn a little about the enormous sensitivity of this great man. He was constantly concerned lest any act on his part should hurt another believer or cause them to stumble. It is in the context of bearing the reproach of Christ that a believer so often finds him or herself tempted to compromise. David was concerned lest any compromise on his part should cause another sincere believer to be ashamed, confounded or to stumble.

As we have seen, the Psalm is describing the reproach of Christ which was primarily directed at the Lord but which indirectly fell on David. It is the **same reproach** which fell directly on the Lord when He was on earth. However, it is good to appreciate that now that the Lord Jesus has returned to heaven the world still holds hatred towards Him. The reproach of Christ is still a very relevant issue. In fact, today, believers are called upon to bear the reproach of Christ – which in some circumstances and countries is every bit as difficult as David found in his day. In Romans 15, Paul quotes from Psalm 69:9 to remind us that just as insults hurled at the Lord in heaven were directed at David, similarly, insults hurled at the Father were directed at Him.

Romans 15:1-4

1 "We then that are strong ought to bear the infirmities of the weak, and not to please ourselves.

2 Let every one of us please *his* neighbour for *his* good to edification.

3 For even Christ pleased not Himself; but, as it is written, **The reproaches of them that reproached Thee fell on Me.**

4 For whatsoever things were written aforetime were written for our learning, that we through patience and comfort of the Scriptures might have hope."

However, the phrase, "Christ pleased not Himself", shows us that just as David was careful that his response to the reproach would not bring discouragement or failure to others, similarly the Lord Jesus was sensitive to the frailty of His own disciples and acted in such a way that they would not stumble in the persecution which would surely surround them because of their association with Him. In this regard we see the gentle way in which He forewarned Peter of his denial but reassured him in advance of this sad episode in Peter's experience by saying: "When thou art converted strengthen thy brethren" (Luke 22:32). We notice as well His concerns for them in the upper room as He gently foretold them about the hatred of the world.

John 16:1

"These things have I spoken unto you, that ye should not be offended (stumble)."

Under the pressure of such reproach, David was careful lest the faithful in his day should be ashamed and stumble. Similarly, the Lord Jesus was concerned lest His own should stumble when faced with the reproach of Christ. How much more then should not we today, when confronted with the reproach of Christ, be vigilant that others are not caused to stumble by our compromising with this world! Let us consider again Paul's continued commentary on this passage in Romans 15.

Romans 15:1-7
> 1 "We then that are strong ought to bear the infirmities of the weak, and not to please ourselves.
> 2 Let every one of us please *his* neighbour for *his* good to edification.
> 3 For even Christ pleased not Himself; but, as it is written, **The reproaches of them that reproached Thee fell on Me.**
> 4 For whatsoever things were written afore time were written for our learning, that we through patience and comfort of the Scriptures might have hope.
> 5 Now the God of patience and consolation grant you to be likeminded one toward another according to Christ Jesus:
> 6 That ye may with one mind *and* one mouth glorify God, even the Father of our Lord Jesus Christ.
> 7 Wherefore receive ye one another, as Christ also received us to the glory of God."

It was in the context of the real danger of a sensitive Jewish believer being stumbled or discouraged by a Gentile believer's dietary liberties, which prompted Paul to remind the Christians in Rome of Psalm 69:9 and David's sensitivity as to how his faithfulness under pressure could impact other believers. However, perhaps, most of all, Paul wanted to remind the believers at Rome that the Lord Jesus was most sensitive and careful in forewarning His own disciples of His sufferings at the hands of men as a result of His rejection by the world. The Lord did not want them to stumble when, subsequent to His resurrection, that same rejection would be directed at the disciples because of their association with the reproach of their rejected Lord.

The message is clear: the world is a hostile environment for believers in our Lord Jesus Christ who are called upon to bear His reproach. We do not live unto ourselves. We do not live to please or to suit ourselves. We should at all times demonstrate the sensitivity David showed to other believers in Psalm 69. However, there is another reason why Psalm 69:9 is quoted in Romans 15 in the context of the weak brother who is at risk of being stumbled by another brother who does not share his dietary scruples. It is that an understanding of Psalm 69 would have **also** solved the weaker brother's dilemma. It is clearly prophesied in verses 22-28 of the Psalm (see later), that the Lord would set aside the Jewish religious system because of their rejection of the true Messiah and that, tragically, they would accept a false Messiah in the future tribulation period. This understanding would have led a Jewish believer in the Lord Jesus Christ to understand that fulfilling God's will would involve a path of moving outside the fold of Israel unto the Good Shepherd and gathering with Jews and Gentiles, all one in Christ. This is the underlying theme of Romans 15. Hence the comment of the Apostle Paul in Romans 15:4 to things "written aforetime" being "written for our learning". This is more than just a general comment. It is a clear example of how contextual and accurate exposition of Old Testament Scripture, including Psalm 69, can answer relevant practical problems in a New Testament assembly. This is a truth that needs to be emphasised again today just as it was in the time of the Apostle Paul.

Romans 15:4

"For whatsoever things were written aforetime were written for our learning, that we through patience and comfort of the Scriptures might have hope."

3 The psalmist's distress is relieved as he prays for the coming of the Messiah

The tone of the Psalm changes from distress to hope as David starts to pray and tells the Lord of an "acceptable time" in verse 13. This was the divine solution to David's depression and it is clear that he had come to grasp this wonderful truth as he prayed.

Psalm 69:13

"But as for me, my prayer *is* unto Thee, O LORD, *in* an acceptable time: O God, in the multitude of Thy mercy hear me, in the truth of Thy salvation…"

An alternative translation for David's prayer in verse 13 could be, "as for me, my prayer unto Thee, O LORD, *is* an acceptable time". The answer to David's troubles would be the arrival of this period known as "an acceptable time". During this time there would be a revelation of "the multitude of Thy mercy" (*chesed* lovingkindness) (verse 13), and the "multitude of Thy tender mercies" (*rachamim*) (verse 16). He refers to the reality of the dawning of this day as "the truth of Thy salvation" (verse 13). In fact, it was the anticipation of the truthfulness of God's pledge regarding the coming of the "acceptable time" which brought the Psalmist his deliverance from the depths of depression which had assailed him earlier in the Psalm. It is the consideration of the glad and inevitable commencement of "the acceptable time" which leads David to claim deliverance from the mire, from the deep waters and from being swallowed up by the pit.

What did David have in mind when he spake of the "acceptable time"? Interestingly, in the Psalms we do not get any guidance as to what this phrase means. However, it is Isaiah who explains it:

Isaiah 49:8

"Thus saith the LORD, In an **acceptable time** have I heard Thee, (Hebrew: I have answered Thee) and in a day of salvation have I helped Thee: and I will preserve Thee, and give Thee for a covenant of the people, to establish the earth, to cause to inherit the desolate heritages;"

This verse refers to the coming of the Messiah, namely Jehovah's Unfailing Servant, Who stands in contrast to Israel who is depicted by Isaiah in Isaiah 49:1-4, as Jehovah's failing servant who feels as if he has laboured for God for "naught". Not merely will Jehovah's Perfect Servant bring Zion again to the Lord, He will bring blessing to the Gentiles.

Isaiah 49:6
> "It is a light thing that Thou shouldest be **My Servant** to raise up the tribes of Jacob, and to restore the preserved of Israel: I will also give Thee for a light to the Gentiles, that Thou mayest be My Salvation ("My *Yeshua*" or "My Jesus") unto the end of the earth."

The period of time in which the Messiah, Jehovah's Perfect Servant, will minister to Israel and to the Gentile nations is called "the acceptable time". The word "acceptable" is elsewhere translated "favour" or "will". The phrase could be translated "in a time of favour have I answered *(anah)* Thee!" What an unparalleled time of favour it was when the Lord was revealed as the Saviour of the world, and was answered by God at Calvary (Psalm 22). This is the very core of the gospel message.

David was a prophet, and he envisaged a time of future outstanding divine favour upon the nation and upon this world in general, but it was Isaiah who **defined this time** as commencing with the arrival of Jehovah's Perfect Servant. The reader may well wonder if we are still living in the time David speaks of as "the acceptable time" or the "time of favour". The answer is an emphatic "yes!" as emphasised in 2 Corinthians 6:2.

2 Corinthians 6:2
> "For He saith, I have heard Thee in a time accepted, and in **the day of salvation** have I succoured Thee: behold, now *is* **the accepted time**; behold, now *is* **the** day of **salvation**."

This passage shows us that we are still in the time of divine favour when God's lovingkindness and mercy are multitudinous.

When will this time end?
A similar phrase is found in Isaiah 61:1-2 when the Lord proclaims the acceptable year or "the year of favour of the Lord".

Isaiah 61:1-2
> 1 "The Spirit of the Lord God *is* upon Me; because the Lord hath anointed Me to preach good tidings unto the meek; He hath sent Me to bind up the brokenhearted, to proclaim liberty to the captives, and the opening of the prison to *them that are* bound;
> 2 To proclaim the **acceptable year** (Hebrew: year of favour) of the Lord, and the day of vengeance of our God; to comfort all that mourn;"

When the Lord read these words in the synagogue of Nazareth and added "this day is this Scripture fulfilled in your ears", everyone should have known that it was the Messiah Who had spoken.

Luke 4:21
> "And He began to say unto them, This day is this Scripture fulfilled in your ears."

This year of divine favour has been graciously stretched out now for almost 2000 years. As we have seen, it was first spoken of by David (Psalm 69:13), further elaborated by Isaiah (49:8) and highlighted again by Paul (2 Corinthians 6:2). However, Isaiah 61:2 makes it clear that one day, the acceptable year (year of favour) of the LORD will give way to the "day of vengeance of our God". Because the day of vengeance was still in the future, the Lord "closed the book" (Luke 4:20) and did not complete His public reading of the sabbath portion in Isaiah 61, indicating powerfully that He had not at that time come as Avenger but as Saviour (*Yeshua*). What favour to a lost human race! Is it any wonder that the Scripture goes on to tell us how they "wondered at the gracious words which proceeded out of His mouth" (Luke 4:22).

Psalm 69:13
> "...O God, in the multitude of Thy mercy hear me, in the truth of Thy salvation."

Several times in the Psalms we read about "Thy Salvation" (*Yishecha* or *Yeshuatcha*). This is the same root word as the Hebrew for Jesus (*Yeshua*). When we come to the New Testament, we discover that Simeon saw "**Thy Salvation**" as a title for the Lord Jesus Christ.

Luke 2:25-32
> 25 "And, behold, there was a man in Jerusalem, whose name was Simeon; and the same man was just and devout, waiting for the consolation of Israel: and the Holy Ghost was upon him.
> 26 And it was revealed unto him by the Holy Ghost, that he should not see death, before he had seen the Lord's Christ.
> 27 And he came by the Spirit into the temple: and when the parents brought in the Child Jesus, to do for Him after the custom of the Law,
> 28 Then took he Him up in his arms, and blessed God, and said,
> 29 Lord, now lettest Thou Thy servant depart in peace, according to Thy Word:
> 30 For mine eyes have seen **Thy Salvation**,
> 31 Which Thou hast prepared before the face of all people;
> 32 A Light to lighten the Gentiles, and the Glory of Thy people Israel."

It would indeed be the truth of "Thy Salvation" (Thy Jesus) which would bring David relief from his soul's distresses. Similarly today, with regard to a believer in a valley experience because of bearing reproach for Christ's sake, it is the meditation of the Lord in His earthly experience under His earthly Name of Jesus (*Yeshua*) which brings comfort to the troubled soul.

The truth of His human Name, Jesus, brings in the doctrine of His incarnation and His humiliation at the hands of men during His earthly sojourn. These key doctrines, which in the New Testament are linked to the

Name of Jesus, are therefore dealt with in some detail in the next section. However, just before David in his prayer goes on to speak of the Kinsman Redeemer he makes an appeal to the Lord for deliverance from the mire, from those who hate him and from the deep waters. The fact is that the powerful Kinsman Redeemer, Who also bears the title "Thy Jesus", would accomplish all of these goals.

Psalm 69:14-17

14 "Deliver me out of the mire, and let me not sink: let me be delivered from them that hate me, and out of the deep waters.
15 Let not the waterflood overflow me, neither let the deep swallow me up, and let not the pit shut her mouth upon me."

Could the mire be the guilt of the sins of the past as referenced in Psalm 40:2? Certainly the Lord Jesus can deliver from this! Could those who hate David be the ones who persecuted him because of his association with the reproach of Christ? Certainly, in the coming day of vengeance at His return, the Lord Jesus will deliver His people. Could the deep waters in verse 14 and the waterflood and the deep in verse 15 allude to the experience of death by analogy to similar language in Psalm 18:4-5 referring to death? Certainly only the Lord Jesus can deliver from the river of death as we saw in Psalm 18:16 when, at His second coming, the Old Testament believers will be raised from the dead. All these aspects of divine deliverance, accomplished by the coming Redeemer, are encompassed in the twin concepts of redemption of **both the soul and body** which will be explained in detail in the next section.

Psalm 69:16-17

16 "Hear me, O Lord; for Thy lovingkindness *is* good: turn unto me according to the multitude of Thy tender mercies.
17 And hide not Thy face from Thy servant; for I am in trouble: hear me speedily."

Faced with a past where there is failure (the mire), a present where there are those characterised by hate, and a future where death and *Sheol* await, David may well have had cause to feel despondent. However, the "truth of Thy Salvation" (Jesus), (Psalm 69:13), changes everything! It is in the Person of the Lord Jesus that the lovingkindness and tender mercies of Jehovah spoken of in verse 16 are revealed. What a revelation! It becomes clear in the next section that this is through the coming into this world of Jesus as the Kinsman Redeemer.

3:1 The pinnacle of David's prayer in Psalm 69 – the coming of the Kinsman Redeemer (Goel)

David appeals to the Lord to come and fulfill the Messianic promise through becoming the Kinsman Redeemer (*Goel*)

Psalm 69:18

"Draw nigh (*karvah*) unto my soul, *and* redeem it (*gealah*, root *gaal*): deliver me (*pedeni*, root *padah* also meaning "to redeem") because of mine enemies."

There are two distinct requests in this verse, which need to be considered. The first is for the Lord to **draw nigh**, and the second is a request for **redemption**. "Draw nigh" means "come near to me". It is the same root word as is used of Boaz in Ruth 2: 20 – "the man is near of kin (*karov*) to us". David is requesting the Lord to come near to him. This nearness is with a view to effecting his redemption. This would necessitate the incarnation of the Lord Himself and it is as a perfect Man that the Lord would come to experience the reproaches against God arising from ungodly men.

The second request should be considered in two parts to reflect the Psalmist's use of two distinct Hebrew words meaning " to redeem" – *gaal* **and** *padah*.

Elucidating the nuances of meaning of these two Hebrew words requires a careful study of their use in the Old Testament. We will first of all determine the contextual meaning of each word and then return to Psalm 69 to understand why both words are used by David here.

Both words require the payment of a price to secure the freedom of the person being redeemed. Where the words differ is in the underlying objective or goal of the action "to redeem". *Gaal* involves the payment of a price **to set the redeemed person on an inheritance** such as, for example, an inheritance of land. *Padah* involves the payment of a price so that **the redeemed persons themselves become God's inheritance,** i.e. to be perpetually the servants of God in worshipful service. This distinction becomes immediately clear in the use of these two words in the story of Israel's redemption from Egypt's bondage.

Examples showing the link between *gaal* and the inheritance

Exodus 6:6-8
> 6 "Wherefore say unto the children of Israel, I *am* the Lord, and I will bring you out from under the burdens of the Egyptians, and I will rid you out of their bondage, and I will **redeem you** (root *gaal*) with a stretched out arm, and with great judgments:
> 7 And I will take you to Me for a people, and I will be to you a God: and ye shall know that I *am* the Lord your God, Which bringeth you out from under the burdens of the Egyptians.
> 8 And I will bring you in unto the land, concerning the which I did swear to give it to Abraham, to Isaac, and to Jacob; and **I will give it you for an heritage**: I *am* the Lord."

The reason why God had drawn near to "redeem" (*gaal*) Israel from Egypt was to set them in their inheritance in the Promised Land. Once the nation was settled, Canaan, their inheritance, was to stay within the family name for future generations. This meant that if the Israelite, years later, fell into debt and had to sell his inheritance of land to pay his debt, he could be redeemed (root *gaal*) provided a kinsman redeemer (*goel*) related to him paid his debt, thus enabling the inheritance to be restored to its original owner. The whole object of the kinsman redeemer's action was to restore the lost inheritance back to its original owner (Leviticus 25).

Leviticus 25:25-34

> 25 "If thy brother be waxen poor, and hath sold away *some* of his possession, and if any of his kin come to redeem it (root *gaal*), then shall he redeem (root *gaal*) that which his brother sold.
>
> 26 And if the man have none to redeem it(*goel* meaning "redeemer" from root *gaal*), and himself be able to redeem it (root *gaal*);
>
> 27 Then let him count the years of the sale thereof, and restore the overplus unto the man to whom he sold it; that he may return unto his possession.
>
> 28 But if he be not able to restore *it* to him, then that which is sold shall remain in the hand of him that hath bought it until the year of jubile: and in the jubile it shall go out, and he shall return unto his possession.
>
> 29 And if a man sell a dwelling house in a walled city, then he may redeem it (root *gaal*) within a whole year after it is sold; *within* a full year may he redeem it (root *gaal*).
>
> 30 And if it be not redeemed (root *gaal*) within the space of a full year, then the house that *is* in the walled city shall be established for ever to him that bought it throughout his generations: it shall not go out in the jubile.
>
> 31 But the houses of the villages which have no wall round about them shall be counted as the fields of the country: they may be redeemed (literally: "a redemption will be his" (root *gaal*), and they shall go out in the jubile.
>
> 32 Notwithstanding the cities of the Levites, *and* the houses of the cities of their possession, may the Levites redeem (literally: "a perpetual redemption shall pertain to the Levites (root *gaal*)") at any time.
>
> 33 And if a man purchase of the Levites, then the house that was sold, and the city of his possession, shall go out in *the year of* jubile: for the houses of the cities of the Levites *are* their possession among the children of Israel.
>
> 34 But the field of the suburbs of their cities may not be sold; for it *is* their perpetual possession."

Similarly, when Isaiah prophesied that Israel would be driven off its earthly inheritance and carried away to Babylon, he also foretold their divine deliverance from the land of their captivity and described their re-establishment in their earthly inheritance as "**redemption**" (root *gaal*) where the Lord was the **Redeemer** (*goel*) (Isaiah 43:1,14; 44:6, 22, 23), Who moved the heart of a heathen King called Cyrus to release the captives to go home to their land.

Of course, Israel was driven off its inheritance subsequent to the return from Babylon. This was because the recovery from Babylon was not an eternal redemption. However, Isaiah goes on to describe an irreversible redemption when the Lord will fit the nation for its earthly inheritance **forever**. The section about this final redemption begins in Isaiah 59:20 describing the Redeemer (*goel*) coming to Zion to set up His Kingdom. The section concludes fittingly in Isaiah 60:19-22 with the declaration of an everlasting inheritance. Here are the relevant quotations:

Isaiah 59:20
> 20 "And the Redeemer (*goel*) shall come to Zion, and unto them that turn
> from transgression in Jacob, saith the Lord.
> 21 As for Me, this *is* My covenant with them, saith the Lord; My Spirit
> that *is* upon thee, and My words which I have put in thy mouth, shall not
> depart out of thy mouth, nor out of the mouth of thy seed, nor out of the
> mouth of thy seed's seed, saith the Lord, from henceforth and for ever."

This is an eternal redemption. The section ends in the next chapter with
an eternal inheritance:

Isaiah 60:21
> "Thy people also *shall be* all righteous: **they shall inherit the land for ever,**
> the Branch of My planting, the work of My hands, that I may be glorified."

An alternative translation could read: "Thy people also shall be all
righteous: **for ever they shall inherit the land** of the Branch of My planting,
the work of My hands that I may be glorified." What a redemption for the
nation it will be when the *Goel* comes to Zion in that future day! Never again
will His people be driven from the inheritance because of their sin.

Examples showing the link between *padah* and the inheritance

The verb "deliver" (*padah*) is the other Hebrew word "to redeem" or
"to ransom". The cognate noun for ransom or redemption is *pidyom* or
sometimes *pidyon*. Gesenius argues that the root meaning of the verb *padah*
in Hebrew is "to cut" in the sense of cutting loose, i.e. setting free. However,
to understand the meaning of this word we can study its contextual use
within the story of deliverance from Egypt's bondage and in the ceremonies
of the tabernacle of ancient Israel.

In Deuteronomy 9:25-29, as Moses recalled the events surrounding the
deliverance from Egypt he spoke of the people being "redeemed" in order
to become **God's inheritance**. This time the word "to redeem" is *padah*.

Deuteronomy 9:25-29
> 25 "Thus I fell down before the Lord forty days and forty nights, as I fell
> down at the first; because the Lord had said He would destroy you.
> 26 I prayed therefore unto the Lord, and said, O Lord God, destroy not Thy
> people and **Thine inheritance, which Thou hast redeemed (root: *padah*)**
> **through Thy greatness**, which Thou hast brought forth out of Egypt with
> a mighty hand.
> 27 Remember Thy servants, Abraham, Isaac, and Jacob; look not unto the
> stubbornness of this people, nor to their wickedness, nor to their sin:
> 28 Lest the land whence thou broughtest us out say, Because the Lord was
> not able to bring them into the land which He promised them, and because
> He hated them, He hath brought them out to slay them in the wilderness.
> 29 Yet they *are* **Thy people and Thine inheritance**, which Thou broughtest
> out by Thy mighty power and by Thy stretched out arm."

When *padah* is used to describe redemption from Egypt, the aspect of redemption emphasised is that **the people will become God's inheritance** thereafter. This is in contrast with the *gaal* aspect of redemption **when the redeemed people obtain an inheritance in the land**. When *padah* is used, it suggests that the people belonged to God and were His servants. As the slave owner, God has a right to service from those whom He owns as His inheritance. When we study the use of the word *padah* in the Law it carries a recurring theme of compensation to the slave owner for work **not rendered** by the slave. If the slave owner is God then the word *padah* involves compensation to God for service **not rendered** to Him. Let's elucidate these nuances of meaning in the occurrences of this word in the Law.

Firstly, consider the slave killed by a runaway ox in Exodus 21:28-32 and how the slave owner was entitled to a payment of redemption money (*pidyom*) as compensation for the loss of service. We could call it a "*padah* redemption".

Exodus 21:28-29
> 28 "If an ox gore a man or a woman, that they die: then the ox shall be surely stoned, and his flesh shall not be eaten; but the owner of the ox *shall be* quit.
> 29 But if the ox were wont to push with his horn in time past, and it hath been testified to his owner, and he hath not kept him in, but that he hath killed a man or a woman; the ox shall be stoned, and his owner also shall be put to death.
> 30 If there be laid on him a sum of money (Hebrew *copher* or "covering" from the root *caphar* "to cover or atone"), then he shall give for the ransom (*pidyom*) of his life whatsoever is laid upon him.
> 31 Whether he have gored a son, or have gored a daughter, according to this judgment shall it be done unto him.
> 32 If the ox shall push a manservant or a maidservant; he shall give unto their master thirty shekels of silver, and the ox shall be stoned."

It is clear from this section that the *pidyom* was paid as **compensation** for the loss of the life ended by the run-away ox. Payment of this compensation meant that the owner of the run-away ox did not, in turn, forfeit his life at the hand of the judges. Interestingly, the value of the *copher* money varied depending on the status of the deceased. Exodus 21:32 shows that the *copher* money for a dead slave was a mere thirty shekels of silver paid to the slave's owner. All of this shows that the *padah* redemption money (*pidyom*) was compensation to the slave owner for service **no longer rendered** by the dead slave in the owner's household.

The verb *padah* is used in several further contexts of compensation, this time to God, where the background is similarly for **loss of service** within the precincts of the tabernacle's sanctuary, God's house. Failure of the people to serve God worshipfully in Egypt required a *padah* redemption. Moses was asked to communicate to Pharaoh that God wanted His people released to be able to worship Him.

Exodus 7:16

"And thou shalt say unto him, The Lord God of the Hebrews hath sent me unto thee, saying, Let My people go, that they may serve Me in the wilderness: and, behold, hitherto thou wouldest not hear."

Freedom from bondage was necessary before the Israelites became God's people and were able to worship God as His great inheritance of emancipated worshippers. They had an obligation to worship Him because they belonged to Him. The place of this worship was the earthly sanctuary. This was at first the tabernacle in the wilderness and later the temple. The *padah* aspect of redemption from Egypt was to fit the nation for this great privilege of worshipfully serving the Lord at His earthly sanctuary.

Sadly, the redeemed nation had not always worshipped and served the Lord so they were therefore not always God's inheritance. This is because prior to their redemption from Egypt they were engaged in idolatrous worship. This becomes clear in Ezekiel 20:5-10 where we discover that in Egypt the people were engaging in the worship of Pharaoh's gods and initially refused God's appeals to them to turn away from this.

Ezekiel 20:5-10

5 "And say unto them, Thus saith the Lord God; In the day when I chose Israel, and lifted up Mine hand unto the seed of the house of Jacob, and made Myself known unto them in the land of Egypt, when I lifted up Mine hand unto them, saying, I *am* the Lord your God;

6 In the day *that* I lifted up Mine hand unto them, to bring them forth of the land of Egypt into a land that I had espied for them, flowing with milk and honey, which *is* the glory of all lands:

7 Then said I unto them, Cast ye away every man the abominations of his eyes, and defile not yourselves with the idols of Egypt: I *am* the Lord your God.

8 But they rebelled against Me, and would not hearken unto Me: they did not every man cast away the abominations of their eyes, neither did they forsake the idols of Egypt: then I said, I will pour out My fury upon them, to accomplish My anger against them in the midst of the land of Egypt.

9 But I wrought for My Name's sake, that it should not be polluted before the heathen, among whom they *were*, in whose sight I made Myself known unto them, in bringing them forth out of the land of Egypt.

10 Wherefore I caused them to go forth out of the land of Egypt, and brought them into the wilderness."

The events of Ezekiel 20:5-10 must refer to Israel's experience in Egypt **before** the wilderness journey since the judgment warning to the nation was for God "to accomplish My anger against them **in the midst of the land of Egypt**" (Ezekiel 20:8). When we recall that in the ancient world it was the firstborn who was involved in priesthood (including idolatrous priesthood) and that firstborn of cattle were involved in idolatrous sacrifices, we now begin to understand why it was the **firstborn of man and beast** which were to be the target of the final judgment of the tenth plague.

Why both *padah* and *gaal* aspects of redemption were necessary for the firstborn of Egypt

Because the nation had deprived Jehovah of priestly worship due to its idolatry in Egypt and, therefore, was not living in the inheritance promised to Abraham so long ago, it is clear that the privileges befitting the firstborn nation of Jehovah (namely that they should be a priestly people and heirs of the inheritance) were completely absent from the enslaved nation. In fact, the nation needed first to transit from a state of being identified with Pharaoh's firstborn and being involved in idolatrous Egyptian worship, and thus under sentence of death, to become the firstborn of Jehovah. The only way this could happen was by the blood of the lamb. Only by this means could they become the firstborn of Jehovah. There is a lovely expression in the New Testament which describes this change – being "born again". The story of how Israel became the firstborn of Jehovah in Egypt by the blood of the lamb is called the story of **redemption**. Both words for redemption, *gaal* and *padah*, are needed to describe this redemption from Egypt because Jehovah wanted Israel to be redeemed to be **His firstborn** and as **Jehovah's inheritance** to enjoy firstborn privileges as **priestly worshippers** in His earthly sanctuary (*padah*) as well as firstborn privileges **as heirs** of the **earthly inheritance** of the Promised Land (*gaal*).

These considerations show that the whole nation, both firstborns and later-born siblings, had all become, in a generic sense, the firstborn of Jehovah by being "born again" through the blood of the Lamb, and as such could enjoy the dual privileges of sanctuary service and heirs of the earthly inheritance.

Further examples of *padah* redemption in the Old Testament

If we focus on the privilege of sanctuary service, namely the fruit of the *padah* aspect of redemption, then it is apparent that ancient Israel saw three levels of privilege. The lowest level of sanctuary privilege was afforded to the eleven non-Levitical tribes who could come in an attitude of worship to the **door of the tabernacle** of the congregation but no further. The highest level of sanctuary service was granted to the consecrated priest (Aaron and his sons) who could serve **within the tabernacle** in the sanctuary at the altar. An intermediate level of sanctuary privilege was enjoyed by the Levites who were effectively, special sanctuary assistants for the fully consecrated priests. Note1

This differing level of privilege is explained in Numbers 3:45-49. It goes back to the desire of the Lord for all the firstborn in Israel to be His sanctuary servants and thus the redeemed inheritance of the Lord (*padah*). Although not all Levites were firstborn, they acted *in lieu* of the firstborn of all Israel and carried out their sanctuary duties in this role. They were, in effect, the acting firstborns of Israel and thus enjoyed sanctuary privileges. However, since there were more firstborns in Israel than Levites, there was a requirement for these excess individuals to be redeemed, so each had to pay five shekels of the sanctuary. The significance of this is important. As not all the firstborns from the non-Levitical tribes could have a Levite *in lieu* of themselves in God's presence there was loss of service to God. The five shekels of the sanctuary were to compensate God for this loss. Otherwise the person's life would have been considered valueless and pointless.

There is more than a hint in Exodus 13:11-15, if we follow the thought flow of that section, that an unredeemed human firstborn's life in Israel would have been at risk of being cut short by God. Certainly, the unredeemed firstborn ass was required to be put to death (Exodus 13:13). Redemption of the firstborn in Israel was *in lieu* of devoting themselves to a life of service by acting as servants in the earthly sanctuary. God wanted ancient Israel to clearly understand that a firstborn, who was not able to function in God's sanctuary, was required to pay compensation to God for the loss sustained to Himself, i.e. the payment of redemption money.

When we recall that the word *padah* is used to describe redemption unto sanctuary service, it is clear then that *padah* must also be used to describe the price paid to exempt an Israelite firstborn from the sanctuary responsibility befitting his firstborn status (Exodus 13:13). Of course, it was not the fault of a firstborn of a non-Levitical tribe that he could not function in the earthly sanctuary and serve the priests there. Nevertheless, he had a responsibility to see to it that God received due compensation for this. Because sin was not in question, this redemption was effected **by silver and not by blood**.

A further use of *padah* is also in the context of compensation to God for service **not rendered** in the sanctuary. In Leviticus 27, an Israelite could sanctify unto the Lord (i.e. dedicate to His service) himself, family members, his house or his lands etc. If for any reason he felt he could no longer dedicate these to the Lord and needed the use again of his house or his field, then he had to redeem these things by payment to the Lord of predetermined sums of silver.

Leviticus 27:19-20

19 "And if he that sanctified the field will in any wise redeem it (*padah*), then he shall add the fifth *part* of the money of thy estimation unto it, and it shall be assured to him.
20 And if he will not redeem (*padah*) the field, or if he have sold the field to another man, it shall not be redeemed (*padah*) any more."

Once again, the word "redeem" is being used in the context of compensating God for work not done in the sanctuary.

These two examples show how the word "to redeem" (*padah*) is applied to tabernacle service and **compensation to God for work not done there**.

However, it was understood even in the Old Testament that redemption from Egypt and the tabernacle service with its attendant customs constituted a picture or pattern of something bigger. In other words, the accounts of redemption from Egypt and the tabernacle service of how man approached God in the earthly sanctuary were illustrative of doctrines central to how man approaches God in His heavenly sanctuary. In Psalm 49 we read of the redemption (*padah*) of the soul. The Psalmist indicates that this subject is a "dark saying" or a riddle.

Psalm 49

1 "Hear this, all *ye* people; give ear, all *ye* inhabitants of the world:

2 Both low and high, rich and poor, together.

3 My mouth shall speak of wisdom; and the meditation of my heart *shall be* of understanding.

4 I will incline mine ear to a parable: I will open my dark saying upon the harp.

5 Wherefore should I fear in the days of evil, *when* the iniquity of my heels shall compass me about?

6 They that trust in their wealth, and boast themselves in the multitude of their riches;

7 None *of them* can by any means redeem his brother, nor give to God a ransom for him:

8 (For the redemption of their soul *is* precious, and it ceaseth for ever:)

9 That he should still live for ever, *and* not see corruption."

The redemption of the soul, therefore, is a challenge to the spiritual mind to elucidate its meaning as, by definition, it is not readily clear at first glance. There were exceptionally godly men in the Old Testament who understood riddles such as Daniel and Joseph, for example. Our task is made much easier by virtue of New Testament exposition which gives us the meaning of the riddle. The first step in solving the meaning of the phrase, "the redemption of the soul", is to understand that this redemption applies to the soul of men in general not just to the firstborns and clearly goes beyond the tabernacle usage of the word.

Psalm 49:8

"For the redemption (*pidyom*, root: *padah*) of their soul *is* precious, and it ceaseth for ever."

It is apparent, however, that the phrase "redemption (*pidyom*) of the soul" presupposes, at the very least, an understanding of the verb *padah* (to redeem) in the tabernacle, where the meaning was of compensating God for **work not done in the earthly sanctuary**. However, since "the redemption of the soul" refers to all men and goes beyond the context of the earthly tabernacle, the question must arise as to why God requires a compensation in the matter of the human soul **which lasts forever**. Clearly, it is not compensation for work not done by a soul in the earthly sanctuary, otherwise the "redemption of the soul" would be irrelevant to those who lived before the tabernacle era or for Gentile nations who lived many miles away from the Promised Land. The meaning of the phrase, "redemption of the soul", becomes apparent once we understand that the matter under consideration is payment of compensation to God for **priestly service not done in the heavenly sanctuary**.

At this point we could reiterate what was noted in Psalm 40 and will be later considered in Psalm 110, namely that priesthood in the **heavenly**

sanctuary was forbidden to men until the Lord Jesus was consecrated a Priest in heaven at His resurrection and ascension. When men of God in the Old Testament prayed, they did not have access to the throne in heaven as do those of us who are saved in this dispensation because they were not priests fitted to function in the **heavenly sanctuary**. They stood on earth and prayed and God heard them. Sometimes they called on God, "hear Thou… in heaven Thy dwelling place" (1 Kings 8:49). They said this because they were speaking on earth outside the heavenly sanctuary as they were not priests of the heavenly sanctuary while they were on earth. This is why in Daniel 9:22, as Daniel is praying, the Lord sends the angel Gabriel who came forth (Hebrew, "came out") from His presence **out of heaven** to come to Daniel. As an aside, it is good to understand that God does something more wonderful than that for His people today! He does not dispatch the Archangel to speak with us. We have access to the throne itself in heaven as fully consecrated New Testament priests.

Furthermore, as we saw in Psalm 16, Old Testament believers who died were still not admitted to the heavenly sanctuary. They were comforted in upper *Sheol* and remained there until the victory of the risen Lord Jesus over the grave was realized. As we saw in Psalm 40, only when the Lord Jesus was consecrated a Priest and entered the heavenly sanctuary on His ascension could those Old Testament believers enter the heavenly sanctuary as priests, where they now are in their unclothed spirits. God still needed to be compensated for all those years spent outside of His heavenly sanctuary in *Sheol,* where those believers remained until their liberation from upper *Sheol.* The sanctuary in heaven was equipped with all the instruments of priesthood for men to serve God in that wonderful place. However, Adam forfeited fellowship with God Note 2 by his fall and stood in need of *padah* redemption as did all the family of Adam. Psalm 49, the great Psalm of the riddle of redemption, shows in verse 20 that the soul of "man (*adam*) that is in honour" needed to be redeemed by a *padah* redemption.

Psalm 49:20
   "Man (*adam*) *that is* in honour, and understandeth not, is like the beasts *that* perish."

God intended the sons of Adam to be fitted for His **heavenly sanctuary**. The redemption of the soul of Psalm 49 is all about this great achievement which is so precious to God, Who for 4000 years following Adam's fall longed for men to be fitted for His house in heaven. Hence Psalm 49 shows how Adam and the sons of Adam can be fitted by *padah* redemption to serve God in His **heavenly sanctuary** and thus rediscover the true "honour" for which man (*adam*) was created in the first place. Men who fail to grasp this, sadly, are like the beasts that perish.

Those Old Testament saints who died were not directly responsible for being unable to enter heaven as priests, **just as the firstborns from the non-Levitical tribes were not responsible for not being priests or Levites**

in the earthly sanctuary. Nevertheless, they had a responsibility to avail themselves of the provision of the five shekels of the sanctuary. Now we begin to understand why the Psalmist says:

Psalm 49:15
> "But God will redeem (*padah*) my soul from the power of the grave (*Sheol*): for He shall receive me. Selah."

The Psalmist in Psalm 49 knew the day would come when his soul would be liberated from upper *Sheol* to be able to serve the Lord in worship in His heavenly sanctuary. This happened on the ascension of the Lord Jesus to heaven and predates the Psalmist's resurrection from the dead which has yet to take place, when his body will be redeemed to enter his earthly inheritance in body, soul and spirit. On the occasion of the Psalmist's redemption from the power of *Sheol* he knew that God would "receive" Him. This carries the idea of welcoming him to heaven. However, the first Human Priest to enter heaven was the Lord Jesus Christ, Who so majestically entered in after His ascension by virtue of His own blood and sat down upon the throne. Only then could the Old Testament saints in their souls enter heaven as redeemed ones (*padah*) who were now constituted not merely Levite-like sanctuary servants but fully consecrated priests able to sing the New Song of Revelation 5, as discussed in Psalm 40. This is what Asaph also speaks of in Psalm 73:24 when he says that "afterward" the Lord will "receive me to glory".

Psalm 73:24
> "Thou shalt guide me with Thy counsel, and afterward receive me *to* glory."

As we saw in Psalm 40, Asaph and all the other Old Testament saints are now around the throne in heaven awaiting the moment when they will be raised from the dead and will return to this earth to reign upon it as their inheritance (*gaal* redemption) .

Hosea also shows us the distinction between *padah* and *gaal* redemption in this same context:

Hosea 13:14
> "I will ransom (*padah*) them from the power of the grave (*Sheol*); I will redeem (*gaal*) them from death: O death, I will be thy plagues; O grave, I will be thy destruction: repentance shall be hid from mine eyes."

Redemption (*padah*) of the souls of the Old Testament saints from *Sheol* has already taken place and they are now able to serve the Lord as priests around the throne in heaven in their disembodied states. However, the day will come when they will be raised from the dead. This is the redemption of the body and the verb is *gaal* to indicate that on resurrection they will enter into their earthly inheritance. This becomes clear in Job 19:25 where it is Job's Redeemer (*Goel*) Who guarantees his resurrection from the dead to enter into his earthly inheritance.

Job 19:25-26

> 25 "For I know *that* my Redeemer (*Goel*) liveth, and *that* He shall stand at
> the latter *day* upon the earth:
> 26 And *though* after my skin *worms* destroy this *body*, yet in my flesh shall
> I see God."

Gaal **redemption guarantees that a believer cannot step unto his inheritance without his resurrected body.** To enter into his inheritance he must be redeemed (*gaal*) from death i.e. be raised from the dead.

In the tabernacle figure, the redemption money of silver was paid to compensate God for service **not rendered** in the **earthly** sanctuary. Indeed, the payment of the redemption money ended any obligation of the Israelite to function as a priestly servant (Levite) in the earthly sanctuary. Redemption in the New Testament is more wonderful. The redemption price is paid once and for all so as to allow a believer to become not merely a priestly servant (Levite) but a fully consecrated priest in the **heavenly** sanctuary and to do so **forever**.

Redemption (*padah*) of the firstborn with the five shekels of the sanctuary is again referred to by Peter in his first epistle where he is reminding us of our privilege as New Testament priests in the heavenly sanctuary.

1 Peter 1:18-19

> 18 "Forasmuch as ye know that **ye were not redeemed with corruptible things, *as* silver and gold**, from your vain conversation *received* by tradition from your fathers;
> 19 But with the precious blood of Christ, as of a Lamb without blemish and without spot:"

In 1 Peter 1-2, we see that by the new birth we as redeemed ones become the firstborn of the Lord. With firstborn comes the dual privilege of being a **priest (God's inheritance)** (***padah* redemption**) and an **heir** to the inheritance (***gaal* redemption**). Redemption in its *padah* and *gaal* aspects brings about both blessings to us!

When we read in Psalm 49 that the redemption of the soul is precious and ceases forever, this shows us that once God is compensated, He will no longer require future compensation. An example from the secular world may help. An oil company may be forced to pay compensation to a government if there is an oil spill leading to environmental damage. This compensation may be adequate for the damage caused but it cannot be said "to cease forever" because there is always a finite possibility that a future oil spill could occur requiring further compensation. However, when the Bible says that the redemption of the soul (*padah*) is precious and ceases forever we learn that no further possibility of a need for future compensation to God is required. In other words, once a believer is consecrated a priest to God, that person can never again be denied access to the throne of God as a priest. This is the underlying concept for the phrase, "the **eternal** redemption" (Hebrews 9:12), which He has obtained for us.

Hebrews 9:11-14

> 11 "But Christ being come an High Priest of good things to come, by a greater and more perfect tabernacle, not made with hands, that is to say, not of this building;
>
> 12 Neither by the blood of goats and calves, but by His own blood **He** entered in once into the holy place, **having obtained eternal redemption *for us.***
>
> 13 For if the blood of bulls and of goats, and the ashes of an heifer sprinkling the unclean, sanctifieth to the purifying of the flesh:
>
> 14 How much more shall the blood of Christ, Who through the eternal Spirit offered Himself without spot to God, purge your conscience from dead works to serve (*latreuein*) the living God?"

This phrase, "eternal redemption" (Hebrews 9:12), answers to the "redemption of the soul" (*padah*) which "ceaseth forever" in Psalm 49, thus fitting a believer for eternal priestly service never to be interrupted again. Notice in Hebrews 9:14 that, purged by the blood of Christ, a New Testament believer can "serve" the living God. This word "serve" (*latreuein*) in the New Testament means the service of worship in the heavenly sanctuary. This is New Testament priestly activity. What a wonderful privilege we have been brought into in this era! As soon as we were saved, immediately we were able to function as priests in the heavenly sanctuary even though we are on earth. When the Lord Jesus redeemed us, He compensated God for the time in our lives prior to salvation when we were not functioning in the sanctuary as firstborn priests. However, *padah* redemption goes further. He has compensated God for any imperfections in our priestly service subsequent to our salvation. Yet there is infinitely more! Before we could begin our priestly service, He paid down in advance the totality of value of what our priestly service means to God not only now but eternally. Our priestly service to God in all its imperfections and limitations is seen by God in all the completeness of the redemptive price pre-paid by the Lord Jesus. Otherwise we could not function as priests because of our intrinsic imperfections. Now we can understand the wonder of Hebrews 9:14

Hebrews 9:14

> 14 "**How much more shall the blood of Christ**, Who through the eternal Spirit offered himself without spot to God, purge your conscience from dead works to serve (*latreuein*) the living God?"

It is good to remember that because of this eternal redemption provided by our Lord Jesus, we (in contrast to tabernacle priests) cannot ever be even temporarily debarred from the heavenly sanctuary through sin, as was considered in our meditations of the sin offering of the priest in Psalm 22.

In summary then, *padah* redemption in its eternal sense involves the redeemed people being made God's inheritance, i.e. priests fitted to function in the heavenly sanctuary. As far as Old Testament believers were concerned, this involved deliverance from *Sheol* to be able to praise the Lord around the throne in heaven. *Gaal* redemption in its eternal sense involves the redeemed people obtaining an inheritance in **their resurrected bodies**. It, therefore, is linked to the redemption of the body which is necessary to be able to receive and enter into the promised inheritance. Both *padah* and *gaal* aspects of redemption are presented in Ephesians chapter 1 where we read of redemption.

Ephesians 1:7
"In Whom we have redemption through His blood, the forgiveness of sins, according to the riches of His grace."

We then read of the redeemed ones obtaining an inheritance i.e. the *gaal* aspect of redemption as illustrated in the Old Testament.

Ephesians 1:11
"In Whom also we have obtained an inheritance, being predestinated according to the purpose of Him Who worketh all things after the counsel of His own will."

Ephesian 1:13-14 goes on to emphasise that *gaal* redemption in the Old Testament also applies to New Testament believers in that our ultimate resurrection from the dead is assured before we enter into the inheritance.

Ephesians 1:13-14
13 "In Whom ye also *trusted*, after that ye heard the Word of truth, the gospel of your salvation: in Whom also after that ye believed, ye were sealed with that Holy Spirit of promise,
14 Which is **the earnest of our inheritance until the redemption of the purchased possession, unto the praise of His glory**."

Ephesians 1:14 is referring to the resurrection from the dead of each believer, when in our new bodies we enter into the inheritance. The indwelling Spirit of God is the guarantee that this will happen!

To complete the teaching on redemption in Ephesians 1, Paul must also allude to the *padah* aspect of redemption i.e. show how that we in the New Testament era also have become God's inheritance. This is made clear in Ephesians 1:17-21 in Paul's prayer for the Ephesian believers.

Ephesians 1:17-21
17 "That the God of our Lord Jesus Christ, the Father of glory, may give unto you the spirit of wisdom and revelation in the knowledge of Him:
18 **The eyes of your understanding being enlightened; that ye may know what is the hope of His calling, and what the riches of the glory of His inheritance in the saints,**
19 And what *is* the exceeding greatness of His power to us-ward who believe, according to the working of His mighty power,
20 Which He wrought in Christ, when **He** raised Him from the dead, and set *Him* at His own right hand in the heavenly *places*,
21 Far above all principality, and power, and might, and dominion, and every name that is named, not only in this world, but also in that which is

to come"

Clearly, an understanding that we as believers are the Lord's inheritance requires divinely granted illumination (Ephesians 1:18). This is needed to grasp the riddle of the *padah* aspect of redemption, namely that we have become priests fitted to function in the heavenly sanctuary (Psalm 49:3-4). As we noted in Psalm 40 and will see in Psalm 110, this required the Lord Jesus first of all to be raised from the dead and to ascend to God's right hand in heaven as our Great High Priest. This is again emphasised in Ephesians 1:19-21 where His resurrection and ascension are vitally linked to our becoming God's inheritance. May our eyes be illuminated by the indwelling Spirit of God to understand and value the immensity of our privileges and responsibilities as recipients of all the privileges of *padah* redemption when, as New Testament priests, we approach the throne of God as the redeemed sons of God. If this is the case, then Paul's prayer will have been fulfilled in our lives. Similarly, this objective for the Lord's people should be a matter of earnest prayer and exercise for shepherds and teachers among the Lord's people whose responsibility it is to teach the wonder of the truth that "we are God's inheritance".

Now let us return to Psalm 69 and inquire as to why David calls on the Lord to redeem him in this two-fold way: *gaal* and *padah* redemption. The question to determine is whether or not David is referring to the eternal redemption of the eternal inheritance, spoken of by Isaiah in Isaiah 60, or referring merely to being restored to his earthly possessions (*gaal*), or once more being given access to the sanctuary entrance (*padah*) after his enforced temporary absence from the city of Jerusalem, such as happened at the Absalom rebellion.

A study of the remainder of the Psalm shows that this redemption was not a temporary thing in David's life. The end of the Psalm shows clearly that the millennial rest is in view when the seed of His servants shall **inherit** the land and have it **in possession** after God has saved Zion.

Psalm 69:34-36
> 34 "Let the heaven and earth praise Him, the seas, and every thing that moveth therein.
> 35 For God will save Zion, and will build the cities of Judah: that they may dwell there, and have it in possession.
> 36 **The seed also of His servants shall inherit it**: and they that love His Name shall dwell therein."

To recap, verse 18 shows how the Lord must become near to David, i.e. become incarnate, in order to redeem (*gaal*) him, as Near Kinsman, to fit him for the future inheritance. Moreover, when David asks the Lord to "deliver (*padah*) " him, it was to fit him for the sanctuary. This relationship of becoming Near Kinsman would be so near that the heavenly *Goel* would

Himself experience at first hand the reproach which David had known.

Psalm 69:19-20

19 "Thou hast known my reproach, and my shame, and my dishonour: mine adversaries *are* all before thee.

20 Reproach hath broken My heart; and I am full of heaviness: and I looked *for some* to take pity, but *there was* none; and for comforters, but I found none."

The phrase, "Thou hast known", in verse 19 is in the short tense in Hebrew. In Hebrew the short tense indicates a completed or closed event. It naturally lends itself to a translation in the past tense in English as in verse 19. However, sometimes in Hebrew the short tense is used to describe the certainty of an event not yet taken place. In other words, even though it hasn't yet happened it is as real in the eyes of God and people of faith as if it already has happened. An example is David's challenge to Goliath when he addressed Goliath in the short tense to indicate the certainty of his victory over this man. In other words, before David defeated Goliath he regarded the defeat of the giant as certain as if it had already happened. This nuance of meaning is somewhat lost in the English translation when the words of David are rendered in the English future tense, even though in the Hebrew David used the short tense indicating an event which was **already** completed – at least in the eyes of God.

1 Samuel 17:46

"This day will the Lord deliver thee into mine hand (long tense: will deliver); and I will smite thee (short tense: I have smitten thee), and take (short tense: I have taken) thine head from thee; and I will give (short tense: I have given) the carcases of the host of the Philistines this day unto the fowls of the air, and to the wild beasts of the earth; that all the earth may know (long tense: will know) that there is a God in Israel."

This understanding shows us how the words, "Thou hast known my reproach" can carry a future meaning of absolute certainty such as, "Thou wilt certainly know my reproach". This flows seamlessly into the next verses where the future coming of the Messiah, "Thy Salvation" or "Thy Jesus", is envisaged in the prophetic poem.

How beautiful is this revelation to David! He realises here that the Lord Himself would become his Kinsman Redeemer (*Goel*) and deliver him through paying the redemption (*pidyon*) price. So near would the Kinsman Redeemer come that He would experience at first hand the reproach, the shame and the dishonour which David had known. The verses which follow then move from becoming an account of David's experiences of bearing the reproach of Christ to a detailed series of prophetic utterances characterising the rejection and reproach which the Lord Himself would surely experience while here as our Kinsman Redeemer.

4 The comfort for David's distress

David received comfort in his distress in a three-fold way. Firstly, it was revealed to him that the Lord Who would come as Kinsman Redeemer (*Goel*) would bear the same reproaches as he was bearing. Secondly, those who hate the coming of the promised Messiah will face divine judgment. Thirdly, this Kinsman Redeemer will issue in Kingdom glory and guarantee the inheritance for the Lord's people.

4.1 Comfort for David's distress: revelation of the experiences of the future Kinsman Redeemer

Psalm 69:20

"Reproach hath broken My heart; and I am full of heaviness: and I looked *for some* to take pity, but *there was* none; and for comforters, but I found none."

David's heart was broken as he bore the reproach of the unborn Messiah. However, this experience would be relived to a much greater extent by the Kinsman Redeemer, Who would know at first hand all the reproach of being rejected by His own people. The phrase, "I am full of heaviness," is one word in the Hebrew Bible (*nosh*) and occurs nowhere else in the canon of Scripture. This renders an exact translation difficult. The Septuagint translates the word *nosh talaiporian,* meaning "affliction". Some have suggested that it is linked to the Hebrew word *enosh* meaning "subject to sickness and mortality" (see Psalm 8) and linked also to a similar sounding Syriac word of that meaning. There are scriptural reasons why the meaning cannot be "sick" since the Lord Jesus was perfect in every way and, unlike us, not subject to illness. That's why the present author is comfortable with the ancient Septuagint rendering of the phrase reflected in the Authorized Version translation, "I am full of heaviness".

When David tells us that he was given gall and vinegar (verse 21) we are not told of any incident in 1 or 2 Samuel where this happened. Nevertheless, in the context of the Lord coming into this world to experience in full the anti-Messianic reproaches which David to some extent experienced, it is apparent that Psalm 69:21 is a prophecy of an experience of reproach which the Kinsman Redeemer would Himself experience.

Psalm 69:21

21 "They gave Me also gall for My meat; and in My thirst they gave Me vinegar to drink."

Nevertheless, it is possible that this refers to an unrecorded incident in David's life when the anti-Messiah movement sought to mock David in this way, possibly pointing to his failures. When we come to Luke 23:36, we discover that it was specifically in mockery that the Lord Jesus was offered vinegar at the cross by the soldiers.

Luke 23:36

"And the soldiers also mocked Him, coming to Him, and offering Him vinegar."

It is unlikely that the soldiers were aware of the language of Psalm 69:21. This makes it perhaps at first difficult to explain how the soldiers felt that offering the Lord vinegar was an act of mockery as Luke contests. However, Luke is careful to show us that the soldiers around the cross did not stand there alone. The rulers of the nation were also there deriding the Lord Jesus (Luke 23:35). When Luke says the soldiers "also mocked Him" the "also" means **in addition** to the rulers who were inciting them on to their cruel act. That would suggest that the mockery arose in the minds of those who were indeed well educated in the Scriptures and Psalm 69 in particular. The flawed reasoning may have been as follows: if vinegar and gall were offered to king David, who by his own confession was marked by failure, then if the King of the Jews hanging on the tree was to be similarly offered vinegar and gall, this would indicate (in their erroneous reasoning) that the Lord was no different from David – a man marked by failures.

If this indeed was their intent, the mockery described by Luke in this act of offering the vinegar was particularly anti-Messianic in its motive and marked complete failure to understand the wonderful truth that the One upon the cross was, in contrast to David, the Unfailing One. Because He was the Unfailing One, He was there, not for His own sins, but as the long-promised sacrificial Victim to bear the sin of the world – "when Thou shalt make His soul an (trespass) offering for sin" (Isaiah 53:10).

Persistence in such anti-Messianic views would lead to certain judgment as is explained in the next section.

4.2 Comfort for David's distress: prospect of judgment on all those who rejected the promise of the coming Messiah

Earlier in the Psalm, David speaks of those who reviled him.

Psalm 69:10-12
10 "When I wept, *and chastened* my soul with fasting, that was to my reproach.
11 I made sackcloth also my garment; and I became a proverb to them.
12 They that sit in the gate speak against me; and I *was* the song of the drunkards."

However, in this section of the Psalm the fate of those who choose to persist in refusing the Messiah is clearly given in verses 22-25.

Psalm 69:22-25

22 "Let their table become a snare before them: and *that which should have been* for *their* welfare, *let it become* a trap.
23 Let their eyes be darkened, that they see not; and make their loins continually to shake.
24 Pour out Thine indignation upon them, and let Thy wrathful anger take hold of them.
25 Let their habitation be desolate; *and* let none dwell in their tents."

If this applied to those who rejected the Messiah, prior to His birth in the city of David, how much more do these verses apply to unbelieving elements within the nation of Israel, in general, and unbelieving individuals, in particular, who say no to the Messiah after He was revealed! It is thus with tremendous accuracy and correct contextual usage that Paul, by the Spirit of God, quotes Psalm 69:22-25 in Romans 11:9-10.

Romans 11:9,10
> 9 "And David saith, Let their table be made a snare, and a trap, and a stumblingblock, and a recompence unto them:
> 10 Let their eyes be darkened, that they may not see, and bow down their back alway."

Judas Iscariot, also, by his rejection of Christ is an example of an unbeliever who falls into this category (Acts 1:20).

Acts 1:20
> "For it is written in the book of Psalms, Let his habitation be desolate, and let no man dwell therein: and his bishoprick let another take."

Let us consider the details of this solemn curse on those who reject the Lord Jesus.

Psalm 69:22
> "Let their table become a snare before them: and *that which should have been* for *their* welfare (*liShlomim*: for peaces), *let it become* a trap."

The table in Scripture on occasions referred to the **altar** in the temple in Jerusalem and the system of sacrifices linked to it, e.g. Malachi 1:7.

Malachi 1:7
> "Ye offer polluted bread upon Mine altar; and ye say, Wherein have we polluted Thee? In that ye say, **The table of the Lord *is* contemptible.**"

How tragic that Israel's altar (no longer the Lord's altar) will one day become a snare to that nation! In fact, the future re-establishing of temple worship on the Temple Mount in Jerusalem will happen in the tribulation period, as prophesied in Daniel 9:26-27. This will become the centre of an anti-God conspiracy greater than that experienced in the time of Antiochus Epiphanes and resisted by the Maccabees in the second century B.C.

Psalm 69:22(b)
> "That which should have been for their welfare (for peaces) let it become a trap"

Israel will obtain a false peace which shall prove to be a trap (Isaiah 28:15-20). In addition to the apostate worship system ("their table") on the future Temple Mount in Daniel 9:26-27, there will be peace guarantees from "the coming prince", a future western leader known as the "Beast" of Revelation

13:1-10 (see Appendix 2). What a tragic alternative to those who refuse the "truth of Thy Salvation (Jesus)" spoken of earlier in the Psalm and accept the lie of 2 Thessalonians 2:11! In fact, it may well be this lie which is referred to in Psalm 69:23 which describes the darkening of the eyes of those who are trapped by the counterfeit table (altar) and spurious peace of the preceding verse.

Psalm 69:23
"Let their **eyes be darkened, that they see not**; and make their loins continually to shake."

It is upon those who have believed the lie of the tribulation that the wrath of God will be poured out. This is made very clear in Psalm 69:24-25.

Psalm 69:24-25
24 "Pour out Thine indignation upon them, and let Thy wrathful anger take hold of them.
25 Let their habitation be desolate; *and* let none dwell in their tents."

The wrath of God is reserved for the tribulation period. Until then it will be withheld as seen in Revelation 6:17.

Revelation 6:17
"For the great day of **His wrath** is come; and who shall be able to stand?"

These solemn truths are considered in further detail in Appendix 2.

4.3 Comfort for David's distress: promise of future restoration of the nation by its Kinsman Redeemer

Psalm 69:29-36
29 "But I *am* poor and sorrowful: let Thy salvation, O God, set me up on high.
30 I will praise the Name of God with a song, and will magnify Him with thanksgiving.
31 *This* also shall please the Lord better than an ox *or* bullock that hath horns and hoofs."

David foresees a day when his destiny will be in complete contrast to those who will be trapped in the false worship at an apostate table, ensnared in a false peace and blinded to accept the terrible lie of the day of God's wrath. David at this point in his experience may well consider himself as "poor and sorrowful" (Psalm 69:29) but he has this confidence that "Thy Salvation" (Thy Jesus) will, in a future day, set him up on high. In that day of glory, David will praise the "Name of God" with a song. The song unto the Name of God will all be about "Thy Jesus".

There is a remarkable parallel in this section to Psalm 40, the Psalm which deals with:
(1) the incarnation of the Lord Jesus to be our Great High Priest

(2) the Psalmist's "New Song" on this wonderful subject

(3) the inadequacy of Old Testament offerings in general but especially in the context of consecration to the Aaronic priesthood.

Psalm 69 also is dealing with:

(1) the incarnation of the Lord Jesus to be our Kinsman Redeemer

(2) the Psalmist's song on this subject

(3) the inadequacy of Old Testament offerings to fully express praise to God for this.

Psalm 69:32-34

32 "The humble shall see *this, and* be glad: and your heart shall live that seek God.

33 For the Lord heareth the poor, and despiseth not His prisoners.

34 Let the heaven and earth praise Him, the seas, and every thing that moveth therein."

The final verses of the Psalm foretell the day when heaven, earth and the seas will be united in praising the Lord. This is a description of the millennial reign of our Lord Jesus Christ as in the later eternal state there will be no more sea. What a day it will be when heaven and earth will be united in the exaltation of the Person of the Lord Jesus Christ, "Thy Jesus"! How this will rejoice the hearts of all the humble ones who, down through the centuries, have borne the reproach of Christ and been persecuted for their association with the One Who bears the Title, "Thy Jesus"!

Notice the play on words in verse 35:"For God **will save** Zion." The One Who will do this is Thy Jesus (Thy Salvation). Moreover it will be those who love His Name – the Name of Jesus (verse 36) – who will enjoy His Kingdom!

Psalm 69:35, 36

35 "For God **will save** Zion, and will build the cities of Judah: that they may dwell there, and have it in possession.

36 The seed also of His servants shall inherit it: and they **that love His Name** shall dwell therein."

However, while it is true that there was a national stumbling 2000 years ago when the nation first encountered her Messiah, the Scripture is clear that this stumbling is not permanent.

Romans 11:11-12

11"I say then, Have they stumbled that they should fall? God forbid: but rather through their fall salvation is come unto the Gentiles, for to provoke them to jealousy.

12 Now if the fall of them be the riches of the world, and the diminishing of them the riches of the Gentiles; how much more their fullness?"

The future "fullness" of Israel is seen in the scenes of unparalleled future blessing which will befall that nation, as described for us beautifully at the end of the Psalm in verses 30-36. If the stumbling of Israel over the truth of her Messiah two thousand years ago has, in God's matchless wisdom, brought unparalleled blessing to Gentiles today, how much more shall the future restoration of Israel to Jehovah bring unparalleled blessing to this world. That will, in fact, be the millennial reign of our Lord Jesus Christ.

While we await this joyful day, in the meantime we know all too well that there is often a reproach to be borne by those who love the as yet rejected Messiah of Israel. However, if waters should overwhelm the soul of a distressed believer today, this Psalm brings the comforting promise of the ever-present nearness to our souls of our Kinsman Redeemer in all the might of His redemption victory, as well as the prospect of the future inheritance He has vouchsafed to His own.

1. Levites, following their loyalty to the Lord at the time of the golden calf incident, were appointed as the acting firstborn of Israel, to perform a special role as servants to the Aaronic priests (Deuteronomy 10:8). As Biblical illustrations of living sacrifices (Romans 12:1-2) (Numbers 8:13-4) they had wonderful sanctuary privileges of nearness to the Lord which exceeded that enjoyed by the rest of the congregation of Israel. This was not a "small thing" (Numbers 16:9)! However, they did not have complete priestly privilege as enjoyed by Aaron and his sons, such as entering into the tabernacle with incense (2 Chronicles 26:17), or approaching the vessels when they were uncovered (Numbers 18:3), a distinction which was rejected by Korah (Numbers 16:3) with tragic consequences. Their role was to 'be joined' (Numbers 18:4) to the priests in sanctuary service and to "go in" to do the service of the tabernacle (Numbers 8:15) and to serve "in the tabernacle" (Numbers 8:19). They also had the sacred duty of bearing the vessels of the tabernacle after these were first prepared for transport by the consecrated priests (Numbers 4). Theirs was a lower order of sanctuary service than that of the consecrated priest. However, it was still a service which required them to "go in" (Numbers 8:15) and to perform duties "in the tabernacle" (Numbers 8:19). In contrast to the limited sanctuary privileges of Levites, New Testament redeemed 'firstborn' priests have no such limitations in approaching the Throne of God in the heavenly sanctuary. Such is the value of the precious blood of the Lord Jesus Christ! There is a practical lesson here for all servants of the Lord. In line with the principle that an Israelite in divine service needed to be 'covered' (see page 101), so the Levite in his special service within the sanctuary, did not flaunt his own Levitical position but rather acknowledged the need for a covering (atonement) for himself, namely the offering of a sin offering and a burnt offering (Numbers 8:12). The lesson of page 101 is again emphasized. The closer the servant is to his Lord the more he eschews attention to himself and longs that only Christ be seen in his life.

2. Adam enjoyed fellowship with God in the Garden of Eden. God came down from heaven to have fellowship with Adam in the Garden. This state of blissful nearness of Adam to his Creator was vandalized by Satan. However, *padah* redemption, by definition, brings redeemed man into the heavenly sanctuary which is infinitely more wonderful than Adam meeting with God in the Garden. The fact that within the heavenly uncreated abode of God, ie the heavenly sanctuary, there are instruments of priesthood (Isaiah 6) even **before** the Lord Jesus was consecrated as a Great High Priest, is quite mind-boggling to us, as it shows that it was ever the divine master-plan (Psalm 40:5) that man should function **within the heavenly sanctuary**, something which is only possible through redemption. This helps us grasp a little of the majesty of the Lord Jesus' Title as "the Lamb foreordained before the foundation of the world"(1 Peter 1:18), where the context is of the eternal divine plan that man should be redeemed (1 Peter 1:18-20).

12

PSALM 72

A Psalm for Solomon.

1 Give the King Thy judgments, O God, and Thy righteousness unto the king's Son.

2 He shall judge Thy people with righteousness, and Thy poor with judgment.

3 The mountains shall bring peace to the people, and the little hills, by righteousness.

4 He shall judge the poor of the people, He shall save the children of the needy, and shall break in pieces the oppressor.

5 They shall fear Thee as long as the sun and moon endure, throughout all generations.

6 He shall come down like rain upon the mown grass: as showers that water the earth.

7 In His days shall the righteous flourish; and abundance of peace so long as the moon endureth.

8 He shall have dominion also from sea to sea, and from the river unto the ends of the earth.

9 They that dwell in the wilderness shall bow before Him; and His enemies shall lick the dust.

10 The kings of Tarshish and of the isles shall bring presents: the kings of Sheba and Seba shall offer gifts.

11 Yea, all kings shall fall down before Him: all nations shall serve Him.

12 For He shall deliver the needy when he crieth; the poor also, and him that hath no helper.

13 He shall spare the poor and needy, and shall save the souls of the needy.

14 He shall redeem their soul from deceit and violence: and precious shall their blood be in His sight.

15 And he shall live, and to him shall be given of the gold of Sheba: prayer also shall be made for him continually; and daily shall he be praised.

16 There shall be an handful of corn in the earth upon the top of the mountains; the fruit thereof shall shake like Lebanon: and they of the city shall flourish like grass of the earth.

17 His Name shall endure for ever: His Name shall be continued as long as the sun: and men shall be blessed in Him: all nations shall call Him blessed.

18 Blessed be the LORD God, the God of Israel, Who only doeth wondrous things.
19 And blessed be His glorious Name for ever: and let the whole earth be filled with His glory; Amen, and Amen.
20 The prayers of David the son of Jesse are ended.

1 Background and context of Psalm 72

This Psalm is about the coming Kingdom of the Son of David and thus is the ultimate vindication of David's claim to be in the line of the Messiah, which was denied by some in Psalm 69. Although not directly quoted in the New Testament, it is recognised as a Messianic Psalm by the prophet Zechariah who quotes Psalm 72:8 in Zechariah 9:10 in a clear reference to the coming Messiah. This shows us that, although the title of the Psalm says "a Psalm for Solomon", it was recognised by the prophet Zechariah as not finding fulfilment in Solomon, but rather the Son of David, i.e. the Lord Jesus of Whom Solomon was but a faint picture. Psalm 72 is not directly quoted in the New Testament. However, principles within this Psalm of how the coming Kingdom is needed to vindicate the righteousness of God are highlighted carefully in the New Testament. This will now become apparent in this overview of the Psalm.

It is helpful to consider the Psalms which lie between Psalm 69 and 72, namely Psalms 70 and 71, since they provide the contextual link between them. Psalm 70:1-5 is almost the same as the end of Psalm 40:13-17 which we have already considered. Both these passages are an expression by David of his tremendous sense of vulnerability and neediness in face of hostility from the evil one and his own failure. Why should both these almost identical sections follow two beautiful Messianic sections – Psalms 40 and 69?

As has been discussed, Psalm 40 presents the Lord Jesus as the Son of David Who would be consecrated as Priest on the basis of His own sacrifice. Psalm 40 was a very noteworthy prophecy given to David since (unlike Uzziah) he would have clearly understood that the offices of Priest and King cannot be afforded to the one person, with the exception of the promised Son of David, Who was unique in that He would bear both offices. Similarly, Psalm 69 presented the coming Messiah as the One Who through birth would become Kinsman Redeemer to the human family and would Himself experience the very reproaches which had become so familiar to David in his life for God. The Messianic revelations of Psalms 40 and 69 amounted to very lofty claims which David had made regarding the Messiah, Son of David, namely that He would be none other than "God manifest in flesh", entering this world by human birth. Moreover, King David had even gone as far as to make these claims the theme of some of Israel's sacred songs of praise! However, it is worth noting that, far from David feeling haughty in his heart regarding the wonderful revelations given to him (Psalm 131:1), his nearness to the Lord made him all the more aware of his own failings before Him. In fact, it is a recurring Biblical principle that nearness to the

Lord causes a heightened awareness of one's own failings before God. It is the expression of this feeling which is given in the repeated sections found within Psalm 40:13-17 and Psalm 70. Perhaps the lesson for us is that the nearer we come in our understanding to the Lord, the more we understand our own weakness and failure and find our only solace in one hundred percent dependence upon Him.

The two long-term messianic prophecies of the coming Messiah in Psalms 40 and 69, combined with the two short-term prophecies of David's preservation at the end of Psalm 40, which is repeated again in Psalm 70 (and amplified further in Psalm 71), constitute an example of a long-term and short-term prophecy. So often a long-term prophecy concerning the Messiah is accompanied by a short-term prophecy, such that the fulfilment of the latter proves the veracity of the former. Another example of this is the prophecy of the coming virgin birth of Christ in Isaiah 7:14 as a long-term prophecy where the accompanying short-term prophecy of the impending death of the two northern kings, who were threatening Judah at that time (Isaiah 7:16), proved the veracity of the promise of the coming Messiah. The long-term prophecies of the coming Messiah in Psalms 40 and 69 are immediately afterwards linked with short-term prophecies at the end of Psalms 40, 70 and 71, to the effect that David cannot be destroyed by the forces of evil. In fact, David was boldly asserting that the same God Who had promised the coming Messiah had also promised that David could not be forsaken by his God. Its fulfilment was to reassure the faithful remnant of Israel that the long-term Messianic promise would also be fulfilled.

Since the content of Psalm 70 has already been considered at the end of Psalm 40, we will move on to Psalm 71. It is dealing with David in the most vulnerable period of his life – old age. Would the God who had promised him security and protection be able to see him through his latter years? In fact, God's promise was clear that David would be protected to the end. Fulfilment of this promise was as sure as the long-term Messianic prophecies he had been given. Psalm 71 is a bold statement of the high spiritual plane David had reached in his final days.

Psalm 71:9

"Cast me not off in the time of old age; forsake me not when my strength faileth."

Psalm 71:17-18

17 "O God, Thou hast taught me from my youth: and hitherto have I declared Thy wondrous works.
18 Now also when I am old and grayheaded, O God, forsake me not; until I have shewed Thy strength unto *this* generation, *and* Thy power to every one *that* is to come."

As an old man facing death, David was rejoicing in the assurance of bodily resurrection on the occasion of the return to the earth of the Messiah.

Psalm 71:20
  "*Thou*, Which hast shewed me great and sore troubles, shalt quicken me
  again, and shalt bring me up again from the depths of the earth."

A more literal translation of Psalm 71:20 shows that David's resurrection
was on the occasion of the Lord's return: "Thou Who hast shown me great
and sore troubles, Thou shalt return, Thou shalt quicken **me**, Thou shalt
return, Thou shalt bring me up from the depths of the earth." (Wigram's
Englishman's Hebrew Concordance).

David is not here speaking of the **first coming** of the Lord Jesus as he did
in Psalms 40 and 69; he is now speaking of His **return to the earth** and is
confident that this shall be the occasion when he will arise from the dead
and enter into the promised Kingdom on earth. When this happens, he
shows that he will be enveloped around with comfort (verse 21) and that
his lips and tongue (physically raised from the dead) shall praise the Lord
(verses 23,24).

Psalm 71:21
  "Thou shalt increase my greatness, and comfort me on every side."

Psalm 71:23-24
  23 "My lips shall greatly rejoice when I sing unto Thee; and my soul, which
  Thou hast redeemed (*padah*).
  24 My tongue also shall talk of Thy righteousness all the day long: for they
  are confounded, for they are brought unto shame, that seek my hurt."

Since it is *padah* redemption which is in view in Psalm 71:23 – my soul
which Thou hast redeemed (*padah*) – David is indicating that he still has
access into the presence of God in heaven even after he is raised from the
dead and has entered into his earthly inheritance.

At the end of Psalm 71, David anticipates that **subsequent to his bodily
resurrection** he will experience the final vindication of his claim to be in the
royal line of the Messiah, something which was contested by his enemies in
Psalm 69. This is the fulfilment of the *gaal* redemption discussed in Psalm
69, which is the redemption of the body. Psalm 72, in its depiction of the
Kingdom of Christ in manifestation, describes this final vindication of
David's faith.

1.1 The themes underlying Psalm 72

Psalm 72 describes the future millennial reign of our Lord Jesus Christ. It
provides some key reasons why He must reign:
  1 to vindicate the reputation of God for righteousness
  2 to vindicate the faithful stand taken by His people (including David)
  3 to vindicate God's verdict on the failure of man
  This threefold theme recurs throughout the Psalm.

2 The righteousness of God displayed in righteous rule

Psalm 72:1

"Give the King Thy judgments, O God, and Thy righteousness unto the king's Son."

In verse 1, the Psalmist is speaking about divine judgments and righteousness. Both these subjects have been questioned by unbelieving men down through the centuries.

In fact, because unbelieving man is "an enemy" in his mind "by wicked works" (Colossians 1:21) and regards the God of heaven as an "austere man" (Luke 19:21 and Matthew 25:24), it is commonplace nowadays in modern literature and the media to hear the righteousness of God in His dealings with men being questioned, especially in the context of His right to judge sinful men. Paul summarises the prevailing philosophy of unbelieving men: "Is God unrighteous Who taketh vengeance?" (Romans 3:5). Of course, everyone who is saved accepts the righteousness of God. In Luke 7, the publicans and sinners accepted the righteousness of God in condemning them. The Biblical language is: "They justified God, being baptized with the baptism of John," in contrast to the Pharisees who "rejected the council of God against themselves being not baptized of him".

Luke 7:29-30

29 "And all the people that heard *Him*, and the publicans, justified God, being baptized with the baptism of John.
30 But the Pharisees and lawyers rejected the counsel of God against themselves, being not baptized of him."

In recent years, some question God's right to be Judge in His dealings with men and even go so far as to blaspheme His righteousness in this matter. Psalm 72 is God's response to this and shows how the good Name of the God of heaven will finally be publicly vindicated.

Of course, by the time we reach the millennial reign, the righteousness and the righteous judgment of God will have already been at least partially displayed in:

1 the **righteous basis of the plan and provision of redemption** already demonstrated in the death, burial and resurrection of our Lord Jesus Christ and His presentation of the Gospel (Romans 3);

2 the **righteous basis of divine judgment in the manifestation** of our Lord Jesus Christ at the end of the tribulation when He will take vengeance on Christ-rejecting men ("...which is a manifest token of the righteous judgment of God" (2 Thessalonians 1:5)).

However, there is one aspect of divine righteousness which remains to be publicly demonstrated. It is **the righteous basis of divine authority** in the setting up and ongoing administration of His Kingdom. Down through the centuries, government was entrusted to man. Even in pre-exilic times, godly kings of Judah so often fell short of the divine will and made mistakes which cost them dearly. Can the Messiah do better? Unlike every ruler on earth who had preceded Him, His Kingdom will be based on **absolute** righteousness. In fact, God the Father has invested the public demonstration of His own righteous character entirely and unreservedly in the King – our Lord Jesus. He is referred to as "the King" and the "king's Son". As the King, He is the Monarch reigning undisputedly and without peer in the earth. As the king's Son, we are reminded that He is the Son of David and that when He reigns in millennial glory He will be finally seated on the throne of His father David. What a change this makes! When our Lord was on earth, He was here as the King-in-waiting. He was not yet seated on the throne of His father David. Moreover, He does not occupy the throne of His father David until His return to the earth. When He does, He will put down all the unrighteousness in government within this earth and will establish righteous authority globally.

This is why it is wrong to blame Christ for unrighteous acts which governments carry out in this world, even if these are done in the Name of Christ, such as happened in the Middle Ages in the times of the so-called Holy Roman Empire and the Crusades etc.

It is important for us to know that our Lord left the earth as a Nobleman (Luke 19:12) but will return as King. When He returns, not just as the King-in-waiting but as the One Who will exercise all the authority of the reigning King, righteousness will prevail. This is why He is referred to as "the king's Son", linking Him with David and confirming His right to reign as King on earth.

In the day-to-day management of the millennial Kingdom, He will be the Judge. In Israel of old, the execution of God's Law was subcontracted to the elders of Israel who were called *elohim* or judges. It was always possible to distinguish when the word *elohim* referred to earthly human judges because the accompanying verb was plural (see Psalms 8 and 82 for more detailed discussion of this). When the word refers to God, the verb is (with one exception) singular.

In the Kingdom, those who once were the *elohim* of Israel are now redundant (see later in Psalm 82). All judgment is committed to the Son (John 5:27). The principles which will govern the judgment of this King will be the Sermon on the Mount. Unlike the judges of Israel who upheld the Law of Moses, this Judge of Israel has the right to read motives and the feelings of the heart (Matthew 5-7). An example of a judge of Israel misjudging a person is Eli who, by looking on the outward appearance only, mistook Hannah for being drunk (1 Samuel 1:14). In fact, Samuel recognised this as he inspected the sons of Jesse: "for *the Lord seeth* not as man seeth; for man looketh on the outward appearance, but the Lord looketh on the heart" (1 Samuel 16:7). No such mistakes will happen when Christ is the Judge because He can see into the heart and judge rightly what is happening there.

3 The vindication of His suffering people

Psalm 72:2

"He shall judge Thy people with righteousness, and Thy poor with judgment."

The millennial reign of Christ is vital to vindicate the faith of those who remained faithful to Him in the time of His rejection. This becomes apparent when we investigate the meaning of the word "to judge" (*yadin*) in verse 2. It carries the meaning of "pleading the cause" of someone who is wrongly treated or downtrodden. Here are some examples of its use which illustrate this meaning:

Proverbs 31:9 "**plead the cause** of the poor and needy"

Genesis 30:6 "And Rachel said, God hath judged me (**pleaded my cause**) and hath also heard my voice, and hath given me a son: therefore called she his name Dan"

Jeremiah 5:28 "…they **judge** not the cause, the cause of the fatherless"

Jeremiah 22:16 "He **judged** the cause of the poor and needy"

Accordingly, this Psalm shows how the righteousness of God will be seen on the occasion of the Lord returning and acting as Judge to plead and defend the cause of His own. In fact, it appears that the first act of the Lord on His return to establish His Kingdom will be to defend the poor and downtrodden believers during the era of His rejection who, during the dark days of the tribulation, had none to speak on their behalf in the anti-Christian tribunals of that dreadful time. What a change it will be when the Lord Himself will come to publicly defend His own. This is the background to the parable of the unjust judge and the widow in Luke 18:1-8. God will avenge the widow from the adversary. The message of Luke 18 is that His delay in avenging the faithful remnant is not because God the Judge is unjust; it is because He is waiting for "faith on the earth", i.e. for more people to believe and be saved.

The designation, "Thy poor," does not necessarily refer to those who are financially in need. Indeed, in the Sermon on the Mount, in the very first beatitude, the Lord speaks of the poor not as those who are financially and materially in poverty but as those who are "poor in spirit." In fact, it is such people who are the objects of divine blessing, "for theirs is the Kingdom of heaven". The determination of the "poor in spirit" requires a Judge Who, unlike Israel's former judges (*elohim*), can see beyond the superficial and material into the inner spiritual recesses of one's being. The judging of the poor involves the identification of those who are poor in spirit and singling such out for blessing in the Kingdom. In fact, it is a prerequisite of the Kingdom to be "poor in spirit", i.e. to depend solely on the Person of Christ for access to that Kingdom. It is the Lord Who will make this judgment because "the Lord knoweth them that are His". Consequently, these persons are called "Thy poor", i.e. they belong to the Lord.

4 Vindication of God's verdict that man is a failure: rebellion of man despite establishing ideal conditions on earth

4.1 Purification of the world's communication systems

Psalm 72:3

"The mountains shall bring peace to the people and the little hills by righteousness."

Mountains were an important part of the communication system of the ancient world (Isaiah 52:7). Nowadays, we might look upon the Biblical mountains as equivalent to the media of today. Alas, the mountains of Israel had often become shrines of idolatry and unrighteousness as highlighted in chapter 6 of Ezekiel.

Ezekiel 6:1-7
1 "And the Word of the Lord came unto me, saying,
2 Son of man, set thy face toward the mountains of Israel, and prophesy against them,
3 And say, Ye mountains of Israel, hear the Word of the Lord God; Thus saith the Lord God to the mountains, and to the hills, to the rivers, and to the valleys; Behold, I, *even* I, will bring a sword upon you, and I will destroy your high places.
4 And your altars shall be desolate, and your images shall be broken: and I will cast down your slain *men* before your idols.
5 And I will lay the dead carcases of the children of Israel before their idols; and I will scatter your bones round about your altars.
6 In all your dwelling places the cities shall be laid waste, and the high places shall be desolate; that your altars may be laid waste and made desolate, and your idols may be broken and cease, and your images may be cut down, and your works may be abolished.
7 And the slain shall fall in the midst of you, and ye shall know that I *am* the Lord."

Clearly, if communication and media systems (whether in ancient or modern times) fall under control of idolatrous ideas, widespread darkness prevails. Psalm 72 shows us that when the Lord reigns, His Word will prevail worldwide and the mountains will be vehicles for the propagation of the truth about God's righteous character.

Isaiah 52:7
"How beautiful **upon the mountains** are the feet of him that bringeth good tidings, that publisheth peace; that bringeth good tidings of good, that publisheth salvation; that saith unto Zion, Thy God reigneth!"

From mountain tops which once hosted sites of idolatrous practice shall go forth a message of peace based on rightousness. It is in this context that "He shall judge (*yishphot;* root *shaphat*) the poor of the people" (Psalm 72:4). This is a different Hebrew word from the word "to judge" (*yadin*) used in verse 2, where the concept is of judging in the sense of vindicating the downtrodden, whereas in verse 4 the idea behind the word "to judge" is of leading and expounding God's word, "when from Zion shall go forth the law and the word of the Lord from Jerusalem" Isaiah 2:3-5.

Isaiah 2:3-5
> 3 "....for out of Zion shall go forth the Law, and the Word of the Lord from Jerusalem.
> 4 And He shall **judge** (*shaphat*) among the nations, and shall rebuke many people: and they shall beat their swords into plowshares, and their spears into pruninghooks: nation shall not lift up sword against nation, neither shall they learn war any more.
> 5 O house of Jacob, come ye, and let us walk in the light of the Lord."

In contrast with today where the internet, radio and television contain so much anti-God material, in that future day communication will be saturated with the truth about the righteousness of God. In this sense, "He shall judge (root *shaphat*) the poor (ones) of the people". They will respond to His guidance in total obedience. A major outcome of this obedience will be in the blessing of their families. Those living saints who enter the millennium from the tribulation will marry and have children. These children stand in need of salvation because they are born sinners. As the Lord judges and guides the "poor of the people", they will learn how to "train up a child in the way he should go" (Proverbs 22:6). In this context "He shall save the children of the needy". The poor of the people will rejoice in this.

It is remarkable that in such an environment there would be any who would dare to oppress the poor (verse 4).

Psalm 72:4
> "He shall judge the poor of the people, He shall save the children of the needy, and shall break in pieces the oppressor."

This is the first hint that during the millennial reign there would be any who would seek to oppress or hinder those who wish to carry out the Lord's will. The word "oppressor" carries the idea of oppression by fraudulence or deceit. An example of its use is in Isaiah 30:12, where the context is the teaching of false prophets in contrast to the faithful teachers who had been elbowed into a corner (Isaiah 30:20). Psalm 72 indicates that this will not be permitted to happen while the Lord is reigning. No persons will openly oppress the people by lies, error or fraudulence. Not only will the devil, who deceived the nations, be bound, but no longer can men act as satanic emissaries in perpetuating lies and deceit. God now has provided this world with ideal conditions for saying 'yes' to the claims of Christ. The only reason why men born during the millennium should refuse to accept the Lord as their Saviour is because of the intrinsic rebellion of their fallen human heart. No longer can they blame the Devil or false teachings and creeds of this world for their unbelief. Any unbelief can now be seen for what it is: open rebellion and enmity against God. In the seven thousandth year (approximately) of this world's existence, Man will now be proven to be a fallen creature in need of redemption.

Psalm 72:5

"They shall fear Thee as long as the sun and moon endure, throughout all generations."

Within the worldwide environment of truth there shall be a wholesome dread of grieving the Lord. The word "fear" here does not mean "terror". It is the word used to describe "the fear of the Lord" which is the "beginning of wisdom" in Proverbs 9:10, and the contextual use of this word includes the reverential awe becoming those who love the Lord. Throughout the entire 1000 year era, this reverential awe shall be maintained from one generation to the next.

Psalm 72:6

"He shall come down like rain upon the mown grass: as showers that water the earth."

The imagery of mown grass is used by Moses in Psalm 90 to describe the death of mankind. At the end of the tribulation there will be many of the human race who will have died and the world will be largely decimated. It will be like a waste wilderness after all the plagues of the tribulation. The presence of the Lord shall bring restoration and productivity.

Psalm 72:7

"In His days shall the righteous flourish; and abundance of peace so long as the moon endureth."

The "flourishing of the righteous" is a horticultural term describing the blossoming or budding of a plant. The Psalmist is, in fact, using the picture of a growing plant or tree to illustrate a righteous person in the future reign of Christ. No longer will there be adverse conditions to stunt such a person's growth. There will be ideal conditions for growth, development and fruit-bearing, such as characterised the "blessed man" in Psalm 1 who is like the tree planted by rivers of living water. When the world will be populated by multitudes of men, such as are found in Psalm 1, it is small wonder that there will be an abundance of peace or "multiplication of peace (*shalom*)". In passing, it is worth reminding ourselves that when Peter says "grace unto you, and peace, be multiplied"(1 Peter 1:2) he is implying growth of these virtues in a believer's life. The phrase, "so long as the moon endureth", reminds us that the sun and the moon will be done away with at the end of the millennium along with the first heaven and earth. This is discussed in detail in Psalm 102.

Psalm 72:8

"He shall have dominion also from sea to sea, and from the river unto the ends of the earth."

This verse confirms for us the universal scope of this dominion. Since it is quoted in Zechariah 9:10, where it refers to the coming Messiah, this is confirmation that Psalm 72 is a Messianic Psalm. Moreover, the verse which precedes Zechariah's quotation from this Psalm (Zechariah 9:9) touchingly reminds us that the King Who reigns supreme and in unrivalled glory in Psalm 72 was the One Who first of all rode into Jerusalem "lowly", "having salvation" and "riding upon an ass, and upon a colt the foal of an ass".

Zechariah 9: 9-10.

9 "Rejoice greatly, O daughter of Zion; shout, O daughter of Jerusalem: behold, thy King cometh unto thee: He is just, and having salvation; lowly, and riding upon an ass, and upon a colt the foal of an ass.

10 And I will cut off the chariot from Ephraim, and the horse from Jerusalem, and the battle bow shall be cut off: **and He shall speak peace unto the heathen: and His dominion shall be from sea even to sea, and from river even to the ends of the earth."**

Even in His glory, the events surrounding the humiliation of His first advent shall never be forgotten by all who love Him.

Psalm 72:9

"They that dwell in the wilderness shall bow before Him; and His enemies shall lick the dust."

This verse solemnly reminds us that there will be areas of planet earth during the millennial reign of our Lord Jesus which will be "wilderness" where drought conditions will prevail. This may seem puzzling to us when we consider the healing and regeneration which shall accompany the onset of the Kingdom of our Lord Jesus Christ. Once more, it is the prophet Zechariah who explains this to us. He tells us in Zechariah 14:16-17 that during the coming Kingdom those who do not "go up from year to year to worship the King, the Lord of Hosts and to keep the feast of tabernacles… even upon them shall be no rain…" In other words, those who begrudgingly obey the Lord but who do not spontaneously worship Him shall be visited upon with drought conditions. Such individuals have entered the millennium through birth but have not obtained salvation and this is evidenced by failure to come and worship the King. They will, however, "bow before Him". Note the precision of Scripture. The word here to bow (*kara*) is simply an act of bowing down. The word is not synonymous with worship and is the word used in Isaiah 45:23 to describe the last great day of judgment when "unto Me every knee will bow…" and includes those who in their hearts had rejected the Lord in their lives.Note 1 Once again, how tragic is this observation that even in the ideal conditions of millennial glory there will be those whom He still regards as His enemies! Let us remember that God is not an enemy of man. Man is an enemy of God (Colossians 1) in his "mind by wicked works". As such, everyone born into the millennial Kingdom is, by birth, an enemy of God and stands in need of salvation, just as everyone born into each preceding age needed salvation.

Psalm 72:10-11

10 "The kings of Tarshish and of the isles shall bring presents: the kings of
Sheba and Seba shall offer gifts.

11 Yea, all kings shall fall down before Him: all nations shall serve Him."

In contrast to those who feign obedience in that coming day and who are
not genuine believers in our Lord Jesus Christ, there shall be a great throng
of people who will worship and serve the King. Whether they are seafaring
peoples, such as those of Tarshish and the isles, or land traders, such as in
Seba and Sheba, there shall be universal obeisance and service to Him. The
exact reasons why people should want to worship the King is explained in
some detail in the next three verses.

Psalm 72:12-14

12 "For (because) He shall deliver the needy when he crieth; the poor also,
and him that hath no helper.

13 He shall spare the poor and needy, and shall save the souls of the needy.

14 He shall redeem (*gaal*) their soul from deceit and violence: and precious
shall their blood be in His sight."

In verse 12, the word "for" means "because". It tells us the reason
why people will want to worship the King as described in the preceding
verses. It is because they were delivered when they cried to the Lord for
salvation (verse 12). They have been spared (verse 13), saved (verse 13) and
redeemed (verse 14). In fact, it is out of appreciation for salvation that they
come in worship to the King. It is the same today. It is only those who have
experienced the joys of salvation from their sin who spontaneously want
to return in thanksgiving and worship to their Redeemer. In verse 14, the
aspect of redemption brought to our attention is *gaal* redemption which was
noted in Psalm 69 to be payment of a price to **enjoy the inheritance,** whereas
padah redemption is the payment of a price to **become God's inheritance** i.e.
functioning in His sanctuary. This verse shows that just because someone
is born into the millennium from saved parents, this does not mean that
they will automatically enjoy the wonderful inheritance within it. In fact,
those who do not get saved, despite the ideal conditions prevailing in the
millennial era, will find themselves in the wilderness (verse 9) away from
the centre of divine blessing. The lie which will lead them into this sad state
will not be from Satan as he is bound. It arises from the hidden recesses
of the fallen human heart itself. This is the ultimate proof of the failure of
fallen man. Hence the necessity to "redeem their soul from deceit". This is
the internal deceit of the heart. "The heart is deceitful" and needs redeemed
to enjoy the inheritance.

Jeremiah 17:9

"The heart *is* deceitful above all *things,* and desperately wicked: who can
know it?"

Unfortunately, in Christendom, this principle was not understood in early Church history and, even today, some believe that children born into Christian families automatically enter into spiritual blessing. This passage shows that apart from personal redemption through faith in Christ this cannot be the case.

For those who have experienced this deliverance, we learn "precious shall their blood be in His sight". This phrase simply means that the King will see to it that they will not experience death. This interpretation arises from a similar contextual use of the verb "to be precious" in 1 Samuel 26:21 when Saul says to David, "My life (Hebrew: my soul) was precious in thine eyes", i.e. David valued Saul's soul so highly that he spared him from death in the cave. The phrase, "precious shall their blood be in His sight", means that those who experience salvation in the millennial reign will not be permitted to die. Only those who do not get saved in the millennium will experience death and then ultimately the second death. For those who get saved in the millennium, there cannot be death as there is no resurrection for the saved at the end of the millennium. The resurrection of the saved occurred at the beginning of the millennium. Only at the end of the millennium is there a resurrection of the lost, which is referred to as the second death in Revelation 20:14 and this will include the lost of all ages.

Psalm 72:15

"And he shall live, and to him shall be given of the gold of Sheba: prayer also shall be made for him continually; and daily shall he be praised."

This verse involves 4 elements:
1 and he shall live
2 to him shall be given of the gold of Sheba
3 prayer also shall be made for (on behalf of) him continually
4 daily shall he be praised

Usually the reader of the Authorized Version understands this verse as referring to the King. The interpretation of the verse would be as follows: "The Lord lives. In response to His claims people shall bring up to Jerusalem their wealth (the gold of Sheba). People in the millennial Kingdom shall daily pray for the King and shall daily praise Him".

While this is the idea which perhaps most accept, the first difficulty with this interpretation is why should the infinite and infallible King need prayer continually for His Kingly rule? Surely the Lord does not need us failing creatures to pray for Him? Clearly, the idea of the Lord needing us to pray for Him cannot be right if we believe in the omnipotence and omniscience of God and His infallibility. Whoever is the object of the prayer in (3) cannot be a divine Person.

To understand this verse, reversion to a literal translation is helpful:
1 He shall live
2 He shall give to him of the gold of Sheba
3 He shall pray for him continually

4 He shall bless him daily (Benjamin Davidson's literal translation).

In the passage it is difficult to identify who the "he" and the "him" signify throughout the verse.

In the context of the preceding verse, where the blood of the saved person is precious, i.e. the saved person is "death resistant", it seems reasonable to allow that the next phrase, "He shall live", refers to the immortality conferred on those who get saved during the millennium. In this regard, the author feels that this phrase is unlikely to refer to the immortality of the King Who has already been risen from the dead for over 2000 years. The next phrase suggests that He (the Messiah King) gives gold of Sheba to the convert, i.e. He not only saves him but keeps and maintains him. As if that were not enough, the King prays for the convert (him) continually and in High Priestly capacity confers upon such a believer a daily blessing (He shall bless him). Accordingly, here is a paraphrase of the verse to show its meaning:

1 the millennial believer shall live

2 the King shall give to him of the gold of Sheba (i.e. provide for his physical needs)

3 the King shall pray for him continually (i.e. provide for his preservation needs)

4 the King shall bless him daily (i.e. provide for his daily spiritual needs)

Psalm 72:16

"There shall be an handful of corn in the earth upon the top of the mountains; the fruit thereof shall shake like Lebanon: and they of the city shall flourish like grass of the earth."

Where the Lord is glorified in His High Priestly ministry, by praying for the millennial saints and blessing the people, there shall be earthly blessing in abundance. This earthly blessing, as in Old Testament days, shall be twofold: firstly abundance of food (the fruit and corn in abundance) and secondly, abundance of children. In contrast to the cut grass of the prayer of Moses in Psalm 90:5-6, referring to people being cut down in death, here we have the inhabitants of **the city** flourishing and multiplying as grass of the earth. Surely this is the city of Jerusalem from where the millennial blessing shall flow globally from the King and which will be the greatest centre of population in that age.

Psalm 72:17

"His Name shall endure for ever: His Name shall be continued as long as the sun: and men shall be blessed in Him:"

In verse 17, the King is acknowledged as the source of all this blessing. "Men shall be blessed in Him". Once more the phrase, "as long as the sun", reminds us that the millennium will come to an end when the sun will cease to be. Psalm 102 tells us of the new universe which will be brought into existence to last unendingly throughout the sin free eternal state.

Psalm 72:17-18

17 "…all nations shall call Him blessed.
18 Blessed be the LORD God, the God of Israel, Who only doeth wondrous things."

In response, all nations without exception shall respond in worship and marvel at the wondrous things the Lord has wrought in this world through His Christ.

Psalm 72:19, 20

19 "And blessed be His glorious Name for ever: and let the whole earth be filled with His glory; Amen, and Amen.
20 The prayers of David the son of Jesse are ended."

This Psalm is the fulfilment of the Messianic promises given to David and for which he suffered so much reproach. David will be filled with joy in that coming day when the glory of king David's Son, referred to at the outset of the Psalm as "the king's Son", shall fill all the earth. This shall be the divine vindication of all those who have borne His reproach throughout the long night of His rejection by this world.

---

1. Of course a true worshipper will bow down (*kara*). However this is not an act of feigned or compulsory obedience to the Lord. It is a genuine display of spontaneously showing worshipful humility before the Lord. When this is the case, Scripture will clarify that the act of bowing down is a genuine act of worship by providing additional words to confirm this e.g. Psalm 95:6; 1 Kings 8:54; 2 Chronicles 7:3; 2 Chronicles 29:29.

13

PSALM 82

A Psalm of Asaph
1 GOD standeth in the congregation of the Mighty; He judgeth among the gods.
2 How long will ye judge unjustly, and accept the persons of the wicked? Selah.
3 Defend the poor and fatherless: do justice to the afflicted and needy.
4 Deliver the poor and needy: rid them out of the hand of the wicked.
5 They know not, neither will they understand; they walk on in darkness: all the
foundations of the earth are out of course.
6 I have said, Ye are gods; and all of you are children of the most High.
7 But ye shall die like men, and fall like one of the princes.
8 Arise, O God, judge the earth: for Thou shalt inherit all nations.

1 Background and introduction

This Psalm is a detailed analysis of the failure of those leaders in Israel who had responsibility for guiding and judging the people. They seemed unaware (Psalm 82:5) that it was God Who was standing in their midst (Psalm 82:1) remonstrating with them. This Psalm is quoted by the Lord Jesus Christ in John 10:34-36 in exactly the same context of the leaders of the nation not knowing that it was the Son of God Who was standing in their midst on that occasion. What breathtaking contextual use of Holy Scripture by the Lord Jesus Christ!

John 10:34-36
> 34 "Jesus answered them, Is it not written in your Law, I said, Ye are gods?
> 35 If He called them gods, unto whom the Word of God came, and the Scripture cannot be broken;
> 36 Say ye of Him, Whom the Father hath sanctified, and sent into the world, Thou blasphemest; because I said, I am the Son of God?"

1.1 The occasion in the New Testament when the Lord quoted from Psalm 82

On that occasion He had been teaching in the temple. It was the Feast of the Dedication known to this day as Hanukkah.

John 10:22
> "And it was at Jerusalem the feast of the dedication, and it was winter."

It was on this day that the Jews had rededicated the temple after its desecration by the evil, anti-God figure, Antiochus Epiphanes, in 167 B.C. Hanukkah is therefore a celebration of truth over deception and a brilliant victory for those who were true to the God of Israel against the wicked anti-God character, Antiochus. Now we know from Daniel 8:9-14 that Antiochus and the circumstances attending his blasphemous attack on the God of Israel in the temple in Jerusalem provide a picture of a future day when a similar anti-God figure, the first beast of Revelation 13:1-8, will likewise claim to be God and force people to worship him. It is hardly surprising, then, that it was a most dramatic event in the temple complex when the Stranger from Nazareth began to set forth His claim that He was, in fact, God manifest in flesh! On a day when people were celebrating victory over the imposter, some must have wondered Who this Person was Who chose such a significant day to publicly claim to be on equality with God. To those who were listening, though, His credentials were flawless.

Firstly, His coming in to the sheepfold of Israel was by the introduction of the "porter" (John 10:1-3).

John 10:1-3
> 1 "Verily, verily, I say unto you, He that entereth not by the door into the sheepfold, but climbeth up some other way, the same is a thief and a robber.
> 2 But He that entereth in by the door is the Shepherd of the sheep.
> 3 To Him the **porter openeth**; and the sheep hear His voice: and He calleth His own sheep by name, and leadeth them out."

Clearly, John the Baptist was the porter, and any who came to Israel claiming to be the Messiah without such an introductory person were decidedly imposters. After all, John's pre-Messianic preparatory ministry was foretold in Isaiah 40:3-4 and Malachi 3:1. However, The Lord Jesus Christ's greatest evidence to be Who He claimed lay in His promise to have power to lay down His life and power to take it again.

John 10:17-18
> 17 "Therefore doth My Father love Me, because I lay down My life, that I might take it again.
> 18 No man taketh it from Me, but I lay it down of Myself. I have power to lay it down, and I have power to take it again. This commandment have I received of My Father."

His death and resurrection were the evidence of His Deity and His claim to be the Son of God. Interestingly, the future world leader in the tribulation, the first beast in Revelation 13:1-8, has a deadly wound which has healed. It is important to note that the Scripture does not say that this individual died. Only one of his heads had a wound unto death while his remaining heads were intact. This man was critically ill but survived. He survives a near-death experience and hence simulates immortality as an anti-God-like figure. He does not simulate resurrection. Resurrection **cannot be simulated** even by satanic power (Appendix 2). This claim of Christ to die and rise again is the proof that He is the Son of God and the true Christ (Messiah). It shows to all that He has the power to save and to keep all who come to Him by faith.

John 10:17-18
17 "Therefore doth My Father love Me, because I lay down My life, that I might take it again.
18 No man taketh it from Me, but I lay it down of Myself. I have power to lay it down, and I have power to take it again. This commandment have I received of My Father."

The second beast of Revelation 13, the anti-Christ figure, can also simulate some Messianic characteristics but not resurrection. Nor can he simulate the voice of Christ. The voice of this second beast is "as a dragon" (Revelation 13:11). However, in John 10, the true sheep recognise the voice of Christ.

John 10:27-30.
27 "My sheep hear My voice, and I know them, and they follow Me:
28 And I give unto them eternal life; and they shall never perish, neither shall any *man* pluck them out of My hand.
29 My Father, which gave *them* Me, is greater than all; and no *man* is able to pluck *them* out of My Father's hand.
30 I and *My* Father are One."

Clearly, a minority in Israel at that time who were sincerely waiting for the Messiah recognised the veracity of His claim to be the Son of God. However, tragically, His statement – "I and the Father are One" – was taken by the majority of the audience that day as blasphemy, and they looked upon Him with the same hostility as they would have reserved for the very memory of Antiochus of old. The result was hostile rejection and an attempt to execute Him by stoning.

John 10:31-33
31 "Then the Jews took up stones again to stone Him.
32 Jesus answered them, Many good works have I shewed you from My Father; for which of those works do ye stone Me?
33 The Jews answered Him, saying, For a good work we stone Thee not; but for blasphemy; and because that Thou, being a man, makest Thyself God."

They tried to stone Him but the Lord was not yet finished with them. He had not just words of evidence, entreaty and life. He had words of warning. Here is John's account:

John 10:34-36
34 "Jesus answered them, Is it not written in your Law, I said, Ye are gods?
35 If He called them gods, unto whom the Word of God came, and the Scripture cannot be broken;
36 Say ye of Him, Whom the Father hath sanctified, and sent into the world, Thou blasphemest; because I said, I am the Son of God?"

The Lord Jesus turned His hostile audience to Psalm 82 and quoted from verse 6:

Psalm 82:6
"I have said, Ye *are* gods; and all of you *are* children of the most High."

Without even raising His voice, He used this Psalm to indicate to His judges – the elders and leaders of Israel at that time – that they would soon be relieved of their duties as the executors of God's Law in Israel and that all judgment would be committed unto Him, the Son. A study of Psalm 82 will show how this passage was chosen by the Lord to powerfully portray this solemn truth.

2 The various meanings of the word *elohim* in the Hebrew Bible

Before considering this Psalm, we need to look at the various meanings of the word God (*elohim*) in the Old Testament, since this word is used with different meanings in the Psalm.

Elohim in the Old Testament is often translated

1 God
2 gods (false)
3 angels
4 judges in Israel (who were in charge of carrying out God's Law)

Please note that *elohim* **always** is a plural noun in the four uses defined above. However, if the accompanying verb is singular, then the word **always** means God and is translated as such. This is not a grammatical error in the Hebrew Bible. Rather the inspired Scriptures are demonstrating the unity of the Godhead. Oh the wonder of God's Word!

2.1 Elohim as God

When the pronoun and/or the verb accompanying the word *elohim* is singular, then the word always means the God of heaven. Almost always when the verb accompanying *elohim* is plural, the meaning is not "God" but either "false gods" (Exodus 32:4), "angels" (Psalm 97:7), or "judges" (Exodus 22:9). There is one notable exception in 2 Samuel 7:23 where we read, "When God (*elohim*) went (plural verb) to redeem for a people to Himself (singular pronoun)".

2 Samuel 7:23
"And what one nation in the earth *is* like Thy people, *even* like Israel, whom **God went (plural verb) to redeem for a people to Himself,** and to make Him a Name, and to do for You great things and terrible, for Thy land, before Thy people, which Thou redeemedst to Thee from Egypt, *from* the nations and their gods?"

Although the verb "went" is plural, the pronoun "Himself" is singular which is why the translators were correct to translate the word *elohim* as "God". As a backup against anyone suggesting another meaning for *elohim* in 2 Samuel 7:23, in the parallel passage in 1 Chronicles 17:21 the verb "went" as well as the pronoun "His" are both **singular** confirming that the meaning of the word *elohim* is definitely God.

1 Chronicles 17:21
> "And what one nation in the earth *is* like Thy people Israel, **whom God (*elohim*) went (singular verb) to redeem** *to be* **His own people**, to make Thee a Name of greatness and terribleness, by driving out nations from before Thy people, whom Thou hast redeemed out of Egypt?"

Why does a plural verb follow the word *elohim* here in 2 Samuel 7:23? It is to remind us that the **Holy Trinity**Note 1 is involved in the matter of redemption. The redemption from Egypt and its gods (as was seen in Psalm 69) involved the Holy Trinity and was a picture of the eternal redemption. Similarly, the eternal redemption required the intervention of the Holy Trinity when He (Christ) "through the Eternal Spirit offered Himself without spot to God" (Hebrews 9:14).

Hebrews 9:14
> "How much more shall the blood of Christ, Who through the Eternal Spirit offered Himself without spot to God, purge your conscience from dead works to serve the living God?"

In summary then, these considerations do not alter the rule that every time *elohim* is followed by a singular verb, the meaning always is God. In 2 Samuel 7:23, the general principle that *elohim* followed by a plural verb does not refer to God finds an exception in the phrase, "**God went (plural verb) to redeem for a people to Himself.....**". Here the use of the singular pronoun "Himself" removes any ambiguity and shows that it is the Holy Trinity which is in view in that unique verse.

Similarly, when God (*elohim*) is being addressed in the Hebrew Bible, the pronoun is generally **Thou**, or **Thee** indicating that it is usual and appropriate to address God in the second person singular pronoun **Thou** or **Thee**. Once again this is illustrated in a further reading of 1 Chronicles 17:21

1 Chronicles 17:21
> "And what one nation in the earth *is* like **Thy** people Israel, **whom God (*elohim*)** went (singular verb) to redeem *to be* His own people, to make **Thee** a Name of greatness and terribleness, by driving out nations from before **Thy** people, whom **Thou** hast redeemed out of Egypt?"

However, even to this generality there is an exception again found in 2 Samuel 7:23!

2 Samuel 7:23
> "And what one nation in the earth *is* like Thy people, *even* like Israel, whom **God (*elohim*) went (plural verb)** to redeem for a people to Himself, and to make Him a Name, and to do **for You** great things and terrible, for Thy land, before Thy people, which Thou redeemedst to Thee from Egypt, *from*

the nations and their gods?"

In this very remarkable verse David addresses God (*elohim*) as "You" in the phrase "to do **for You** (plural) great things and terrible". Now this is consistent with the verb "went" being plural, as earlier considered, indicating the distinctive roles of the Persons of the Godhead (the Holy Trinity) in the matter of redemption. David now in this prayer, unique in all of Holy Scripture, addresses the Holy Trinity directly using the plural pronoun "You" rather than the singular pronoun "Thee". To remove any ambiguity as to Whom the "You" refers in 2 Samuel 7:23, the parallel passage of 1 Chronicles 17:21 indicates that the "You" of 2 Samuel 7:23 has been changed to "Thee" i.e. God (*elohim*) by the phrase "to make **Thee** a Name of greatness and terribleness". Thus 2 Samuel 7:23 differs from the rest of Scripture in that *elohim*, meaning God, is used with a plural verb "went" and a plural pronoun "You". A parallel study of the differences between 2 Samuel 7:23 and 1 Chronicles 17:21 will helpfully show that the doctrine of the Holy Trinity is as much Old Testament doctrine as New Testament teaching.

Is it appropriate for believers today to address God as "You" as David does in 2 Samuel 7:23? In other words is it right for a believer today to address the Holy Trinity directly? It is the New Testament pattern that we as New Testament priests and as ones filled with the Spirit (Ephesians 5:18) approach the Father (Ephesians 5:19) in our thanksgiving in the Name of our Lord Jesus Christ (Ephesians 5:19). By so doing the several roles of the Holy Trinity are honoured in our prayer and praise to Him.

Ephesians 5:18-20
> 18 "And be not drunk with wine, wherein is excess; but be filled **with the Spirit**;
> 19 Speaking to yourselves in psalms and hymns and spiritual songs, singing and making melody in your heart **to the Lord**;
> 20 Giving thanks always for all things **unto God and the Father** in the Name of our **Lord Jesus Christ**."

As we approach our Father in this way, the Lord Jesus receives His portion as was already considered in Psalm 16. To address the Holy Trinity directly is outside of the New Testament way of approach for New Testament priests on earth.

2.2 *Elohim* as gods (false)

Some may argue that there is one exception in Genesis when Abraham, under intense emotional pressure from the heathen king Abimelech, tells him "When *elohim* caused (plural) me to wander from my father's house".

Genesis 20:13
> "And it came to pass, when God (*elohim*) caused me to wander (plural verb) from my father's house, that I said unto her, This *is* thy kindness which thou shalt shew unto me; at every place whither we shall come, say of me, He *is* my brother."

The plural verb (caused to wander) indicates that *elohim* here means "the gods". Unfortunately, in our Authorised Version this is translated, "When God caused me to wander from my father's house." This hides from the English non-Hebrew reader the Peter-type denial which Abraham did of His God before the Philistine King. What Abraham was saying was: "When the gods caused me to wander from my father's house". Abraham, in fear, was denying the monotheistic God, Jehovah, Who called him out of idolatry. It was perhaps Abraham's lowest moment when he denied his God and yet God graciously gave Abraham one more opportunity to prove his love for Him in Genesis 22 when, on Mount Moriah, Abraham passed the test of faithfulness to God.

When Aaron told the children of Israel at the golden calf incident: "These be thy gods, O Israel, which brought thee up out of the land of Egypt," the verb "brought up" is plural showing that *elohim* on this occasion means "gods" (false).

Exodus 32:4

"And he received *them* at their hand, and fashioned it with a graving tool, after he had made it a molten calf: and they said, These *be* thy gods (*elohim*), O Israel, which brought (verb is plural) thee up out of the land of Egypt."

2.3 Elohim as judges

In Exodus 22:9, the judges of Israel are called *elohim* but the verb is plural to indicate that the word *elohim* does not refer to God.

Exodus 22:9

"For all manner of trespass, *whether it be* for ox, for ass, for sheep, for raiment, *or* for any manner of lost thing, which *another* challengeth to be his, the cause of both parties shall come before the judges (*elohim*); *and* whom the judges (*elohim*) shall condemn (plural verb), he shall pay double unto his neighbour."

2.4 Elohim as angels

If the word means angels, the verb or pronoun is plural indicating that the word does not refer to the God of heaven.

Psalm 97:7

"Confounded be all they that serve graven images, that boast themselves of idols: worship him, all *ye* gods (*elohim*, angels)."

We know from Hebrews 1:6 that the word *elohim* in Psalm 97:7 refers to angels.

Hebrews 1:6

"And again, when He bringeth in the First Begotten into the world, He saith, And let all the angels of God worship Him."

3 A prophecy of God standing in the midst of the nation's leaders

Psalm 82:1

> "God (*elohim*) standeth (singular) in the congregation of the Mighty (*El*);
> He judgeth among the gods (*elohim*, judges)."

In this Psalm, God (*elohim*) is reviewing the faithfulness of the elders and leaders of Israel to whom He had subcontracted the responsibility of executing Moses' Law in Israel. The verbs "standeth" and "judgeth" are in the singular form indicating that it is God Who is judging. Whom is He judging? We read that He "judgeth among the gods" (*elohim*). However, when we read the ensuing verses we see that He asks them in plural verbal forms why they, the *elohim*, judge unjustly etc. This indicates to us that the word translated "gods" in verse 1 is better translated "judges", i.e. earthly judges in Israel. They were the leaders of the nation who were tasked with carrying out and enforcing God's Law given to Moses. The verse could be translated thus: "God (*elohim*) standeth (singular) in the congregation of the Mighty (Hebrew *el* meaning God); He judgeth **among** the **judges** (*elohim*)".

The scenario envisaged by the prophet is clearly not the last judgment in a coming day, since God is exhorting the judges to judge righteously in the future. Remarkably, the verse tells us that God (*elohim*) is standing **within** the congregation and judging **among** the judges. The fact that *elohim* is standing and not seated shows that this is not the great white throne judgment (Revelation 20:11) or the judgment of the living nations (Matthew 25:31) at the end of the tribulation, when on both occasions the Lord will be **seated**. Surely, the literal meaning of this verse is a prophecy which only would find its fulfilment on the occasion or occasions when God (i.e. the Lord Jesus incarnate) would stand **within** the congregation of Israel, known as the congregation of God, and remonstrate with them regarding their failure as executors of God's Law. Some expositors have suggested that the verse is referring to the great white throne judgment, but to hold this view they have had to somehow try to dilute the literal meaning of the word "to stand" to suggest that it is not "standing," in contrast to "sitting," but rather the idea of "taking a stand." Unfortunately, this argument is not supported by the many uses of the word in the Old Testament, where the meaning of the verb as "standing" in contrast to "sitting" is repeatedly confirmed. A clear example is Joseph's sheaf which arose and **"stood upright"**.

Genesis 37:7

> "For, behold, we *were* binding sheaves in the field, and, lo, my sheaf arose, and **also stood upright**; and, behold, your sheaves stood round about, and made obeisance to my sheaf."

All who acknowledge the precision of Scripture will readily understand that the phrase, "God standeth in the congregation of the Mighty", cannot refer to the great white throne judgment or the judgment of the living nations where the Lord is seated.

In this context, it is worth noting that the verb "to judge" (*shaphat*), already encountered in Psalm 72:4, carries the idea of expounding God's Word, "when from Zion shall go forth the Law and the Word of the Lord from Jerusalem" (Isaiah 2:3-5). This is exactly what the Lord was doing in the great temple discourses of the New Testament eg John 8 and John 10.

4 The message God incarnate brought to the nation: failure of judgment

Psalm 82:2-5

2 "How long will ye (plural) judge unjustly, and accept the persons of (show partiality to) the wicked (ones)? Selah.
3 Defend (plural) the poor and fatherless: do justice (plural) to the afflicted and needy.
4 Deliver (plural) the poor and needy: rid (plural) *them* out of the hand of the wicked (ones)."

Their problem was one of a long catalogue of failures of discernment. They were accepting (showing partiality to) the wicked (ones) and failing to do justice to (justify or recognise as just) the afflicted and needy. Throughout John's Gospel, the Lord Jesus charged the nation's leaders with such flawed judgment (John 7:24; 8:15). Furthermore, in Matthew, the Lord charged the leaders of His own nation with condemning the guiltless ones, i.e. His disciples.

Matthew 12:7

"But if ye had known what *this* meaneth, I will have mercy, and not sacrifice, ye would not have condemned the guiltless."

4.1 The underlying cause of this failure: inability to recognise God in their midst

Psalm 82:5

"They know not, neither will they understand; they walk on in darkness."

In the New Testament, the underlying reason for failure of the leaders to judge accurately is seen in John 10. On that momentous occasion within the temple and its congregation of devout Jews, the divine Judge, Christ Himself, stood in the midst of the leaders (*elohim*) of the people and remonstrated with them regarding their failure to recognise Who He was. When we read, "they know not, neither will they understand", the question may be asked: "What is it that they **do not know and understand**?" The Psalm does not directly tell us the answer to this question. However, the context of Psalm 82, and its use by the Lord Jesus in John 10, suggests strongly that what they did not **know and understand** in Psalm 82:5 is the statement of fact given earlier in Psalm 82:1, namely **that it was the Lord Himself** Who was standing in their midst.

This lack of understanding would lead them to "walk on in darkness". This would be the judicial blindness which would descend on the nation for its failure to recognise the Messiah (John 9:39-41).

Please read carefully the following verses from John 8 as the Lord **stood** and taught in the temple. It is the occasion when the Lord dramatically raised Himself up to a standing position after writing with His finger on the ground. He charged them that they **didn't know Him**.

John 8:15-20
> 15 "Ye judge after the flesh; I judge no man.
> 16 And yet if I judge, My judgment is true: for I am not alone, but I and the Father that sent Me.
> 17 It is also written in your Law, that the testimony of two men is true.
> 18 I am One that bear witness of Myself, and the Father that sent Me beareth witness of Me.
> 19 Then said they unto Him, Where is Thy Father? Jesus answered, **Ye neither know Me, nor My Father: if ye had known Me, ye should have known My Father also**.
> 20 These words spake Jesus in the treasury, as He taught in the temple: and no man laid hands on Him; for His hour was not yet come."

Notice, firstly, that in John 8:15 He charges them with flawed judgment as He does also in Psalm 82. Then notice how He shows the cause of this flawed judgment: they did not **know Him as God** (John 8:19), exactly as He does in Psalm 82 where He declares, **"they know not"**.

Please note that although the Psalm prophesies the general response of the nation in rejecting the claims of the Lord Jesus to be the Son of God, this prophecy did not doom all members of the Jewish people at that time to fail to recognise Him. John 8:30 tells us that "many" of them "believed on Him". What divine grace!

4.2 God's response to this failure to recognise the Son of God in their midst

Psalm 82: 5
> "All the foundations of the earth are out of course."

(Literally: "all the foundations of the earth will be moved"). The occasion of the moving of the foundations of the earth is identified as the Lord's return to reign in Isaiah 24:18-19.

Isaiah 24:18-19
> 18 "And it shall come to pass, *that* he who fleeth from the noise of the fear shall fall into the pit; and he that cometh up out of the midst of the pit shall be taken in the snare: for the windows from on high are open, and the foundations of the earth do shake.
> 19 The earth is utterly broken down, the earth is clean dissolved, the earth is moved exceedingly."

It is apparent, therefore, that significant elements within the nation who rejected Him will be walking in darkness **until the return** of the Lord Jesus Who will shake the very ground underneath the feet of the unbelieving nation.

However, although the Lord Jesus did not quote Psalm 82:7, the Jews listening to Him would have known it and it would have reminded them of something they had forgotten, namely that they were mortal and subject to the immortal Judge, God Himself.

Psalm 82:6-7

6 "I have said, Ye (plural) *are* gods; and all of you (plural) *are* children of the Most High.
7 But ye shall die like men, and fall (plural) like one of the princes."

God is telling them, "I have said Ye are *elohim* (judges in Israel) … but ye shall die like men and fall…" In other words, these leaders in Israel who considered themselves to be the judges would themselves die and face the judgment of God Himself. The Psalm is carrying a warning that these earthly judges were about to be relieved of their legal duties, and God would take over the job of enforcing His Law Himself in the coming Kingdom of Christ.

Psalm 82:8

"Arise (singular), O God (*elohim*), judge (singular) the earth: for Thou (singular) shalt inherit (singular) all nations."

This time the verb "to arise" is singular indicating that it is God Himself (*elohim*) Who will arise and judge. Is this a reference to His arising in resurrection or to His arising from His seated position upon the throne in heaven to come to judge? From the context, it is the latter idea which is in view in this Psalm. However, we know that the One Who arises from the throne to scatter His enemies (Psalm 68:1) has already risen from amongst the dead (please see chapter on Psalm 110). How will these events unfold? The next statement tells us. The judgment is carried out by the One Who is the Heir of all nations – God. This has already been considered in Psalm 2 where the inspired writer shows that it is God's Son Who is the Heir, Who takes to Himself His rightful inheritance on the occasion of His return to reign. This brings us back to John 10 and the tense confrontation between those who were actively rejecting the Lord Jesus as the Son of God to be their Lord and Saviour. The Lord's quotation from Psalm 82, reminding them that He is ultimately the divine Heir to the universe, was yet another scriptural proof of His Sonship to a sophisticated audience who understood the link between Sonship and being the Heir. The Lord Jesus had, in effect, shown them that because He is the Son and Heir He will be their final Judge if they reject Him.

A common misunderstanding of John 10:35-6 should be addressed.

John 10:35-6
> 35 "If He called them gods, unto whom the Word of God came, and the
> Scripture cannot be broken;
> 36 Say ye of Him, Whom the Father hath sanctified, and sent into the world,
> Thou blasphemest; because I said, I am the Son of God?"

Some think that the Lord was merely saying that if the judges were
called *elohim*, which sometimes means "gods", why should the temple
worshippers that day have got upset when the Lord Jesus claimed to be the
Son of God, i.e. *elohim* Himself? That is not the meaning of the verse. The
Lord was indicating by the phrase, "the Scripture (not Scriptures (plural))
cannot be broken", that the occasion of John 10 was, in fact, a fulfilment of
a specific single scriptural prophecy which could not be broken. Since the
Lord quotes from Psalm 82, He Himself indicates that this is the Scripture
(singular not plural) He had specifically in mind. Moreover, that Scripture
was familiar to His audience that day, and by reminding them that they
were all of them individuals "unto whom the Word of God came", the Lord
Jesus was challenging them with their added responsibility arising from
their special privilege of having the original Hebrew Scriptures in their
hands and being so very familiar with them. This shows the magnitude
of their sin of unbelief in not recognising the Lord Jesus for Who He was,
despite such clear Biblical knowledge. Had they by faith accepted the truth
of Psalm 82, they would not have accused the Lord Jesus of blasphemy for
claiming to be God in their midst. Rather, they would have understood
that the very confrontation between themselves, as the judges of Israel, and
God Incarnate was prophesied in their own Scriptures and that, solemnly,
the outcome of their unbelief was also prophesied, namely walking on in
darkness and facing eternal judgment. An understanding of the Psalm
would have shown them that they were the *elohim* (judges) who would
meet God incarnate (*elohim*) standing in their midst (sent into the world in
fulfilment of Psalm 82:1) to challenge them with their unbelief.

How solemn a way to end a gospel message! In John 10:1-18, He had
given to all gospel preachers a model gospel message of how to preach to
an antagonistic audience. He shows how to begin the message and how
to conclude it. He lovingly presents the need for salvation and how it is
obtained through Him by His death and resurrection. He reasons with His
audience again and again from Holy Scripture as to why He is worthy of
their faith because His resurrection is proof of His power to save. Down
through the centuries, many enemies of the Lord Jesus have been captivated
and convinced by such words of divine love! Then He presents the fact
based on Holy Scripture that He will "arise" and "judge the earth". The
Lord Jesus did not need to raise His voice in threatening tones to warn His
audience. He quotes the Scriptures from Psalm 82 to convict His religious
and self-righteous audience of the sin of rejecting the risen One Who will
one day become their Judge (Acts 17:31). What divine dignity He showed

that day as He unfolded these solemn realities in Jerusalem!

Acts 17:31
> "Because He hath appointed a day, in the which He will judge the world in righteousness by *that* Man Whom He hath ordained; *whereof* He hath given assurance unto all *men*, in that He hath raised Him from the dead."

Psalm 82 is clearly a Messianic Psalm. Its use by the Lord Jesus in John 10 demonstrates a clear lesson on how to preach a balanced Gospel. The loving description by the Lord in John 10 of the divine provision of salvation for the lost sheep through His death and resurrection is balanced by the Lord's earnest warning of future divine judgment at His own hands for all those who do not accept Him. Everything is meticulously backed up by Holy Scripture. This is the example of how to preach a Christ-exalting gospel which rightly represents the God of heaven.

1. The word "Trinity" does not occur in the Holy Scriptures. However, the truth of this word is found in the Old and New Testaments. When the word refers to the Godhead (the Father, the Son and the Holy Spirit), it is often referred to as the "Holy Trinity". This is accurate language and is used in *Meditations in the Messianic Psalms*. The phrase, "Holy Trinity", stands in contrast to the "Trinity of Evil" discussed in Appendix 2, which is a Satanic counterfeit to the Holy Trinity and it is made up of the dragon, the beast and the false prophet.

14

PSALM 89

Maschil of Ethan the Ezrahite.
1 I Will sing of the mercies of the Lord for ever: with my mouth will I make known Thy faithfulness to all generations.
2 For I have said, Mercy shall be built up for ever: Thy faithfulness shalt Thou establish in the very heavens.
3 I have made a covenant with My chosen, I have sworn unto David My servant,
4 Thy Seed will I establish for ever, and build up thy throne to all generations. Selah.
5 And the heavens shall praise Thy wonders, O Lord: Thy faithfulness also in the congregation of the saints.
6 For who in the heaven can be compared unto the Lord? who among the sons of the mighty can be likened unto the Lord?
7 God is greatly to be feared in the assembly of the saints, and to be had in reverence of all them that are about Him.
8 O Lord God of hosts, who is a strong Lord like unto Thee? or to Thy faithfulness round about Thee?
9 Thou rulest the raging of the sea: when the waves thereof arise, Thou stillest them.
10 Thou hast broken Rahab in pieces, as One that is slain; Thou hast scattered Thine enemies with Thy strong arm.
11 The heavens are Thine, the earth also is Thine: as for the world and the fullness thereof, Thou hast founded them.
12 The north and the south Thou hast created them: Tabor and Hermon shall rejoice in Thy Name.
13 Thou hast a mighty arm: strong is Thy hand, and high is Thy right hand.
14 Justice and judgment are the habitation of Thy throne: mercy and truth shall go before Thy face.
15 Blessed is the people that know the joyful sound: they shall walk, O Lord, in the light of Thy countenance.
16 In Thy Name shall they rejoice all the day: and in Thy righteousness shall they be exalted.
17 For Thou art the glory of their strength: and in Thy favour our horn shall be

exalted.

18 *For the Lord is our defence; and the Holy One of Israel is our King.*

19 *Then Thou spakest in vision to Thy holy one, and saidst, I have laid help upon one that is mighty; I have exalted one chosen out of the people.*

20 *I have found David My servant; with My holy oil have I anointed him:*

21 *With whom My hand shall be established: Mine arm also shall strengthen him.*

22 *The enemy shall not exact upon him; nor the son of wickedness afflict him.*

23 *And I will beat down his foes before his face, and plague them that hate him.*

24 *But My faithfulness and My mercy shall be with him: and in My Name shall his horn be exalted.*

25 *I will set his hand also in the sea, and his right hand in the rivers.*

26 *He shall cry unto Me, Thou art my Father, my God, and the Rock of my salvation.*

27 *Also I will make him My firstborn, higher than the kings of the earth.*

28 *My mercy will I keep for him for evermore, and My covenant shall stand fast with him.*

29 *His Seed also will I make to endure for ever, and his throne as the days of heaven.*

30 *If his children forsake My Law, and walk not in My judgments;*

31 *If they break My statutes, and keep not My commandments;*

32 *Then will I visit their transgression with the rod, and their iniquity with stripes.*

33 *Nevertheless My lovingkindness will I not utterly take from him, nor suffer My faithfulness to fail.*

34 *My covenant will I not break, nor alter the thing that is gone out of My lips.*

35 *Once have I sworn by My holiness that I will not lie unto David.*

36 *His Seed shall endure for ever, and his throne as the sun before Me.*

37 *It shall be established for ever as the moon, and as a faithful witness in heaven. Selah.*

38 *But Thou hast cast off and abhorred, Thou hast been wroth with Thine anointed.*

39 *Thou hast made void the covenant of Thy servant: Thou hast profaned his crown by casting it to the ground.*

40 *Thou hast broken down all his hedges; Thou hast brought his strong holds to ruin.*

41 *All that pass by the way spoil him: he is a reproach to his neighbours.*

42 *Thou hast set up the right hand of his adversaries; Thou hast made all his enemies to rejoice.*

43 *Thou hast also turned the edge of his sword, and hast not made him to stand in the battle.*

44 *Thou hast made his glory to cease, and cast his throne down to the ground.*

45 *The days of his youth hast Thou shortened: Thou hast covered him with shame. Selah.*

46 *How long, Lord? wilt Thou hide Thyself for ever? shall Thy wrath burn like fire?*

47 *Remember how short my time is: wherefore hast Thou made all men in vain?*

48 What man is he that liveth, and shall not see death? shall he deliver his soul from the hand of the grave? Selah.

49 Lord, where are Thy former lovingkindnesses, which Thou swarest unto David in Thy truth?

50 Remember, Lord, the reproach of Thy servants; how I do bear in my bosom the reproach of all the mighty people;

51 Wherewith Thine enemies have reproached, O Lord; wherewith they have reproached the footsteps of Thine anointed.

52 Blessed be the Lord for evermore. Amen, and Amen.

Introduction

In this Psalm, Ethan the Ezrahite[Note 1], under the inspiration of the Spirit of God, provides a commentary on the revelation of the Davidic covenant to David through Nathan in 2 Samuel 7:1-17 and describes how the seed and throne of David will be established forever.

At this point it is worth summarising key aspects of the Davidic covenant as revealed in this and other Old Testament passages.

1 David was promised that after his death kings would arise who would reign from Jerusalem sitting "upon the throne of David".

2 He was told that they would not be perfect and if and when they failed God would punish them. These kings who failed, subsequent to David, were known as the children of David, namely "his children" or "thy children".

Psalm 89:30-32

30 "If **his children** forsake My Law, and walk not in My judgments;

31 If they break My statutes, and keep not My commandments;

32 Then will I visit their transgression with the rod, and their iniquity with stripes."

Psalm 132:12

"If **thy children** will keep My covenant and My testimony that I shall teach them, their children shall also sit upon thy throne for evermore."

3 The ultimate punishment meted out upon these kings of the Davidic line was to cast "to the ground" the crown and throne of David, i.e. to carry off into captivity the royal line of David (Psalm 89:39;44).

Psalm 89:38-44

38 "But Thou hast cast off and abhorred, Thou hast been wroth with Thine anointed.

39 Thou hast made void the covenant of Thy servant: **Thou hast profaned his crown** *by casting it* **to the ground.**

40 Thou hast broken down all his hedges; Thou hast brought his strong holds to ruin.

41 All that pass by the way spoil him: he is a reproach to his neighbours.

42 Thou hast set up the right hand of his adversaries; Thou hast made all his enemies to rejoice.

43 Thou hast also turned the edge of his sword, and hast not made him to stand in the battle.

44 Thou hast made his glory to cease, **and cast his throne down to the ground.**"

4 In contrast to David himself and to the children of David, who all had intrinsic failure, there would arise One called "his Seed", i.e. the Seed of David Who would reign and sit upon a restored throne of David forever.

Psalm 89:29;36
> 29 "**His Seed** also will I make *to endure* for ever, and his throne as the days of heaven...
> 36 **His Seed** shall endure for ever, and his throne as the sun before Me (Hebrew literally: in My presence)."

We should be careful to distinguish this divine One, referred to as David's Seed, from Solomon, spoken of as "thy seed **after thee**".

2 Samuel 7:12-14
> 12 "And when thy days be fulfilled, and thou shalt sleep with thy fathers, I will set up **thy seed after thee**, which shall proceed out of thy bowels, and I will establish his kingdom.
> 13 He shall build an house for My Name, and I will stablish the throne of his kingdom for ever
> 14 I will be his Father, and he shall be My son. If (Hebrew literally: when) he commit iniquity, I will chasten him with the rod of men, and with the stripes of the children of men."

Solomon is described as, "thy seed after thee", which lets us know that he arose **immediately after** David to sit on David's throne. This is in contrast to the One referred to as the Seed of David Who would arise at the end of a long line of the children of David who failed so tragically. Another point which helps justify this distinction is the observation in 2 Samuel 7:14 that the one spoken of as "thy seed after thee", namely Solomon, would inevitably fail ("if (when) he commit iniquity I will chasten him" etc) (see comments on this verse in Psalm 2:7). Solomon spectacularly fulfilled this sad prophecy. However, Solomon is surpassed by the ultimate Seed of David, Christ, Who never failed because He is God.

5 This One, Who is called David's "Seed", would be truly Man, because He would arise from the body of David!

Psalm 132:11
> "The Lord hath sworn *in* truth unto David; He will not turn from it; Of **the fruit of thy body** will I set upon thy throne."

6 However, He is also truly God and bears the Title Jehovah *Tsidkenu* (Jehovah our Righteousness).

Jeremiah 23:5-6
> 5 "Behold, the days come, saith the Lord, that I will raise unto David a righteous Branch, and a King shall reign and prosper, and shall execute judgment and justice in the earth.
> 6 In His days Judah shall be saved, and Israel shall dwell safely: and this *is* His Name whereby He shall be called, **THE LORD OUR RIGHTEOUSNESS**."

The One referred to as David's Seed ("his Seed") in Psalm 89 is God manifest in flesh. This is further emphasised to us in the prophecy describing the ultimate location of His throne. It is in the immediate presence of God.

Psalm 89:36
"His (David's) Seed shall endure for ever, and his (David's) throne as the sun before Me (*negdi* literally: in My presence)". This word *negdi* is the same as the Hebrew word *le-negdi* (before Me) in Psalm 16:8.

Psalm 16:8
"I have set the Lord always (Hebrew literally: as an equal) before Me (*negdi*): because *He is* at My right hand, I shall not be moved."

The significance of the Seed of David being seated upon a throne in the presence of the Lord is made even more apparent in Psalm 89:37 when, as regards the throne of David, we read that ultimately "it shall be established for ever as the moon, and *as* a faithful witness in heaven. Selah".

The expression, "in heaven", means literally, "in the cloud" (singular). The scene is in heaven but the language chosen is highly instructive. The Lord Jesus shall be seated on the throne of David within the *Shechinah* cloud. This privilege can only be for One Who is divine. In Isaiah 14:14, Lucifer had an ambition to ascend above the cloud (singular) and be like the Most High.

Isaiah 14:13-14
13 "For thou hast said in thine heart, I will ascend into heaven, I will exalt my throne above the stars of God: I will sit also upon the mount of the congregation, in the sides of the north:
14 I will ascend above the heights of the clouds (Hebrew: *av* cloud (singular)); I will be like the most High."

Lucifer did not succeed, of course. How wonderful when the Seed of David, namely the Lord Jesus, shall reign supreme as God manifest in flesh within the *Shechinah* cloud itself in the heavens!

The major message of this Psalm is that, although the Davidic throne would be "cast down **to the ground**" and would remain unoccupied for many years, there would be a time when God would re-establish the throne of David.

Psalm 89:44
"Thou hast made his glory to cease, and cast his throne down to the ground."

However, this time God would put His throne out of harm's way completely. It would be re-established **in heaven**.

Psalm 89:36-37
36 "His Seed shall endure for ever, and his throne as the sun before Me (Hebrew: in My presence).

37 It shall be established for ever as the moon, and *as* a faithful witness **in heaven.** Selah."

Now this aspect of truth was quite new. Old Testament believers must surely have wondered how the future throne of David would be located in heaven. This heavenly aspect of government of the future earthly Kingdom, whereby the Son of David from His throne in heaven would govern this world, was very difficult for the Old Testament saints to grasp. This is because the heavenly dimension to the administration of the future earthly Kingdom was not fully revealed in the Old Testament. However, with the illumination of New Testament teaching it all becomes so clear. The **deity** of the Seed of David (Christ) is again confirmed to us by Gabriel in his message to Mary.

Luke 1:32-33
32 "He shall be great, and shall be called the **Son of the Highest**: and the Lord God shall give unto Him the throne of His father David:
33 And He shall reign over the house of Jacob for ever; and of His Kingdom there shall be no end."

However, the **destiny** of the One Who bears the title of "Seed of David" is given in 2 Timothy 2:8-12. It is that we in this Church era should reign with Him.

2 Timothy 2:8-12
8 "Remember that Jesus Christ of **the seed of David** was raised from the dead according to my gospel:
9 Wherein I suffer trouble, as an evil doer, *even* unto bonds; but the Word of God is not bound.
10 Therefore I endure all things for the elect's sakes, that they may also obtain the salvation which is in Christ Jesus with eternal glory.
11 *It is* a faithful saying: For if we be dead with *Him,* we shall also live with *Him:*
12 If we suffer, **we shall also reign with *Him:*** if we deny *Him,* He also will deny us:"

Now this aspect of Biblical truth regarding the Church, the Bride of Christ, reigning with the Lord Jesus in coming Kingdom glory was not clearly revealed in the Old Testament. It is alluded to, as we have seen in Psalms 18, 19 and 45 but not clearly expounded. In retrospect, with New Testament revelation we have now revealed to us the divine key to understanding these passages. However, to Old Testament saints this truth was hidden by an all-wise God. This concept has already been considered in the study of the "babes and sucklings" of Psalm 8. Peter tells us that Old Testament writers were aware that God had secrets He did not fully reveal to them regarding believers who would later be on this scene.

1 Peter 1:10-12
10 "Of which salvation the prophets have inquired and searched diligently,

who prophesied of the grace *that should come* unto you:

11 Searching what, or what manner of time the Spirit of Christ Which was in them did signify, when It testified beforehand the sufferings of Christ, and the glory that should follow.

12 Unto whom it was revealed, **that not unto themselves, but unto us** they did minister the things, which are **now reported unto you** by them that have preached the gospel unto you with the Holy Ghost sent down from heaven; which things the angels desire to look into."

No doubt, one of the difficulties these Old Testament believers and angels "desired to look into" was how and why it should be that the promised Seed of David should reign from heaven. We now know why it is. We, the heavenly people, shall be with Him, the heavenly One, reigning with Him from the heavenly city over the millennial earth. This aspect of truth is revealed in the mystery doctrines of the New Testament having been kept secret in God's heart throughout the Old Testament period. At this point, we shall mention the big surprise in this Psalm which just fills every true believer with wonder at the inspiration of Scripture and the harmony of divine revelation throughout Old and New Testaments: **there is a direct reference to mystery doctrine (albeit not explained) in the Psalm**. Now read on!

The divisions of the Psalm

The Psalm is easily divided into 3 parts.

All three parts consider different aspects of how the **mercies** and **faithfulness** of God are demonstrated by the manner in which God will eventually establish **the Seed** and **throne of David** forever. This is despite the unfaithfullness of the Davidic line of kings, culminating in the cessation of David's throne on earth which caused the Psalmist to raise his lament heavenwards to God Who had "cast his (David's) throne down to the ground!"

PART 1 (verses 1-18)

Ethan discusses the **lovingkindness of God** and **His faithfulness** in bringing to fulfilment the Davidic covenant. This section emphasises how this great achievement of God will bring to Him worship, wonder and reverential awe.

PART 2 (verses 19-37)

Ethan reports *verbatim* to us an historic conversation which God had with at least two of His servants, possibly including David and while the latter was yet alive, in which God personally guaranteed a promise to David regarding **His lovingkindness** and **faithfulness** in fulfilling the Davidic covenant in its entirety.

PART 3 (verses 38-52)

Ethan once again discusses **the lovingkindness** and **faithfulness** of God despite the failure of the nation and the monarchy who are described as

"David's children".

PART 1(verses 1-18)

1 The principles underlying the Davidic covenant: God's lovingkindness and faithfulness

Psalm 89:1-4

"I will sing of the **mercies** of the Lord for ever: with my mouth will I make known **Thy faithfulness** to all generations.

2 For I have said, Mercy shall be built up for ever: **Thy faithfulness** shalt Thou establish in the very heavens.

3 I have made a covenant with My chosen, I have sworn unto David My servant,

4 Thy Seed will I establish for ever, and build up thy throne to all generations. Selah."

This section begins with an emphasis on the **duration** of God's mercies and faithfulness. It is unending. It lasts unto eternity – "forever" and "to all generations" (from generation to generation). This is found to be all the more wonderful when in the Psalm we read of the rebellion of men against the mercies and faithfulness of God, and of the opposition of Satan and his hosts against the Lord's plan to fulfill the Davidic covenant. These apparent obstacles will not prevent future fulfilment of God's promise to David. His promise is confirmed by an oath (verse 3). It cannot be rescinded. In this the peerless glory of God is displayed, evoking worship from the saints eternally.

Of particular importance to the understanding of the Psalm is that the place where God's faithfulness is going to be established is "in the very heavens" (Psalm 89:2).

Psalm 89:2

"For I have said, Mercy shall be built up for ever: Thy faithfulness shalt Thou establish in the very heavens (Hebrew: *shamayim* – stellar and atmospheric)."

This might seem at first a puzzling statement, since one might have expected earth to be the preferred location for establishing the faithfulness of God in relation to restoring the throne of David. Moreover, the re-establishment of the throne of David is an event which will lead the Lord Jesus, as Jehovah *Tsidkenu*, to "execute judgment **on the earth**" (Jeremiah 23:5). However, the next few verses will show how a display of God's faithfulness **in the heavens** is inextricably linked to establishing obedience to David's throne **on the earth**. In fact, the verses show that before God's faithfulness in establishing obedience to David's throne **on earth** can be displayed, it is necessary that God's faithfulness **in the heavens** be confirmed first of all. Moreover, it becomes apparent later in the Psalm that the display of God's faithfulness in the heavens will take place when the throne of David will be "a faithful witness **in the heavens**" (Psalm 89:37). In other words, David's throne, which today has been cast to the ground (Psalm 89:44), will in that day be a "faithful witness in the heavens" (Psalm 89:37). When that happens, God's faithfulness will be established "in the very heavens". The very fact that God's faithfulness needs to be established in the heavens suggests to us that, at the present time, the heavens are not a place where the faithfulness of God is displayed. In fact, the opposite is the case. It is the sphere of the "prince of the power of the air" (Ephesians 2:2).

1.1 The establishing of God's faithfulness in the heavens

Psalm 89:5

> 5 "And the heavens (*shamayim*) shall praise Thy wonders, O Lord: Thy faithfulness also in the congregation of the saints.
> 6 For (*ki:* because) who in the heaven (Hebrew: *haShshachak:* the cloud) can be compared (Hebrew root: *arach*) unto (Hebrew preposition: *le*) the Lord? *who* among the sons of the mighty can be likened unto the Lord?"

What a day it will be when the created heavens (*shamayim*), where the prince of the power of the air and his lying hosts have access today, shall once more be a public stage for displaying divine faithfulness and truth (verse 5). Verse 6 begins with the word "for", which literally means "because", thus alerting us to be aware that the phrases immediately following actually constitute the grand reason for this great celestial outpouring of praise to God for His wonders and faithfulness. Therefore, a detailed study of the literal meaning of the question: "Who in the cloud can be compared (Hebrew root: *arach*) unto (Hebrew: *le*) the Lord?", is most useful. It emerges that the word *arach* followed by the proposition *le* means: "to set in array (*arach*) against (*le*)". A clear example of this appears in Jeremiah 50:9:

Jeremiah 50:9

> "For, lo, I will raise and cause to come up against Babylon an assembly of great nations from the north country: **and they shall set themselves in array** (Hebrew root: *arach*) **against** (*le*) **her;** from thence she shall be taken: their arrows *shall be* as of a mighty expert man; none shall return in vain."

It can now be understood how a literal rendering of the first part of Psalm 89:6 reads as follows:

"Who in the cloud will set himself in (hostile) array against the Lord?"

This literal translation of the verse shows why the created heavens in that day will resound in praise to God. It is because the long era of any created being, especially Satan, daring to compare himself with or arrange himself in hostile array against the One dwelling in **"the cloud",** has ended. Satan will have been excluded from the created heavens at last. We are reminded of an event in the distant past when such a hostile satanic comparison was made against the God of heaven in Isaiah 14.

Isaiah 14:13-14
> 13 "For thou hast said in thine heart, I will ascend into heaven, I will exalt my throne above the stars of God: I will sit also upon the mount of the congregation, in the sides of the north:
> 14 I will **ascend above the heights of the clouds (cloud singular)**; I will be like the Most High."

Satan himself will yet again attempt this anti-God insurgency in the created heavens before being cast down to the earth during the coming tribulation (Revelation 12:7-8).

Revelation 12:7-8
> 7 "And there was war in heaven: Michael and his angels fought against the dragon; and the dragon fought and his angels,
> 8 And prevailed not; neither was their place found any more in heaven.
> 9 And the great dragon was cast out, that old serpent, called the devil, and Satan, which deceiveth the whole world: he was cast out into the earth, and his angels were cast out with him."

Psalm 89 is showing us that this future event, when Satan and his hosts will be excluded from the created heavens, will trigger an outpouring of praise from the hosts of heaven in God's dwelling place. This is also confirmed in the following verses in Revelation:

Revelation 12:10-12
> 10 "And I heard a loud voice saying in heaven, Now is come salvation, and strength, and the Kingdom of our God, and the power of His Christ: for the accuser of our brethren is cast down, which accused them before our God day and night.
> 11 And they overcame him by the blood of the Lamb, and by the word of their testimony; and they loved not their lives unto the death.
> 12 **Therefore rejoice, ye heavens, and ye that dwell in them**. Woe to the inhabiters of the earth and of the sea! for the devil is come down unto you, having great wrath, because he knoweth that he hath but a short time."

Shortly after this event comes the millennium, when Satan's long-time dominion within the created atmospheric and stellar heavens will be denied him. Moreover, earth will be denied him too, as for 1000 years he and his infernal hosts are confined to the bottomless pit. Throughout this long period of time there will be none to challenge the throne of David in the heavens (the cloud).

It should be pointed out at this juncture that later in the Psalm we encounter "**the cloud**" again.

Psalm 89:36-37
> 36 "His (David's) Seed shall endure for ever, and his (David's) throne as the sun before Me.
> 37 It (David's throne) shall be established for ever as the moon, and *as* a faithful witness in heaven (**the cloud**). Selah."

In verse 6 we learn that the Lord is "in the cloud" and in verse 36 we see that He is seated on David's throne. Taking together these two verses, it becomes clear that it is David's Seed, i.e. the Person of the Lord Jesus, Who is the One seated on David's throne **in the cloud**. Some may wonder if this reference to "the cloud" suggests that during the millennium the Lord Jesus shall be above the heavens, i.e. in the third heaven, known also as the heaven of heavens, the heavenly tabernacle not of this creation. Psalm 89 does not clarify this issue. It merely affirms that He will be **in the *Shechinah* cloud**. The metaphor comparing this restored throne of David to "the sun" and to "the moon" strongly suggests that this throne in that day will be in the created heavens. However, it is good to find other Scriptures to clarify this. Clarity comes when we reconsider Psalm 19 where the appearance of the sun in the sky is compared to the rejoicing Bridegroom orbiting the earth in His heavenly tabernacle. Comparing Scripture with Scripture it becomes apparent that David's restored throne, enveloped in the *Shechinah* cloud, is occupied by the divine Seed of David, the Person of Christ in the heavens He Himself created.

How would first-century A.D. Christians have understood this? They would have understood New Testament teaching regarding the final conclusion of satanic activity in the air when the created heavens, which are today his sphere of activity as prince of the power of the air (Ephesians 2:2) and the present domain of the "spiritual wickedness in high places" (Ephesians 6:12), will at last be liberated from this evil dominion when Satan and his hosts will be bound in the bottomless pit for the 1000 years of the millennium (Revelation 20:2). When the Lord Jesus, in the company of His Bride, is reigning from the heavenly city in the created heavens the question could be asked: "Who in the heaven (cloud) can be compared unto (set himself in array against) the Lord?" A triumphant answer: "No one!" is the only response. The next question, "*Who* among the sons of the mighty can be likened unto the Lord?" similarly begs the answer: "No one!" God Jehovah is peerless and cannot be simulated. The first beast of Revelation 13, under satanic empowerment, shall simulate immortality and thus try to present himself as an anti-God figure (Appendix 2). Of course, in this he will be confounded and destroyed on the occasion of the return of the Lord Jesus Christ. The order is as follows: if the one who in the created heavens (Satan) sets himself in array against the God of heaven and fails, similarly his emissary on earth (the first beast of Revelation 13), who claims to be a God-like figure, will also face certain defeat. Only when the enemies of God have been defeated will God's final programme of glory be revealed and at its centre is God's great masterpiece hidden in His heart from before times eternal.

The destiny of the Church **in the very heavens** will be to faithfully administer His coming earthly Kingdom. The Church's location in the heavens will be where the prince of the power of the air holds sway today. Small wonder that Satan opposes the Church of God today since he knows very well that it will one day reign in the aerial sphere where he now operates! Only when the Church is revealed in its inheritance in the heavens does the New Testament indicate that there is fulfilment of the promises to Abraham of an earthly inheritance and to David of an everlasting covenant (Hebrews 11). This is consistent with the teaching of this Psalm that only **after the heavens declare the faithfulness of God** will the Davidic covenant come to fruition. This is also consistent with what was considered in Psalms 18 and 19, where it was seen that subsequent to the resurrection from the dead of David and the Old Testament saints (Psalm 18), the Bridegroom King with His Bride in the created heavens will orbit an earth in total obedience to the will of God, which will be declared from those created heavens (Psalm 19).

Of course, this perspective is not apparent to the Old Testament reader without New Testament revelation. This is because this is mystery doctrine, i.e. hidden in the Old Testament and not revealed until the descent of the Spirit of God in the New Testament. However, with New Testament revelation, a renewed study of Psalms 18 and 19 leads to understanding where the Church fits into the programme of God and how her identity was veiled in those Old Testament passages. Moreover, New Testament revelation further elaborates how the faithfulness of God, awaiting heavenly display in Psalm 89, will come to pass. It will find fulfilment when the Church, the Bride of Christ in the heavens, will hold sway in the place where once the prince of the power of the air held dominion. It should therefore be a matter of breathtaking wonder to us that in the next verse there is an allusion made (lacking any explanation of course) to mystery doctrine in relation to the gathering together of the people of God.

1.2 The mystery of the saints

Psalm 89:7

"God is greatly to be feared in the assembly **(Hebrew: *sod* mystery)** of the saints, and to be had in reverence of all *them that are* about Him."

Please note that the word "assembly" could be translated "secret" or "mystery". In fact, it is this word *sod* which is used in the modern Hebrew New Testament for "mystery".

Here are some uses of the word *sod* to illustrate this principle:

Genesis 49:6 Come not thou into their secret (*sod*)

Job 15:9 Hast thou heard the secret (*sod*) of God

19:19 All the men of my secret (*sod*) (Wigram) abhorred me

29:4 When the secret (*sod*) of God was upon my tabernacle

Psalm 25:14 The secret (sod) of the Lord is with them

55:14 We took sweet counsel (*sod)* together

64:2 Hide me from the secret counsel (*sod*) of

83:3 taken crafty counsel (*sod*) against Thy people

89:7 to be feared in the assembly (*sod*) of the saints

111.1 in the assembly (*sod*) of the upright

Proverbs 3:32 His secret (*sod*) is with the righteous
11:13 A talebearer revealeth secrets (*sod*)
15:22 Without counsel (*sod*) purposes are disappointed
20:19 A talebearer revealeth secrets (*sod*)
25:9 Discover not a secret (*sod*) of another (Wigram)
Jeremiah 6:11 upon the assembly (*sod*) of young men together
15:17 I sat not in the assembly (*sod*) of the mockers
23:18 who stood in the counsel (*sod*) of the Lord
23:22 If they had stood in My counsel (*sod*)
Ezekiel 13:9 They shall not be in the assembly (*sod*) of My...
Amos 3:7 He revealeth His secret (*sod*) unto His servants

A study of the use of the word *sod* shows that its primary meaning is "secret", and as a secondary meaning there is "secret counsel" which has come to mean an "assembly", possibly where the circumstances are secret.

In the references to the *sod* (secret) of God as revealed to His servants in the Old Testament, nowhere is the **content** of the secret given. Only **the context** is revealed, and in each of these passages the **context** is consistent with the **content** of the mysteries as revealed in the New Testament (note similarity to the New Song in Psalm 40). For example, in Psalm 89 the context shows that in the eventual revealing of the "secret" or "mystery" God is greatly to be feared. However, revelation of the content of the "secret" or "mystery" must await the New Testament.

1.3 How a first century Christian would understand Psalm 89:7

Today's reader should imagine a first century A.D. Christian reading Psalm 89:7 in his Hebrew Bible, still rejoicing in the freshly revealed mystery doctrines of the New Testament and how they have brought into perspective the overall divine programme hidden in the Old Testament.

Perhaps the first lesson they grasped was that, although mystery doctrines (*sod*) were alluded to in the Old Testament, only their context was discussed there. The content of the mysteries had to await New Testament revelation.

Ephesians 3:3-7
> 3 "How that by revelation He made known unto me **the mystery**; (as I wrote afore in few words,
> 4 Whereby, when ye read, ye may understand my knowledge in the mystery of Christ)
> 5 **Which in other ages was not made known unto the sons of men, as it is now revealed unto His holy apostles and prophets by the Spirit;**
> 6 That the Gentiles should be fellowheirs, and of the same body, and partakers of His promise in Christ by the gospel:
> 7 Whereof I was made a minister, according to the gift of the grace of God given unto me by the effectual working of His power."

What a day that will be when the congregation of the saints will be fully seen! There will be the heavenly people in the Church and the earthly people

(Israel) on the earth all in harmony and involved in the administration and service of His Kingdom. In that day, **Christ will be the Head of the Church in the heavens, and Israel the head of the nations on the earth, as quoted below.**

Ephesians 1:9-10
> 9 "Having made known unto us **the mystery of His will**, according to His good pleasure which He hath purposed in Himself:
> 10 **That in the dispensation of the fullness of times He might gather (head up) together in one all things in Christ, both which are in heaven, and which are on earth;** *even* **in Him:**"

Psalm 89 does not specifically tell us what is meant by the phrase, "the mystery of the saints". No doubt Old Testament readers would have been greatly exercised as to what was the secret God had in His heart. Could they have wondered why it was that the restored throne of David and its divine Throne-sitter would be in the heavens? The fact is, He did not reveal it to them in those days. However, the New Testament makes it clear that in future glory, when the Church is in its heavenly inheritance, it will judge the millennial world through the media of the angels.

1 Corinthians 6:2-3
> 2 "Do ye not know that the saints shall judge the world? and if the world shall be judged by you, are ye unworthy to judge the smallest matters?
> 3 Know ye not that we shall judge angels? how much more things that pertain to this life?"

The angels will ascend and descend from heaven to earth communicating the will of Christ through His Church to Israel on earth (John 1:51).

John 1:51
> "And He saith unto him, Verily, verily, I say unto you, Hereafter ye shall see heaven open, and the angels of God ascending and descending upon the Son of man."

In the Old Testament, God uses angels to teach Israel. In contrast, in this era He uses the Church to teach the angels (Ephesians 3:10) general principles regarding His wisdom, with a specific emphasis on the truth of headship (1 Corinthians 11:10). This is because it is the principle of headship which underlies the mechanisms of future government in that day of righteous administration, with Christ the Head of the Church in the heavens and Israel the head of the nations on the earth. This is why angels have such an interest in the truth of headship expressed in the godly order displayed in assembly gatherings of believers today (1 Corinthians 11:10), a matter to be discussed in further detail in Psalm 95.

1.4 How the New Testament harmonises the prophecies of the earthly inheritance for Old Testament believers with the heavenly inheritance of the Church

The fact that the future throne of David is in the heavens may lead some to suggest that all the Old Testament prophecies of a future earthly Kingdom have been commuted to a heavenly or spiritual Kingdom and that there is no future for Israel. Scripture does not support this view as the following considerations will show.

Genesis 22, as expounded in Psalm 24, shows that Abraham looked forward to an earthly Kingdom when his Seed would inherit the **gate of His enemies**.

Genesis 22:17
> "That in blessing I will bless thee, and in multiplying I will multiply thy seed as the stars of the heaven, and as the sand which *is* upon the sea shore; and thy Seed shall possess **the gate of His enemies;**"

Old Testament believers would have been very familiar with the concept of the gate being the place of administration. Thus, when the Seed of Abraham inherits the gate of His enemies this is **the city gate** and place of administration. They may well have wondered where the city was whose gate is referred to in Genesis 22:17. It would have been clear that this could not be the heavenly city since there are enemies there and there are no enemies in the heavenly city. Nothing "that defileth" can enter in there. The gate of Genesis 22 and Psalm 24 must, therefore, be at the earthly city of Jerusalem, in whose gates and places of administration enemies of God have maintained a presence over many millennia. This is why the heads of the gates of this city are hanging in shame today (Psalm 24), but when the King of Glory returns to reign, they will be lifted up in dignity once again (Psalm 24) when, for the first time, the Jerusalem centre of earthly government will be characterised by all the dignity pertaining to the reign of the King of kings and Lord of lords. In that day, Mount Moriah (Teacher of Jehovah) shall be the place from whence shall "go forth the Law and the Word of the Lord from Jerusalem" (Isaiah 2:3).

However, first century Hebrew Christians would have had special insights, which had been withheld from the Old Testament writers, namely that the earthly city could only be enjoyed **after** the revelation of the Church in the heavens. They would have been led to this conviction by the very clear commentary in Hebrews 11:10 regarding the inauguration of the city sought after by Abraham "whose builder and maker is God".

Hebrews 11:10
> "For he looked for a city which hath foundations, whose builder and maker is God."

A careful examination of the context of this verse shows that the city Abraham looked for was, in fact, the millennial earthly city of Jerusalem

whose "gate" his Seed would one day possess in Genesis 22. God will build
it and secure it. However, many will ask: "Is not this the city in 'the heavenly
country' referred to in Hebrews 11:16?"

Hebrews 11:15-16

> 15 "And truly, if they had been mindful of that *country* from whence they
> came out, they might have had opportunity to have returned.
> 16 But now they desire a better *country*, that is, an heavenly: wherefore
> God is not ashamed to be called their God: for He hath prepared for them
> a city."

A superficial reading may suggest (wrongly) that the "better country, that
is an heavenly" is the country where the city, which God "hath prepared for
them", is located. However, any confusion on this issue is dispelled at the
end of the chapter where we read in Hebrews 11:40 that the "better thing"
(i.e. the heavenly inheritance as defined in Hebrews 11:16) is "provided...
for us", i.e. saints of this Church era **in contrast** to the Old Testament saints.

Hebrews 11:39-40

> 39 "And these all, having obtained a good report through faith, received
> not the promise:
> 40 God having provided some **better thing for us**, that they **without us
> (apart from us)** should not be made perfect."

Why then do the Old Testament saints "now" (i.e. now that their spirits
are in heaven awaiting their future resurrection and entry into the earthy
Kingdom) "desire a better country that is an heavenly" (Hebrews 11:16) even
though it is clear in Hebrews 11:40 that it is not provided for them but rather
for us, i.e. the Church, "apart from" them? The reason is that these saints
in their lifetime did not know about the heavenly inheritance or indeed the
Church, the Bride of Christ, and her role in the administration of the future
millennial Kingdom which they looked forward to. They only knew about
the earthly city and the day that her gates would be lifted up in dignity when
the King, the Son of Abraham, would return to reign. However, now that
they are in heaven in their souls and spirits, they understand the mystery
doctrines of the New Testament, which have now been fully revealed. They
now understand that only when the "better thing", namely the heavenly city
(the Church), is revealed in the heavens will the promises, given to them in
their lifetimes regarding the earthly inheritance, be literally fulfilled. This
is why they **now** desire the heavenly city, i.e. the Church, to be revealed in
the heavens so that they can experience fulfilment of the promises of glory
on the millennial earth. Only when "the better thing, that is "the heavenly"
(Hebrews 11:16), is inaugurated for us (the Church) in the heavens will the
city which "He hath prepared for them" (Hebrews 11:16) be inaugurated
on earth.

This is New Testament understanding of the future Kingdom and shows
that the promises to the Old Testament saints of an earthly Kingdom will

be literally fulfilled but that before this can happen the Church must be revealed in the heavens. The revelation of that which is new, i.e. the Church, and its attendant doctrines regarding the heavenly inheritance does not in any way dilute, neutralise or replace the Old Testament promises. It is in this context that the Lord taught the disciples not to mix or amalgamate the old with the new.

Matthew 9:17
> "Neither do men put new wine into old bottles: else the bottles break, and the wine runneth out, and the bottles perish: but they put new wine into new bottles, **and both are preserved**."

When He indicated that both old and new bottles will be "preserved", He was showing His disciples that the promises to the Old Testament saints of an earthly inheritance and future for Israel will be literally fulfilled and will neither be replaced nor annulled by the New Testament revelations of the heavenly. In Christendom, the ideas have been mixed. Sadly, "new wine" has been put "into old bottles" in modern exposition. For any who mistakenly have done this, Old Testament promises have become like "bottles" which "break" and are no longer to be regarded as literal. What a sad mistake to make in exposition, since significant sections of Old Testament Scripture regarding the future Kingdom of our Lord Jesus would become remote, irrelevant and incomprehensible! How sad this is! Happily, however, for those who have grasped the mystery doctrines of the New Testament this would not happen.

A first century Christian, rejoicing in these truths, would have understood at once from Psalm 89 that the faithfulness of God must be asserted in the heavens **before** the covenant with David is fulfilled on earth. It is in a similar context that Paul raises a doxology, in which we could, at this point, with bowed hearts worshipfully join:

Romans 11:33-36
> 33 "O the depth of the riches both of the wisdom and knowledge of God! how unsearchable are His judgments, and His ways past finding out!
> 34 For who hath known the mind of the Lord? or who hath been His counsellor?
> 35 Or who hath first given to Him, and it shall be recompensed unto Him again?
> 36 For of Him, and through Him, and to Him, are all things: to Whom be glory for ever. Amen."

With this missing piece of the jigsaw in place, we now understand clearly how it is that God will be **"feared"** in that Day and will be "held in awe of all them that are about Him" (Psalm 89:7). However, this response of holding God in awe and reverence for His wonderful plan should not await the coming day of glory. It should already be the response of the heart of each believer today. In fact, in Romans 11, as the mystery is taught of how

Israel will be set aside and the Gentiles grafted in, those of us in this Church era are warned to **fear**. It is indeed a healthy state of soul to fear the Lord, i.e. to have a holy dread of grieving Him, and this should be the practical result of any study of God's dealings with Israel, her temporary setting aside and her future blessing and, in the meantime, His present blessings to us in the Church (see Romans 11:20-25).

Romans 11:20-25
> 20 "Well; because of unbelief they were broken off, and thou standest by faith. **Be not highminded, but fear:**
> 21 For if God spared not the natural branches, *take heed* lest He also spare not thee.
> 22 Behold therefore the goodness and severity of God: on them which fell, severity; but toward thee, goodness, if thou continue in *His* goodness: otherwise thou also shalt be cut off.
> 23 And they also, if they abide not still in unbelief, shall be graffed in: for God is able to graff them in again.
> 24 For if thou wert cut out of the olive tree which is wild by nature, and wert graffed contrary to nature into a good olive tree: how much more shall these, which be the natural *branches*, be graffed into their own olive tree?
> 25 **For I would not, brethren, that ye should be ignorant of this mystery**, lest ye should be wise in your own conceits; that blindness in part is happened to Israel, until the fullness of the Gentiles be come in."

1.5 The effect of this heavenly display of divine faithfulness on the millennial earth

Psalm 89:8
"O Lord God of hosts, who *is* a strong Lord like unto Thee? or to **Thy faithfulness** round about Thee?"

In that day, when the mystery of the saints will be fully revealed, the strength of the Lord will be fully displayed along with "**His faithfulness**". An evidence of this will be a demonstration of the very creation obeying Him in the finest details.

Psalm 89:9
"Thou rulest the raging of the sea: when the waves thereof arise, Thou stillest them."

We recall that on His way across the sea of Galilee in the boat to liberate the man of Gadara from the bondage of Satan, there was a terrible storm on the sea with the waves seeking to engulf the boat (Mark 4:36-41). Of course, this was not possible because Christ, the omnipotent One, was in the boat. However, that didn't deter the unseen forces of evil from attempting to sink it. One **rebuke** from the Lord to the waves – "Peace, be still" – effected a great calm (Mark 4:39). What a contrast there will be in a coming day! He will "rule the raging of the sea". This could also be translated, "He will rule in majesty the sea". Either way, it is clear that the sea and its waves will be completely subservient to Him. The next phrase is beautiful: "When the waves thereof arise, thou stillest (**dost praise**) them." The word "stillest" also means "to praise". In that coming day of universal dominion, the Lord shall no longer have cause **to rebuke** the waves. They will rise and fall to His pleasure. When the waves thereof arise He will approvingly "**praise them**". What a day that will be!

How has such a transformation been made possible? The next verse traces the reason for this to the victory over Satan at Calvary. This is the basis of the victory and why the promise to David will finally be fulfilled.

Psalm 89:10

"Thou hast broken Rahab in pieces, as One that is slain (rendered correctly "wounded" in Young's literal translation); Thou hast scattered Thine enemies with Thy strong arm."

Rahab is spelled differently in the original text from Rahab the harlot and should not be confused with her. Commentators vary on the meaning of "Rahab", most correctly identifying it with the ancient nation of Egypt who held the children of Israel in bondage. Others have wondered if it is some kind of mythical sea creature (J. Flanigan). However, clear guidance as to the meaning of this word comes in Isaiah 51:9 where Rahab is also identified with "the dragon" in the Exodus story.

Isaiah 51:9-10

9 "Awake, awake, put on strength, O arm of the Lord; awake, as in the ancient days, in the generations of old. Art Thou not it that hath cut Rahab, and wounded the dragon?
10 Art Thou not it which hath dried the sea, the waters of the great deep; that hath made the depths of the sea a way for the ransomed to pass over?"

If we allow Scripture to interpret Scripture and pursue the use of the title "dragon" in the Old and New Testaments it becomes apparent that this is a title used of Satan in Revelation 12:3 and Psalm 91:13 (see later). This would suggest strongly that Rahab must surely be the god of Egypt and therefore a reference to Satan himself. If that is the case, as the present author believes, then Psalm 89:10 is referring to the defeat of Satan by the Lord Jesus at Calvary.

The word order in the original arrests the attention of the careful reader: "Thou hast broken in pieces, **as One that was wounded**, Rahab…" While most translators assume that the "One that was wounded" is Rahab or Satan, the order of the verse leads to the opposite understanding. It is as One **Who was wounded** that our Lord has broken in pieces Satan Himself. That is the victory of Calvary when the Lord Jesus "was wounded for our transgressions" (Isaiah 53:5). It is as a result of the victory over Rahab, the ruler of darkness, that the Lord is declared the rightful Ruler of the heavens and the earth.

Psalm 89:11

"The heavens are Thine, "the earth also is Thine: as for the world and the fullness thereof, Thou hast founded them."

Verse 11 is a reference to Psalm 24:1-2 already considered. We saw there how it referred to the coming day of glory when the Lord is finally acknowledged as the final and unrivalled "Owner" of this universe.

Psalm 89:12

"The north and the south Thou hast created them: Tabor and Hermon shall rejoice in Thy Name."

The literal translation of this verse is: "The north and the right hand Thou hast created them."

When we consider Rahab as the evil being opposing the Exodus, and the Lord calling His people to Him by means of sacrifice as the only way of approach, we may see a reason why the north is linked with the right hand in this verse. When the Israelite stood facing the entrance to the tabernacle, such was the orientation of the tabernacle, with the door looking towards the east, that the Israelite on his way into the presence of God had to stand with his face to the west and his right hand toward the north. That was the only way which God created for man to enter into His presence.

Later in the Psalm, Ethan describes the sad state of the monarchy when both crown and throne are cast to the ground (verses 39 and 44). The first stage in this was the division of Solomon's kingdom into the kingdom of Judah in the South under Rehoboam and the kingdom of Israel in the North under Jeroboam (1 Kings 12). In general, the northern kingdom persisted in apostasy and unwillingness to recognise and come to the House of God in Jerusalem. As Ethan describes the way which God has created, i.e. entering in God's way by facing west, he envisages a day when Tabor and Hermon in the North, which for so long have been lands of "the shadow of death" (Isaiah 9:2), will rejoice in God's only way of approach into His presence, namely the Sacrifice of the victorious One Who was wounded.

Psalm 89:13-14

13 "Thou hast a mighty arm: strong is Thy hand, *and* high is Thy right hand.
14 Justice and judgment *are* the habitation of Thy throne: mercy and truth shall go before Thy face."

It will be a wonderful day when the strength of the Lord will be displayed as well as His faithfulness to His Word. The elevated right hand is so often taken as the picture of the hand uplifted in solemn oath or pledge.

Ezekiel 20:5-6

5 "And say unto them, Thus saith the Lord God; In the day when I chose Israel, and **lifted up Mine hand** unto the seed of the house of Jacob, and made Myself known unto them in the land of Egypt, **when I lifted up**

Mine hand unto them, saying, I am the Lord your God;
6 In the day that I **lifted up Mine hand unto them**, to bring them forth of
the land of Egypt into a land that I had espied for them, flowing with milk
and honey, which is the glory of all lands:"

God's mighty arm and strong hand are seen in bringing about the
restoration of the throne of David under the Messiah. However, "high is
Thy right hand" reminds us that all of this is consistent with the promises
of God sworn to David in the Davidic covenant. When this is seen, Israel
will be a united land, and the character of the Lord will be universally
expressed on this earth in His justice, judgment, mercy and truth. In fact,
it is the substance of the Gospel message to present the Lord in His justice,
judgment, mercy and truth. For all who recognise the truth of this it could
be said that they **knew or acknowledged** this message as good news. Of
such it can be said:

Psalm 89:15
"Blessed *is* the people that know the joyful sound: they shall walk, O Lord,
in the light of Thy countenance."

The joyful sound is the victory over Rahab (Satan) through the One
Who was wounded, providing the way into God's presence, all of which
illustrates God's justice, judgment, mercy and truth. These truths form
the main ingredients of the gospel message. It is no surprise that this is a
"joyful sound" because those who have believed it are assured of walking
in the light of the Lord's countenance. The joyful sound is not diminished
by insecurity, as those who are blessed thereby acknowledge that their
confidence is exclusively resting on the Lord and not on themselves. He is
their strength and defence.

Psalm 89:16-18
16 "In Thy Name shall they rejoice all the day: and in Thy righteousness
shall they be exalted.
17 For Thou *art* the glory of their strength: and in Thy favour our horn shall
be exalted.
18 For the Lord *is* our defence;"

How secure is this defence? David, while he was upon the throne in
Jerusalem, defended his realm to the best of his ability. In that future day,
when the Son of David reigns, His realm is secure because of Who He is;
He is the Son of David, the King, none other than the Holy One of Israel
Himself.

Psalm 89:18
"...and the Holy One of Israel *is* our King."

This is the fulfilment of the Davidic Covenant. Then the principles
underlying the Davidic covenant will be seen by the wondering universe:

God's lovingkindness and His faithfulness displayed in the victorious Son of David, the Lord Jesus.

PART 2

2 The lovingkindness and faithfulness of the Lord in David's experience both in his lifetime and in subsequent fulfilment of prophecy

The Psalm now gives a detailed account of the *verbatim* promise Jehovah gave to David and possibly contemporaries of his, such as Nathan the prophet, regarding the eternal establishing of the throne of David. Other servants of God may have been involved in receiving the vision in relation to the Davidic covenant, as suggested by the word "holy one" in verse 18 which is in the plural form in the original text. This should not surprise us, as a vision as important as this needed the witness of two or more servants of God to corroborate it. After all, the issue at stake is the faithfulness of God, so the contemporaneous and independent testimony to it by several of God's faithful servants demanded acceptance by all men of faith from that day forwards. Doubtless, for similar reasons the doctrines of the New Testament mysteries were delivered to Paul and then to others of the apostles and prophets in the New Testament (Ephesians 3:5). He recounted to His servants, and especially to David, the details of His covenant with him regarding the coming King, Who would one day emerge from his descendants. Early in this amazing conversation with David, the Lord was careful to warn him that being in the line of the coming King would attract to him personal animosity from any who hated the news of this covenant. Accordingly, the Lord reveals to him that he would need to learn about the Lord's lovingkindness and faithfulness not just in the greater prophetic scheme of things, but in the here and now, in the day-to-day trials of living for God. The practical lesson for Christians today is that we too, as those who are linked with the rejected King, may similarly attract the hostility of the world. However, in the trial we can always draw upon the ever present lovingkindness and tender mercies of the Lord.

2.1 God's promise of mercy and faithfulness to David in his life

Verses 19-24 bring before us God's faithfulness to David in giving him victory over his known enemies. We know that some of these enemies were dealt with by his son Solomon shortly after David's death. However, their judgment, even under Solomon, was in fulfilment of the promise to David that his enemies would be destroyed. Interestingly, this section closes in verse 24 with a statement of God's lovingkindness and mercy to David:

Psalm 89:24

"But My faithfulness and My mercy *shall be* with him: and in My Name shall his horn be exalted."

2.2 God describes David

Psalm 89:19-21

19 "Then thou spakest in vision to **thy holy one** (*chasid*, - plural in Hebrew), and saidst, I have laid help upon *one that is* **mighty**; I have exalted *one* **chosen** out of the people.

20 I have found David **My servant**; with My holy oil have I **anointed him**:

21 With whom My hand shall be established: Mine arm also shall strengthen him."

In this section, David is described in detail as God sees him, in a five-fold way. Three descriptions describe David's character: " holy one" (*chasid*), a "mighty" man (*gibbor*), "my servant" (*avdi*) . Two expressions present to us David's special calling: God's "chosen" or elect (*bachur* chosen) one and God's "anointed" (*mashiach*).

1 God's holy one

In this section of the Psalm we learn why David was special. He is referred to in our Authorised Version as God's holy one (*chasid*). This is here translated "holy one" but as we see in Psalm 16, the word *chasid* is used to describe the "saints". Elsewhere, it carries the meaning of "godly ones". However, the root meaning of the word is "merciful one" (Psalm 18:25). The word does not imply sinless perfection. It describes David as one who was godly and given to lovingkindness and mercy. This is illustrated in his life in his treatment of Saul and his kindness to the house of Saul. Some may argue that showing kindness and mercy is a sign of weakness. On the contrary, the next description of him is as a "mighty one (*gibbor*)".

"Thy gentleness has made me great" (Psalm 18:35).

2 God's mighty one (gibbor)

He is seen as a strong man. However, his strength is attributed to his willingness to be helped of God. His strength did not emanate from himself but rather from God. "I have laid help upon *one that is* mighty (*gibbor* mighty man)." Interestingly, the word "I have laid" (*shiviti*) means literally, "I have laid help **equal** to one that is mighty" (this word has already been discussed in Psalm 16:8). How beautiful this is! The divine help is given equal to the task or role demanded of the Lord's servant. Moreover, David's greatness was only in the measure in which he depended and acted upon divine help and enabling. What a lesson to all believers today!

3 God's servant

God "found" him. This does not suggest a random act but rather the result of a detailed search for one with servant characteristics. God is still searching for servants who rely on Him and reflect God's character of lovingkindness.

4 God's anointed one

As the anointed one, David's mission was to keep alive the hope of the coming Messiah. David knew, through God's promises to him, that this Coming One would be of his lineage.

5 God's chosen or elect one

This brings before us David's mission and destiny to which he was called and chosen, not by men but by God: "I have exalted *one* chosen out of the people."

This description sets David apart from all others in his generation. It was the claim to be in the line of the Messiah which attracted such hostility to him. We find this in other Psalms considered in this book, especially Psalms 40, 41, and 69. The New Testament shows us that also in our modern day, being linked with the rejected Christ can be costly. Increasingly in the twenty-first century there are parts of the world where this principle is, sadly, being proven by many suffering and persecuted Christians. The next section shows how David, the anointed and chosen one of Jehovah, finds himself confronting "the enemy", "the son of wickedness", "foes" and "them that hate him". The encouraging promise given to him was that despite this formidable array of opposition, God had pledged that His faithfulness and His mercy would be with him.

2.3 God reassures David of victory in his lifetime

Psalm 89:22-24

22 "The enemy shall not exact upon him; nor the son of wickedness afflict him.
23 And I will beat down his foes before his face, and plague them that hate him.
24 But My faithfulness and My mercy *shall be* with him: and in My Name shall his horn be exalted."

So, just as in the previous section, God's **faithfulness** and **mercy** will be seen in a future day when Christ reigns supreme, so in David's historical experience God's **faithfulness** and **mercy** would be proven in his day-to day life and be demonstrated to David in the repeated victories God gave him over his enemies. This is a matter of tremendous encouragement to us today. God's faithfulness and lovingkindness in a coming day of victory will be publicly displayed by the One Who was wounded. However, God does not wait until then to allow His lovingkindness and faithfulness to be displayed! In David's experience, God's lovingkindness and faithfulness were displayed in his lifetime in the victories he enjoyed over his enemies. In fact, the only time David faced defeat was in his lack of dependence upon the Lord. The practical lesson for us today is clear. In the measure in which we depend on Him alone, we too can be mighty in His strength, not our own, and enjoy His faithfulness and lovingkindness displayed in every trial and difficulty of life.

2.4 God's promise of mercy and faithfulness to David in the coming Kingdom

Verses 25-28 describe promises to David which go beyond his experience while alive and must therefore find their fulfilment in a coming day when he enters into the earthly Kingdom.

2.5 The scope of His future authority

Psalm 89:25

"I will set his hand also in the sea, and his right hand in the rivers."

David's hand is "in the sea, and his right hand in the rivers", so this would suggest that his hand will have unfettered access to the resources of the seas and rivers of earth. This suggests freedom, wealth and prosperity which go beyond his experience in life. In other words, when the throne of David is occupied by David's Son, the Messiah, David will be in a place of administration then in that Kingdom. The man who once longed for a drink of water from the well of Bethlehem (2 Samuel 23:15) will have unlimited access to the many waters supplying the healed earth. In that day, David will call God "My Father".

2.6 David's future new relationship to God

Psalm 89:26

"He shall cry unto Me, Thou *art* my Father, my God, and the Rock of my Salvation."

In the Old Testament, no one ever directly called God "my Father" or "our Father" in their lifetimes such as we do in this New Testament era. Note 2 However, the Old Testament envisaged the future tribulation period, described as "the day of vengeance" (Isaiah 63:4), when believers of the remnant of Israel and believing Gentiles, redeemed from the tribulation chaos, would call God "our Father" in this prayer:

Isaiah 63:15-16

15 "Look down from heaven, and behold from the habitation of Thy holiness and of Thy glory: where is Thy zeal and Thy strength, the sounding of Thy bowels and of Thy mercies toward me? are they restrained?
16 **Doubtless Thou art our Father**, though Abraham be ignorant of us, and Israel acknowledge us not: Thou, **O Lord, art our Father**, our Redeemer; Thy Name is from everlasting."

Isaiah 64:8

"But now, **O Lord, Thou art our Father**; we are the clay, and Thou our Potter; and we all are the work of Thy hand."

The context of Isaiah 63-4 shows that the believers who express this prayer will be alive on this earth at the end of the tribulation period when the Lord will come to the earth to put down all rebellion in what He describes as "the day of vengeance" (Isaiah 63:4). Moreover, the future aspect of their lives is shown by the remark that they are unknown to Abraham and not acknowledged by Israel.

Old Testament believers must have wondered when it would be possible for them to learn to address God as Father like the tribulation believers of Isaiah 63-4. This moment had to await that momentous day when the Lord Jesus taught the disciples to pray using "our Father" in Luke 11:2. The disciples must have been so surprised by this. They were not in the tribulation, yet the Lord was teaching that they could soon address God as "our Father" in a non-tribulation era context. This was completely new. It was a wonderful **secret** in God's heart from before the foundation of the world. It has at its centre the amazingly close relationship to God of Church believers who, as adopted sons of God, are indwelt by the Holy Spirit in this Church era! Appreciation of this helps us understand why, in the preceding chapter, in Luke 10:21, the Lord rejoices at the imminent revelation of the Father to the babes (Old Testament saints, as explained in Psalm 8). This would come by the revelation in Luke 11 that those who trust Christ will be indwelt by the Spirit of God (Luke 11:13), i.e. receive the **divine nature** and thus become true sons of God. This is why today we call Him Father. No one in the Old Testament could do this even though they knew that God was the Father, as stated in Isaiah 63 and 64 and also in Malachi:

Malachi 1:6
"If then I *be* a Father, where *is* Mine honour?"

Therefore, when the Lord spoke of the Father in the New Testament, the Jews understood about Whom He was speaking. However, to personally address God as "my Father" or "our Father" would have to await the coming of the Lord Jesus and His direct revelation that we could speak to God in prayer as "our Father". As a result of His ascension to heaven, the Holy Spirit descended "whereby we cry, Abba Father".

Romans 8:15
"Ye have received the Spirit of adoption, whereby we cry, Abba, Father."

In that coming day of glory, David will cry unto God: "Thou *art* My Father, My God, and the (bed) Rock of my salvation" (see Appendix 3).

David as firstborn

Psalm 89:27
"Also I will make him (Hebrew: give him as) *My* **firstborn**, higher than the kings of the earth."

Many acknowledge that verse 27 affords a dignity to David which goes well beyond the historical experience of his lifetime. In consideration of this, some valued commentators suggest that this could be a reference to the Lord Jesus in a future day as "firstborn, higher than the kings of the earth". Whilst it is true that Revelation 1:5 makes it clear that the Lord Jesus will be "**the** (note definite article) Firstborn from amongst the dead, and **the** (note definite article) Prince of the kings of the Earth", this should be seen **in contrast** with Psalm 89:27 where David is spoken of as "firstborn (definite article omitted), higher than the kings of the earth".

Revelation 1:5

"And from Jesus Christ, *Who is* **the** faithful Witness, *and* **the** First Begotten (Greek: the Firstborn) of the dead, and **the** Prince of the kings of the earth. Unto Him that loved us, and washed us from our sins in His Own blood."

The use of the definite article highlights to us that the Lord Jesus is **the** Firstborn and **the** Prince of the kings of the earth. This also shows that He stands uniquely without peer and **distinct from David**. Revelation 1:5 goes beyond Psalm 89:27 which promises David that he will be given as "firstborn" (article omitted in Hebrew) and "high one" (article omitted in Hebrew) to the kings of the earth. Whilst David in his lifetime did not see fulfilment of this honoured role, he will enjoy being a future firstborn in the coming Kingdom. However, this respected status falls well short of the peerless role held exclusively by the Lord Jesus of being "**the** Firstborn, **the** Prince of the kings of the earth", as spoken of in Revelation 1:5. When that day comes, David will remember God's promise to Him of His mercy and His faithfulness:

Psalm 89:28

"My mercy will I keep for him for evermore, and My covenant shall stand fast (be faithful) with him."

2.7 The pledge of God's faithfulness and lovingkindness in future generations of David's descendants

Psalm 89:29-37

29 "His Seed also will I make *to endure* for ever, and his throne as the days of heaven.

30 If his children forsake My Law, and walk not in My judgments;

31 If they break My statutes, and keep not My commandments;

32 Then will I visit their transgression with the rod, and their iniquity with **stripes**.

33 Nevertheless My lovingkindness will I not utterly take from him, nor suffer My faithfulness to fail.

34 My covenant will I not break, nor alter the thing that is gone out of My lips.

35 Once have I sworn by My holiness that I will not lie unto David.

36 **His Seed** shall endure for ever, and his throne as the sun before Me.

37 It shall be established for ever as the moon, and *as* a faithful witness in heaven. Selah."

In these verses, Ethan distinguishes between David's "Seed" and David's "children". Verse 32, speaking of the punishment of David's unfaithful progeny, does not refer to the Lord Jesus, Who is defined exclusively as "the Seed of David". Verse 32 refers only to David's erring children down through the centuries. In verses 30-32, we read the sad prediction of David's children forsaking God's Law, not keeping His commandments and requiring to be visited with the rod and with stripes (plural). This word "stripes" is the same word as "stricken" in Isaiah:

Isaiah 53:8
> "For the transgression of my people was He stricken" (Hebrew: was the blow (singular) upon Him).

When it was a case of David's children, God dealt to them **many blows** in His judgments upon the erring kings of Judah. However, it is not so with the Person of Christ. In Isaiah 53:5, it was one stripe:

Isaiah 53:5
> "By His stripe we are healed."

Similarly:

Isaiah 53:8
> "For the transgression of my people was the blow (singular) upon Him".

When He suffered at the hands of God, once was enough and never needed to be repeated (see Psalm 22).

Regarding David's Seed (singular, not seeds but Seed), this will endure for ever and His throne as the days of heaven. This is on the basis of Jehovah's **lovingkindness** and His **faithfulness** (verse 33). Clearly, the "Seed" referred to is none other than the Lord Jesus Christ Himself. Only through Him will all God's mercies and lovingkindnesses come to fruition. It is lovely to see that God's promise to David was unconditional. Unlike the Law of Moses, which required compliance for its blessings to be enjoyed, this promise to David was independent of men. It was based only on God's lovingkindness and mercy which is seen only in the promised Seed.

The eternal state

The preceding section shows us that His Kingdom shall endure as the days of heaven (Psalm 89:29). Psalm 72:7 tells us that during His reign, men will fear him as long as the sun and moon endure. This suggests that the existing sun and moon will cease. We know this is the case from Psalm 102:25-28 (see later) where we learn that the heavens and the earth will cease and be exchanged for a new heaven and new earth (please see chapter on Psalm 102). Does this mean that the Kingdom will end at that great event? On the contrary, Psalm 89:36-7 shows that his Seed and His throne shall endure **forever**. In that great forever, His throne shall be **as** the Sun and the Moon. Note it does not say that His throne shall be the sun and the moon. In other words, He is the overwhelming light source in that future day of endless morning. This does not mean that there will be no sun or moon in the new heavens of that eternal state. In fact, Psalm 89:36-7 indicates that there will be a sun and moon into perpetuity. It is just that the light of these two heavenly objects will be redundant, so bright will be the light emanating from the Lord Jesus. This will be a constant reminder of the excelling glories of Christ eternally

Psalm 89:36-7

36 "His Seed shall endure for ever, and His throne as the sun before Me (in My presence).
37 It shall be established for ever as the moon, and *as* a faithful witness in heaven (Hebrew: in the cloud (singular)). Selah."

This is a good time just to refresh ourselves on what is known of the eternal state and the heavenly city. When we read the description of the heavenly city, which descended from God down to the new earth in the eternal state, we are clearly told that it has only one street and one river yet its perimeter is square and its height is the same as its length and breadth (Revelation 21:16).

Revelation 21:16

"And the city lieth foursquare, and the length is as large as the breadth: and he measured the city with the reed, twelve thousand furlongs. The length and the breadth and the height of it are equal."

The idea of a pyramidal structure answers this description given in Revelation 21:16, and in that day the throne of the Lamb will be at the pinnacle of the pyramid with the single street and tree-lined river winding downwards to the surrounding walls with the twelve gates. It is apparent that the city retains its heavenly character even though it is on earth, having come down from God out of heaven. For the first time, "the tabernacle of God" is on earth (Revelation 21:3). In other words, the third heaven, the eternal abode of God, in the future eternal state will be on earth. It is literally heaven on earth. The heavenly city, the Church, situated then on the new earth will remain the home of the Church eternally. However, tribulation, Old Testament and millennial saints will mingle at its gates with the heavenly inhabitants of the city, namely those who make up the Church, the heavenly people. At the centre and pinnacle of this temple city is the King seated upon His throne. This will be so bright that the light of the sun and the moon will not be needed. This does not mean that there will not be a sun and moon in the New Heavens. The language used in Revelation 21:23-25 and later in Revelation 22:5 does not support such a conclusion. Rather the meaning is that the light of the sun and the moon is not needed for illumination, so intensely bright is the light emanating from the Lamb Himself. Here are the two quotations from Revelation 21 and 22.

Revelation 21:23-25

23 "And the city had **no need of the sun, neither of the moon, to shine in it**: for the glory of God did lighten it, and the Lamb *is* the light thereof.
24 And the nations of them which are saved shall walk in the light of it: and the kings of the earth do bring their glory and honour into it.
25 And the gates of it shall not be shut at all by day: for there shall be no night there."

Revelation 22:5
> "And there shall be no night there; and they need no candle, neither light
> of the sun; for the Lord God giveth them light: and they shall reign for ever
> and ever."

Now let us return to Psalm 89. What a lovely observation is revealed to
the Psalmist! "His throne... shall be... a faithful witness in heaven (in **the**
cloud)". Evidently, the *Shechinah* cloud shall surround that throne in all
its brightness. What an amazing Old Testament revelation of the ultimate
eternal and divine character of the Davidic throne!

3 PART THREE

3.1 A description of the judgments on the disobedient children of David

Psalm 89:38-45

38 "But Thou hast cast off and abhorred, Thou hast been wroth with Thine
anointed.
39 Thou hast made void the covenant of Thy servant: Thou hast profaned
his crown *by casting it* to the ground.
40 Thou hast broken down all his hedges; Thou hast brought his strong
holds to ruin.
41 All that pass by the way spoil him: he is a reproach to his neighbours.
42 Thou hast set up the right hand of his adversaries; Thou hast made all
his enemies to rejoice.
43 Thou hast also turned the edge of his sword, and hast not made him to
stand in the battle.
44 Thou hast made his glory to cease, and cast his throne down to the
ground.
45 The days of his youth hast Thou shortened: Thou hast covered him with
shame. Selah."

Now Ethan returns to address the Lord Himself and reminds Him in
his prayer of His judgments on the disobedient children of David. He
accurately describes and predicts the cessation of the throne of David in
Jerusalem (verse 44), the end of the monarchy (verse 39), the breakdown of
the hedges (verse 40, i.e. the walls of Jerusalem) and the apparent victory of
the enemies of the Lord, who rejoiced at the destruction of the Temple by
Nebuchadnezzar (verses 41-42).

3.2 The miracle of the lovingkindness of God being displayed despite the collapse of David's dynasty

In the final section of the Psalm, Ethan looks at the reality of what was
happening to the nation as it underwent divine discipline in its captivity
and defeat, and yet it soars above this to ask the Lord in verse 49:

Psalm 89:49

> "Where are Thy former lovingkindnesses which Thou swarest unto David
> in Thy truth (Hebrew: faithfulness)?"

The reason for his request is not that he is in any doubt as to the certainty of God fulfilling His promise to David in establishing the throne of David. The issue perplexing Ethan is that he has a sneaking worry that the fulfilment will come after he (Ethan) has died.

Psalm 89:46-48

46 "How long, Lord? wilt Thou hide Thyself for ever? shall Thy wrath burn like fire?
47 Remember how short my time is: wherefore hast Thou made all men in vain?
48 What man *is he that* liveth, and shall not see death? shall he deliver his soul from the hand of the grave? Selah."

He argues that life would have been "in vain" if one were to miss this wonderful event of the Davidic Kingdom on earth. This idea comes out more clearly in Mr Darby's helpful alternative translation to Psalm 89:47: "Remember, as regards me, **what life is**. Wherefore hast Thou created all the children of men to be vanity?"

This is a rhetorical question to which the unspoken answer is that God has not created man to vanity. God has created man to a true purpose and that is ultimately to realize fullness of life in seeing the King in His beauty. It is a tragic emptiness (vanity) to miss this. The Psalmist, facing death, calls on the Lord to remember what real life is. That is surely an appeal to resurrection and to personally enter into that coming Kingdom and enjoy it in its reality in a future day. This is the opposite of emptiness. This is fullness. "In Thy presence is fullness of joy" (Psalm 16:11).

Psalm 89:49

"Lord, where *are* Thy former lovingkindnesses, *which* Thou swarest unto David in Thy truth?"

In anticipation of personally entering into the wonderful blessings of the future Davidic covenant, the Psalmist has placed his personal confidence in the same "former loving-kindnesses, which Thou swarest unto David in Thy truth". In other words, he realises that when God pledged His lovingkindness and faithfulness to David by assuring him of the day when the Son of David would rule supreme, that promise had an application not just to David but **also** to Ethan the Psalmist and, by implication, **to all God's servants** (verse 50) who claim by faith that same lovingkindness and truth. In fact, when we come to study the lovingkindness of the Lord in Psalm 117 we will see that it has been wonderfully extended out to the Gentiles!

Psalm 89:50,51

50 "Remember, Lord, the reproach of Thy servants; *how* I do bear in my bosom *the reproach of* all the mighty people;
51 Wherewith Thine enemies have reproached, O Lord; wherewith they have reproached the footsteps of Thine anointed."

God will not forget the departed saints! He will never forget what life is. That is because He is the God of resurrection. He will also never forget (verse 50) the reproach each one bore for the Lord while on this earth (verse 51). What a solace to know that long after the memory of a believer is lost in the mists of time, and long after their faithfulness to the Lord has been forgotten on earth, there is One Who remembers, and that remembrance brings added impetus to hasten the day when the King reigns supreme. Then the aspirations of the saints will have been satisfied. In that day all those who bore the reproach of Christ (verses 50-51) will find public vindication. Then will the great doxology burst forth:

Psalm 89:52

"Blessed *be* the Lord for evermore. Amen, and Amen."

1. Ethan the Ezrahite is a contemporary of David and Solomon, and noted for his exceptional wisdom in the things of God (1 Kings 4:31) surpassed only by Solomon. This Psalm and the truth contained within it testify to the spiritual wisdom of this remarkable man.

2. Jeremiah 3:19 describes the Lord's aspiration that in a coming day the nation could address Him as "My Father" and "shall not turn away from" the Lord. This will be fulfilled when the remnant nation is restored after the rapture (see Appendix 3).

Jeremiah 3:4 shows how the apostate elements of the nation in Jeremiah's day said to the Lord: "My Father, Thou art the guide of my youth". However, this address to God was hypocritical and impudent and invoked a claim to a relationship which was entirely spurious. Jeremiah 3:19 describes the day when that relationship of being **genuinely** able to address God as "my Father" will be enjoyed by the restored nation.

15

PSALM 90

A Prayer of Moses the man of God.

1 LORD, Thou hast been our dwelling place in all generations.

2 Before the mountains were brought forth, or ever Thou hadst formed the earth and the world, even from everlasting to everlasting, Thou art God.

3 Thou turnest man to destruction; and sayest, Return, ye children of men.

4 For a thousand years in Thy sight are but as yesterday when it is past, and as a watch in the night.

5 Thou carriest them away as with a flood; they are as a sleep: in the morning they are like grass which groweth up.

6 In the morning it flourisheth, and groweth up; in the evening it is cut down, and withereth.

7 For we are consumed by Thine anger, and by Thy wrath are we troubled.

8 Thou hast set our iniquities before Thee, our secret sins in the light of Thy countenance.

9 For all our days are passed away in Thy wrath: we spend our years as a tale that is told.

10 The days of our years are threescore years and ten; and if by reason of strength they be fourscore years, yet is their strength labour and sorrow; for it is soon cut off, and we fly away.

11 Who knoweth the power of Thine anger? even according to Thy fear, so is Thy wrath.

12 So teach us to number our days, that we may apply our hearts unto wisdom.

13 Return, O Lord, how long? and let it repent Thee concerning Thy servants.

14 O satisfy us early with Thy mercy; that we may rejoice and be glad all our days.

15 Make us glad according to the days wherein Thou hast afflicted us, and the years wherein we have seen evil.

16 Let Thy work appear unto Thy servants, and Thy glory unto their children.

17 And let the beauty of the Lord our God be upon us: and establish Thou the work of our hands upon us; yea, the work of our hands establish Thou it.

Introduction

Psalm 90 is not generally considered to be a Messianic Psalm because it does not directly refer to the Lord Jesus or the coming Messiah. However, it is included in this book on the Messianic Psalms for the following reasons:

1 It provides a conceptual bridge between the Messianic Psalms which immediately precede and follow it, namely Psalms 89 and 91. Psalm 89 considers the failure of the Davidic monarchy in particular and how God would react through the promised Messiah to completely overcome this. Psalm 90 is considering the failure of **humanity in general** and what God would do to undo this tragedy. This then provides a perfect lead in to Psalm 91 which considers a dependent man who brings pleasure to God.

2 Psalm 90 is written by Moses, the man of God. Accordingly, it is based around some key events recorded by Moses in the historical account of the Pentateuch. It thus deals with man's sin, man hiding from God (as did Adam in the garden), and the frailty and death which result. However, it also deals with how God can reverse the effects of man's sin, namely the resultant disease and death, and create a new thing: human beings clothed in the very beauty of God. Moses shows in his prayer that this is based on God being "comforted". It will be seen in the detailed study that this is a reference to Moses' intercessory prayer for the people of Israel after the golden calf episode, when he pleaded with God to have mercy on the people in light of the promise given to Abraham in Genesis 22. Since that promise was **specifically about the coming of the Lamb of God's providing,** namely the Person of the Lord Jesus, it follows therefore that this Psalm could be regarded as a Messianic Psalm.

The beginning

Psalm 90 opens with the beginning (Psalm 90:1-2) as does Moses in Genesis 1:1.

Psalm 90:1-2

1 "LORD, Thou hast been our dwelling place in all generations.

2 Before the mountains were brought forth, or ever Thou hadst formed the earth and the world, even from everlasting to everlasting, Thou *art* God."

It describes the goal and desire of God that men should dwell in Him and be "at home" in God's company. This was the delightful state of bliss our first parents enjoyed for such a short time before sin entered in and spoiled it all. The next part of the Psalm tells us of the disastrous tragedy of sin entering into this world.

The entry and effects of sin

Here human frailty and mortality are described by Moses. This is fitting as it was he who gave the Biblical account of how man (Adam) sinned and became subject to mortality. The choice of word used to describe man in Psalm 90:3 emphasises this theme:

Psalm 90:3

"Thou turnest man (*enosh*) to destruction; and sayest, Return ye children of men (sons of Adam)."

This sequence was already noted in Psalm 8 in the words: "What is man (*enosh*) that Thou art mindful of him or the son of man (*adam*) that Thou visitest him?" As discussed in Psalm 8, the word used for man, *enosh*, means "frail, mortal man". Thus it is that the Psalm contrasts the eternality of God the Creator (Psalm 90:1-2) with man, a creature of time with a lifetime limited to 70 or 80 years (Psalm 90:10). "If by reason of strength" this is 80 years "yet is their strength (pride) labour and sorrow". Moses must surely have marvelled how a creature of such frailty and weakness should be characterised by pride, especially when the reason for God's **anger and wrath** against humanity is elaborated in verses 7 and 8.

Psalm 90:7

"For we are consumed by Thine anger, and by Thy wrath are we troubled."

We know from the New Testament that the wrath of God comes on men not merely because of their sin alone, but also because of their unbelief or disobedience:

Ephesians 5:6

"Because of these things cometh the wrath of God on the children of **disobedience**."

It is, therefore, consistent with New Testament teaching that the next verse addresses not so much the problem of man's sin alone, as his **iniquity and hidden sins**.

Psalm 90:8

"Thou hast set our **iniquities** before Thee, our **secret** *sins* in the light of Thy countenance."

Iniquity has as its core meaning in Hebrew an inner **twistedness and perversion**. The idea of "secret" sins is a feature of fallen man, as this was the very first action of our fallen first parents, as described by Moses, who sought to hide their nakedness from God. Moses has thus put his finger on the problem. Men are lost not only because they are sinners but also because they refuse to admit this to God. Men are unwilling to accept the guilty verdict against them and thus benefit from a loving God's provision for fallen humanity. Man has an intrinsic rebellious spirit which takes him away from God and causes him to deny his sin to God. It is this which merits God's wrath. God is grieved in His innermost being by man's unbelief and disobedience. God's wrath and anger arise from a feeling of being hurt or aggrieved through His love being spurned by men. Even in human experience, a person who has been hurt or aggrieved craves a remedy or some form of compensation which will bring comfort and closure. Ignoring God and His loving provision for such sons of Adam leads to the irreversible outcome of death and eternal loss. In verses 3-6, Moses uses the imagery of a current of death washing away generation after generation like a great unending tsunami wave of destruction (see similar imagery in Psalm 18).

How is it that Moses speaks of God's wrath in verse 7 and then speaks of God's mercy (Hebrew: lovingkindness) in verse 14? This is not a contradiction within the passage. God's wrath is upon men who hide from Him and rebel against Him through refusing His lovingkindness. How offensive to God is such human pride!

What a contrast, then, in Psalm 91 when it is not the secret sins of man which are being considered but an ideal man, acting in complete dependence on God, abiding in the secret place of the Most High. How can such a human rebel in Psalm 90 be so radically changed to become a being who is content to abide in God (Psalm 90:1) and in the secret place of the Most High (Psalm 91:1) in contrast to secret sins of Psalm 90? The second half of Psalm 90 shows how this is possible.

Moses describes God's plan for human deliverance

Moses, the man of God, who described man's fall and the devastating effect of this on humanity in the first half of the Psalm, also describes in detail how such a fallen man can be brought back into fellowship with his God and once again feel comfortable abiding in God and able to say from the depths of his soul:

Psalm 90:1
"O Lord Thou hast been our dwelling (abiding) place in all generations (from generation to generation)."

This is the ideal situation described in verse 1 of the Psalm but, sadly, forfeited due to sin.

The pathway to blessing

Psalm 90:11-12

11 "Who knoweth the power of Thine anger? even according to Thy fear, *so is* Thy wrath.
12 So teach *us* to number our days, that we may apply *our* hearts unto wisdom."

Verse 11 inquires as to the power of God's anger and its underlying rationale. Remarkably, the subject of divine anger is misunderstood by fallen man. Following the fall, men have become "enemies" of God in their "mind by wicked works" (Colossians 1:21) and regard God as such. However, the Psalmist tells us that "according to Thy fear, so is Thy wrath". The word here used for "fear" is elsewhere used in a good sense as "the fear of the Lord is the beginning of wisdom"(Psalm 111:10). This is a holy dread of grieving God. Fear of God is not proportional to His wrath but rather **inversely**

proportional to it. Those who do not hold God in reverential fear and thus disregard God and His divine claims merit His wrath. It is apparent from verse 12 that this realisation is not intuitive. It needs to be taught of God by His Spirit. Thus the Psalmist prays, "So **teach us** to number our days, that we may apply our hearts unto wisdom". Verse 11 is all about fearing God in an **intelligent** way. Verse 12 is about the wisdom which this fear of the Lord engenders. The next verses detail for us this divinely imparted wisdom.

The revelation of God's wisdom in the matter of redemption

Psalm 90:13

"Return, O Lord, how long? and let it repent Thee (Hebrew "be comforted") concerning Thy servants."

Verse 13 shows how this wisdom reveals the means whereby God **is comforted** in respect of His erring servants. Firstly, there is a recognition of the enormity of the grief which sin has caused to God. Then we can just begin to appreciate, by divinely imparted wisdom, the greatness of the payment God requires to effect the restitution and satisfaction He needs with respect to the matter of our sin. Before God can be comforted in this matter, He and only He can intervene to bring about the answer. To this end Moses prays, "Return O Lord, how long?" Moses was longing for the intervention of God to deal with the root cause of man's problems: his sin.

Next, he appeals to the Lord to intervene in the affairs of men in such a way as to bring about comfort to His own soul in respect of His servants' sins. This understanding of the verse emerges from realising that the phrase, "let it repent Thee", is literally translated as "be comforted". A well known illustration of the same verb being used in the sense of "to be comforted" is found in Jeremiah 31:15 when Rachel "refused to be comforted". How then is God comforted in the matter of human guilt? In Scripture, God is comforted, in respect of the grief which sin has caused Him, through the sin-expiating Sacrifice of Christ alone, on the basis of which He can provide forgiveness to all who avail of this provision. This principle has been considered in Psalm 22 and, as will be explained in the next paragraph, is raised again by Moses in this section in the context of the sacrificial death of Christ as the Lamb of God's providing, as prophesied in Genesis 22. However, for those who do not accept this as the only remedy for sin, i.e. the adversaries of God, judgment on such individuals will be inevitable and this brings comfort to God. It is in this latter context of God punishing His adversaries that in Isaiah 1:24 God declares, "I will ease me of (Hebrew: be comforted of) My adversaries", meaning, "I will be comforted through exacting vengeance upon them."

Isaiah 1:24

"Therefore saith the Lord, the Lord of hosts, the Mighty One of Israel, Ah, I will ease Me of Mine adversaries, and avenge Me of Mine enemies:"

A word of clarification is needed here. The punishment of the adversaries of God does not bring about expiation of sin, nor does it propitiate God's throne. It must be emphasised that the punishment of the adversaries of God **does not comfort God** in the matter of **sin**. **Only the death of the Lord Jesus** can do this, as considered in Psalm 22. However, for those who reject God's provision in Christ, an eternal punishment will ensue, which is eternal because, by definition, it cannot be sin-expiating (see Psalm 22). This is the righteous judgment of God. It brings comfort to the heart of a righteous and holy God in respect of **persons** who have refused God's righteous offer of full forgiveness and who, by so doing, have disbelieved and set at naught the infinite comfort given to God in the propitiatory work of Christ.

In Isaiah 57:5-7, in the context of heathen idolatrous sacrifices, God asks: "Should I receive comfort (be comforted) in these?"

Isaiah 57:5-7
> 5 "Enflaming yourselves with idols under every green tree, slaying the children in the valleys under the clifts of the rocks?
> 6 Among the smooth *stones* of the stream *is* thy portion; they, they *are* thy lot: even to them hast thou poured a drink offering, thou hast offered a meat offering. **Should I receive comfort (be comforted) in these**?
> 7 Upon a lofty and high mountain hast thou set thy bed: even thither wentest thou up to offer sacrifice."

The implication is that a sacrifice brings comfort to God in the matter of sin but **not** an idolatrous counterfeit sacrifice. Only the Sacrifice of the Lord Jesus brings ultimate and eternal comfort to God's heart in the matter of **sin**. This glorious principle is illustrated in the story of the nation's sin at the time of the golden calf apostasy in Exodus 32 when Moses interceded with God on their behalf.

Exodus 32:11-14
> 11 "And Moses besought the Lord his God, and said, Lord, why doth Thy wrath wax hot against Thy people, which Thou hast brought forth out of the land of Egypt with great power, and with a mighty hand?
> 12 Wherefore should the Egyptians speak, and say, For mischief did He bring them out, to slay them in the mountains, and to consume them from the face of the earth? Turn from Thy fierce wrath, and repent of this evil against Thy people.
> 13 Remember Abraham, Isaac, and Israel, Thy servants, **to whom Thou swarest by Thine own Self,** and saidst unto them, I will multiply your seed as the stars of heaven, and all this land that I have spoken of will I give unto your seed, and they shall inherit *it* for ever.
> 14 And **the Lord repented (Hebrew: was comforted) of the evil** which He thought to do unto His people."

It was the fact that Moses reminded God of **His oath to Abraham** which brought about the deliverance that day. What was this oath by **"His own Self"**? The phrase in Exodus 32:13, **"by Thine own Self"**, is the key to understanding the basis of Moses' intercessory prayer because it recalls the

specific promise of God to Abraham confirmed **through an oath by Himself** in Genesis 22:13-18, which we studied in Psalm 24. It was when Abraham was **offering up Isaac his son** upon the altar that God revealed to him the promise of the Seed Who was destined for the altar, **the Lamb of God's providing, i.e. Christ.**

Genesis 22:13-18

13 "And Abraham lifted up his eyes, and looked, and behold behind *him* a ram caught in a thicket by his horns: and Abraham went and took the ram, and offered him up for a burnt offering in the stead of his son.

14 And Abraham called the name of that place Jehovah-jireh: as it is said *to* this day, In the mount of the Lord it shall be seen.

15 And the Angel of the Lord called unto Abraham out of heaven the second time,

16 And said, **By Myself have I sworn**, saith the Lord, for because thou hast done this thing, and hast not withheld thy son, thine only *son:*

17 That in blessing I will bless thee, and in multiplying I will multiply thy seed as the stars of the heaven, and as the sand which *is* upon the sea shore; and **thy Seed shall possess the gate of His enemies;**

18 And in thy Seed shall all the nations of the earth be blessed; because thou hast obeyed My voice."

It was thus with tremendous spiritual intelligence that Moses prayed for the people in Exodus 32 that God might have mercy upon them, pleading alone this specific promise to Abraham given in Genesis 22:17 regarding the promised Seed, namely this One unique Person Who is the promised sacrificial Lamb of God. A difficulty may arise in the minds of some, as to why Moses quotes this occasion of God swearing by Himself to Abraham and why he indicates that this oath was **also** given to Isaac and Jacob, even though such an oath being repeated to Isaac and Jacob is not specifically recorded in Genesis. The answer is that God **confirmed** to Isaac and Jacob the promises which He gave to Abraham, singling out for special attention the promise and oath to Abraham in Genesis 22:17. We read of these confirmatory promises to Isaac regarding the oath to his father Abraham in Genesis 26:3.

Genesis 26:3

"Sojourn in this land, and I will be with thee, and will bless thee; for unto thee, and unto thy seed, I will give all these countries, and **I will perform the oath which I sware unto Abraham thy father;**"

Similarly, in Jacob's experience, God confirmed to him **the content of the promise** to Abraham and Isaac in Genesis 35:12.

Genesis 35:12

"And the land which I gave Abraham and Isaac, to thee I will give it, and to thy seed after thee will I give the land."

However, the fact that this was based on an oath to Abraham was not restated to Jacob. It seems that this was already clearly understood by Jacob, as Moses infers in Exodus 32:13 where he indicates that the oath of Genesis 22:16 was to Abraham, Isaac **and** Jacob.

It was Moses' mention of this specific promise and oath to Abraham which led God that day to "repent" concerning the evil, or literally "to be comforted" with regard to His judgment on the people. What divine wisdom! If anticipation of the promised Sacrifice of Christ brought God comfort of heart on that occasion, how much more did not Christ at Calvary forever satisfy God in the matter of sin!

There is no doubt as Moses wrote Psalm 90 and pleaded for the Lord to be comforted regarding His servants, that he must have been recalling those dramatic events of Exodus 32 when he pleaded with God on the basis of the future sacrificial Lamb of God.

The idolatrous sacrifice of the golden calf brought judgment on the people. No animal sacrifice could bring forgiveness to the people in light of such a great sin. Only pleading the merits of the promised Sacrifice of Christ, the Lamb Whom God would provide, brought forgiveness.

The outcome of the Sacrifice

Psalm 90:14

"O satisfy us early with Thy mercy; that we may
rejoice and be glad all our days."

What a change has taken place now in the Psalm! Frail, mortal man in all his perversity and rebellion, depicted as abiding under divine anger, is now being satisfied "with Thy mercy". Here the word for mercy is "lovingkindness" (*chesed*). The moment a sinner is satisfied with the lovingkindness of God in His provision of salvation through the sacrificial death of the Lamb of God, is the moment of salvation by faith! From that moment forwards a saved man or woman is now basking in the warmth of the love of God and rejoicing with joy unspeakable and full of glory! Man, who was earlier depicted as frail and mortal (*enosh*) is now satisfied in God!

One is reminded of the beginning of the beautiful hymn by Henry Bennett (1813-1868):

Satisfied with Thee Lord Jesus I am blessed
Peace which passeth understanding on Thy breast
No more doubting, no more trembling.
No more trembling
O what rest!

Only then, can God reveal Himself to man in His work, His glory and His beauty.

Psalm 90:16

"Let Thy work appear unto Thy servants, and Thy glory (Hebrew: *hadar*)
unto their children."

One cannot but remember the occasion, subsequent to the golden calf incident, when Moses desired to behold the glory (Hebrew: *cavod*) of the Lord.

Exodus 33:17-23

> 17 "And the Lord said unto Moses, I will do this thing also that thou hast spoken: for thou hast found grace in My sight, and I know thee by name.
> 18 And he said, I beseech Thee, **shew me Thy glory (Hebrew: *cavod*)**.
> 19 And He said, I will make all My goodness pass before thee, and I will proclaim the Name of the Lord before thee; and will be gracious to whom I will be gracious, and will shew mercy on whom I will shew mercy.
> 20 And He said, Thou canst not see My face: for there shall no man see Me, and live.
> 21 And the Lord said, Behold, *there is* a place by Me, and thou shalt stand upon a rock:
> 22 And it shall come to pass, while My glory passeth by, that I will put thee in a clift of the rock, and will cover thee with My hand while I pass by:
> 23 And I will take away Mine hand, and thou shalt see My back parts: but My face shall not be seen."

Hidden in the cleft of the rock by the hand of God, Moses waited as the glory of the Lord passed by. Then the Lord took away His hand and Moses beheld the back parts of the Lord but not His face. In the Psalm, Moses prays that one day God's work will appear unto His servants and His glory (*hadar*) unto their children. We have already considered in Psalm 8 this word *hadar*. It was veiled by the Lord Jesus while He was upon earth (Isaiah 53:2), but is fully revealed in His **resurrection** body (Psalms 8, 45 and 110). The answer to Moses' prayer will come when the redeemed nation, indeed all the redeemed, will see the Person of Christ in all His resurrection *hadar*.

When that happens, the redeemed themselves will have been changed and will, in bodies of resurrection, be marked by the "beauty of the Lord".

Psalm 90:17

"And let the **beauty** (Hebrew: *noam*) of the Lord our God be upon us..."

What a transformation for human beings who had become so ugly through sin! It has all been made possible through the Lamb of God's providing and His death and resurrection which have satisfied (comforted) the heart of God and satisfied all who have put their faith in Him throughout the ages of human history.

The practical aspect of Moses' Prayer

Psalm 90:17

"...and establish Thou the work of our hands upon us; yea, the work of our hands establish Thou it."

Here we have the longing desire of each redeemed soul. It is that he or she should not be idle in the things of God but that redeemed hands should be active in His service. However, it is most instructive to note the exact wording of this prayer of Moses who has the distinction of being a man of God. It is that the **Lord establish the work of our hands** and **not** that our hands establish the work of the Lord. What a counter-intuitive prayer, at least as far as human fleshly ambition is concerned! Nevertheless, this is the prayer of a saint who recognises that it is not oneself or ones efforts which count but rather the Lord being pleased to work **through** us. The Lord does not need us to work for His objectives to be met. However, it is His good pleasure to allow His servants to worshipfully work for Him, not in their own power but in as far as they wholly depend on Him. Only such believers are servants that God can use because all glory accrues to the Lord alone.

May this prayer of Moses the man of God be on the lips of every servant of God both now and in the days to come.

16

PSALM 91

1 HE that dwelleth in the secret place of the most High shall abide under the shadow of the Almighty.

2 I will say of the Lord, He is my refuge and my fortress: my God; in Him will I trust.

3 Surely He shall deliver thee from the snare of the fowler, and from the noisome pestilence.

4 He shall cover thee with His feathers, and under His wings shalt thou trust: His truth shall be thy shield and buckler.

5 Thou shalt not be afraid for the terror by night; nor for the arrow that flieth by day;

6 Nor for the pestilence that walketh in darkness; nor for the destruction that wasteth at noonday.

7 A thousand shall fall at thy side, and ten thousand at thy right hand; but it shall not come nigh thee.

8 Only with thine eyes shalt thou behold and see the reward of the wicked.

9 Because Thou hast made the Lord, which is my refuge, even the Most High, Thy habitation;

10 There shall no evil befall Thee, neither shall any plague come nigh Thy dwelling.

11 For He shall give His angels charge over Thee, to keep Thee in all Thy ways.

12 They shall bear Thee up in their hands, lest Thou dash Thy foot against a stone.

13 Thou shalt tread upon the lion and adder: the young lion and the dragon shalt Thou trample under feet.

14 Because He hath set His love upon Me, therefore will I deliver Him: I will set Him on high, because He hath known My Name.

15 He shall call upon Me, and I will answer Him: I will be with Him in trouble; I will deliver Him, and honour Him.

16 With long life will I satisfy Him, and shew Him My salvation.

Introduction

Psalm 91 continues the theme of Psalm 90 where Moses described the triumph of the Sacrifice of Christ, as promised to Abraham in Genesis 22, allowing man in all his fallen state to become invested in the very beauty of the Lord. Accordingly, Psalm 91 considers the remarkable phenomenon of men, now saved and redeemed and who are once again in fellowship with God, appearing to be completely resistant to the lying attacks of Satan and his emissaries. This phenomenon is a divine masterpiece, arguably even more wonderful than the first creation which was marred by Adam's fall. In the garden, Adam in ideal conditions succumbed to Satan's lies. In contrast, in the first part of Psalm 91 we meet men in horrendous conditions who, due to their complete dependence on God and reliance on His protection, refuse to deny their Lord.

The period of time chosen to illustrate this is one of widespread evil ("noisome pestilence", Hebrew meaning: epidemic of evil), under the influence of an individual known as "the snare of the fowler", an expression elsewhere used to describe a false prophet. This period of time is limited by a grand conclusion when the faithful to the Lord will witness with their own eyes "the reward (Hebrew: recompense) of the wicked (ones)" (Psalm 91:8). This verse is the key to understanding the section, as it indicates that those who refuse to bow to the false prophet will, in their lifetimes, behold the judgment of the wicked ones. This identifies the period of time being considered by the Psalm as the future tribulation, when Satan and his emissaries will find themselves powerless to shake the steadfastness of the faithful remnant, despite the fiercest of persecution imaginable directed against this godly band of believers. At the end of this time, the remnant will see the judgment of their enemies. This has never happened in its fullness at any time in the past, as wicked men throughout history have never been fully recompensed for their wickedness by human courts of justice. This will not be the case when the divine Judge, the Lord Jesus, on His return fully recompenses righteous judgment upon the heads of all those wicked rebels against God (as outlined in detail in Psalm 68). The New Testament comments on this time of recompense:

2 Thessalonians 1:6-9

> 6 "Seeing *it is* a righteous thing with God to **recompense tribulation** to them that trouble you;
> 7 And to you who are troubled rest with us, when the Lord Jesus shall be revealed from heaven with His mighty angels,
> 8 In flaming fire taking vengeance on them that know not God, and that obey not the gospel of our Lord Jesus Christ:
> 9 Who shall be punished with everlasting destruction from the presence of the Lord, and from the glory of His power."

The second part of the Psalm (verses 9-16) is an analysis of the reason for this defeat of the forces of evil. It is traced to the Person of the Lord Jesus Christ Who by His life, death, resurrection and ascension defeated Satan and all his hosts.

Part 1 of the Psalm (Psalm 91:1-8)

The faithful remnant in the tribulation

This section does not refer primarily to the Lord Jesus because verse 7 describes a single individual standing unscathed while multitudes perish right beside him. This clearly cannot refer to the Lord Jesus in His first advent to this earth, where such an event did not happen.

Psalm 91:7

> "A thousand shall fall at thy side, and ten thousand at thy right hand; *but* it shall not come nigh thee."

However, this prophecy is consistent with the experience of the remnant in the future tribulation. The first part of the Psalm is set during a period of extreme persecution of those who love the Lord. Despite this, the believer who is simple enough to abide in the Lord stands unscathed spiritually. This is the wonderful claim and boast of verses 1 and 2.

The security of abiding in Him

Psalm 91:1-2

> 1 "He that dwelleth (Hebrew: abides) in the secret place of the most High shall abide (Hebrew: lodge or spend the night) under the shadow of the Almighty.
> 2 I will say of the Lord, *He is* my refuge and my fortress: my God; in Him will I trust."

In contrast to the first man Adam, who did not abide, we have a dependent man who abides in the secret place. What does it mean to abide in Him? According to John it means:

1 to keep His commandments

John 15:10

> "If ye keep My commandments, ye shall abide in My love; even as I have kept My Father's commandments, and abide in His love."

1 John 3:24

> "And he that keepeth His commandments dwelleth (abideth) in Him, and He in him. And hereby we know that He abideth in us, by the Spirit Which He hath given us."

2 to confess that Jesus is the Son of God

1 John 4: 15

> "Whosoever shall confess that Jesus is the Son of God, God dwelleth (abideth) in him, and he in God."

3 to abide in love

1 John 4:16

> "And we have known and believed the love that God hath to us. God is love; and he that dwelleth in love dwelleth in God, and God in him."

If, today, in peaceful and congenial circumstances, we fail sometimes in the principles of abiding in Him, as outlined above, how much more pleasing to the Lord will it be in that day when against a maelstrom of severe persecution these believers will indeed "abide in Him". In the matter of abiding in Him, it is worth bearing in mind that there seems to be a desire in every human being, apart from the Lord Jesus, to act independently of the Lord. In this matter, Abraham failed when he went down to Egypt rather than depending on the Lord to feed him. Likewise, David failed when he numbered the people rather than relying on the Lord of Hosts to protect him. It is not a natural thing for a man to abide in the Lord. Only when we are redeemed and walking closely with the Lord do we enjoy the blessings of abiding in Him.

In a sense, the Psalm is the answer to the opening line of the prayer of Moses:

Psalm 90:1
"Lord, Thou hast been our dwelling (abiding) place in all generations (from generation to generation)."

It depicts the blessed experience of a person now abiding in the Lord. Anyone who is acting in dependence on the Lord will find that this is challenged by the forces of evil. In a very special way in a coming day, those members of the redeemed remnant of Israel in the tribulation will be cast upon the Lord in those extreme days of trial. Just as Psalm 90 depicts the miseries of the man who is acting independently of the Lord, this Psalm assures us of the security of the person who does depend on Him even despite the challenges of Satan.

In this Psalm, the dependent man constantly is abiding in the secret place of the Most High. In Psalm 89, mention was made of the reference to the secrets or mysteries which are alluded to in the Old Testament but fully revealed in the New Testament. The dependent man is in the very inner secret place of God and understands His hidden counsels even into eternity past. The application to us is that if we are dependent on Him, the Lord is pleased to reveal to us the hidden places of the Most High, including the mystery doctrines of the New Testament. Access to this secret resort is precluded to all natural men.

Ultimately, the example of dependent manhood has only been **fully** told out in the perfect life of the Lord Jesus Christ. He lived here and those who come into relationship with Him come into the sublime environment of the One Who dwelled in the environment of heaven, even though He was physically on earth:

John 1:38-9
38 " They said unto Him, Rabbi ... where dwelleth Thou?
39 He saith unto them, Come and see!"

Paul shows that every believer should have access to this hidden place of spiritual security:

Colossians 3:3
"Ye are dead and your life is hid **with Christ in God**."

This secret place of the Most High is a secure place of lodging and affords protection from the hostile intent of the unseen spirit world. The use of the word "lodge" suggests someone on a pilgrim journey who every night needs a place in the dangerous hours of night to find rest, protection and food. The Almighty (Hebrew: *Shadday*, meaning the "All Sufficient One") has the full resources to meet the needs of the travelling pilgrims who have cast themselves on Him for protection and sustenance. This applies to every person who depends on the Lord, but will apply most especially to the tribulation remnant in the darkest hours of the night of the Lord's absence just before the dawn of His return.

"The shadow of the Almighty (Shadday: the All Sufficient One)"

If the picture is of a person who is lodging during the night, the question may be asked why it is that the All Sufficient Lord is needed to provide a protecting **shadow** under which to lodge. The answer is that during the long night of the Lord's absence there are hostile light sources from which a believer needs to be protected in the divine shadow. This is consistent with New Testament teaching where we learn that Satan is transformed into an "angel of light" (2 Corinthians 11:14) and his followers, who seek to give others an erroneous moral compass, are called "wandering stars" (Jude 15). The suggestion is that the believer, seeking protection under the shadow of the Almighty, is claiming asylum from the attentions of hostile, possibly satanically-energised, light sources. One is also reminded of the night the Lord Jesus was betrayed, when the hostile crowd came searching for the Light of the World with "lanterns, torches and weapons" (John 18:3). His disciples, however, were secure. He said simply, "If ye therefore seek Me, let these go their way" (John 18:8). This was because the disciples' security that night was guaranteed by the Lord Himself:

John 18:9
"That the saying might be fulfilled, which He spake, Of them which Thou gavest Me have I lost none."

The believer who abides in Him is secure from all attacks of the evil one.

The promise of protection from hostile evil forces

Psalm 91:3-4

3 "Surely He shall deliver thee from the snare of the fowler, *and* from the noisome pestilence.
4 He shall cover thee with His feathers, and under His wings shalt thou trust: His truth *shall be thy* shield and buckler."

A man, acting in dependence on the Lord, arouses much hostility under several images:

The snare of the fowler – out to trap and to kill, thus robbing the victim of freedom and life

The noisome pestilence (literally: an epidemic of wicked desires) – to rob the victim of fellowship with God

If we study the phrase, "snare of the fowler", we discover that Hosea likens a false prophet in Israel to the snare of the fowler:

Hosea 9:8
"The watchman of Ephraim *was* with my God: *but* the prophet *is* a **snare of a fowler** in all his ways, *and* hatred in the house of his God."

Once we understand that the metaphor of a "snare of a fowler" is used to describe a false prophet, it is clear that the "snare" refers to the prophet, and the "fowler" to the being who handles and controls the prophet. It is in the context of false teaching that we meet the phrase in 2 Timothy 2:24-26, "snare of the devil".

2 Timothy 2:24-26
24 "And the servant of the Lord must not strive; but be gentle unto all *men*, apt to teach, patient,
25 In meekness instructing those that oppose themselves; if God peradventure will give them repentance to the acknowledging of the truth;
26 And *that* they may recover themselves out of **the snare of the devil**, who are taken captive by him at his will."

A consideration of these two passages could lead to the conclusion that the "snare" in view is the false prophet and that the "fowler" is his handler, namely Satan himself.

In Proverbs 6:1-5, we discover that the man who strikes an agreement with a stranger needs to be delivered as a bird from the hand of the fowler.

Proverbs 6:1-5
1 "My son, if thou be surety for thy friend, *if* thou hast stricken thy hand with a **stranger,**
2 Thou art snared with the words of thy mouth, thou art taken with the words of thy mouth.
3 Do this now, my son, and deliver thyself, when thou art come into the hand of thy friend; go, humble thyself, and make sure thy friend.
4 Give not sleep to thine eyes, nor slumber to thine eyelids.
5 Deliver thyself as a roe from the hand *of the hunter*, and as a bird from the **hand of the fowler.**"

In John 10:5, it is clear that the "stranger" is the counterfeit to the true shepherd, i.e. the false shepherd, whom the sheep will not follow. So the very similar Old Testament terms, **"snare of the fowler"** and **"hand of the fowler"**, depict for us the false prophet and the stranger (identified as the false shepherd in John 10:5) respectively (see Appendix 2). Of course, the false prophet and the false shepherd are one and the same person, a man who will yet arise under the control of the "fowler", i.e. Satan. This false-prophet, false-shepherd figure will be a counterfeit to the Person of Christ, Who is the true Prophet and the true Shepherd. In a special way, this will be fulfilled in a future day when the true remnant of Israel will act in complete dependence on the Lord and not fall for the lie of the false prophet/shepherd/antichrist counterfeit to Christ (Appendix 3). Notice that the protection against the snare of the fowler is **truth**: "His truth shall be thy shield and buckler" (verse 4). The conflict underlying this Psalm is between truth and falsehood, righteousness and wickedness, Christ and the devil. The reign of this evil person, the "snare of the fowler", is accompanied by "the noisome pestilence: (literally the pestilence of wickedness)". A pestilence is an epidemic which swallows up whole populations. A "pestilence of wicked desires" is an epidemic of wickedness. This will find its fulfilment in the man of sin (2 Thessalonians 2:3) who will champion wickedness globally in the tribulation. For those who dare to stand against this evil there is a promise: "He shall cover thee with His feather (singular)" (Psalm 91:4). What resources of divine protection! All that is required to protect us safely is one feather while there is the reserve protection of the entire wing. This removes all fear from the pilgrim. Moreover, there is the prospect of seeing the defeat and the punishment (reward) of the wicked ones.

A complete peace –"thou shalt not be afraid" – in the heart of the hidden believer

Psalm 91:5-7

> 5 "Thou shalt not be afraid for the terror by night; *nor* for the arrow *that* flieth by day;
> 6 *Nor* for the pestilence *that* walketh in darkness; *nor* for the destruction (Hebrew: *ketev*) *that* wasteth at noonday.
> 7 A thousand shall fall at thy side, and ten thousand at thy right hand; *but* it shall not come nigh thee."

Verses 5-7 list for us the punishment of the "wicked ones" which the dependent man will witness. These are the people who have fallen for the snare of the fowler and the pestilence of wickedness.

"The destruction (*ketev*) that wasteth" is a phrase employing an unusual word for destruction. Moses used it in Deuteronomy 32:22-24 to describe the future judgment on the nation.

Deuteronomy 32:22-24

> 22 "For a fire is kindled in Mine anger, and shall burn unto the lowest hell, and shall consume the earth with her increase, and set on fire the foundations of the mountains.
> 23 I will heap mischiefs upon them; I will spend Mine arrows upon them.
> 24 They shall be burnt with hunger, and devoured with burning heat, and with bitter destruction (Hebrew *ketev*): I will also send the teeth of beasts upon them, with the poison of serpents of the dust."

Similarly, "the pestilence that walketh in darkness" and the "fear by night" may be allusions to the many dreadful judgments of Revelation 6:8.

Revelation 6:8
"And I looked, and behold a pale horse: and his name that sat on him was Death, and Hell followed with him. And power was given unto them over the fourth part of the earth, to kill with sword, and with hunger, and with death, and with the beasts of the earth."

While thousands shall fall, seized with fear in that coming day, the "Dependent Man" will be strengthened in the Lord. This dreaded period of tribulation, when satanic power shall attain its zenith, will swiftly come to an end with the return of the Lord Jesus Christ in glory. This will bring about the recompense of divine judgment meted out upon the wicked ones. This will be witnessed by the tribulation saints.

Psalm 91:8
"Only with thine eyes shalt thou behold and see the reward of the wicked (ones)."

The reason why the "Dependent Man" in this dark period is enabled to withstand the persecutions and trials of that day is because Satan was defeated over 2000 years earlier by the Lord Jesus Christ. This is the subject matter of the second part of the Psalm.

Part 2 of the Psalm (Psalm 91:9-16)

The victory of the Lord Jesus over Satan 2000 years ago
This part of the Psalm is all about the Lord Jesus and His victory over Satan. At the time of writing, it was obviously a prophecy. A literal translation of verse 9 shows that the Psalmist is addressing the Lord Jesus directly under His title of "Jehovah". This is another evidence of the deity of Christ within the Old Testament.
Literal translation of Psalm 91:9-10:

Psalm 91:9-10
9 "Because Thou, O Lord (Jehovah), my refuge, hast made the Most High Thy habitation;
10 There shall no evil befall Thee, neither shall any plague come nigh Thy dwelling."

Verse 9 shows that it is the Lord, the Psalmist's refuge, Who makes the Most High His habitation. With this translation accords the English Revised version.

Psalm 91:9 (English Revised Version)
"For Thou, O LORD, art my refuge! Thou hast made the Most High Thy habitation."

Here the Psalmist is addressing Deity as "Thou, O Lord". This Divine

Person to Whom he speaks is the Psalmist's refuge. However, this divine Person abides in (or has made for His habitation) the Most High God. This, along with Psalm 110:1, is yet another Old Testament proof of the equality of the Lord Jesus to His Father:

Psalm 110:1
> "The Lord said unto my Lord..."

The ascension and entrance into heaven

Psalm 91:11-12
> 11 "For He shall give His angels charge over Thee, to keep Thee in all Thy ways.
> 12 They shall bear Thee up in *their* hands, lest Thou dash Thy foot against a stone."

The Psalm now moves to the occasion of the ascension of the Lord Jesus when the angels would bear Him up heavenwards.

Luke tells us that He was "carried" up into heaven.

Luke 24:50
> 50 "And He led them out as far as to Bethany, and He lifted up His hands, and blessed them.
> 51 And it came to pass, while He blessed them, He was parted from them, and **carried up into heaven**."

When He came to earth He came alone. When He returned He was carried up as the Victor into heaven.

What a sight! The Dependent Man Who lived a perfect life of total pleasure to God is now carried up into heaven where He is now the Man in the Glory.

The reason why Satan did not quote the whole section

During our Lord's temptation, the devil quotes verses 11 and 12; not surprisingly, he leaves out Psalm 91:9-10 as these verses prove so clearly the Deity of Christ. He also leaves out verse 13 since it describes the defeat of Satan by the Lord Jesus. Satan only quotes verses 11 and 12 and does so completely out of context. The lesson is that most doctrinal error emerges from passages which have been taken out of context. Since this passage is quoted by the devil during the temptation in the wilderness it is worthwhile reminding ourselves of that event.

Matthew 4:3-4
> 3 "And when the tempter came to Him, he said, If Thou be the Son of God, command that these stones be made bread.
> 4 But He answered and said, It is written, Man shall not live by bread alone, but by every word that proceedeth out of the mouth of God."

Satan first of all tried to question the Deity of the Lord Jesus by saying: "If Thou be the Son of God, command that these stones be made bread". Perhaps a paraphrase might be: "What better way to show Thy Deity than changing stones into bread!" The Lord reminded him that He was not only God but also Man with these words: "Man shall not live by bread alone, but by every word that proceedeth out of the mouth of God". Apparently accepting that the Lord was indeed God, he now asks Him to demonstrate His Dependent Manhood by bringing Him up into the holy city, setting Him on a pinnacle of the Temple (Matt 4:5-6) and inviting Him to cast Himself down, backing up his request with an incomplete quotation from Psalm 91:

Matthew 4:6
"He shall give His angels charge concerning Thee: and in *their* hands they shall bear Thee up, lest at any time Thou dash Thy foot against a stone." (Matthew 4:6).
The Lord replies with a statement of His deity:

Matthew 4:7
"Jesus said unto him, It is written again, Thou shalt not tempt the Lord thy God."

Satan was attempting to separate the truth of His Dependent Manhood from His deity. Herein is the wonder of the Person of Christ. He was truly the Dependent Man but was still wholly God. As such, He would not and could not step outside of God's will as to the manner in which His Perfect Dependent Manhood would be displayed universally. God had a plan to display the perfection of the Dependent Manhood of His Son but it would most certainly not be in the scheme suggested by Satan. Here we see the error of partially quoting a verse of Scripture. When we complete the verse we find out exactly how God the Father would glorify and display the wonder of the Perfect Dependent Man to the universe. It was in death, burial, resurrection, ascension and exaltation.

Psalm 91:13
"Thou shalt tread upon the lion and adder: the young lion and the dragon shalt Thou trample under feet."

The victory over Satan would occur when He would bruise the serpent's head. Herein is the promise to our fallen first parents fulfilled. It would be the last Adam (1 Corinthians 15:45) Who would tread on the lion, the adder, the young lion and the dragon. These are all pictures of Satan and, not surprisingly, Satan did not complete the verse in his quotation.

God's declares His pleasure in Christ
How would the Perfect Dependent Man win such a victory over the dragon? From verse 14 to the end of the Psalm, the speaker is now God the Father Who declares His pleasure in the life and death and resurrection of Christ.

Psalm 91:14
"Because He hath set His love upon Me, therefore will I deliver Him: I will set Him on high, because He hath known My Name."

Verse 14 declares the love of the Lord Jesus for God His Father. In this regard He fulfilled absolutely the first five commandments. We should remind ourselves that the ten commandments within the Law of Moses are divided in two. The first five commandments are God-ward and are summarised by, "Thou shalt love the Lord thy God". They end with the promise, "that thy days might be long". The second five commandments are man-ward and are summarised by, "thou shalt love thy neighbour as thyself". This is the basis of the incident in the life of the Lord Jesus recorded by Matthew.

Matthew 22:35-40
> 35 "Then one of them, *which was* a lawyer, asked *Him a question*, tempting Him, and saying,
> 36 Master, which *is* the great commandment in the Law?
> 37 Jesus said unto him, **Thou shalt love the Lord thy God with all thy heart, and with all thy soul, and with all thy mind**.
> 38 This is the first and great commandment.
> 39 And the second *is* like unto it, **Thou shalt love thy neighbour as thyself**.
> 40 On these two commandments hang all the Law and the Prophets."

Psalm 91:14 makes clear that the Lord Jesus fulfilled the first five commandments. He loved His Father in heaven and fulfilled His will in full. In this He was the Perfect Dependent Man Who always did those things which pleased the Father. Why then did His life end at 33 ½ years of age, if the promise at the end of the fifth commandment was to be fulfilled – "that thy days should be long" ? The answer is that **this promise was fulfilled in resurrection** when the prophecy in Isaiah 53:10 was also fulfilled: "He shall see His seed, He shall prolong His days."

Isaiah 53:10
> "Yet it pleased the Lord to bruise Him; He hath put *Him* to grief: when Thou shalt make His soul an offering for sin, He shall see *His* seed, **He shall prolong *His* days**, and the pleasure of the Lord shall prosper in His hand."

Fulfilment of the first five commandments, i.e. His perfect love Godwards, demanded the **resurrection** of the Lord Jesus. Fulfilment of the second five commandments demanded that He love His neighbour as Himself. In this He became neighbour to man, His creature, and loved Him to the extent that **He died for man** on account of His creature's sin. The second five commandments **demanded His death** to make propitiation for sin because He loved His neighbour as Himself. The first five commandments **demanded His resurrection** because He loved the Lord His God. This is the argument being presented in this Psalm where the death, resurrection and ascension of the Lord are being set forth.

Psalm 91:14
> "Because **He hath set His love upon Me**, therefore will I deliver Him: I will set Him on high, because He hath known My Name."

The deliverance in verse 14 is not a deliverance from death but a deliverance right through death, to the other side of death i.e. resurrection and ascension. This is the meaning of **Hebrews 5:7.**

Hebrews 5:6-10
6 "As He saith also in another *place,* Thou *art* a Priest for ever after the order of Melchisedec.
7 Who in the days of His flesh, when He had offered up prayers and supplications with strong crying and tears unto Him that was able to **save Him from** (Greek: *ek* meaning "out of") **death,** and was heard in that He feared;
8 Though He were a Son, yet learned He obedience by the things which He suffered;
9 And being made perfect, He became the Author of eternal salvation unto all them that obey Him;
10 Called of God an High Priest after the order of Melchisedec."

In Hebrews 5:7, the Lord Jesus prays unto Him Who "was able to save Him from death". The word "from" (Greek: *ek)* means "out of" implying going right through to the other side of this experience. It is, in fact, a reference to His impending resurrection which was the basis of the intercessory prayer of Hebrews 5:7 (see Psalm 2). This is what is in view in Psalm 91:14 where the One Who loved His God is delivered even to the extent of ascension and to sitting on the throne "set on High".
    The next verse is a further elaboration on how God would deliver Him.

Psalm 91:15
"He shall call upon Me, and I will answer Him: I *will be* with Him in trouble; I will deliver Him, and honour Him."

God will answer Him when He calls. We have seen in Psalm 22 that the word to "answer" here carries the meaning of the sacrifice being answered by fire. It was at Calvary when the Sacrifice of the Lord Jesus was accepted by the divine judgment falling upon Him. This was how God would show His pleasure in the Dependent Man. This was His deliverance and it was right through death i.e. in resurrection. In resurrection God would honour Him.
    This is what is being referred to in the next verse.

Psalm 91:16
"With long life will I satisfy Him, and shew Him My salvation."

In the context, this is salvation from death, i.e. resurrection, in the same sense as in Hebrews 5:7 when He prayed to Him Who would "**save** Him from death". It was in this that Satan was defeated and he who had the power of death, that is the devil, was destroyed (Hebrews 2:14).
    Thus the Psalm concludes with a risen Man Who has defeated Satan and death. What a triumphant contrast with the start of the preceding Psalm,

Psalm 90, where man is described in all his *enosh* weakness following the disaster of the fall in Eden's garden!

Conclusion

Whilst this Psalm describes the hostility of the powers of darkness against the believer in our Lord Jesus Christ, it emphasises the security to be found hiding under the feather of the overarching wing of the Almighty. This is a place of provision and peace amidst all the frightening chaos outside. Central to this security is the death, burial, resurrection and ascension to glory of the Perfect Dependent Man, the Lord Jesus Himself.

17

PSALMS 92-94

Introduction

Psalms 92-94 are not quoted in the New Testament and are not Messianic Psalms.

They are situated in the Psalter between two Messianic Psalms, both of which are quoted in the New Testament (Psalms 91 and 95). Therefore, Psalms 92-94 must be considered along with Psalm 91 to understand the significance of the position of Psalm 95 in the Psalter as well as its contextual use within the New Testament in Hebrews 3 and 4.

Psalms 91-94 form the introduction to Psalm 95. Psalms 91-93 are prophetic Psalms set during the future tribulation period (Psalm 91), at the end of the tribulation period (Psalm 92) and at the start of the millennium (Psalm 93).

They are then followed by Psalm 94 which is a cry or prayer to God that the prophecies of Psalms 91-93 be expedited to an early fulfilment. There is a poignancy in the prayer of Psalm 94 as the Psalmist confesses his perplexity at the apparent delay in the fulfilment of Psalms 91-93, particularly when the godly are being persecuted. This leads to Psalm 95 which is the divine answer to this quandary – the provision of **divine rest** to the perplexed believer in the midst of his adversity. There are three different Hebrew words for "rest" in this cluster of Psalms:

1 Shabbat rest in Psalm 92

Psalm 92 is entitled, "A Psalm *or* Song for the Sabbath (Hebrew: *shabbat* meaning 'rest') day". This is because it anticipates the imminent dawn of the millennial Sabbath. One could call this Psalm a song in anticipation of that coming day of millennial rest. Psalm 93 goes on to describe the conditions that will pertain during that great period of millennial rest for this world.

2 Hashkatah rest in Psalm 94

Psalm 94 looks into the heart of a believer who is not entirely at rest in the midst of the persecutions and shows how the instruction (chastening) of the Lord and the teaching of the Lord out of His Law (Psalm 94:12) can give such a believer a blessed rest (*hashkatah*) of soul (Psalm 94:13).

Psalm 94:12-13

12 "Blessed *is* the man whom Thou chastenest, O Lord, **and teachest him out of Thy Law;**
13 That thou mayest **give him rest** (Hebrew: *lehashkit*) from the days of adversity, until the pit be digged for the wicked."

3 Mnuchah rest of Psalm 95

Psalm 95 is the Lord teaching from His Law how a believer can rest in glorious anticipation of the certainty of the coming Kingdom. In Psalm 95, the rest is at a higher level than the *hashkatah* rest revealed in Psalm 94:13. It is a *mnuchah* rest, which the context shows is a rest which God Himself enjoys in anticipation of the fulfilment of the prophecies which He Himself has given. The three passages of the Law which form the basis of this instruction are detailed in Psalm 95. They are the *Massah* and *Meribah* incidents in Exodus 17 and Numbers 20, and the *Kadesh* incident (Numbers 14) when the Lord's **power** in the signs and wonders was questioned. A study of these three incidents will show the security of those who rest in God.

The doctrinal progression within Psalms 91-93

Psalm 91 primarily describes the security which will be afforded to those who refuse the lies of the false prophet in the tribulation period. It traces this to the victory of the risen Lord Jesus Christ over the Lion and the Adder, firstly during His perfect life when Satan was ineffective in the temptation and then His victory of resurrection and ascension.

PSALM 92

(A Psalm or Song for the sabbath day.)
1 It is a good thing to give thanks unto the LORD, and to sing praises unto Thy Name, O most High:
2 To shew forth Thy lovingkindness in the morning, and Thy faithfulness every night,
3 Upon an instrument of ten strings, and upon the psaltery; upon the harp with a solemn sound.
4 For Thou, LORD, hast made me glad through Thy work: I will triumph in the works of Thy hands.
5 O LORD, how great are Thy works! and Thy thoughts are very deep.
6 A brutish man knoweth not; neither doth a fool understand this.
7 When the wicked spring as the grass, and when all the workers of iniquity do flourish; it is that they shall be destroyed for ever:
8 But Thou, LORD, art most high for evermore.
9 For, lo, Thine enemies, O LORD, for, lo, Thine enemies shall perish; all the workers of iniquity shall be scattered.

10 But my horn shalt Thou exalt like the horn of an unicorn: I shall be anointed with fresh oil.

11 Mine eye also shall see my desire on mine enemies, and mine ears shall hear my desire of the wicked that rise up against me.

12 The righteous shall flourish like the palm tree: he shall grow like a cedar in Lebanon.

13 Those that be planted in the house of the LORD shall flourish in the courts of our God.

14 They shall still bring forth fruit in old age; they shall be fat and flourishing;

15 To shew that the LORD is upright: He is my Rock, and there is no unrighteousness in Him.

Psalm 92 is set further along the prophetic time line and focuses on the events of the end of the tribulation, when not just some but **all** the workers of iniquity will be scattered.

Psalm 92:9

"For, lo, Thine enemies, O Lord, for, lo, Thine enemies shall perish; all the workers of iniquity shall be scattered."

This identifies the timing of the Psalm as subsequent to the great tribulation, i.e. the start of the millennium. Then the remnant believers in the tribulation, who are the central subject matter of the Psalm, will say:

Psalm 92:11

"Mine eye also shall see *my desire* on mine enemies, *and* mine ears shall hear *my desire* of the wicked that rise up against me."

These saints will have just come through the dreaded tribulation period when the anti-God propaganda shall have saturated this world's philosophies and thought-systems. They will truly rejoice to be able to freely and safely declare aloud the great truth that God is characterised by "lovingkindness" and "faithfulness" (Psalm 92:2) and that He is "upright (dependable) " and "no unrighteousness is in Him" (Psalm 92:15). As they review the divine programme they will exclaim:

Psalm 92:5

"O Lord, how great are Thy works! *and* Thy thoughts are very deep."

What a contrast to the natural or "brutish" man (Psalm 92:6) who rejected the Lord and in his lifetime never got beyond the miserable status of being unable to know God!

Psalm 92:6

"A brutish man knoweth not; neither doth a fool understand this."

Their destruction is "forever" (Psalm 92:7). In contrast to these ungodly ones, there is given to the godly the promise of ageless youth:

Psalm 92:14

"They shall still bring forth fruit in old age; they shall be fat (fresh) and flourishing."

Age shall not spoil enjoyment of Him by those who love Him. What a lovely prophecy of what life will be like in the glorious millennial era! What a contrast to the lie of Satan to our first parents in the garden! Their spiritual and physical death was first manifested in the aging process, followed by disease, frailty and death. These considerations now show why the title of the Psalm is: "A Psalm or Song for the sabbath day (*shabbat* meaning 'rest')". The Sabbath in view is that great millennial Sabbath when God shall rest in the midst of His people in a healed earth when Christ reigns supreme. This leads on to the next Psalm which beautifully describes that event.

PSALM 93

1 The Lord reigneth, He is clothed with majesty; the Lord is clothed with strength, wherewith He hath girded Himself: the world also is stablished, that it cannot be moved.
2 Thy throne is established of old: Thou art from everlasting.
3 The floods have lifted up, O Lord, the floods have lifted up their voice; the floods lift up their waves.
4 The Lord on high is mightier than the noise of many waters, yea, than the mighty waves of the sea.
5 Thy testimonies are very sure: holiness becometh Thine house, O Lord, for ever.

Psalm 93 is a further progression on the prophetic theme of God's programme, this time focussing on God's perspective on these events. We read that the result is: "Holiness becometh Thine House, O LORD forever" (Psalm 93:5). The Word "becometh" suggests "dwelling comfortably". Note 1 The fact that now in the millennial temple the Holiness of God can "dwell comfortably" means that the outward display of the *Shechinah* glory in the House of the Lord in Jerusalem will not be conditional as it was in the time of the kings of Israel. Ezekiel saw in his vision the glory of the Lord leaving the temple in Jerusalem, effectively because God could not dwell comfortably among His ancient people amidst all their sin and defilement. What a day that will be when the promise of the Lord dwelling in the midst of His people, and they dwelling around Him, shall no longer be conditional, but guaranteed into perpetuity! This will arise only when the truth of God has triumphed in human hearts. What a defeat this event will mean for Satan! When this happens the conditions within Moses' Law of granting tenure of the land have been satisfied and replaced by the unconditional tenure of the land in the covenant with Abraham. This, of course, is only made possible through Christ. The realisation of this calls for the worship and praise of Psalm 93.

Psalms 91-93 deal with three sequential prophetic time periods. Psalm 91 considers the dark days of tribulation. Psalm 92 considers the end of the tribulation and the scattering of **all** God's enemies. Psalm 93 considers the glad day when the Lord Jesus is reigning supreme. Accordingly, Psalms 91-93 are Psalms of **prophecy**. This leads to a perplexing problem in the minds of many believers down through the centuries. Why does God seem to delay the fulfilment of His prophecies? The implications of and answers to this question form the basis of Psalm 94.

PSALM 94

1 O LORD God, to Whom vengeance belongeth; O God, to Whom vengeance belongeth, shew Thyself.

2 Lift up Thyself, Thou Judge of the earth: render a reward to the proud.

3 Lord, how long shall the wicked, how long shall the wicked triumph?

4 How long shall they utter and speak hard things? and all the workers of iniquity boast themselves?

5 They break in pieces Thy people, O Lord, and afflict Thine heritage.

6 They slay the widow and the stranger, and murder the fatherless.

7 Yet they say, The Lord shall not see, neither shall the God of Jacob regard it.

8 Understand, ye brutish among the people: and ye fools, when will ye be wise?

9 He that planted the ear, shall He not hear? He that formed the eye, shall He not see?

10 He that chastiseth the heathen, shall not He correct? He that teacheth man knowledge, shall not He know?

11 The Lord knoweth the thoughts of man, that they are vanity.

12 Blessed is the man whom Thou chastenest, O Lord, and teachest him out of Thy Law;

13 That Thou mayest give him rest from the days of adversity, until the pit be digged for the wicked.

14 For the Lord will not cast off His people, neither will He forsake His inheritance.

15 But judgment shall return unto righteousness: and all the upright in heart shall follow it.

16 Who will rise up for me against the evildoers? or who will stand up for me against the workers of iniquity?

17 Unless the Lord had been my help, my soul had almost dwelt in silence.

18 When I said, My foot slippeth; Thy mercy, O Lord, held me up.

19 In the multitude of my thoughts within me Thy comforts delight my soul.

20 Shall the throne of iniquity have fellowship with Thee, which frameth mischief by a law?

21 They gather themselves together against the soul of the righteous, and condemn the innocent blood.

22 But the Lord is my defence; and my God is the Rock of my refuge.

23 And He shall bring upon them their own iniquity, and shall cut them off in their own wickedness; yea, the Lord our God shall cut them off.

The perplexity of delays in the fulfilment of prophecy

Psalm 94 follows directly on from the prophecies of Psalms 91-93 and is a Psalm of **prayer** for the prophecies of Psalms 91-93 to be fulfilled. This is clear in the first two verses which are a prayer for the Kinsman Avenger to arise and be manifested (appear) and avenge the adversary.

Psalm 94:1-2

1 "O LORD God, to Whom vengeance belongeth; O God, to Whom vengeance belongeth, shew Thyself (Hebrew: cause Thyself to appear).
2 Lift up Thyself, Thou Judge of the earth: render a reward to the proud."

This is a prayer for the appearing in glory of the Lord Jesus at the end of the tribulation. The truth of the "appearing" is revealed elsewhere in the Old Testament (Malachi 3:2).

Malachi 3:2

"But who may abide the day of His coming? and who shall stand when He **appeareth**? for He *is* like a refiner's fire, and like fullers' soap."

It was recognised in the Old Testament that this "appearing" will spell judgment to the enemies of the Lord and bring comfort and relief to the remnant at that time.

Similarly, in the New Testament this same occasion is spoken of in 2 Thessalonians 2:8 when the wicked one (lawless one) shall be consumed before the appearing (*epiphaneia*) of the Lord Jesus Christ.

2 Thessalonians 2:8

"And then shall that Wicked be revealed, whom the Lord shall consume with the spirit of His mouth, and shall destroy with the brightness (**appearing** *epiphaneia*) of His coming (*parousia*)."

This same event is also described in 2 Thessalonians 1:7 when the Lord Jesus shall "be revealed" from heaven.

2 Thessalonians 1:7-9

7 "…when the Lord Jesus shall **be revealed** from heaven with His mighty angels,
8 In flaming fire taking vengeance on them that know not God, and that obey not the gospel of our Lord Jesus Christ:
9 Who shall be punished with everlasting destruction from the presence of the Lord, and from the glory of His power."

The event prompting the prayer of Psalm 94:1-2 is the apparent delay in the Lord bringing to fulfilment the events prophesied in Psalms 91-94. In fact, this delay has led the Psalmist to question how long it can continue.

Psalm 94:3-4

3 "Lord, how long shall the wicked, how long shall the wicked triumph?
4 How long shall they utter and speak hard things? and all the workers of iniquity boast themselves?"

There is nothing wrong with a believer wondering how long it will be until God fulfils His promises. However, in such circumstances there is the possibility of even faithful saints, prior to the appearing and manifestation of our Lord Jesus, being beset with perplexities as to why there are divine delays in this matter. Any apparent delay in the arrival of the Kinsman Avenger is all the more difficult to explain when the ongoing suffering of the widow, the stranger and the fatherless is considered.

Psalm 94:5-7
> 5 "They break in pieces Thy people, O Lord, and afflict Thine heritage.
> 6 They slay the widow and the stranger, and murder the fatherless.
> 7 Yet they say, The Lord shall not see, neither shall the God of Jacob regard it."

Interestingly, it is the same dilemma in Luke 18:1-8 when the Lord told the parable of the unjust judge who was slow to avenge the widow of her adversary.

Luke 18:1-8
> 1 "And He spake a parable unto them to this end, that men ought always to pray, and not to faint;
> 2 Saying, There was in a city a judge, which feared not God, neither regarded man:
> 3 And there was a widow in that city; and she came unto him, saying, Avenge me of mine adversary.
> 4 And he would not for a while: but afterward he said within himself, Though I fear not God, nor regard man;
> 5 Yet because this widow troubleth me, I will avenge her, lest by her continual coming she weary me.
> 6 And the Lord said, Hear what the unjust judge saith.
> 7 And shall not God avenge His own elect, which cry day and night unto Him, though He bear long with them?
> 8 I tell you that He will avenge them speedily. Nevertheless when the Son of man cometh, shall He find faith on the earth?"

The slowness of the unjust judge was because he was unjust and did not care. The purpose in the Lord telling this parable was to show that the delay in the appearing of Himself as future Kinsman Avenger was not because the Lord is unjust. He **will** avenge His elect who cry to Him day and night (Luke 18:7). Believers can be reassured regarding the Lord's delays and have no cause to doubt His Word. The parable of the unjust judge in Luke 18:1-8 is essentially a New Testament commentary on Psalm 94:3-7, when the elect are also crying for the Judge to arise and avenge: "O LORD God, to Whom vengeance belongeth; O God, to Whom vengeance belongeth, shew Thyself (Hebrew: cause Thyself to appear)".

Psalm 94:19 shows how thoughts of perplexity and disquiet can arise in the minds of true believers in circumstances of persecution when there may be a perception of an apparent delay in the Lord's appearing to judge the adversaries of God.

Psalm 94:19

"In the multitude of my (perplexed) thoughts (Hebrew: *sarap*) within me
Thy comforts delight my soul."

The word for thought is an unusual word which carries the idea of
perplexity (Gesenius' Hebrew and English Lexicon of the Old Testament).
God's answer to these perplexing thoughts is to comfort His people through
His Law and give them **rest** in the midst of the trial (verse 13) throughout
those long dark days "until" such times as "the pit be digged for the wicked".

Psalm 94:12-14

12 "Blessed *is* the man whom Thou chastenest, O Lord, and teachest him
out of Thy Law;
13 That Thou mayest give him rest from the days of adversity, until the pit
be digged for the wicked.
14 For the Lord will not cast off His people, neither will He forsake His
inheritance."

Psalm 94:18-19

18 "When I said, My foot slippeth; Thy mercy, O Lord, held me up.
19 In the multitude of my thoughts within me Thy comforts delight my
soul."

The gracious reason for God's delay

There is a reason for God's delay. In the delay, the believer learns seven
things about the power of the Lord regarding His people.
We learn how the Lord:
1 chastises (instructs) us (verse 12)
2 teaches us (verse 12)
3 pacifies us (gives us rest in the **midst** of the trouble) (verse 13)
4 pledges never ever to cast us off (verse 14)
5 pledges never ever to forsake us (verse 14)
6 sustains us (holds us up) (verse 18)
7 delights us with His comforts (verse 19)
These precious lessons concerning the power of God are only learned in
the experiences of life. The Lord's delays are not denials.

Examples of how the Lord ministers to His own in the midst of the delay

1 Lazarus and the family in Bethany

A lovely example of a divine delay is in John 11:6 when the Lord delayed
His journey to the home of Lazarus in Bethany.

John 11:4-6

4 "When Jesus heard *that*, He said, This sickness is not unto death, **but for
the glory of God, that the Son of God might be glorified thereby.**
5 Now Jesus loved Martha, and her sister, and Lazarus.

6 When He had heard therefore that he was sick, He abode two days still in the same place where He was."

This delay was not out of lack of love for Mary, Martha and Lazarus. On the contrary! It was that the Lord should be glorified in the experience of these believers (John 11:4-6) and that the disciples should believe in Him (John 11:15). May we take courage from this.

The delay in this Psalm, as with all divinely ordered delays, is of strictly limited duration. It is only **"until** the pit be digged for the wicked" (Psalm 94:13).

Although God's delays are not denials, they do constitute tests for our faithfulness to Him, allowing the Lord to prove to the universe, including Satan, that we are faithful to Him (remember the conversation Satan had with God about Job in Job 1:8-12). Before God causes His power to appear in avenging judgment, He wants to make manifest His great power to help us, sustain us and give us **rest** (verse 13). The rest occurs **during** the trial and arises from the reassurance within that the Lord hears and sees everything and will eventually avenge.

2 John the Baptist in prison

Perhaps it is John the Baptist who provides the best known example in Scripture of a servant of God being overcome with perplexity of mind in the context of intense suffering for Christ's sake and an apparent delay in direct divine intervention.

> Matthew 11:1-6
> 1 "And it came to pass, when Jesus had made an end of commanding His twelve disciples, He departed thence to teach and to preach in their cities.
> 2 Now when John had heard in the prison the works of Christ, he sent two of his disciples,
> 3 And said unto Him, Art Thou He that should come, or do we look for another?
> 4 Jesus answered and said unto them, Go and shew John again those things which ye do hear and see:
> 5 **The blind receive their sight, and the lame walk, the lepers are cleansed, and the deaf hear, the dead are raised up, and the poor have the gospel preached to them.**
> 6 And blessed is *he*, whosoever shall not be offended in Me."

In Matthew 11:5, the Lord reminded John of **His preaching the gospel to the poor** and **His miraculous works of healing**. John was very familiar with Isaiah and preached from Isaiah 40, which begins with the comforts of God. He would immediately have understood that the Lord's words were intended to direct his mind to Isaiah's prophecy and especially the passage in Isaiah 61:1-2 where the prophet tells of the coming Messiah **preaching the gospel to the poor** and **performing miraculous works of healing**. Indeed, it was in advance of performing these works that the Lord gave notice in Luke

4:18-19 that Isaiah 61:1-2 was about to be fulfilled in Himself.

Luke 4:18-19

> 18 "The Spirit of the Lord *is* upon Me, because he hath anointed Me **to preach the gospel to the poor**; He hath sent Me to heal the brokenhearted, to preach deliverance to the captives, **and recovering of sight to the blind**, to set at liberty them that are bruised,
> 19 To preach the acceptable year of the Lord."

However, in Luke 4:19 the Lord closed the book and did not complete the reading in Isaiah 61:2 to proclaim "the day of vengeance of our God; **to comfort all that mourn**". The reason was that He had not **yet** come to avenge the adversary and declare the "day of vengeance of our God". This too was the reason for the Lord's non-intervention in John's situation to free him from evil king Herod. As John would have contemplated that the Lord was "preaching the gospel to the poor", he would have understood from Isaiah 61:1 that it was a message of blessing and **not yet** of judgment and vengeance. Nevertheless, the words which had remained unread by the Lord Jesus that day in the synagogue must have come with freshness to his soul: "to comfort those that mourn". We are not told what impact the Lord's reference to Isaiah 61:1-2 in Matthew 11:5 had on this tried servant of God in the prison of Herod. However, it is appropriate to anticipate that the outcome would have been exactly as given in Psalm 94:

Psalm 94:18-19

> 18 "When I said, My foot slippeth; Thy mercy, O Lord, held me up.
> 19 In the multitude of my (perplexed) thoughts within me Thy comforts delight my soul."

The proof of faith's reality during the delay

Backsliding may well begin with doubting God's faithfulness. Unless this is averted early, there is a further step away in the believer's life – it is losing one's identity and separation from the world and may even end in having fellowship with (literally: "joining up with") the throne of iniquity.

Psalm 94:20-22

> 20 "Shall the throne of iniquity have fellowship with Thee, which frameth mischief by a law?
> 21 They gather themselves together against the soul of the righteous, and condemn the innocent blood.
> 22 But the Lord is my defence; and my God *is* the Rock of my refuge."

In the Psalm, the test in the tribulation is so severe that only a true believer will resist the temptation to join up with the beast and the false prophet, who make up "the throne of iniquity". Like Psalm 91, this is another Psalm of testing. Here we see that even if a believer may be beset with perplexity at the apparent delay in the Lord's intervention under the intensity of persecution, he or she is preserved by the Lord from taking the step of joining up with the throne of iniquity. This divine preservation is mighty and is seen in a practical way in the divine comfort and upholding of a believer throughout that trial of faith. It is this divine comfort which not only banishes any doubts and perplexity from a believer's heart but which also "delights" his "soul". Note 2

In the epistle to the Hebrews, the writer emphasises that the delay in the fulfilment of the Old Testament promises of the coming Kingdom was part of the divine plan:

Hebrews 1:13
"Sit on My right hand, **until** I make Thine enemies Thy footstool."

Hebrews 2:8
"Now we see **not yet** all things put under Him."

Hebrews 12:26
"**Yet once more** I shake not the earth only, but also heaven."

The repeated use of the words "**yet**" and "**until**" by the writer of the epistle to the Hebrews refers to the time delay between the Lord's first advent and His coming in glory. Clearly, this was an important aspect of truth, particularly needed to encourage and strengthen the Hebrews believers. Indeed their hands were hanging down and their knees had become feeble during this time delay (Hebrews 12). In fact, the cause of their perplexity is very akin to that affecting the Psalmist in Psalm 94 – distress as to why persecution continues against the Lord's people without His immediate intervention to come and fulfill prophecy through setting up His Kingdom. The answer to this very problem, afflicting an anxious saint in Psalm 94, comes in the ensuing Psalms – Psalms 95-110. Similarly, the problem of the anxious Hebrew believer in the epistle to the Hebrews is solved by an understanding of Psalms 95-110. Not surprisingly, therefore, it is in this very same context that Psalms 95, 97, 102 and 110 are quoted in the epistle to the Hebrews.

1. In Psalm 93:5, the word "becometh" (Hebrew: *naavah*) is derived from a primitive root, meaning "to be at home" (Strong's Exhaustive Concordance), hence the sense of "to dwell comfortably".

2. Psalm 94:19 shows how "Thy comforts" delight the soul of the perplexed believer. "Thy conforts" refer not only to how God comforts a believer, but also include how God Himself is "comforted" in relation to the problem of sin in His universe. We saw in Psalm 90, that in this matter God is fully "comforted" and satisfied through the sacrificial death of the Lord Jesus. How soothing for a perplexed believer to contemplate how God has found "comfort" in Christ. It is this realisation which will "delight the soul."

18
PSALM 95

1 O come, let us sing unto the Lord: let us make a joyful noise to the Rock of our salvation.
2 Let us come before His presence with thanksgiving, and make a joyful noise unto Him with psalms.
3 For the Lord is a great God, and a great King above all gods.
4 In His hand are the deep places of the earth: the strength of the hills is His also.
5 The sea is His, and He made it: and His hands formed the dry land.
6 O come, let us worship and bow down: let us kneel before the Lord our Maker.
7 For He is our God; and we are the people of His pasture, and the sheep of His hand. To day if ye will hear His voice,
8 Harden not your heart, as in the provocation, and as in the day of temptation in the wilderness:
9 When your fathers tempted Me, proved Me, and saw My work.
10 Forty years long was I grieved with this generation, and said, It is a people that do err in their heart, and they have not known My ways:
11 Unto whom I sware in My wrath that they should not enter into My rest.

Introduction

This Psalm is not generally taken as a Messianic Psalm because it does not directly refer to the Lord Jesus Christ. However, it is quoted in Hebrews 3 and 4 in the context of warning the believers of losing their expectancy of the Lord's future Kingdom glory. In this sense it is a Messianic Psalm as to its doctrinal content and is therefore included in this book.

Psalm 95 is divided in two parts: the **worship** of the sheep and the **warning** of the shepherd

1 The worship of the sheep (Psalm 95:1-10)

This section begins with the **worship of the sheep** (verses 1-7). The worshippers in this section refer to themselves as "the people of His pasture, and the sheep of His hand" (verse 7). The section summarises their worship with regard to **Whom they are worshipping** – Jehovah, the Rock of our Salvation (Psalm 95:1) – and **why they are worshipping** – Jehovah's greatness in creation (Psalm 95:3-6) as well as His greatness in caring (shepherding) for His people, who are referred to as "the people of His pasture". (The Hebrew word for "pasture" shares the same root as the Hebrew word for "shepherd").

One might have expected that the Lord's response to such warm words of worship would have been an expression of appreciation. This is not the case. The Lord responds to His people with a warning. They had omitted in their worship to praise Him for His greatness in faithfully carrying out His divinely promised programme of glory.

2 The warning of the Shepherd (Psalm 95:7-11)

This section is entirely devoted to the response of the divine Shepherd to the worship of His sheep. Far from praising His sheep for their words of worship, His response is one of warning and entreaty. He Who can see into the inner recesses of the heart observes that the worshipping "sheep" are at risk of developing "hardness of heart". How solemn that saints engaged in worship should be seen by the Lord to be in great danger of developing hearts which are hard and unresponsive to the voice of the Shepherd! The Shepherd outlines the concerns in His heart, regarding His beloved sheep, with illustrative references to two Old Testament incidents of failure in the history of Israel in the wilderness. These will be discussed in detail later in this chapter but are outlined at this point by way of introduction.

These incidents are firstly (Psalm 95:8-9), the **Massah** and **Meribah** incident of Exodus 17 when Moses smote the bedrock for the water to flow, and secondly (Psalm 95:10), the Kadesh Barnea incident of Numbers 14. In the Massah and Meribah incident, the root cause of the problem was a failure to appreciate the **presence** of the Lord in the midst of the people as they questioned: "Is the Lord among us or not?" (Exodus 17:7). In the Kadesh Barnea incident (Numbers 14) the people questioned the **power of the Lord** to be able to bring them into the Land. Failure to grasp the significance of the **presence** and **power** of the Lord in the midst of His people would have a deleterious effect upon the flock and render any outward expression of worship as insincere. A believer who is consciously enjoying the **presence** of the Lord in his or her life, will not doubt the **power** of the Lord to fulfill His promises. Sadly, however, a believer who has backslidden in heart and is not enjoying the **presence** of the Lord could easily proceed to doubt the **power** of the Lord to fulfill His promises. The thought-flow in the Psalm indicates that these difficulties, which are deep within the heart of a believer, can happen even to someone who is outwardly "making a joyful noise unto the Lord" in a public display of worship to Him. The challenge of this Psalm to each believer is to evaluate one's own life to determine if one is so enjoying the **presence of the Lord in one's life** as to rest in the **power of the Lord to fulfill God's purpose for one's life.** Only a believer in this state of soul can bring worship to the Lord which is pleasing to Him.

The context of this warning

Let us remember that the position of Psalm 95 in the Psalter, coming as it does immediately after Psalm 94 with all its anxiety and perplexity, might just suggest that the worshippers of Psalm 95 are not entirely enjoying their **rest in God** as perhaps they should. The context of the perplexity of Psalm 94 was the delay in the Lord fulfilling His promised prophetic programme of Psalms 91-93. Not surprisingly, then, worship with regard to the Lord carrying out His programme of glory is missing from the worship section of Psalm 95:1-6. The Lord must address this deficit in His people's appreciation of Him.

The second part of the Psalm brings before us God's rest in **anticipation** of the future glorious Kingdom of His Son, and His longing desire that His people of all ages similarly **rest together with Him** in anticipation of that great event being brought to fruition. The point is that a believer who is sharing with God the restful anticipation of the future Kingdom glory of His Son is engaging in fellowship with God regarding prophetic matters, and from that place of nearness to Him feels worship spontaneously arising within a heart softened by the wonder of the wisdom of God. The believer who is **resting together with God** in anticipation of the fulfilment of the divine promises of the Lord Jesus' future glory is enjoying the **presence** of the Lord in his or her life. The outcome of this will be a restful confidence in the **power of God** to ultimately fulfill His prophetic promises.

These two incidents from the wilderness experience of the children of Israel were to teach His worshipping people of their vulnerabilities and need to always keep close to the Lord.

The Massah and Meribah incident where the people lightly esteemed the presence of the Lord

The Psalm brings before us the Shepherd's first warning to the sheep which is based on the *Massah* and *Meribah* incidents in the Law.

Psalm 95:8
> "Harden not your heart, as in the **provocation (Meribah)**, and as in the day of **temptation (Massah)** in the wilderness:"

That was the occasion in Exodus 17:6-7 when the people murmured: "Is the Lord among us or not?"

Exodus 17:6-7
> 6 "Behold, I will stand before thee there upon the (bed)rock in Horeb; and thou shalt smite the (bed)rock, and there shall come water out of it, that the people may drink. And Moses did so in the sight of the elders of Israel.
> 7 And he called the name of the place **Massah**, and **Meribah**, because of the chiding of the children of Israel, and because they tempted the Lord, saying, Is the Lord among us, or not?"

On that occasion, Moses stood beside the bedrock while the Lord stood upon it above and Moses smote the rock. It is, of course, a picture of the Lord Who bears the title of "Bedrock". It was He Who presented Himself to the nation of Israel as God manifested in flesh. The majority of the people questioned His claim of deity. Their response could be paraphrased by the ancient question of their forefathers: "Is the Lord among us or not?" God's response to this question in the experience of His Son many years later was shown illustratively and prophetically in His response to Moses in the wilderness when, in the same context, God asked Moses to smite the bedrock while He stood upon it. Christ the Bedrock was smitten at Calvary, not by Moses, the symbol of the Law, but by God as He bore the judgment of a broken Law.

The significance of the Lord as Bedrock in the Psalm

The Psalm juxtaposes the Lord bearing His title of "Bedrock of our salvation" in verse one with the later reference in verse 8 to the *Massah* incident, when the bedrock on which the Lord stood was smitten by Moses. There is an important lesson here. Were the worshippers in verse one, who acknowledged the Lord as the "Bedrock of our Salvation", at risk of making the same mistake as their forefathers in Exodus 17, who lightly esteemed the **Presence of that same Lord in their midst** as He stood upon the smitten bedrock in the wilderness? The incident in Exodus 17 of the smiting of the bedrock with the Lord upon it, is a picture or type of the Lord Jesus Who bears the title of "Bedrock of our Salvation", when He was smitten at Calvary, not by Moses but by God, so that we who believe in Him as Saviour and Lord might be able to drink of the water of life freely. How important for us to recognise today that this same Lord, Who is the Bedrock of our Salvation and the Bedrock of the ages, longs for us to enjoy and value His presence!

The juxtaposition of the truths of the Lord as the **once**-smitten Bedrock and as Creator and Possessor of this world (Psalm 95:1-6) also reminds us that the result of His being smitten at Calvary by God will be to allow Him to take to Himself undisputed possession of this universe.

When the Lord Jesus reigns supreme, He will be recognised as the rightful owner of this world. It is His by creation and also His by redemption. Resting in calm, certain anticipation of this event is called the *mnuchah* rest of verse 11. It is in this aspect of worship that the Lord does not want His people to fail.

The Kadesh incident (Numbers 13 and 14) when the people lightly esteemed the power of the Lord in His signs and wonders

Having warned the people from the Massah and Meribah incident of the dangers of lightly esteeming the **presence** of the Lord, the Shepherd now extends His warning to the danger of undervaluing the **power** of the Lord in His signs and wonders. In Psalm 95:9-10, He does this by calling to their remembrance the Kadesh Barnea incident of Numbers 14.

Psalm 95:9-10

9 "When your fathers tempted Me, proved me, and saw My work.
10 **Forty years long was I grieved** with *this* generation, and said, It *is* a people that do err in their heart, and they have not known My ways:"

At a first glance we may think that Psalm 95:9-10 also refers to Massah and Meribah. However, let us look at the Spirit of God's commentary on Psalm 95:10 in Hebrews 3:17.

Hebrews 3:17

"But with whom was **He grieved forty years?** *was it* not with them that had sinned, **whose carcases fell in the wilderness?**"

Hebrews 3:17 links the phrase from Psalm 95:10, "forty years long was I grieved with this generation", to the phrase in Numbers 14:29, "whose carcases fell in the wilderness", thus showing that Psalm 95:9-10 refers to the Kadesh failure of Numbers 14 when the people refused to believe Joshua and Caleb, the faithful spies. It was then that God declared that their "carcases would fall by the wilderness".

Numbers 14:28-29

28 "Say unto them, *As truly as* I live, saith the Lord, as ye have spoken in Mine ears, so will I do to you:
29 **Your carcases shall fall in this wilderness**; and all that were numbered of you, according to your whole number, from twenty years old and upward, which have murmured against Me..."

The failure of the people to believe the good report of the two faithful spies, Joshua and Caleb, arose from unbelief (Numbers 14:11) of the signs God had shown them. The people had undervalued the **power of God** in their midst.

Numbers 14:11

"And the Lord said unto Moses, How long will this people provoke Me? and how long will it be ere they believe Me, **for all the signs** which I have shewed among them?"

These "signs", we discover, were demonstrations of "My glory and My miracles" (Numbers 14: 22-23).

Numbers 14:22-23

22 "Because all those men which **have seen My glory, and My miracles**, which I did in Egypt and in the wilderness, and have tempted Me now these ten times, and have not hearkened to My voice;
23 Surely they shall not see the land which I sware unto their fathers, neither shall any of them that provoked Me see it"

The phrase in Numbers 14:22, "those men which have seen My glory and My miracles", suggests strongly that the reference in Psalm 95:9 to the fathers seeing "My work" refers to this incident at Kadesh.

At the Kadesh incident the people lost sight of the **power of the Lord** as revealed in His **signs and wonders and miracles**. This led to them becoming powerless to enter into the Promised Land.

There is a very obvious application of this to the first century A.D. Hebrew Christians. They had witnessed **the signs and wonders and divers miracles** of the Spirit of God following Pentecost. These miracles all carried meaning. Hebrews calls them the "powers of the world (age) to come" (Hebrews 6:5). The "world (age) to come" is the millennium and the "ages to come" are the eternal state (Ephesians 2:7). The New Testament miracles proved God's sincerity in the offer of a literal Kingdom to the nation. The doctrinal basis of this was unveiled in the mystery doctrines of the New Testament which formed the subject matter of the New Testament tongues, as is made clear in 1 Corinthians 14:2 which says, regarding the content of the miraculous tongues, "Howbeit in the Spirit he speaketh mysteries" (1 Corinthians 14:2). Just as the Old Testament children of Israel lightly esteemed the signs and wonders of God in Egypt and the wilderness, so these New Testament Hebrew believers seemed to have missed the doctrinal significance of the New Testament miracles, even to the extent of querying the reality of the coming Kingdom.

Failure to grasp the mysteries meant that they were locked into "babyhood" and were not mature (Hebrews 5:13). (Please see again the explanation for the word "babe" in Psalm 8.) The practical application to us today is simple. Do we understand the mystery doctrines of the New Testament? Do we understand or, perhaps more importantly, do we by faith accept the clear difference between the destiny of Old Testament saints (who have an earthly future) and saints of this Church era (who have a heavenly destiny)? If we do, we are no longer "babes tossed to and fro and carried about with every wind of doctrine" (Ephesians 4:14). If we despise doctrine or think it isn't relevant, or if we imbibe the wrong doctrine such as, for example, denying a future Kingdom on earth of the Lord Jesus, then spiritual loss and cessation of usefulness for God will be sustained. Above all, such a limited perception of the Lord's ability to bring to fruition His programme of glory would compromise the acceptability of any worship to the Lord.

Those who failed to appreciate the truths of the **presence** and **power** of the Lord were penalised by not being allowed to enter into the Lord's rest.

What is the nature of this divine rest which a believer is called upon to share with the Lord?

Psalm 94 brings before us a rest (*hashkatah*) (Psalm 94:13) in the midst of the most intense trial possible. It comes from the Lord Who is instructing His suffering saints from His Law. It is a rest from doubt and fear based on the comforts of God's Word and His upholding hand. It is a rest experienced by believers **on earth** and will be particularly evident during the dark days of tribulation which lie ahead. Psalm 95 lifts this idea of rest to a higher plane. It is of the Lord speaking of His own divine rest – "My rest" (*mnuchah*) (Psalm 95:11). However, what is so beautiful about this Psalm is that this divine rest is one into which the Lord longs for His own saints to enter. Reading about the *mnuchah* rest of Psalm 95:11 in isolation might not, at first, lead to an understanding of this rest as having anything to do with God's rest on completion of creation in Genesis 2. However, this is the interpretation which is provided by the Spirit of God in the New Testament commentary of Psalm 95, given in Hebrews 3 and 4, which shows that this divine rest commenced from creation's morning and continues undisturbed since then.

Hebrews 4:3
> "For we which have believed do enter into rest, as He said, As I have sworn in My wrath, if they shall enter into My rest: although the works were finished from the foundation of the world."

With the benefit of this New Testament exposition, which identifies the divine rest of Psalm 95:11 as dating back to the foundation of the world, we can appreciate the relevance of creation being spoken of at the beginning of Psalm 95 when the Lord is called "the Lord our Maker". It was on completion of His perfect creation that God "rested". However, this Psalm indicates that thousands of years later, God **continues** to rest even to the extent of inviting His creatures to share His rest with Him. This is the crucial point of the passage. The fact that God still continues in His creation rest indicates that it is a rest which **anticipates** the fulfilment of His grand plan for creation.

Bible students sometimes differ as to their understanding of the word "rest" in Psalm 95:11. This is because in various passages this word *mnuchah* can have different meanings and the exact meaning on each occasion must be determined from the context.

The *mnuchah* rest is used in other passages in a three-fold way:

1 Anticipatory (prophetical) rest

This is a rest experienced in **anticipation** (prophetically) of the coming Kingdom of our Lord Jesus Christ. This rest occurs before the Kingdom is actually set up and is caused by the calm confidence of the certainty of this coming event. This rest is a present rest based on unwavering dependence on the promises of God. From the beginning of time, every believer who accepts the certainty of the coming Kingdom and rejoices in this has entered into this **anticipatory rest**. Moreover, Hebrews 4 indicates that God rested from the foundation of the world. When we read, "**before** the foundation of the world", the context is of God's thoughts regarding the Church – "Chosen in Him before the foundation of the world" (Ephesians 1:4). However, when we read, "**from** the foundation of the world", the context is of God's thoughts of the remnant and Israel entering the Kingdom –"inherit the Kingdom prepared for you from the foundation of the world" (Matthew 25:36). (God's thoughts about the Church **precede** His thoughts about the Kingdom. This is because the Kingdom is the arena where Christ and His

Church will be displayed. He that built the house has more honour than the house.) From the foundation of the world God was resting (Hebrews 4:3-4). This is in anticipation of the assured glorification of His Son on this earth. God invites us to enter into this anticipatory rest.

2 Analagous or allegorical rest (pictorial)

A Biblical allegory is an earthly story or event with a prophetical/spiritual meaning. For example, the journey of the Ark of the Covenant from the tabernacle of David to its *mnuchah* (rest) in Solomon's temple constitutes an Old Testament allegory of the return journey of the Lord Jesus Christ to this earth to reign.

Psalm 132:8
"Arise, O LORD, into Thy rest; Thou and the ark of Thy strength."

A careful study of Psalms 96:1- Psalm 105:15 shows that these verses together are a commentary on the journey of the Ark of the Covenant from the house of Obed-Edom the Gittite through a period residing in the tabernacle of David before eventually moving up to Solomon's temple. We know this because the celebratory song in **1 Chronicles 16:7-33**, written by David on the occasion of the Ark being moved to the tabernacle of David, is partially requoted in Psalm 96 (**which is the same as 1 Chronicles 16:23-33**) and Psalm 105:1-15 (**which is the same as 1 Chronicles 16:7-22**). The Ark of the Covenant is the symbol of the Throne of God, and its journey from the temple of Dagon, through the house of Obed-Edom the Gittite, then through the tabernacle of David, and on to its final rest in Solomon's temple becomes an **allegorical picture** of the Lord Jesus' "journey" from the place of the power of death (temple of Dagon), to the house of Obed -Edom the Gittite (the Church today), to the tabernacle of David (the tribulation saints), to Solomon's temple (the millennium). The details of the allegory will be discussed later in Psalm 96.

3 Actual rest (publicly displayed)

This is the fulfilment of the **anticipated** and **allegorical** rests when the Lord actually reigns in millennial glory. This is the second use of the word *mnuchah* in Psalm 132 when it is referring to the actual future rest:

Psalm 132:13-14
"For the LORD hath chosen Zion; He hath desired it for His habitation.
This is My **rest** forever: here will I dwell; for I have desired it."

We know that the rest in Psalm 132:14 cannot be a reference to Solomon's kingdom as it was not forever. Since the rest in Psalm 132:14 is forever, this refers to the **actual** Kingdom rest. It is the *mnuchah* spoken of by Isaiah in Isaiah 11:6-10, where we read that **His rest** shall be glorious (literally: "His rest shall be glory").

Isaiah 11:6-10

> 6 "The wolf also shall dwell with the lamb, and the leopard shall lie down with the kid; and the calf and the young lion and the fatling together; and a little child shall lead them.
> 7 And the cow and the bear shall feed; their young ones shall lie down together: and the lion shall eat straw like the ox.
> 8 And the sucking child shall play on the hole of the asp, and the weaned child shall put his hand on the cockatrice' den.
> 9 They shall not hurt nor destroy in all My holy mountain: for the earth shall be full of the knowledge of the Lord, as the waters cover the sea.
> 10 And in that day there shall be a root of Jesse, which shall stand for an ensign of the people; to it shall the Gentiles seek: **and His rest (*mnuchah*) shall be glorious."**

We can see from the discussion on the meaning of the word "rest" above, that the "rest" in question in Psalm 95 is the **anticipatory**, present and restful enjoyment of the certainty of the Lord Jesus' manifestation in glory. This is clear because the rest in question is entered upon during a person's lifetime (Hebrews 4). Accordingly, the rest of Psalm 95 cannot be the **actual rest**, since that couldn't be entered into in the lives of the wilderness people. Moreover, it couldn't be the **analogous rest**, because Solomon's temple wasn't built for many centuries after Moses. The fact is that this **anticipatory rest** was something that God wanted the people to enjoy amidst the hardships of their wilderness life. Similarly, today, He wants us to be enjoying this rest in our daily Christian lives.

Does failure to enter the rest mean that someone is not saved? No! Failure to enter into the full grasp of the Lord's future Kingdom glory retards spiritual development and is detrimental to spiritual balance and productivity. Above all, the lesson of this Psalm is that failure to enter into the rest greatly robs a believer of his ability to worship the Lord fully. However, this does not mean that eternal security is in question. Even Moses didn't enter Canaan due to unbelief (Numbers 20:12) but we know he was saved.

Numbers 20:12

> "And the Lord spake unto Moses and Aaron, Because **ye believed Me not**, to sanctify Me in the eyes of the children of Israel, therefore ye shall not bring this congregation into the land which I have given them."

However, there is no doubt that although Moses did not enter into the Promised Land he had entered into the anticipatory *mnuchah* of the Lord during his long life of faith.

Failure to enter into the rest was evidenced outwardly by failing to enter Canaan with Joshua. Hebrews 4 makes that clear. Failure to enter into the rest had already occurred **internally** in the hearts of the wilderness people, even before they died in the wilderness. They had failed to anticipate by faith the future promised glory of the Messiah. Failure to enter the rest appears to mean that there is uncertainty in the heart in relation to the divine revelations regarding the future glory of the Lord Jesus Christ. Herein lies the solemn implication of our passage. Those who lightly esteem the **presence and power** of the exalted Lord in the midst of His people are unlikely to understand the underlying reason as to why there must be a millennium. Those who appreciate the **presence and power** of the Lord in their personal and assembly lives can grasp the need for the public demonstration of the **presence and power** of the Lord in the future millennial Kingdom.

It is in New Testament-based assembly gatherings that the **presence** and **power** of the Lord are owned and His glory revered in the godly order of the gatherings with the head-coverings and silence of sisters (1 Corinthians 11). Moreover, such gatherings regularly teach the doctrines relating to the coming again and reign of our Lord Jesus Christ. It is interesting that the rediscovering of the New Testament pattern of Church gatherings in the mid 1800s, and the solemn truth of the **presence of the Lord** in the midst of the public gatherings of His people, happened in parallel with a rediscovery of the truths of the Lord's coming to the air before the great tribulation which precedes His future millennial reign.

However, for those who enjoy the blessings of meeting in assembly fellowship there is no room for **spiritual complacency or pride** in contemplation of this wonderful privilege. It is possible to have a theoretical grasp of the truth of the Lord Jesus' future millennial reign, and indeed the truths relating to the ordering of New Testament assemblies, and perhaps not be guided in one's own personal life by the twin doctrines of the **presence and power** of the Lord. May we as individual believers be ever preserved from such a state of soul!

The importance of Psalm 95 in Old and New Testaments

1 We have already seen how this Psalm provides a clear warning to us from the two Old Testament incidents of Exodus 17 (*Massah* and *Meribah*) and Numbers 14 (*Kadesh*) as discussed above.

2 We have already alluded to this Psalm forming a lead-in to a series of Psalms depicting the journey of the Ark of the Covenant through the wilderness to the tabernacle of David and eventually to Solomon's temple. This will be further considered in Psalm 96.

3 We have touched on how this Psalm forms a key element of the argument developed in Hebrews 3-4. This is an appropriate point in our meditations to re-acquaint ourselves with Hebrews 3 and 4 and consider why its exposition of Psalm 95 is so effective and relevant in the circumstances of the Hebrew believers of first century AD.

Hebrews 3 where the Psalm is quoted

Hebrews 3:1-6
"1 Wherefore, holy brethren, partakers of the heavenly calling, consider the Apostle and High Priest of our profession, Christ Jesus;
2 Who was faithful to Him that appointed Him, as also Moses *was faithful* in all his house.

3 For this *Man* was counted worthy of more glory than Moses, inasmuch as He Who hath builded the house hath more honour than the house.
4 For every house is builded by some *man;* but He that built all things *is* God.
5 And Moses verily *was* faithful in all his house, as a servant, for a testimony of those things which were to be spoken after;
6 But Christ as a Son over His own house; Whose house are we, if we hold fast the confidence and the rejoicing of the hope firm unto the end."

Hebrews 3 is in two parts. Verses 1-6 consider the **faithfulness of Christ,** using a comparison with the faithfulness of Moses. The remainder of the section considers the **unfaithfulness of the people of God,** using a comparison with the people of Israel in the wilderness.

Verses 1 and 2 emphasise the faithfulness of Christ Jesus. If He cannot be faithful in the matter of fulfilling all the Old Testament prophecies regarding future millennial glory, as outlined in Hebrews 1 and 2, how can He be faithful as our High Priest today? Moses, in Numbers 12:7, was declared as "faithful in all Mine House" in the context of Miriam and Aaron's railing on him for marrying a Gentile bride. The faithfulness of Moses was not altered when he married this woman. Is there a possibility that the Hebrew believers were querying the faithfulness of Christ to the Old Testament promises to Israel in the context of His taking to Himself His largely Gentile Bride, the Church? In this context, Miriam and Aaron both had to learn that in this Moses was faithful. Let us not question the faithfulness of Christ to the Old Testament promises, just because He is now bringing Gentiles into blessing. Let us remember that when we read that Moses was faithful in all His house this does not mean that Moses never made mistakes. He did. However, he was absolutely meticulously faithful in delivering the plans of the tabernacle to the people, and supervising its construction and the commencement of ceremonial worship therein. Moses was faithful in delivering the "plans" to the people. The Lord Jesus was faithful in delivering the "plan" of the Church to His own.

Hebrews 3:3

"For this *Man* was counted worthy of **more glory than Moses,** inasmuch as He Who hath builded the house hath more honour than the house."

We read of the **glory of Moses** on the occasion of his **second** descent from Mount Sinai. On his first descent, there is no record of Moses' face shining. However, it is on his second descent that his face shone and we learn from 2 Corinthians 3:7 that this was Moses' **glory.** Interestingly, the revelation of the Law given on the first visit to the mountain top did not cause his face to shine. It was the second time that this happened, and we should ask ourselves what was different about the second descent from Sinai when compared with the first descent. The answer lies in the very special revelation Moses received on the second visit to Mount Sinai. It was a vision of the **grace and mercy** of God. Jehovah revealed Himself to Moses as the gracious and merciful Lord Who forgives iniquity, transgression and sin (Exodus 34:7).

The word "to forgive" in Exodus 34:7 means "to bear away" – the same word as is used of the scapegoat bearing away the iniquities "unto a land not inhabited" in Leviticus 16:22. God revealed to Moses that a divine Sin-bearer would one day bear away the sin of the world. Is it any wonder his face shone before such a vision of the glory of His grace (Exodus 34:29)? Moses' face showed a **reflected glory** which also diminished with time. It was, nevertheless, so awesome that Moses veiled his face so that the children of Israel could not see it in its entirety. The glory of the Lord Jesus is seen as **greater than that of Moses**. Firstly, Moses' face shone after seeing a revelation of divine grace (Exodus 34:29). The Lord Jesus is not merely a messenger of divine grace, He is the embodiment of divine grace. "Grace and truth came by Jesus Christ" (John 1:17).

Secondly, Moses' face shone after receiving the plans for the tabernacle. The Lord Jesus came down, not from Mount Sinai but from heaven, to manifest plans, not of a physical tabernacle but rather of the Church which is the dwelling place of God, a "habitation of God through the Spirit" (Ephesians 2:22). It is significant that after He revealed to the disciples in Matthew 16 the truth of the Church, in Matthew 17 we see Him on the Mount of Transfiguration with His face shining beyond the brightness of the sun in conversation with Moses! Apart from that incident on the Mount of Transfiguration, throughout the rest of His pre-Calvary sojourn He veiled His glory – "He hid as it were His face from us" (Isaiah 53:3). Isaiah also shows us the significance of hiding His face: "He hath no form nor comeliness (*hadar* outward splendour)" (Isaiah 53:2). Thirdly, Moses was merely the messenger with the plans. Although it is called Moses' house (Hebrews 3:5), this is synonymous with the House of God of Numbers 12:7, just as God's Law is synonymous with Moses' Law. Moses was part of this House. He was a servant in this House. Christ is more worthy of honour than Moses because He is the Architect of both the House of God in the wilderness as well as Architect of the Church today. "He Who hath builded the House hath more honour than the House" (Hebrews 3:3).

It is worth noting that Moses on his first visit to Mount Sinai spent 40 days there, so much so that the people wondered what had befallen him, and this led them to question the reliability and faithfulness of Moses. We should remember that at the time of writing the epistle to the Hebrews, the Lord Jesus had ascended to heaven less than 40 years previously. Now that there was no sign on the horizon of His return to reign, the question may have been troubling some Hebrew believers if God had remembered His promises to the nation. What a lesson for them to learn! The God of heaven is a God of mercy and grace, and this remains despite the unfaithfulness of His people.

Moses was a servant **in** his House **(Hebrews 3:5)**. As the servant, he delivered the pattern and plan of the house. Christ is Son **over** His House

(Hebrews 3:6). As the Son **over** the House, it suggests that He left His Father (in heaven) and His Mother (Israel) and cleaved to His wife. This alludes to the Church as the Bride of Christ. God's plan for the Church was not just revealed by Christ, it is centred in Christ Himself ,"Whose House are we" (Hebrews 3:6).

It is solemn to see that despite the vision of the reflected glory of God in Moses' face, and the **visible presence** of the Lord in the congregation, that the children of Israel in the wilderness developed a heart problem – a hardened heart and an erring heart. A detailed analysis of this heart problem is provided in the second part of Psalm 95 and, as we have just seen, it involves lightly esteeming the **presence** and **power** of the Lord in the midst.

A meditation of the incident of Massah and Meribah in Exodus 17 would be incomplete without a consideration of the second visit of the people to Meribah in Numbers 20:8 when they murmured again. This time Moses was asked to speak, not to the bedrock but rather to the crag-rock (Hebrew *sela*), to bring forth the water. It is faithfully taught by Bible teachers that on that occasion he was not asked to smite the crag-rock, just to speak to it. Sadly, Moses disobeyed and smote the crag-rock twice. The crag-rock, in contrast to the bedrock, speaks of Christ in exaltation and no longer in humiliation:

Isaiah 32:1-2
> 1 "Behold, a King shall reign in righteousness, and princes shall rule in judgment.
> 2 And a Man shall be as an hiding place from the wind, and a covert from the tempest; as rivers of water in a dry place, as the shadow of a great **(Crag-)Rock** in a weary land."

The water flowed from the once-smitten bedrock. However, thereafter the crag-rock is only spoken to for the blessing to flow. No further smiting is required. The judgment of God meted out upon His Son at Calvary was **once** only and that was enough. Moses broke a type and by so doing failed to sanctify the Lord among the people.

Numbers 20:12
> "And the Lord spake unto Moses and Aaron, Because ye believed Me not, to **sanctify Me** in the eyes of the children of Israel, therefore ye shall not bring this congregation into the land which I have given them."

Resurrection and exaltation (the meaning of the Crag-Rock) have "set apart" or "sanctified" the Lord Jesus in contrast to all others who preceded Him. The problem which beset the ancient people of Israel in the wilderness was a failure to recognise that the Lord was **among** them in Exodus 17 (i.e. **His presence**) and that the **glory of His presence** is unsurpassed and peerless (sanctified and set apart) (Numbers 20:12). The whole point of the tabernacle was for the Lord to dwell in the midst of His people. Similarly, the One Who is in our midst in the Church today stands "set apart or sanctified" not just in His death, which has made propitiation for sin, but also **in His glory** (the meaning of the Crag-Rock). Moses learned that the Lord is very careful to protect the glory of His presence. We have often been taught these things by faithful teachers in assembly fellowship today but can we lose the impact of this warning?

There are several New Testament examples of where these truths can be neglected:

1 Head-coverings and silence of sisters (1 Corinthians 11)

A modern application of this truth in the Church today is the teaching of the head-covering of sisters. Head-covering by the sister (being the emblem of the glory of man) indicates that only that which speaks of the glory of Christ (the male's head) is visible.

2 The flesh coming into prominence

1 Corinthians 1:29: "That no flesh should glory in **His presence.**" A fleshly or carnal person glories in the flesh and glories in division. **Nothing of the flesh can be present when the glory of the Lord's presence is there**. Acting in the flesh in an assembly could lead to the Lord **being grieved** that the glory of His presence is being lightly esteemed. How solemn it is to be in assembly fellowship where the glory of the Lord is present!

It was failure to recognise the presence of the Lord's glory in their midst which caused the Lord to grieve (literally: "to loathe") "this generation" in Psalm 95:10 and declared them to be "a people which do err in their heart, and they have not known My ways". A hard heart is insensitive to the feelings of the Lord. The next step for such a heart is to become an erring heart, leading to an "ignorant (not knowing) heart", which is unaware of the Lord's ways. God then is grieved with such a person.

Conclusion

The subject matter of Psalm 95 is applied in Hebrews 3 and 4 to believers today in assembly fellowship as a very powerful warning to always treasure the wonder of the Lord's **presence and power** in our midst. May the lesson from this Psalm, written approximately 3000 years ago, come to our souls with solemn freshness and cause us to rediscover the Lord's **presence and power** in our lives, so as to be able to worship Him daily as we are led along this wilderness pathway by His freshly experienced presence and power. If that were the case, then the **warning of the Shepherd** would refine and purify the **worship of the sheep**.

19

PSALM 96

1 *O sing unto the Lord a New Song: sing unto the Lord, all the earth.*
2 *Sing unto the Lord, bless His Name; shew forth His salvation from day to day.*
3 *Declare His glory among the heathen, His wonders among all people.*
4 *For the Lord is great, and greatly to be praised: He is to be feared above all gods.*
5 *For all the gods of the nations are idols: but the Lord made the heavens.*
6 *Honour and majesty are before Him: strength and beauty are in His sanctuary.*
7 *Give unto the Lord, O ye kindreds of the people, give unto the Lord glory and strength.*
8 *Give unto the Lord the glory due unto His Name: bring an offering, and come into His courts.*
9 *O worship the Lord in the beauty of holiness: fear before Him, all the earth.*
10 *Say among the heathen that the Lord reigneth: the world also shall be established that it shall not be moved: He shall judge the people righteously.*
11 *Let the heavens rejoice, and let the earth be glad; let the sea roar, and the fullness thereof.*
12 *Let the field be joyful, and all that is therein: then shall all the trees of the wood rejoice*
13 *Before the Lord: for He cometh, for He cometh to judge the earth: He shall judge the world with righteousness, and the people with His truth.*

Introduction

Psalm 96 is not a Messianic Psalm in as far as it is not directly quoted in the New Testament. However, it provides an important introduction to Psalm 97, which is a Messianic Psalm, and thus is included in this book.

1 The position of this Psalm in the Psalter

Psalm 96 was composed by David and sung on the occasion of the setting up of the tabernacle of David in 1 Chronicles 16:1-6.

1 Chronicles 16:1-6

1 "So they brought the ark of God, and set it in the midst of the **tent that David had pitched for it:** and they offered burnt sacrifices and peace offerings before God.

2 And when David had made an end of offering the burnt offerings and the peace offerings, he blessed the people in the Name of the Lord.

3 And he dealt to every one of Israel, both man and woman, to every one a loaf of bread, and a good piece of flesh, and a flagon *of wine.*

4 And he appointed *certain* of the Levites to minister before the ark of the Lord, and to record, and to thank and praise the Lord God of Israel:

5 Asaph the chief, and next to him Zechariah, Jeiel, and Shemiramoth, and Jehiel, and Mattithiah, and Eliab, and Benaiah, and Obed-Edom: and Jeiel with psalteries and with harps; but Asaph made a sound with cymbals;

6 Benaiah also and Jahaziel the priests with trumpets continually before the Ark of the Covenant of God."

On that joyful occasion, David composed and taught the people a Psalm (1 Chronicles 16:8-36), the latter part of which (1 Chronicles 16:23-33) is almost identical to Psalm 96:2-13. This linking of Psalm 96 to the historical events of 1 Chronicles 16 and the setting up of the tabernacle of David is most instructive, particularly when we note the two other occurrences of the **rebuilding of the** "tabernacle of David" in the Scriptures in **Amos 9:11-15** and **Acts 15:13-18.**

Here is the Old Testament passage:

Amos 9:11-15

11 "**In that day will I raise up the tabernacle (Hebrew: *sukkah*) of David that is fallen,** and close up the breaches thereof; and I will raise up his ruins, and I will build it as in the days of old:

12 That they may possess the remnant of Edom, and of all the heathen, which are called by My Name, saith the Lord that doeth this.

13 Behold, the days come, saith the Lord, that the plowman shall overtake the reaper, and the treader of grapes him that soweth seed; and the mountains shall drop sweet wine, and all the hills shall melt.

14 And I will bring again the captivity of My people of Israel, and they shall build the waste cities, and inhabit *them;* and they shall plant vineyards, and drink the wine thereof; they shall also make gardens, and eat the fruit of them.

15 And I will plant them upon their land, and they shall no more be pulled up out of their land which I have given them, saith the Lord thy God."

Here is the New Testament passage:

Acts 15:13-18

13 "And after they had held their peace, James answered, saying, Men *and* brethren, hearken unto me:

14 Simeon hath declared how God at the first did visit the Gentiles, to take out of them a people for His Name.

15 **And to this agree the words of the prophets; as it is written,**

16 **After this I will return, and will build again the tabernacle of David, which is fallen down; and I will build again the ruins thereof, and I will set it up:**

17 **That the residue of men might seek after the Lord, and all the Gentiles, upon whom My Name is called, saith the Lord, Who doeth all these**

things.
18 Known unto God are all His works from the beginning of the world."

A combined study of 1 Chronicles 16, Acts 15 and Amos 9 is required to eludicate the doctrinal and prophetical significance of the tabernacle of David and the rebuilding of the tabernacle of David. It is 1 Chronicles 16 which describes the building up of the tabernacle (*ohel*) of David and Psalm 96 is the Psalm which was sung on that occasion. The passages in Amos 9 and Acts 15 refer to a future latter-day event – the building up **again** of the tabernacle (*sukkah*) of David in a coming day. Please note that the word for "tabernacle" in Amos 9:11 is *sukkah,* whereas the word for "tabernacle" in 1 Chronicles 16:1 is *ohel*. This suggests that Amos 9:11 is not describing the future literal rebuilding of the same actual tabernacle (*ohel*) which David built in 1 Chronicles 16:1, but rather the future rebuilding of collective worship for the remnant Jewish people before the millennial temple worship is instituted. The rebuilding of the *sukkah* of David, as foreseen by Amos, indicates this major development for the remnant, and the fact that the word *sukkah* is different from *ohel* reminds us that the principle of worship in that coming day will be different. No longer are believers under Law since this was satisfied at Calvary.

The significance of the building up **again** of the tabernacle of David was alluded to in Psalm 95 when we saw that the progress of the Ark of the Covenant in its long journey to its "rest" (*mnuchah*) in the temple of Solomon formed an allegory, depicting the journey of the Lord Jesus from Calvary through this Church era and eventually back to the earth to reign in glory. Psalms 96-99 form a continuation of that allegory.

2 The allegory of the journey of the Ark of the Covenant

The Ark of the Covenant was lost to the nation of Israel and ended up in the hands of the Gentile Philistines in the days of Eli the priest in 1 Samuel 4. In the place of satanic dominion, i.e. the heathen temple of Dagon, the power of God was seen when Dagon fell to the ground with his head and hands severed (1 Samuel 5:1-5). This part of the allegory foretells how the Messiah would one day be lost to the nation of Israel, be handed over to the Gentiles and in the place of "him who had the power of death, that is the devil", defeat that evil foe (Hebrews 2:14). Subsequent to that event, the Ark of the Covenant made its way to the house of Abinadab on the hill (1 Samuel 7:1), where it resided for many years until it was moved from there (2 Samuel 6:3) to the care of Obed-Edom the Gittite, where it remained for three months (2 Samuel 6:11). From there it was moved to the tabernacle (*ohel*) of David which was situated in the city of David. The ark was then eventually moved to Solomon's temple after David's death.

Now it is clear that the spiritual songs of Psalms 94-100 provide a divine commentary on this journey of the Ark of the Covenant to its final resting place in Solomon's temple. This journey was understood by the Psalmist to be pictorial of the Lord Jesus' return to take up His Kingdom, since this cluster of Psalms concentrate on the future millennial reign of Christ. However, the references to the future rebuilding of the tabernacle (*sukkah*) of David in Acts 15 and Amos 9 add very clear detail to the prophetical and allegorical significance of the historical journey of the Ark of the Covenant. In Acts 15:13-14, James speaks of this **present era of grace** when God is calling out of the nations a people for His Name.

Acts 15:13-14
> 13 "And after they had held their peace, James answered, saying, Men *and* brethren, hearken unto me:
> 14 Simeon hath declared how God at the first did visit the Gentiles, to take out of them a people for His Name."

God's visitation to the Gentiles, to take out of them a people for His Name, is a clear reference to this Church era from Pentecost to the rapture of the saints.

Then James tells us that it is "**after this**" that the Lord returns and builds up **again** the tabernacle of David (Acts 15:16-18).

Acts 15:16-18
> 16 "**After this** I will return, and will build again the tabernacle of David, which is fallen down; and I will build again the ruins thereof, and I will set it up:
> 17 That the residue of men might seek after the Lord, and all the Gentiles, upon whom My Name is called, saith the Lord, Who doeth all these things.
> 18 Known unto God are all His works from the beginning of the world."

The return of the Lord, which is envisaged in Acts 15:16 and which must happen before the building up again of the tabernacle of David, cannot be His return to the earth to reign, since Amos 9 makes clear that **subsequent** to the re-erection of the tabernacle (*sukkah*) of David millennial conditions will prevail. This suggests that the "return" which is alluded to in Acts 15:16-18 is the return of the Lord Jesus to the air, i.e. the rapture of the Church to heaven, which precedes the tribulation. Acts 15 thus defines the building up again of the tabernacle of David as subsequent to God's visitation of blessing to the Gentiles, which is a term referring to this Church era of grace, stretching from Pentecost to the rapture of the Church. This means that the building up **again** of the tabernacle (*sukkah*) of David is an event that must happen **after the end** of this Church era, i.e. subsequent to the rapture of the Church. However, Amos 9:14 shows us that the rebuilding of the tabernacle of David occurs **before** the onset of the millennial reign of our Lord Jesus Christ, when the Lord will have reversed (restored) the captivity of the people of Israel.

Amos 9:14
> "And I will bring again (restore) the captivity of My people of Israel."

These Scriptures show us that the rebuilding of the tabernacle of David is a picture of the conditions pertaining immediately prior to and during the tribulation period **between** the rapture of the Church and the coming of the Lord Jesus to the earth to reign (see Appendices 2 and 3).

Interestingly, the phrase, "after this I will return", in Acts 15:16, depicting the return of the Lord prior to the re-establishing of the tabernacle of David, is not found in Amos 9:11. This should not surprise us as the return of the Lord Jesus prior to the tribulation era, i.e. the coming of the Lord Jesus to the air for His Church, is a truth which **was hidden in the Lord's heart** in the Old Testament era but now revealed as one of the New Testament "mystery doctrines"(1 Corinthians 15:51).

Now, if the rebuilding of the tabernacle of David speaks of the worshipping remnant during the tribulation period, as is clear from Amos 9 and Acts 15, then we can deduce that the historical **pre-tabernacle-of-David era**, namely the time when the Ark of the Covenant abode in the house of Abinadab on the hill and the short time that it remained in the care of Obed-Edom the Gittite, correlates in the allegory **to this present Church era.**

A detailed study of the historical events in the experience of the nation of Israel during the Abinadab years and the three months with Obed-Edom is outside of the scope of this present book. However, such a study will show some important events which find parallels in 2000 years of Church history. For example, the tabernacle remained devoid of the Ark of the Covenant and had become a centre of ritual but lacked the divine presence. Does this refer, in the allegory, to the past two thousand years of Jewish religious rituals which lack the Lord's presence, in contrast to what was enjoyed during the days of Solomon and the kings of Judah? Perhaps the national putting away of the idols in 1 Samuel 7 and the rediscovery of the value of the Lamb in that chapter, after 20 years of backsliding by the people, find a parallel in the story of the reformation in the 1500s, when the truth of justification by faith was rediscovered, and the homage of images was forsaken by many. Sadly, the long era of the custody of the Ark by Abinadab ended in failure by the error of Uzzah, the son of Abinadab, who lifted his hand to steady the Ark of the Covenant in 2 Samuel 6:6. Uzzah clearly felt that the Ark of the Covenant was vulnerable to falling or failing.

2 Samuel 6:7
"And the anger of the Lord was kindled against Uzzah; and God smote him there for *his* **error**; and there he died by the ark of God."

Is there a modern equivalent to the error of Uzzah which we do well to avoid as the end of the dispensation of grace approaches? One example of an equivalent error today may be a teaching by some of a supposed vulnerability of the Lord during His sojourn on earth as a Man. Such expositors have attributed finite limits to the One Who never ceased to be God while being fully and perfectly human. Even at this late stage of the dispensation of grace we need to be careful to avoid becoming influenced by such arguments.

We should not be unmindful that there was special divine blessing on the household of Obed-Edom during the brief period of the ark, the symbol of the throne of God residing at his home (2 Samuel 6:11). This leads to an important and urgent practical lesson for every Christian today. **It is for exercised believers in this the final chapter of the era of grace to be prepared and willing for a similar revival, as a result of the Lordship of Christ being owned and revered in our personal and assembly lives.**

3 The prophetic programme in this cluster of Psalms

These observations show how Acts 15 and Amos 9 identify Psalm 96 as describing the events which occur **immediately before** the Lord returns to this earth to reign (Amos 9) but **after** the rapture of the Church (Acts 15).

Hebrews 1 identifies Psalm 97 as describing the events which occur **on the occasion** of the Lord Jesus returning to this earth to reign.

A study of the content of Psalms 98 and 99 shows that both Psalms describe what will happen **immediately after** the Lord Jesus comes back to reign. Thus we see how these Psalms have been placed in a specific order.

4 A detailed look at Psalm 96: the tribulation Psalm

A The gospel of the Kingdom: a world-wide invitation to learn the New Song

Psalm 96:1-2

1 "O sing unto the Lord a New Song: sing unto the Lord, all the earth.
2 Sing unto the Lord, bless His Name; shew forth His salvation from day to day."

It is delightful to note in Psalm 96 that the tribulation saints of the era of the rebuilt tabernacle of David will sing the "New Song" which was considered in our chapter on Psalm 40. As part of the New Song they will be looking forward to the day when they will reign on the earth with the Lord Jesus, as is consistent with the content of the New Song given in Revelation 5:9-10. Appendix 3 looks in more detail at the restoration of the remnant of Israel after the rapture of the Church, before the tribulation commences, and their role in that tribulation.

In this Psalm, there is an appeal for "all the earth" to become acquainted with the "New Song". This will particularly be the case in the tribulation, when, worldwide, the gospel of the Kingdom will be proclaimed by the redeemed remnant. Those who will be candidates for salvation and those who will not be eligible are considered in Appendix 2. In fact, the phrase, "show forth His salvation", means, "declare as good news His salvation". This is truly the gospel or good news of the Kingdom. It is important also to note that the Hebrew word here used for "salvation" is the lovely word *Yeshua* which, in fact, is the Name "Jesus". The verse could be translated "tell out the gospel of His Jesus from day to day". This shows us that central to the gospel message in that day will be the preaching of the Person of Jesus to the people. We are reminded of Philip telling the gospel to the Ethiopian eunuch in the wilderness in Acts 8:35. We learn in that passage how that from Isaiah 53 "he preached unto him Jesus". In other words, he told the Ethiopian the good news about *Yeshua* (Acts 8:35). The preaching of *Yeshua* or Jesus will tell of His earthly sojourn and all the sufferings He encountered in His life here. It will also tell of His death which made propitiation for sin. Since the message is linked with the New Song, it will show that *Yeshua* is the One Who was slain and has provided redemption by His precious blood. We noted in Psalm 40 that a key element of the New Song is thanksgiving to the Lord for being made "kings and priests". It is interesting that, later on in this Psalm, there is a call to the singers of the New Song, irrespective of their nationality, to enter the courts of the sanctuary, thus indicating that they are enjoying the privilege of priestly access there.

Psalm 96:3
"Declare His glory among the heathen, His wonders among all people."

Not only will the tribulation gospel preachers speak of the suffering and death of *Yeshua*, they will speak of His glory. This will involve declaring His resurrection and exaltation. These verses form a beautiful summary of the gospel of the Kingdom. It is the proclamation of the Person of Christ (*Yeshua*) first in His humiliation and death and then in His glory.

Psalm 96:4
"For the Lord *is* great, and greatly to be praised: He *is* to be feared above all gods."

The passage now provides some very good reasons why it is wise to believe and act on the message. Against the background in the tribulation period of general anti-God sentiments and idolatry, the tribulation preachers will be reminding their hearers of the greatness of God, which is in contrast to the idols of earth.

Psalm 96:5-6
"For all the gods of the nations *are* idols: but the Lord made the heavens."

When we recall that in the ancient world many deities of idolatrous worship were linked with the constellations in the sky, it is noteworthy that the Psalmist shows that the Lord "**made** the heavens". The pathogenesis of atheism begins with rejection of a Creator God and into this void man places his worthless idols. Clearly, in the tribulation period, atheism and denial of a Creator God will be rampant. Atheism is already a major part of western thinking even today, but no doubt this will intensify even more in the tribulation. How wonderful it is to know that even in that day there will be the tribulation preachers who will proclaim the truth about the Creator God Who has provided salvation for fallen humanity!

B The result of the gospel of the Kingdom: worshipping in the heavenly sanctuary as priests

Psalm 96:6

"Honour and majesty *are* before Him: strength and beauty *are* in His sanctuary."

At the time of David's composition of this Psalm, the tabernacle was in disarray. The Ark of the Covenant was missing from the tabernacle and thus there was no glory in that place, which was characterised by *Ichabod*, meaning "the glory has departed" (1 Samuel 4:22). Clearly, the sanctuary about which David was speaking was not the earthly tabernacle since the Ark of the Covenant was missing. Nor was he referring to the temple of Solomon since it was not yet built. He must, therefore, have been referring to the heavenly sanctuary of God which is "above the heavens". In the tribulation there will be no earthly sanctuary to which the tribulation saints can go. The temple of Jerusalem will be a scene of horrendous idolatry. The "place of worship" of the tribulation saints will be the heavenly sanctuary which they will enter by faith while physically on earth. This will be the basis of the worship of the rebuilt *sukkah* of David foreseen by Amos. This leads us to the next verses which depict for us the nature of the worship to the Lord in that coming day.

C The basis of worship of tribulation saints

Psalm 96:7

7 "Give unto the Lord, O ye kindreds of the people, give unto the Lord glory and strength.
8 Give unto the Lord the glory *due unto* His Name: bring an offering, and come into His courts.
9 O worship the Lord in the beauty of holiness: fear before Him, all the earth."

Verse 7 shows us that "the kindreds (families) of the peoples (plural in Hebrew)" will be engaged in this worship. No longer is approach to the presence of God restricted to the Jewish nation. In the tribulation, the Jew takes the message globally initially, but the great throng of the redeemed in that era will be made up of Jews and Gentiles, all functioning as priests before God (see Psalm 40). Verse 8 shows that this great international company shall be made up of priestly men and women who can come into His heavenly courts. No doubt many of these saints will be martyrs for Christ's sake in the tribulation and will swell the New Song of the heavenly company, which we considered in Psalm 40 to be the "four and twenty elders" of Revelation 5:8. We noticed in Psalm 40 that the "four and twenty elders" represented deceased saints from Old Testament times, who are functioning as priests before the throne of God in heaven (Revelation 5:8) but awaiting their return to earth to continue serving the Lord there. Verse 9 in its appeal to "worship the Lord in the beauty of holiness" is an encouragement to tribulation believers, in all the dignity of priesthood, to swell the song of the "four and twenty elders" in worshipping the Lord on earth. Interestingly, it is only after worshipping the Lord in the beauty of holiness that these believers move outward to call on "all the earth" to fear the Lord. Moreover, it is this worshipping band of preachers who will herald to the world the solemn ultimatum of the Lord's impending reign:

D The worshippers go forth to preach

Psalm 96:10

"Say among the heathen *that* the Lord reigneth: the world also shall be established that it shall not be moved: He shall judge the people righteously."

We may learn a practical lesson here. God wants His servants who preach the gospel to do so out of hearts which have first been engaged in worship to God. This is a further statement of the principle that worship always precedes service. In verse 10, the statement, "the Lord reigneth", does not mean that the Lord is actually reigning on earth at that moment. The tense is in the Hebrew short tense which can be used, on occasions, to express the certainty of an event to take place in the future which has not yet taken place. It could be read with the meaning: "say among the heathen that the Lord will certainly reign…"

E A positive and joyful message

The remaining verses of the Psalm bring before us the anticipation of tribulation preachers of the dramatic changes which the impending millennial reign will have.

Psalm 96:11

11 "Let the heavens rejoice, and let the earth be glad; let the sea roar, and the fullness thereof.
12 Let the field be joyful, and all that *is* therein: then shall all the trees of the wood rejoice."

There will be effects on the heavens, earth and sea (verse 11) and unprecedented agricultural productivity will be seen as Eden-garden conditions will once more prevail. This shows us that the gospel of the Kingdom is an attractive message which comes across positively to the hearer. We can learn from this example in our gospel preaching today to present the message positively and with joy.

F The prospect of the Lord putting every wrong right

An important aspect of the attractiveness of the gospel of the Kingdom in the tribulation era is the great comfort that it brings to those who believe and receive it. This will be particularly sweet to those who are persecuted for Christ's sake during that dreadful period of anti-God rebellion.

Psalm 96:13

"Before the Lord: for He cometh, for He cometh to judge the earth: He shall judge the world with righteousness, and the people with His truth."

This verse shows us that the Psalm is anticipating the coming again of the Lord Jesus. This confirms the Psalm as pertaining to the tribulation era when the intervention of the Judge is an eagerly anticipated relief from intense persecution.

This now leads to Psalm 97, which goes beyond the pre-return events as described in Psalm 96, to depict in detail that actual return.

Conclusion

Psalm 96 particularly applies to future saints between the rapture and the end of tribulation era, and shows the triumph of the message of the gospel of the Kingdom during that period of unprecedented global wickedness and anti-God rebellion. The lesson for us today is that the Lord will always triumph, even in the darkest hour of human rebellion against Him and that **we, in this the closing era of the dispensation of grace,** should be deeply and prayerfully exercised about immediate Obed-Edom-type revival in our personal and assembly lives. May this be the case for His Name's sake!

20

PSALM 97

1 *The Lord reigneth; let the earth rejoice; let the multitude of isles be glad thereof.*
2 *Clouds and darkness are round about Him: righteousness and judgment are the habitation of His throne.*
3 *A fire goeth before Him, and burneth up His enemies round about.*
4 *His lightnings enlightened the world: the earth saw, and trembled.*
5 *The hills melted like wax at the presence of the Lord, at the presence of the Lord of the whole earth.*
6 *The heavens declare His righteousness, and all the people see His glory.*
7 *Confounded be all they that serve graven images, that boast themselves of idols: worship Him, all ye gods.*
8 *Zion heard, and was glad; and the daughters of Judah rejoiced because of Thy judgments, O Lord.*
9 *For Thou, Lord, art high above all the earth: Thou art exalted far above all gods.*
10 *Ye that love the Lord, hate evil: He preserveth the souls of His saints; He delivereth them out of the hand of the wicked.*
11 *Light is sown for the righteous, and gladness for the upright in heart.*
12 *Rejoice in the Lord, ye righteous; and give thanks at the remembrance of His holiness.*

Introduction

This Psalm describes the events which characterise the return of our Lord Jesus Christ to the earth to reign. We are left in no doubt that this is the meaning of the Psalm by a similar, albeit not identical, quotation of the final part of Psalm 97:7 in Hebrews 1:6.

Hebrews 1:6
"And again, when He bringeth in the Firstbegotten into the world, He saith,
And let all the angels of God worship Him."

1 Questions regarding the difference between Hebrews 1:6 and Psalm 97:7

A.

It may be queried, firstly, as to why the Hebrew text in Psalm 97:7 is "worship Him, all ye gods (Hebrew: *elohim*)", and the parallel ancient Greek Septuagint translation is "worship Him all ye **angels**", which is consistent with the phrase in Hebrews 1:6, "let all the angels of God worship Him". The reason why the word "gods" in Psalm 97:7 becomes "angels of God" in the Septuagint Greek translation of the original Hebrew text of Psalm 97:7 lies in the meaning of the word *elohim*. This has already been discussed in detail in the chapter dealing with Psalm 82. There it was noted how the word *elohim* should be translated as "God" if the accompanying verb and any identifying pronoun are singular. However, if the accompanying verb and pronoun are plural, the word *elohim* must be determined from the context of the passage to be one of either gods, angels or judges. Because the Hebrew verb for "worship Him" in Psalm 97:7 is in the plural, the word *elohim*, which is the subject of that verb, means either gods, angels or judges. It is clear that the ancient translators of the Septuagint Greek version of the Hebrew Bible grasped this and in Psalm 97:7 showed that they understood the phrase to mean "worship Him, all ye angels".

B.

There is a further question. Why should the quotation in Hebrews 1:6, "and let all the angels of God worship Him", be a *verbatim* quotation of part of the Septuagint rendering of Deuteronomy 32, which is not present in the original Hebrew manuscript, rather than a *verbatim* quotation of the Septuagint translation of Psalm 97:7? The answer to this question is not given to us in Scripture so any attempt to explain this would only be speculation. We should note that the writer to the Hebrews does not reference the 97th Psalm in his quotation, nor does he reference the book of Moses as to the source either. One thing is clear: by using the phrase, "and let all the angels of God worship Him", the Spirit of God is giving His seal of approval to the truth contained in the phrase. As far as the Hebrew Masoretic text is concerned, the only reference to angels worshipping the Lord Jesus on His return is in Psalm 97:7. Hence, the fact that the reference to this in Deuteronomy 32 is omitted from the Masoretic text available to us today should not alarm us. The truth of this statement is enshrined in both the Septuagint and the Masoretic witnesses to Psalm 97:7, where both testify to the angels of God worshipping the Lord Jesus on His return. It is, therefore, safe to regard Psalm 97 as a Messianic Psalm which deals specifically with the occasion of the Lord Jesus' return to this earth to reign since Hebrews 1:6 states that this specific truth is relevant on the occasion of His return.

C.

Another reason why we know that Psalm 97 refers to the occasion of the Lord Jesus' return to this earth in glory is because the literal translation of Hebrews 1:6 is, "And when He bringeth in **again** the Firstbegotten into the world…". The word "again" refers to the bringing in of the Lord Jesus to this world **a second** time, i.e. His return.

2 The Lord's return in Glory

A The description of the moment of the Lord's return in glory

Psalm 97:1 shows how the commencement of His reign will cause universal joy to those faithful ones scattered throughout the earth, who are eagerly awaiting His return.

Psalm 97:1

"The Lord reigneth; let the earth rejoice; let the multitude of isles be glad *thereof.*"

The next two verses are reminiscent of the scenes of glory already described by the Psalmist in Psalm 18 and discussed there.

Psalm 97:2-3

2 "Clouds and darkness *are* round about Him: righteousness and judgment *are* the habitation of His throne.
3 A fire goeth before Him, and burneth up His enemies round about."

The clouds surrounding Him on His return are also mentioned by John in the Apocolypse:

Revelation 1:7

"Behold, He cometh with clouds; and every eye shall see Him, and they *also* which pierced Him: and all kindreds of the earth shall wail because of Him. Even so, Amen."

His enemies shall be engulfed in flames emerging from His Person (Psalm 97:3). This is the same event as is described in 2 Thessalonians 2:8 when the wicked one and his followers will be "consumed at the brightness of His coming".

2 Thessalonians 2:8

"And then shall that Wicked be revealed, whom the Lord shall consume with the Spirit of His mouth, and shall destroy with the brightness (*epiphaneia*) of His coming (*parousia*):"

The fire emerging from His Person, which engulfs and destroys His enemies, is like lightning. It will target His enemies specifically, bringing instant destruction. This is clear in Psalm 97:4

Psalm 97:4

"His lightnings enlightened the world: the earth saw, and trembled."

Now the Lord turns His attention to the hills. In Psalm 72, we saw that the hills in the Old Testament were used pictorially to describe ancient communication systems. Once again, this is addressed in Psalm 97:5.

Psalm 97:5

"The hills melted like wax at the presence of the Lord, at the presence of the
Lord of the whole earth."

This verse can be literally translated: "the hills melted like wax away from
the face of the Lord". We considered in Psalm 72 that the hills were the
communication systems of the ancient world. Even today hills are used for
radio masts and communication antennae. At the end of the tribulation.
this world's communication systems will have a lot to be ashamed of, as
during this dreaded period the beast and the false prophet will likely have
had largely unrestricted dominion over airwaves and internet. In contrast
to the corrupted earthly communication systems, the divine message will
then have unrestricted distribution when God's righteousness and glory
will be universally seen in the heavens (Psalm 97:6), as already considered
in Psalms 19 and 89.

Psalm 97:6

"The heavens declare His righteousness, and all the people see His glory."

We considered in Psalms 19 and 89 that the concept of the heavens
declaring the righteousness and glory of God means more than just the glory
of the Creator in creation being once more recognised by man, His creature.
When we consult other passages showing that the Church, visible in the
heavens, will be involved in the administration of that coming Kingdom, it
can be appreciated that, in a special way in that day of glory, the heavens
shall declare His righteousness through the display of the Church therein.
This, of course, could not have been understood by the Psalmist as he wrote
"the heavens declare His righteousness", since Church truth was, at that
time, still a hidden unrevealed mystery known only to God .

B The future impact of the return of the Lord Jesus on believers and unbelievers

As for those who have worshipped the beast and his image there shall be
consternation and dread to discover that they have been deceived (Psalm
97:7).

Psalm 97:7

"Confounded be all they that serve graven images, (image (singular in
Hebrew)) that boast themselves of idols: worship Him, all *ye* gods (angels)."

Verse 7 considers the awful terror which will fill the hearts of the earth-
dwellers involved in the worship of the image (singular). Their scheme
to eliminate God has been found to have totally failed. The Lamb has at
last prevailed. It is this which provokes the worship from the hosts of
angels. Angels cannot sing the New Song of Psalm 96, because it is about
personal redemption by the blood of the Lamb, something angels can never
experience and only witness. However, they can and will worship Him for

His triumph over evil which will be demonstrated in that coming day.

Interestingly, in Hebrews 1:5 the writer quotes from Psalm 2, "Thou art My Son, this day have I begotten Thee", to show us that the grand cause of worship to the Lord from redeemed mankind is because of His resurrection and victory over death (see Psalm 2). It is immediately after this that the Hebrews writer (Hebrews 1:6) quotes from Psalm 97 to say on the occasion of the Lord Jesus' return, "let all the angels of God worship Him". To the great delight of the Father not only will redeemed humanity worship the Son, but unfallen angels worship Him too. When that happens, it can be said that the "Lord's prayer" has been fulfilled: "Thy will be done, as in heaven, so in earth". (Luke 11:2) The joy of the angels may be one thing. However, the joy of the redeemed shall be indescribable. This is what Psalm 97:8-9 is considering.

Psalm 97:8-9

8 "Zion heard, and was glad; and the daughters of Judah rejoiced because of Thy judgments, O Lord.
9 For Thou, Lord, *art* high above all the earth: Thou art exalted far above all gods (angels)."

The sight of the heavenly hosts worshipping Him on His return to earth will fill the waiting saints with joy. On the occasion of His condescension to become a little lower than the angels, these heavenly beings worshipped Him from heaven (Luke 2:13-14). That was a sight which filled the wondering shepherds with awe. How much more magnificent will it not be to see the Lord Jesus exalted "above all the earth" – not just "above all angels" but "far above all angels" (Psalm 97:9) – and worshipped by those august creatures! It is this sight which causes the remnant to rejoice and be glad.

C The present impact such meditations should have on believers today

Of course, such meditations must have a practical application. Doctrine without practical application is **pointless** and practical application without underlying doctrine is **powerless**. Accordingly, the Psalmist brings to us the divinely inspired application in Psalm 97:10.

(i) Preservation from evil

Psalm 97:10

"Ye that love the Lord, hate evil: He preserveth the souls of His saints; He delivereth them out of the hand of the wicked."

Literally, this could be translated, "Lovers of Jehovah, hate ye evil". There must surely be a practical application of any consideration of the Lord Jesus returning to reign. It is that all who love the Lord should depart from iniquity and hate the evil. Can this be done through natural strength? Clearly, divine help is needed to protect all believers' affections against evil influence, which is particularly intense as the last of the days approach. It is here where the keeping power of God is described. We learn that it is the Lord Who "preserveth the **souls** of His saints". The soul is the seat of perception, as emphasised in Leviticus 5 where we read, "if a soul see.., hear…, touch.. etc" and is "guilty…". The message of Leviticus 5 is that it is in the things we "see, hear and touch" that we can contract defilement in our souls. How important it is, then, to learn that the Lord "preserveth the **souls** of His saints". Note 1 He not only saves, He keeps His own and, above all, guards their affections. Since such an inexpressibly glorious future lies before us, how important it is that our souls, i.e. the affections of our hearts, are divinely protected to be wholly and exclusively taken up with the All-worthy One Who is the theme of the unending New Song of redemption. May those of us who are saved always crave from the Lord this constant divine protection of our souls' affections.

(ii) A constant exercise regarding future reward

Psalm 97:10
"Light is sown for the righteous, and gladness for the upright in heart."

There is a textual variant on the word "sown" in verse 11, where a change of only one letter in the Hebrew verb "to sow" changes the meaning of the phrase to, "light will dawn for the righteous and gladness for the upright in heart". This textual variant is supported by the Septuagint, and some scholars prefer this rendering, finding it difficult to understand how "light is sown". However, just because, superficially, a phrase in the Masoretic Hebrew text is at first glance difficult to understand, it does not necessarily mean it is not authentic. In fact, such conceptual difficulties may dissolve in consideration of the context of the exhortation "to hate evil" (verse 10), where the rendering, "light is sown", emerges as an **outcome** from such godly exercise of heart. Accordingly, the present author feels the Authorised Version rendering is contextually meaningful. In fact, this rendering brings much encouragement to us when we recall that for the righteous and upright ones God has prepared a wonderful and bountiful harvest, where the "fruit" to be reaped will be "light" and "gladness". In preparation for this, God has already sown the seeds of "light" and "gladness", and it is only a matter of time until the harvest will come. When a seed is sown it disappears from view and dies before it can produce fruit for the harvest (1 Corinthians 15:36).

In the valley experiences of life, at times there are overcast experiences when light is distant and gladness faint. In the valley of the shadow of death, it could be truly said that "light is sown", and in life's bereavement "gladness" seems to be an invisible "seed". Psalm 97:11 assures us that because it is God Who has sown the seed of light and gladness, the harvest is assured and the beneficiaries of this harvest of light and gladness will be the "righteous and upright in heart". Let us look forward, even in the valley of the shadow of death and the vale of tears, to that wonderful morning lying ahead when He will return in Glory and then we will not only see the light and gladness of His divine presence but we ourselves, His Bride, will become part of that light and gladness.

(iii) This prophetic study will bring joy to a believer today

However, do we have to await the great harvest of light and gladness to rejoice in Him? How wonderful to know that in the meantime, even in the vale of tears, the saints of all ages can rejoice and give thanks in remembrance of His holiness!

Psalm 97:11

"Rejoice in the Lord, ye righteous; and give thanks at the remembrance of His holiness."

Conclusion

Psalm 96 considered the tribulation era. Psalm 97 considered the events around the Lord Jesus' return to the earth to reign. This now leads into Psalms 98 and 99 which once again look joyfully at the characteristics of that future Kingdom. Let us too rejoice in anticipation of that day of glory.

---

1. In Psalms 8, 69 and 110 it is discussed how man, made in the image of God, has the capacity to love God (see Psalm 69 pages 269- 270). The redeemed human soul loves God (Psalm 110 pages 448-449). It is thus to these who love the Lord (Psalm 97:10) (lovers of Jehovah) that we read, "He preserveth the **souls** of His saints". The Lord jealously preserves His people's love for Him.

21

PSALM 98

A Psalm
1 O sing unto the Lord a New Song; for He hath done marvellous things: His
right hand, and His holy arm, hath gotten Him the victory.
2 The Lord hath made known His Salvation: His righteousness hath He openly
shewed in the sight of the heathen.
3 He hath remembered His mercy and His truth toward the house of Israel: all
the ends of the earth have seen the salvation of our God.
4 Make a joyful noise unto the Lord, all the earth: make a loud noise, and rejoice,
and sing praise.
5 Sing unto the Lord with the harp; with the harp, and the voice of a psalm.
6 With trumpets and sound of cornet make a joyful noise before the Lord, the
King.
7 Let the sea roar, and the fullness thereof; the world, and they that dwell therein.
8 Let the floods clap their hands: let the hills be joyful together
9 Before the Lord; for He cometh to judge the earth: with righteousness shall He
judge the world, and the people with equity.

Introduction

Psalm 98 is not a Messianic Psalm since it is not quoted directly in the New
Testament. However, it deals with the transformation which happens to this
earth immediately after the events of Psalm 97 have come to pass, namely
the Lord's return to reign. Because Psalm 98 follows on so directly from
Psalm 97, which is a Messianic Psalm, it is included in this book. The Psalm
speaks of the joy attending the Lord's return to the earth in manifested glory
when the earth will have been healed from the ravages of sin.

The worship in the coming Kingdom

It is in this context that the worshippers take up once more the priestly
song of Psalm 40 – "the New Song".

Psalm 98:1

"O sing unto the Lord a New Song; for He hath done marvellous things:
His right hand, and His holy arm, hath gotten Him the victory."

The language of the Psalm indicates that the victory has already been accomplished: "for He hath done marvellous things". The Psalm is effectively the future language of a people looking back to the victory of the Person of Christ over His enemies on the occasion of His return in Psalm 97. The words, "marvellous things", are used to describe the victory of the Lord over the hosts of Pharaoh in the Passover story.

Micah 7:14-15

14 "Feed Thy people with Thy rod, the flock of Thine heritage, which dwell solitarily *in* the wood, in the midst of Carmel: let them feed *in* Bashan and Gilead, as in the days of old.

15 According to the days of thy coming out of the land of Egypt will I shew unto him marvellous *things*."

The association with priesthood is emphasised to us by the words, "marvellous things", since the objective of the Passover and subsequent Exodus was to call out of Egypt a priestly people. However, this victory is infinitely more marvellous than the ancient victory over Pharaoh in Egypt. The phrase, 'hath gotten Him the victory', is the word *hoshiah* which forms the first part of the *hoshiah...* in *hoshiah-na* (meaning "save now") in Psalm 118 (see later). The *hoshiah-na* of Psalm 118 is a call to the Lord to come and "save" His remnant people from the horrors of the great tribulation. The *hoshiah* of Psalm 98:1 ("gotten Him the victory") is looking back at the great victory of the One Who has come and saved His people from their distresses.

Psalm 98:2

"The Lord hath made known His salvation: His righteousness hath He openly shewed in the sight of the heathen."

An intrinsic part of this deliverance will be the making known of His salvation. We saw in Psalm 96 that the remnant preachers of that era will "preach as good news *Yeshua* (salvation)". That was the only message which could bring deliverance to the people. However, in Psalm 98 the consideration is no longer of the tribulation preachers declaring their message of "Jesus". Rather it is of the public declaration and revelation **by God** to the whole world of "His Jesus" (His Salvation).

Psalm 98:3

"He hath remembered His mercy and His truth toward the house of Israel: all the ends of the earth have seen the Salvation of our God."

What a day that will be when the Lord Jesus shall be revealed in all His glory to a wondering world! When that happens, it can be said that the Lord has remembered His mercy and His faithfulness to the house of Israel and publicly demonstrated this globally.

Psalm 98:4-8

4 "Make a joyful noise unto the Lord, all the earth: make a loud noise, and rejoice, and sing praise.

5 Sing unto the Lord with the harp; with the harp, and the voice of a psalm.

6 With trumpets and sound of cornet make a joyful noise before the Lord, the King.

7 Let the sea roar, and the fullness thereof; the world, and they that dwell therein.

8 Let the floods clap *their* hands: let the hills be joyful together."

The universal recognition by the dwellers on earth of the claims of the Person of Christ will lead to unparalleled prosperity and productivity in the natural world. Verses 4-5 describe the spontaneous praise from the inhabitants of earth, and verses 7-8 show the parallel productivity of healed creation. The picture of the rivers clapping their hands is a delightful description of the sounds emerging from streams and rivers where copious fast flowing water, tumbling over stones and waterfalls, causes the sound of clapping of hands to be heard in what was once wilderness and drought-cursed land.

Psalm 98:9

"Before the Lord; for He cometh to judge the earth: with righteousness shall He judge the world, and the people with equity."

This great response is to the Lord, Who has come to "judge the earth". This word "to judge" means to administer and govern it. When that happens there will be unparalleled peace and prosperity globally.

22

PSALM 99

1 *"The Lord reigneth; let the people tremble: He sitteth between the cherubims; let the earth be moved.*
2 The Lord is great in Zion; and He is high above all the people.
3 Let them praise Thy great and terrible Name; for it is holy.
4 The King's strength also loveth judgment; Thou dost establish equity, Thou executest judgment and righteousness in Jacob.
5 Exalt ye the Lord our God, and worship at His footstool; for He is holy.
6 Moses and Aaron among His priests, and Samuel among them that call upon His Name; they called upon the Lord, and He answered them.
7 He spake unto them in the cloudy pillar: they kept His testimonies, and the ordinance that He gave them.
8 Thou answeredst them, O Lord our God: Thou wast a God that forgavest them, though Thou tookest vengeance of their inventions.
9 Exalt the Lord our God, and worship at His Holy Hill; for the Lord our God is holy."

Introduction

Psalm 99 continues the theme of Psalm 98 and further elaborates the New Song which will be sung in millennial glory. Like Psalm 98, it is not a Messianic Psalm as it is not quoted directly in the New Testament. However, since it forms part of a series of Psalms dealing with the story of the Lord Jesus coming back to reign, it is included in this book. The Psalm gives more details as to how worship will be conducted in the millennial Kingdom.

Psalm 99:1-4

1 "The Lord reigneth; let the people tremble: He sitteth *between* the cherubims; let the earth be moved.
2 The Lord *is* great in Zion; and He *is* high above all the people.
3 Let them praise Thy great and terrible Name; *for it is* holy.
4 The King's strength also loveth judgment; Thou dost establish equity, Thou executest judgment and righteousness in Jacob."

Worship of the Lord in the millennial Kingdom

Psalm 99:1-4 graphically describes the unversal reverential awe in which the Lord will be held in that coming day. The people will tremble (verse 1). This is a healthy fear of the Lord which is a reverential dread of grieving Him. The application for each believer today is that in our individual lives such a reverential fear of grieving Him will bring divine blessing upon us.

Where will the Lord be during the millennial reign? We know that the Church will be in the heavens. However, where will He be? Verse 2 tells us that He is high above all the people. Verse 5 calls on the earth-dwellers in that coming day to "worship at His footstool".

Psalm 99:5

"Exalt ye the Lord our God, and worship at His footstool; *for* He *is* holy."

This is most illuminating as Isaiah identifies for us the meaning of the Lord's "footstool" in this statement:

Isaiah 66:1

"Thus saith the Lord, The heaven is My throne, and the earth is My footstool: where is the house that ye build unto Me? and where is the place of My rest?"

If the inhabitants of the millennial earth are worshipping at His footstool, that would suggest that there is **an earthly sanctuary (the house that ye build unto Me (Isaiah 61:1))** where this worship takes place. However, the **throne will be in the heavens** and it is to the Throne-Sitter that the worship is directed. This shows us that the Lord Jesus will be with the Church in the heavenly city in the heavens, while the Old Testament and tribulation saints will mingle with the millennial inhabitants, and in priestly capacity they will worship before Him at His footstool, i.e. at His earthly sanctuary, which will be the wonderful millennial temple described by Ezekiel at the end of his prophecy. Although Ezekiel's temple will be the physical location on earth of their collective worship, by faith as priests who are able to sing the New Song, they will have access to the heavenly throne, just as we as priests on earth today have access to the heavenly throne, even though we are physically upon this earth.

Psalm 99:6-8 brings before us some famous people who will be on earth in that coming day worshipping the Lord Jesus.

Psalm 99:6-8

6 "Moses and Aaron among His priests, and Samuel among them that call upon His Name; they called upon the Lord, and He answered them.
7 He spake unto them in the cloudy pillar: they kept His testimonies, and the ordinance *that* He gave them.
8 Thou answeredst them, O Lord our God: Thou wast a God that forgavest them, though Thou tookest vengeance of their inventions."

Moses, Aaron and Samuel will no longer be around the throne in heaven singing the New Song, as in Revelation 5, but are now on earth at the Lord's **footstool,** worshipping Him and continuing their priestly ministry. Verse 6 brings before us the reason for their worship in that coming day. It is because in the past they had "called upon the Lord, and He answered them". This is the same word for "answer" as was discussed in Psalm 22:2, i.e. the "answer" which God gives to the "Sacrifice" indicating His acceptance of it. In a sense, these servants of God were familiar with the Lord "answering" them with fire upon the altar to demonstrate divine acceptance of their sacrifices in their lifetime. However, as was considered in Psalm 22:2, the ultimate "answer" to all the needs of the Old Testament saints came when God answered the Lord Jesus at Calvary in the hours of darkness. This important doctrinal matter was discussed at length in Psalm 22:2. In Psalm 22:21, it was the divine answer to the sacrificial Person of Christ at Calvary which is the theme of the praise in the "great congregation". In fact, the reference in Psalm 98:8 to God's forgiveness (Hebrew: "bearing away" sins) being based on God "answering" His servants strongly suggests that the "answer", envisaged in this verse, goes beyond the divine answer of fire upon animal sacrifices to the ultimate Sacrifice of the Lord Jesus, which was answered in the "night season" in Psalm 22:2.

The sins of Old Testament believers which were "passed over" before Calvary have now been borne by Christ (see Psalm 22 and Appendix 5). On the basis of this, these Old Testament saints can now be made fit for the heavenly sanctuary (Revelation 5:8-9) and the millennial earthly sanctuary.

Herein, then, is the revelation of the New Song. It is a song about personal redemption and of the triumph of the suffering One of Golgotha Who bore away iniquity that a priestly people may be fitted to serve Him eternally. How fitting then that this Psalm ends with a call to these millennial saints to "exalt the Lord our God and worship at His Holy Hill" in millennial Jerusalem, which is the "footstool" of the Lord!

Psalm 99:9

"Exalt the Lord our God, and worship at His Holy Hill; for the Lord our God *is* holy."

Conclusion

We have seen how the perplexities of Psalm 94 are all solved when, after the return of the Lord Jesus to the earth, every wrong is put to right and divine authority is established. This Psalm shows that in that day of glory, Old Testament saints, risen from the dead, will once again be walking on this earth, singing the New Song of priests who have access to the throne in heaven.

23

PSALM 102

A Prayer of the afflicted, when he is overwhelmed, and poureth out his complaint before the Lord.

1 Hear my prayer, O Lord, and let my cry come unto Thee.

2 Hide not Thy face from me in the day when I am in trouble; incline Thine ear unto me: in the day when I call answer me speedily.

3 For my days are consumed like smoke, and my bones are burned as an hearth.

4 My heart is smitten, and withered like grass; so that I forget to eat my bread.

5 By reason of the voice of my groaning my bones cleave to my skin.

6 I am like a pelican of the wilderness: I am like an owl of the desert.

7 I watch, and am as a sparrow alone upon the house top.

8 Mine enemies reproach me all the day; and they that are mad against me are sworn against me.

9 For I have eaten ashes like bread, and mingled my drink with weeping,

10 Because of Thine indignation and Thy wrath: for Thou hast lifted me up, and cast me down.

11 My days are like a shadow that declineth; and I am withered like grass.

12 But Thou, O Lord, shalt endure for ever; and Thy remembrance unto all generations.

13 Thou shalt arise, and have mercy upon Zion: for the time to favour her, yea, the set time, is come.

14 For Thy servants take pleasure in her stones, and favour the dust thereof.

15 So the heathen shall fear the Name of the Lord, and all the kings of the earth Thy glory.

16 When the Lord shall build up Zion, He shall appear in His glory.

17 He will regard the prayer of the destitute, and not despise their prayer.

18 This shall be written for the generation to come: and the people which shall be created shall praise the Lord.

19 For He hath looked down from the height of His sanctuary; from heaven did the Lord behold the earth;

20 To hear the groaning of the prisoner; to loose those that are appointed to death;

21 To declare the Name of the Lord in Zion, and His praise in Jerusalem;

22 When the people are gathered together, and the kingdoms, to serve the Lord.

23 He weakened my strength in the way; He shortened my days.
24 I said, O my God, take me not away in the midst of my days: Thy years are throughout all generations.
25 Of old hast Thou laid the foundation of the earth: and the heavens are the work of Thy hands.
26 They shall perish, but Thou shalt endure: yea, all of them shall wax old like a garment; as a vesture shalt Thou change them, and they shall be changed:
27 But Thou art the same, and Thy years shall have no end.
28 The children of Thy servants shall continue, and their seed shall be established before Thee.

Introduction

While it is possible that the writing of this Psalm took place at a time of personal trouble in the experience of the Psalmist, there is a clear indication in verse 18 that a primary prophetic significance to the Psalm was intended: "This shall be written for the **generation to come**: and the people which shall be created shall praise the Lord."

We may well ask which generation and which people are referred to in the Psalm?

The people are the people of Zion (verse 13), i.e. the nation of Israel, and the generation is a future generation (verse 18) facing an impending time period of extreme adversity.

Psalm 102:1-2

1 "Hear my prayer, O Lord, and let my cry come unto Thee.
2 Hide not Thy face from me in the day (Hebrew: a day) when I am in trouble; incline Thine ear unto me: in the day (Hebrew: a day) when I call answer me speedily."

The supplicant in the Psalm is imploring the Lord not to hide His face from him in **a day** when he is in trouble. The fact that the day being described here is depicted in indefinite language as "a day", and not "this day" or "the day", suggests that it is a day yet future and that the timing of its onset is unclear or indefinite to the speaker. This observation is important, as further details of the day under consideration here point to it as being the tribulation period yet to be seen on this earth, a day of "trouble" or perhaps literally "a day of tribulation".

As the supplicants in the Psalm face this impending day of uncertain onset, they recognise the underlying problem that God has hidden His face from them.

Psalm 102:2

"Hide not Thy face from me in the day (Hebrew: a day) *when* I am in trouble."

Evidently, the Psalmist in the Psalm, who is speaking on behalf of the estranged nation of Israel, is facing the prospect of a day of tribulation just lying ahead. However, even before this happens the supplicant is already experiencing a tragic valley experience of loneliness and despair (verses 3-11) where God's face seems to be hidden from them. How sweet then that the Psalm ends with the restored nation once again beholding **the face** of the Lord:

Psalm 102:28
"The children of Thy servants shall continue, and their seed shall be established before Thee (literally: before Thy face)."

1 Israel's condition under the metaphor of a serious illness
Before the day of tribulation comes on the nation, it has come to recognise its own desolation in verses 3-11.

Psalm 102:3-9
3 "For my days are consumed like smoke, and my bones are burned as an hearth.
4 My heart is smitten, and withered like grass; so that I forget to eat my bread.
5 By reason of the voice of my groaning my bones cleave to my skin.
6 I am like a pelican of the wilderness: I am like an owl of the desert.
7 I watch, and am as a sparrow alone upon the house top.
8 Mine enemies reproach me all the day; *and* they that are mad against me are sworn against me.
9 For I have eaten ashes like bread, and mingled my drink with weeping."

The recovery of the remnant of Israel occurs after the rapture of the Church but before the tribulation starts, and it begins with a recognition of their absolute helplessness and desolation as those from whom God's face has been hidden. The timing of the spiritual rebirth of the nation of Israel's remnant is considered in Appendices 2 and 3. There it is shown that following the rapture of the Church there will be a move of God among those of the Jewish nation who, at the time of the rapture, were too young to be among those who "believe not the truth" and "have pleasure in unrighteousness" (2 Thessalonians 2:12). The recovery will begin with a recognition that their position is desperate.

A Time is running out

Psalm 102:3
"My days –consumed like smoke."

When the underlying flame which generates the smoke is petering out, the smoke is most dense. This is in parallel with verse 11: "My days are like a shadow that declineth (literally: lengthened)". The longer the shadow, the later the hour. This is Israel's final and darkest hour.

B Strength is running out
My bones – burned as an hearth (literally: burned as fuel) (Psalm 102:3)

My heart – smitten and withered like grass (Psalm 102:4)

My bones – cleaving to my skin (muscles have wasted away, i.e. no strength) (Psalm 102:5) because of my groaning

My drink – mingled with weeping (Psalm 102:9) (a picture of mourning and sadness having eaten ashes like bread and mingled his drink with tears)

The Psalmist depicts a complex medical disease involving hyper-metabolism of the bones (bones burning as fuel), severe muscle wasting (bones cleaving to skin with no muscle between) and severe heart disease such that the heart is "smitten" and then withers (i.e. dead tissue within the heart such as a healed and fibrosed myocardial infarction). There is also profound accompanying depression. This, to the author's knowledge, is the first ever-recorded description of the symptoms of hyperparathyroidism in the world – a condition which, until the advent of modern medicine, was universally fatal. In hyperparathyroidism, the calcium in the bones is liberated into the blood (bones burn like fuel) and the bones become weaker and more easily fractured. Frequently, these patients develop abdominal pain and lose appetite (I forget to eat my bread (Psalm 102:4)). There is also profound depression at times. There is resulting weight loss and muscle atrophy. The excessive calcium in the blood can predispose to heart attacks, where blood supply to an area of the heart is disrupted and the resulting damaged area of heart becomes fibrosed and dysfunctional (withered like grass). Of course, thankfully, not all sufferers from hyperparathyroidism experience the totality of these symptoms and complications! However, in this Psalm we are brought to consider a worst case scenario to depict the helpless situation of the remnant of Israel looking forward to the dreadful days of tribulation, and longing for the God of Israel to reveal His face to them before the day of tribulation starts.

C Support is running out

Psalm 102:6-8 describes the complete helplessness, isolation and desolation of the nation in that future day.

Psalm 102:6-8

6 "I am like a pelican of the wilderness: I am like an owl of the desert (Hebrew: wastelands).

7 I watch, and am as a sparrow alone upon the house top.

8 Mine enemies reproach me all the day; *and* they that are mad against me are sworn against me."

A pelican eats fish so it is in trouble if it finds itself in the wilderness. Similarly, the owl is in difficulty if it is in wastelands where the small animal life, which it needs for survival, is nowhere to be found. A sparrow alone upon the house top is exposed, vulnerable and possibly has lost its only mate. "I watch" (Psalm 102:7) depicts the constant second by second vigilance of this tiny creature which is always concerned with approaching danger. In the Psalmist's case, he is similarly looking around at the constant threat from those who have "sworn against me". In the post-rapture pre-tribulation period there will be none to whom Israel can turn for true protection. Those who form part of the apostate segment of the nation will turn to the man of sin, in whom so many will have placed their trust for protection (see Appendix 2). This evil individual will stand together with Israel's apostate leader, the false prophet, to promote his own self worship and seek (unsuccessfully) to fulfil his aim to exterminate the nation.

2 The awakening

The next section considers Israel's future awakening and revival. It begins with a deep conviction as to why the Lord has been grieved with His people.

Psalm 102:10

"Because of Thine indignation and Thy wrath: for Thou hast lifted me up, and cast me down."

There is a recognition that the extreme circumstances, into which the nation has fallen, have come from God Himself. God in the past had "lifted up" the nation, and it is He Who has cast them down. There is a realisation that God has been grieved by the nation's independence of Him and has allowed them to go on with His face hidden from them (Psalm 102:2) until they noticed that something was wrong. The "casting down" of the nation, as described here, is discussed in Romans 11:1: "Hath God cast away His people? God forbid." God may have cast **down** the nation (Psalm 102), following the rejection of her Messiah, but He has not cast her **away** (Romans 11:1-2).

Romans 11:1-2
1 "Say then, Hath God cast away His people? God forbid. For I also am an Israelite, of the seed of Abraham, of the tribe of Benjamin.
2 God hath not cast away His people which He foreknew."

There is a very bright future, but this dawn cannot happen until the remnant nation acknowledges that it is *in extremis* and realises that their problem throughout two millennia of wanderings and sufferings at the hands of the Gentiles has directly arisen from **God hiding His face** (verse 2) from His own beloved people. What joy there will be in heaven when the prayer goes forth from Israel:
"Hear my prayer, O Lord, and let my cry come unto Thee. **Hide not Thy face** from me in the day *when* I am in trouble" (verses 1-2).
Sadly, for over 2000 years the nation has been estranged from her Messiah and blind to His mercy and grace. His constant longing has been that they will be reconciled to Him. To this day, the veil has been upon their heart (2 Corinthians 2:12-16), and they have been blinded to the wonderful **face of Christ** and His mercy and grace.

2 Corinthians 3:12-16
12 "Seeing then that we have such hope, we use great plainness of speech:
13 And not as Moses, *which* put a vail over his face, that the children of

Israel could not steadfastly look to the end of that which is abolished:
14 But their minds were blinded: for until this day remaineth the same vail
untaken away in the reading of the Old Testament; which *vail* is done away
in Christ.
15 But even unto this day, when Moses is read, the vail is upon their heart.
16 Nevertheless when it shall turn to the Lord, the vail shall be taken away."

Herein lies the first hint of hope: a recognition that the **Lord's face** has
been hidden from them for many years. The next step in the revival is the
discovery that, although the Lord's face has been hidden from them, He has
never forgotten them and, despite all their failure, His heart has remained
full of longings towards them of mercy and grace.

Psalm 102:12-13

12 "But Thou, O Lord, shalt endure for ever; and Thy remembrance unto
all generations.
13 Thou shalt arise, *and* have mercy upon Zion: for the time to favour her
(Hebrew: be gracious to her), yea, the set time, is come."

Realising that her circumstances have been allowed of God, there comes
a **remembrance** in the heart of the distressed remnant people of God's
unchangeable character, especially His mercy and His grace. In verse 10, the
nation has encountered His **indignation and wrath** but in verse 13 they are
reminded of His **mercy and His grace!** Why for so long have they been blind
to a remembrance of His mercy and grace? It is in the next Psalm, Psalm
103, that we are reminded that God's mercy and grace were in a special way
revealed to Moses in Exodus 34. Indeed, this section must form a central
part of this national remembrance of the Lord's mercy and grace.

Psalm 103:7-12

7 "He made known His ways unto Moses, His acts unto the children of
Israel.
8 The Lord *is* merciful and gracious, slow to anger, and plenteous in mercy.
9 He will not always chide: neither will He keep *His anger* for ever.
10 He hath not dealt with us after our sins; nor rewarded us according to
our iniquities.
11 For as the heaven is high above the earth, *so* great is His mercy toward
them that fear Him.
12 As far as the east is from the west, *so* far hath He removed our
transgressions from us."

In fact, the reference in Psalm 103:8 to the **mercy and grace** of the Lord calls
to remembrance the incident in Exodus 34:6-8 when, after the golden calf
apostasy, the Lord revealed Himself to Moses as the gracious and merciful
God (Exodus 34:6). This incident has already been considered in detail in
the prayer of Moses, the Man of God, in Psalm 90, again in Psalm 95 and
its citation in Hebrews 3. However, some points need to be reconsidered as
they are important to the understanding of Psalm 102 and the Lord's face

being hidden from His people for so long.

One is reminded of Moses' first descent from Mount Sinai. It was a revelation of God's **indignation and wrath** on the people for breaking His Holy Law. However, it was following Moses' second visit to Mount Sinai and the revelation of Jehovah as the **merciful and gracious One** that Moses descended with a revelation of the forgiveness of God (Exodus 34:6) based on God's mercy and grace through the divine Sin-Bearer. This is clear because the phrase in Exodus 34:7, "the Lord God…forgiving iniquity, transgression and sin…" means literally in Hebrew, "the Lord God… bearing away iniquity, transgression and sin". This revelation of the **Sin-Bearing One** made Moses' face to shine, and he veiled his face (Exodus 34:33).

Two thousand years ago, the Son of God came down, not from Mount Sinai but from heaven's throne, with a revelation, not of judgment but of mercy and grace. Moses' face shone with a reflected glory which he veiled. The Lord's glory was intrinsic because He is the embodiment of divine Grace. He is the divine Sin-Bearing One prophesied by Moses in Exodus 34. This is consistent with John the Baptist's comment on the Lamb of God Who had come to bear away the sin of the world in John's Gospel 1:17. "The Law was given by Moses, but grace and truth came by Jesus Christ." The Lord Jesus did not veil the glory of His grace and mercy while on earth. This was fully revealed to the people as the apostle Paul points out:

2 Corinthians 8:9:
"For ye know the grace of our Lord Jesus Christ, that, though He was rich, yet for your sakes He became poor, that ye through His poverty might be rich."

John the Baptist made it very clear that He was the Sin-Bearing Lamb. Surely the nation should have responded with gladness and relief at such wondrous grace! Alas, only a minority did! Unbelief characterised the majority. Paul continues to parallel the Exodus 34 story with Israel's present condition. He shows us that just as Moses' veiled face meant that the ancient people were unable to see the glory of God's grace in the face of Moses, so today this veil remains upon the heart of the unbelieving nation of Israel:

2 Corinthians 3:15-16
15 "But even unto this day, when Moses is read, the vail is upon their heart.
16 Nevertheless when it shall turn to the Lord, the vail shall be taken away."

In Psalm 102, the nation claims that the **Lord's face is hidden** from them, so they are missing the revelation of the glory of the grace and mercy of God in the face of Christ. Likewise, in Exodus 34, they were missing the reflected glory of the mercy and grace of God in Moses' face.

Sadly, to this day perhaps the majority of Jews remain blind to the glory of the mercy and grace in the face of Christ. This is because of their 2000-year period of unbelief in their Messiah. What a day it will be when they realise that there is more to the face of God than a face of indignation and wrath! When they ask the Lord to no longer hide His face from them, the face of His mercy and His grace will be revealed to them. Surely this is the revelation of Christ Himself to the nation!

Salvation comes when they discover that the one and only way to personally receive this mercy and grace, is to come as one empty-handed and destitute claiming that very mercy and grace as indicated in this Psalm:

Psalm 102:17
"He will regard the prayer of the destitute, and not despise their prayer."

As considered in Appendix 3, this great awakening and spiritual rebirth of the nation will take place after the rapture of the Church and before the tribulation starts during an undefined period of time between the rapture of the Church and the onset of the seven-year tribulation period.

3 The result of Israel's acceptance of the Lord's grace and mercy through Christ

The turning again to the Lord will lead His people to look upon the desolate land of Israel before and during the tribulation with anticipation of its impending transformation under Messiah's rule (Psalm 102:14)

Psalm 102:14
"For Thy servants take pleasure in her stones, and favour the dust thereof."

When the set time is reached that Zion becomes the object of divine grace and mercy (verse 13), then the Lord's servants will similarly have cause to take pleasure in her stones and dust. The stones and dust of Zion today speak of Israel's desolations and judgments. This cannot bring pleasure to the Lord's servants. It is a cause of sorrow. What brought them joy was the prospect of the day of Zion's rebuilding by her Messiah when the stones and dust will be transformed by Him into a royal city suitable for the King. Then the nations who enter into the millennium shall fear the Lord.

Psalm 102:15-16
15 "So the heathen (nations) shall fear the Name of the Lord, and all the kings of the earth Thy glory.
16 When the Lord shall build up Zion, He shall appear in His glory."

This will be the earthly city we considered in Psalm 24, the gates of which shall be the place of administration of the King. His glory will be seen then in Zion. This will mark the answer to the prayers of the destitute remnant during the horrors of the tribulation months a short time earlier, of whom it can be said,

Psalm 102:17
"He will regard the prayer of the destitute, and not despise their prayer."

The Psalmist is conscious that he is describing momentous events of a coming day and therefore says,

Psalm 102:18

"This shall be written for the generation to come: and the people which shall be created shall praise the Lord."

4 The praise of the Lord

A The reason for the praise

We considered in Psalm 72 that praise unto the King shall be for His salvation and grace. In this Psalm, the same theme is emphasised. The people shall praise the Lord (verse 18) for considering them, hearing them and loosing them from bondage:

Psalm 102:19-20

19 "For He hath looked down from the height of His sanctuary; from heaven did the Lord behold the earth;
20 To hear the groaning of the prisoner; to loose those that are appointed to death;"

B The location of the praise

This song of praise shall take place in Jerusalem which will become the centre of worship of the Lord on earth, not just for Israel but for all the nations:

Psalm 102:21-22

21 "To declare the Name of the Lord in Zion, and His praise in Jerusalem;
22 When the people are gathered together, and the kingdoms, to serve the Lord."

C The duration of the praise

The Psalm ends with a consideration of the duration of this blessed state of Israel's future fellowship with her God. Will it come to an end? Can it end in tears like the former time the *Shechinah* cloud was present among the children of Israel in the Land, from the Exodus up until the time of Ezekiel the prophet? In this context, the Psalmist is reminded of former days of weakness and premature death of Israel's kings due to their unfaithfulness to God.

Psalm 102:23

"He weakened my strength in the way; He shortened my days."

What a contrast is the situation of the restored nation in that day of glory! They have no cause to fear a repeat of the nation's many failures as happened in the days of the kings. At this point, the Psalmist remembers the prayer of the remnant in its hour of distress in the tribulation. It is a prayer of someone subject to mortality.

Psalm 102:24

"I said, O my God, take me not away in the midst of my days."

God answered that prayer and delivered the captive and preserved the dying. The God Who answers the prayers of His people, who are subject to death, is eternal and unchanging. What a comfort to us! Thus we read at the end of verse 24, "Thy years *are* throughout all generations". This means that those who experience the deliverance of Christ cannot lose His security no matter what era of time (generation) he or she lives in, even if and when the universe ends! We now come upon a beautiful statement of the unchanging character of God.

5 The unchanging character of God

Psalm 102:25-27

25 "Of old hast Thou laid the foundation of the earth: and the heavens *are* the work of Thy hands.
26 They shall perish, but Thou shalt endure: yea, all of them shall wax old like a garment; as a vesture shalt Thou change them, and they shall be changed:
27 But Thou *art* the same, and Thy years shall have no end."

These verses bring before us a future day when this world and the heavens shall be changed. The word "changed" is the same root word as is used of Joseph changing the garments of his brothers in Egypt (Genesis 45:22). Joseph didn't patch up the old worn clothes! He gave them new clothing – the best in his palace. This is the underlying meaning of the word "to change" here. It really means "to replace". The old creation will pass away. The earth and the heavens will be no more and they will be replaced. Therefore, Psalm 102 is an Old Testament prophecy of new heavens and a new earth. John's vision in Revelation 21:1 of the new heaven and a new earth accords with this.

Interestingly, Psalm 72, which is the Psalm of the millennium, limits the duration of the earthly Kingdom to the duration of the sun and moon.

In Psalm 72:5, we read, "They shall fear Thee as long as the sun and moon endure, throughout all generations". Again, in Psalm 72: 17 we read, "His Name shall be continued as long as the sun".

Psalm 102 helps us to understand these verses in Psalm 72. The significance of Psalm 72 verses 5 and 17 is that the present sun and moon will eventually cease to exist. Psalm 72 implies a day when the universe will end. Psalm 102 goes further and states that it will end and be replaced by a new earth and heaven. However, the Kingdom of our Lord Jesus shall not cease! This is because, "Thou art the same, and Thy years shall have no end". However, the question may be asked, what will become of the saints in that great event when the universe will pass away and the new heavens and the new earth be brought in? Is their security in jeopardy? Of course not! Their entire well-being is bound up in the God of mercy and grace Whose glorious face they have come to behold. Thus we read these reassuring and blessed words:

Psalm 102:28

"The children of Thy servants shall continue, and their seed shall be
established before Thee (literally: before Thy face)."

What a wonderful way to end the Psalm! Heaven and earth have passed
away. The memory of the wicked is gone. That **face of mercy and grace,**
which so moved the believing remnant at the time of their restoration, will
continue to be their occupation forever as "the children of Thy servants shall
continue and their seed shall be established before Thy face".

Let us not forget that this Psalm is quoted in Hebrews chapter one.

Hebrews 1:10-12

10 "And, Thou, Lord, in the beginning hast laid the foundation of the earth;
and the heavens are the works of Thine hands:
11 They shall perish; but Thou remainest; and they all shall wax old as doth
a garment;
12 And as a vesture shalt Thou fold them up, and they shall be changed:
but Thou art the same, and Thy years shall not fail."

It comes at the end of a series of Old Testament passages reaffirming
the certainty of the future earthly Kingdom of Christ. The reason for this
was that there were those within that early Jewish Christian community
who were doubting the literal meaning of these Old Testament promises,
and this was casting doubt on the faithfulness of God. If God is not able to
bring to fruition His promises of an earthly Kingdom to His ancient people
Israel, how can our Lord Jesus be faithful as our Great High Priest today?
Before expounding the truth of the faithfulness of Christ, the writer of the
Hebrews must show that none of the Old Testament promises to Israel
would be watered down. Psalm 102 is thus an important passage for him
to quote, to show that even after this universe passes away, "the children
of Thy servants and their seed will be established" in the new heavens and
the new earth. This means that Israel will retain her identity not only in
the millennium but right through into the eternal state. This has already
been considered in Psalm 8. Similarly, the Church will retain its identity
eternally, but that is left to the New Testament to explain to us, since Church
teaching, as we saw in Psalm 89, is a mystery doctrine hidden in the Old
Testament and only fully expounded in the New.

Conclusion

This Psalm shows that the nation of Israel, once distressed through finding
God's face hidden from them for two thousand years, will once more see the
face of their Messiah in a renewed Peniel experience like Jacob of old. Their
new-found relationship with Him will never be interrupted again. Their
salvation is eternal and goes out into the eternal state.

24

PSALM 110

A Psalm of David.
1 The Lord said unto my Lord, Sit Thou at My right hand, until I make Thine enemies Thy footstool.
2 The Lord shall send the rod of Thy strength out of Zion: rule Thou in the midst of Thine enemies.
3 Thy people shall be willing in the day of Thy power, in the beauties of holiness from the womb of the morning: Thou hast the dew of Thy youth.
4 The Lord hath sworn, and will not repent, Thou art a Priest for ever after the order of Melchisedec.
5 The Lord at Thy right hand shall strike through kings in the day of His wrath.
6 He shall judge among the heathen, He shall fill the places with the dead bodies; He shall wound the heads over many countries.
7 He shall drink of the brook in the way: therefore shall He lift up the head.

Introduction

We are left in no doubt that this is a Messianic Psalm by the Lord's referring to the first verse of this Psalm in a discourse with the Pharisees in Matthew 22:44. All other subsequent quotations in the New Testament underline an understanding by the New Testament writers that this Psalm refers to the Lord Jesus.

The Psalm readily divides into two. Verses 1-4 are focussed mainly on the **"day of Thy power"** (Psalm 110:3). This present era is the day of His power, when His power is seen in the preaching of the gospel of the risen Christ.

The remainder of the Psalm considers **"the day of His wrath"** (Psalm 110:5). This will be the future manifestation of the wrath of God in the events leading up to and including the return of the Lord Jesus to reign.

The day of His power

The first demonstrations of the day of His power are the occasions of the resurrection and ascension to glory of the Lord Jesus Christ.

Each of the three clauses which make up the first verse are given sequential exposition in the New Testament.

Psalm 110:1

"The Lord said unto my Lord, Sit Thou at My right hand, until I make Thine enemies Thy footstool."

Firstly, it is the Lord Who expounds the first clause, "The Lord said unto my Lord" in Matthew 22:44.

Then it is Peter, subsequent to the resurrection of the Lord Jesus in Acts 2:34, who explains the second clause, "Sit Thou at My right hand."

Finally, it is the writer of the Hebrews who tells us the significance of the third clause, "Until I make Thine enemies Thy footstool" in Hebrews 1:13. The verse is then given detailed exposition throughout the rest of the Hebrews epistle.

1 "The Lord said unto my Lord" – man's reluctance to accept the Lordship and Deity of Christ

When the Lord in Matthew 22:24 quoted to His temple audience from Psalm 110, He was bringing to a conclusion a discourse on the subject of God's analysis of and response to the rejection by man of the Messiah. The purpose of the Lord's discourse was to show that man rejects the Messiah, despite irrefutable evidence for His legitimate claim upon men for their obedience and faith. The Lord shows that they reject Him despite the witness of John the Baptist, the presence of the Lord Jesus Himself during His life on earth and even despite the ideal conditions of the future millennial Kingdom. Here is a summary of His teaching that day:

His rejection despite the message of John

In Matthew 21:28-32, in the parable of the two sons who were asked by their father to work in the vineyard, the context is the rejection of the message of John by the elite elements of the Jewish nation.

His rejection despite being present on earth Himself

Later, in Matthew 21:33-46 in the parable of the husbandmen of the vineyard, who slew the son of the owner, He is showing that even the very presence of Christ in the midst does not prevent some of His own people rejecting Him.

His future rejection by some individuals even in the day of His millennial glory

The parable of Matthew 22: 1-14 is of a wedding feast. Moreover, there are people present who are not true believers and have wandered in without a wedding garment. The wedding feast cannot be a picture of heaven as there cannot be anything which defiles in heaven. When we recall that the millennial reign of our Lord Jesus Christ is in fact the marriage supper of the Lamb on earth, then we understand how there can be false professors at the wedding feast on earth but no false professors at the great supper of Luke 14:16-24 which is a picture of heaven. How do the false professors gain access to the millennial scene in Matthew 22:1-14? The answer is that they have been born into it. Everyone who is born into the millennium still requires a fitness to remain in it, in fellowship with God (see Psalm 72). In other words, they need to be saved. Despite absence of any influences to discourage the truth of God, there will be those who will still reject the "garments of salvation" (Isaiah 61:10). This parable is the Lord's final argument proving the total failure of man as illustrated by the future rejection of the Messiah, despite the ideal conditions which will prevail in the millennium.

A The Lord's reasons why fallen man is still special to God

Having established that man is a failure despite (i) the testimony of John the Baptist, (ii) the direct challenge of the Lord Himself and (iii) the ideal conditions of millennial glory, the Lord proceeds to give detailed reasons why man is still very special to God.

(i) Man is made in the image and likeness of God – in this he differs from angels (Matthew 22:15-22)

This is a status which is not given to any other created being, including angels. This matter has already been considered in the discussion on the human soul in Psalm 69, where it was noted that as one made in the **image of God**, man is a creature which **uniquely can love God**. When the Lord asked them to show Him a penny, He inquired, "Whose **image** and superscription is written?" They replied, "Caesar's". He responded, "Render to Caesar the things that are Caesar's and to God the things that are God's" (Matthew 22:21). The Lord was illustrating that because the coin bore the image of Caesar, those who possess the coin have a legal obligation to render the coin to Caesar. It belongs to Caesar because it bears his image. Similarly, if we bear the image of God, we have an obligation to render ourselves lovingly to Him since we are made in His image. God expects no less from His creature. Sadly, human refusal to render to God the things that are God's, i.e. our loving obedience and faith, has arisen out of the satanic vandalism of the human heart at the fall. This has left man as an enemy of God rather than a creature who loves God. How contrary this is to the Creator's original divine intention! Furthermore this tragedy has led to man being subject to death.

(ii) The Lord can reverse Eden's tragedy through raising believing man from the dead to a status even higher than that in which he was originally created – resurrected redeemed man will be similar to angels (Matthew 22:23-33)

In the next section (Matthew 22:23-33), He responds to the Sadducees' questions about whose wife in the resurrection would be the woman who married the seven brothers who died. The lesson for the hearers was that God is the God of Abraham, Isaac and Jacob. This means that, although physically dead, all three men are consciously alive at this moment and will one day be raised from the dead in genderless bodies. The Lord adds that, in this regard, resurrected redeemed humankind will be "as the angels of God in heaven (Matthew 22:30)".

What is the significance of the argument about the coin (man-made in God's image) and the teaching of resurrected man being like unto angels in their genderless bodies? We have already considered in Psalms 8 and 69 that man was made a little lower than the angels, yet despite this he was made in the image of God, i.e. with a capacity to love God his Creator. Isaiah 14:14 indicates that Satan (Lucifer) wished also to be in the **likeness of God,** a status which was only afforded to man.

Isaiah 14:14
"I will be like (*eddameh*) the most High."

The word *eddameh,* meaning "I will be like", is from the same root as *dmut,* meaning "likeness" in Genesis 1:26.

Genesis 1:26
"And God said, Let Us make man in Our image, **after Our likeness**: and let them have dominion over the fish of the sea, and over the fowl of the air, and over the cattle, and over all the earth, and over every creeping thing that creepeth upon the earth."

If Satan envied man in his status of being in the image and likeness (*dmut*) of God, he devised an attack on man which would rob man of the unique position of being in the likeness of God, i.e. being a God-loving creature. Instead, as a result of the fall, man ceased to love God and became an enemy of God, eventually doomed to death. The "coin" was terribly defaced by the fall but not forgotten by the One to Whom it belonged or in Whose image it was originally made.

The other aspect of Satan's insurrection was an aspiration to become **higher than the** *Shechinah* **cloud, i.e. higher than God Himself.**

Isaiah 14:14
"I will ascend above the heights of the clouds (Hebrew *av* meaning 'cloud' singular);"

These considerations show that Satan was envious of God **and** man and thus became the enemy of both.

In the discourse about the coin, the Lord indicated that man, as originally created in the image of God, was still an object of divine concern despite his fall and the resulting sentence of death. In the next section about the woman and her seven husbands, the Lord by His breathtaking divine mastery redirects the conversation to **the reversal of the effects of that fall** through the future resurrection of the dead of those who are believers in Him. He goes further, however. He shows that not only in resurrection are believers delivered from death, but in addition they arise in bodies which, in fact, are of a higher order than that in which Adam was created. They are comparable to angelic beings at least in this regard that they are genderless. The amazing net outcome of the Lord's intervention in redemption is that humankind who are saved through faith in Him end up in resurrection in a status higher than even Adam enjoyed when he was created. This means that Satan's attack on man ultimately has been a complete failure. Not only is man restored to his status of loving God, i.e. made in God's image, but he is now in a higher role than before the fall itself.

The Lord challenged His hearers with not being familiar with these truths and said:

Matthew 22:29
> "Ye do err, not knowing the Scriptures, nor the power of God."

When He spake of "the Scriptures", He was referring to the complete canon of Old Testament Scripture which makes up three scrolls. First, the scroll of the Law (*Torah*) which comprises the five books of Moses. Then, there is the scroll of the Prophets (*Neviim*) which combines the historical and doctrinal Prophets. Thirdly, there is the scroll of the Writings (*Ctuvim*) which begins with the Psalms and is sometimes just referred to as the Psalms since it was the first book in that particular scroll. In Luke 24:44-45 these distinctions are clear.

Luke 24:44-45
> 44 "And He said unto them, These *are* the words which I spake unto you, while I was yet with you, that all things must be fulfilled, which were written **in the Law of Moses, and** *in* **the Prophets, and** *in* **the Psalms,** concerning Me.
> 45 Then opened He their understanding, that they might understand **the Scriptures**,"

Sadly, the Lord's audience that day by their very questions were indicating their blindness to the teachings of the three scrolls of the Old Testament Scriptures in a general way (Matthew 22:29). The Lord now would show how they were ignorant of the Law and the Prophets in a particular way.

(iii) Man has the capacity to love God

Matthew 22:34-40
> 34 "But when the Pharisees had heard that He had put the Sadducees to silence, they were gathered together.
> 35 Then one of them, *which was* a lawyer, asked *Him a question,* tempting Him, and saying,
> 36 Master, which *is* the great commandment in the Law?
> 37 Jesus said unto him, Thou shalt love the Lord thy God with all thy heart, and with all thy soul, and with all thy mind.
> 38 This is the first and great commandment.
> 39 And the second *is* like unto it, Thou shalt love thy neighbour as thyself.
> 40 On these two commandments hang all **the Law** and **the Prophets**."

This aspect of truth complements the earlier teaching about the coin and man being made in the image and likeness of God. As one made in God's image, man has the unique potential to love God his Creator, as discussed in Psalm 69. The first book of the scroll of the **Law (Torah)** is Genesis, and it shows how this was lost when Adam sinned in the Garden of Eden. The second scroll of the **Prophets (Neviim)** unveiled God's wonderful plan to reverse the effects of the fall through the intervention of the Lord Jesus.

Only the Lord Jesus could fulfill the Law in its God-ward aspect in loving God His Father perfectly. Only He could fulfill it in its manward aspect in loving His neighbour as Himself – something which became apparent when He died for us at Calvary. Thus the Lord indicates that "on these two commandments hang all the **Law** and the **Prophets**" (Matthew 22:40). In fact, only when **the Law** would be fulfilled by the Lord Jesus can all the promises to Abraham and David be fulfilled as outlined in **the Prophets**.

The Lord then challenges His audience with the Psalms

As the Lord was remonstrating with His critics in Matthew 22, He showed them their lack of knowledge of the Law and the Prophets regarding God's great programme of redemption. These great teachers needed challenged as to their ignorance of the third scroll of the Old Testament which begins with the Psalms. How fitting, then, that at this point (verse 44) the Lord takes control of the debate and ceases to be the One Who is asked the questions and now challenges His audience from the Psalms. He introduces Psalm 110 and uses its first verse to press home His right to be Lord of the life of every human being.

Matthew 22:41-46
41 "While the Pharisees were gathered together, Jesus asked them,
42 Saying, What think ye of Christ? whose Son is He? They say unto Him, *The Son* of David.
43 He saith unto them, How then doth David in Spirit call Him Lord, saying,
44 **The LORD said unto my Lord, Sit Thou on My right hand, till I make Thine enemies Thy footstool?**
45 If David then call Him Lord, how is He his Son?
46 And no man was able to answer Him a word, neither durst any *man* from that day forth ask Him any more *questions*."

The theme of His day of teaching was that man is a failure. Even in the most congenial of circumstances he will rebel against his Creator and seek to refuse the Lordship and Deity of Christ. Despite this, man is special to God and can, unlike fallen angels, be redeemed and realise the purpose for which he was created namely (1) to reflect the image of God (like the coin) as a loving creature, (2) to exist eternally in the divine presence (like Abraham Isaac and Jacob) with death defeated and (3)to love God spontaneously from his heart. God's great rescue plan to deliver man from a state of rebellious failure to a state of realising God's three-fold divine purpose depends entirely on the intervention of the Lord Himself Who, as the Son of David, came to deliver the human family. We will see shortly from Psalm 110 that He achieves this through becoming the Mediator and Guarantor of the New Covenant as the Priest forever after the order of Melchisedec. Upon this aspect of truth, mentioned in the Psalm, the Lord did not elaborate on that occasion. He undoubtedly knew that this was beyond the acceptance of their unbelieving hearts. However, to His audience that day the Lord was presenting a very simple introductory lesson from the Psalm. If David called the Son of David "Lord", He must therefore be divine, a truth which David consciously acknowledged. Accordingly, Psalm 110:1 is a proof of the divinity of the Messiah. It was this truth which the elite among the leaders of Israel could not grasp that day. However, there was to be another opportunity for them. Peter would take up again the next clause of the same Scripture from Psalm 110 after the resurrection and ascension of the Lord Jesus. Then the rest of the Psalm would be expounded in the Epistle of the Hebrews.

2 "Sit Thou at My right hand"

This is expounded for us in Acts 2:32-36 by Peter in his preaching regarding the risen and exalted Christ to the nation of Israel in Jerusalem.

Acts 2:32-36

32 "This Jesus hath God raised up, whereof we all are witnesses.
33 Therefore being by the right hand of God exalted, and having received of the Father the promise of the Holy Ghost, He hath shed forth this, which ye now see and hear.
34 For David is not ascended into the heavens: but he saith himself, **The Lord said unto my Lord, Sit Thou on My right hand,**
35 **Until I make Thy foes Thy footstool.**
36 Therefore let all the house of Israel know assuredly, that God hath made that same Jesus, Whom ye have crucified, both Lord and Christ."

Peter, when preaching in Jerusalem shortly after the resurrection and ascension, wanted his audience to know that the One they rejected was indeed indisputably Lord, "being by the right hand of God exalted". It is therefore the central part of Psalm 110:1 which he seeks to emphasise: "Sit Thou at My right Hand". Peter did not emphasise the significance of His seated position –"Sit Thou". This has to await the exposition of Hebrews chapter 10 when the clause, "Sit Thou at My right Hand", is given in contrast to the standing position of the earthly priests of the Aaronic order, whose daily work was never over and who couldn't sit in the sanctuary:

Hebrews 10:11-12

11 "And every priest standeth daily ministering and offering oftentimes the same sacrifices, which can never take away sins:
12 But This Man, after He had offered one sacrifice for sins for ever, sat down on the right hand of God;"

The writer to the Hebrews explains that the seated position of Christ at the right hand of God shows that the work of putting away sin is over forever: "But this Man after He had offered one Sacrifice for sins forever sat down at the right hand of God". This is an important truth which will be dealt with later.

3 "Until I make Thine enemies Thy footstool"

The emphasis in Hebrews is, firstly, on the word "until", which suggests a period of time between the Lord sitting at God's right hand and His return to make His enemies His footstool.

A The "until" argument in Hebrews

When we come to the epistle to the Hebrews, the writer emphasises the word "until" in the Psalm. He is quoting from a range of Old Testament passages which state the certainty of the Lord Jesus coming again in manifestation to reign. The absence of any sign on the horizon in first century A.D. of the ancient promises to Israel being fulfilled must have led those early Jewish believers to wonder if those promises of future glory for the nation were literal. By restating some key Old Testament passages regarding the return of the Lord in glory to earth and the establishing of His earthly Kingdom, the writer firstly reassures His readers that God never fails to fulfill His promises. However, by emphasising the word "until" he is showing that there was going to be a delay between the Lord's ascension to heaven and the fulfilment of the Old Testament promises of manifested glory. In fact, in this "until" period the writer is showing his Jewish Christian readership that they will have the wonderful opportunity to come to know and appreciate the value of the Lord Jesus as their Great High Priest in the midst of a hostile world. Moreover, they would be able to prove His faithfulness in a way that could never have been possible had the Kingdom been issued in shortly after His ascension in glory. The writer continues the theme of this "delay" in the divine programme of God glorifying His Son in the following passages:

Hebrews 2:8
> "Now we see **not yet** all things put under Him."

Hebrews 10:16
> "This *is* the covenant that I will make with them **after those days**, saith the Lord, I will put My Laws into their hearts, and in their minds will I write them."

Visitors to the treasures of Pharaoh Tutankhamun in the Cairo museum in Egypt will notice that on his throne was a footplate on which is depicted the faces of his defeated enemies. By this means the ancient monarch celebrated his victory over his foes. What a day it will be when the Person of Christ will return to earth to destroy His enemies! **Until** this happens He is seated at God's right hand in glory. The next verse (Psalm 110:2) is a brief summary to explain the preceding metaphor of His enemies being made His footstool.

Psalm 110:2
> "The Lord shall send the rod of Thy strength out of Zion: rule Thou in the midst of Thine enemies."

This verse describes for us how He will move out from Zion and will establish His rule, i.e. make His enemies His foostool. The Psalm is concentrating, however, on the events before the Lord makes His enemies His footstool, i.e. the "until" period and what it will mean for believers who live through this long period of time.

B The faithfulness of believers during the present "until" period

The faithfulness of believers during the present "until" period is now brought to the reader and the underlying basis of their confidence which is in the truth of the resurrection of the Lord Jesus (Psalm 110:3).

Psalm 110:3(a)

"Thy people *shall be* willing (literally: free will offerings) in the day of Thy power ..."

This verse brings before us the "day of Thy power". When is the day of His power? Some would think that this is a reference to the occasion when His enemies will be made His footstool. However, when we understand that the phrase, "Thy people shall be willing", literally means, "Thy people shall be free will offerings", it seems singularly inappropriate that genuine followers of the Lord Jesus should come out from their closet and present themselves as free will offerings to Him in the moment of His triumph over His enemies. That is surely much too late to claim loyalty to Him. The tenor of Scripture is clear that loyalty to Him in the day of His rejection is what matters. "The day of Thy power" is today – even in this the day of His rejection. This is supported by New Testament passages such as:

Matthew 28:18-19

"All **power** is given unto Me in heaven and in earth. Go ye therefore..."

Romans 1:16

"I am not ashamed of the Gospel of Christ: for it is the **power** of God unto salvation."

Today is the day of His power. What is the proof of His power? It is seen in His resurrection from the dead. This One has power over death. Let us see how this unfolds in the verse.

If the Day of His power is today, even in this era of His rejection, then the response of His people to Him by presenting themselves to Him as free will offerings must be on the basis of a major triumph to draw out such unconditional and total loyalty. In fact, the presentation of one's self as a free will offering is the truth of Romans 12:1–2 in presenting our bodies as living sacrifices to Him which is our "reasonable service". The rest of Psalm 110:3 gives us the reason for such devotion: the triumph of His resurrection from the dead. Let's look at the way in which the resurrection is described for us here.

C The resurrection: the basis of the display of His power today even during the "until" period of His absence

Psalm 110:3(b)

"in the beauties of holiness from the womb of the morning: Thou hast the dew of Thy youth (Hebrew: *yaldutecha* meaning 'Thy youthfulness')."

The occurrence of *yaldutecha* in Ecclesiastes 11:9-10 confirms that this word in Psalm 110 means 'Thy youthfulness' rather than 'Thy youths' as many non-literal translations inaccurately suggest. The word "beauties" is the plural of the word *hadar*, which was discussed in Psalm 8 and Psalm 45. It refers to the outward splendour of the Lord Jesus, which He had veiled while on earth. Isaiah 53:2 reminds us that while on earth, He had "no form nor comeliness (*hadar*)" and that "He hid as it were His face from us" (Isaiah 53:3). The Lord, while on earth, veiled His *hadar* lest men be consumed by His glory. The only occasion prior to His resurrection when it was seen or unveiled was on the Mount of Transfiguration when His face shone beyond the brightness of the sun (Matthew 17:2). However, in this Psalm His *hadar* emerges forth from the "womb of the morning (dawn)". What does this phrase mean? It occurs nowhere else in our Bible. However, its likely meaning becomes clearer when we consider several passages which depict the joy attending the birth of a baby as pictorial of the joy attending the resurrection from the dead.

John 16:19-22
> 19 "Now Jesus knew that they were desirous to ask Him, and said unto them, Do ye inquire among yourselves of that I said, A little while, and ye shall not see Me: and again, a little while, and ye shall see Me?
> 20 Verily, verily, I say unto you, That ye shall weep and lament, but the world shall rejoice: and ye shall be sorrowful, but your sorrow shall be turned into joy.
> **21 A woman when she is in travail hath sorrow, because her hour is come: but as soon as she is delivered of the child, she remembereth no more the anguish, for joy that a man is born into the world.**
> 22 And ye now therefore have sorrow: but I will see you again, and your heart shall rejoice, and your joy no man taketh from you."

In this passage, the Lord Jesus was referring to the "little while" He would be separated from His disciples during His three days and three nights in the tomb. However, the joy which they would experience on the occasion of the birth of a baby would fade into insignificance when compared with the joy which would be theirs on the morning of His resurrection when the "little while" of weeping and lamenting turned into unparalleled joy .

John 19:20
> "Then were the disciples glad when they saw the Lord."

The Lord's use of the joy attending a birth to illustrate the joy of His resurrection is no doubt based on Psalm 139:15, where the womb is compared to "the lowest parts of the earth", a phrase later used by Paul when referring to the death of the Lord Jesus in Ephesians 4:9: "the lower parts of the earth". Also, a similar phrase, "the heart of the earth", is used by the Lord Jesus to describe His death in Matthew 12:40.

These three relevant passages are given below:

Psalm 139:13

> 13 "For Thou hast possessed my reins: Thou hast covered me in my mother's womb.
>
> 14 I will praise Thee; for I am fearfully *and* wonderfully made: marvellous *are* Thy works; and *that* my soul knoweth right well.
>
> 15 My substance was not hid from Thee, when I was made in secret, *and* curiously wrought in the **lowest parts of the earth**.
>
> 16 Thine eyes did see my substance, yet being unperfect; and in Thy book all *my members* were written, *which* in continuance were fashioned, when *as yet there was* none of them.
>
> 17 How precious also are Thy thoughts unto me, O God! how great is the sum of them!"

Ephesians 4:9

> "Now that He ascended, what is it but that He also descended first into the **lower parts of the earth**?"

Matthew 12:39

> 39 "But He answered and said unto them, An evil and adulterous generation seeketh after a sign; and there shall no sign be given to it, but the sign of the prophet Jonas:
>
> 40 For as Jonas was three days and three nights in the whale's belly; so shall the Son of man be three days and three nights **in the heart of the earth**."

When we consider these three passages, together with John 16:19-22, it is clear that the phrase, "womb of the morning (dawn)" refers to the triumph of the morning of His resurrection. As He stood in the garden in His resurrection body He bore the "dew of His youth". What a sight of beauty, power and triumph. The morning dew reminds us of freshness. The theme of His resurrection triumph shall ever remain fresh eternally.

How fitting that we are reminded of the triumph of resurrection here! It is on this basis that His enemies will one day be put under His feet, and, as we are reminded in 1 Corinthians 15:26, the last enemy to be destroyed and to be put under Him is death. The Psalm now moves to the ascension of the Lord Jesus and the truths attending His Melchisedec Priesthood.

4 His Melchisedec Priesthood in Hebrews chapters 5-10

Psalm 110:4

> "The Lord hath sworn, and will not repent, Thou *art* a Priest for ever after the order of Melchisedec."

The first and most important aspect of declaring His triumph in resurrection is that the Melchisedec Priest has conquered death and abides forever. Hence the reason why the verse describing resurrection must precede the section about His Melchisedec priesthood.

The first New Testament references to the Melchisedec priesthood of our Lord Jesus Christ are found in Hebrews 5. We will study this chapter in some detail to take the first steps in grasping the significance of this grand title of our Lord Jesus: "A Priest forever after the order of Melchisedec". The Hebrews' writer in chapter 5 takes up the word "forever" and emphasises that His priesthood stands in contrast to that of Aaron. Christ's priesthood is unchanging and everlasting

Hebrews 5

1 "For every high priest taken from among men is ordained for men in things *pertaining* to God, that he may offer both gifts and sacrifices for sins:
2 Who can have compassion on the ignorant, and on them that are out of the way; for that he himself also is compassed with infirmity.
3 And by reason hereof he ought, as for the people, so also for himself, to offer for sins.
4 And no man taketh this honour unto himself, but he that is called of God, as *was* Aaron.
5 So also Christ glorified not Himself to be made an High Priest; but He that said unto Him, Thou art My Son, to day have I begotten Thee.
6 As He saith also in another *place*, **Thou** *art* **a Priest for ever after the order of Melchisedec.**
7 Who in the days of His flesh, when He had offered up prayers and supplications with strong crying and tears unto Him that was able to save Him from death, and was heard in that He feared;
8 Though He were a Son, yet learned He obedience by the things which He suffered;
9 And being made perfect, He became the Author of eternal salvation unto all them that obey Him;
10 Called of God an High Priest after the order of Melchisedec.
11 Of Whom we have many things to say, and hard to be uttered, seeing ye are dull of hearing.
12 For when for the time ye ought to be teachers, ye have need that one teach you again which *be* the first principles of the oracles of God; and are become such as have need of milk, and not of strong meat.
13 For every one that useth milk *is* unskilful in the word of righteousness: for he is a babe.
14 But strong meat belongeth to them that are of full age, *even* those who by reason of use have their senses exercised to discern both good and evil."

A Simple but profound contrasts between the Aaronic priesthood and that of Melchisedec

A recurring theme is that the Melchisedec priesthood is unchangeable by death (Hebrews 5:1), unlimited by weakness (Hebrews 5:2) and unaffected by sin (Hebrews 5:3).

(i) In Hebrews 5: 1, we read that every high priest is continually being taken from among men and continually being ordained. This constant line of high priests was needed because death always defeated the Aaronic priest. In contrast, as the writer later points out, the Melchisedec Priest defeated death.

(ii) In Hebrews 5: 2, we read how the Aaronic priest can have "compassion on the ignorant and on them that are out of the way". The literal meaning of "compassion" is " limited compassion". Even Aaron's compassions were limited. In contrast, our Melchisedec Priest is of unfailing compassion.

(iii) In Hebrews 5:3, the Aaronic priest had to make an offering for his own sin. Not so our Melchisedec Priest. He stands alone in His sinless perfection.

B Comparison of the honour of the Aaronic priesthood with that of Melchisedec's priesthood

In Hebrews 5:4-5, Aaron considered it an honour to be high priest among his people. It is beautiful to observe that the Lord Jesus likewise is honoured to be our Great High Priest. This suggests that each time we come to the Father through the Son, as we praise the Father in the Name of the Lord Jesus Christ, we are bringing glory and honour to the Lord Jesus.

C The doctrinal significance of His resurrection

We have already seen from Psalm 110 that the Melchisedec Priest Who emerges forth from the womb of the dawn is the Victor over death in resurrection. As we continue to study this exposition of His High Priestly ministry in Hebrews 5, it should not be a surprise to us that the passage also moves to focus on His resurrection triumph.

Hebrews 5:5-6

> 5 "So also Christ glorified not Himself to be made an High Priest; but He that said unto Him, Thou art My Son, to day have I begotten Thee.
> 6 As He saith also in another *place*, Thou *art* a Priest for ever after the order of Melchisedec."

Hebrews 5:5 shows us that the conferring upon Him of this office of High Priest must be subsequent to His resurrection. We have already considered in Psalm 40 that this also involved His ascension so that He could enter as a Priest into the heavenly temple to sit down at God's right hand. However, verse 5 shows that He was called "an High Priest after the order of Melchisedec" by His Father, Who had already said to Him, "Thou art My Son, this day have I begotten Thee". We have already seen in Psalm 2 that this phrase, "this day have I begotten Thee", refers to the occasion of His resurrection from amongst the dead and constitutes the evidence to the world that He is the Eternal Son. Some have argued that Hebrews 5:5 refers to His being begotten at Bethlehem and that His becoming Man at Bethlehem is what is meant by the quotation from Psalm 2 in Hebrews 5:5, "Thou art My Son, to day have I begotten Thee". The reasoning is that in order to be a Priest He must become a Man and therefore Bethlehem is what is meant here. The passage acknowledges that to be our High Priest He must be a Man. However, the teaching of Hebrews 5:5 is that to be our High Priest He must be a **risen Man** Who has defeated death. Hebrews 8:6 goes a step further to show us from Psalm 110 that He must be a risen, ascended and exalted Man to be our High Priest.

In Hebrews 5:7-9, we see the Lord's ministry upon earth and are given a unique insight into His prayer life.

Hebrews 5:7-9

7 "Who in the days of His flesh, when He had offered up prayers and supplications with strong crying and tears unto Him that was able to save Him from death, and was heard in that He feared;

8 Though He were a Son, yet learned He obedience by the things which He suffered;

9 And being made perfect, He became the Author of eternal salvation unto all them that obey Him;"

In the days of His flesh, in His intense intercessory prayers, He addressed Him Who was "able to save Him from death". Now this is not the idea of the Lord cowering in weakness in contemplation of His impending Sacrifice at Calvary. Rather, the meaning is: "Him that was able to save Him right through death", i.e. into death, through death and out the other side in resurrection power! In fact, the only time in the Gospels that we find the verbal root (*deomai*) of the word for prayer in Hebrews 5:7 being used of the Lord is in Luke 22:32, when He prayed for Peter that his faith would not fail. This passage gives us a unique insight into the Lord's intercession for Peter. We learn that it was on the basis of His soon coming victory over death in resurrection that He prayed that Peter's faith would not fail. The lesson for us is as follows: if on the basis of His impending resurrection He was able to intercede for Peter how much the more can He not perform this ministry of intercession for us now that He is alive and seated at God's right hand. Some have argued from this verse that the Lord Jesus was already functioning as a Melchisedec Priest in the days of His flesh. We will see later that His Melchisedec priesthood could not be practised while He was on earth. It required the ascension to glory of a risen Man Who had defeated death. His experiences on earth were to **qualify Him** for His Melchisedec priesthood. This is what is meant by His "being made perfect". How wonderful for us to know that we cannot be called upon to endure any trial (with the exception of sin, of course) that He has not already experienced Himself at first hand. He is fully qualified – "made perfect" – to become this Melchisedec Priest.

D An aspect of Melchisedec priesthood-truth that the Hebrew believers were too immature to understand

Now after these basic lessons on the Melchisedec priesthood, the writer would have longed to tell them more. As we will shortly see, He wanted to show them that the Melchisedec Priest, with His "forever priesthood", has put an end to their connection with ancient Judaism and temple worship and indeed any claim they might still retain to an earthly inheritance under the Old Covenant. However, such truths were not for babes in Christ. Such truth is for more mature believers, and they were certainly not there yet. In fact, they were being distressed at the possibility of the Old Testament earthly promises, for which they longed, not being realised in their lives. However, it is **precisely because His priesthood is forever, and hence unchangeable, that the Hebrew believers must face the practical application to their lives that their associations with the earthly sanctuary in Jerusalem were**

finished. Such a conclusion was by no means intuitive to them! Arriving at such an understanding of Scripture would require some very sensitive and clear exposition. This is now the lead-in to Hebrews chapter 6.

Hebrews chapter 6 is a parenthetical chapter to provide remedial teaching to help bring the Hebrew believers up to a level of maturity which would enable them to understand that the Melchisedec Priest was the only basis of the literal fulfilment of the Old Testament promises of an earthly inheritance to Israel. They had to learn that for Hebrew and non-Hebrew believers of this Church age there is not an earthly inheritance to be possessed. Instead, there is a heavenly one. Accordingly, the writer must first show that the nation has at present rejected Him and that all believers of this era, whether Jew or Gentile, are looking forward to a heavenly inheritance, no longer an earthly one. Let's see how this truth unfolds in Hebrews 6.

Hebrews 6:1-3

1 "Therefore leaving the principles of the doctrine of Christ, let us go on unto perfection; not laying again the foundation of repentance from dead works, and of faith toward God,

2 Of the doctrine of **baptisms**, and of **laying on of hands**, and of **resurrection of the dead**, and of **eternal judgment**.

3 And this will we do, if God permit."

E The nation's first encounter with their Messiah

Hebrews 6:1-3 deals with the reasons why the nation of Israel rejected Christ and why God had to set that nation aside temporarily until it will be taken up again by divine power.

"The principles (literally: the beginning) of the doctrine of Christ" refer to the teachings of the Lord Jesus to the nation of Israel while upon earth. The rest of verse 1 and verse 2 gives us the reasons why, in a general way, those teachings were rejected by the nation's leaders at that time.

(i) Dead works and faith toward God

The Lord remonstrated with them for neglecting "judgment, mercy and faith" (Matthew 23:23). This is the foundation of repentance from dead works and of faith toward God.

(ii) Baptisms

In Mark 7, He challenged them for their obsession with external washings (plural) (baptisms) which had no spiritual cleansing value.

(iii) Laying on of hands

This always speaks of identification, and the Lord did not shirk from contact with lepers and sinners, allowing the woman of the city to touch His feet (Luke 7:38).

(iv) Resurrection of the dead and eternal judgment

In John 5, He indicated that He had power to raise the dead and judge the living and the dead.

For these claims He was at first resented and eventually rejected by the leaders of the Jewish nation at that time.

F The nation's second encounter: the challenge of the risen Christ

Hebrews 6:4-6

4 "For *it is* impossible for those who were once enlightened, and have tasted of the heavenly gift, and were made partakers of the Holy Ghost,
5 And have tasted the good Word of God, and the powers of the world to come,
6 If they shall fall away, to renew them again unto repentance; seeing they crucify to themselves the Son of God afresh, and put *Him* to an open shame."

In the Acts of the Apostles, the nation of Israel was once again offered their Messiah, this time in resurrection. Peter informed them that it was in ignorance that the Messiah had been put to death (Acts 3:17). This is what we might understand as culpable homicide or manslaughter. It was in recognition of this that the Lord on the cross prayed, "Father forgive them for they know not what they do" (Luke 23:34). Crucifying Him the first time was done in ignorance. However, to reject Him the second time was much more serious. This is "to crucify to themselves the Son of God afresh" (Hebrews 6:6). The reason why rejecting Him the second time could not be regarded as an action of ignorance was because of the overwhelming evidence of the power of the Spirit of God on earth following the resurrection and ascension of Christ.

In a special way, the nation of Israel was privileged to witness at first hand those amazing events following Pentecost and the descent of the Spirit of God. The **"powers of the world to come"** (Hebrews 6:5) which they witnessed in those days were all the miracles which caused widespread amazement. Now, it is worth pointing out that the miracles in the Acts of the Apostles attested to the certainty of the coming Kingdom. In fact, all New Testament miracles carried this significance. So, the lame man at the beautiful gate of the temple is seen "walking and leaping" (Acts 3:8). This was to remind people of Isaiah's prophecy: "Then shall the lame man leap as an hart" (Isaiah 35:6).

Moreover, the tongues were not just a collection of meaningless syllables. They carried a meaning and special doctrinal significance: "Howbeit in the Spirit he speaketh mysteries" (1 Corinthians 14:2), i.e. New Testament mystery doctrines. These teachings were full of meaning as to the setting aside of the nation in this Church era and the role of the Church today, culminating in its removal at the rapture and the taking up of the nation of Israel subsequent to that.

All of this goes to show that the powers of the age to come Note 1 (the millennium) attested powerfully to the sincerity of God's offer to the nation of future glory should they change their mind and accept their risen Messiah. Sadly, however, this was not to be. Persistence in rejecting their Messiah in face of such evidence provided by God would lead to the nation and its religious system stepping into a wilderness era of estrangement from her Messiah.

G The significance of the Melchisedec priesthood for the manslayer

Against this background, the writer is challenging his Jewish Christian readership to recognise the provision which God has made for the "manslayer" so as to escape from the avenger of blood.

In the Old Testament, when someone became a manslayer, i.e. killed a person in ignorance, they were permitted to flee for refuge to cities of refuge, which were strategically placed throughout the land of Israel. The person could remain there in safety while the high priest lived, and when the high priest died then he could safely go back to his inheritance, to the little tract of land which he had inherited from his forefathers (Numbers 35:11-28). The writer is now using this picture for us.

Hebrews 6:18-20

> 18 "That by two immutable things, in which *it was* impossible for God to lie, we might have a strong consolation, **who have fled for refuge** to lay hold upon the hope set before us:
>
> 19 Which *hope* we have as an anchor of the soul, both sure and stedfast, and which entereth into that within the veil;
>
> 20 Whither the Forerunner is for us entered, *even* Jesus, made an High Priest for ever after the order of Melchisedec."

The nation of manslayers can find refuge by fleeing to the heavenly city where there is a High Priest Who will guarantee their security from the avenger of blood. What a lovely picture of the eternal security of the person who trusts Christ!

Now, it is here where the Melchisedec priesthood of Christ takes on a special significance. In the Old Testament, the manslayer was allowed to return to his little farm on his earthly inheritance as soon as the high priest died (Numbers 35:28). No one could legally harm him then; he was a free man. The contrast between those Old Testament times and now is that **our Melchisedec Priest can never die**. That means that for those manslayers (i.e. those who were involved in the crucifixion of the Lord Jesus) who repent and by faith flee to the heavenly city, there is no return to their earthly patch of land. Those Jews, or indeed Gentiles, who have fled for refuge to the heavenly city of refuge have, by so doing, indicated cessation of interest in this world or any claim to a future **earthly inheritance**.

Now, it was the understanding of the difference between **the earthly inheritance** for ancient Israel and future tribulation saints, and **the heavenly inheritance**, which is exclusively the portion of His saints in this Church era, which defines the difference between babyhood and perfection (maturity). By using the picture of the city of refuge, from which there is no return to one's former **earthly inheritance** while the High Priest lives, the writer to the Hebrews in chapter 6 is bringing these Jewish "babes" into the truths of "perfection" or "maturity", which he longed for them to grasp at the end of Hebrews chapter 5.

Let us once again restate the distinction between the saints of this Church era (Pentecost to the Rapture) and the saints of the Old Testament period and the tribulation. Ours is a heavenly hope, a heavenly inheritance and a heavenly city. Theirs is an earthly hope, an earthly inheritance and an earthly city as prophesied in the Old Testament.

The realisation of this truth must have caused genuine disquiet to these Jewish saints. Have they kissed farewell forever to their earthly inheritance? In Christ have they forfeited everything on earth they held so dear? It was clear, as far as they were concerned, that they had said farewell to temple worship, an earthly sanctuary and any claim to an earthly inheritance. They had thrown their lot in with the heavenly city, their city of refuge, and the High Priest Who now has entered there. Moreover, they had their eye set on a heavenly inheritance which He will guarantee for them. It is in realisation of this truth that first century Jewish believers sold their property and laid it at the apostles' feet (Acts 4:34-35). It was wrong to sell ones inheritance in ancient Israel as the incident of Naboth and his vineyard illustrates (1 Kings 21:3). But once those early believers learned that their inheritance was heavenly, they had no problem with parting with their links to the land of Israel. For this reason, Barnabas, a Levite, sold his parcel of land (Acts 4:36-37). He, by this action publicly and boldly declared that he understood that the prohibition to a Levite to sell his parcel of land in Leviticus 25:34 no longer applied in the Church era, since it was the heavenly land to which he was going.

Leviticus 25:33,34
> 33 "And if a man purchase of the Levites, then the house that was sold, and the city of his possession, shall go out in *the year of* jubile: for the houses of the cities of the Levites *are* their possession among the children of Israel.
> 34 But the **field of the suburbs of their cities may not be sold**; for it *is* their perpetual possession."

Some must have started to wonder if these developments meant that the ancient Old Testament prophecies were no longer on offer and had somehow been replaced by the promises to the Church. Such thoughts would have filled these believers with disquiet. It might even have caused such babes to "be tossed to and fro with every wind of doctrine". It is here, therefore, that the writer brings in another beautiful aspect of the Melchisedec priesthood. He actually **guarantees the literal fulfilment of the promises of an earthly future to the nation!**

At this point the writer reminds his Hebrew believing readers of the promise made to Abraham:

Hebrews 6:13-18
> 13 "For when God made promise to Abraham, because He could swear by no greater, He sware by Himself,
> 14 Saying, Surely blessing I will bless thee, and multiplying I will multiply thee.
> 15 And so, after he had patiently endured, he obtained the promise.
> 16 For men verily swear by the greater: and an oath for confirmation *is* to them an end of all strife.
> 17 Wherein God, willing more abundantly to shew unto the heirs of

promise the immutability of his counsel, confirmed *it* by an oath:
18 That by two immutable things, in which *it was* impossible for God to lie,
we might have a strong consolation, who have fled for refuge to lay hold
upon the hope set before us:"

By the immutability of God's counsel and His oath, **God had assured
Abraham of a literal future for the nation** that would emerge from him.
This passage in Genesis 22 was considered in Psalm 90 and Psalm 24. The
new revelation of the one-way flight to the heavenly city of refuge does not
abrogate this fact.

One can imagine how those Jewish believers would have struggled
with this. Almost in response to such queries we enter Hebrews 7 where
we are reminded that Melchisedec, King of Salem (peace) and King of
righteousness, comes out from Salem (Jerusalem) to bless Abraham and his
seed in his loins after the slaughter of the kings. What an amazing picture!
The Melchisedec Priest, Who has provided this heavenly city of refuge for
the manslayer today, will come out and after the slaughter of the kings will
bless the nation of Israel **on earth**.

> **H The Hebrews exposition of the significance of the oath in Psalm 110:
> His priesthood is infallible**

Psalm 110:4

"The Lord **hath sworn, and will not repent**, Thou *art* a Priest for ever after
the order of Melchisedec."

Hebrews 6 ends by reminding the Hebrew believers that the covenant
with Abraham was guaranteed by an oath. God never breaks His Word.
There is guaranteed a future for Israel. Is there going to be some kind of
contradiction between the oath to Abraham, guaranteeing an **earthly** future
for Israel, and the Melchisedec priesthood, offering a **heavenly** city of
refuge for the manslayer today in this Church era? Since some of the Jewish
believers were still at the level of "babes", they may have wondered if there
was a contradiction between the oath to Abraham, referred to in Hebrews
5, and the oath of Psalm 110:4, declaring the Lord Jesus as "a Priest forever
after the order of Melchisedec". It is fitting, therefore, at this point that the
Hebrews writer should expound the significance of Psalm 110:4: "The Lord
hath sworn, and will not repent…" and plainly establish that there is no
contradiction between the oath to Abraham and the oath of Psalm 110:4.

He approaches this subject by reminding his readers that, unlike Aaron
whose priesthood was not guaranteed by an oath, the Melchisedec
Priesthood is guaranteed by an oath.

Hebrews 7:20-21

20 "And inasmuch as not without an oath He was made Priest:
21 (For those priests were made without an oath; but This **with an oath** by
Him that said unto Him, **The Lord sware and will not repent, Thou *art* a
Priest for ever after the order of Melchisedec**:)"

Interestingly, in Hebrews 5 when the declaration from Psalm 110, "Thou *art* a Priest **for ever** after the order of Melchisedec", is quoted there is no mention of the oath: "The Lord sware and will not repent". This is because in Hebrews 5, the theme was the "forever" aspect of His priesthood, i.e. it cannot be limited by death since He is risen. In other words, His priesthood is **unchanging**. In Hebrews 7, the theme has moved on to establish that His priesthood is **infallible**. This is the significance of the oath. No one can challenge His priesthood since it is confirmed by an oath. Now, the fact that the Aaronic order of priests was never confirmed by an oath shows that God never intended the Aaronic priestly order to be permanent (unchanging) or infallible. It was designed to cease.

I The Hebrews exposition of the significance of the relationship between Aaronic priests and the Old Covenant versus the Melchisedec Priest and the New Covenant

Old Testament priests could not keep the nation on the parcel of land promised to Abraham under the Abrahamic covenant. Sadly, when that Old Covenant was broken by the nation, the priests were carried off into captivity along with their people. The broken Mosaic covenant and its priests could do nothing to bring about the Abrahamic covenant which offered the nation a guaranteed future in the Land of Promise. In fact, one of the great expositional problems facing Jewish expositors today is how to bring about the Covenant to Abraham while the Mosaic Covenant of Law is being perpetually broken. The past 2000 years of exposition by Jewish sages has failed to answer this problem so long as they exclude from their deliberations the intervention of the Lord Jesus in His sin-expiating death and resurrection. He is the answer to this problem and a New Covenant is required which deals with sin forever to allow the covenant with Abraham to be fulfilled and to provide for the fulfilment and putting to silence of all the demands of a broken Mosaic Covenant. It is here where the Melchisedec Priest comes in. Old Testament believers would have understood the need for a New Covenant to replace the Old Covenant of Moses, if ever the oath to Abraham and the Covenant with him could be fulfilled.

The question may still be legitimately asked as to why the New Covenant is not mentioned in Psalm 110. The answer is that Psalm 110 should be read in conjunction with Psalm 111 where there are two references to the Covenant-keeping God. In fact, it is impossible to read Psalm 111, and the references therein to the Covenants of Jehovah, and not consider that it is the New Covenant of Jeremiah 31 which is in mind. In Psalm 111:5 we read, "…He will ever be mindful of His covenant". And, later in verse 9, "He hath commanded His covenant for ever". The fact that it is an everlasting covenant in Psalm 111 certainly excludes the Mosaic Covenant. The reference to sending "redemption (root *padah*) unto His people" (Psalm 111:9) would link the references to the covenants in Psalm 111 to the New Covenant of Jeremiah 31 which forms the basis of redemption. Moreover, the two references to the covenant in Psalm 111 are consistent with two aspects given in Hebrews, namely the Lord Jesus as both Mediator and Guarantor of the New Covenant. Note 2

5 The Melchisedec Priest and the New Covenant

A The Melchisedec Priest is the Guarantor and Mediator of the New Covenant.

He is the Mediator of the New Covenant ("He hath commanded His covenant forever" (Psalm 111:9)).

He is also the Guarantor of the New Covenant ("He will ever be mindful of His covenant" (Psalm 111:5)).

These important truths form the basis of the doctrines of Hebrews 7-9.

Hebrews 7:22
   "By so much was Jesus made a Surety (Guarantor) of a better Testament."

When, in Hebrews 7, we learn that the Lord Jesus is the Surety (Guarantor) of the better (New) Covenant, the concept here is quite different from our modern concept of a guarantee. If we buy a car today, the guarantee pledges that if there is a breakdown it will be fixed. The guarantee in Hebrews 7:22 is that there will never be a breakdown because of the infallibility of Christ. In Hebrews 7, He is the Guarantor of the New Covenant by virtue of His endless life (i.e. His resurrection). Later, in chapter 9, He is the Mediator of the New Covenant. We must distinguish the parallel truths of the Lord Jesus' being the Guarantor of the New Covenant and His being the Mediator of the New Covenant.

He is the **Guarantor** of the New Covenant in Hebrews 7:22 by virtue of **His Life taken up again in resurrection (Hebrews 7:23-25)**.

Hebrews 7:23-25
   23 "And they truly were many priests, because they were not suffered to continue by reason of death:
   24 But this *Man*, because He continueth ever, hath an unchangeable priesthood.
   25 Wherefore He is able also to save them to the uttermost that come unto God by Him, seeing He ever liveth to make intercession for them."

He is the **Mediator** of the New Covenant (Hebrews 9:13-15) by virtue of **His Life laid down by the shedding of His Blood**.

Hebrews 9:13-15
   13 "For if the blood of bulls and of goats, and the ashes of an heifer sprinkling the unclean, sanctifieth to the purifying of the flesh:
   14 How much more shall the blood of Christ, Who through the eternal Spirit offered Himself without spot to God, purge your conscience from dead works to serve the living God?
   15 And for this cause He is the **Mediator of the New Testament (Covenant)**, that by means of death, for the redemption of the transgressions that were under the first Testament (Covenant), they which are called might receive the promise of eternal inheritance."

As if to further emphasise the importance of the link between the Melchisedec priesthood of the Lord Jesus and the New Covenant, we find that in both **Hebrews 8 and 10** these two Old Testament passages (Psalm 110 and Jeremiah 31) are placed side by side.

B The Melchisedec Priest and the New Covenant in Hebrews 8

In Hebrews 8:1, the writer refers to Psalm 110:1 when he states that the High Priest (the Melshisedic Priest – the Lord Jesus) is "set on the right hand of the throne of the Majesty in the heavens". Then in verses 8-13, he quotes directly from Jeremiah 31 and the New Covenant.

Hebrews 8:8-13

8 "For finding fault with them, He saith, Behold, the days come, saith the Lord, when I will make a New Covenant with the house of Israel and with the house of Judah:

9 Not according to the Covenant that I made with their fathers in the day when I took them by the hand to lead them out of the land of Egypt; because they continued not in My Covenant, and I regarded them not, saith the Lord.

10 For this *is* the Covenant that I will make with the house of Israel after those days, saith the Lord; I will put My Laws into their mind, and write them in their hearts: and I will be to them a God, and they shall be to Me a people:

11 And they shall not teach every man his neighbour, and every man his brother, saying, Know the Lord: for all shall know Me, from the least to the greatest.

12 For I will be merciful to their unrighteousness, and their sins and their iniquities will I remember no more.

13 In that He saith, A New *Covenant*, He hath made the first old. Now that which decayeth and waxeth old *is* ready to vanish away."

C The Melchisedec Priest and the New Covenant in Hebrews 10

Similarly, in Hebrews 10, the writer refers to the Melchisedec Priest in verses 12-13 and the New Covenant in verses 15-18.

Hebrews 10:12-13 *(a reference to the Melchisedec Priest)*

12 "But this Man, after He had offered one Sacrifice for sins for ever, sat down on the right hand of God;

13 From henceforth expecting till His enemies be made His footstool."

Hebrews 10:15-18 *(a reference to the new covenant)*

15 "*Whereof* the Holy Ghost also is a Witness to us: for after that He had said before,

16 This *is* the Covenant that I will make with them after those days, saith the Lord, I will put My Laws into their hearts, and in their minds will I write them;

17 And their sins and iniquities will I remember no more.

18 Now where remission of these *is*, *there is* no more offering for sin."

Hebrews 8 and 10 are presenting two parallel aspects of the same truth. Hebrews 8 establishes **in a general way** how the Melchisedec Priest has instituted the New Covenant by virtue of being its "Mediator" (Hebrews 8:6) and thus renders the former (Mosaic) Covenant "old" and "ready to vanish away".

Hebrews 10 is focussing **in a specific way** on the sin offering of the Old Covenant and shows that because in Psalm 110 the Melchisedec Priest is seated, having completed the offering for sin, the Day of Atonement is abolished and no more remembrance of sin is found in Jeremiah 31. This will be discussed later.

If the Hebrews epistle in the New Testament is so emphatic in linking the Melchisedec Priest in Psalm 110 with the New Covenant of Jeremiah 31, is it reasonable to suspect that Old Testament believers, in their lifetimes, could have noticed the doctrinal link between Psalm 110 and Jeremiah 31, even though neither passage directly refers to the other? Here are some considerations which point to the idea that thoughtful Old Testament believers could indeed have easily noticed the doctrinal link between the two passages.

6 Old Testament priests and the Old Covenant; Melchisedec Priest and the New Covenant

A Old Testament priests were the guarantors of the Old Covenant

Firstly, Old Testament believers would have been very aware of the link between the existing Aaronic priesthood and the Old Covenant. They would have been aware that under the Old Covenant, the persons charged with upholding it were those of the Levitical priesthood (Deuteronomy 17:8-13, Malachi 2:1-9).

Deuteronomy 17:8-13

> 8 "If there arise a matter too hard for thee in judgment, between blood and blood, between plea and plea, and between stroke and stroke, *being* matters of controversy within thy gates: then shalt thou arise, and get thee up into the place which the Lord thy God shall choose;
> **9 And thou shalt come unto the priests the Levites, and unto the judge that shall be in those days, and inquire; and they shall shew thee the sentence of judgment:**
> **10 And thou shalt do according to the sentence, which they of that place which the Lord shall choose shall shew thee; and thou shalt observe to do according to all that they inform thee:**
> **11 According to the sentence of the Law which they shall teach thee, and according to the judgment which they shall tell thee, thou shalt do: thou shalt not decline from the sentence which they shall shew thee, *to* the right hand, nor *to* the left.**
> 12 And the man that will do presumptuously, and will not hearken unto the priest that standeth to minister there before the Lord thy God, or unto the judge, even that man shall die: and thou shalt put away the evil from Israel.
> 13 And all the people shall hear, and fear, and do no more presumptuously."

Malachi 2:4-9

> 4 "And ye shall know that I have sent this commandment unto you, that My covenant might be with Levi, saith the Lord of hosts.
>
> 5 My covenant was with him of life and peace; and I gave them to him *for* the fear wherewith he feared Me, and was afraid before My Name.
>
> 6 The Law of truth was in his mouth, and iniquity was not found in his lips: he walked with Me in peace and equity, and did turn many away from iniquity.
>
> 7 **For the priest's lips should keep knowledge, and they should seek the Law at his mouth: for he** *is* **the messenger of the Lord of hosts.**
>
> 8 But ye are departed out of the way; ye have caused many to stumble at the Law; ye have corrupted the covenant of Levi, saith the Lord of hosts.
>
> 9 Therefore have I also made you contemptible and base before all the people, according as ye have not kept My ways, but have been partial in the Law."

Old Testament believers would have been all too aware that the priests' failure led to the exile of the people of Judah along with their priests and finally to the dreadful curse upon the priests and their seed in Malachi 2, effectively indicating the impending end of the earthly priesthood.

Malachi 2:1-3

> 1 "And now, O ye priests, this commandment *is* for you.
>
> 2 If ye will not hear, and if ye will not lay *it* to heart, to give glory unto My Name, saith the Lord of hosts, **I will even send a curse upon you, and I will curse your blessings: yea, I have cursed them already, because ye do not lay** *it* **to heart.**
>
> 3 Behold, I will corrupt your seed, and spread dung upon your faces, *even* the dung of your solemn feasts; and *one* shall take you away with it."

Moreover, if the priests, who guaranteed the Old Covenant, belonged to a priesthood which was not intended to last forever and would be eventually cursed, because of its rejection of the Lord, it follows that the Old Covenant, for which they were the guarantors, would itself pass away.

B The New Covenant of Jeremiah 31 required a Priest to be its Guarantor

Old Testament believers, being familiar with the Aaronic priestly order guaranteeing the Old Covenant, would have wondered Who, in priestly role, would guarantee the New Covenant of Jeremiah 31. Clearly, it could not be the Aaronic priesthood which, as Malachi points out, was intrinsically flawed. For the New Covenant to be mediated and guaranteed, a Priest of a completely different order was required. This knowledge would have been well within the grasp of spiritually intelligent Old Testament believers. The only One Who could fulfill such a role was the promised Melchisedec Priest of Psalm 110.

C The New Covenant of Jeremiah 31 required that the Day of Atonement and a standing priest would be ended

By linking the seated Priest of Psalm 110 with the prophesied end of the

Day of Atonement in Jeremiah 31, the Hebrews writer has proven the finality of the death of Christ in the matter of putting away sin forever, allowing it to be forgiven forever. However, thoughtful Old Testament believers would also have understood this. Since the putting away of sins forever is a key element of the New Covenant of Jeremiah 31, there was a requirement for a new order of Priest Who could be seated, since there would no longer be a need to offer up sacrifices. Old Testament believers could have seen how this stipulation was fulfilled in the Melchisedec Priest Who was described as "seated" in Psalm 110.

Old Testament believers understood that there is an order to the Psalms. They are not randomly ordered. Psalm 111, following Psalm 110, refers twice to the Covenant. It would have been readily appreciated that the priestly Guarantor of such a covenant must be the divine Melchisedec Priest.

D The Melchisedec Priest is Guarantor and Mediator of the New Covenant

We have already observed that He is Guarantor of the New Covenant on the basis of the oath and His endless life. However, to be Mediator of the New Covenant He must die and His blood must be shed.

Hebrews 8:6

"But now hath He obtained a more excellent ministry, by how much also He is the **Mediator** of a better Covenant, which was established upon better promises."

Hebrews 9:13-17

13 "For if the blood of bulls and of goats, and the ashes of an heifer sprinkling the unclean, sanctifieth to the purifying of the flesh:

14 How much more shall the blood of Christ, Who through the eternal Spirit offered Himself without spot to God, purge your conscience from dead works to serve the living God?

15 **And for this cause He is the Mediator of the New Testament, that by means of death, for the redemption of the transgressions** *that were* **under the first Testament, they which are called might receive the promise of eternal inheritance**.

16 For where a Testament (Covenant) *is*, there must also of necessity be the death of the Testator (Covenant victim).

17 For a Testament (Covenant) *is* of force after men are dead: otherwise it is of no strength at all while the Testator (Covenant victim) liveth."

Hebrews 9:15 shows us that the Melchisedec Priest, by virtue of His precious blood previously shed at Calvary, is now the Mediator of the New Covenant and that this has a twofold effect :

Firstly, He dealt with the sins of the Old Testament saints which until Calvary were only covered and not put away.

Secondly, He provided them with **an eternal inheritance**, something which the Old Covenant could only withhold from them (please see Introduction of Psalm 22).

The reference to "the redemption of the transgressions that were under the first Covenant" reminds us of the ending forever of the Day of Atonement already alluded to in Jeremiah 31 as well as the ending of the era when God covered over (made atonement for) the sins of Old Testament believers. Please see pages 91-103 where this has been discussed. The reference to the **eternal inheritance** reminds us that the New Covenant was made to Israel and is the basis exclusively on which all the promises of earthly blessings to that nation can be fulfilled. The blood of Christ guarantees a future for Israel. Any denial of the future earthly Kingdom and a future role for Israel is a denial of the value of the precious blood of Christ.

Once more, we return to the theme of Hebrews 6 and 7. The Melchisedec Priest has opened a city of refuge in heaven with a one-way ticket for the manslayer today. However, by virtue of His death, blood-shedding, resurrection and ascension, He now is the Mediator and Guarantor of the New Covenant, thus guaranteeing and effecting all the earthly Old Testament promises to Israel. That was the consolation for first century A.D. Jewish Christians. The entire programme of God relies on this victory.

7 Is the New Covenant effective today?

The New Covenant is already operative with the nation in the experience of Old Testament believers, whose sins prior to Calvary were only covered but which now, following the resurrection, are taken away (Hebrews 9:15). However, the promise of the eternal inheritance which is pledged in the New Covenant will not be fulfilled in the experience of these saints until their bodily resurrection and their entering in to the earthly Kingdom. These Old Testament saints have **not yet** received their eternal inheritance which is pledged to them under the terms of the New Covenant (Hebrews 9:15).

A What is the role of the Church in the New Covenant?

This issue is not addressed in Jeremiah 31 or in Hebrews 8 and 10. In all of these passages, it is confirmed that the New Covenant is made with Israel and not with the Church, the Bride of Christ. This should not confuse a believer today since in God's sight we, in this Church era, are seen positionally "in Christ" and therefore it is not possible that He can make a covenant with us seeing that we are "in Him" positionally. The answer comes in 2 Corinthians 2:5-6.

2 Corinthians 2:5-6
> 5 "Not that we are sufficient of ourselves to think any thing as of ourselves; but our sufficiency *is* of God;
> 6 Who also hath made us able **ministers of the New Testament**; not of the letter, but of the Spirit: for the letter killeth, but the Spirit giveth life."

The New Covenant is made with Israel and by the blood of the Covenant Victim it guarantees forgiveness, puts an end to the old order of Covering over sin on the Day of Atonement (*Yom Cippur*) and allows the Kingdom on earth to be instituted. However, in the Old Testament, the means by which this future earthly Kingdom is to be administered is not revealed. We know that in the New Testament it is shown that the Church, the Bride of Christ, will reign with Him over His Kingdom (see Psalms 19 and 45). We will be involved in administering the earthly Kingdom from our heavenly city through the service of the angels. In this sense, we of this Church era will be the "ministers of the New Covenant". In the measure in which we minister unto the needs of the Church today, we are being tested for our roles of administration (ministering) in that coming day. However, let us never forget that being in a position of administering that future Kingdom was not merited through anything of ourselves. It is exclusively on the basis of the blood of the divine Covenant Victim Who has brought us into such unparalleled blessings.

B Will the New Covenant ever grow old or come to an end?

Since the Melchisedec Priest, by virtue of the power of His endless life, is the Guarantor of the New Covenant it can never be annulled. That means that there is no risk in the ages to come that our sins or iniquities can ever be called to remembrance again. This shows us clearly that when He is called a Priest "forever" after the order of Melchisedec, "forever" means for eternity. If His Melchisedec priesthood were to ever come to an end, our sins could be called again to remembrance. However, praise His Name, His is an **eternal** priesthood guaranteeing the eternal security of every blood-bought one!

8 The Hebrews explanation of the timing of the oath of Psalm 110

Hebrews 7:28
> "For the Law maketh men high priests which have infirmity; but the Word of the oath, which was **since the Law**, maketh the Son, Who is consecrated for evermore."

Here we discover that the oath was made "since the Law".
When did the Lord Jesus become a Priest after the order of Melchisedec?

A It must be subsequent to His **death** or **"after the Law was finished"** or "since the Law" (Hebrews 7:28). We know from other passages that it required the death of the Lord Jesus Christ to end the Law of Moses. His consecration as the Melchisedec Priest must be **subsequent** to His death since the oath by which He was consecrated was "since the Law" (Hebrews 7:28). Moreover, just as the Aaronic priesthood required sacrifice for consecration, (see Psalm 40) similarly, "This Man should have somewhat also to offer".

Hebrews 8:3
> "For every high priest is ordained to offer gifts and sacrifices: wherefore *it is* of necessity that this Man have somewhat also to offer."

Prior to Calvary, the Lord could not function as a Melchisedec Priest because He had not yet offered Himself. His death was necessary for His priestly consecration (see Psalm 40).

B It must be subsequent to His **resurrection**. To be a Melchisedec Priest, death must first be defeated. This can only happen in resurrection.

Hebrews 7: 15-16
> 15 "...after the similitude of Melchisedec there ariseth another Priest,
> 16 Who is made, not after the Law of a carnal commandment, but after the power of an endless life."

This shows us that to be our High Priest it is not enough to be a Man. He must be a **risen** Man.

C It must be subsequent to His **ascension. He must be a risen and ascended Man.**

Hebrews 8: 4-6
> 4 "**For if He were on earth, He should not be a Priest**, seeing that there are priests that offer gifts according to the Law:
> 5 Who serve unto the example and shadow of heavenly things, as Moses was admonished of God when he was about to make the tabernacle: for, See, saith he, *that* thou make all things according to the pattern shewed to thee in the mount.
> 6 But now hath He obtained a more excellent ministry, by how much also He is the Mediator of a better Covenant, which was established upon better promises."

It is appropriate at this point to reiterate what was considered in Psalm 40, that status of priesthood was not required to offer sacrifice in the Old Testament. Accordingly, David could offer sacrifice even though he was not a Levitical priest. This is why the Lord Jesus could offer Himself a Sacrifice to God before He is consecrated as a Priest in resurrection. However, **status of priesthood is necessary to be able to enter into the sanctuary**. Thus, it is in resurrection that the Lord Jesus is consecrated as Priest and ascends up to enter into the heavenly temple by virtue of His own blood, His work of putting away sin finished forever.

9 The pivotal role of Psalm 110 in Hebrews

The underlying error afflicting the Hebrew believers was a hankering after the temple worship and its sacrificial system, not in order to have their sins forgiven but to somehow bring about the earthly Kingdom promised in the Old Testament for which they longed. The linking of the Melchisedec Priest of Psalm 110 and the New Covenant of Jeremiah 31 in Hebrews chapters 8 and 10 provides the answer to this difficulty. The reasoning is as follows.

A The Day of Atonement is finished as well as the temple system

If the Lord Jesus as the Melchisedec Priest has sat down and, as the New Covenant Mediator (Hebrews 9:15, 12:24) and Guarantor (Hebrews 7:22), has brought about a situation whereby sins and iniquities are remembered no more forever (Hebrews 10:17), then it is clear that the Day of Atonement is finished, since on that day a remembrance of sin was made every year (Hebrews 10:3). As was shown in Psalm 22, it was on the Day of Atonement that every sin offering of the preceding year was validated. If the Day of Atonement is done away with, then it follows that the entire system of offerings under the Old Covenant is obsolete. The application of this doctrinal fact is that there is no profit in pursuing the temple worship system.

B The temple system is powerless to bring about the Kingdom

If the New Covenant is mediated by the blood of Christ (Hebrews 9:14-15), which promises to Israel a Kingdom and an eternal forgiveness for their sins, then any attempt to advance the coming of that Kingdom by pursuing temple rituals is a denial of the efficacy of the blood of Christ. In fact, it is preposterous to claim that the blood of an animal sacrifice can bring about the Kingdom, when Scripture makes it clear that this prospect has been vouchsafed by the precious shed blood of Christ (Hebrews 12:24). In fact, any dependence on the temple system with its shedding of animal blood to somehow bring about the Kingdom "rest" is the equivalent of counting "the blood of the Covenant.... an unholy thing" (Hebrews 10:28-9).

Hebrews 10:28-29

28 "He that despised Moses' Law died without mercy under two or three witnesses:

29 Of how much sorer punishment, suppose ye, shall he be thought worthy, who hath trodden under foot the Son of God, **and hath counted the blood of the Covenant, wherewith he was sanctified, an unholy thing**, and hath done despite unto the Spirit of grace?"

C How this fits into the thought-flow of Hebrews

Having established these principles in Hebrews 10, the writer in Hebrews 11 provides a long list of heroes of faith. Interestingly, most of the heroes of faith mentioned in Hebrews 11 had no access to the temple in Jerusalem. Either they died **before it was built** or they lived **away from Israel** making temple rituals impossible. This shows that even in Old Testament times, inability to adhere to temple worship did not in any way compromise the faithful in the prospect of participating in the future Kingdom. Hence, Hebrews 11 selects witnesses to faith who had no access to a temple in Jerusalem to reinforce the argument of Hebrews 10, that it is alone **through the blood of Christ** that the divine programme is effected.

Hebrews 12 continues this theme under the image of runners in a race (Hebrews 12:1) being tutored and coached by their Father, in this case their heavenly Father (Hebrews 12:5-13). The idea of this race was already introduced in Hebrews 6:18. The finishing point of the race is heaven, the city of refuge (Hebrews 6:18) where the Lord Jesus has already entered and sat down as a Priest forever (Hebrews 6:18, 12:2). Clearly, the effectiveness of the runners would be compromised if unnecessary burdens were laid upon them. There is more than a hint that the unnecessary burdens which could hinder the athlete in his journey to the finishing line would be getting entangled in the futile temple religious system. The chastening (Hebrews 12:5-11) or coaching which the Father applied to His beloved Hebrew Christian children in the race would have had the effect of distancing them from the burdens of an obsolete and ineffective religious system. The chastening was, in fact, the onslaught of persecutions which caused them to physically flee from Jerusalem, the earthly temple city. Perhaps, this was to remind them that they had indeed spiritually made their flight to the heavenly city of refuge (Hebrews 6:18).

In this context it is worth remembering that the temple in the millennium will not have a Day of Atonement. This means that it is not a continuation of the Old Testament temple system of worship which relied on the Day of Atonement to validate all its sin offerings of the previous year as being sin-atoning. The millennial temple is something completely new – a system of commemorative worship which looks back to the once-and-for-all sin-expiating Sacrifice of the Lord Jesus. Because the sin offerings in Ezekiel's temple do not have a Day of Atonement to validate them as sin-atoning sacrifices, they do not contradict the finality of Hebrews 10:17-18 that "where remission of these is, there is no more offering for sin."

Hebrews 10:17-18
> 17 "And their sins and iniquities will I remember no more.
> 18 Now where remission of these *is, there is* no more offering for sin."

10 The Day of His Wrath

The Psalm now moves from the "Day of His power" to the "Day of His wrath".

Psalm 110:5
> "The Lord at Thy right hand shall strike through kings in the day of His wrath."

Hebrews 7 reminds the Jewish readership that the Melchisedec of Genesis came out to bless Abraham after the slaughter of the kings. Those early Jewish believers would have immediately understood the connection with the future Melchisedec Priest in Psalm 110:5, Who will Himself come out from His heavenly throne to "strike through" the kings of the earth.

In the day of His wrath He will be the King Priest Who has come to put right all the wrongs on this earth. This is His role as King of righteousness Who is going to institute a Kingdom of peace (King of Salem).

A Judgment of the Nations

Psalm 110:6
> "He shall judge among the heathen, He shall fill *the places* with the dead bodies; He shall wound the heads over many countries."

"He shall judge among the heathen" could be translated, "he shall plead the cause among the nations".

We have already encountered this particular verb "to judge" (*yadin*) in Psalm 72, when we noticed that "to judge" (*yadin*) carries the meaning of "pleading the cause" of someone who is wrongly treated or downtrodden, for example:

1 "plead the cause of the poor and needy" (Proverbs 31:9)

2 "and Rachel said, God hath judged me (pleaded my cause) and hath also heard my voice, and hath given me a son: therefore called she his name Dan" (Genesis 30:6)

3 "...they judge not the cause, the cause of the fatherless..." (Jeremiah 5:28)

"he judged the cause of the poor and needy" (Jeremiah 22:16).

When the Melchisedec Priest comes again into this world, it will be in the context of His wrath that He will plead the cause of His own among the nations. This idea of "pleading the cause" strongly implies the righting of a great wrong. This is the divine response to the persecutions of the beleaguered remnant during the tribulation, many of whom will be scattered among the nations awaiting His intervention. Just as we saw in Psalm 18 that the Lord is angry because of the impact of death on His suffering people, similarly in Psalm 110 He is also angry because of the injustices this world has meted out to His own during the tribulation. We saw in Psalm 72 that the Lord must intervene to establish justice in this earth. Similarly, here in Psalm 110 He must intervene to recompense the great injustice caused by this world persecuting His own. He is a merciful and faithful High Priest and measures accurately every drop of suffering His people endure. This verse brings before us the face of His wrath responding now to the suffering of His beloved people. The merciful and faithful One is also the righteous One. His righteousness demands that He intervene again in this world in judgment. He will plead their cause and that will mean judgment to their enemies.

Psalm 110:6

"...He shall fill *the places* with the dead bodies; He shall wound the heads (Hebrew: head (singular)) over many countries."

His intervention will lead to instant death of His enemies on an unprecedented scale. However, chief of them is one individual known as the "head over many countries". This must surely be the future world leader known as the "beast" in Revelation 13:1-10 (for more details on this please see Appendix 2).

B The world is once again reminded of the humanity of Christ

Psalm 110:7

"He shall drink of the brook in the way: therefore shall He lift up the head."

The Psalm ends with this description of the Lord pausing to drink from the brook in the midst of His work of avenging Himself on His enemies.

How fitting that this should be the case! The last this world saw of the Lord Jesus on the cross was a suffering Man saying, "I thirst" and shortly thereafter bowing His head and dismissing His Spirit in death. On His return, He drinks of the brook in the way and then lifts up His head. What a contrast! However, this simple act of drinking from the brook carries an even greater significance. It shows that this Melchisedec Priest Who, **at the start of the Psalm**, is acknowledged as being divine by the title, "My Lord", is still truly human **at the end of the Psalm**, even after 2000 years seated on the throne in heaven interceding for His own. That lovely head which once was bound with thorns is now lifted high in honour, while His feet which ascended the hill of Golgotha in humiliation have now His defeated enemies as their footstool.

11 Does the Melchisedec King remain on earth throughout the millennium?

A question remains in the minds of some as to how it is that the Lord Jesus, on the immediate occasion of His return to this earth, will (1) have His feet stand upon the Mount of Olives (Zechariah 14:4), (2) will ride on the wastes of this earth (Psalm 68:4) (3) will drink of the brook in the way— possibly the brook Cedron (Psalm 110:7) — and (4) will then enter the gates of the city (Psalm 24:7) and yet it is prophesied that He will sit upon His throne in the heavens during the millennium, as considered at length in Psalm 89, in the company of His Bride (Psalm 19). When will He return again to His throne in the heavens? Possibly this was also a question in the minds of Old Testament believers who had noted this matter. The solution to this question, as offered by some Bible teachers today, is to teach that the Lord Jesus remains upon this earth during the entire period of the millennium. However, that view has to discount the many passages considered in Psalm 89 and elsewhere, showing that the ongoing government of His Kingdom, once it is established, will be from the heavens. However, there is a good reason why the details of the Lord Jesus' returning to His throne in the heavens are given only sparingly in the Old Testament. It is because the Church and her heavenly inheritance comprised a mystery, held in God's heart as a secret and not revealed until the New Testament era. This is part of the mystery doctrines considered in Psalm 89.

However, it is worth reflecting once more on the details of the historical account of Melchisedec coming out of the ancient city of Salem and blessing Abraham after the slaughter of the kings (Genesis 14:17-20), since the Hebrews writer uses this historical event as an allegorical picture of the heavenly Melchisedec coming out of His heavenly city in a coming day to bless the earthly nation of Israel in Hebrews 7:1-3.

Genesis 14:17-20

17 "And the king of Sodom went out to meet him after his return from the slaughter of Chedorlaomer, and of the kings that *were* with him, at the valley of Shaveh, which *is* the king's dale.

18 And Melchisedec king of Salem **brought forth** bread and wine: and he *was* the priest of the Most High God.
19 And he blessed him, and said, Blessed *be* Abram of the Most High God, Possessor of heaven and earth:
20 And blessed be the Most High God, Which hath delivered thine enemies into thy hand. And he gave him tithes of all."

In Genesis 14:18, when Melchisedec "brought forth (brought out)" bread and wine, the verb "to bring out" is in the short tense indicating it was a single and completed act. In other words, the reader of the Hebrew text in Genesis 14 would be clear that Melchisedec did not stay outside the city of Salem after he had brought out the bread and wine to Abraham. This supports the idea that after the Lord Jesus has come out from His heavenly city to earth to bless Israel with the earthly Kingdom, He returns to the city of the Melchisedec Priest in heaven to administer that same Kingdom. This is consistent with Psalm 47:5 which shows us how the Lord will "go up (ascend up)" to "sit upon the throne of His holiness" (Psalm 47:8). How wonderful is God's Word in its detail and clarity! This is a wonderful example of the unity of divine authorship throughout all of Scripture, in both Old and New Testaments. Old Testament believers must have struggled as to the meaning of Psalm 47:5, but now with New Testament revelation it is clear that having established His Kingdom on earth on the occasion of His physical return to this planet (Psalm 47:2-4), He then returns to His Bride in the heavens to continue the management of His Kingdom (Psalm 47:5).

Psalm 47:2-6

2 "For the **LORD Most High** *is* terrible; *He is* a great King over all the earth.
3 He shall subdue the people under us, and the nations under our feet.
4 He shall choose our inheritance for us, the excellency of Jacob whom He loved. Selah.
5 **God is gone up (ascended up) with a shout, the LORD with the sound of a trumpet.**
6 Sing praises to God, sing praises: sing praises unto our King, sing praises."

In this context, attention should be directed to Zechariah 12:6 where we read that Jerusalem shall be inhabited again in her own place (literally: Jerusalem shall yet dwell under herself), even in Jerusalem".

This literal translation of Zechariah 12:6 shows in a remarkable way that the millennial city of Jerusalem will be inhabited "under herself (*tachteha*)", i.e. under Jerusalem, that is the heavenly Jerusalem which will be above it in the heavens.Note 3 This is discussed in Psalms 18, 19 and 89. Once again it can be said that these matters may not have been clear to Old Testament readers, but with the clear illumination of the New Testament these details come together as a unified whole showing the perfection of divine revelation.

Conclusion

Psalm 110 forms the basis of major doctrinal sections in the synoptic Gospels, Acts 2 and the Epistle to the Hebrews. The theme is that while the Lord Jesus in resurrection power is seated in heaven on His throne, His people in this **the day of His power** have fled for refuge to the heavenly city where, as an eternal and undying High Priest, He guarantees their eternal security and eternal heavenly inheritance. The second aspect of the Psalm is that **in the day of His wrath** He will come out once more from His heavenly city to this earth to guarantee the promises of an earthly Kingdom to the restored nation of Israel.

1. "This age" is the age of His rejection (Matthew 24). "The age to come" (Hebrews 6:5) is the millennium. "The ages to come" refer to the eternal state (Eph 1-2).

2. The reference in Psalm 111:4 to the Lord being "gracious and full of compassion (Hebrew *rachum*)" reminds us of that first occasion when God was described by the Hebrew word *rachum* in Exodus 34:6. There the context was of God **Himself** forgiving (Hebrew: bearing away) iniquity, transgression and sin (Exodus 34:7). This again links Psalm 111 with the truth of the New Covenant in Jeremiah 31:34 which is all about iniquity being forgiven and sin being remembered no more forever.

3. In Zechariah 14:10, we read that Jerusalem "shall be lifted up and inhabited in her place (*tachteha* under herself)." The Hebrew word *tachteha* means literally "underneath her or it," where "it" (denoted by the ending ....*ha*) is a pronoun of feminine gender in Hebrew grammar. This is clear in Jonah 4:5 when after Jonah made himself a booth (feminine in Hebrew), he sat "under it," where "it" is feminine in the Hebrew to agree in gender with the Hebrew word for booth (*sukkah*) indicated by the ending "..*ha*" in *tachteha*.

> *Jonah 4:5*
> "So Jonah went out of the city, and sat on the east side of the city, and there made him a booth (feminine in Hebrew), and sat under it (*tachteha*) in the shadow, till he might see what would become of the city."

Now the translation of *tachteha* with "in her place" in Zechariah 14:10 is perfectly accurate, but it is worth considering how the literal meaning of "under herself" has come to mean "in her place" in this and similar passages. Perhaps the best Biblical example to illustrate this is found in Judges 7:21 where we read how Gideon's men held their ground during the attack on the camp of Midian.

> *Judges 7:21*
> "And they stood every man in his place (Hebrew: *tachtav* under himself) round about the camp".

The phrase in Judges 7:21, "in his place", means literally "under himself". This is the Hebrew way of emphasisng that the area on which each man stood, referred to as "under himself", was not vacated in the heat of battle. In other words, Gideon's 300 men stood firm. When Zechariah tells us that Jerusalem shall be inhabited "under herself", he is indicating that its inhabitants will not lose their territory again, in other words they have security of tenure in the millennial Kingdom. However, we have on several occasions in these meditations noted how a verse in the Hebrew

Bible can have more than one interpretation, both of which are correct. When we reflect that the literal meaning of Jerusalem dwelling in its own place is, in fact, that Jerusalem is dwelling under itself, we can understand how the Hebrew construction allows for the portrayal of the earthly Jerusalem being located under the heavenly Jerusalem above it.

Below are several further examples where "in her (or its) place" (*tachteha*) mean literally "under her or it", and perhaps would be better translated by "under her or it".

Consider Leviticus 13:23

Leviticus 13:23

"But if the bright spot stay in his place (*tachteha*) , and spread not, it is a burning boil; and the priest shall pronounce him clean."

It should be noted that in these verses when *tachteha* is rendered "in his place", the literal meaning is still "underneath it" or "her".

Let us now review a literal translation of Leviticus 13:23, when, this time the word *tachteha* is rendered with its literal meaning "underneath it" or "her."

Leviticus 13:23

"But if the bright spot (Hebrew: feminine) stay (Hebrew: stand up) under itself (*tachteha*) (feminine), and spread not, it is a burning boil; and the priest shall pronounce him clean."

This literal translation shows that when the "bright spot" "stands up under itself", the diagnosis is "a burning boil". How can the "bright spot" "stand up under itself"? Clearly, the picture is of a bright spot, deep in the flesh, pressing up on the skin above. It is an accurate description of a boil, "pointing" to a head prior to its discharge. A similar construction is found in Daniel 8:8 where the literal translation of *tachteha* as "under it" is quite clear.

Daniel 8:8

"Therefore the he goat waxed very great: and when he was strong, the great horn was broken; and for it (Hebrew: *tachteha* "under it") came up four notable ones toward the four winds of heaven."

These verses show that while it is a legitimate translation of Zechariah 12:6 and 14:10 to render *tachteha* with "in her place", it is also correct to render *tachteha* with "under herself". Below is a literal translation of these two passages.

Zechariah 12:6 (author's literal translation)

"In that day will I make the governors of Judah like an hearth of fire among the wood, and like a torch of fire in a sheaf; and they shall devour all the people round about, on the right hand and on the left: and Jerusalem shall dwell again under herself (*tachteha*), even in Jerusalem."

Zechariah 14:10 (author's literal translation)

"All the land shall be turned as a plain from Geba to Rimmon south of Jerusalem: and it (*Jerusalem*) shall be lifted up, and dwell under herself (*tachteha*), from Benjamin's gate unto the place of the first gate, unto the corner gate, and from the tower of Hananeel unto the king's winepresses."

The only way this alternative literal translation from Zechariah 12:6 and 14:10 can be understood doctrinally, is to recognise that the heavenly Jerusalem shall be in the heavens as the dwelling place of the heavenly Bridegroom-King and His Church the Bride. Meantime, "under it" (*tachteha*) will be the earthly Jerusalem, the seat of divine government on the millennial earth.

25

PSALM 116

1 I love the Lord, because He hath heard my voice and my supplications.
2 Because He hath inclined His ear unto me, therefore will I call upon Him as long as I live.
3 The sorrows of death compassed me, and the pains of hell gat hold upon me: I found trouble and sorrow.
4 Then called I upon the Name of the Lord; O Lord, I beseech Thee, deliver my soul.
5 Gracious is the Lord, and righteous; yea, our God is merciful.
6 The Lord preserveth the simple: I was brought low, and He helped me.
7 Return unto thy rest, O my soul; for the Lord hath dealt bountifully with thee.
8 For Thou hast delivered my soul from death, mine eyes from tears, and my feet from falling.
9 I will walk before the Lord in the land of the living.
10 I believed, therefore have I spoken: I was greatly afflicted:
11 I said in my haste, All men are liars.
12 What shall I render unto the Lord for all His benefits toward me?
13 I will take the cup of salvation, and call upon the Name of the Lord.
14 I will pay my vows unto the Lord now in the presence of all His people.
15 Precious in the sight of the Lord is the death of His saints.
16 O Lord, truly I am Thy servant; I am Thy servant, and the son of Thine handmaid: Thou hast loosed my bonds.
17 I will offer to Thee the sacrifice of thanksgiving, and will call upon the Name of the Lord.
18 I will pay my vows unto the Lord now in the presence of all His people,
19 In the courts of the Lord's house, in the midst of thee, O Jerusalem. Praise ye the Lord.

1 Introduction

This Psalm is not generally regarded as a Messianic Psalm because it is not directly quoted in the New Testament. It is included in this book because it has strong parallels with Psalm 18, which is a Messianic Psalm, and provides an important lead-in to Psalm 118, which is also Messianic.

It begins with a succinct and confident statement of personal faith by the Psalmist in his God, especially in the matter of delivering him from death (Psalm 116:8). Specifically, it is about deliverance from death of Old Testament believers. This is because he speaks in verse 3 of *Sheol*, the temporary abode of the departed Old Testament believers, as discussed in Psalms 16, 18, 22 and 69. The language in the first part of the Psalm, regarding deliverance from death (Psalm 116:3-9), is very similar to Psalm 18:4-6 which has already been studied in this book.

1.1 Authorship and similarity to Psalm 18

The name of the author is not given and the reference at the end of the Psalm to the Psalmist paying his vows unto the Lord "in the courts of the Lord's house in the midst of thee, O Jerusalem" lead some to think that the author could not be David, since in David's lifetime the Lord's house was not yet built in Jerusalem by Solomon. In fact, at the end of David's life, the Ark of the Covenant was residing in Mount Zion in the "tabernacle of David" which was a tent and not a house. This has already been considered in our meditations of Psalms 95 and 96.

However, it is worth comparing the description of death in Psalm 116:3-4 with a very similar prophetic description by David of his own impending death in Psalm 18:4-6 and major events subsequent to his death, namely his resurrection and future Kingdom role.

Psalm 116:8-9
> 8 "For Thou hast delivered my soul from death, mine eyes from tears, *and* my feet from falling.
> 9 I will walk before the Lord in the land of the living."

As in Psalm 18, the Psalmist here describes death as if it has already happened, and then goes on to triumphantly exult in the divine deliverance from that death.

The deliverance from death of his soul must be a reference to resurrection since the Psalmist ultimately died. How could Psalm 116:8 mean resurrection since it is in the past tense in our English Bible? The Hebrew perfect (past) tense, as found in verse 8 ("Thou hast delivered my soul from death"), can sometimes denote the certainty of an event which has not yet taken place, i.e. a future event. This grammatical phenomenon was considered in Psalm 69. In other words, the perfect tense can be used to describe a future event which is as certain as if it has already happened as far as the eternal perspective is concerned. This is likely the sense of the verse here and, if we read it with that understanding, then it becomes clear that the Psalmist is considering his certain future deliverance from death (i.e. his resurrection) and the assurance that one day he will in resurrection "walk before the Lord in the land of the living". Furthermore, the Psalmist speaks of the Lord delivering his "eyes from tears". This can only happen after a believer has left this sad world of sin behind, as tears remain the lot of each one, all the while we are in this "vale of tears". This resonates with the words of John in Revelation 8:17, where he tells us that the martyred believers of the dreaded tribulation period will be personally comforted by the Lamb in the midst of the throne, as God shall wipe away all tears from their eyes – something which happens even before they are raised from the dead at the end of the tribulation.

Revelation 8:17
> "For the Lamb which is in the midst of the throne shall feed them, and shall lead them unto living fountains of waters: and **God shall wipe away all tears from their eyes.**"

The Psalmist also links his deliverance from death and the wiping away of his tears with an assurance that he can never ever again fall morally. What a day it will be when the flesh is finished with forever, and each believer can say that the Lord has indeed "delivered my feet from falling"!

Identifying the end of the Psalm as future events in the Psalmist's experience **after** his resurrection will help us to understand why he, in his resurrection body, is looking forward to entering into the Lord's house in millennial Jerusalem to praise the Lord. It is from a similar eternal perspective that David tells us that he "will dwell in the house of the Lord forever" (Psalm 23:6). All of these themes point to David as being the likely author.

Accordingly, the Psalm gives us delightful insights into how and why this Psalmist in particular and Old Testament believers in general, when raised from the dead in the coming Kingdom, will praise the Lord in His temple in Jerusalem.

1.2 Other interpretations of this section
At this point it is appropriate to acknowledge some other main interpretations of this section.

A
One idea is that the Psalmist, likely to be David, had a near-death experience, possibly on the battlefield, from which God delivered him and his life was spared, hence prompting the writing of this Psalm. Against this interpretation is the observation that the experience described in Psalm 116:3 goes beyond a near-death experience. It is an accurate description of what death was like for Old Testament believers who passed to upper *Sheol*, as discussed in detail in Psalm 16.

Psalm 116:3
> "The sorrows (literally: cords) of death compassed me, and the pains (literally: straits) of hell (*Sheol*) gat hold upon me (literally: found me)…"

Note that the word "sorrows" is more accurately translated "cords", and the word "pains" is more accurately translated "straits" or "narrows". Old Testament believers' souls did not suffer in upper *Sheol*. However, it was a place of restriction, hence the suitability of the words "cords" and "straits". It is only when an Old Testament believer's soul actually entered **into** the gates of upper *Sheol* that they experienced the restrictions (straits and cords) which it necessitated, but there was no suffering there. The fact that the Psalmist speaks of the "straits" of *Sheol* finding him and the "cords" of death surrounding him suggests that he is describing his literal death before it happened. It was anticipation of these restrictions which caused the Psalmist to feel "trouble and sorrow" and not the experience of being there. It was this which prompted him to cry to the Lord.

Psalm 116:4

"Then called I upon the Name of the Lord; O Lord, I beseech Thee, deliver my soul."

Another well known example of a faithful Old Testament believer experiencing sorrow in anticipation of going into the restrictions of upper *Sheol* is Hezekiah in Isaiah 38

Isaiah 38:10

"I said in the cutting off of my days, I shall go to (literally: in) the gates of the grave (*Sheol*): I am deprived of the residue of my years."

The answer to the Psalmist's "trouble and sorrow" was the knowledge that he would be delivered and loosed from *Sheol*, as discussed in Psalm 116:8.

B

Another interpretation of Psalm 116:3 is that the Psalmist is here speaking of conviction of sin, or some other cause of spiritual distress, using metaphorical imagery of death for literary effect. However, it cannot be the case that the description of death here is metaphorical of a spiritual experience when we recall that every human being born into the world is **already** spiritually dead. We do not become spiritually dead at some time in our life's experience. Those who are saved have the glad experience of passing from spiritual death to life in their lifetime and not of passing from spiritual life to spiritual death!

2 More detailed consideration of the Psalm

2.1 Why the Psalmist loves the Lord (Psalm 116:1-11)

In Psalm 116:1-4, the Psalmist recalls the days when he cried unto the Lord out of the trouble and sorrow of impending death. He was concerned about facing death and *Sheol*. He cried for deliverance of soul. He claims the promise that the Lord is "**gracious** and **merciful**" (Psalm 116:5). This great reassurance came to Him as he was considering the reality of death. This reference to the **gracious** and **merciful** Jehovah is a recurring theme throughout the Old Testament. It has already been considered in detail in Psalms 22, 90, 95, 102 and can be traced back to the revelation of God's **grace** and **mercy** given to Moses on his second visit to Mount Sinai in Exodus 34:7. Here God showed Moses that the basis of His grace and mercy lies in His being able to forgive iniquity, transgression and sin (Exodus 34:7).

As we have already observed, the word to "forgive" is the word used of the scapegoat "bearing away" the iniquities into the land not inhabited in Leviticus 16:22 on the Day of Atonement. It means forgiveness through sacrificially bearing away sin by the promised divine Sin-Bearer. It is faith which brings deliverance from trouble and sorrow. This alone brings the soul rest: "Return unto thy rest O my soul" (verse 7). The word here for rest is *mnuchah,* considered in detail in Psalm 95. Death would not rob the Psalmist of enjoyment of the *mnuchah* of Psalm 95! Confidently and on this basis he can now exclaim in advance of his actual death the prospect of his soul being delivered from death itself:

Psalm 116:8-9
8 "Thou hast delivered my soul from death, mine eyes from tears, *and* my feet from falling.
9 I will walk before the Lord in the land of the living."

How can he be so sure? The answer is simple:

Psalm 116:10
"I believed, therefore have I spoken."

It is faith in the merciful and gracious Lord and acceptance of His grace and mercy, namely the Sacrifice of the divine Sin-Bearer as revealed to Moses in Exodus 34, which bring about such confident boasting in the Lord of resurrection. In fact, it is in this context that the Psalmist declares that "all men are liars" (Psalm 116:11). Perhaps this is a difficult phrase to understand initially. However, we should remember that everyone born into this world, including the Psalmist, is, prior to salvation, an unbeliever and thus makes God a liar (1 John 5:10). This is because all who remain in unbelief of God are confessing, whether intentionally or otherwise, that they do not consider God's Word to be reliable enough to put their faith in Him. Therefore, those who through unbelief make God a liar are, by transmission of this false idea about God, judged by God as being liars themselves. Thus, when the Psalmist declares that all men are liars, he is merely showing the status before God of every unregenerate person. This was once his own standing before he exited from that condition by faith. In light of this he can say, "I believe therefore have I spoken!"

Not all men are passive in their unbelief of divine testimony through the lips of His servants. The Psalmist discovered this when he was "greatly afflicted". This is in the context of the unbelief of men. How comforting for believers down through the epochs of time to know that, irrespective of hostility to them from unbelievers, their eternal future is secure in the gracious and merciful God of resurrection in Whom they have placed their trust for eternity!

2.2 What will be the Psalmist's response?

Psalm 116:12-19

12 "What shall I render unto the Lord *for* all His benefits toward me?

13 I will take the cup of salvation, and call upon the Name of the Lord.

14 I will pay my vows unto the Lord now in the presence of all His people.

15 Precious in the sight of the Lord *is* the death of His saints.

16 O Lord, truly I *am* Thy servant; I *am* Thy servant, *and* the son of Thine handmaid: Thou hast loosed my bonds.

17 I will offer to Thee the sacrifice of thanksgiving, and will call upon the Name of the Lord.

18 I will pay my vows unto the Lord now in the presence of all His people,

19 In the courts of the Lord's house, in the midst of thee, O Jerusalem. Praise ye the Lord."

From verse 12 to the end, the Psalmist wishes to express his love to the Lord by a spontaneous response of worshipful service. Evidently, he may have done this in his lifetime before his death. However, there is no record of this in the historical sections of Scripture. The language goes beyond the Psalmist's lifetime to his experience on the other side of resurrection when he will be in the midst of the millennial city of Jerusalem. The picture is of the fulfilment of a vow (verses 14 and 18). When a vow is fulfilled, the work is done. In Psalm 22:25, the Lord Jesus in His coming Kingdom will "repay His vows", i.e. declare to the "great congregation" that His work for God is finished and completed.

Similarly, in Psalm 116, the Psalmist is looking back on his life's work which is, of course, finished after resurrection, so he too can fulfill his vows. This will involve offering "the sacrifice of thanksgiving" (verse 17) in the Lord's house in Jerusalem. This is not in the tent or tabernacle of David but "in the courts of the Lord's house" in Jerusalem (verse 19).

If David is the author of the Psalm, this means that the scene of praise must be millennial Jerusalem when, "in the presence of **all His people**" (verses 14 and 18), David will praise the Lord. The phrase, "**all His people**", indicates a collective gathering of all the Lord's people when death is no longer able to detract from the numbers of the redeemed! This shows that these verses in the Psalm can only find complete fulfilment in the context of the future millennial Kingdom. It may be asked why the Psalmist says, "I will pay my vows unto the Lord **now** in the presence of all His people". What is meant by the word "now" (*na*) if the event in question is future? We should note that the word *na*, meaning "now", can refer to a future event, where an immediate action is being called for. A clear example is in Psalm 118:25, where the call *hoshiah-na* or, in the New Testament, *hosan-na* meaning "save **now**", goes forth. We know this refers to the future cry of the remnant on the occasion of our Lord Jesus' return. Similarly, the statement, "I will pay my vows unto the Lord **now** in the presence of all his people", refers to that future day of assembly of **all** the Lord's people.

What a gathering that will be! **All** the Old Testament saints will be there. Not one will be missing. Psalm 118 shows that, in addition, **all** the tribulation saints will be there. Not one will be missing. Psalm 117 tells us of the Gentiles who will be praising the Lord for His lovingkindness. Romans 15:11 identifies Psalm 117 as referring to the believers of this Church era. Taken together then, Psalms 116, 117 and 118 are looking at the saints of all ages, Old Testament, Church era and tribulation era who will be praising the Lord in the Kingdom. As we have seen earlier, the Old Testament and tribulation saints will be "in the courts of the Lord's house, in the midst of thee, O Jerusalem" (verse 19). The Church-era believers will be with the Lord Jesus in the heavenly city (Psalm 19). All will be involved in the "sacrifice of thanksgiving" (verse 17). As was noted in Psalm 40, the word "sacrifice" in the Old Testament refers to the peace offering of praise. In Scripture, the peace offering was offered after the sin offering and burnt offering of worship. It formed the climax of ritual sacrifices on the completion of the Nazarite vow (Numbers 6:17).

After resurrection, all believers will have finished their life's work. The praise of the Nazarite is a sacrifice of thanksgiving. He does not thank God for what he himself has done. He makes no mention of this. He is only presenting to God that which speaks of what Christ has done. This now brings us to the theme of the praise.

Psalm 116:14-15

14 "I will pay my vows unto the Lord now in the presence of all His people.
15 Precious in the sight of the Lord *is* the death of His saints."

Verse 15 has puzzled expositors over many years. Why should the Psalmist speak of the death of a saint as being valuable and precious in a chapter which openly celebrates the deliverance of a saint from death and the pains of death through salvation?

The widely held understanding of this verse is that the death of each saint is a special event to the Lord because each saint is precious to Him. This thought has brought much comfort to believers who are grieving for loved ones who were saved. It should be noted, however, that the verse is not speaking about the preciousness of the saints to the Lord, but the preciousness of the death. Most of us regard death as being sad, as being an enemy, and even something which leads the Lord to be "troubled" as He contemplates the sorrow it engenders in the hearts of His own (John 11:33). Why then does He say, "Precious in the sight of the Lord is the death of His saints"? When we consider that the Psalm is bringing before us the triumph of a believer over death, it seems fair to suspect that there is much more to this verse than merely bringing before us the undoubted special interest and care which God has for His dying children and those of their loved ones who grieve for them.

The word "precious" means more than being of interest or meriting special care. It actually means of **great value**. We are told in Psalm 49:8 that the redemption of the soul is precious (same root word). We know what effected the redemption of the soul. This was the precious blood of Christ. There is no preciousness comparable to that of the blood of Christ, which was required to provide the precious redemption of the soul (Psalm 49:8). Most of us understand that the verse ("Precious in the sight of the Lord *is* the death of His saints") reminds us of how precious each blood-bought saint is to the Lord. This is absolutely true but this is not the primary meaning of the verse. This becomes apparent in a literal translation:

"Precious in the sight of the Lord is the death **for** His saints".

Herein lies the the reason for the triumph over death, so emphatically announced in this Psalm. It is because of the preciousness of the death **for** His saints. The word "death" is in a grammatical form which attributes emphasis. This suggests the special value of **this death** for His saints. We know that this is the death of the Lord Jesus Christ, as it is the only death in Scripture which is intrinsically precious and of such value that it avails for His saints. This realisation leads the Psalmist to bow in the Lord's presence as the servant of the Lord. As we observed in Psalm 68, His service is perfect freedom. In acknowledgement of this, the Psalmist says, "Thou hast loosed my bonds."

Psalm 116:16

"O Lord, truly I *am* Thy servant; I *am* Thy servant, *and* the son of Thine handmaid: Thou hast loosed my bonds."

His praise to the Lord is directed to Him from the courts of the Lord's house in the midst of Jerusalem (please see Psalms 98-9). This will be the theme of the redeemed Old Testament saints in their earthly inheritance as they rejoice in the preciousness of the death of the Lord Jesus Christ for His saints!

Psalm 116:17-19

"17 I will offer to Thee the sacrifice of thanksgiving, and will call upon the Name of the Lord.
18 I will pay my vows unto the Lord now in the presence of all His people,
19 In the courts of the Lord's house, in the midst of thee, O Jerusalem. Praise ye the Lord."

3 Conclusion

This Psalm foresees a future day of glory when Old Testament believers, raised from the dead, will, in resurrection bodies, praise the Lord in the millennial temple in Jerusalem. This leads on to Psalm 117 which considers believers (mainly Gentile) of this Church era who would be brought into eternal relationship with God on the basis of divine lovingkindness. This brings us to Psalm 118 which describes the revival of the remnant of Israel on the eve of the future tribulation period and how they will be restored to their Messiah to praise Him eternally.

26

PSALM 117

1 O praise the Lord, all ye nations: praise Him, all ye people.
2 For His merciful kindness is great toward us: and the truth of the Lord endureth
for ever. Praise ye the Lord.

Introduction
This little Psalm is quoted in the New Testament

Romans 15:11
"And again, Praise the Lord, all ye Gentiles; and laud Him, all ye people."

Here the context is of the Gentiles being brought into blessing in this
Church age.

The display of the merciful kindness of the Lord
This Psalm is all about the display of the merciful kindness of the Lord.
Verse 2 presents to us the reason: "For His merciful kindness is great toward
us: and the truth of the Lord endureth for ever." The word translated
"merciful kindness" is the Hebrew word *chesed*. Scholars debate the meaning
of *chesed*, some suggesting it means "grace" (N.H. Snaith). However, if we
confine ourselves to its use and application by New Testament writers, we
are reassured that the Authorised Version translation –"merciful kindness"
– beautifully captures the meaning of the word. The argument in support of
the Authorised Version rendering goes as follows: *chesed* is translated into
Greek in the Septuagint by the Greek word *eleos*, both in this passage and
also in Hosea:

Hosea 6:6
"For I desired mercy *(chesed)*, and not sacrifice; and the knowledge of God
more than burnt offerings…"

When this verse is quoted in the New Testament, mercy is again translated
eleos:

Matthew 9:13
> "I will have mercy *(eleos)* and not sacrifice…"

Moreoever, mercy *(eleos)* is distinct from grace *(charis)* in several New Testament passages where we read of "grace *(charis)*, mercy *(eleos)* and peace (2 Timothy 1:2)."

We learn that the Lord's merciful kindness has prevailed (literally: is great) over the Gentiles without any compromise in divine truth. This surely is a summary of God's dealings with the nations in this era of His grace, when His merciful kindness has been offered globally to all nations. The result is a response of universal praise from these nations. In fact, the theme of the New Testament is that in this present era, the age of grace, God has chosen to highlight the wonder of His grace "in His kindness toward us through Christ Jesus" (Ephesians 2:7). The spiritual significance of *chesed* is more fully explained in Micah 7. This is considered in Appendix 5.

The question could well be asked: "Where is the Jewish nation in Psalm 117 amongst all this universal praise to God from the nations (Gentiles)?" The Psalm is silent with respect to worship from the nation of Israel in response to Jehovah's great merciful kindness. Why is the nation of Israel not thanking the Lord for His merciful kindness *(chesed)* in Psalm 117? Could this be telling us that the nation of Israel is estranged temporarily from her God during the time that the Gentiles are rejoicing in His mercy? What a wonderful contrast we are going to find in Psalm 118 when the nation of Israel is at last thanking God for His merciful kindness *(chesed)*!

Conclusion

This Psalm is brief because it is touching on an aspect of truth which has required the entire New Testament to be expounded to us. The bringing into blessing of Gentiles in this Church era was mystery doctrine hidden in God's heart in the Old Testament, but only fully revealed in the New Testament. In retrospect, when we line up Psalms 116, 117 and 118 we can see that Psalm 117 points to this Church era, although at the time the Psalmist could not have elucidated its significance. Perhaps Psalm 117 is one of those passages to which Peter refers in 1 Peter 1:10-12 as he writes of how the Old Testament writers recognised that some of their own inspired writings pointed to future blessing stretching beyond their own nation, in a way that they did not fully understand.

1 Peter 1:10-12
> 10 "Of which salvation the prophets have inquired and searched diligently, who **prophesied of the grace *that should come* unto you:**
> 11 Searching what, or what manner of time the Spirit of Christ Which was in them did signify, when It testified beforehand the sufferings of Christ, and the glory that should follow.
> 12 Unto whom it was revealed, **that not unto themselves, but unto us** they did minister the things, which are now reported unto you by them that have preached the gospel unto you with the Holy Ghost sent down from heaven; which things the angels desire to look into."

27

PSALM 118

1 O give thanks unto the Lord; for He is good: because His mercy endureth for ever.

2 Let Israel now say, that His mercy endureth for ever.

3 Let the house of Aaron now say, that His mercy endureth for ever.

4 Let them now that fear the Lord say, that His mercy endureth for ever.

5 I called upon the Lord in distress: the Lord answered me, and set me in a large place.

6 The Lord is on my side; I will not fear: what can man do unto me?

7 The Lord taketh my part with them that help me: therefore shall I see my desire upon them that hate me.

8 It is better to trust in the Lord than to put confidence in man.

9 It is better to trust in the Lord than to put confidence in princes.

10 All nations compassed me about: but in the Name of the Lord will I destroy them.

11 They compassed me about; yea, they compassed me about: but in the Name of the Lord I will destroy them.

12 They compassed me about like bees; they are quenched as the fire of thorns: for in the Name of the Lord I will destroy them.

13 Thou hast thrust sore at me that I might fall: but the Lord helped me.

14 The Lord is my strength and song, and is become my salvation.

15 The voice of rejoicing and salvation is in the tabernacles of the righteous: the right hand of the Lord doeth valiantly.

16 The right hand of the Lord is exalted: the right hand of the Lord doeth valiantly.

17 I shall not die, but live, and declare the works of the Lord.

18 The Lord hath chastened me sore: but He hath not given me over unto death.

19 Open to me the gates of righteousness: I will go into them, and I will praise the Lord:

20 This gate of the Lord, into which the righteous shall enter.

21 I will praise Thee: for Thou hast heard me, and art become my salvation.

22 The Stone which the builders refused is become the Head Stone of the corner.

23 This is the Lord's doing; It is marvellous in our eyes.

24 This is the day which the Lord hath made; we will rejoice and be glad in it.

25 Save now, I beseech Thee, O Lord: O Lord, I beseech Thee, send now prosperity.
26 Blessed be He that cometh in the Name of the Lord: we have blessed you out of the house of the Lord.
27 God is the Lord, which hath shewed us light: bind the sacrifice with cords, even unto the horns of the altar.
28 Thou art my God, and I will praise Thee: Thou art my God, I will exalt Thee.
29 O give thanks unto the Lord; for He is good: for His mercy endureth for ever.

Introduction

We have seen that Psalm 117 is a doxology, rejoicing that not just the nation of Israel but also the Gentiles worldwide are being brought into blessing. It is a Psalm which applies particularly to this present Church era. It will find its complete fulfilment when, in the future Kingdom, the Church, which includes all those saved throughout this dispensation of grace, will praise the Lord in their heavenly city over the millennial earth.

Psalm 118 follows on with the story of how the nation, which for two millennia has been estranged from her Messiah, is brought back into relationship with Him and proclaims, "Blessed be He that cometh in the Name of the Lord" (Psalm 118:26). This aspect of the Psalm will be fulfilled at the end of the tribulation when the once-estranged nation of Israel welcomes back her Messiah before entering into the earthly Kingdom. The Psalm goes on to describe the first great celebratory Passover of the millennial Kingdom.

In contrast to the previous Psalm, which is about the nations, Psalm 118 refers specifically to the nation of Israel and the God-fearers within it – Israel (verse 2), the house of Aaron (verse 3) and those that fear the Lord (verse 4).

1 The time period referred to in the Psalm

To understand this Psalm, we must figure out the event in prophecy to which it refers. The Psalm projects forward in time to a period in the history of the nation of Israel specifically when it will thank God for His merciful kindness (*chesed*). This period will be characterised by an urgent appeal both to Israel and to the Lord to act "now" (*na*) which recurs throughout the Psalm. The Hebrew word "*na*" is known in Hebrew Grammar as the "particle of entreaty" and is usually translated by the phrase, "I pray thee" or the word "now". Because it denotes a call or entreaty, it is sometimes translated "I pray thee", and because it is used in a context where an urgent response is intended, it is frequently translated "now".

In verses 1-4, the Psalmist addresses Israel, the house of Aaron and them that fear the Lord, calling upon them to **now** say, that His mercy (*chesed*) endureth forever (literally: even to the age).

Psalm 118:1-4

1 "O give thanks unto the Lord; for He is good: because His mercy (*chesed*) endureth for ever.
2 Let Israel now say, that His mercy (*chesed*) endureth for ever.

3 Let the house of Aaron now say, that His mercy (*chesed*) endureth for ever.
4 Let them now that fear the Lord say, that His mercy (*chesed*) endureth for ever."

It is worth noting that the word "now" (*na*), which occurs three times in the opening verses, is the same word in verse 25:

Psalm 118:5
"Save now, (*hoshiah-na*) I beseech Thee, O Lord: O Lord, I beseech Thee, send now (*na*) prosperity."

It was from Psalm 118 that the multitudes were singing as the Lord entered Jerusalem in Matthew 21:9, presenting Himself so meekly to them as their future King. *Hosanna* is the Greek transliteration of the Hebrew *hoshiah-na*.

Matthew 21:9
"And the multitudes that went before, and that followed, cried, saying, Hosanna to the Son of David: Blessed *is* He that cometh in the Name of the Lord; Hosanna in the highest."

As the people that day cried, "*Hoshiah-na*" (save now) they meant *na* to be an urgent appeal for action, i.e. an immediate "now". Sadly, this was not to be the case. We know from our Lord's own words in Matthew 23:37-9 that the *na* in *hoshiah-na* will not be fulfilled until He comes back to this earth to set up His Kingdom.

Matthew 23:37-39
37 "O Jerusalem, Jerusalem, *thou* that killest the prophets, and stonest them which are sent unto thee, how often would I have gathered thy children together, even as a hen gathereth her chickens under *her* wings, and ye would not!
38 Behold, your house is left unto you desolate.
39 For I say unto you, **Ye shall not see Me henceforth, till ye shall say, Blessed *is* He that cometh in the Name of the Lord.**"

This observation clarifies for us that the timing of the urgent appeals in Psalm 118, both to Israel and to the Lord, to act "**now**" refers to the future **after** the nation has been reconciled to her Messiah (see Appendix 3).

Already we can see that even though the Gentiles have for many years been thanking God for His mercy (*chesed*), Israel in a general way is largely unimpressed by the mercy of the Lord. What a joyful day it will be in the history of this world when the remnant nation of Israel, following its restoration after the rapture, will at last attain the sense of urgency of response required of them by the Lord, as implied by the "**now**" referred to in the Psalm, and publicly recognise and confess God's wonderful *mercy* to them after so many long, lonely and sad years of estrangement from Him (see Appendix 3)!

Indeed, the period of Israel's estrangement is referred to in verse 13:

Psalm 118:4

"Thou hast thrust sore at me that I might fall: but the Lord helped me."

In Romans 11, we read of Israel's fall through rejecting her Messiah two thousand years ago and that this brought much blessing to the Gentiles.

Romans 11:11-12

11 "I say then, Have they stumbled that they should fall? God forbid: but *rather* **through their fall salvation** *is come* **unto the Gentiles**, for to provoke them to jealousy.

12 Now if the fall of them *be* the riches of the world, and the diminishing of them the riches of the Gentiles; how much more their fullness?"

Romans 11:12 envisages the rise again of the once-fallen nation and how Israel's restoration to her Messiah will bring unparalleled blessing to this sad world ("how much more their fullness"). Similarly, Psalm 118 describes that wonderful future time when the nation will be gloriously restored to her God through putting her faith in their Messiah Lord and His provision for all their need. As discussed in Psalm 102, the great revival of the nation begins with a recognition that her distress is primarily an internal, spiritual one rather than some external, political or military threat. The restoration of the nation of Israel is considered in more detail in Appendix 3. It happens after the rapture of the church and before the tribulation begins.

2 Israel's distress call and her salvation

In the next section the Psalm moves to the first person with repeated references to "I, me, my".

Psalm 118:5-9

5 "I called upon the Lord in distress: the Lord answered me, *and set me* in a large place.

6 The Lord *is* on my side; I will not fear: what can man do unto me?

7 The Lord taketh my part with them that help me: therefore shall I see *my desire* upon them that hate me.

8 *It is* better to trust in the Lord than to put confidence in man.

9 *It is* better to trust in the Lord than to put confidence in princes."

A Who is the distressed person referred to in this Psalm?

Firstly, it cannot be the Messiah because in Psalm 118:17 we read, "I shall not die, but live, and declare the works of the Lord". This excludes the Lord Jesus from being the "I" referred to in this section since He did die. Moreover, we see this again confirmed to us in Psalm 118:18 "The Lord hath chastened me sore: but He hath not given me over unto death". Clearly, the Lord Jesus was given over unto death, so these verses cannot refer to Him. Rather, the "I" is referring to someone who will enter into the gates of righteousness. We know from Psalm 24 that the gates refer to the administration of the Kingdom and the unnamed person in this Psalm is calling for the gates of righteousness to open. In verse 20, we discover that the "I" of verse 19 is, in fact, **collectively referring to a body of people,** since in verse 20 when we read of "this gate of the Lord, into which the righteous shall enter", the word righteous is in the plural, meaning "righteous ones". This careful attention to detail shows us that the "I", "me" and "my" references in the Psalm are, in fact, the language of the remnant believing nation in distress, speaking as one person longing for the gates of righteousness to be opened to them, i.e. access to the Kingdom.

Psalm 118:19-21

19 "Open to me the gates of righteousness: I will go into them, *and* I will praise the Lord:
20 This gate of the Lord, into which the righteous (ones) shall enter.
21 I will praise Thee: for Thou hast heard me, and art become my salvation."

B What is the nature of their distress?

Psalm 118:5

"I called upon the Lord in distress: the Lord answered me, *and set me* in a large place."

This word "distress" (*metsar*) carries the literal idea of a straitened circumstance or place rather than distress as already noted in Psalm 116:3. This is why, when the people are delivered from this, they are placed in "a large place" which means the exact opposite to "a straitened place". It denotes a narrowed or confined closed-in space which is why it is sometimes translated "distress". The word "in" is actually the preposition "from" (*min*). Moreover, the definite article is present so the literal translation is: "I called upon the Lord from **the** straitened place". This is the only occurrence of the word distress (*metsar*) in the singular, and its only occurrence with the definite article.

If, as we have seen above, the "I" in this verse is the united confession of the remnant nation in a future day, then the occurrence of "distress" with the definite article and in the singular suggests to us a uniquely specific distress in the experience of the restored remnant nation of Israel when they truly feel hemmed in by deadly enemies from every direction, as described in Appendix 3. In the context, this surely is the tribulation period, the time of Jacob's trouble. In contrast to the straitened circumstances of this distress, God places the nation in a "large place". Again, the definite article is present. God places Israel in "the large (or wide) place". It speaks of definite relief from a very definite distress.

C The answer to the distress

Psalm 118:6-7

6 "The Lord *is* on my side; I will not fear: what can man do unto me?
7 The Lord taketh my part with them that help me: therefore shall I see *my desire* upon them that hate me."

The next verse, "The Lord is on my side", literally means, "The Lord is for me; I will not fear; what can man do unto me?" The following verse, "The Lord taketh my part...", is again identical in Hebrew to the start of the preceding verse and also means, "The Lord is for me…" This is echoed in Romans 8:31,"If God be for us, who can be against us?". How wonderful it must be for the Lord in that day to see this little remnant of Jewish believers so dependent upon Him! In fact, the next two verses (Psalm 118:8-9) describe this trust.

Psalm 118:8-9

8 "*It is* better to trust in the Lord than to put confidence in man.
9 *It is* better to trust in the Lord than to put confidence in princes."

The remnant of believers in the nation of Israel will be marked by complete dependence and trust in the Lord. This, we learn, is better than "to put confidence in man (*ba-adam*: Hebrew literal meaning "in the man")". The phrase, "confidence in man", suggests confidence in human strength and humankind in a general sense, and indeed where the word *ba-adam* occurs this general sense is always clear from the context. Whilst this is indeed the case, we know that during the tribulation the apostate elements of the nation will put their trust not just in man in a general sense but in one specific man, i.e. the first beast of Revelation 13 (see Appendix 2). This man is the personification of all that is anti-God and is the one man the apostate nation will trust for their security. In contrast to the apostate nation, which tragically will be trusting in man in general and in the leader of global humanity in particular, namely "**the** man", i.e. the man of sin of 2 Thessalonians 2:3, this little remnant is united in its trust in the Lord alone. Similarly, they will not be depending on princes, those earthly leaders which, for a time, will have given their authority over to this man, also known as "the beast" (Revelation 17:13). It is to such dependent ones that the gates of the Kingdom will swing open once the King comes to take up His authority and reign. How beautiful this is!

The distress-call arises from those who have called upon the Lord in **the** distress, who earlier received His salvation (verses 14 and 21) and who are now longing for the manifestation of the King in righteousness.

3 Victory over hostile armies

This godly remnant of Israel finds itself surrounded by hostile nations who are intent on its destruction. However, the tables will be turned when the tiny remnant of Israel will become the instrument in the Lord's hand for the destruction of these murderous armies. The key to this change of events is the "Name of the Lord (Jehovah)" as emphasised in Psalm 118:10-12. (Details of the confrontation between the remnant in Jerusalem and the surrounding armies who will wish to exterminate them are considered in Appendices 2 and 3). Now the remnant is acting in the **Name of the Lord** and in fellowship with Him.

Psalm 118:10-12

10 "All nations compassed me about: but in the **Name of the Lord** will I destroy them.

11 They compassed me about; yea, they compassed me about: but in the **Name of the Lord** I will destroy them.
12 They compassed me about like bees; they are quenched as the fire of thorns: for in the **Name of the Lord** I will destroy them."

Even in the midst of the impending victory, the nation will be constantly in remembrance of the Lord's sovereign dealings with them throughout the ages of their estrangement from Him. This brings us to the next section.

4 Memories of Jehovah's dealings with the once estranged nation

Psalm 118:13-18

13 "Thou hast thrust sore at me that I might fall: but the Lord helped me.
14 The Lord *is* my strength and song, and is become my salvation.
15 The voice of rejoicing and salvation *is* in the tabernacles of the righteous: the right hand of the Lord doeth valiantly.
16 The right hand of the Lord is exalted: the right hand of the Lord doeth valiantly.
17 I shall not die, but live, and declare the works of the Lord.
18 The Lord hath chastened me sore: but He hath not given me over unto death."

In Psalm 118:13, there are vivid memories of the "fall of Israel". We know from Romans 11 that this fall refers to the rejection by the nation of the Person of Christ so many years ago. However, despite this, the Lord helped the fallen nation (Psalm 118:13) and protected her against the waves of anti-semitism down through the centuries. The section ends in verse 18 with memories of the Lord chastening the nation severely. Down through the years, the experience of the nation in its estrangement from her God has been "sore" (Psalm 118:13). Nevertheless, she has been the subject of divine protection. "He hath not given me over to death" (Psalm 118:18) and it is to death that anti-semitic leaders down through the centuries have sought to consign the nation of Israel. God had a greater plan than the destruction of His sometimes wayward people. It was their salvation. As anti-semitism intensifies to alarming levels in recent times, it is reassuring for all Bible-believing Christians who love the Jewish people to see that both Old and New Testament Scriptures pledge divine protection to the nation of Israel even right through the tribulation persecutions which lie ahead. We know that bringing in the Gentiles to blessing after the fall of Israel in Romans 11:12 was for the express purpose of provoking the Jewish nation to jealousy to effect their recovery (Romans 11:11-14). One of the many reasons why true Christians repudiate anti-semitism is because we understand from Scripture that Israel's fall and **temporary** estrangement from her God have brought us unworthy Gentiles into blessing.

Romans 11:15
"For if the casting away of them *be* the reconciling of the world, what *shall*

the receiving *of them be*, but life from the dead?"

This should cause those of us who are Gentile believers in the Lord Jesus to have a sense of humble indebtedness to the Jewish people, because through them the Messiah came to us, and as Paul tells us, "as touching the election, *they are* beloved for the fathers' sakes"(Romans 11:28).

In Psalm 118, when the moment of the "now" appeals is reached, the remnant nation has already been recovered and saved. This national revival happens after the Church is called away at the rapture. The matter of Israel's national rebirth is considered in detail in Appendix 3. Each young Jewish believer in the tribulation will be able to say, "The Lord is become my salvation" (verse 14).

5 Longing for the Kingdom

These newly-saved Jewish believers in the Lord Jesus Christ, the so-called "sucklings" considered in Psalm 8, will eventually endure the most horrendous persecution imaginable. They will intensely long for the Lord Jesus' return in manifested glory. The following verses articulate their prayer:

Psalm 118:19-21

19 "Open to me the gates of righteousness: I will go into them, *and* I will praise the Lord:
20 This gate of the Lord, into which the righteous shall enter.
21 I will praise Thee: for Thou hast heard me, and art become my salvation."

The redeemed remnant are longing for the gates of righteousness to open. We know from Psalm 24 that the gates speak of the place of administration of the Kingdom, under the righteous government of Christ. Only the righteous will enter into this millennial era and offer endless praise to the Lord. Their song is sweet, "Thou hast heard me, and art become my salvation" (Psalm 118:21). The final section of the Psalm is a beautiful preview of the sublime praise which Israel will present to her God in that day of victory, when she beholds for the first time her beloved Messiah, Who so lovingly suffered for her redemption all those years ago.

6 Israel prepares for her first Passover since her salvation

Psalm 118:22-23

22 "The Stone Which the builders refused is become the Head Stone of the corner.
23 This is the Lord's doing; it is marvellous in our eyes."

We are left in no doubt in Matthew 21:42 that this verse refers to the humiliation of the Lord Jesus on the occasion of His presenting Himself to the nation for acceptance as their King just prior to Calvary.

Matthew 21:42

> "Jesus saith unto them, Did ye never read in the Scriptures, The Stone which the builders rejected, the Same is become the Head of the corner: this is the Lord's doing, and it is marvellous in our eyes?"

On that occasion, the people had earlier (Matthew 21:9) been quoting from further down the Passover Psalm, as they excitedly called out, "Save now (*hoshiah-na*)" (verse 25) and "Blessed is He that cometh in the Name of the Lord" (verse 26). Calmly, in Matthew 21:42, the Lord reminded them that they had gone too far down the Psalm in their excitement and religious fervour and had omitted to notice the earlier verses, 22 and 23, about "the Stone which the builders refused" becoming "the Headstone of the corner".

The Lord, in His teaching, was showing His audience that before He will be received by the nation with the **official and genuine** welcome of, "Blessed is He Who cometh", there must first be an **official rejection** of the Lord Jesus by the leaders (the builders). How literally this prophecy was fulfilled. It would only be a matter of hours until the multitude who were crying, "Save now (Hosanna)" would be shouting, "Away with this Man" (Luke 23:18) under the encouragement of their leaders.

"The Stone" (even) is a Messianic title.

A

Zechariah prophesied that Zerubbabel would be legitimately in the Messianic line and that he would bring forth (out) the "Stone" shouting, "Grace, Grace unto (pertains to) It" This is a picture of Christ in **incarnation**.

Zechariah 4:7

> "Who *art* thou, O great mountain? before Zerubbabel *thou shalt become* a plain: and he shall bring forth **the Headstone** *thereof with* shoutings, *crying*, Grace, grace unto It."

B

In Isaiah, we see Him as a Stone of stumbling and Rock of offence, a picture of Christ in **humiliation**.

Isaiah 8:14

> "And He shall be for a sanctuary; but for a **Stone of stumbling and for a Rock of offence** to both the houses of Israel, for a gin and for a snare to the inhabitants of Jerusalem."

C

In Daniel, we read of "the Stone cut out without hands" which felled the huge humanistic image seen by Nebuchadnezzar in his dream. This is a picture of Christ in **exaltation**.

Daniel 2:34

> "Thou sawest till that **a Stone was cut out without hands**, Which smote the image upon his feet *that were* of iron and clay, and brake them to pieces."

D

In Psalm 118:22, the "Stone", Who is Christ, is presented to us **in humiliation and then in exaltation,** where first we see His humiliation at the hands of the builders (the nation at the time of His earthly sojourn) and then a vision of His exaltation – He will become "the Head Stone of the corner."

The next verse tells us how the truth of the Lord Jesus' one time humiliation, followed by His glorification, will be perceived by the saved remnant of believers at His manifestation. They will confess their feelings in the words of Psalm 118:23.

Psalm 118:23

"This (feminine) is the Lord's doing; It *is* marvellous (feminine) in our eyes."

The phrase, "This is the Lord's doing", literally means, "From Jehovah has been this (feminine)".

There are perhaps two ways of understanding this verse, both of which are right. Firstly, we could consider that the humiliation and exaltation of Christ, described in the preceding verse, had been "from Jehovah", i.e. from His heart and part of His great master plan of redemption. All of this is "marvellous". "This" is seen as being a general view of the Lord's programme of redemption through Christ. This is a legitimate understanding of the verse.

There is a second equally legitimate view which Hebrew grammar permits, and it is also very sweet. The word "Stone" in Hebrew is of the feminine (f) gender. Also, in the next verse, the word "this" is feminine, and the word "marvellous" is also feminine. Thus, when we read the literal rendering, "From Jehovah has been this (f)" and "it (f) is marvellous (f) in our eyes", we discover that verse 23 is referring specifically to the "Stone". A literal rendering of the verse could be as follows: "from Jehovah has been This (i.e. the Stone)" and "It (i.e. the Stone) is marvellous in our eyes". This then is an acknowledgement that the "Stone", i.e. the Person of the Messiah, had come out from Jehovah. What a journey! Can it be that such a divine Being had come to this earth to be rejected of the builders? Yes! But look again. It (f) (*the Stone*) is marvellous (f) in **our** eyes. The word "marvellous" is from the root word *pele* meaning "wonderful" – one of the titles of our Lord Jesus (Isaiah 9:6). The meaning of the verse is very beautiful. In contrast to the eyes of the first builders, who rejected the "Stone" (Christ at His first advent), in "our eyes", i.e. specifically in the eyes of the remnant, the "Stone", i.e. the exalted Christ, is "wonderful" or "marvellous".

One is reminded of the hymn by J. Denham Smith (1817-1889),

"Rise my soul behold 'tis Jesus,
Jesus fills thy wondering eyes!
See Him now in glory seated,
Where thy sins no more can rise."

The remnant goes on to acknowledge that the day of the Lord Jesus' exaltation is the goal of the divine master plan and that they are at its very centre (Psalm 118:24).

Psalm 118:24

"This *is* the day *which* the Lord hath made; we will rejoice and be glad in it."

The day of the exaltation of Christ is truly the work of the Lord. God has made this day. We are reminded of the words of the Lord Jesus: "The Sabbath was made for Man, and not Man for the Sabbath" (Mark 2:27).

The remnant of Israel will be longing for this day. Psalm 118:25 once again is a further plea for the Lord to speed the arrival of that day of glory:

Psalm 118:25

"Save now (*hoshiah-na*), I beseech Thee, O Lord: O Lord, I beseech Thee, send now (*na*) prosperity."

The cry of the remnant to their Messiah is twofold: (1) "Save now" and (2) "Prosper now".

Already the remnant will have been saved by faith. It is too late at His second coming to cry for salvation from sin (see Appendix 3). This is a cry for salvation from their intense persecutions and "the distress". The call to "prosper now" will be seen when the King, as envisaged in Psalm 45:4, will "ride prosperously". This is the opening up of the unparalleled and unrivalled prosperity which will characterise the Kingdom of Christ in that day. The remnant is craving for the dawn of this millennial morning. It is no surprise, then, that they offer a heartfelt "welcome" to the returning King:

Psalm 118:26

"Blessed *be* He that cometh *(Baruch haBba)* in the Name of the Lord: we have blessed you out of the house of the Lord."

"*Baruch haBba*", the ancient Hebrew phrase for "welcome", is still a frequently used greeting to all who have been privileged to be guests in a Hebrew-speaking, Jewish home. This is exactly the phrase used in verse 26 and is literally translated: "Blessed is He Who cometh". In contrast to the first "builders" of 2000 years ago who refused to welcome Christ to the nation, the believing remnant of Israel will simply say to Him, "*Baruch haBba*", "Welcome!" (Blessed is He Who comes).

The verse ends with a blessing or welcome extended not just to the coming Messiah, but to others unnamed and undefined in the Psalm: "We have blessed (welcomed) **you** (plural) out of the house of the Lord". Who can these people be who are referred to by the pronoun "you" (plural)? Evidently, they are not partaking in the Passover festivities in the house of the Lord since the blessing is: "We bless you **from** the house of the Lord". We know that they cannot be Old Testament believers since they, in their resurrection bodies, will be **in the house of the Lord** at Jerusalem (Psalms 23, 99, 116). Old Testament believers must have found this difficult to understand. The question was, if those being blessed are not Old Testament believers and not tribulation believers, who can they be?

As was noted in Psalm 117, there were aspects of truth in some passages of the Old Testament, regarding future blessings falling to an unidentified group, which went beyond the boundaries of Israel. Peter shows us that Old Testament believers identified these passages as not applying to them but to others (1 Peter 1:12). Could those receiving the blessing of the remnant be the Church, the Bride of Christ, who will return with Him from beyond the heavens, (where we have been with Him since the rapture) to take up residence with the King in the heavenly city as it orbits above the earth (see Psalm 19) throughout the millennial reign? After the Lord has defeated His enemies on the earth and established the Kingdom there, He will return to His Bride in the heavenly city from where the millennial Kingdom will be administered. When He came to redeem us, He came alone. When He comes in glory, we (the Church) shall accompany Him then. What mercies He has shown to us!

7 Israel keeps the first millennial memorial Passover

It was Passover when the Lord Jesus presented Himself to the nation the first time. No one in the leadership of Israel at that memorable Passover occasion made the connection that the true Passover Lamb was in their midst and was about to die and shed His blood to bring deliverance from the bondage of sin. The Psalm ends with a reference to the Passover and a call to keep it.

Psalm 118:27

"God is the Lord, Which hath shewed us light: bind the sacrifice with cords, even unto the horns of the altar."

This will be a Passover even greater than that of Josiah the reformer in 2 Chronicles 36, although Josiah's Passover is no doubt a picture of this one.

On this occasion, the people's hearts will have been illuminated to understand the meaning of the Passover. They will bind the festive sacrifice (the Lamb) to the horns of the altar. We know from Ezekiel that the Passover will be kept in the millennium. As was considered in Psalm 22 and Psalm 110, there will be no Day of Atonement in the millennium with the result that sacrifices during that period are only commemorative. Accordingly, this will be a grand remembrance Passover feast which will be characterised by intense praise to the Lord (see Psalm 22), Who is the Lamb provided by God. This is the theme on which our Psalm ends. They will look to Christ and say:

Psalm 118:28

"Thou *art* my God, and I will praise Thee: *Thou art* my God, I will exalt Thee."

In contrast to two thousand preceeding years of national darkness, "now" with hearts which have been illuminated by the God "Who gives us light" can they thank God for His wondrous mercy:

Psalm 118:29

"O give thanks unto the Lord; for *He is* good: for His mercy *endureth* for ever."

8 The practical lesson

What is the practical lesson of this Psalm for us today?

The doctrine of the **mercies of Jehovah** in His dealings with Gentiles (Psalm 117), and then His taking up the nation of Israel (Psalm 118) after the rapture, should not be just something to fill us with wonder. There is a response required. Paul challenges us with this in Romans 12:1-2.

Romans 12:1-2

1 "I beseech you therefore, brethren, **by the mercies of God**, that ye present your bodies a living sacrifice, holy, acceptable unto God, which is your reasonable service.

2 And be not conformed to this world: but be ye transformed by the renewing of your mind, that ye may prove what is that good, and acceptable, and perfect, will of God."

To each believer in this Church era of grace, the question comes afresh, in light of the mercies of the Lord in His dealings with men: "Am I willing to present myself to Him as a living sacrifice in His service?"

This brings us to Psalm 110:3 again. "Thy people shall be free will offerings in the day of His power."

Conclusion

Psalm 118 tells us of the restoration of the nation of Israel to her Messiah after an era of unparalleled blessing to Gentiles (Psalm 117). So great is the divinely wrought transformation in the heart of the nation of Israel, whose "builders" once rejected the Stone, that around 2000 years later they will joyfully extol Him as "wonderful in our eyes". What a day of joy that will be for the nation of Israel! What joy will it be for us, the Bride of Christ, to witness that great reunion from our heavenly city and to enter into the feelings in His soul as His own nation, at long last, welcomes Him to their heart!

FROM ETERNITY TO ETERNITY

As we review all of the Psalms considered in this book, it is clear that the Person of Christ is central to each one. In this chapter, some key doctrines, touching our Lord Jesus Christ in the Psalms, are summarised. Since the verses quoted in this summary have already been discussed at length in *Meditations in the Messianic Psalms,* they are not considered again in detail. A useful exercise for the reader would be to identify and add yet more examples from the Psalms to each of the sections given below.

The doctrine of the Deity of the Lord Jesus

In **Psalm 2:7,** the Lord Jesus is spoken of as the Son of God.

"I will declare the decree: the LORD hath said unto Me, Thou *art* My Son; this day have I begotten Thee." As the Son of God He was understood by the Jews in New Testament times as claiming equality with God His Father (John 10:32-33).

John 10:32-33
> 32 "Jesus answered them, Many good works have I shewed you from My Father; for which of those works do ye stone Me?
> 33 The Jews answered Him, saying, For a good work we stone Thee not; but for blasphemy; and because that Thou, being a Man, makest Thyself God."

This was indeed correct, as Isaiah 9:6 makes clear, that the Child born (at Bethlehem) was the Son Who was given and that the Son given was the "Father of Eternity", i.e. eternal and thus God.

Isaiah 9:6
> "For unto us a Child is born, unto us a Son is given: and the government shall be upon His shoulder: and His Name shall be called Wonderful, Counsellor, The Mighty God, The everlasting Father (Father of eternity) , The Prince of Peace."

The equality of the Lord Jesus to His Father is made clear in **Psalm 16:8** where we read, "I have set the Lord always (as an Equal) before Me."

Psalm 16:8
> "I have set the LORD always (as an Equal) before Me: because He is at My right hand, I shall not be moved."

These words were spoken by the Lord Jesus prior to Calvary. The One on equality with God had come to die. Again, in **Psalm 82:1** we learn how the One Who stood in the Temple Mount in Jerusalem, remonstrating with the judges of Israel, was *elohim*.

Psalm 82:1
> "God (*elohim*) standeth (singular) in the congregation of the Mighty; He judgeth among the gods (judges)."

Again, in **Psalm 110:1** we read David's inspired words: "The Lord said unto my Lord sit Thou at My right hand". Here David speaks of the future Son of David as his own Lord, i.e. indicating that David considered Him to be God.

The doctrine of His incarnation

In **Psalm 8:4,** we read how God would "visit" frail mortal man.

Psalm 8:4
> "What is man, that Thou art mindful of him? and the son of man, that Thou visitest him?"

This visitation was with the objective of delivering man from death and therefore required the incarnation of the Messiah. Psalm 8 emphasises God's plan as to how man, who was intended by God to head His creation but who lost this role through sin, would be restored to pre-fall dignity through the visitation of the incarnate Christ.

Psalm 68:20 refers to the purpose of incarnation when we read that "unto God the Lord *belong* the goings out (unto) death."

This is a further explanation of Micah 5:2, where we read of the preincarnate Christ "Whose goings forth (out) *have been* from of old, from everlasting…" The incarnation was a key step in Christ's movements out from the eternal throne of God to undergo death itself (Psalm 68:20). **Psalm 40:7** shows that the Lord Jesus must be incarnate in order to achieve God's purpose of fitting men to become priests of the Lord, able to function in God's immediate presence in this capacity. "Then said I, Lo, I come: in the volume of the book *it is* written of Me" (Psalm 40:7). Once again, the goal of His incarnation was to die, but this time to die in order to be consecrated Priest so that all the redeemed could, as a result, be constituted priests before the throne of God. **Psalm 69** shows that the Lord Jesus must draw near to His servants as Kinsman Redeemer (*goel*) to deliver them and restore the inheritance lost through sin.

Psalm 69:18
> "Draw nigh (as near Kinsman) unto my soul, *and* redeem it (as a *goel*):

deliver me (*padah*) because of mine enemies."

The *goel* (Kinsman Redeemer) must be related to the one he comes to deliver. This happened at Bethlehem when He became Man, i.e. became related to us. Once again, Psalm 69 shows that the purpose of incarnation, i.e. becoming our *goel* at Bethlehem, was ultimately to die for us.

The doctrine of His perfect and sinless life

The life of the Lord Jesus was unique to all other human beings. He was perfect and sinless. Unlike faithful servants of God, who could not fully keep God's Law, the Lord Jesus could say in Psalm 40:8, "Thy Law is in the midst of My bowels".

In Psalm 45:7 we read, "Thou lovest righteousness, and hatest wickedness". This is also emphasised in Psalm 24:3-4.

Psalm 24:3-4
> 3 "Who shall ascend into the Hill of the LORD? or Who shall stand in His holy place?
> 4 He that hath clean hands, and a pure heart; Who hath not lifted up His soul unto vanity, nor sworn deceitfully."

This was uniquely fulfilled in Him. **Psalm 22:21** shows that God's pleasure and satisfaction in the perfect life of Christ were when He, as Sacrifice, was "answered" at Calvary.

Psalm 22:21
> "Save Me from the lion's mouth: for Thou hast heard (**answered**) Me from the horns of the unicorns."

The satisfaction of God in the perfect life of Christ is again emphasised in **Psalm 16:10**, where we read "neither wilt Thou suffer Thine **Holy One** to see corruption". In fact, Psalm 16:10 shows that **resurrection** was the proof of His holiness. Psalm 91:9 shows Him as the Perfect and Dependent Man Who had made "the most High His abiding place". A literal translation of Psalm 91:9 reads as follows: "Because Thou O Lord, my refuge, hast made the most High Thy habitation…" As the One Who never failed in His dependence upon God, He is seen in Psalm 91 as the Perfect Dependent Man. This is the One Who would defeat Satan in the temptation.

The doctrine of His rejection by men

In Psalm 2:1, we read that "the heathen rage, and the people imagine a vain thing". This is in the context of the rejection of the Lord Jesus. Psalm 22 considers His rejection by Jews and Gentiles together. Psalms 41 and 69 show that hatred directed against David, for being in the line of the promised Messiah, would ultimately be directed at the Lord Jesus when He finally would come. Thus, the reproaches of them that reproached the Lord in heaven fell on David first of all, but when the Lord came He would come to personally experience these same reproaches. Accordingly, as David spoke of the divine *Goel,* Who was yet to be revealed, he said "Thou wilt know my reproach" (Psalm 69:19). This was fulfilled in the finest of details in the events leading up to His death, as prophesied in Psalms 22, 41 and 69. In fact, David's betrayal in Psalm 41 was based on a resentment to his being in the line of the Messiah, and hence would be replayed in the experience of the Lord Jesus, Who would relive these same Davidic reproaches in His own experience. Remarkably, the aspect of human rejection in the run-up to the death of the Lord Jesus was not understood by the disciples prior to His death. They never questioned the many occasions that the Lord Jesus spoke of His impending death. However, in the gospels, they questioned the manner of His death, that is, a death of reproach and rejection by His own nation (Matthew 16:22). It was in this context, however, that the Lord emphasised that the Scriptures must be fulfilled (Mark 9:12). Included in the Scriptures to which the Lord alludes in Mark 9:12 must surely be the passages from the Psalms discussed above.

The doctrine of His death

The death of the Lord Jesus is referred to in many Messianic Psalms. The circumstances leading up to His death were characterised by rejection by the political and religious leaders of the day. This is clearly described in Messianic Psalms and discussed in the paragraph above. However, the Psalms tell us about the supernatural divine aspect of His death. In **Psalm 116:15** we read, "Precious in the sight of the Lord is the death **for** His saints". This shows that His death was on behalf of fallen humanity. **Psalm 90:13** shows that when Moses prays, "Repent Thee concerning Thy servants", he is referring to the occasion in his own life (Exodus 32:12) when he prayed for his own wayward nation on the basis of the promise of God to Abraham regarding the coming Lamb of God's providing, as revealed in Genesis 22. On the basis of the future death of Christ, God was able to forgive the nation. Similarly, in Psalm 90, on the same basis God is able to forgive His servants. This shows that the death of the Lord Jesus was of sin-expiating value. Psalm 24:3 also foresaw the day when the Lamb of God would ascend "the Hill of the Lord", i.e. Calvary. When we understand that Christ, the promised Lamb of God in Genesis 22, is alluded to in Psalms 90 and 24, it becomes clear that the death of the coming Messiah must be a sacrificial death. This matter is discussed in detail in Psalm 90.

Psalm 40 shows that His death was necessary for Him to be consecrated as a Priest so that redeemed ones of all ages can sing either the New Song (Revelation 5:9) or the "as it were" New Song (Revelation 14:3), "Thou art worthy, for Thou wast slain and hast redeemed us to God by Thy Blood…". **Psalm 22** shows that at His death He was "answered" by God, alone in the darkness (referred to in verse 2 as "the night season") "from the horns of the high ones" (Psalm 22:21). This showed divine satisfaction in His death and declared that His was a propitiating death when sin was borne away, as typified by the scapegoat, who bore away the sin into the land "cut off" on the Day of Atonement. **Psalm 89:10** shows that the Messiah will destroy Satan (Rahab) through the wounding of Himself. Here is the literal translation of the verse which makes this clear.

Psalm 89:10
> "Thou as One that is wounded hast broken Rahab in pieces; Thou hast scattered Thine enemies with Thy strong arm."

This refers to His victory over Satan at Calvary. This shows that the aerial heavens, which are the sphere of satanic dominion, will be liberated from this as a result of the death of the Lord Jesus.

The doctrine of His resurrection

His being begotten from amongst the dead in resurrection is referred to in Psalm 2:7, "Thou art My Son; this day have I begotten Thee". Again, the idea of being begotten from the womb of death is mentioned in Psalm 110:3, where we read in the context of His "forever" priesthood: "from the womb of the dawn; Thou hast the dew of Thy youth". As the One Who has burst forth from the domain of death, His priesthood is forever and can never be terminated by death. Perhaps, the clearest reference to His resurrection is in Psalm 16:10-11 where we read: "Neither wilt Thou suffer Thine holy One to see corruption. Thou wilt show Me the path of life". Here we see that resurrection is the proof that the One Who died was holy, i.e. He did not die for sins of His own. He was holy, spotless and pure. Resurrection is the proof that His was a victorious, effective and once-for-all sin-expiating death. **In Psalm 91:14**, we read that it is "because He hath set His love upon Me", that "with long life will I satisfy Him" (Psalm 91:16). In other words, because of His perfect love God-ward He fulfilled the Law God-ward. Accordingly, the blessings uniquely attending the One Who fulfilled the Law God-ward must be fulfilled, namely that His days be long: "That thy days may be long upon the land which the LORD thy God giveth thee" (Exodus 20:12). In the case of the Lord Jesus, this was fulfilled in His resurrection from the dead as explained by Isaiah:

Isaiah 53:10
> "He shall see *His* seed, He shall prolong *His* days."

The doctrine of His ascension to God's right hand

His ascension is mentioned in **Psalm 68:18**: "Thou hast ascended on high".

It is also referred to in **Psalm 91**, when it states that after defeating the lion, adder, young lion and dragon (i.e. Satan) God will "set Him on high" (Psalm 91:13-14). In fact, this Psalm also shows that the angels shall bear "up in their hands" the Victor over Satan (Psalm 91:12). We know that the victory over Satan was at Calvary. **Psalm 24:3** shows that the One Who ascended the Hill of the Lord (i.e. Calvary) to die is the One Who would "stand in His Holy place". This is the Holy place in heaven where He entered and is seated in **Psalm 110:1**, but is seen **standing** on two occasions: to welcome martyred Stephen into His presence (Acts 7:56) and to return to this earth in Revelation 5:6.

The doctrine of the delay from ascension to His coming to the earth to reign

In Psalm 110:1 we read: "Sit Thou at My right Hand, **until** I make Thine enemies Thy footstool". The Scriptures thus envisage a delay between His ascension and sitting down and His return to reign. This period is the "day of His power" (Psalm 110:3) when the gospel of His grace is proclaimed. The Psalms do not reveal how long this period will last. However, Psalms 96-99 and later Psalm 132 describe the journey of the Ark of the Covenant from the house of Obed-Edom the Gittite to the tabernacle of David and eventually to the temple of Solomon as an allegory of the events describing the circumstances in the lead-up to the Lord's return to this earth to reign.

In Acts 15:16, the re-erection of the tabernacle of David is described by James as pictorial of the events which will happen in this world **after** the Lord has called out of the nations a people for His Name, i.e. **after** this Church period, which ends with the rapture of the Church. Amos 9:11-15 defines the re-erection of the tabernacle of David as a term to describe the revival of the nation of Israel just prior to the Lord's return to the earth to reign. It follows, therefore, that Psalm 96, which was written by David to provide a spiritual commentary on the erection of the tabernacle of David, carries a major prophetical significance depicting the conditions of revival which will characterise the nation of Israel in that coming day. The brief three-month period when the ark remained in the house of Obed-Edom the Gittite (1 Chronicles 13:13), preceding the erection of the tabernacle of David, was characterised by tremendous spiritual blessing, so there is, therefore, every reason to expect that the final years of this Church era, immediately prior to the rapture, will be characterised by unprecedented spiritual revival and gospel blessing worldwide. This matter is discussed at length in Psalm 96. Let us be before the Lord in prayerful exercise should it be that this happens in our lifetimes.

During the "until" period, Israel has "fallen" (Psalm 118:13).

Psalm 118:13
"Thou hast thrust sore at me that I might fall: but the LORD helped me."

Moreover, Israel seems to be blind to the beautiful doctrines of the lovingkindness of God (Psalm 117). Meantime, the Gentiles in this Church era are praising God for His lovingkindness and His mercy (Psalm 117). During this period, the Bride is being called out of the nations (Psalm 45). She is unknown to the Old Testament believers (i.e. the friends of the Bridegroom in Psalm 45:7), but she will be known to the tribulation believers after the Church has gone, who are known as "the virgins which come **after** her" (Psalm 45:14). The role of the Church is not given in the Old Testament. This is part of the mystery doctrine referred to but not explained in Psalm

89:7, "God is greatly to be feared in the mystery of the saints". Nevertheless, Psalm 40:10 foresees a day when the Lord Jesus will have explained and will continue to explain all the hidden things (mystery doctrines) to all the saints in the millennium and eternal state.

Psalm 40:10

"I have not hid Thy righteousness within My heart; I have declared Thy faithfulness and Thy salvation: I have not concealed Thy lovingkindness and Thy truth from the great congregation."

How wonderful an era is this dispensation of grace, when the secrets of God's heart have already been revealed to us in the New Testament through the Holy Spirit (1 Peter 1:12)! The end of the Church period, which concludes with the rapture of the Church, is not revealed in the Old Testament. This is because it is a mystery doctrine. Nevertheless, in Acts 15:16 James shows that the re-erection of the tabernacle of David, i.e. the spiritual revival of the nation of Israel, will happen **after** the Lord has finished calling out of the nations a people for His Name. This was not apparent in the Old Testament. However, the New Testament harmonises perfectly with Old Testament passages.

The doctrine of the tribulation period

This is the time of **the** distress (Psalm 118:5). It is also the period when the epidemic of evil (noisome pestilence) will stalk this world (Psalm 91:3). The false prophet, who is the "snare of the fowler" (Psalm 91:3), will be a central character in Israel at that time. There will be a great deceit which will descend upon the apostate nation of Israel with their table, i.e. their system of temple worship, becoming "a snare before them" (Psalm 69:22), and "their eyes will be darkened that they cannot see" (Psalm 69:23). In other words, they will believe the lie of 2 Thessalonians 2:11 as will indeed the rest of the inhabitants of the world who, before the rapture of the Church, were among those who "believed not the truth, but had pleasure in unrighteousness" (2 Thessalonians 2:12). As part of this deception, ungodly men will trust in **"the** man" of Psalm 118:8, i.e. the future Gentile world leader, but the true remnant will not be trapped into this great deception. The New Testament clearly distinguishes the future activities of these two wicked men. This is described in **Appendix 2**.

In the midst of all of this intense globalised moral wickedness there will be a great spiritual revival among the nation of Israel, who are spoken of as "sucklings" in Psalm 8:2. The term "sucklings" possibly reflects their youthfulness, i.e. they were too young to be among those who received the strong delusion of 2 Thessalonians 2:12, and who, in their lifetimes prior to the rapture of the Church, "believed not the truth and had pleasure in unrighteousness". This remnant of "sucklings" will be greatly persecuted and distressed during the tribulation. How they are brought to faith in Christ is described in Psalm 102 and also commented on in Psalm 118 (see

Appendix 3). The end of the tribulation will be characterised by the Lord having His enemies "in derision" (Psalm 2:4). The details of this derision are alluded to in Psalm 2:5-7 as the resurrection from the dead of the Lord Jesus.

During the tribulation, Satan has two main players on the world scene – the beast and the false prophet (Revelation 13). The former is an anti-God type figure of Gentile origin and the latter is an anti-Christ type figure of Jewish origin. The beast has a deadly wound which heals (Revelation 13:3). To onlookers it seems as if he is indestructible and resistant to death itself. This suggests a simulation of immortality, hence his anti-God characteristic. The point is that he cannot simulate resurrection. Resurrection cannot be simulated by the powers of darkness. This is why in Psalm 2, the great Psalm about the resurrection of the Lord Jesus, the Lord "shall have them in derision" as He declares "the decree" regarding the resurrection from the dead of the Lord Jesus. The book of Revelation shows that in the second half of the tribulation, just as Satan has two main men, so God has two men who faithfully serve Him, known as the two witnesses in Revelation 11. Their service, according to Revelation 11:2-3, is in the second half of the tribulation period. These men will be martyred for Christ at the end of their period of service and their dead bodies will lie in the streets of Jerusalem (Revelation 11:8). These two men of God will be opposed to Satan's two men, the issue at stake being the truthfulness of the account of the resurrection from the dead of the Lord Jesus. On this truth, all testimony to Him hangs. God's two witnesses will be called upon to provide the ultimate evidence to this world that God is the God of resurrection. They will die and be raised from the dead in the full view of the people of Jerusalem (Revelation 11:11). This will trouble the people of the earth with a "great fear" (Revelation 11:11). Psalm 2:5 tells us that the Lord will speak unto the earth dwellers "in His wrath, and vex them **(terrify them)** in His sore displeasure". Revelation 11:11 shows us that it is the public demonstration of the resurrection from the dead of these two witnesses which will terrify the world of unbelievers, who will then recognise that it is too late to change sides and get right with God.

The doctrine of the return of the Lord Jesus to reign

Psalm 97:7 charts His movement downward to this earth to reign and calls upon all the angels to worship Him as He returns. Psalm 18 describes the gradual descent of the Lord Jesus to the earth to reign as the arrows fly forth from His presence, consuming His adversaries (Psalm 18:14). This is further described in Psalm 68:1-2 as the wicked will flee away from His face. **Psalm 68:4** shows that on reaching this earth "He will ride on the wastes". **Psalm 110:7** describes how He crosses the brook Cedron on the way to the city, and **Psalm 24:7** describes how He enters the gates of the city in triumph. **Psalm 45:3-4** also describes this journey and tells us that on His return, He will ride "in majesty" destroying His enemies. These Psalms show that He physically stands on this earth to set up His Kingdom.

Psalm 18:16 and Psalm 71:20 refer to the resurrection from the dead of Old Testament believers and martyred tribulation believers on the occasion of the return to the earth of the Lord Jesus. Obviously, the Psalms do not refer to the rapture of the Church to heaven prior to the tribulation period, because this is mystery doctrine (I Corinthians 15:51), which, by definition, is something not fully revealed in the Old Testament (Ephesians 3:5). Nevertheless, the doctrine of the rapture of the Church, prior to the tribulation, fits in perfectly with the overall unity of scriptural truth since it is clear that the heavenly people (the Church) with their heavenly inheritance cannot be on earth when the gospel of the Kingdom, proclaiming again an imminent earthly inheritance, is on offer.

The doctrine of the maintenance of His Kingdom

The Psalms show that having established His Kingdom He will govern it from the heavens. For example, **Psalm 89:37** confirms that His throne will be in the heavens. **Psalm 99:5** shows that the millennial earth is like "the footstool" of His throne. **Psalm 19:4-6** describes Him as the "Sun" orbiting the earth in His Bridegroom's tent. This clearly indicates that throughout the coming Kingdom He will rule this world from the heavens in the company of His people, the Church believers of this era. During this time there will be unparalleled blessing in the world (Psalm 72). Is there any reference in Scripture to the Lord moving to His throne in the heavens, having established the millennial Kingdom on the earth? Psalm 46 describes how the Lord will cause "wars to cease" as He establishes His Kingdom. Psalm 47 continues this theme, describing how He will continue His reign. Then Psalm 47:5 describes how the Lord will "go up (ascend up)" to "sit upon the throne of His holiness" (Psalm 47:8). This remarkable verse shows that having established His Kingdom on earth on the occasion of His physical return to this planet, He then returns to His Bride in the heavens to continue the management of His Kingdom.

Psalm 47:2-6
> 2 "For the LORD most high is terrible; He is a great King over all the earth.
> 3 He shall subdue the people under us, and the nations under our feet.
> 4 He shall choose our inheritance for us, the excellency of Jacob whom He loved. Selah
> **5 God is gone up (ascended up) with a shout, the LORD with the sound of a trumpet.**
> 6 Sing praises to God, sing praises: sing praises unto our King, sing praises."

What a day it will be when, in the coming Kingdom, the restored nation of Israel, symbolised by the "sons of Korah" (as discussed in Psalm 45) gladly confesses the deity of Christ and calls Him "our King"!

The doctrine of the eternal state

The millennial Kingdom will have to give way to the sin-free eternal state. Psalm 102:25-28 speaks of the new heavens and new earth under the metaphor of setting aside an old garment and replacing it with a completely new one. Psalm 8:6 shows that "all things" will be put "under His feet" and that includes death and sin, according to 1 Corinthians 15:27.

Concluding remarks

The Psalms have, as their central and unifying theme, the Lord Jesus Christ. Failure to see Him in the Psalms renders a study of Israel's divinely given songbook a dry and meaningless exercise. May our eyes be opened, as were the eyes of the two disciples on the road to Emmaus when the Lord opened "their understanding that they might understand the Scriptures" (Luke 24:45). The Lord showed them that this would allow them to grasp the things "which were written in the Law of Moses and in the Prophets and in the Psalms concerning Me" (Luke 24:44).

If my reader has not yet trusted the Lord Jesus Christ, revealed in these Psalms as Lord and Saviour, then these meditations will be distant and irrelevant to you. The riches of the Scriptures will be beyond your grasp because they can only be spiritually discerned. To really understand the Psalms you must have first come to personally know the Messiah of the Psalms and this is only possible through coming to Him by faith, trusting Him as Lord and Saviour to experience the forgiveness of sins and the promise of heaven forever. It should not surprise us, then, that it is in the first Messianic Psalm, Psalm 2:12, that the exhortation to trust in Him as Saviour goes forth.

Psalm 2:12
> "Kiss the Son, lest He be angry, and ye perish *from* the way, when His wrath is kindled but a little. Blessed *are* all they (whosoever) that put their trust in Him."

If this exhortation in the first Messianic Psalm is heeded, then the rest of the Messianic Psalms will be opened up to you by the Spirit of God. Heaven will become near to you on a daily basis!

Now, in conclusion, it is the author's sincere prayer that *Meditations in the Messianic Psalms*, even though incomplete and imperfectly presented, might bring glory to God and rich spiritual blessing to each reader. Amen

Appendix 1

The Messiah in the New Testament spoken of as "Christ" and "the Christ"

Those who are familiar with the detail of Scripture understand and are very comfortable with the principle that even tiny "jot and tittle" differences, such as the presence or absence of the definite article, carry significance. For example, a careful student of Scripture can readily distinguish between "Church" and "the Church", "faith" and "the faith", "Son" and "the Son", "word" and "the Word" etc. Similarly, we should know how to distinguish between "heaven" and "heavens", "sin" and "sins", "suffering" and "sufferings", "offering" and "offerings", "seed" and "seeds" etc.

Similarly, we should distinguish between "Christ" and "the Christ" in the rest of Scripture. Christ is the Greek translation of the Hebrew word *Mashiach,* meaning "messiah" or "anointed one". For example, this word is used of David and Aaron when they were anointed to the offices of king and priest respectively. The Hebrew *HaMmashiach* means "the Anointed One" or "the Messiah." "*HaMmashiach*" or "the Messiah" is widely used in modern Hebrew today to describe the expected Messiah Whom they hope will soon come to deliver Israel. Surprisingly, though, "*HaMmashiach*" is never used of the Lord Jesus in the Hebrew Old Testament. Rather it is "**His** Anointed" (*Meshicho*) in Psalm 2. We have to wait to the New Testament to meet the phrase "the Christ" or "the Messiah".

In the Gospels and the Acts of the Apostles, the Lord Jesus is recognised by Israel as "the Messiah" (the Christ). In this context, we should note that the high priest did not say, "Art Thou Christ?" but rather, "Art Thou the Christ?" (Mark 14:61). This was the One Israel had been looking for following the exile of Babylon – "The Christ" or "The Messiah". It was in the context of the two on the road to Emmaus, who were puzzling over their hope "that it had been He Who should have redeemed Israel" (Luke 24:21), that the Lord Jesus explained: "Ought not **the** Christ to have suffered these things, and to enter into His Glory?" (Luke 24:26). When Peter, in Acts 2, is showing the Lord Jesus as the One through Whom Old Testament prophecy is fulfilled, and the One Who will sit on the throne of His father David, he refers to Him as **the** Christ in Acts 2:30, saying, "Therefore, being a prophet and knowing that God had sworn with an oath to him, that of the fruit of his loins, according to the flesh, He (God) would raise up **the** Christ (Textus Receptus) to sit on his (David's) throne…". he refers to Him as "**the** Christ". Similarly, (and of relevance to 2 Thessalonians 2:2), when Paul entered the Jewish synagogue in Thessalonica in Acts 17 to preach the gospel to a largely Jewish audience, he reasoned "that **the** Christ must needs have suffered, and risen again from the dead; and that this Jesus Whom I preach unto you, is **the** Christ". Even to this day, the Jew recognises the phrase "the Christ" or "the Messiah" (*HaMmashiach*) as the coming One.

It appears that the occurrence of "the Christ" in the Epistles carries the significance of reminding the reader of the primary presentation of Christ to the nation of Israel, which in grace has now moved beyond to reach Gentiles. For example, on those special occasions when we read of "the Christ" in relation to the Church, as in Ephesians 5:24-25, we in the Church are to be gently reminded that it was indeed the "Jewish" Christ Who came forth from that nation to find us Gentiles and make us His own. Hence, when the Spirit of God wants to emphasise to us the wonder of the love of the Lord Jesus Christ, we read that it was "**the** Christ" Who loved the Church and gave Himself for her (Ephesians 5:25). Similarly, we read of the "Gospel of **the** Christ" (Romans 1:16) (Textus Receptus). It certainly is wonderful "good news" that "the Christ" does not limit His blessing to Jews only but moves out to Gentiles. This calls forth worship when we remember that He did not restrict His love to the Jewish people only, but that it went out even to Gentiles. Such is the wonder of the Love of "the Christ".

Moreover, the Church is subject to (i.e. dependent on) **the** Christ (Ephesians 5:24 and 1 Corinthians 11:3). This suggests that in this Church era we cannot arrogantly discount the Old Testament and the doctrine therein as some kind of irrelevancy. We should know the Old Testament and its truths intimately. In the context of Gentile believers eating foods which may be unacceptable to a recently saved Jew, Paul reminds Gentile believers in Rome that sensitivities of other (Jewish) believers should be respected. In this special context he reminds them that we must one day stand before the judgment seat of **the** Christ (the Messiah) (Romans 14:10). That prospect should cause a Gentile believer to think twice before despising the foibles of his weaker Jewish brother. Similarly, in 2 Corinthians 5:10 Paul reminds the Corinthians that we must be manifested before the judgment seat of "the Christ". Once again, this was in the context of our conduct being appropriate to the propagation of "the gospel of the Christ" (2 Corinthians 4:4), which trumpets the wonder of how Gentiles can be recipients of blessings which, under grace, are no longer limited to Israel.

In the context of the great mystery of Christ and the Church in Ephesians 5:32, the definite article is omitted. It is simply "Christ and the Church". Similarly, in multiple passages in the Epistles to do with Christ and the Church, the definite article is omitted, showing us the equally important truth that in the Church there is neither Jew nor Greek and that the middle wall of partition has come down.

It now becomes clearer that there is much spiritual worth in exploring the contexts of "Christ" and "the Christ", especially noting a peculiar emphasis in the latter to the Lord Jesus in his primary presentation to Israel and then His outward movements to Gentiles in grace. These considerations become important when we consider the doctrinal difference between "day of Christ" and "the day of the Christ" in Appendix 2.

Appendix 2

The two evil world leaders of end times spoken of in the Psalms

The Psalms speak of the tribulation as "**the** distress" (Psalm 118:5) and the period of the "epidemic of evil (noisome pestilence)" (Psalm 91:3). The false prophet, who is the "snare of the fowler" (Psalm 91:3), will be a central character in Israel at that time. A great deceit will descend upon the apostate nation of Israel with their table, i.e. their system of temple worship, becoming "a snare before them" (Psalm 69:22), and "their eyes will be darkened that they cannot see" (Psalm 69:23). Another key player on the world stage at that time will be "**the** man" of Psalm 118:8, i.e. the future Gentile world leader. The New Testament clearly distinguishes the future activities of these two wicked men.

Summary of 2 Thessalonians 2:1-12

2 Thessalonians chapter 2

1 "Now we beseech you, brethren, by the coming of our Lord Jesus Christ, and *by* our gathering together unto Him,

2 That ye be not soon shaken in mind, or be troubled, neither by spirit, nor by word, nor by letter as from us, as that the day of Christ is at hand (literally "in progress").

3 Let no man deceive you by any means: for *that day shall not come* (or be in progress), except there come a falling away (apostasy) first, and that man of sin be revealed, the son of perdition;

4 Who opposeth and exalteth himself above all that is called God, or that is worshipped; so that he as God sitteth in the temple of God, shewing himself that he is God.

5 Remember ye not, that, when I was yet with you, I told you these things?

6 And now ye know what withholdeth that he might be revealed in his time.

7 For the mystery of iniquity doth already work: only He Who now letteth *will let*, until He be taken out of the way.

8 And then shall that Wicked (Lawless one) be revealed, whom the Lord shall consume with the spirit of His mouth, and shall destroy with the brightness of His coming:

9 *Even him*, whose coming is after the working of Satan with all power and signs and lying wonders,

10 And with all deceivableness of unrighteousness in them that perish; because they received not the love of the truth that they might be saved.

11 And for this cause God shall send them strong delusion, that they should believe a lie:

12 That they all might be damned who believed not the truth, but had pleasure in unrighteousness."

Background

Before considering 2 Thessalonians 2, it is important to have a clear understanding of the two separate evil leaders of the end times known in Revelation 13 as:

1 the beast out of the sea
2 the beast out of the earth

1 The beast out of the sea ("first beast") Revelation 13:1-10

This first beast comes out of the "sea" suggesting his Gentile origins. The fierce character of this creature, complete with his ten horns, is reminiscent of the fourth ten- horned beast of Daniel 7:7, identified as the ancient Roman Empire, suggesting strongly that the first beast of Revelation 13 is a future Roman Emperor-type figure. However, his physical description also bears the characteristics of a leopard, a bear and a lion, showing that all the worst aspects of the three great pre-Roman empires of the ancient world, depicted as beasts in Daniel 7, will characterise this man:

the pre-Roman ancient Greek Empire is seen as a leopard,

the Medopersian Empire preceding it is seen as a bear,

the Babylonish Empire, which came before the Medopersian Empire, is seen as a lion.

Thus, the main evil aspect of the ancient Greek Empire is seen in the leopard characteristic of the "first-beast" of Revelation 13, while the fullness of Medopersian wickedness will be seen in his bear-like character, while that which was most prominent in Babylonish wickedness will be seen in his lion-like appearance.

It is important for us to identify in Daniel's prophecy the chief aspects of wickedness which particularly characterised each ancient empire (Roman, Grecian, Medopersian and Babylonish) in order to understand how each of these aspects will be seen together, personified in this future wicked world leader.

Perhaps the worst aspect of the ancient Roman Empire was its cruelty and military prowess.

The worst aspect of the Greek Empire was that of temple desecration (historically prefigured in the actions of Antiochus Epiphanes, the little horn of Daniel 8:9).

The worst aspect of the Medopersian Empire was emperor worship (Darius banning all prayer to God except to himself in Daniel 6).

The worst aspect of the ancient Babylonish Empire was enforced image worship (Daniel 3).

All of the above will characterise this wicked individual. The first beast of Revelation 13 operates in a specific anti-God manner. In this regard, he accepts worship and blasphemes against God. However, one important detail is given in Revelation 13:5: he operates in this anti-God capacity for forty-two months (three and a half years), i.e. the latter half of the seven-year tribulation period. This does not suggest that he only becomes a public figure for this time. He is operating as a public figure before this (Revelation 17:3), in the first half of the tribulation period, acting in collaboration with the harlot (false) bride known as Mystery Babylon the Great (Revelation 17:5). Babylon was known in the Old Testament, but the mystery aspect of its character as the counterfeit bride (harlot) had to await the New Testament mystery revelation in Ephesians 5:32 of the true Bride (the Church); hence its designation as the "Mystery Harlot" in contrast to the New Testament mystery of the true Bride, i.e. the New Testament Church. It is with regard to the counterfeit (harlot) religious system that the "first beast" acts as the supporter and promoter. In this role he is **not yet** acting as the counterfeit against God and all that is worshipped. That must await the forty-two month designated period of his open anti-God rebellion. Until that happens, he is tacitly allowing the religious activities of the harlot Church system to continue with his overt support. These observations cause us to distinguish between the first beast's initial political activities and his later religious anti-God activities.

It is worth reiterating that his anti-religious actions are restricted to a forty-two month (three and a half year) period in the second half of the tribulation, whereas his political prominence precedes this. However, during his time as a political world leader, in the first half of the tribulation, he has not yet manifested his true objectives. His manifestation as a religious anti-God figure awaits the 42 month period stipulated in Revelation 13:5, i.e. the second half of the seven-year tribulation period. This manifestation as the anti-God figure spells the end of Mystery Babylon and the brutal cessation of Jewish temple worship in Jerusalem with the unparalleled genocide against the people of Israel. It is only then that the true combined "leopard-bear-lion-ten-horned beast" character is manifested as the emperor-image worship and temple desecration are seen.

The "first beast" is seen personified in the description of the last anti-God world leader, namely the "little horn" arising from the last beast (Roman Empire-figure) of Daniel 7. To help us understand how he will perform in practice, we have an historical prefiguring of his actions in another "little horn" figure in Daniel 8:9. Arising from the fierce Grecian he-goat comes a little horn (Antiochus Epiphanes), who historically desecrated the temple, the victory over which is celebrated to this day in the feast of the Dedication or *Hanukkah* (John 10) and formed the background to Psalm 82. This "little horn" of Daniel 8 constitutes an historic prefiguring of the, as yet, prophetic "little horn" of Daniel 7:8, just as the historical worship of the image (Daniel 3) and the emperor (Daniel 6) constitutes an historic prefiguring of the anti-God activities of this final Gentile leader. However, this happens only **after** his anti-God agenda is manifested in the final three and a half years of the tribulation. The onset of this dreadful time is spoken of in Matthew 24 as "the time of the end". As regards the period of the tribulation which precedes this, it is said that "the end is not yet" (Matthew 24:6). The Lord's account in Matthew of the "time of the end" being heralded by the "abomination of desolation spoken of by Daniel the prophet" (Matthew 24:15) in the temple fits exactly with:

1 The time span of forty-two months at the second half of the tribulation (Revelation 13:5).

2 The decree to forcibly end the "sacrifice and the oblation" in the "midst of the week" (Daniel 9:27).

Accordingly, the "time of the end" (Matthew 24) is the period of the manifestation of the first beast in his anti-God campaign.

To confirm this further, let us briefly consider Daniel 9:24-27. In that section, sixty-nine weeks are numbered from the command to rebuild the city to the death of Messiah the Prince. In Hebrew, in Genesis 29:28, a week can mean seven years, so with this in mind it is clear that Daniel's prophecy referred to 483 years from the command to rebuild the city to the death of the Lord Jesus, Whose death was "not for Himself...". However, in verse 27, Daniel envisages the events of the final week or seven-year period. This period commences with the confirming of a covenant between Israel and the "prince that shall come." Who is the prince that shall come? He is clearly a future Roman emperor-like figure, because Daniel speaks of the "people of the prince that shall come" and tells us that they would destroy the temple in Jerusalem. Historically, this happened in A.D. 70, carried out by the people of the Roman Empire, although the **coming prince** was unheard of at that time. This is because the "coming prince" is **a future Roman emperor-type figure**. Accordingly, the title of "the coming prince" aptly describes the first beast of Revelation 13, but is a title which encompasses his astute political activities before his anti-God religious activities become apparent with his blasphemous image and emperor worship going forth from the desecrated temple in Jerusalem in the last three and a half years of the tribulation.

Before leaving this "first beast", we must give attention to Revelation 13:3: "And I saw one of his heads as it were wounded to death; and his deadly wound was healed: and all the world wondered after the beast". Later, in verse 14, he is described as "the beast which had the wound by a sword and did live". Surely, some may argue (in my view wrongly), this is a picture of death and resurrection and as such this first beast is a counterfeit to Christ rather than to God, i.e. is an anti-**Christ** figure rather than an anti-**God** figure. Note 1 The incident referred to is a literal traumatic injury sustained by this man (wounded by a sword). To all reasonable observers, the magnitude of the injury and wound sustained would have been sufficient to cause death. The man is "**as it were** wounded to death", not **actually** wounded to death. This means that this man **did not** die. The world will see him as one who had miraculously survived what would, ordinarily, have been understood as a fatal injury. In this regard, this man does not simulate the death and resurrection of Christ which was a genuine death proven by three days and three nights in the tomb before His resurrection. The significance of the deadly wound which was healed lies in the demonstration of **apparent immortality**. In other words, it will be understood by earth that this amazing man is not vulnerable or susceptible to death. The world will then think that he is immortal.

Now this designation of being "immortal" places him in the category of the ancient Greek, heathen, gods who were known as the "immortals", i.e. not susceptible to death, even if wounded. As taking his place among the ancient Greek heathen "immortal" deities he is seen as an "anti-God figure" rather than an anti-Christ figure.Note 1 It is comforting for us to note that the Biblical evidence attesting to Who the Lord Jesus Christ is (the Son of God) and the holiness of His character lies in His resurrection from the dead (Romans 1:4, Psalms 2 and 16). Satan specialises in devising multiple counterfeits of reality but he is unable to simulate the resurrection from the dead of the Lord Jesus. In this connection, he cannot simulate the voice of the Lord Jesus either (Revelation 13:11). It is by the voice of the Lord Jesus that His own recognise and follow Him (John 10). Secondly, in John 10 it is resurrection which defines Him as the Shepherd with power to lay down His life and power to take it again. No one else can or ever will exercise or simulate this power!

In summary, then, the first beast of Revelation chapter 13 is **at first** a Gentile political figure in league with the false Gentile (harlot) Church and false Jewish religious systems for the first half of the seven-year "week" of tribulation. However, in the middle of the tribulation seven-year "week", he casts off all toleration of nominal worship of God (both Gentile and Jewish) and demands all such worship to be directed to himself. This is his manifestation as the anti-God figure and lasts forty-two months (three and a half years) – a set period of time emphasised in several passages.

2 The beast out of the earth (Revelation 13:11) also known as the false (*pseudo*) prophet (Revelation 16:13; Revelation 19:20)

While on earth, the Lord Jesus was the fulfilment of the Old Testament **Prophet** foretold by Moses in Deuteronomy 18:18. He was not a Priest on earth (Hebrews 8:4) "seeing that there are priests that offer gifts according to the Law". However, He is a **Priest** in Heaven today. While on earth, the Lord Jesus was here as a King-in-waiting but was not yet in open manifestation as King. However, when He comes back again it will be to sit upon the throne of His father David as the **King**. Then, for the first time, He will be seen as **Prophet, Priest and King**. Let us remember, therefore, that while on earth He was not yet manifested as Priest or King. He was only manifested as Prophet. That was why when the people desired to make Him a King He withdrew. When He is manifested as the King, there will be no injustice in this world. What was the role of a prophet in the Old Testament and thus what was the role of the Lord Jesus as **the** Prophet?

The Old Testament prophet reminded the people constantly of a broken Law and prophesied of the penalties that would have to be carried out because of this. Every true Old Testament prophet based his ministry firmly on the Law of God. **It is an important principle of Biblical exposition that the Law is only understood through the Prophets and the Prophets are only understood through the Law**. In the New Testament, this relationship is emphasised in the phrase "the Law and the Prophets".

Similarly, the Lord Jesus reminded the people of the broken Law, but unlike the prophets of the Old Testament, the Lord Jesus fulfilled the Law and made it honourable to the extent of bearing its curse in love to lawbreaking sinners and thus providing a means of escape from divine judgment.

Let us consider the false or *pseudo*-prophet of Revelation 16:13 and Revelation 19:20. Will he base his wicked ministry on the Law of God? On the contrary, his entire ministry will be in opposition to the Law of God. There is one word therefore to describe this man – "lawless" or "the lawless one".

In Revelation 13, the "first beast" is clearly a Gentile leader because he comes out of the sea (of the nations). The second so-called "other beast" in Revelation 13:11-18 comes "out of the earth". In the Old Testament, the Hebrew word *erets*, often translated "earth", is also often used specifically for the "land", i.e. the land of Israel itself. This second leader emerging out of the earth or "the land" is evidently of Jewish origin. In Revelation 13:11-18 he is not yet referred to as the false prophet. Nevertheless, it is clear from his close working relationship with the "first beast" that the title "false (*pseudo*)prophet", mentioned later in Revelation 16:13 and 19:20, is simply another title used to describe the second "other" beast of Revelation 13:11-18. Moreover, his special trade mark miracle in Revelation 13:13 of calling down fire from heaven to earth identifies him as a counterfeit Elijah prophet-like figure (it was Elijah in the Old Testament in 2 Kings 1:14 who called down fire from heaven), although it is later in chapters 16 and 19 that he is actually described as the "false (*pseudo*) prophet".

Summary of the two future world leaders

The first is a Gentile, who commences as a future world Roman Emperor-type figure who happily engages in a three and a half year symbiotic relationship with a Christless religious harlot Church system as well as a Christless Jewish system of worship in Jerusalem. In this role, he provides security guarantees to the nation of Israel, which has somehow managed to rebuild its temple and establish temple sacrifice worship. After three and a half years, this Gentile leader breaks off his security guarantees to Israel and establishes or "manifests" himself as God, demanding all worship to himself. He is thus **an anti-God** figure.

The second leader is a future Jewish leader or "false (*pseudo*)prophet". In this regard, he is acting as a counterfeit to the Lord Jesus, Who on earth was **the** Prophet foretold by Moses. For this reason we are right in regarding this man, described as the false prophet, as being also the false Messiah or **anti-Christ** type figure (in Hebrew Messiah = Christ = anointed one).

As the counterfeit to the Lord Jesus, he is at one and the same time:

1 false (*pseudo*) prophet – counterfeit to the Lord Jesus as **the** Prophet

2 lawless (wicked) one because as the false prophet he rejects the Law of God

3 anti-Christ because he is the counterfeit to the Lord Jesus as the Anointed

One or Christ

4 idol–shepherd (Zechariah 11:17) because he is the counterfeit to the Lord Jesus as the divine "Good Shepherd" of John 10

5 "like a Lamb" (Revelation 13:11) because he is the counterfeit to the true Lamb of God

Interestingly, the false "lamb" can be distinguished from the true Lamb by his voice –"He spake as a dragon". Moreover, he also has "horns" which a real lamb does not have.

It is important to note that the second beast directs attention to the first beast. In this regard, the second beast is acting as a counterfeit to the Lord Jesus Christ Who, throughout His public ministry, directed men to the Father (John 8:54, John 7:18).

In Revelation 13:12, we read that "He exerciseth all the power (authority) of the first beast before him…". This does not mean that the first beast came chronologically before the second "other beast". The word "before" means "in the presence of" or "with the approval of". This simply tells us that the second "other beast" operates with the full political approval and support of the first beast. This is consistent with the teaching of Daniel 9 where the "prince that shall come", i.e. the first beast, provides the security guarantees for the Jewish leader to develop temple worship and to practise his lying (*pseudo*) wonders with impunity. However, after the first beast claims his godhood status in the middle of the week, the false prophet will back up this claim fully and champion the worship of the image of the first beast.

Although the first beast manifests his anti-God activities along with the desecration of the temple after three and a half years of political activity (i.e. the middle of the week), the second "other" beast operates as a *pseudo*-prophet and *pseudo*-Messiah figure well before this. (Note his false prophet activities are not limited to forty-two months, in contrast to the first beast). Moreover, he shores up his position by deceiving "wonders" (Revelation 13:13-14). We have already mentioned above his most impressive wonder in making "fire come down from heaven on the earth in the sight of men". It is this *pseudo*-Elijah prophet-like activity which especially identifies him as **the** false prophet of Revelation 16 and 19. Critically, however, unlike Elijah who based his ministry wholly on the Law given at Horeb (1 Kings 19:8), we will see later that this man is, in fact, lawless as far as God's Law is concerned.

The trinity of evil

We have seen how that the first beast of Revelation 13 is the counterfeit to God and how the second beast is the counterfeit to the Lord Jesus. Is there a counterfeit to the Holy Spirit of God in Revelation? In Luke 3:22 we read how the Holy Ghost descended in a bodily shape like a dove upon the Lord Jesus on the occasion of His baptism by John.

Luke 3:22

"And the Holy Ghost descended in a bodily shape like a dove upon Him, and a voice came from heaven, which said, Thou art My beloved Son; in

Thee I am well pleased."

For those who refuse the gentle, dove-like Spirit of God, the alternative is the cruel dragon (the devil), who empowers the first beast (Revelation 13:4). Please note that, in contrast to the Holy Spirit, Who in bodily shape like a dove descended from heaven, the dragon (the devil) is cast out from heaven to earth (Revelation 12:7-12).

The problem disturbing the Thessalonian assembly (2 Thessalonians 2:1-12)

In 2 Thessalonians 2, we discover that the Thessalonian believers were troubled by some who were teaching that the "day of Christ" was in progress. This is not "day of Christ", as in Philippians 2:16 (judgment seat of Christ), but rather "the day of the Christ" or "the day of the Messiah". The distinction between "Christ" and "the Christ" has been discussed in Appendix 1. "The day of the Christ" is, therefore, a quite different phrase from "day of Christ" in Philippians and should be distinguished from it. "The day of *the* Christ", which we have in this verse, is the fulfilment of the day of vengeance of our God of Isaiah 61:1-2, when the One Who was anointed as Messiah, ("The Lord hath anointed Me to preach good tidings unto the meek…") is now taking charge of "the day of vengeance" when, not now as Kinsman Redeemer (having become near relative to us at Bethlehem), but rather as Kinsman Avenger, the Messiah returns to exact vengeance and avenge the adversary (Luke 18:7) – "these be the days of vengeance (Luke 21:22)".

The point is that He is not yet avenging the adversary. We are still in the acceptable year of the Lord. The avenging of the adversary must await the rapture of the Church and the taking up again in divine purpose of the nation of Israel. At the present time, there is no distinction between saved Jew and saved Gentile. All who are saved, whether Jew or Gentile, are one in Christ (Galatians 3:28). After the Church has gone, there is again a distinction between the saved of the Jewish nation and the saved of the Gentile nations. This is a very clear reason why the Church cannot go through the tribulation, because while the Church is on earth no such distinction exists between Jew and Gentile believers. All of this is part of "the faith", i.e. New Testament doctrine.

Now just imagine the impact on "the faith" of these believers when someone is suggesting that "the day of the Christ" is "at hand" or, more literally in meaning, "already in progress". Such an assertion would mean that the tribulation was in progress and that there was once more a distinction between saved Jews and saved Gentiles. This erroneous teaching regarding "the day of the Christ" happening in their experience, and the Lord taking up the nation of Israel while the Church was still on earth, was in direct confrontation to the New Testament mystery doctrines (mystery means unrevealed in the Old Testament) regarding the oneness of Jewish and Gentile believers in Christ. In fact, such teaching would have rendered obsolete all passages regarding New Testament assembly gathering. It is worth noting that Christian groupings who are unclear on these distinctions are often also unclear on principles of assembly gathering. Errors on these doctrines are ultimately destructive of assembly gathering and therefore must be discerned and corrected by truth. It was too serious for Paul to ignore.

The doctrinal answer to the problem facing the Thessalonian assembly

The Apostle appeals to their understanding of the pre-tribulation rapture by these words:

2 Thessalonians 2:1
> "We beseech you, brethren, by the coming of our Lord Jesus Christ, and *by* our gathering together unto Him."

Had they grasped the necessity for the rapture of the Church before the events of the tribulation, they would easily have been able to defend this assault on "the faith".

Clearly, "the day of the Christ" does not commence until several key prophetic events take place. The apostle delineates these for us.

Firstly, there must be the apostasy (falling away) and *then* the revelation of the "man of sin" promoting himself as God. The day of the Christ begins after the open revelation of the "man of sin" as God. In Psalm 118:8, we read that the godly remnant will not "put confidence in **the** man".

The man of sin, being manifested as God, identifies very clearly with the first beast of Revelation 13. As we have noted above, this event takes place halfway through the seven-year tribulation and, according to 2 Thessalonians 2:3, **the day of the Messiah (Christ)** cannot be in operation until the public manifestation of this man declaring himself to be God. This observation shows that "the day of the Christ" is quite different from **"the day of the Lord"**, because the latter occurs well before the public manifestation of the man of sin, immediately subsequent to the rapture (1 Thessalonians 5:2). The man of sin is referred to as "the son of perdition". This title is also used of Judas Iscariot in John 17:12 and thus carries the significance of treachery and breach of trust. We know from Daniel 9:27 that the "coming prince" (the other title for the first beast of Revelation 13 and the man of sin) provides security guarantees for the nation of Israel to practise their temple worship in Jerusalem in what is called "the covenant confirmed with the many". Israel (with the exception of the remnant) will foolishly place their trust in this man (**the** man of Psalm 118:8), but then suddenly in the middle of the seven year "week" of the tribulation he will treacherously break that covenant and ban all worship of any God apart from himself. In this act of treachery and betrayal of the nation he is indeed the "son of perdition".

Before his public manifestation as (false) God, there is envisaged a period of an apostasy. Clearly, this apostasy is well in progress in the first half of the tribulation period, well before the public revelation of the man of sin as God. For this reason, **it is most important** to see that the apostasy must be understood **as prior to and distinct from** the activities of the man of sin, albeit providing the climate in which he can present himself as God in the midst of the tribulation.

Apostasy involves the following process:

1 an original profession of truth

2 turning away from that truth and acceptance of error

3 refusal to return to the truth when challenged regarding the error

The use of the word "apostasy" sadly indicates that those who imbibe the error of the "*apostasia*" should have known better. They have earlier, at least nominally, professed truth although the reality of that profession failed the test. In verse 3, the exact nature of the error is not defined for us, but shortly it is defined as "the lie (*pseudos*)" and linked with the "mystery of **lawlessness**".

2 Thessalonians 2:6

"And now ye know what withholdeth that he might be revealed in his time."

This "man of sin" cannot be revealed yet, because of that which "withholdeth".

After that which "withholdeth" goes, the "man of sin" will be revealed, but not immediately; he is revealed "in his time". This detail is most important. The cessation of the withholding power of God does not precipitate the immediate revelation of the man of sin in his blasphemous claim to be God. He appears in all his blasphemous activity "in his time", i.e. later. What is meant by the phrase "what withholdeth"? Let us look at the clues. The withholding power of God is something which the Thessalonian believers then knew, and they were very familiar with the truth – "**now** ye know what withholdeth". It is not something future awaiting coming revelation. Moreover, it is something which is going to be removed and "taken out of the midst" (2 Thessalonians 2:7). There can be only one thing which fits this description: the Church, the "habitation of God through the Spirit (Ephesians 2:22)", as we know it, will be "taken out of the way" at the rapture. The Church is spoken of as "salt" (Mathew 5:13) and once the "salt" has gone, its preservative effect has ended. Accordingly, this verse tells us that the rapture will not precipitate the immediate revelation of the "man of sin" as God – that will happen later "in his time", i.e. after the first three and a half years of tribulation foretold by Daniel and before the forty-two months specified in Revelation 13.

2 Thessalonians 2:7-8

7 "For the mystery of iniquity (lawlessness = *anomia*) doth already work: only He Who now letteth will let, until He be taken out of the way.

8 And then shall that Wicked be revealed, whom the Lord shall consume

with the Spirit of His mouth, and shall destroy with the brightness of His coming."

The passage now leaves the idea of the "man of sin" and moves to the "mystery of lawlessness".

We noted earlier that every true Biblical **prophet** based his message on **the Law** of God. Moreover, everything pertaining to the Messiah, the Prophet foretold by Moses, is entirely consistent with and based on the Law of God. The idea of driving a wedge between the Law of God and the credentials of the Messiah is lawlessness (*anomia*). One of the reasons why the Law was given was to preserve the identity of the promised Seed. "Wherefore then serveth the Law? It was added because of transgressions till the Seed should come to Whom the promise was made" (Galatians 3:19). Many Jews today are anticipating the Messiah's coming and say they will accept him if he brings peace to the land, regathers the nation and rebuilds the temple. They say there is no need for a proven genealogy because that was destroyed in A.D. 70 when the temple records were burned. How amazing that the nation to which the Law was given and who preserved it down through the centuries should, in these last days, depart from its central significance in seeking a Messiah who lacks a proven genealogy! This is in fulfilment of the Lord's words, "If another will come in his own name, him ye will receive" (John 5:43). In contrast, the Lord can trace His earthly genealogy right back to Adam. This is a vital qualification of the true Messiah. However, the mystery of lawlessness is already working and is especially seen in those elements within Judaism today who have opened their arms wide to accept any Messiah at all who fulfills their own wish list of political and religious emancipation irrespective of his moral character or genealogical credentials. It is against this background of lawlessness that Paul tells us that "He Who now letteth (withholdeth) *will let (withhold),* until He be taken out of the way and then shall the lawless one be revealed".

Although the mystery of lawlessness is at present simmering away, its effects are curtailed by Him "Who now withholdeth." This refers to the withholding power of God in the indwelling Spirit of God in the Church today. Once "He be taken out of the way", **then** shall the lawless one be revealed. It is vital to notice the timing. The lawless one is not revealed "in his time", unlike the man of sin. In contrast, he is revealed **immediately after** the removal of Him "Who now withholdeth." The word "then" in the phrase, "and **then** shall the lawless one be revealed", tells us that this event takes place immediately after the removal of the Church in the rapture, and with the Church the indwelling Spirit of GodNote 2. The rapture will allow the lawless man, i.e. the Jewish leader who completely ignores the Law of God, to come to the fore. In this regard, he stands in contrast to the Lord Jesus Who, as the true Prophet, acted according to God's Law. This is why it is appropriate to identify this lawless man as the false (*pseudo*)prophet of Revelation 16 and 19 and the "other" or second beast of Revelation 13 who will perform counterfeit wonders in the style of Elijah the prophet, such as calling down fire from heaven. These considerations make it very clear that just as the **man of sin** in this section is an **anti-God** counterfeit figure, operating openly in this capacity from the middle of the tribulation, similarly the **lawless man** in this section is an **anti-Christ** counterfeit figure operating much earlier than the man of sin, i.e. immediately after the rapture. He is, therefore, well established as a world leader acting in full anti-Christ and *pseudo*-prophet capacity in the first three and a half years of the tribulation. The likelihood of a delay between the rapture and the start of the tribulation is discussed in Appendix 3.

This man shall be the master of counterfeit. He promulgates the lie (*pseudos*) and backs this up with lying (*pseudo*) wonders. What is the *pseudos*? Just as the Lord Jesus told the truth and was Himself "the Truth", this man shall present himself as an object of faith as the true Messiah and millions will believe in this imposter as if he were true, not knowing that they have believed a lie (*pseudos*) and have trusted in the *pseudo* (false or lying) prophet. Once again, let us notice the timing of this blasphemous and lying prophet. It is immediately after the rapture and well before the manifestation of the man of sin as God.

One might be tempted to suppose that most people on earth would see through the lying wonders of this false prophet and refuse to recognise him. Sadly, this is not the case. Many will unquestioningly believe the lie (*pseudos*) "that they all might be damned".

It has been suggested by some that the lie is linked with the second half of the tribulation and those who believe it are those who reject the gospel which is preached in the first half of the tribulation. The implication of this argument is that those who are not saved, and thus left behind at the rapture, will have an opportunity to believe the gospel in the first half of the tribulation.

This idea fails under scriptural scrutiny, once we understand that the lie is linked with the lawless man and is **already** in full swing before the first half of the tribulation.

Who are those who believe the lie?

2 Thessalonians 2:10-12
> 10 "And with all deceivableness of unrighteousness in them that perish; because they received not the love of the truth, that they might be saved.
> 11 And for this cause God shall send them strong delusion, that they should believe a lie:
> 12 That they all might be damned who believed not the truth, but had pleasure in unrighteousness."

Those who believe the lie are those who are perishing because
1 they received not the love of the truth
2 they believed not the truth but had pleasure in unrighteousness

The phrase, "them that perish", is a present participle carrying the significance of "them that are continuously perishing". The question arises:

Are these individuals irreversibly in a state of perishing, i.e. doomed, or are they reversibly in a state of perishing, i.e. have the opportunity of believing and getting saved?

If these individuals are in a reversible state of perishing, i.e. have opportunity to be saved, the verse would read like this:

"...in them that perish because they receive (present tense) not the love of the truth etc". However, this is not the case and the careful reader will observe that this state of perishing arises from an earlier, past, once-and-for-all act (aorist tense) of receiving not the love of the truth: "they received not the love of the truth". This observation leads to the sad conclusion that they are irreversibly perishing. In 1 Corinthians 1:18 we read that the "preaching of the cross is to them that perish (are perishing) foolishness..." The significance of the verb "perishing" in 1 Corinthians 1:18 is, clearly, reversible perishing. These individuals can still be saved through the preaching of the cross. Alas, those who are "perishing" in 2 Thessalonians 2:10 are irreversibly perishing. They have been previously exposed to the truth, have had pleasure in unrighteousness and have, as a once-and-for-all act, "received not" the truth. Once the rapture takes place and the lie is unleashed on this world, they will swallow the lie unquestioningly and will accept the false messiah, the lawless man or the false prophet. The sad conclusion from this consideration is that there can be no second chance after the rapture for those who believe not the truth of the gospel in this Church era.

Why there cannot be a mid-tribulation rapture

Some teach (erroneously) that the Church is raptured halfway through the tribulation. Such teaching is called "mid-tribulation rapture". This idea arises from one of two arguments which we will now see are, in fact, in themselves mutually contradictory!

Argument 1
Replacing the phrase, "day of Christ," in 2 Thessalonians 2:2 with "day of the Lord."

Argument 2
Allowing the phrase, "day of Christ", in 2 Thessalonians 2:2 to remain in the text but seeing no difference between the meaning of "day of Christ" in Philippians 2:16, which refers to the rapture, and "the day of the Christ" in 2 Thessalonians 2:2, which refers to the middle of the tribulation.

Let us explore these two lines of thought.

Argument 1

This idea requires the phrase, "day of the Christ", to be replaced with "day of the Lord". If this change is made, it leads to the erroneous idea that the day of the Lord cannot commence until after the Apostasy and the man of sin is revealed. Since the man of sin is revealed only in the second half of the week, this, therefore, suggests that the day of the Lord only starts in the second half of the week. Since the day of the Lord in 1 Thessalonians 5:2 comes as a thief in the night, and other passages link "the thief in the night" with the return of the Lord Jesus for His own (Luke 12:39), some who teach mid-tribulation rapture argue that the rapture must occur in the middle of the tribulation to allow the day of the Lord to commence.

Author's Comment

It is true that the day of the Lord commences at or immediately after the rapture of the Church (1 Thessalonians 5). The confusion of 2 Thessalonians 2:2 arises from choosing a non-Authorised Version (A.V.) translation which requires the reader to date the commencement of the day of the Lord to halfway through the tribulation. This is because, according to non-A.V. translations, the day of the Lord starts after the manifestation of the man of sin, which, as we have shown, happens in the middle of the seven-year tribulation. Please note that Mr. Newberry supports the A.V. rendering: the day of Christ in 2 Thessalonians 2:2. Argument 1 cannot be sustained if we follow the text on which the A.V. is based.

Argument 2

These believers who hold mid-tribulation rapture ideas are quite content with the A.V. rendering that it is "the day of the Christ", which starts halfway through the tribulation and follows the manifestation of the man of sin. Their difficulty arises from a failure to notice the difference between the "day of Christ" in Philippians 2:16 and "the day of the Christ" in 2 Thessalonians 2:2. All are agreed from the context of Philippians 2:16 that "day of Christ" in that section is linked with **the rapture of the Church and the judgment seat of Christ**. In the original Greek text, the phrase, "the day of Christ" in Philippians 2:16, reads "day of Christ" (definite articles omitted). A careful examination of the original text in 2 Thessalonians 2:2 shows that, unlike Philippians 2:16, both definite articles are included so that the literal meaning of the phrase, "the day of Christ" in 2 Thessalonians 2:2, should read "the day of the Christ". Those who hold argument 2 must contend that there is no doctrinal difference between the phrase "day of Christ" (Philippians 2:16) and "the day of the Christ" (2 Thessalonians 2:2). Indeed, if these two phrases are synonymous (which they are not) then the rapture must take place halfway through the tribulation if we follow the Authorised Version rendering in 2 Thessalonians 2! This is because "the day of the Christ" **must be preceded** by the manifestation of the man of sin, and as we have already considered this happens in the **second half** of the tribulation.

Author's comment

The occurrences of "the Christ" (*HaMmashiach* or the Messiah) in the New Testament emphasise to the reader the coming into the world of Christ through Israel and the wonder of why He moved out in love beyond the boundaries of Israel to bring Gentiles into relationship with Himself. This title also reminds us of His coming again as Kinsman Avenger. (See

Appendix 1 for more details.)

"The Day of the Christ" and "Day of Christ", cannot be synonymous (Appendix 1).

"The Day of the Christ" in the context of 2 Thessalonians 2:2, is the public vindication of Israel's once rejected Messiah by the destruction of the false Messiah whom Israel has chosen and the vindication of the faithful remnant, who always hoped in "the Christ" to redeem Israel (Luke 24:26). "Day of Christ" (Philippians 2:16), in contrast, is not calling to mind Israel. It is a celebration of the unity of Jew and Gentile in the raptured Church. Let us not miss a distinction which has been put there by the Spirit of God.

The implications of these considerations

2 Thessalonians 2:13-14

> 13 "But we are bound to give thanks alway to God for you, brethren beloved of the Lord, because God hath from the beginning chosen you to salvation through sanctification of the Spirit and belief (faith) of the truth:
> 14 Whereunto He called you by our gospel, **to the obtaining of the glory** of our Lord Jesus Christ."

Escaping these dreadful events requires "faith of the truth". Where is the truth to be found? It is found within what Paul calls "our gospel". This is the message of salvation obtainable through faith in the risen Son of God. It is a wonderful message because it guarantees eternal security, "sanctification of the Spirit" and the promise of a wonderful destiny, **"the obtaining of the glory of our Lord Jesus Christ"**. This phrase includes all the New Testament revelation regarding the heavenly aspect of our destiny, something not mentioned in the Old Testament. There the prophets preached salvation by faith, as do we today, and spoke much of the future earthly Kingdom of our Lord Jesus, but they had no direct revelation of the heavenly destiny (1 Peter 1:4; Colossians 1:5), as proclaimed in the gospel message of this Church era and defined as "Paul's Gospel" or, as in this passage, "our gospel". When the gospel will be preached during the tribulation, the destiny presented to those who believe will once again be an earthly Kingdom, and those who believe it will enter into the earthly millennial Kingdom of our Lord Jesus Christ (Matthew 25:34).

After the rapture, the gospel proclaimed will no longer present a heavenly destiny. This means that those who hear the gospel of today, proclaiming its heavenly destiny, will not be able to believe it retrospectively once the Church has gone. The offer of the heavenly destiny will have been withdrawn with the departure of the Church. Some may argue that God could give those who have refused the offer of the heavenly destiny before the rapture the offer of the earthly destiny after the rapture as an act of grace, in the same way as those who heard the offer of the earthly Kingdom under John the Baptist before Pentecost were free to accept the offer of the heavenly destiny proclaimed subsequent to the descent of the Spirit of God at Pentecost (1 Peter 1:12). This cannot be the case, as God never downgrades His offer to the same individuals. Those who refused the offer of an earthly Kingdom under John were offered something "better", i.e. heavenly (Hebrews 11:16), after Pentecost. Having offered the better thing (heavenly) in the Gospel of today, God is not going to offer something less (i.e. earthly) to the same group. Rather, for those who today refuse the wondrous offer of salvation, and who will not therefore **obtain the glory of our Lord Jesus Christ** which is on offer today, there will be no option but to believe the lie (*pseudos*).

For those who believe the Gospel today and accept the Lord Jesus Christ as Saviour, what a wonderful prospect awaits them! They will obtain the very glory of the Lord Jesus Himself. This will be seen in a spectacular way when the Church comes down from God out of heaven "having the Glory of God" (Revelation 21:11).

Should there be one reading these pages who would earnestly desire to know peace with God, assurance of heaven as home and deliverance from these solemn coming events then do not tarry! You must accept God's verdict that you are guilty before Him and that the problem of your sin will debar you from the heavenly land unless a way is found for it to be dealt with. There is a way! This is the gospel message. It declares a means whereby you can obtain justification – that is the righteous declaration by God that you have been constituted **(absolutely legally)** righteous before Him, i.e. saved and forgiven. "How can this be?" you may ask. The answer is clearly summarised in Romans 4:23-Romans 5:1, where we learn that the justification and salvation you long for can be **immediately** obtained "if we believe in Him that raised up Jesus our Lord from the dead, Who was delivered for our offences and raised again for our justification" (Romans 4:24-25).

Hurry and by simple faith accept God's verdict on the **all-sufficiency** of the Sacrifice of the Lord Jesus to meet your need when God raised Him from the dead.

If you do, then "being justified by faith you will have peace with God through our Lord Jesus Christ" (Romans 5:1).

---

1. The first beast of Revelation 13 is elsewhere described as "the beast that thou sawest was, and is not: and shall ascend out of the bottomless pit, and go into perdition..." (Revelation 17:8). This reference to the beast ascending "out of the bottomless pit" should not be understood as a description of resurrection, whether real or simulated. This beast rose "out of the sea" (Revelation 13:1), i.e. from among the nations. However, he also arose out of the abyss. As one who arose from the sea, he has gentile origins. As one who arose from the abyss, the same satanic power which empowered the old Roman Empire will empower him in an unprecedented way (Revelation 17:8).

2. Some have suggested that the removal of the Spirit of God from "the midst", as happens during the rapture of the Church, means that the Spirit of God will not indwell believers during the tribulation. It will be shown in Appendix 3 that believers, subsequent to the rapture and in the tribulation period, will as individuals be indwelled by the Holy Spirit just as the Spirit of God indwells each person who is saved during this Church era. However, it is apparent from Ephesians 2:21-22 that the Church collectively is a Holy Temple, in which God through His Spirit

dwells today. This is unique to this dispensation of grace.

> Ephesians 2:21, 22
>
> *21 In Whom all the building fitly framed together groweth unto an holy temple in the Lord*
>
> *22 In Whom ye also are builded together for an habitation of God through the Spirit.*

These verses indicate that there is a special Church-related ministry of the Spirit of God, whereby the Spirit of God inhabits the Church on earth in a very unique way, just as the glory of the Lord filled the temple of old. This ceases at the rapture, after which the Spirit of God indwells individuals, as will be discussed in Appendix 3. It is the author's understanding that it is the cessation of the Spirit of God inhabiting the Church in this collective way which is referred to in the phrase, "He Who now letteth will let, until He be taken out of the way" (2 Thessalonians 2:7).

Appendix 3

The restoration of the remnant

The future restoration of the remnant of Israel, following the rapture of the Church, is central to an understanding of Psalms 91, 96, 102 and 118 but is touched upon in many of the other Messianic Psalms. New Testament revelation throws much light on this aspect of prophetic truth and some of these matters are discussed in this section.

Introduction and summary of the key events

The Bible appears to distinguish between:

1 the salvation of the remnant nation of Israel **after the rapture but before the start** of the tribulation

2 the outpouring of the Spirit of God upon the saved nation **subsequent to their salvation but before** the great and terrible day of the Lord and

3 their purification and sanctification at **the very end of the tribulation** to prepare them for the impending Kingdom of Christ

It is at an undefined time **after the rapture, but before the start of** the tribulation, that the remnant of the nation of Israel is (1) saved, i.e. born again and indwelt by the Spirit of God. Later, before the great and terrible day of the Lord, i.e. before the most intense part of the tribulation seven-year period, they have (2) an outpouring of the Spirit of God. However, it is **at the end of** the tribulation, just prior to the millennial Kingdom of our Lord Jesus Christ, that they undergo (3) a specific sanctification and purification from all the defilement of the tribulation to prepare them for entering into the Kingdom and participating in the gathering centre of the millennium, namely Ezekiel's temple.

It is this purification and sanctification at the end of the tribulation which some Bible teachers hold to be a national salvation. The difficulty with this view is that a national salvation for Israel at the end of the tribulation would mean that these supposed Jewish converts to Christ at the end of the tribulation would somehow have managed to avoid believing the lie of 2 Thessalonians 2:11-12, which would have earlier sealed their eternal doom. However, there is nothing in 2 Thessalonians 2:11-12 to suggest that the entire Jewish nation, after the rapture and before the start of the tribulation, is exempted from the effects of the "strong delusion" and from believing "the lie" which will take hold **immediately after the rapture,** even before the tribulation starts (see Appendix 2).

Tragically, along with the millions of Gentiles "who believed not the truth, but had pleasure in unrighteousness" (2 Thessalonians 2:12), there will be elements of the Jewish nation who will, similarly, welcome the strong delusion immediately after the rapture. The only ones, both Jew and Gentile, who will be exempt from the strong delusion, and thus potential candidates for salvation after the rapture, are those who do not fall into the category of persons who, prior to the rapture, "believed not the truth" and "had pleasure in unrighteousness". This category must include the many millions who, at the time of the rapture, will be under the age of accountability and thus are not part of the population who "believed not the truth" and "had pleasure in unrighteousness" prior to the rapture. This requires there to be an undefined period of time between the rapture and the onset of the tribulation to allow those who at the rapture will be under the age of accountability to reach an age when they can consciously believe and be saved.

The fact that during the tribulation there will be "old men" among the worldwide company of believers, upon which the Spirit is poured (Joel 2:28), suggests strongly that the undefined period of time between the rapture and the start of the tribulation must be of sufficient length for someone who was a babe at the rapture to reach an age consistent with being an "old man" of Joel 2:28. This is confirmed in Joel where we learn that it is "after" the remnant has come to know the Lord by faith (Joel 2:28) that the Lord will dramatically pour upon them His Spirit in circumstances akin to Acts chapter 2. In Acts 2, all who were saved, including the Apostles, received the Spirit, having already come to know the Lord Jesus by faith prior to this and at individually differing times. Similarly, the collective body of both old and young believers who will get saved subsequent to the rapture will, at a single event, have poured upon all of them the Spirit of God (Joel 2:28). The exact timing of this outpouring of the Spirit of God is not fully specified in Joel 2:28. We are just told that it is before the great and terrible day of the Lord which, we know, takes place in the latter and most intense part of the tribulation period.

The nation will experience salvation prior to the tribulation (Revelation 7). This is the same event as is mentioned in Isaiah 66:7-14 when the nation will be "born in a day". However, it is at the end of the tribulation that the believing remnant of the nation will experience purification in preparation for meeting their Messiah.

A New Testament believer will understand the analogous principle how that on the occasion of our salvation we were cleansed from all our iniquity, as far as God was concerned. However, subsequent to our salvation, before we come to remember the Lord on the first day of every week, the Bible reminds us to engage in self-examination and preparation to meet the Lord at the remembrance feast.

1 Corinthians 11:27-30
27 "Wherefore whosoever shall eat this bread, and drink *this* cup of the Lord, unworthily, shall be guilty of the body and blood of the Lord.
28 But let a man examine himself, and so let him eat of *that* bread, and drink of *that* cup.
29 For he that eateth and drinketh unworthily, eateth and drinketh damnation to himself, not discerning the Lord's body.
30 For this cause many *are* weak and sickly among you, and many sleep."

This preparation before gathering to remember the Lord on the first day of the week should involve confession of sin to the Lord and realisation of cleansing from the defilement of the way (1 John 1:9). This is not salvation. It is preparation for meeting with the Lord. Similarly, the remnant who are saved after the rapture, but before the onset of the tribulation, and those who come of age during the tribulation and get saved during its seven long years, will at its end prepare themselves for meeting their Messiah at His return. The details of the salvation of Israel, prior to the onset of the tribulation, and the later purification of these believers, in preparation for the return of the Lord Jesus at the end of the tribulation, will now be described.

1 The salvation of Israel

The illustration of Israel's salvation by the metaphor of the mother nation bringing forth children

In Revelation 12, Israel is described in the vision as a woman or mother nation in travail (Revelation 12:2). Suddenly, she as the mother nation delivers the Man Child, Who is clearly the Lord Jesus Christ, Who is caught up to heaven well away from the persecutions of the dragon, who is the devil. However, the dragon in the vision persists in persecuting the "remnant of her seed" (Revelation 12:7). This indicates that in addition to delivering the Man Child, at a later date she gives rise to a body of people referred to as "the remnant of her seed" (Revelation 12:17) who are subject to the fiercest of persecution. It is clear that the "remnant of her seed" are those of the Jewish remnant who get saved prior to the tribulation, since it is throughout the period of the tribulation, in particular the latter part of it, that these Jews are so dreadfully persecuted (Revelation 12:7-17). The fact that the Jewish remnant who are born to the "woman" in Revelation 12 are persecuted during the tribulation shows that they must be saved, i.e. born to Israel, the mother nation, either prior to or early in the tribulation, so as to be able to experience the tribulation as persecuted believers. Those who get saved during the tribulation will be those who were born shortly before the tribulation and who came to the age of accountability during this dreadful time and choose Christ as Saviour rather than the beast and the false prophet.

This consideration alone shows that the idea of the entire nation being saved and born again at the end of the tribulation cannot be sustained. Now, Revelation 12 does not specify when the "remnant of her seed" is born. It concentrates on how these people will be treated by this world during those seven long, dark years of tribulation. However, Revelation 12 does not need to specify when the remnant of her seed is spiritually born as this has already been clearly spelled out in Revelation 7:1-8 when representatives of all the twelve tribes of Israel, known as the 144,000, are saved and sealed before the tribulation starts.

This New Testament understanding of Israel, the mother nation, being in travail before the birth of the Messiah seems at first to be in contrast with Isaiah 66:7, where we read concerning mother Israel, that "before she travailed she brought forth; before her pain came, she was delivered of a Man Child", i.e. Christ. As was noted in the introduction to this book, the entire Bible is God-breathed and there cannot be contradictions within it. Recourse to a literal translation of Isaiah 66:7-14 is helpful.

Isaiah 66:7-14

7 "Before she travailed (continuously), she brought forth; before her pain came (continuously), she was delivered of a Man Child.
8 Who hath heard such a thing? who hath seen such things? Shall the earth be made to bring forth in one day? *or* shall a nation be born at once? for as soon as Zion travailed (finished travailing) , she brought forth her children.
9 Shall I bring to the birth, and not cause to bring forth? saith the LORD: shall I cause to bring forth, and shut *the womb*? saith thy God.
10 Rejoice ye with Jerusalem, and be glad with her, all ye that love her: rejoice for joy with her, all ye that mourn for her:
11 That ye may suck, and be satisfied with the breasts of her consolations; that ye may milk out, and be delighted with the abundance of her glory.
12 For thus saith the LORD, Behold, I will extend peace to her like a river, and the glory of the Gentiles like a flowing stream: then shall ye suck, ye shall be borne upon *her* sides, and be dandled upon *her* knees.
13 As one whom his mother comforteth, so will I comfort you; and ye shall be comforted in Jerusalem.
14 And when ye see *this,* your heart shall rejoice, and your bones shall flourish like an herb: and the hand of the LORD shall be known toward His servants, and *His* indignation toward His enemies."

Every labour is characterised at first by non-continuous travail (first stage), which then becomes continuous (second stage) before the baby arrives. Isaiah 66:7 shows that the birth of the Man Child, i.e. Christ, to the mother nation came (miraculously) at stage 1, i.e. before the onset of continuous labour (stage 2) by that nation. It will be a continuous and severe labour (stage 2) which will give rise to the new-born spiritual sons and daughters of the nation prior to the tribulation. As considered in Psalms 8 and 118, the restored nation is spoken of as "sucklings", which answers to the similar metaphorical description given of them in Isaiah 66:12. Israel is seen in Revelation 12 and Isaiah 66 as the mother nation who has given rise to the Messiah for the whole world. It is part of **the same labour,** albeit the **second stage of it,** which gives rise to the new birth of the nation. It is in addressing the nation as a "barren woman", having been set aside by her Husband (Jehovah) at the time of the captivity, that Isaiah in Isaiah 54 says, "Awake O barren O thou that didst not bear". Isaiah is speaking to the nation in anticipation of her desolate state, which was about to be realized in the soon-coming Babylonish captivity, when Israel would be set aside by her Husband Jehovah. Isaiah indicates that it is as a nation, barren and set aside by her Husband Jehovah, that she will undergo a labour which would **first of all give rise to the Messiah, and then a prolonged second stage which will bring forth a spiritual remnant** in that future day. Realisation of this was enough to cause Isaiah and spiritually intelligent members of the captivity to rejoice. Sadly, the bringing forth of the Messiah did not end Israel's spiritual travails. There is a sense in which Israel's spiritual travails are continuing and will intensify until the remnant is brought forth after the rapture but prior to the tribulation. As that day draws nearer, waves of satanically energized anti-Semitism will no doubt intensify.

In Ephesians 5:31-32, we read, "For this cause shall a man leave his father and mother, and shall be joined unto his wife, and they two shall be one flesh. This is a great mystery: but I speak concerning Christ and the Church". The author recalls the late Mr Albert Leckie speaking on this "great mystery" and helpfully showing that the Lord Jesus left His Father in Heaven and left His mother (Israel) to be joined unto His wife, the Bride, i.e. the Church. The true Church should always look upon Israel with affection and care as the mother nation who gave the Messiah to the world, even in these days of her long, albeit temporary, estrangement from her Husband Jehovah. Again, in this context, in Galatians 4:26 the mother nation is spoken of as "the mother of us all" in the allegory. How can this be? Galatians 3:28 makes clear that believers are, as to their position, "in Christ" in this Church era. Because Israel is the mother nation of Christ and we who are in the Church are "in Christ", Israel is therefore the "mother of us all". Forever, the Church will respectfully and affectionately regard Israel as such. This understanding helps us appreciate the significance of the description given of the remnant nation at the end of the tribulation in Psalm 68:12 as "the beautiful woman of the house".

In the New Testament, this event is referred to indirectly in several passages. For example, when the Lord indicated to Nicodemus, the elderly Bible teacher in Israel, in John 3:7, "Marvel not that I said unto thee, Ye must be born again", He was using language which should have been familiar to Nicodemus from his knowledge of Isaiah 66:7-14. It was appropriate, then, for the Lord to go further to challenge Nicodemus for his lack of knowledge on the necessity for new birth in John 3:9-10.

John 3:9-10
> 9 "Nicodemus answered and said unto Him, How can these things be?
> 10 Jesus answered and said unto him, Art thou a master of Israel, and knowest not these things?"

Clearly, Nicodemus understood from Isaiah 66 that there was a need for national new birth. It had not occurred to him that he needed this experience personally if he was ever to see the Kingdom of God. Hence the significance of the singular pronoun "thee" in the Lord's words, "Marvel not that I said unto thee (singular), Ye (plural) must be born again".

The Holy Spirit indwells each post-rapture believer who can also address God as "Father"

The Lord indicated something in John 3 which was not made clear in

Isaiah 66. It is that this new birth is a work of the Spirit of God: "That which is born of the flesh is flesh; and that which is born of the Spirit is spirit" (John 3:6). One of the features of being born of God is possession of the divine nature through the indwelling Holy Spirit, Who is received on the moment of believing (Ephesians 1:13-14).

Ephesians 1:13-14
> 13 "In Whom ye also *trusted*, after that ye heard the Word of truth, the gospel of your salvation: in Whom also after that ye believed (literally: on believing), ye were sealed with that Holy Spirit of promise,
> 14 Which is the earnest of our inheritance until the redemption of the purchased possession, unto the praise of His glory."

It is the indwelling Holy Spirit which then leads the new born-again believer to address God spontaneously as "Abba Father" (Galatians 4:6).

Galatians 4:6
> "And because ye are sons, God hath sent forth the Spirit of His Son into your hearts, crying, Abba, Father." Note 1

Now, in the Old Testament, it does not directly indicate that the tribulation believers are "indwelt" by the Spirit of God. However, there are many references to the Spirit of God being "upon" them. Here are some examples:

Isaiah 32:15
> "Until the Spirit be **poured upon us** from on high, and the wilderness be a fruitful field, and the fruitful field be counted for a forest."

Isaiah 44:3
> "For I will pour water upon him that is thirsty, and floods upon the dry ground: **I will pour My Spirit upon thy seed**, and My blessing upon thine offspring:"

Isaiah 59:21
> "As for Me, this *is* My covenant with them, saith the LORD; **My Spirit that *is* upon thee,** and My words which I have put in thy mouth, shall not depart out of thy mouth, nor out of the mouth of thy seed, nor out of the mouth of thy seed's seed, saith the LORD, from henceforth and for ever."

Joel 2:28-9
> 28 "And it shall come to pass afterward, *that* **I will pour out My Spirit upon all flesh**; and your sons and your daughters shall prophesy, your old men shall dream dreams, your young men shall see visions:
> 29 And also upon the servants and upon the handmaids in those days will **I pour out My Spirit**."

However, although there is a pouring out of the Spirit "upon" tribulation believers and evidence that the Spirit of God will be "upon" them, the fact that they are able to address God as "Father" in Isaiah 63:16 and Isaiah 64:8 indicates that they must have the divine nature, i.e. be indwelt by the Spirit of God to do so. This is clear in Romans 8:15.

Romans 8:15
> "For ye have not received the Spirit of bondage again to fear; but ye have received the Spirit of adoption, whereby we cry, Abba, Father."

There is a further mention of this in Galatians 4:6.

Galatians 4:6
> "And because ye are sons, God hath sent forth the Spirit of His Son into your hearts, crying, Abba, Father."

Since the indwelling Spirit is necessary for a believer to cry unto God "Abba Father" and tribulation believers address God as "Father" in Isaiah 63 and 64, then it follows that they must be indwelt by the Spirit of God from the moment they are born of God.

Now it is clear in the Old Testament that when deceased Old Testament believers and tribulation believers arise from the dead, they will arise from the dead indwelt by the Spirit of God as they enter into the earthly Kingdom.

Ezekiel 37:13-14
> 13 "And ye shall know that I *am* the LORD, when I have opened your graves, O My people, and brought you up out of your graves,
> 14 And shall put My Spirit **in** you, and ye shall live, and I shall place you in your own land: then shall ye know that I the LORD have spoken *it*, and performed *it*, saith the LORD."

This is why David, when raised from the dead in Psalm 89:26, can cry unto God as "Father", something he could not do directly while alive.

Psalm 89:26
> "He shall cry unto Me, Thou *art* my Father, my God, and the Rock of my salvation."

Old Testament believers thus understood that one day they, on resurrection ground, would be indwelt by the Spirit of God and be able to address God as "Father".

It was, therefore, a wonderful moment in the lives of the disciples in Luke 11:2 when the Lord taught them that they could address God in their lifetimes as "our Father" even **before** they would arise from the dead. This was, of course, possible because they were about to be indwelt by the Holy Spirit (Luke 11:13). Similarly, in James 1:18 when we read that we in this Church era are "a kind of first-fruits of His creatures", as "begotten ones" we are the first of the redeemed of all ages who can enjoy on earth what it means to be Spirit-indwelt sons of God.

James 1:18
> "Of His own will begat He us with the Word of truth, that we should be a kind of firstfruits of His creatures."

Some may infer from Ezekiel 36:26-27 that when God promises that He will put His Spirit "within" His restored people, at the outset of the millennial reign, that this is a reference to their being indwelt by the Holy Spirit.

Ezekiel 36:26-27
> 26 "A new heart also will I give you, and a new Spirit will I put **within you (Hebrew: among you)**: and I will take away the stony heart out of your flesh, and I will give you an heart of flesh.
> 27 And I will put My Spirit **within you (Hebrew: among you)**, and cause you to walk in My statutes, and ye shall keep My judgments, and do *them.*"

At first glance, these verses may appear to mean that Ezekiel is speaking of the Spirit of God indwelling millennial believers. However, the phrase "within you" in these verses means literally "among you" and is used in that context elsewhere to describe the Lord dwelling in the midst of His people during the Exodus story.

Joshua 3:10
> "And Joshua said, Hereby ye shall know that the living God *is* **among** you, and *that* He will without fail drive out from before you the Canaanites, and the Hittites, and the Hivites, and the Perizzites, and the Girgashites, and the Amorites, and the Jebusites."

During the millennial reign, the Spirit of God will be **among** the people of God in the millennial temple in Jerusalem even after the Lord Jesus has returned to His throne with His Bride in the heavens. Now, a study of these verses shows an absence of a reference to tribulation believers being indwelt by the Spirit of God in their lifetime. The emphasis is on the Spirit of God being "upon" them. This may lead some expositors to suppose that these believers only have the Spirit of God coming upon them from time to time, as was often recorded in the experience of some Old Testament characters. As we have already indicated, this view cannot be sustained in light of the clear revelation in Scripture that these believers will address God as "Father", something which can only be done through the **indwelling** Spirit of God (Romans 8:15). This argument from Romans 8:15 is perhaps an indirect route to the conclusion that tribulation believers are **indwelt** by the Spirit as well as the Spirit being **upon** them. However, we can find direct and clear scriptural support for these believers being **indwelt** by the Spirit of God in their lifetimes, when we remember that **oil** is used as a symbol of the Spirit of God.

Zechariah 4:12
> "And I answered again, and said unto him, What *be these* two olive branches which through the two golden pipes empty the golden *oil* **out of themselves**?"

In Zechariah 4:12, the oil came from **within** the branches of the two olive trees. In Revelation 11:4, we discover that the two olive trees of Zechariah 4:12 are the two witnesses who serve the Lord in Jerusalem in the latter half of the tribulation. It is clear, then, from the New Testament that the two witnesses, as the two most prominent remnant believers of the tribulation era, are indwelt by the Holy Spirit in as far as the "oil" is "within them". Furthermore, the New Testament also shows that all true believers in the tribulation era will have "oil in their vessels" (Matthew 25:4), i.e. be indwelt by the Holy Spirit.

In the riches of the wisdom and knowledge of God (Romans 11:33), the Word of God waits until New Testament revelation to clearly present the fact that living tribulation believers will be indwelt by the Spirit of God, while in the Old Testament this truth is alluded to, using the metaphor of "oil". It appears that the teaching of Spirit-indwelt believers being the sons of God in their lifetime was something which is not on the surface in the Old Testament. It is a truth which has to be searched out and is clear when revealed in the New Testament. It is part of what Paul exclaims in Romans 11:33.

Romans 11:33
"O the depth of the riches both of the wisdom and knowledge of God! How unsearchable *are* His judgments, and His ways past finding out!"

2 The pouring out of the Spirit of God upon the remnant

Whilst it is true that every believer after the rapture will be indwelt by the Spirit of God, i.e. have oil in his or her vessel, there will also be an outpouring of the Spirit of God **upon** them (Joel 2:28-9). In the Old Testament, when the Spirit came "upon" an individual, it was generally to enable them to carry out a specific task. In Joel 2:28-9, the effect of the pouring out of the Spirit on these believers will be miraculous visions, dreams and prophecies but, of note, tongues are not mentioned. We know from 1 Corinthians 14:22 that tongues were for a sign, and since it is the Jews who "require a sign" (1 Corinthians 1:22), the tongues were specifically directed to the unbelieving Jew in the early Church years. They seem to be omitted in the events foreseen by Joel. However, since "visions, dreams and prophecies" are for the preservation and edification of believers rather than unbelievers, it is not surprising that the Lord will supply His people with this Spirit-given resource during the dreadful years of tribulation. Surely, this degree of divine guidance on how to conduct their day-to-day lives will be important to enable them to carry out the task of preaching the gospel of the Kingdom worldwide.

The preaching of the remnant during the tribulation

They will indeed preach the gospel of the Kingdom worldwide. It was the "fall" of Israel which brought salvation to the Gentiles almost two thousand years ago (Romans 11:11). How much more, then, will not their future restoration bring global spiritual blessing in the tribulation! This is Paul's argument under divine inspiration in Romans 11:11-12.

Romans 11:11-12

11 "I say then, Have they stumbled that they should fall? God forbid: but *rather* through their fall salvation *is come* unto the Gentiles, for to provoke them to jealousy.

12 Now if the fall of them *be* the riches of the world, and the diminishing of them the riches of the Gentiles; how much more their fullness?"

They will be subject to intense global persecution. However, it appears that there will be areas where they will find protection. Moab and Bozrah (modern day Jordan) will fulfill this role (Isaiah 16:4; Micah 2:12).

Isaiah 16:4

"Let Mine outcasts dwell with thee, Moab; be thou a covert to them from the face of the spoiler: for the extortioner is at an end, the spoiler ceaseth, the oppressors are consumed out of the land."

Micah 2:12

"I will surely assemble, O Jacob, all of thee; I will surely gather the remnant of Israel; I will put them together as the sheep of **Bozrah**, as the flock in the midst of their fold: they shall make great noise by reason of *the multitude of* men."

In addition, there will be areas in Jerusalem where remnant believers will live right up until the end of the tribulation. Their leaders (governors) will be able to consume with fire any who dare to attack them.

Zechariah 12:6

"In that day will I make the governors of Judah like an hearth of fire among the wood, and like a torch of fire in a sheaf; and they shall devour all the people round about, on the right hand and on the left: and Jerusalem shall be inhabited again in her own place (literally: Jerusalem shall yet dwell under herself),Note 2 *even* in Jerusalem."

Who are these governors of Judah during the tribulation period? In Revelation 11:3-5, we have already considered how God has two servants, called "two witnesses", who shall minister during the second half of the tribulation in Jerusalem. Like the governors of the remnant in Jerusalem in Zechariah 12:6, the "two witnesses" are able to destroy anyone who comes against them by fire emanating from their bodies.

Revelation 11:3-5

3 "And I will give *power* unto My two witnesses, and they shall prophesy a thousand two hundred *and* threescore days, clothed in sackcloth.

4 These are the two olive trees, and the two candlesticks standing before the God of the earth.

5 And if any man will hurt them, fire proceedeth out of their mouth, and devoureth their enemies: and if any man will hurt them, he must in this manner be killed."

It is possible that the two witnesses of Revelation 11 and the governors of Judah in Zechariah 12 are the same people. It is truly remarkable that while the great apostasy, involving worship of the beast and his image, is being perpetrated on the Temple Mount, just a short distance away in a secluded quarter of Jerusalem will be a group of the remnant believers who are dwelling under supernatural divine protection under the leadership of these unnamed governors or witnesses. Revelation 11:7 adds the interesting detail that it is only at the end of the tribulation that the first beast of Revelation 13 declares war on the two witnesses and, in fact, overcomes them. Now, it is clear that there will have been many attempts earlier in the tribulation to harm the two witnesses before this final declaration of war by the beast against them at the very end of the tribulation. These early attempts will all fail as deadly fire emanates from the bodies of the two witnesses to consume their enemies. During this time, there appears to be a standoff between the beast and the two witnesses, but eventually the beast formally opens up a final campaign to try to destroy them. The military might of the beast appears to be ineffective against the two witnesses and the enclave of believers sheltering close to them.

It is clear that if military might is ineffective against them, then sorceries are the only weapon left to employ. This is the final weapon of the beast and the false prophet (Revelation 16:13-14). How startling an event it will be when the two witnesses are overcome and killed by Satan's men, namely the beast and his emissary, the false prophet! We have earlier considered that neither the beast nor the false prophet can simulate resurrection. How fitting, then, that an apparent defeat in divine testimony, in the murder of the Lord's two witnesses, should redound to a global demonstration of the peerless might of Jehovah in raising those same two witnesses from the dead!

One would have thought that this very public and irrefutable show of divine power in resurrection would have caused those who have believed "the lie" to re-evaluate their loyalty and worship to the beast. God is showing now that even a public and live viewing of His resurrection power will not shift human unbelief and rebellion against Him. This becomes clear when Zechariah shows that the armies of the ungodly, which we know are the forces in the beast's alliance, will commence an invasion of the remnant's safe area in Jerusalem, something they could not do while the two witnesses were there. It seems that, emboldened by the departure heavenwards of the two witnesses, the armies surrounding Jerusalem are so satanically deceived that they will prepare to move in for the kill, the target being the Jewish remnant quarter referred to in Zechariah 14:1-3 as "the residue of the people" (Zechariah 14:2).

This will be the moment of the Lord's return to deliver the remnant nation!

The purification of the remnant nation at the end of the tribulation

Purification and cleansing of a believer from the defilement of the way is distinct from the cleansing of salvation, as is clear in 2 Corinthians 7:1 where

Paul, speaking to New Testament believers, exhorts us to "cleanse ourselves from all filthiness of the flesh and spirit..." (2 Corinthians 7:1).

2 Corinthians 7:1

"Having therefore these promises, dearly beloved, let us **cleanse ourselves** from all filthiness of the flesh and spirit, perfecting holiness in the fear of God."

New Testament believers are familiar with this truth. However, this is not a doctrine peculiar to New Testament revelation. Several Old Testament passages show that believers **at the end of the tribulation** will be "purified" to prepare them for the service awaiting them in the coming Kingdom of Christ. A selection of these will be considered here.

For example, Daniel 12:8-10 shows how tribulation believers will be "purified and made white". This refining and purification is not salvation because, from the context in Daniel, it is clear that it is the "wise" who are "purified, and made white and tried" whereas those who are "wicked" (i.e. unbelievers), "do wickedly" and do not "understand".

Daniel 12:8-10

8 "And I heard, but I understood not: then said I, O my Lord, what shall be the end of these things?

9 And he said, Go thy way, Daniel: for the words *are* closed up and sealed till the time of the end.

10 Many shall be **purified, and made white, and tried**; but the wicked shall do wickedly: and none of the wicked shall understand; but the wise shall understand."

More specifically, Malachi is concerned with the purification of the subset of remnant believers who are of the tribe of Levi and who will have a special role in the service of the millennial earthly sanctuary. He shows how the Lord will personally supervise their purification for this important work.

Malachi 3:3

"And He shall sit *as* a refiner and purifier of silver: and He shall purify the sons of Levi, and purge them as gold and silver, that they may offer unto the LORD an offering in righteousness."

This special setting apart of tribulation believers who are of Levitical lineage for priestly service in the **earthly sanctuary** in Jerusalem should not be confused with the ability of all millennial believers, without exception, Levite or non-Levite, Jew or Gentile, to enter in spirit into the **heavenly sanctuary** as a priestly people at all times. This right will become theirs from the moment of salvation onwards, as is the case with every New Testament believer today.

Isaiah considers both the salvation and sanctification of the remnant together in one verse in **Isaiah 1:25** where we read, "And **I will turn My hand** upon thee, and purely purge away thy dross, and take away all thy tin:"

When Zechariah repeats the same phrase in Zechariah 13:7 (**I will turn Mine**

hand upon the little ones), it is in the same context of the believing element within the nation being purified for the coming Kingdom.Note 3 This time it is not the moment of their salvation which is being emphasised, but rather their **sanctification**, when the redeemed nation will be **preparing for that first sight** of their Redeemer "Whom they pierced". It should be acknowledged at this point that many hold a differing view, namely that it is on the occasion of the nation seeing the Lord Jesus on His return that they will get saved. However, the problem with this view, as discussed earlier, is that it is too late then to be saved. It should also be remembered from Psalm 68 that only those who are saved will be able to behold the face of the Lord at His return and not be consumed. It will be too late then to get right with God. The question then arises as to why is it that this first sight of the glorified Lord in Zechariah 12:10 will be accompanied by intense grief and mourning? Surely the first sight of the Saviour should bring unparalleled joy?

Zechariah 12:10

> "And I will pour upon the house of David, and upon the inhabitants of Jerusalem, the Spirit of grace and of supplications: and they shall look upon Me Whom they have pierced, and they shall mourn for Him, as one mourneth for *his* only *son*, and shall be in bitterness for Him, as one that is in bitterness for *his* firstborn."

Those who hold that the remnant only get saved when they see the Lord on His return, argue that the sorrow expressed on that occasion will arise from conviction of sin, especially the sin of crucifying the Lord, which will become very vivid in their consciences when "they shall look upon Me Whom they have pierced". Indeed, this occasion has been linked by valued Bible teachers over the years to a prophetic aspect to the Day of Atonement, when the nation "afflicted their souls" as a sign of repentance for sin (Leviticus 23:27-32). There is indeed a prophetic aspect to the Day of Atonement, especially that yearly ritual of the faithful elements of the nation who, in repentance, "afflicted their souls". This annual afflicting of the soul in repentance for past sins is a picture of the future occasion of the rebirth of the nation when the nation will be born in a day (Isaiah 66:8-9). However, this future affliction of the soul and national repentance for sin will not take place **at the end** of the tribulation. It will have taken place before the tribulation begins, as we have already seen, when the nation "is born at once" (Isaiah 66:8-9). In that day of spiritual national rebirth, the remorse will be for the great sin of rejecting the Lord Jesus over so many centuries. What a transformation will happen in their lives when they trust Him for salvation! The sin of unbelief will have been forgiven! As those who now are saved and indwelt by the Holy Spirit, they go forward into the dark days of tribulation.

At the end of the tribulation, these believers will know of the imminent return of the Lord Jesus. They will be expecting Him and earnestly longing for His coming to the earth. It is in parallel with this that the Lord will "pour upon the house of David, and upon the inhabitants of Jerusalem, the Spirit of grace and of supplications…" (Zechariah 12:10). As we have earlier seen, these believers are already indwelt by the Spirit of God. The Oil is in their vessels. If the Oil (the Spirit) is not already in their vessels it is, sadly, then too late to obtain It (Matthew 25:1-12). However, God will pour upon them an aspect of the Spirit's ministry which will mark them in a special way in those momentous days. It will be a manifestation of Spirit-led and Spirit-empowered grace and supplication. It may be inquired as to what will be the subject matter of their Spirit-led supplication. The next phrase gives the answer, where we read "and they shall look **upon** Me (*hibbitu elay*) Whom they have pierced" (Zechariah 12:10). Now it must be acknowledged that most Bible teachers assume from this English translation of Zechariah 12:10, quoted above, that the verse is describing the moment when the earthly remnant will actually **see the One Whom the nation once pierced**. It must be said that the grammatical construction does allow this interpretation, as is clearly the case in Exodus 3:6 when Moses was afraid to "look upon God (*habbit el haelohim*)". However, a careful examination of the phrase, "and they shall look upon Me", shows that this phrase does not **always** mean to physically behold Him. It sometimes means to "look to Him" or "look unto Him" in the sense of looking trustingly to Him, **even if He is not necessarily physically visible**.

Here are some examples of this phrase being used in the sense of looking to the Lord trustingly, where direct visualization of Him is not in question.

Psalm 34:4-5
> 4 "I sought the Lord, and He heard me, and delivered me from all my fears.
> 5 They **looked unto Him** (*hibbitu elav*), and were lightened: and their faces were not ashamed".

In this example, the phrase "looked upon…" (*hibbitu el…*) carries the sense of looking trustingly to the Lord by the eye of faith in time of need. Another example is the experience of Jonah in the belly of the whale when he said, "I will look again toward Thy holy temple" (Jonah 2:4). It follows then, that it must be determined **from the context** whether the phrase "to look upon" in Zechariah 12:10 means "to look directly at" or "to look towards" Christ in faith, even when a physical view of Christ is not the case. Does the New Testament quotation of Zechariah 12:10 help clarify this question?

John 19:37
> "And again another Scripture saith, they shall look (*opsontai*: root *horao*) on (*eis*) Him Whom they pierced."

This quotation in the Greek New Testament from Zechariah 12:10 uses a rare construction of the verb *horao*, "to look", by combining it with the preposition *eis* (meaning into or unto). Usually the verb *horao* occurs in the New Testament without the preposition *eis*, when it refers to **direct vision** of a person or object. For example, in Revelation 1:7, when we read how every eye shall see Him, the preposition *eis* is not present indicating that it is referring to a physical sight of Christ.

Revelation 1:7

"Behold, He cometh with clouds; and every eye shall see (root *horao*) Him, and they *also* which pierced Him: and all kindreds of the earth shall wail because of Him. Even so, Amen."

Because the occurrence of the verb *horao* in combination with the preposition *eis* (John 19:37) is so rare, it could be argued that it is difficult to be sure as to whether looking upon Him Whom they pierced means looking to Him by faith, or looking at Him physically. Happily, there is one occurrence of the verb *aphorao* (a combination of *apo* meaning "away" and *horao* meaning "to look") in the New Testament in combination with the preposition *eis* (Hebrews 12:2). This verb *aphorao* means "to look away". If used in combination with *eis* it means "to look away unto". Thus, in Hebrews 12:2 it means "to look away **unto Christ**". Does *aphorao eis* in Hebrews 12:2 carry the significance of looking away unto Christ physically or looking away to Him by faith?

Hebrews 12:2

"Looking (root *aphorao*) unto (*eis*) Jesus the Author and Finisher of *our* faith; Who for the joy that was set before Him endured the cross, despising the shame, and is set down at the right hand of the throne of God".

Clearly, in Hebrews 12:2 the verb *aphorao eis* carries the significance of looking unto Jesus by the eye of faith and not physically looking at Him. By evaluating these Scriptures, it appears reasonable to understand that Zechariah 12:10 also describes an expectant look of faith by the waiting remnant, who will be looking away unto Him with intense longing and supplication. In other words, the Spirit of grace and supplication poured upon them leads them to look expectantly for their Lord's return. This understanding helps us to see why they are mourning in the verse. Clearly, if they were looking into the physical face of the Lord Jesus, they would not be mourning. They would be rejoicing in His presence as we saw in Psalm 68:3. Again it must be pointed out that sin is not identified as the primary cause of the mourning in Zechariah 12:10. Note 4 Rather it is a Spirit-begotten sensitivity to the absence of the Only One and the Firstborn, which has led to this intense mourning. These believers are longing for His presence with them and this is the cause of their mourning. Such an emotion can only emerge from the movements of the Spirit of God in their hearts. In this same context, the Lord spake of the **mourning of the tribulation believers for the absent Christ**.

Matthew 9:15

"And Jesus said unto them, Can the children of the bridechamber mourn, as long as the Bridegroom is with (*meta*) them (see Appendix 4 for significance of *meta*)? but the days will come, when the Bridegroom shall be taken from them, and then shall they fast."

Once again this verse shows that the mourning of Zechariah 12:10 could not happen if these believers were in the immediate presence of Christ or if they even felt His **spiritual presence** in the "*meta*" sense of the word (see

Appendix 4) such as is promised to us in Matthew 28:20: "Lo I am with (*meta*) you alway." If the children of the Bridechamber (tribulation saints) in Matthew 9:15 felt that the Lord was with (*meta*) them, as promised in Matthew 28:20, they would not be mourning. Why then are they mourning? What has happened to prevent them from enjoying the Lord's spiritual presence with (*meta*) them even in the period of His physical absence? Clearly there is a problem. The enjoyment of His presence has been compromised and this needs to be corrected in anticipation of His *parousia* to the earth. This suggests that the "looking upon Him" in Zechariah 12:10 must be in the sense of looking to Him in earnest, dependent and expectant prayer for restoration and cleansing of defilement. This is not salvation. Rather, this is sanctification and preparation for the impending return to the earth of the Lord Jesus by the waiting remnant. This leads on to the divine solution to their problem when, in Zechariah 13:1, we find that "there shall be a fountain opened to the house of David and to the inhabitants of Jerusalem for sin and for uncleanness".

Zechariah 13:1
> "In that day there shall be a fountain opened to the house of David and to the inhabitants of Jerusalem for sin and for uncleanness."

This is laver truth. It is in the same context as the purification and cleansing available to believers in Daniel 12:8-10 and Malachi 3:3, discussed above. It is the cleansing of the defilement encountered during the tribulation period, rather than the putting away of sin which will have already happened at their salvation. The Lord will not only have saved His people from the guilt of their sin, but He will purify and sanctify them for the holy service of His Kingdom. There is a practical lesson from these meditations. We discover how the remnant believers will be exercised to make things right with their Lord and be restored to Him in preparation for His return. We do well to remember the exhortation of the Lord Jesus to the disciples that we should be like these tribulation believers in their exercise of heart to be morally ready for the coming of their Lord to the earth for them after the wedding (Luke 12:35-36). The Lord indicated that the tribulation believers are waiting for the Lord **to return from the wedding**. We in this church era are not waiting for the Lord to return from the wedding for us. We are waiting for Him to come to the air before this **to take us into the wedding in heaven!** This is the rapture of the church. After this, He comes to the earth at the end of the tribulation, i.e. He **returns** from the wedding. However, the lesson for us in this church era is very important and relevant today. We must and should be **like the tribulation believers** in being exercised and prepared for His coming to the air for us at any time.

Luke 12:35-36
> "Let your loins be girded about, and *your* lights burning; And **ye yourselves like unto men that wait for their Lord**, when He will return from the wedding; that when He cometh and knocketh, they may open unto Him immediately."

1. When we speak of the Spirit of God continuously and forever **indwelling** a believer today, this is scriptural language based on John 14:16-17.

John 14:16-17

16 "And I will pray the Father, and He shall give you another Comforter, that He may abide with you **for ever;**

17 Even the Spirit of truth; Whom the world cannot receive, because it seeth Him not, neither knoweth Him: but ye know Him; for He **dwelleth** *with you, and shall be* **in you."**

However, this was not the case in the Old Testament. The Spirit of God **entered into** His servants the prophets only on distinct and repeated occasions (Ezekiel 2:2;3:24) rather than abiding (dwelling) continuously within them as in John 14:16-17. In 1 Peter 1:11 we again read of the Spirit of Christ being **in the Old Testament prophets** as they prophesied and were "Searching what, or what manner of time the Spirit of Christ **which was in** them did signify, when It testified beforehand the sufferings of Christ, and the glory that should follow."

Some may think that because Joshua is spoken of as a man "in whom is the spirit" (Numbers 27:18), that he was continuously indwelled by the Holy Spirit in the Old Testament. However, the phrase "in whom is the spirit" cannot refer to the Holy Spirit for the following combination of reasons. In Numbers 27:18 the word 'spirit' is not preceded by the definite article in the original text, nor is it the Spirit of God Which is described in the verse. Rather, the phrase 'in whom is spirit" can be understood by comparing it with the opposite scenario described in 1 Kings 10:6, where we read of the Queen of Sheba's response to beholding Solomon's glory, such that 'there was no more spirit in her'. This shows that the phrase 'in whom is spirit' describes the strength of character of Joshua.

It was because the Spirit of God did not **indwell Old Testament believers continuously** that they could not in their lifetimes address God as "Abba Father" as we do today.

2. This literal translation of Zechariah 12:6 shows that the millennial city of Jerusalem will be inhabited "under herself", i.e. under Jerusalem, that is the heavenly Jerusalem which will be above it in the heavens. This is discussed in Psalm 89.

3. The full quotation of Zechariah 13:7 is as follows: "Awake, O sword, against My Shepherd, and against the Man that is My Fellow (Hebrew: My Equal), saith the LORD of hosts: smite the Shepherd, and the sheep shall be scattered: and I will turn Mine hand upon the little ones." This remarkable verse spans a time period of over 2000 years. It calls us to look back to when the Shepherd was smitten at Calvary by Jehovah, and the sheep of Israel were scattered, leading to the dispersion of 2000 years. However, it looks forward to the day when there will be a regathering and restoration of the "little ones" under the hand of God. Not surprisingly, then, the tribulation believers are referred to in the Gospels as the "little ones" (eg Matthew 10:42).

4. When Zechariah indicates that "they shall look unto Me (Hebrew "unto Me" is *elay*"), Whom they have pierced" (Zechariah 12:10), he is showing how remnant believers of the nation will be looking **in faith unto** (*elay*) the Man of Calvary, in contrast to their forefathers in Psalm 22:16-17 who looked (*yabbitu* is same verb as *hibbitu*) and stared **in unbelief at** (Psalm 22:17 "at Me" is *vi* rather than *elay*) the pierced hands and feet of Christ at Golgotha.

Appendix 4

More examples of *sun* and *meta* meaning "with" in the same passage

We have observed in Psalm 68 how *sun* **generally** carries the idea of "with" in the sense of "in close physical proximity to". *Meta* indicates "with" where a sense of a moral or spiritual proximity is being emphasised. This can happen sometimes in a context where close physical proximity is also being described and sometimes where close physical proximity is not the case. Accordingly, one can only determine from the context whether or not *meta* involves close physical proximity. Matthew 28:20 is a classic example of *meta* being used in a context where close physical proximity is not meant. It was the Lord's final benediction to His disciples when He said, "Lo I am with (*meta*) you" (Matthew 28:20). Clearly, the Lord was referring to the time of His physical absence from earth after He ascended to heaven. However, His use of "*meta*" in "Lo I am with (*meta*) you alway" (Matthew 28:20) indicates that, despite being absent from them in a physical sense, He has pledged His presence with them **spiritually**.

In summary then, while *meta* **sometimes** is used in the context of close physical proximity (e.g. John 15:27) it does **not always** carry this significance. Accordingly, the New Testament reader who comes across *meta* must determine from the context if close physical proximity is or is not involved. Whether or not the use of *meta* in a passage involves physical proximity, the meaning will include either nearness spiritually or nearness of moral character. It follows, then, that on the occasions in Scripture where *meta* is used in **combination** with *sun,* the presence of *meta* denotes spiritual nearness or similarity of moral character.

The story of the two on the road to Emmaus

In Luke 24:15, the two on the road to Emmaus had the wonderful experience of the risen Lord coming to walk with (*sun*) them.

Luke 24:15
> "And it came to pass, that, while they communed together and reasoned, Jesus Himself drew near, and went with (*sun*) them."

As they listened to the Lord expounding to them the Scriptures, this sense of being "with" (*sun*) Him had intensified to "*meta*". Thus they request the Lord, "Abide with (*meta*) us".

Luke 24:28
> 28 "And they drew nigh unto the village, whither they went: and He made as though He would have gone further.
> 29 But they constrained Him, saying, Abide with (*meta*) us: for it is toward evening, and the day is far spent."

Luke shows that the Lord's response to their desire for Him to abide with (*meta*) them was for Him to first enter their home to be with (*sun*) them.

Luke 24:29
   "...And He went in to tarry with (*sun*) them."

It was clear that the Lord wished them to be with Him in the *meta* sense of the word, but to achieve this goal He must be with them physically first in the *sun* sense of "with". This was because the Lord wished them to understand that He was physically risen from the dead. This required Him to be physically with (*sun*) them to prove this truth. Their ability to have spiritual fellowship with (*meta*) the Lord would have been compromised if they had not fully grasped the truth of His physical resurrection from the dead. As they watched the Lord breaking the bread – and no doubt they saw His nail-pierced hands – they were not only with the Lord Jesus physically in the *sun* sense of "with", but they recognised that this was the risen, glorified Lord Who was with them spiritually (the *meta* sense of with).

Luke 24:30-35
   30 "And it came to pass, as He sat at meat with (*meta*) them, He took bread, and blessed *it*, and brake, and gave to them.
   31 And their eyes were opened, and they knew Him; and He vanished out of their sight.
   32 And they said one to another, Did not our heart burn within us, while He talked with us by the way, and while He opened to us the Scriptures?
   33 And they rose up the same hour, and returned to Jerusalem, and found the eleven gathered together, and them that were with (*sun*) them,
   34 Saying, The Lord is risen indeed, and hath appeared to Simon.
   35 And they told what things *were done* in the way, and how He was known of them in breaking of bread."

The crucifixion of the Lord Jesus with the two thieves

Matthew 27:38
   "Then were there two thieves crucified with (*sun*) Him, one on the right hand, and another on the left."

This verse shows that the Lord Jesus was crucified in close physical proximity with (*sun*) the thieves.

Mark 15:27-28
   27 "And with (*sun*) Him they crucify two thieves; the one on His right hand, and the other on His left.
   28 And the Scripture was fulfilled, which saith, And He was numbered (reckoned) with (*meta*) the transgressors (lawless ones)."

Mark 15:27 reiterates that the Lord's crucifixion was in close proximity with (*sun*) the thieves but verse 28 shows that, in addition, He was reckoned (by those around Him) as being with (*meta*) "lawless ones" (definite article omitted before "lawless ones"). The use of *meta* in verse 28 shows that the

Lord Jesus was reckoned by the execution squad, and indeed their masters, as being "with (*meta*) lawless ones". This phrase indicates a categorisation much wider than being reckoned with the two thieves who were crucified alongside Him. They reckoned the Lord Jesus to be "with (*meta*) lawless ones" in a general way, in the sense of being morally categorized along with people of such character. What a blasphemous attitude of mind to have against the Holy Son of God Who was the only One who fulfilled the Law of God in all its aspects. Remarkably, the centurion (Luke 23:47) who headed the execution squad that day changed his mind radically as He confessed on the event of the Saviour's death that "certainly this was a righteous Man".

Luke is careful to emphasise how the Lord Jesus stood morally distinct from the two thieves

Luke 23:32
> "And there were also two other (*heteroi* meaning "others of a different kind"), malefactors, led with (*sun*) Him to be put to death".

Luke gives us the Lord's perspective of what happened that day. The thieves were *heteroi*, i.e. "others of a different kind" morally to the Lord Jesus. Accordingly, they were crucified with (*sun*) Him but not in the *meta* sense of "with" in as far as they were in no way morally comparable to Him.

John's account of the crucifixion seems at first glance to contradict Luke 23:32.

John 19:17-18
> 17 "And He bearing His cross went forth into a place called *the place* of a skull, which is called in the Hebrew Golgotha:
> 18 Where they crucified Him, and two other (*allous* meaning "others of the same kind") with (*meta*) Him, on either side one, and Jesus in the midst".

In John 19:18, John tells us that the two thieves were "others of the same kind" (*allous*) in comparison to the Lord Jesus. Moreover, the thieves were crucified with (*meta*) Him suggesting that they were of similar moral character as the central Prisoner. Clearly, this flatly contradicts Luke 23:32 where the thieves are "others of a different kind" in comparison with the Lord Jesus. Secondly, in Luke, they were with Him in the *sun* sense of the word, where no moral comparison could be inferred. How can the reader resolve this apparent contradiction?

We have a helpful clue to the answer in Mark 15:27:

Mark 15:27
> 27 "And with (*sun*) (i.e. in immediate proximity to) Him they crucify two thieves; the one on His right hand, and the other on His left.
> 28 And the Scripture was fulfilled, which saith, And He was numbered (reckoned) with (*meta*) the transgressors (lawless ones)."

A study of the relevant Scriptures shows that it was **men** who reckoned the Lord Jesus to be on the same moral level (*meta*) as the thieves. Here is a synopsis of the argument in support of this view:

Now there is a view that the quotations from Isaiah 53:12 in Luke 22:37 and Mark 15:28 – "He was numbered (reckoned) with (*meta*) the transgressors (numbered with lawless ones)" – refer to God's perspective of events that day rather than what men thought of the Lord Jesus. Those who hold this view teach that God, in fact, reckoned the Lord Jesus as identified "with or among" other lawless ones as part of the work of putting away sin. The difficulty with this view is that a sin-expiating death cannot be effective if God regards it as merely "with" (*meta*) other condemned sinners who equally share the same condemnation. In contrast to this idea, the death which makes propitiation for sin must be "for", i.e. "on behalf of" or "instead of", sinners in order to have saving power (see Psalm 22). When in Levitcus 16, on the Day of Atonement, Aaron cast in his own teeth the sins of the people and attributed these to himself, he was not standing with the people. He stood as one lonely man taking to himself the guilt of the nation so that they, unlike him, went out free. It was only through the death of the scapegoat that Aaron, as the sin-bearing priest, escaped the death which sin bearing would have uniquely entailed for him (see Psalm 22). In this very connection, Hebrews 7:26 emphasises that our Lord Jesus was "separate from sinners".

Hebrews 7:26

"For such an High Priest became us, *Who is* holy, harmless, undefiled, separate from sinners, and made higher than the heavens;"

Accordingly, then, being "numbered with lawless ones" is the perspective of **ungodly men** who did not understand the uniqueness of the Lord Jesus.

Mark specifies that the exact moment when Scripture was fulfilled, regarding the Lord Jesus being "reckoned with (*meta*) lawless ones", was not when the Lord was crucified but when the two thieves were crucified **shortly after** the Lord's crucifixion. This shows that the reckoning of the Lord Jesus to be with the transgressors was directly dependent on the crucifixion of the two thieves subsequent to the Lord's crucifixion. Those who hold that the Lord Jesus being "reckoned with the transgressors" describes God starting to treat His Son as a transgressor, for the sake of lost sinners, should note that being "reckoned with the transgressors" arose as a result of the crucifixion of the two thieves, and was not simultaneous with the crucifixion of the Lord Jesus. Being "reckoned with the transgressors" could not be part of the propitiatory work of the Lord Jesus, since this reckoning was dependent on the suffering of the two malefactors, as Mark confirms.

Mark 15:27

27 "And with (*sun*) (i.e. in immediate proximity to) Him they crucify two thieves; the one on His right hand, and the other on His left.
28 And the Scripture was fulfilled, which saith, And He was numbered (reckoned) with (*meta*) the transgressors (lawless ones)."

Evaluation of all the gospel accounts shows that it could only be ungodly men who branded the Lord Jesus as being reckoned with (*meta*) lawless ones. Since this is clarified in Mark, when John repeats this perspective in John 19:17-18, and uses the word *meta* we can be confident that John is bringing before us sinful men's perception of that event.

Accordingly, John 19:18 is describing the **innermost thoughts** of the soldiers who set about crucifying the Lord Jesus that day. They considered, erroneously, that the central Prisoner was in the same moral category (*meta*) as the two thieves. How wonderful, then, is the change wrought in the heart of the centurion, as considered in Psalm 22, who, after witnessing the Lord Jesus' hours of suffering and death, exclaimed, "Certainly this was a righteous Man!" (Luke 23:47).

Appendix 5

The lovingkindness (*chesed*) of God defined in Micah 7

In Micah 7, the prophet takes a panoramic view of God's dealings with the nation of Israel from a twofold viewpoint.

In Micah 7:1-17, he has projected his mind forwards to the experience of the remnant nation of Israel subsequent to the rapture of the church and prior to the onslaught of the tribulation period. During that future time, they will be looking to their present circumstances of moral darkness on every hand, remembering the sad occasion of their rejection of Christ and the resultant cascade of national tragedy emerging from this. In verses 1-17, the prophet is using the exact language such future remnant believers will use in that coming day. We could regard this section as a prophecy of the **future confession** of the remnant.

In Micah 7:18-20, the prophet is looking forward from his own time period as he grapples with the challenge to faith of the impending Assyrian invasion and the Babylon captivity. He rests in the conclusion that God will bring to fruition His purposes and promises to the patriarchs. Moreover, he outlines **the way** in which God will do this. It is alone dependent on the Person of Christ. We could consider this section as a statement of the **present confession** of faith of true believers in Micah's own time period.

The future confession of the remnant

Micah 7:1-7

1 WOE is me! for I am as when they have gathered the summer fruits, as the grapegleanings of the vintage: *there is* no cluster to eat: my soul desired the firstripe fruit.

2 The good *man* is perished out of the earth: and *there is* none upright among men: they all lie in wait for blood; they hunt every man his brother with a net.

3 That they may do evil with both hands earnestly, the prince asketh, and the judge *asketh* for a reward; and the great *man*, he uttereth his mischievous desire: so they wrap it up.

4 The best of them *is* as a brier: the most upright *is sharper* than a thorn hedge: the day of thy watchmen *and* thy visitation cometh; now shall be their perplexity.

5 Trust ye not in a friend, put ye not confidence in a guide: keep the doors of thy mouth from her that lieth in thy bosom.

6 For the son dishonoureth the father, the daughter riseth up against her mother, the daughter in law against her mother in law; a man's enemies *are* the men of his own house.

7 Therefore I will look unto the Lord; I will wait for the God of my salvation: my God will hear me.

The scene depicted in Micah 7:1 is of **the end** of the time of harvest. The narrator says, "Woe is me". It is as if he feels there has been a curse upon him. He says, "My soul desired the first ripe fruit", which surely strikes the reader as an unusual statement at the **end** of harvest. The key to understanding this passage is that the first ripe fruit referred to here is the first ripe (early) figs of the fig tree. This passage becomes clear in the New Testament. Two thousand years ago the Lord Jesus, in the last week of His public ministry, desired the first ripe fruit of the fig tree and found none. The result was His curse upon the fig tree (Mark 11:12-14) causing it to wither up (Mark 11:20-21). This withered fig tree was a picture of the nation which, as a result of rejecting Christ, has been withered up spiritually as far as bearing fruit for God is concerned. Of course, this is not a permanent state. Micah 5 shows that God has given up the nation only temporarily because it smote "the Judge of Israel with a rod upon the cheek" two thousand years ago. God only "gave them up **until** she which travaileth hath brought forth". We know this will be when the nation is born at once (Isaiah 66).

Micah 5:1-3

1 "NOW gather thyself in troops, O daughter of troops: He hath laid siege against us: they shall smite the Judge of Israel with a rod upon the cheek.
2 But thou, Beth-lehem Ephratah, *though* thou be little among the thousands of Judah, *yet* out of thee shall He come forth unto Me *that is* to be Ruler in Israel; Whose goings forth *have been* from of old, from everlasting.
3 Therefore will He give them up, **until the time** *that* **she which travaileth hath brought forth**: then the remnant of His brethren shall return unto the children of Israel."

In Micah 7, the narrator is speaking on behalf of the remnant element of faithful ones within the nation of Israel at the end of the harvest period. During this long period of harvest time, Israel has largely been fruitless for God. However, now after around two thousand years it is desiring fruit. "My soul desired the first ripe fruit" (of the fig tree) even though it is clear from the passage that the time of harvest has now reached an advanced stage. It would be imprudent to expect fruit from the fig tree if it were fully withered up. However, the Lord Jesus indicated that in a coming day the fig tree (Israel) would put forth leaves as a precursor to producing fruit.

Matthew 24:32-22

32 "Now learn a parable of the fig tree; When his branch is yet tender, and putteth forth leaves, ye know that summer *is* nigh:
33 So likewise ye, when ye shall see all these things, know that it is near, *even* at the doors."

Today, after almost two thousand years, Israel is regathered as a nation state. The fig tree, after almost two thousand years of being withered up, has put forth leaves. However, spiritual **fruit** for God is still awaited to the spectacular degree, yet to be seen, when the remnant nation is spiritually restored after the rapture of the church. In that coming day, even though the great harvest from the days of Luke 10:2 will be approaching its final stages (i.e. after the rapture of the church), there will be a longing from within this nation for the first ripe fruit of the fig tree! This divinely begotten exercise in the hearts of the Jews of that future day will be fulfilled when they experience enlightenment and salvation: at long last the first ripe fruit of the fig-tree will have come. The nation will have been born at once (Isaiah 66).

Sadly, even to this day from a spiritual perspective, Israel in a general sense is not characterised by fruit bearing. In fact, Micah describes major elements within the nation at this time as being "as a brier" and "sharper than a thorn hedge" (Micah 7:4). In Micah 7:6, we learn that at this time "a man's enemies are the men of his own house". This verse is quoted by the Lord Jesus in Matthew 10:36, again in the context of the tribulation period.

Matthew 10:36
"And a man's foes *shall be* they of his own household."

A study of the context of Matthew 10:36 shows that it is the tribulation period which is being considered in that passage, since the Lord indicates that those He is speaking about will be **alive** when the Son of man comes, which is in the future.

Matthew 10:23
"For verily I say unto you, Ye shall not have gone over the cities of Israel,
till the Son of man be come."

Clearly then, Matthew 10:23 could not refer to the apostles as those who would "not have gone over the cities of Israel till the Son of man be come". This is because, as far as the apostles were concerned, they did not at that time have to wait for His coming. He was already there. This shows that Matthew 10:23 is referring to the tribulation believers who await the Lord's coming. By implication, if Matthew 10:23 is referring to the future tribulation period, then Matthew 10:36 and the passage from which it is quoted, Micah 7:6, also refer to the same time period.

These considerations place Micah 7:1-7 as a confession suitable for the lips of remnant believers when the nation will be miraculously brought to faith in Christ subsequent to the rapture. There will be a note of triumph in their confession.

Despite the moral darkness of this period, the narrator has a confidence that although Israel may have fallen, it will arise again (Micah 7:8).

Micah 7:8
Rejoice not against me, O mine enemy: when I fall, I shall arise; when I sit
in darkness, the Lord *shall be* a light unto me.

Israel stumbled and fell (Romans 11:11) almost two thousand years ago in its rejection of Christ. This happened at the same time as the fig tree failed to produce its fruit and Israel, the nation of divine blessing, fell (temporarily) under the judgmental curse of God (the curse of the fig tree). Nevertheless, the narrator of this great confession is confident that the Lord will enlighten him (Micah 7:8).

There is a recognition that the nation, over many years, has borne "the indignation of the Lord". Clearly this is due to the rejection of her Messiah in Micah 5. However, this is for a limited period only. It is "until He plead my cause". This limited period has lasted for almost two thousand years.

Micah 7:9
> "I will bear the indignation of the Lord, because I have sinned against Him, until He plead my cause, and execute judgment for me: He will bring me forth to the light, *and* I shall behold His righteousness".

This illumination of the remnant nation is also described in Psalm 118:27, "God is the Lord, Which hath shewed us light".

Psalm 118:27
> "God *is* the Lord, Which hath shewed us light: bind the sacrifice with cords, *even* unto the horns of the altar".

In our considerations of Psalm 118, it was seen how this was on the occasion of the nation's turning to the Lord, when Israel is born in a day (Isaiah 66) (see Appendix 3). The recovery of the remnant at that time shall be noticed by the rest of the world, including "she that is mine enemy". Sadly, the world, under the inspiration of the dragon, will seek to persecute the remnant of her seed (Revelation 12).

Micah 7:10
> "Then *she that is* mine enemy shall see *it*, and shame shall cover her which said unto me, Where is the Lord thy God? mine eyes shall behold her: now shall she be trodden down as the mire of the streets".

During this time there will be a rebuilding of the walls.

Micah 7:11
> "*In* the day that thy walls are to be built, *in* that day shall the decree be far removed."

There will be immigration to the land of Jews from Assyria (Iraq).

Micah 7:12
> " *In* that day *also* he shall come even to thee from Assyria, and *from* the fortified cities, and from the fortress even to the river, and from sea to sea, and *from* mountain to mountain."

Despite these signs of political prosperity and stability, moral poverty, "the fruit of their doings", fills the land.

Micah 7:13
> "Notwithstanding the land shall be desolate because of them that dwell therein, for the fruit of their doings".

These passages suggest a regathering of the nation in unbelief which is a prerequisite to the restoration of the nation spiritually. Within this environment of a politically stable Israel, albeit morally in transgression of God's Laws, there will be a remnant. The Lord will care for them as a Shepherd will care for His sheep.

Micah 7:14
> "Feed Thy people with Thy rod, the flock of Thine heritage, which dwell solitarily *in* the wood, in the midst of Carmel: let them feed *in* Bashan and Gilead, as in the days of old."

The remnant within Israel at that future time will experience the Lord's direct dealings in a similar way to the experiences of the nation of Israel coming through the wilderness.

Micah 7:15
> "**According to the days of Thy coming out of the land of Egypt** will I shew unto him marvellous *things*."

We have already seen, in Psalm 95, that the experience of Israel in Egypt carries a prophetic import. For example, Massah and Meribah answer to the rejection of Christ at Calvary. Kadesh Barnea answers to the rejection of Christ in the Acts of the Apostles. The Korah, Dathan and Abiram apostasy answers to the future rejection of Christ in favour of the beast and the false prophet. The Massah and Meribah incident and the Kadesh Barnea incident have already found fulfilment. It is the Korah, Dathan and Abiram apostasy which still awaits its prophetic fulfilment. The remnant of Israel are like the sons of Korah who distance themselves from their own kinsmen, who have fallen for the apostasy (see Psalm 45).

The next section describes the discomfiture of the nations who, likewise, will be confounded when it is clear that earth's last great apostasy under the beast is about to be judged.

Micah 7:16-17
> 16 "The nations shall see and be confounded at all their might: they shall lay *their* hand upon *their* mouth, their ears shall be deaf.
> 17 They shall lick the dust like a serpent, they shall move out of their holes like worms of the earth: they shall be afraid of the Lord our God, and shall fear because of Thee".

The present confession of the prophet

The section then closes with the prophet Micah reflecting on how it is possible that his own beloved nation should be eventually recovered unto their God. He describes how the members of the nation **in his own time can experience a present salvation and forgiveness.** Not surprisingly, Micah 7:18-20 forms a succinct summary of the doctrines considered in Psalm 22 on the matter of how Old Testament believers were saved!

Micah 7:18

"Who *is* a God like unto Thee, that pardoneth (**beareth away**) iniquity, and passeth by the transgression of the remnant of His heritage? He retaineth not His anger for ever, because He delighteth *in* mercy (Hebrew: lovingkindness)."

As considered in Psalm 22, all Old Testament believers enjoyed the truth that it is God Who bears away their iniquities (Micah 7:18) and that the scapegoat on the Day of Atonement provided a picture of this. While these believers enjoyed forgiveness of their sins, they were aware that God had merely "passed by" their transgressions and not yet dealt with them. This is what is meant by "the remission (passing over) of sins that are past" in Romans 3:25.

Romans 3:25

"Whom God hath set forth *to be* a propitiation through faith in His blood, to declare His righteousness for the remission (passing over) of sins that are past, through the forbearance of God;"

During those times, God "passed by" their transgressions. He had not yet dealt with them in judgment. This was already understood by all Old Testament believers. Until the sins were dealt with by Christ, God "retained His anger" in respect of these sins, even though the sinner in the Old Testament was now saved and delivered from personally bearing any eternal punishment. However, Old Testament believers understood that, in this matter, God did not retain "His anger **forever**". This, we are told in Micah 7:18, is because of the **lovingkindness** (Hebrew: *chesed*) of God. It is a rewarding study to seek to define the lovingkindness (*chesed*) of God in this context, since the lovingkindness of God means He does not have to retain "His anger **forever**". Indeed, in contrast, we discover that the lovingkindness (*chesed*) of God is forever (Psalm 18:1-4).

Psalm 118:1

"O give thanks unto the Lord; for *He is* good: because His mercy (lovingkindness) *endureth* for ever."

What is this lovingkindness of God (*chesed*) which enables the wrath of God in the matter of sin to be ended forever? In other words, sin is no longer merely passed over, or passed by, but dealt with forever. Micah 7:20 defines it for us!

Micah 7:20

"Thou wilt perform the truth to Jacob, and the mercy (*chesed*: lovingkindness) to Abraham, which Thou hast sworn unto our fathers from the days of old."

The "truth to Jacob" and the "lovingkindness (*chesed*) to Abraham" are not referred to as such in the accounts of their lives in the book of Genesis.

However, these terms are defined in Micah 7:20 as synonymous with the divine oath sworn unto the fathers from the days of old. Indeed, a study of this divine oath sworn to Abraham in Genesis 22 shows that it is all about the **promised Seed, namely the Lord Jesus**.

Genesis 22:15-18
> 15 "And the Angel of the Lord called unto Abraham out of heaven the second time,
> 16 And said, **By Myself have I sworn, saith the Lord**, for because thou hast done this thing, and hast not withheld thy son, thine only *son:*
> 17 That in blessing I will bless thee, and in multiplying I will multiply thy seed as the stars of the heaven, and as the sand which *is* upon the sea shore; **and thy Seed shall possess the gate of His enemies;**
> 18 And in thy Seed shall all the nations of the earth be blessed; because thou hast obeyed My voice."

Accordingly, Micah 7:20, by linking lovingkindness (*chesed*) with the oath to Abraham, helpfully **defines the word *chesed*** (lovingkindness) as being embodied in the Person of Christ, the promised Seed of Abraham. In fact, this linking of the *chesed* of Micah 7 with the promised Seed, namely the Lord Jesus, is key to understanding Micah 7. It helps us to understand why it is that the Lord "retaineth not His anger for ever, because He delighteth *in* mercy (Hebrew *chesed:* lovingkindness)". It is God's delight in the Person of Christ and His finished work which allows God to righteously end retaining His anger for sin, because justice has been fully satisfied in the shedding of the precious blood of Christ.

Micah 7 reveals that the *chesed* (lovingkindness) of Jehovah is displayed in the Person and work of the promised Seed, the Lamb of God's providing, i.e. the Lord Jesus. This leads the prophet to confidently claim that all those in his generation who, in saving faith, claimed the lovingkindness of God through the promised sin-bearing Messiah would experience the Lord "turning again" to them and they have the assurance that the Lord would "cast all their sins into the depths of the sea".

Micah 7:19
> "He will turn (Hebrew: return) again, He will have compassion upon us; He will subdue our iniquities; and Thou wilt cast all their sins into the depths of the sea."

When we read, "He will turn (return) again", in the context it is not the Lord's return to reign which is in consideration but rather the Lord "returning" in the same sense as in Zechariah 1:3, where the Lord returns spiritually to establish a relationship with those who were formerly rebelling against Him.

Zechariah 1:3
> "Therefore say thou unto them, Thus saith the LORD of hosts; Turn (Hebrew: return) ye unto me, saith the LORD of hosts, and I will turn (Hebrew: return) unto you, saith the LORD of hosts."

In Micah 7:19, those who experience the Lord "turning again" have "all their sins cast into the depths of the sea". As discussed in Psalm 22, casting sins into the depths of the sea was a **provisional act** of God to cover over the sins of Old Testament believers until the Lord should bear them away, once and for all, at Calvary. This was the basis of their saving faith in the Old Testament. However, this act of faith of Old Testament believers was based in the eventual fulfilment of the promises to the Fathers, namely the coming of the Lamb of God, the promised Seed, revealed in the divine oath to Abraham. It is the promised Seed, the coming Messiah, **Who** would deal with sin once and for all. Convinced of this wonderful truth, the prophet can confidently exclaim:

Micah 7:20
"Thou wilt perform the truth to Jacob, *and* the mercy to Abraham, which Thou hast sworn unto our fathers from the days of old".

How fitting that the prophet's name Micah should mean, "Who is like God?"!